Praise for
Rails 3 in Action

Takes you on an excellent Rails 3 adventure!

—Anthony J. Topper, Penn State Harrisburg

Conversational and current. A wellspring of information.

—Jason Rogers, Dell Inc.

An essential roadmap for the newest features of Rails 3.

—Greg Vaughn, Improving Enterprises

Essential, effective Rails techniques and habits for the modern Rubyist.

—Thomas Athanas, Athanas Empire, Inc.

A holistic book for a holistic framework.

—Josh Cronemeyer, ThoughtWorks Studios

The API chapter was an absolute lifesaver, and if I hadn't read it I wouldn't have been able to write my application that I have now deployed.

—Leo Cassarani

I think I've learned more about Rails in the first five chapters than I did in all the other resources I've tried … combined!

—J.K. Wood

The writing in the book is natural and relaxed, and it takes us through the process of developing an application. In doing so, it references and shows us how to use specific non-base Rails gems that really help in achieving our goals.

—Mario Alberto Chávez Cárdenas

Rails 4 in Action

RYAN BIGG
YEHUDA KATZ
STEVE KLABNIK
REBECCA SKINNER

MANNING
Shelter Island

For online information and ordering of this and other Manning books, please visit
www.manning.com. The publisher offers discounts on this book when ordered in quantity.
For more information, please contact

> Special Sales Department
> Manning Publications Co.
> 20 Baldwin Road
> PO Box 761
> Shelter Island, NY 11964
> Email: orders@manning.com

 Manning Publications Co.
20 Baldwin Road
PO Box 761
Shelter Island, NY 11964

Development editor:	Susan Conant
Technical editor:	Steven Jenkins
Copyeditor:	Andy Carroll
Proofreader:	Katie Tennant
Technical proofreader:	Doug Warren
Typesetter:	Gordan Salinovic
Cover designer:	Marija Tudor

ISBN 9781617291098
Printed in the United States of America
1 2 3 4 5 6 7 8 9 10 – EBM – 20 19 18 17 16 15

brief contents

1 ▪ Ruby on Rails, the framework   1

2 ▪ Testing saves your bacon   25

3 ▪ Developing a real Rails application   39

4 ▪ Oh, CRUD!   84

5 ▪ Nested resources   124

6 ▪ Authentication   148

7 ▪ Basic access control   170

8 ▪ Fine-grained access control   215

9 ▪ File uploading   283

10 ▪ Tracking state   325

11 ▪ Tagging   382

12 ▪ Sending email   420

13 ▪ Deployment   448

14 ▪ Designing an API   468

15 ▪ Rack-based applications   496

contents

preface *xv*
acknowledgments *xvii*
about this book *xx*

1 Ruby on Rails, the framework 1

1.1 Ruby on Rails overview 2

Benefits 2 ▪ *Ruby gems* 3 ▪ *Common terms* 4 ▪ *Rails in the wild* 5

1.2 Developing your first application 6

Installing Rails 6 ▪ *Generating an application* 6 ▪ *Starting the application* 7 ▪ *Scaffolding* 8 ▪ *Migrations* 9 ▪ *Viewing and creating purchases* 11 ▪ *Validations* 14 ▪ *Routing* 17
Updating 18 ▪ *Deleting* 21

1.3 Summary 23

2 Testing saves your bacon 25

2.1 Using TDD and BDD to save your bacon 26

2.2 Test-driven development basics 27

Writing your first test 27 ▪ *Saving bacon* 29

2.3   Behavior-driven development basics   31
        *Introducing RSpec   31 • Writing your first spec   32 • Running
        the spec   33 • Much more bacon   34 • Expiring bacon   35*

2.4   Summary   38

3 *Developing a real Rails application   39*

3.1   First steps   41
        The application story   41 • Laying the foundations   41

3.2   Version control   42
        Getting started with GitHub   43 • Configuring your Git client   44

3.3   Application configuration   46
        The Gemfile and generators   47 • Database configuration   50

3.4   Beginning your first feature   51
        *Creating projects   52 • Defining a controller action   55
        RESTful routing   57 • Committing changes   74 • Setting a
        page title   74 • Validations   77*

3.5   Summary   83

4 *Oh, CRUD!   84*

4.1   Viewing projects   85
        Introducing Factory Girl   85 • Adding a link to a project   87

4.2   Editing projects   88
        The edit action   88 • The update action   92

4.3   Deleting projects   94

4.4   What happens when things can't be found   97
        *Visualizing the error   98 • Handling the
        ActiveRecord::RecordNotFound exception   99*

4.5   Styling the application   102
        *Installing Bootstrap   103 • Improving the page's header   104
        Improving the show view   106 • Semantic styling   107 • Using Simple
        Form   113 • Adding a navigation bar   117 • Responsive styling   120*

4.6   Summary   123

5 *Nested resources   124*

5.1   Creating tickets   124
        *Nested routing helpers   126 • Creating a tickets controller   127
        Demystifying the new action   128 • Defining a has_many
        association   129 • Creating tickets in a project   131 • Finding
        tickets scoped by project   133 • Ticket validations   135*

5.2   Viewing tickets   136

Listing tickets   138 ▪ *Culling tickets   139*

5.3   Editing tickets   141

The ticket-editing spec   141 ▪ *Adding the edit action   144*
Adding the update action   144

5.4   Deleting tickets   145

5.5   Summary   147

6   **Authentication   148**

6.1   Using Devise   149

6.2   Adding sign-up   152

6.3   Adding sign-in and sign-out   154

Adding sign-in   154 ▪ *Adding sign-out   157* ▪ *Styling the*
Devise views   159

6.4   Linking tickets to users   161

Fixing the failing four features   167

6.5   Summary   168

7   **Basic access control   170**

7.1   Turning users into admins   171

Adding the admin field to the users table   172 ▪ *Creating the first*
admin user   173

7.2   Controller namespacing   174

Generating a namespaced controller   174 ▪ *Testing a namespaced*
controller   177 ▪ *Moving functionality into the admin namespace   180*

7.3   Hiding links   187

Hiding the "New Project" link   187 ▪ *Hiding the delete link   189*

7.4   Namespace-based CRUD   191

The index action   193 ▪ *The new action   195* ▪ *The create action   196*
Creating admin users   197 ▪ *Editing users   199* ▪ *The edit and update*
actions   203 ▪ *Archiving users   205* ▪ *Ensuring that you can't archive*
yourself   210 ▪ *Preventing archived users from signing in   211*

7.5   Summary   214

8   **Fine-grained access control   215**

8.1   Project-viewing permission   216

Assigning Roles in specs   217 ▪ *Creating the Role model   219* ▪ *Setting*
up Pundit   220 ▪ *Testing the ProjectPolicy   223* ▪ *Fixing what you*
broke   227 ▪ *Handling authorization errors   230* ▪ *One more thing   232*

8.2   Project-updating permission   236

*Testing the ProjectPolicy again   236 ▪ Applying the
authorization   238 ▪ Hiding the "Edit Project" link   240*

8.3   Ticket-viewing permission   242

*Refactoring policy specs   243 ▪ Testing the TicketPolicy   246
Refactoring policies   249*

8.4   Ticket-creation permission   250

*Testing the TicketPolicy … again   250 ▪ Applying the
authorization   252*

8.5   Ticket-updating permission   256

*Testing the TicketPolicy … turbocharged   256 ▪ Implementing
controller authorization   258 ▪ Hiding the "Edit Ticket"
link   259*

8.6   Ticket-destroying permission   262

*Testing the TicketPolicy … for the final time   262 ▪ Implementing
controller authorization   264*

8.7   Ensuring authorization for all actions   266

8.8   Assigning roles to users   269

*Planning the permission screen with a feature spec   270 ▪ The roles
screen   271 ▪ Building a list of projects in a select box   271
Processing the submitted role data   278 ▪ Saving roles of new
users   280*

8.9   Summary   282

9   **File uploading   283**

9.1   Attaching a file   284

*A feature featuring files   285 ▪ Enter, stage right:
CarrierWave   286 ▪ Using CarrierWave   287 ▪ Persisting
uploads when redisplaying a form   290*

9.2   Attaching many files   293

*Testing multiple-file upload   293 ▪ Implementing multiple-file
upload   294 ▪ Using nested attributes   298*

9.3   Serving files through a controller   302

*Testing existing functionality   303 ▪ Protecting attachments   304
Showing your attachments   306 ▪ Public attachments   307
Privatizing attachments   308*

9.4   Using JavaScript   310

*JavaScript testing   310 ▪ Cleaning the database   312 ▪ Introducing
jQuery   314 ▪ Adding more files with JavaScript   316*

9.5 Responding to an asynchronous request 317

Appending new content to the form 320 ▪ *Sending parameters for an asynchronous request 322*

9.6 Summary 324

10 Tracking state 325

10.1 Leaving a comment 326

The comment form 328 ▪ *The comments controller 332*

10.2 Changing a ticket's state 342

Creating the State model 343 ▪ *Selecting states 345* ▪ *Setting a default state for a comment 352* ▪ *Seeding your app with states 352*

10.3 Tracking changes 353

Ch-ch-changes 353 ▪ *Another c-c-callback 355* ▪ *Displaying changes 356* ▪ *Styling states 358*

10.4 Managing states 361

Adding additional states 361 ▪ *Defining a default state 367 Applying the default state 371* ▪ *Setting a default state in seed states 373*

10.5 Locking down states 373

Hiding a select box 373 ▪ *Defining the change_state permission 375 Hacking a form 376* ▪ *Ignoring a parameter 378*

10.6 Summary 381

11 Tagging 382

11.1 Creating tags 384

The tag-creation feature 384 ▪ *Showing tags 386* ▪ *Defining the tags association 387* ▪ *The Tag model 387* ▪ *Displaying a ticket's tags 388*

11.2 Adding more tags 391

Adding tags through a comment 392

11.3 Tag restriction 396

Testing tag restriction 396 ▪ *Tags are allowed, for some 401*

11.4 Deleting a tag 402

Testing tag deletion 403 ▪ *Adding a link to delete the tag 404 Removing a tag from the page 408*

11.5 Finding tags 409

Testing search 409 ▪ *Searching by tags 412* ▪ *Searching by state 416* ▪ *Search, but without the search 417*

11.6 Summary 419

12 **Sending email   420**

12.1   Sending ticket notifications   421

*Automatically watching a ticket   421 ▪ Using service classes   423
Defining the watchers association   427 ▪ Introducing Action
Mailer   429 ▪ An Action Mailer template   432 ▪ Testing with
mailer specs   434*

12.2   Subscribing to updates   437

*Testing comment subscription   437 ▪ Automatically adding the
commenter to the watchers list   439 ▪ Unsubscribing from ticket
notifications   440*

12.3   Summary   446

13 **Deployment   448**

13.1   What is deployment?   449

13.2   Simple deployment with Heroku   450

Signing up   450 ▪ Provisioning an app   450

13.3   Twelve-factor apps   452

*Configuration   452 ▪ Processes   453 ▪ Combining Heroku
and S3   454*

13.4   Deploying Ticketee   457

*Fixing deployment issues   458 ▪ Fixing CarrierWave file
uploads   460 ▪ Deploying is hard   462*

13.5   Continuous deployment with Travis CI   462

Configuring Travis   462 ▪ Deployment hooks   463

13.6   Sending emails   465

13.7   Summary   467

14 **Designing an API   468**

14.1   An overview of APIs   469

A practical example   470

14.2   Using ActiveModel::Serializers   471

Getting your hands dirty   473

14.3   API authentication and authorization   476

*The API namespace   477 ▪ A small tangent on inflections   481
Getting back to your API   483*

14.4   It's not a party without … HTTParty   486

14.5   Handling errors   487

Authenticating with a blank token   488 ▪ *Permission denied   489*
Validation errors   491

14.6   A small refactoring   494

14.7   Summary   495

15 Rack-based applications   496

15.1   Building Rack applications   497

A basic Rack application   498 ▪ *Let's increase the heartbeat   499*
You're not done yet   501

15.2   Building bigger Rack applications   502

You're breaking up   503 ▪ *Running a combined Rack
application   505*

15.3   Mounting a Rack application with Rails   506

Mounting Heartbeat   507 ▪ *Introducing Sinatra   508* ▪ *The
API, by Sinatra   509* ▪ *Basic error-checking   515*

15.4   Middleware   517

Middleware in Rails   518 ▪ *Crafting middleware   519*
Using middleware   520

15.5   Summary   521

appendix A   Installation guide   523
appendix B   Why Rails?   535

index   541

preface

I came to be an author on this book back in April 2010, and then spent about a year and a half writing it from scratch while working full-time. The first edition, *Rails 3 in Action,* was published in September of 2011. It's now 2015 and the revised edition is finally here, this time focusing on Rails 4.2 instead of Rails 3.1.

During this time, many changes have come to pass in the Ruby and Rails community, with almost 40 new versions of Rails since 3.1. The way we whitelist data attributes received from the outside world has moved from the models to the controllers. The popularity of Cucumber (a staple in the first edition) has faded, and it has been replaced by RSpec and Capybara. Validation syntax has morphed. The find_by_* finders have been deprecated. And so much more.

By the time this book goes to print, Rails 5 will be due for release. Rails changes much faster than other frameworks, and with good reason—the community around it is actively evolving the best ways to write web applications. Other frameworks (or even languages, *cough* Java), evolve much more slowly. My thoughts about publishing this book, even though Rails 5 is coming soon, are these: It's worthwhile to know Rails 4 and to have a good grasp of how applications are built. This book is a good indication of where the community is in terms of getting started with Rails at this particular point in time.

Days (here and there) and nights (mostly) have gone into updating this book. Not one page has gone without review. It's our utmost pleasure to bring you a book that is up to date after such a long wait. Never did I think it would take this long between publications, but that's how things played out. "Good feels" is an apt expression to explain what it's like to finally have this book done.

So here's the book you've all been waiting for. Use it well. Capture the knowledge within its pages. Know this: This book has been used by many people to jump-start their careers in Rails, and you could be next. Skimming through these pages won't get you there, but reading it thoroughly and applying the lessons in it just might. Good luck.

RYAN BIGG

acknowledgments

This book has been a long time coming, so I would like to say thanks to you, the reader, for waiting as long as you have for this revised edition.

I'd like to thank Steve Klabnik for taking over as an author after I left the project. He got the book a long way toward being compatible with Rails 4, and without his efforts this would have taken even longer to do. Thanks to my other coauthor, Rebecca Skinner, for joining the project and helping tremendously with updating the book. Rebecca rewrote at least three chapters and has pored over the others for many hours to make this book as good as it can be.

Along with Rebecca, special mention goes to Justin Lane and Ivan Polchenko, who put in an excellent effort on reviewing this book. They showed great dedication by providing feedback nearly every day on IRC or by email.

We'd also like to thank the other reviewers who volunteered to help out with the book: Andrew Grimm, Andrew Hoffman, Andy Henson, Ben Woodall, Bredan Murtagh, Cory Simmons, Dana Jones, D. Deryl Downey, Eduardo Bautista, Jimmy Beaudoin, Harry Moreno, Paulo Toro, Sushruth Sivaramakrishnan, Johnneylee Jack Rollins, Tamara Temple, David Workman, and Yaw Boakye. These reviewers span the globe: America, Australia, India, the UK, and Ghana. To be able to collaborate with such a diverse group of people is fantastic.

The creators of the tools that we use to publish books also deserve a mention: The wonderful people at GitHub, for providing a service that lets people worldwide collaborate with ease on projects such as these. Stuart Rackham, the creator of AsciiDoc, for proving that there's a better way to write books than in Microsoft Word,

XML, or Markdown. Dan Allen, for writing Asciidoctor, which we used to compile the HTML and PDF versions of the book that we shared with our reviewers.

Thanks to everyone at Manning, from my development editor Susan Conant to technical editor Steven Jenkins to technical proofreader Doug Warren to everyone on the production team to the marketing folks—and to many more who worked behind the scenes.

Also thanks to the following peer reviewers who read the manuscript at various stages of its development: Alex Perucchini, Michele Bursi, Damien White, Eddie Welker, Gavin Whyte, Greg Helton, Jared Hirsch, Justin Wiley, Lee Allen, Mike Gehard, Nathan Bean, Paul Hollyer, Robert O'Connor, Steve Robertson, William E. Wheeler, and William Ko. Your comments and insights made this a better book!

Finally, I thank my wife, Sharon, for putting up with all the time that I've spent on this book, *obsessing* about this book, and so on. Thanks for being as wonderful as you are, my love.

RYAN BIGG

I can say with confidence that this book, much like *Rails 3 in Action,* would not exist without the hard, tireless work of Ryan Bigg. It was Ryan's idea to focus both books around real-world testing from the ground up, and it makes them the best books for Rails practitioners that teach Rails the way professional Rails developers do it.

Ever since Merb was merged with Rails, I have had the benefit of not insignificant support from friends and family, who helped keep me on course in the long process that eventually delivered Rails 3.0, and then went beyond. I want to especially call out Aaron Patterson, José Valim, Santiago Pastorino, and Xavier Noria, who stepped up and brought life back to a community that was starting to show signs of age. And Carl Lerche, who helped me keep focus on doing things right, even when it was tempting not to.

Finally, I would be remiss if I didn't thank my wife, Leah, who has been there for me through the amazing trajectory of my development career, through good times and bad. Without her, I would have given up long ago.

YEHUDA KATZ

I should know better than to give estimates.

When I first started to work on this book, I thought updating it would take me three months. Oh, how foolish I was! In the end, I worked hard for about eighteen, I think. I don't want to look back at that calendar!

After this book chewed me up and spit me out, Ryan and Rebecca came on and took it over the finish line. I'm deeply indebted to them for helping pull me out of the quicksand.

I'd like to thank everyone who gave me support during that time. My partners, friends, Twitter followers, those who gave me feedback and encouragement, and everyone who bought an advance copy, even though I kept repeating "It's almost done, I swear." Writing a book is a family affair, and I'm lucky enough to have a large, geographically distributed family.

STEVE KLABNIK

Wow, we've reached the end of this journey. This has been an amazing experience, from start to end.

I would like to thank all of you, the readers, who have entrusted us with teaching them about this awesome, awesome framework. While it's a little warty in parts, I truly believe it's a masterpiece of a framework that's easy to extend, easy to customize, and easy to write powerful web applications in. You won't regret taking the time to learn the framework, and I sincerely hope you won't regret spending the time to read this book.

I'd like to thank Ryan Bigg for giving me the opportunity to contribute to this book. Initially I was only here to support him and do a bit of technical proofreading; he encouraged me to help out more, change the parts I didn't like, make the book better, and he supported me throughout the entire process.

Thanks also to everyone at Manning who worked with me during development, review, and production, especially Susan Conant, Katie Tennant, Kevin Sullivan, Janet Vail, and Mary Piergies.

But most importantly, thanks to the man who encourages me to follow my dreams, and aim to accomplish things I never thought possible but always wanted to do. Thuc, this is for you.

Well, it's for the boys too. But mostly for you.

REBECCA SKINNER

about this book

Ruby on Rails is a leading web application framework built on top of the fantastic Ruby programming language. Both the language and the framework place a strong emphasis on conforming to the principle of least surprise and getting out of the way of the developers using it.

Ruby on Rails has been growing at a rapid pace, with large internet companies such as Yellow Pages and Groupon using it for their core functionality. The latest release of Rails, version 4.2, includes a set of changes that improves the already brilliant framework constructed over the past 11 years. The fantastic community around the framework has been growing at a similar pace.

This book is designed to take you through developing a full-featured Rails application from step one, showing you exactly how professionals in the real world are developing applications right now.

Who should read this book

This book is primarily for those who are looking to work with the Ruby on Rails framework and who have some prior experience with Ruby, although that's not entirely necessary. The chapters become more advanced as you go along, and they provide a smooth learning curve to teach you how Rails applications are built.

If you're looking for a book that teaches you the same practices that are used in the real world, then this is the book you're looking for.

What's new in the revised edition

Wow, 11 years of Rails. That's a long time in software!

There have been a lot changes in the Ruby and Rails community over this time. There have been almost 40 new versions of Rails since 3.1—when the last edition of this book was published—and a lot has changed in that time. The way we whitelist data attributes received from the outside world has moved from the models to the controllers (attr_accessible versus strong parameters). The popularity of Cucumber (a staple in the first edition) has faded, and it has been replaced by RSpec and Capybara. Validation syntax has morphed. The find_by_* finders have been deprecated. And so much more.

You can find out what's changed since the first edition by reading all the release notes from 3.2 (http://guides.rubyonrails.org/3_2_release_notes.html), 4.0 (http://guides.rubyonrails.org/4_0_release_notes.html), 4.1 (http://guides.rubyonrails.org/4_1_release_notes.html), and 4.2 (http://guides.rubyonrails.org/4_2_release_notes.html).

Creating a revised edition of a Rails book is not just a matter of fixing up typos, images, and other things. It almost requires an entire rewrite of the whole thing. In fact, we rewrote chapters 6, 7, 8, and most of 9 for this book. Other chapters received less extensive touchups. Everything has been pored over and vetted by authors and volunteer reviewers.

We have spent hundreds of hours updating this book, all just for you. We hope you like it.

Roadmap

Chapter 1 introduces the Ruby on Rails framework and shows how you can develop the beginnings of an application.

Chapter 2 shows off test-driven development and behavior-driven development, two core concepts that you'll use throughout the remainder of this book and that can be applied instantly to any Ruby and Rails code you may write in the future. By testing the code you write, you can be assured that it's always working.

Chapters 3 and 4 discuss the application you'll develop in this book (Ticketee—a project-management app for issue-tracking tickets) and delve into the core concepts of a Rails application. They also look at developing the first core features of the Ticketee application.

Chapter 5 introduces nested resources, building on top of the features developed in the previous two chapters.

Chapter 6 introduces authentication and uses the Devise gem to implement features such as requiring users to sign in to the application before they can perform certain tasks.

Chapter 7 builds on the work in chapter 6 by adding new areas of the application that are accessible only to users with a certain flag set in the database. You'll also use namespaces for the first time.

Chapter 8 builds on the basic authorization created in chapter 7, fleshing it out into something neater and more fine-grained.

In chapter 9 you'll learn about file uploading using the CarrierWave gem. You'll also learn about testing parts of your application that use JavaScript, and about CoffeeScript, a neater language that compiles down to JavaScript.

Chapter 10 builds not one but two new features for the application, adding the ability to comment on a ticket as well as track the ticket's lifecycle through varying states. You'll also use the lessons you learned in chapter 8 about fine-grained access control.

In chapter 11 you'll add a feature that lets users assign tags to tickets so they can be easily grouped. You'll also add a feature to allow users to search for tickets matching a certain state, tag, or both.

Chapter 12 begins our foray into dealing with email in a Rails application. You'll see how Rails makes it easy to send email using a part of its framework called ActionMailer.

Chapter 13 involves deploying the application to Heroku, a well-established hosting provider that offers a free service. This chapter also introduces a CI service called Travis CI, which will run the tests for the application and deploy the application to Heroku if all the tests are passing.

Chapter 14 covers designing parts of an API for Ticketee so that other applications can interact with the application that you've built.

Chapter 15 shows how to use Rack-based applications to serve requests without having to use Rails at all, and also how to combine these applications within your Rails applications.

Code conventions and downloads

Code conventions in the book follow the style of other Manning books in the *In Action* series. All code in listings and in text appears in a `monospaced font like this` to differentiate it from ordinary text. In some cases, the original source code has been reformatted to fit on the pages. In general, the original code was written with page-width limitations in mind, but sometimes you may find a slight formatting difference between the code in the book and that provided in the source download. In a few rare cases, where long lines could not be reformatted without changing their meaning, the book listings contain line-continuation markers that look like this ➥. Code annotations accompany many of the listings, highlighting important concepts. In many cases, numbered bullets link to explanations that follow in the text.

Source code for all the working examples in this book is available for download from the publisher's website at www.manning.com/rails-4-in-action.

Author Online

The purchase of *Rails 4 in Action* includes free access to a private forum run by Manning Publications where you can make comments about the book, ask technical questions, and receive help from the authors and other users. To access and subscribe to the forum, point your browser to www.manning.com/rails-4-in-action, and click the Author Online link. This page provides information on how to get on the forum once you are registered, what kind of help is available, and the rules of conduct in the forum.

Manning's commitment to our readers is to provide a venue where a meaningful dialogue between individual readers and between readers and the authors can take place. It's not a commitment to any specific amount of participation on the part of the authors, whose contribution to the book's forum remains voluntary (and unpaid). We suggest you try asking the authors some challenging questions, lest their interest stray!

The Author Online forum and the archives of previous discussions will be accessible from the publisher's website as long as the book is in print.

About the cover illustration

The figure on the cover of *Rails 4 in Action* is captioned "A Soldier." The illustration is taken from a nineteenth-century edition of Sylvain Maréchal's four-volume compendium of regional and military dress customs published in France. Each illustration is finely drawn and colored by hand. The rich variety of Maréchal's collection reminds us vividly of how culturally apart the world's towns and regions were just 200 years ago. Isolated from each other, people spoke different dialects and languages. In the streets or in the countryside, it was easy to identify where they lived and what their trade or station in life was just by their dress.

Dress codes have changed since then, and the diversity by region, so rich at the time, has faded away. It is now hard to tell apart the inhabitants of different continents, let alone different towns or regions. Perhaps we have traded cultural diversity for a more varied personal life—certainly for a more varied and fast-paced technological life.

At a time when it is hard to tell one computer book from another, Manning celebrates the inventiveness and initiative of the computer business with book covers based on the rich diversity of regional life of two centuries ago, brought back to life by Maréchal's pictures.

Ruby on Rails,
the framework

1

This chapter covers

- Introducing Ruby on Rails
- Benefits of Rails
- Developing an example Rails application

Welcome aboard! It's great to have you with us on this journey through the world of Ruby on Rails. Ruby on Rails is known as a powerful web framework that helps developers rapidly build modern web applications. In particular, it provides lots of niceties to help you in your quest to develop a full-featured, real-world application, and be happy doing it. Great developers are happy developers.

If you're wondering who uses Rails, there are plenty of companies that do: Twitter, Hulu, and Urban Dictionary, just to name a few. This chapter will teach you how to build a very small and simple application, right after we go through a brief description of what Ruby on Rails actually *is*. Within the first couple of chapters, you'll have the solid foundations for an application, and you'll build on those throughout the rest of the book.

1.1   Ruby on Rails overview

Ruby on Rails is a framework built on the Ruby language—hence the name *Ruby on Rails*. The Ruby language was created back in 1993 by 松本行弘 (Yukihiro "Matz" Matsumoto) of Japan and was released to the general public in 1995. Since then, it has earned both a reputation and an enthusiastic following for its clean design, elegant syntax, and wide selection of tools available in the standard library and via a package management system called *RubyGems*. It also has a worldwide community and many active contributors continuously improving the language and the ecosystem around it. We're not going to go into great depth about the Ruby language in this book though, because we'd rather talk about Ruby on Rails.

> **RUBY LANGUAGE**   For a full treatment of the Ruby language, we highly recommend *The Well-Grounded Rubyist* by David A. Black (Manning, 2014).

The foundation for Ruby on Rails was created during 2004 when David Heinemeier Hansson was developing an application called Basecamp. For his next project, the foundational code used for Basecamp was abstracted out into what we know today as Ruby on Rails, released under the MIT License (http://en.wikipedia.org/wiki/MIT_License).

Since then, Ruby on Rails has quickly progressed to become one of the leading web development frameworks. This is in no small part due to the large community surrounding it, contributing everything from documentation to bug fixes to new features for the framework.

This book is written for version 4.2 of the framework, which is the latest version of Rails. If you've used Rails 3.2, you'll find that much feels the same, but Rails has learned some new tricks as well.

> **RAILS VERSION DIFFERENCES**   The upgrade guides and release notes provide a great overview of the new features, bug fixes, and other changes in each major and minor version of Rails. They can be found under "Release Notes" on the RailsGuides page: http://guides.rubyonrails.org/.

1.1.1   Benefits

Ruby on Rails allows for the rapid development of applications by using a concept known as *convention over configuration*. A new Ruby on Rails application is created by running the application generator, which creates a standard directory structure and the files that act as a base for every Ruby on Rails application. These files and directories provide categorization for pieces of your code, such as the app/models directory for containing files that interact with the database and the app/assets directory for assets such as stylesheets, JavaScript files, and images. Because all of this is already there, you won't be spending your time configuring the way your application is laid out. It's done for you.

How rapidly can you develop a Ruby on Rails application? Take the annual Rails Rumble event. This event brings together small teams of one to four developers around the world to develop Ruby on Rails[1] applications in a 48-hour period. Using

Rails, these teams deliver amazing web applications in just two days.[2] Another great example of rapid development of a Rails application is the 20-minute blog screencast recorded by Yehuda Katz (http://vimeo.com/10732081). This screencast takes you from having nothing at all to having a basic blogging and commenting system.

Once learned, Ruby on Rails affords you a level of productivity unheard of in other web frameworks, because every Ruby on Rails application starts out the same way. The similarity between the applications is so close that the paradigm shift between different Rails applications isn't tremendous. If and when you jump between Rails applications, you don't have to relearn how it all connects—it's mostly the same. The Rails ecosystem may seem daunting at first, but Rails conventions allow even the new to seem familiar very quickly, smoothing the learning curve substantially.

1.1.2 Ruby gems

The core features of Rails are split up into many different libraries, such as *Active Record, Active Support, Action Mailer,* and *Action Pack.* These are called *Ruby gems,* or *gems* for short. These gems provide a wide range of methods and classes that help you develop your applications. They eliminate the need for you to perform boring, repetitive tasks—such as coding how your application hooks into your database—and let you get right down to writing valuable code for your business.

> **GEM VERSIONS** The libraries that make up Rails share the same version number as Rails, which means that when you're using Rails 4.2, you're using the 4.2 version of the sub-gems. This is helpful to know when you upgrade Rails, because the version number of the installed gems should be the same as the version number of Rails.

Ever wished for a built-in way of writing automated tests for your web application? Ruby on Rails has you covered with *MiniTest,* which is part of Ruby's standard library. It's incredibly easy to write automated test code for your application, as you'll see throughout this book. Testing your code saves your bacon in the long term, and that's a fantastic thing. We'll touch on MiniTest in the next chapter before moving on to RSpec, which is the testing framework preferred over MiniTest by the majority of the community, and is a little easier on the eyes, too.

In addition to testing frameworks, the Ruby community has produced many high-quality gems for use in your day-to-day development with Ruby on Rails. Some of these libraries add functionality to Ruby on Rails; others provide ways to turn alternative markup languages such as Markdown (see the redcarpet gem at https://rubygems.org/gems/redcarpet) and Textile (see the RedCloth gem at https://rubygems.org/gems/RedCloth) into HTML. Usually, if you can think of it, there's a gem out there that will help you do it.

---

[1] And now other Ruby-based web frameworks, such as Sinatra.

[2] To see an example of what's come out of previous Rails Rumbles, take a look at the alumni archive: http://railsrumble.com/entries/winners.

Noticing a common pattern yet? Probably. As you can see, Ruby on Rails (and the great community surrounding it) provides code that performs the trivial application tasks for you, from setting up the foundations of your application to handling the delivery of email. The time you save with all of these libraries is immense! And because the code is open source, you don't have to go to a specific vendor to get support. Anyone who knows Ruby will help you if you're stuck. Just ask.

1.1.3   Common terms

You'll hear a few common Ruby on Rails terms quite often. This section explains what they mean and how they relate to a Rails application.

MVC

The *model-view-controller* (MVC) paradigm isn't unique to Ruby on Rails, but it provides much of the core foundation for a Ruby on Rails application. This paradigm is designed to keep the logically different parts of the application separate while providing a way for data to flow between them.

In applications that don't use MVC, the directory structure and how the different parts connect to each other are commonly left up to the original developer. Generally, this is a bad idea because different people have different opinions about where things should go. In Rails, a specific directory structure encourages developers to conform to the same layout, putting all the major parts of the application inside an app directory.

This app directory has three main subdirectories: models, controllers, and views:

- *Models* contain the *domain logic* of your application. This logic dictates how the records in your database are retrieved, validated, or manipulated. In Rails applications, models define the code that interacts with the database's tables to retrieve and set information in them. Domain logic also includes things such as validations or particular actions to be performed on the data.

- *Controllers* interact with the models to gather information to send to the view. They're the layer between the user and the database. They call methods on the model classes, which can return single objects representing rows in the database or collections (arrays) of these objects. Controllers then make these objects available to the view through instance variables. Controllers are also used for permission checking, such as ensuring that only users who have special permission to perform certain actions can perform those actions, and users without that permission can't.

- *Views* display the information gathered by the controller, by referencing the instance variables set there, in a developer-friendly manner. In Ruby on Rails, this display is done by default with a templating language known as *Embedded Ruby* (ERB). ERB allows you to embed Ruby into any kind of file you wish. This template is then preprocessed on the server side into the output that's shown to the user.

The assets, helpers, and mailers directories aren't part of the MVC paradigm, but they're also important parts of Rails:

- The *assets* directory is for the static assets of the application, such as JavaScript files, images, and Cascading Style Sheets (CSS), for making the application look pretty. We'll look more closely at this in chapters 3 and 4.
- The *helpers* directory is a place to put Ruby code (specifically, modules) that provide helper methods for just the views. These helper methods can help with complex formatting that would otherwise be messy in the view or is used in more than one place.
- Finally, the *mailers* directory is a home for the classes of your application that deal with sending email. In previous versions of Rails, these classes were grouped with models, but they have since been given their own home. We'll look at them in chapter 12.

REST

MVC in Rails is aided by *Representational State Transfer* (REST; see http://en.wikipedia.org/wiki/Representational_state_transfer for more information). REST is the convention for *routing* in Rails. When something adheres to this convention, it's said to be *RESTful.* Routing in Rails refers to how requests are routed within the application—how URLs map to the controller actions that should process them. You'll benefit greatly by adhering to these conventions, because Rails provides a lot of functionality around RESTful routing, such as determining where a form can submit data.

1.1.4 *Rails in the wild*

One of the best-known sites that runs Ruby on Rails is GitHub. GitHub is a hosting service for Git repositories. The site was launched in February 2008 and is now the leading Git web-hosting site. GitHub's massive growth was in part due to the Ruby on Rails community quickly adopting it as their de facto repository hosting site. Now GitHub is home to over a million repositories for just about every programming language on the planet. It's not exclusive to programming languages, either; if it can go in a Git repository, it can go on GitHub. As a matter of fact, this book and its source code are kept on GitHub!

You don't have to build huge applications with Rails, either. There's a Rails application that was built for the specific purpose of allowing people to review the previous edition of this book, and it was just over 2,000 lines of code. This application allowed reviewers during the writing of the book to view the book's chapters and leave notes on each element, leading to a better book overall.

Now that you know what other people have accomplished with Ruby on Rails, it's time to dive into creating your own application.

1.2   Developing your first application

We covered the theory behind Rails and showed how quickly and easily you can develop an application. Now it's your turn to get an application going. This will be a simple application that can be used to track items that have been purchased: it will track the name and the price for each item.

First you'll learn how to install Rails and use the scaffold generator that comes with it.

1.2.1   Installing Rails

To get started, you must have these three things installed:

- Ruby
- RubyGems
- Rails

If you're on a UNIX-based system (Linux or Mac), we recommend that you use ruby-install (http://github.com/postmodern/ruby-install) to install Ruby and RubyGems. For Windows, we recommend the RubyInstaller application (http://rubyinstaller.org). There's a complete installation guide for Ruby and Rails on Mac OS X, Linux, and Windows in appendix A.

Before proceeding, let's check that you have everything. Type these commands, and check out the responses:

```
$ ruby -v
ruby 2.2.1p85 (2015-02-26 revision 49769) [x86_64-linux]
$ gem -v
2.4.6
$ rails -v
Rails 4.2.0
```

If you see something that looks close to this, you're good to go! You might see [x86_64-darwin14] instead of [x86_64-linux], or a slightly different patch (p number), but that's okay. These particular values are the ones we're using right now and we've tested everything in the book against them; as long as you have Ruby 2.1 or later, Rails 4.2 or later, and RubyGems 2.2 or later, everything should be fine.

If you don't get these answers, or you get some sort of error message, please be sure to complete this setup before you try to move on; you can't just ignore errors with this process. Certain gems (and Rails itself) only support particular versions of Ruby, so if you don't get this right, things won't work.

1.2.2   Generating an application

Now that Rails is installed, to generate an application, you run the `rails` command and pass it the `new` argument and the name of the application you want to generate: `things_i_bought`. When you run this command, it creates a new directory called things_i_bought, which is where all your application's code will go.

Don't use reserved words for application naming

You can call your application almost anything you wish, but it can't be given a name that's a reserved word in Ruby or Rails. For example, you wouldn't call your application *rails*, because the application class would be called `Rails`, and that would clash with the `Rails` constant within the framework. Names like *test* are also forbidden.

When you use an invalid application name, you'll see an error like one of these:

```
$ rails new rails
Invalid application name rails, constant Rails is already in use.
Please choose another application name.

$ rails new test
Invalid application name test. Please give a name which does not match
one of the reserved rails words.
```

The application you'll generate will be able to record purchases you've made. You can generate it using this command:

```
$ rails new things_i_bought
```

The output from this command may seem a bit overwhelming at first, but rest assured, it's for your own good. All the directories and files generated provide the building blocks for your application, and you'll get to know each of them as we progress. For now, you'll learn by doing, which is the best way. Let's get rolling.

1.2.3 Starting the application

To get the server running, you must first change into the newly created application's directory and then start the application server:

```
$ cd things_i_bought
$ rails server
```

The rails server command (or `rails s`, for short) starts a web server on your local address on port 3000 using a Ruby standard library web server known as WEBrick. It will say "starting in development on http://localhost:3000", which indicates that the server will be available on port 3000 on the loopback network interface of this machine. To connect to this server, go to http://localhost:3000 in your favorite browser. You'll see the Welcome Aboard page, which is famous in Rails (see figure 1.1).

On the right side of the Welcome Aboard page are four links to more documentation for Rails and Ruby. The first link takes you to the official Rails Guides page, which will give you great guidance that complements the information in this book. The second link takes you to the Rails API, where you can look up the documentation for classes and methods in Ruby. The final two links take you to documentation about Ruby itself.

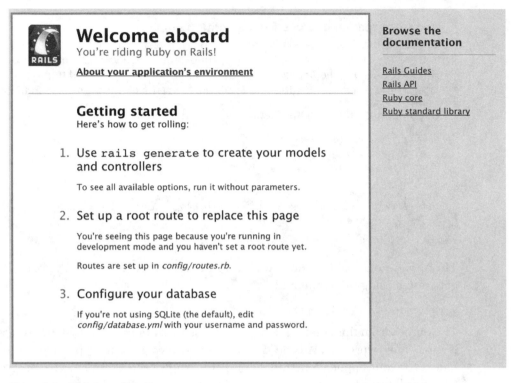

Figure 1.1   Welcome aboard!

If you click the About Your Application's Environment link, you'll find your Ruby, RubyGems, Ruby on Rails, and Rack versions and other environmental data. One of the things to note here is that the output for Environment is "development." Rails provides three environments for running your application: *development*, *test*, and *production*. How your application functions can depend on the environment in which it's running. For example, in the development environment, classes aren't cached, so if you make a change to a class when running an application in development mode, you don't need to restart the server. The same change in the production environment would require a restart.

1.2.4   *Scaffolding*

To get started with this Rails application, you can generate a *scaffold*. Scaffolds in Rails provide a lot of basic functionality and are generally used as temporary structures for getting started, rather than for full-scale development. Generate a scaffold by running this command:

```
$ rails generate scaffold purchase name:string cost:decimal
```

When you used the `rails` command earlier, it generated an entire Rails application. You can use this command within an application to generate a specific part of the application by passing the generate argument to the rails command, followed by what it is you want to generate. You can also use rails g as a shortcut for rails generate.

The scaffold command generates a model, a controller, views, and tests based on the name passed after scaffold in this command. These are the three important parts needed for your purchase tracking. The model provides a way to interact with a database; the controller interacts with the model to retrieve and format its information and defines different actions to be performed on this data; and the views are rendered by the controller and display the information collected within them.

Everything after the name for the scaffold defines the *fields* for the database table and the *attributes* for the objects of this scaffold. Here you tell Rails that the table for your purchase scaffold will contain name and cost fields, which are a string and a decimal, respectively.[3] To create this table, the scaffold generator generates what's known as a *migration*. Let's look at what migrations are.

1.2.5 Migrations

Migrations are used in Rails as a form of version control for the database, providing a way to implement incremental changes to the database schema. They're usually created along with a model or by running the migration generator. Each migration is timestamped right down to the second, which provides you (and anybody else developing the application with you) an accurate timeline of your database. When two developers are working on separate features of an application and both generate a new migration, this timestamp will stop them from clashing.

Let's open the only file in db/migrate now and see what it does. Its contents are shown in the following listing.

Listing 1.1   db/migrate/[date]_create_purchases.rb

```
class CreatePurchases < ActiveRecord::Migration
  def change
    create_table :purchases do |t|
      t.string :name
      t.decimal :cost

      t.timestamps null: false
    end
  end
end
```

Migrations are Ruby classes that inherit from ActiveRecord::Migration. Inside the class, one method is defined: the change method.

Inside the change method, you use database-agnostic commands to create a table. When this migration is run forward, it will create a table called purchases with a name

---

[3] Alternatively, you can store the amount in cents as an integer and then do the conversion back to a full dollar amount. For this example, we're using decimal because it's easier to not have to define the conversion. It's worth noting that you shouldn't use a float to store monetary amounts, because it can lead to incorrect rounding errors.

column that's a string, a `cost` column that's a decimal, and two timestamp fields. These timestamp fields are called `created_at` and `updated_at`, and are automatically set to the current time when a record is created or updated, respectively. This feature is built into Active Record. If there are fields present with these names (or `created_on` and `updated_on`), they'll be automatically updated when necessary.

When the migration is reverted, Rails will know how to undo it because it's a simple table creation. The opposite of creating a table is to drop that table from the database. If the migration was more complex than this, you'd need to split it into two methods—one called up and one called `down`—that would tell Rails what to do in both cases. Rails is usually smart enough to figure out what you want to do, but sometimes it's not clear and you'll need to be explicit. You'll see examples of this in later chapters.

RUNNING THE MIGRATION
To run the migration, type this command into the console:

```
$ bundle exec rake db:migrate
```

Because this is your first time running migrations in your Rails application, and because you're using a SQLite3 database, Rails first creates the database in a new file at db/development.sqlite3 and then creates the purchases table inside that. When you run `bundle exec rake db:migrate`, it doesn't just run the `change` method from the latest migration, but runs any migration that hasn't yet been run, allowing you to run multiple migrations sequentially.

Your application is, by default, already set up to talk to this new database, so you don't need to change anything. If you ever wanted to roll back this migration, you'd use `bundle exec rake db:rollback`, which rolls back the latest migration by running the `down` method of the migration (or reverses the steps taken in the `change` method, if possible).

> **ROLLING BACK MULTIPLE MIGRATIONS** If you want to roll back more than one migration, use the `bundle exec rake db:rollback STEP=3` command, which rolls back the three most recent migrations.

Rails keeps track of the last migration that was run by storing it using this line in the db/schema.rb file:

```
ActiveRecord::Schema.define(version: [timestamp]) do
```

This version should match the prefix of the migration you just created, where `[time-stamp]` in this example is an actual timestamp formatted like `YYYYmmddHHMMSS`. Rails uses this value to know what migration it's up to. The remaining content of this file shows the combined state of all the migrations to this point. This file can be used to restore the last known state of your database if you run the `bundle exec rake db:schema:load` command.

You now have a database set up with a purchases table in it. Let's look at how you can add rows to it through your application.

1.2.6 *Viewing and creating purchases*

Ensure that your Rails server is still running, or start a new one by running rails s or rails server again. Start your browser now, and go to http://localhost:3000/purchases. You'll see the scaffolded screen for purchases, as shown in figure 1.2.

No purchases are listed yet, so you can add a new purchase by clicking New Purchase.

In figure 1.3, you'll see two inputs for the fields you generated.

This page is the result of rendering the new action in the PurchasesController controller. What you see on the page comes from the view located at app/views/purchases/new.html.erb, and it looks like the following listing.

Listing Purchases

Name Cost

New Purchase

Figure 1.2   Purchases

New Purchase

Name

Cost

Create Purchase

Back

Figure 1.3   A new purchase

> **Listing 1.2   app/views/purchases/new.html.erb**

```
<h1>New Purchase</h1>

<%= render 'form' %>

<%= link_to 'Back', purchases_path %>
```

This is an ERB file, which allows you to mix HTML and Ruby code to generate dynamic pages. The <%= beginning of an ERB tag indicates that the result of the code inside the tag will be output to the page. If you want the code to be evaluated but not output, you use the <% tag, like this:

```
<% some_variable = "foo" %>
```

If you were to use <%= some_variable = "foo" %> here, the some_variable variable would be set and the value output to the screen. When you use <%, the Ruby code is evaluated but not output.

The render method, when passed a string, as in this example, renders a *partial*. A partial is a separate template file that you can include in other templates to repeat similar code. We'll take a closer look at these in chapter 4.

The link_to method generates a link with the text of the first argument ("Back") and with an href attribute specified by the second argument (purchases_path), which is a routing helper that turns into the string /purchases. How this works will be explained a little later when we look at how Rails handles routing.

THE FIRST HALF OF THE FORM PARTIAL

The form partial is at app/views/purchases/_form.html.erb, and the first half of it looks like the following listing.

Listing 1.3   The first half of app/views/purchases/_form.html.erb

```erb
<%= form_for(@purchase) do |f| %>
  <% if @purchase.errors.any? %>
    <div id="error_explanation">
      <h2><%= pluralize(@purchase.errors.count, "error") %> prohibited
      ➥ this purchase from being saved:</h2>

      <ul>
      <% @purchase.errors.full_messages.each do |message| %>
        <li><%= message %></li>
      <% end %>
      </ul>
    </div>
  <% end %>
...
```

This half is responsible for defining the form by using the form_for helper. The form_for method is passed one argument—an instance variable called @purchase— and with @purchase it generates a form. This variable comes from the new action of PurchasesController, which is shown next.

Listing 1.4   The new action of PurchasesController

```ruby
def new
  @purchase = Purchase.new
end
```

The first line in this action sets up a new @purchase variable by calling the new method on the Purchase model. This initializes a new instance of the Purchase class, but doesn't create a new record in the database. The @purchase variable is then automatically passed through to the view by Rails.

So far, all this functionality is provided by Rails. You've coded nothing yourself. With the scaffold generator, you get an awful lot for free.

Going back to the app/views/purchases/_form.html.erb partial, the block for the form_for is defined between its do and the <% end %> at the end of the file. Inside this block, you check the @purchase object for any errors by using the @purchase .errors.any? method. These errors will come from the model if the object doesn't pass the validation requirements set in the model. If any errors exist, they're rendered by the content inside this if statement. Validation is a concept covered shortly.

THE SECOND HALF OF THE FORM PARTIAL

The second half of this partial looks like the following listing.

Listing 1.5   The second half of app/views/purchases/_form.html.erb

```erb
...
  <div class="field">
    <%= f.label :name %><br>
    <%= f.text_field :name %>
  </div>
```

```
<div class="field">
  <%= f.label :cost %><br>
  <%= f.text_field :cost %>
</div>
<div class="actions">
  <%= f.submit %>
</div>
<% end %>
```

Here, the f object from the form_for block is used to define labels and fields for your form. At the end of this partial, the submit method provides a dynamic Submit button.

Let's fill in this form now and click the Submit button. You should see something similar to figure 1.4. This is the result of your posting: a successful creation of a Purchase. Let's see how it got there.

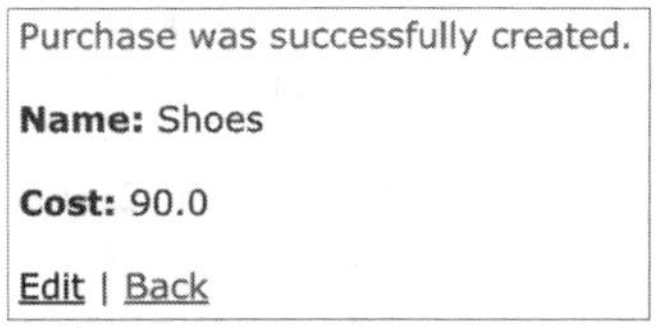

The Submit button posts the data from the form to the create action, which looks like this.

> Purchase was successfully created.
>
> **Name:** Shoes
>
> **Cost:** 90.0
>
> Edit | Back

Figure 1.4   Your first purchase

Listing 1.6   The create action of PurchasesController

```
def create
  @purchase = Purchase.new(purchase_params)

  respond_to do |format|
    if @purchase.save
      format.html { redirect_to @purchase, notice: 'Purchase was successfully
      created.' }
      format.json { render :show, status: :created, location: @purchase }
    else
      format.html { render :new }
      format.json { render json: @purchase.errors, status:
      ➥ :unprocessable_entity }
    end
  end
end
```

Here, you use the same Purchase.new method you first saw in the new action. But this time you pass it an argument of purchase_params, which is actually another method. That method calls params (short for *parameters*), which is a method that returns the parameters sent from your form in a Hash-like object. We'll talk more about why you need this little dance later (in chapter 3); this is a feature called *strong parameters*. When you pass this params hash into new, Rails sets the *attributes* (the Rails word for *fields*) to the values from the form.

Inside respond_to is an if statement that calls @purchase.save. This method *validates* the record; and if it's valid, the method saves the record to the database and returns true.

If the return value is true, the action responds by redirecting to the new @purchase object using the redirect_to method, which takes either a path or an object that it turns into a path (as seen in listing 1.6). The redirect_to method inspects the @purchase object and determines that the path required is purchase_path because it's an instance of the Purchase model. This path takes you to the show action for this controller. The :notice option passed to redirect_to sets up a *flash message*, which is a message that can be displayed on the next request. This is the green text at the top of figure 1.4.

You've seen what happens when the purchase is valid, but what happens when it's invalid? Well, it uses the render method to show the new template again. We should note here that this doesn't call the new action again, it only renders the template.

> **REDIRECTING VS. RENDERING** To call the new action again, you'd call redirect_to new_purchase_path, but that wouldn't persist the state of the @purchase object to this new request without some seriously bad hackery. By re-rendering the template, you can display information about the object if the object is invalid.

You can make the creation of the @purchase object fail by adding a validation. Let's do that now.

1.2.7 *Validations*

You can add validations to your model to ensure that the data conforms to certain rules, or that data for a certain field must be present, or that a number you enter must be greater than a certain other number. You'll write your first code for this application and implement both of these things now.

Open your Purchase model, and change the entire file to what's shown in the following listing.

Listing 1.7 app/models/purchase.rb

```
class Purchase < ActiveRecord::Base
  validates :name, presence: true
  validates :cost, numericality: { greater_than: 0 }
end
```

You use the validates method to define a validation that does what it says on the box: validates that the field is present. The other validation option, :numericality, validates that the cost attribute is a number and then, with the :greater_than option, validates that it's greater than 0.

Let's test these validations by going back to http://localhost:3000/purchases, clicking New Purchase, and clicking Create Purchase. You should see the errors shown in figure 1.5.

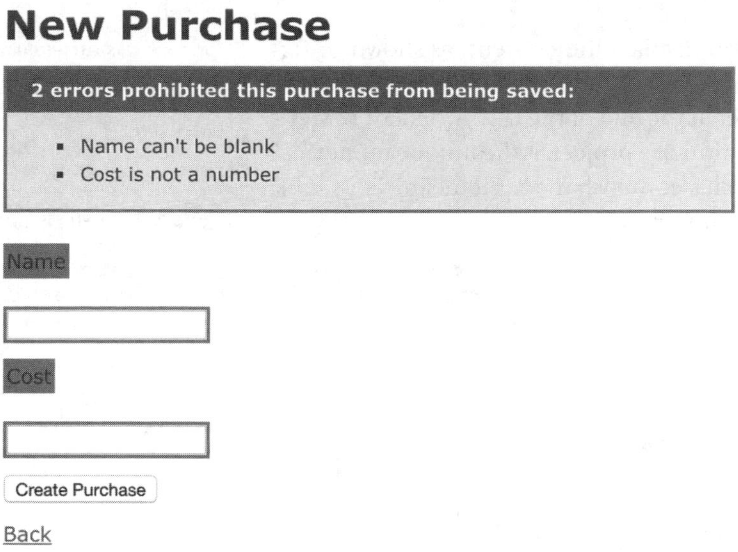

New Purchase

2 errors prohibited this purchase from being saved:

- Name can't be blank
- Cost is not a number

Name

Cost

[Create Purchase]

Back

Figure 1.5   Cost must be greater than 0

Great! Here you're told that name can't be blank and that the value you entered for cost isn't a number. Let's see what happens if you enter foo for the Name field and -100 for the Cost field, and click Create Purchase. You should get a different error for the Cost field now, as shown in figure 1.6.

Good to see! Both of your validations are working. When you change Cost to 100 and click Create Purchase, the value should be considered valid by the validations and take you to the show action. Let's look at what this particular action does now.

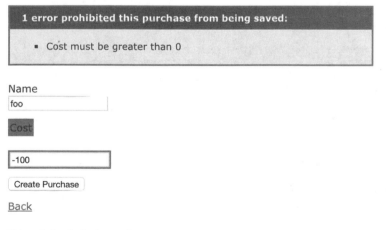

New Purchase

1 error prohibited this purchase from being saved:

- Cost must be greater than 0

Name
foo

Cost

-100

[Create Purchase]

Back

Figure 1.6   A single purchase

SHOWING OFF

The show action displays the content, as shown in figure 1.7.

The number at the end of the URL, when we're viewing the show action of a project, is the unique numerical ID for this purchase. But what does it mean? Let's look at the view for this show action.

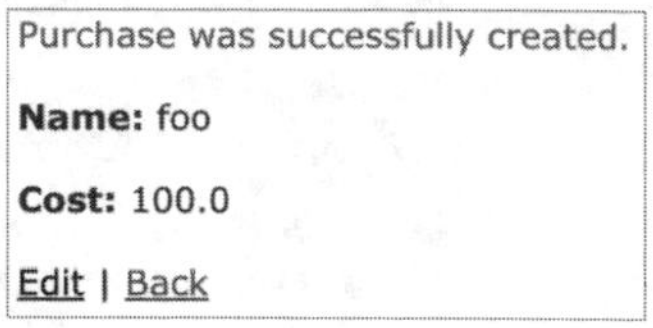

Purchase was successfully created.

Name: foo

Cost: 100.0

Edit | Back

Figure 1.7   A single purchase

Listing 1.8   app/views/purchases/show.html.erb

```erb
<p id="notice"><%= notice %></p>

<p>
  <strong>Name:</strong>
  <%= @purchase.name %>
</p>

<p>
  <strong>Cost:</strong>
  <%= @purchase.cost %>
</p>

<%= link_to 'Edit', edit_purchase_path(@purchase) %> |
<%= link_to 'Back', purchases_path %>
```

On the first line is the notice method, which displays the notice set on the redirect_to from the create action. After that, field values are displayed in p tags by calling them as methods on your @purchase object. This object is defined in the show action of PurchasesController, as shown in the following listing.

Listing 1.9   The show action of PurchasesController

```ruby
def show
end
```

Or is it? It turns out that it's not actually defined here. A before_action is defined.

Listing 1.10   The set_purchase before_action in PurchasesController

```ruby
class PurchasesController < ApplicationController

  before_action :set_purchase, only: [:show, :edit, :update, :destroy]

  ...

  # Use callbacks to share common setup or constraints between actions.
  def set_purchase
    @purchase = Purchase.find(params[:id])
  end

  ...
end
```

This code will be executed before every action given: hence the name before_action. The find method of the Purchase class is used to find the record with the ID of params[:id] and instantiate a new Purchase object from it, with params[:id] being the number on the end of the URL.

Going back to the view (listing 1.8, app/views/purchases/show.html.erb), at the end of this file is link_to, which generates a link using the first argument as the text value, and the second argument as the href for that URL. The second argument for link_to is a method: edit_purchase_path. This method is provided by a method call in config/routes.rb, which we'll look at next.

1.2.8 Routing

The config/routes.rb file of every Rails application is where the application routes are defined in succinct Ruby syntax. The methods used in this file define the pathways from requests to controllers. If you look in your config/routes.rb file, ignoring the commented-out lines for now, you'll see what's shown in the following listing.

Listing 1.11   config/routes.rb

```
Rails.application.routes.draw do
  resources :purchases
end
```

Inside the block for the draw method is the resources method. Collections of similar objects in Rails are referred to as *resources*. This method defines the routes and routing helpers (such as the edit_purchase_path method) to your purchases resources. Look at table 1.1 for a list of the helpers and their corresponding routes. You can see similar output in your terminal if you run the rake routes command inside your things_i_bought directory.

Table 1.1   Routing helpers and their routes

Helper	Route
purchases_path	/purchases
new_purchase_path	/purchases/new
edit_purchase_path	/purchases/:id/edit
purchase_path	/purchases/:id

In this table, :id can be substituted for the ID of a record. Each routing helper has an alternative version that will give you the full URL to the resource. Use the _url extension rather than _path, and you'll get a fully qualified URL such as http://localhost:3000/purchases for purchases_url.

Two of the routes in this table will act differently depending on how they're requested.

The first route, /purchases, takes you to the index action of PurchasesController if you do a GET request. GET requests are the standard type of requests for web browsers, and this is the first request you did to this application. If you send a POST request to this route, it will go to the create action of the controller. This is the case when you submit the form from the new view.

The second route that will act differently is /purchases/:id. If you do a GET request to this route, it will take you to the show action. If you do a PATCH request, it will take you to the update action. Or you can do a DELETE request, which will take you to the destroy action.

Let's go to http://localhost:3000/purchases/new now and look at the source of the page. The beginning tag for your form should look like this.

Listing 1.12　HTML source of app/views/purchases/new.html.erb

```
<form accept-charset="UTF-8" action="/purchases"
  class="new_purchase" id="new_purchase" method="post">
```

The two attributes to note here are action and method. The action attribute dictates the URL to where this form goes, and method tells the form what kind of HTTP request to make.

How was this tag rendered in the first place? Well, as you saw before, the app/views/purchases/new.html.erb template uses the form partial from app/views/purchases/_form.html.erb, which contains this as the first line:

```
<%= form_for(@purchase) do |f| %>
```

This one simple line generates that form tag. When we look at the edit action shortly, you'll see that the output of this tag is different, and you'll learn why.

The other route that responds differently is /purchases/:id, which acts in one of three ways. You already saw the first way: it's the show action to which you're redirected (via a GET request) after you create a purchase. The second of the three ways is when you update a record, which we'll look at now.

1.2.9　Updating

Let's change the cost of the foo purchase now. Perhaps it only cost 10. To change it, go back to http://localhost:3000/purchases and click the "Edit" link next to the foo record. You should see a page that looks similar to the new page, as shown in figure 1.8.

This page looks similar because it reuses the app/views/purchases/_form.html.erb partial that was also used in the template for the new action. Such is the power of partials in Rails: you can use the same code for two different requests to your application.

Editing Purchase

Name

`foo`

Cost

`100.0`

[Update Purchase]

Show | Back

Figure 1.8　Editing a purchase

The template for this action is shown in the following listing.

Listing 1.13 app/views/purchases/edit.html.erb

```
<h1>Editing Purchase</h1>

<%= render 'form' %>

<%= link_to 'Show', @purchase %> |
<%= link_to 'Back', purchases_path %>
```

For this action, you're working with a preexisting object rather than a new object, which you used in the new action. This preexisting object is found by the edit action in PurchasesController, as shown here.

Listing 1.14 The edit action of PurchasesController

```
def edit
end
```

Oops: it's not here! The code to find the @purchase object is identical to what you saw earlier in the show action: it's set in before_action, which runs before the show, edit, update, and destroy actions.

Back in the view for a moment, at the bottom of it you can see two uses of link_to. The first creates a "Show" link, linking to the @purchase object, which is set up in the edit action of your controller. Clicking this link would take you to purchase_path(@purchase) or /purchases/:id. Rails will figure out where the link needs to go according to the class of the object given. Using this syntax, it will attempt to call the purchase_path method because the object has a class of Purchase, and it will pass the object along to that call, generating the URL.

> **NOTE** This syntax is exceptionally handy if you have an object and aren't sure of its type but still want to generate a link for it. For example, if you had a different kind of object called Order, and it was used instead, it would use order_path rather than purchase_path.

The second use of link_to in this view generates a "Back" link, which uses the routing helper purchases_path. It can't use an object here because it doesn't make sense to. Calling purchases_path is the easy way to go back to the index action.

Let's try filling in this form—for example, by changing the cost from 100 to 10 and clicking Update Purchase. You'll now see the show page but with a different message, as shown in figure 1.9.

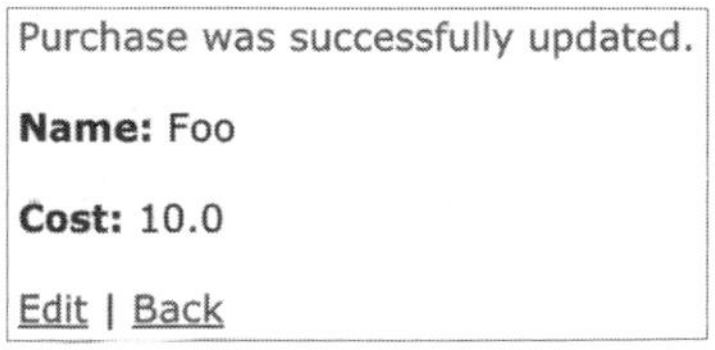

Clicking Update Purchase brought you back to the show page. How did that happen? Click the Back button on your browser, and view the source of this page, specifically the form tag and the tags directly underneath, shown in the following listing.

Purchase was successfully updated.

Name: Foo

Cost: 10.0

Edit | Back

Figure 1.9 Viewing an updated purchase

Listing 1.15 Rendered HTML for app/views/purchases/edit.html.erb

```
...
<form accept-charset="UTF-8" action="/purchases/2" class="edit_purchase"

id="edit_purchase_2" method="post">
  <input name="utf8" type="hidden" value="&#x2713;" />
  <input name="_method" type="hidden" value="patch" />
...
```

The action of this form points at /purchases/2, which is the route to the show action
in PurchasesController. You should also note two other things. The method attribute
of this form is a post, but there's also the input tag underneath.

The input tag passes through the _method parameter with the value set to patch.
Rails catches this parameter and turns the request from a POST into a PATCH. This is
the second (of three) ways /purchases/:id responds according to the method. By
making a PATCH request to this route, you're taken to the update action in Purchases-
Controller. Let's look at this next.

Listing 1.16 The update action of PurchasesController

```
def update
  respond_to do |format|
    if @purchase.update(purchase_params)
      format.html { redirect_to @purchase, notice: 'Purchase was successfully
      updated.' }
      format.json { render :show, status: :ok, location: @purchase }
    else
      format.html { render :edit }
      format.json { render json: @purchase.errors, status:
      ➥ :unprocessable_entity }
    end
  end
end
```

Just as in the show and edit actions, the @purchase object is first fetched by the call to
before_action :set_purchase. The parameters from the form are sent through in
the same fashion as they were in the create action, coming through as
purchase_params. Rather than instantiating a new object by using the new class
method, you use update on the existing @purchase object. This does what it says:
updates the attributes. What it doesn't say, though, is that it validates the attributes
and, if the attributes are valid, saves the record and returns true. If they aren't valid, it
returns false.

THE PATCH METHOD The PATCH HTTP method is implemented by Rails by
affixing a _method parameter on the form with the value of PATCH, because
the HTML specification doesn't allow the PATCH method for form elements. It
only allows GET and POST, as stated here: http://www.w3.org/TR/html401/
interact/forms.html#adef-method.

Editing Purchase

1 error prohibited this purchase from being saved:

- Name can't be blank

Name

Cost

100.0

Update Purchase

Show | Back

Figure 1.10   Update fails!

When update returns true, you're redirected back to the show action for this particular purchase by using redirect_to. If the update call returns false, you're shown the edit action's template again, just as back in the create action where you were shown the new template again. This works in the same fashion and displays errors if you enter something wrong.

Let's try editing a purchase, setting Name to blank, and then clicking Update Purchase. It should error exactly like the create method did, as shown in figure 1.10.

As you can see in this example, the validations you defined in your Purchase model take effect automatically for both the creation and updating of records.

What would happen if, rather than updating a purchase, you wanted to delete it? That's built into the scaffold, too.

1.2.10 Deleting

In Rails, *delete* is given a much more forceful name: *destroy.* This is another sensible name, because to destroy a record is to "put an end to the existence of."[4] Once this record's gone, it's gone, baby, gone.

You can destroy a record by going to http://localhost:3000/purchases and clicking the "Destroy" link shown in figure 1.11 and then clicking OK in the confirmation box that pops up.

Listing Purchases

Name	Cost			
Shoes	90.0	Show	Edit	Destroy
foo	100.0	Show	Edit	Destroy

New Purchase

Figure 1.11   Destroy!

---

[4] As defined by the Mac OS X Dictionary application.

When that record's destroyed, you're taken back to the Listing Purchases page. You'll see that the record no longer exists. You should now have only one record, as shown in figure 1.12.

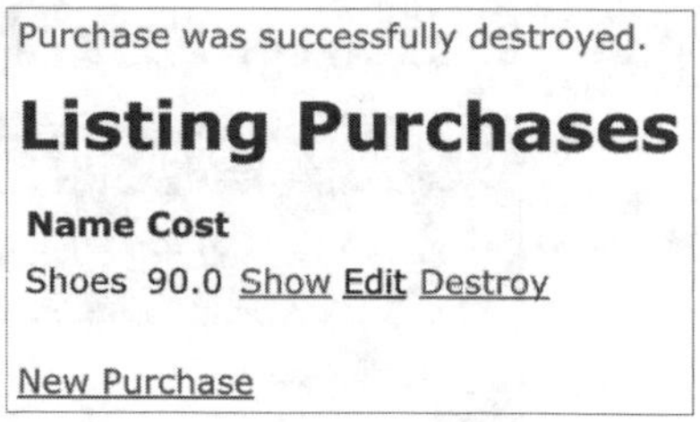

How does all this work? Let's look at the index template in the following listing to understand, specifically the part that's used to list the purchases.

Purchase was successfully destroyed.

Listing Purchases

Name Cost

Shoes 90.0 Show Edit Destroy

New Purchase

Figure 1.12 Last record standing

Listing 1.17   app/views/purchases/index.html.erb

```
<% @purchases.each do |purchase| %>
  <tr>
    <td><%= purchase.name %></td>
    <td><%= purchase.cost %></td>
    <td><%= link_to 'Show', purchase %></td>
    <td><%= link_to 'Edit', edit_purchase_path(purchase) %></td>
    <td><%= link_to 'Destroy', purchase, method: :delete, data:

{ confirm: 'Are you sure?' } %></td>
  </tr>
<% end %>
```

In this template, @purchases is a collection of all the objects from the Purchase model, and each is used to iterate over each, setting purchase as the variable used in this block.

The methods name and cost are the same methods used in app/views/purchases/show.html.erb to display the values for the fields. After these, you see the three uses of link_to.

The first link_to passes in the purchase object, which links to the show action of PurchasesController by using a route such as /purchases/:id, where :id is the ID for this purchase object.

The second link_to links to the edit action using edit_purchase_path and passes the purchase object as the argument to this method. This routing helper determines that the path is /purchases/:id/edit.

The third link_to links seemingly to the purchase object exactly like the first, but it doesn't go there. The :method option on the end of this route specifies the method :delete, which is the third and final way the /purchases/:id route can be used. If you specify :delete as the method of this link_to, Rails interprets this request as a DELETE request and takes you to the destroy action in the PurchasesController. This action is shown in the following listing.

Listing 1.18   The destroy action of PurchasesController

```
def destroy
  @purchase.destroy
  respond_to do |format|
```

```
        format.html { redirect_to purchases_url, notice: 'Purchase was
        ➡ successfully destroyed.' }
        format.json { head :no_content }
    end
end
```

This action destroys the record loaded by `before_action :set_purchase` by calling `destroy` on it, which permanently deletes the record. Then it uses `redirect_to` to take you to `purchases_url`, which is the route helper defined to take you to http://localhost:3000/purchases. Note that this action uses the `purchases_url` method rather than `purchases_path`, which generates a full URL back to the purchases listing.

That wraps up our application run-through!

1.3 Summary

In this chapter, you learned what Rails is and how to get an application started with it: the absolute bare, bare, *bare* essentials of a Rails application. But look how fast you got going! It took only a few simple commands and an entire two lines of your own code to create the bones of a Rails application. From this basic skeleton, you can keep adding bits and pieces to develop your application, and all the while you get things for free from Rails. You don't have to code the logic of what happens when Rails receives a request or specify what query to execute on your database to insert a record—Rails does it for you.

You also saw that some big-name players—such as Twitter and GitHub—use Ruby on Rails. This clearly answers the question "Is Rails ready?" Yes, it very much is. A wide range of companies have built successful websites on the Rails framework, and many more will do so in the future. Rails also has been around for a decade, and shows no signs of slowing down any time soon.

Still wondering if Ruby on Rails is right for you? Ask around. You'll hear a lot of people singing its praises. The Ruby on Rails community is passionate not only about Rails but also about community building. Events, conferences, user group meetings, and even camps are held around the world for Rails. Attend these, and discuss Ruby on Rails with the people who know about it. If you can't attend these events, you can explore the IRC channel on Freenode *#rubyonrails* and the mailing list *rubyonrails-talk* on Google Groups, not to mention Stack Overflow and a multitude of other areas on the internet where you can find experienced people and discuss what they think of Rails. Don't let this book be your only source of knowledge. There's a whole world out there, and no book could cover it all!

The best way to answer the question "What is Rails?" is to experience it for yourself. This book and your own exploration can eventually make you a Ruby on Rails expert.

When you added validations to your application earlier, you manually tested that they were working. This may seem like a good idea for now, but when the application grows beyond a couple of pages, it becomes cumbersome to manually test it. Wouldn't it be nice to have some automated way of testing your applications? Something to ensure that all the individual parts always work? Something to provide the peace of mind that you crave when you develop anything? You want to be sure that your application is continuously working with the least effort possible, right?

Well, Ruby on Rails does that too. Several testing frameworks are available for Ruby and Ruby on Rails, and in chapter 2 we'll look at the two major ones: MiniTest and RSpec.

Testing saves your bacon

2

This chapter covers

- Introducing testing approaches
- Test-driven development with MiniTest
- Behavior-driven development with RSpec

Chapter 1 presented an extremely basic layout of a Rails application and an example of using the scaffold generator. One question remains, though: how do you make your Rails applications maintainable?

> **ABOUT THE SCAFFOLD GENERATOR** We won't use the scaffold generator for the rest of the book because people tend to use it as a crutch, and it generates extraneous code. There's a thread on the rubyonrails-core mailing list where people have discussed the scaffold generator's downsides: http://mng.bz/g33u.

The answer is that you write automated tests for the application as you develop it, and you write these all the time. By writing automated tests for your application, you can quickly ensure that your application is working as intended. If you don't write tests, your alternative is to check the entire application manually every time you make a change, which is time consuming and error prone. Automated testing saves you a ton of time in the long run and leads to fewer bugs. Humans make mistakes; programs (if coded correctly) don't. We'll do it correctly from step one.[1]

---

[1] Unlike certain other books.

In the Ruby world, a huge emphasis is placed on testing, specifically on *test-driven development* (TDD) and *behavior-driven development* (BDD). This chapter covers two testing tools—MiniTest and RSpec—in a basic fashion so you can quickly learn their formats.

By learning good testing techniques now, you'll have a solid way to make sure nothing is broken when you start to write your first real Rails application. If you don't write tests, there'll be no automatic way of telling what might be going wrong in your code.

A cryptic yet true answer to the question "Why should I test?" is "Because you're human." Humans—the large majority of this book's audience—make mistakes. It's one of our favorite ways to learn. Because humans make mistakes, having a tool to inform us when we make one is helpful, isn't it? Automated testing provides a quick safety net to inform developers when they make mistakes. And by *they*, of course, we mean *you*. We want you to make as few mistakes as possible. We want you to save your bacon!

2.1 *Using TDD and BDD to save your bacon*

In addition to catching errors, TDD and BDD give you time to think through your decisions before you write any code. By first writing a test for the implementation, you are (or, at least, you should be) thinking through the implementation: the code you'll write *after* the test and how you'll make the test pass. If you find the test difficult to write, then perhaps the implementation could be improved. Unfortunately, there's no clear way to quantify the difficulty of writing a test and working through it, other than to consult with other people who are familiar with the process.

Once the test is implemented, you should go about writing some code that your test can pass. If you find yourself working backward—rewriting your test to fit a buggy implementation—it's generally best to rethink the test and scrap the implementation. Test first, code later.

TDD is a methodology consisting of writing a failing test case first (usually using a testing tool such as MiniTest), then writing the code to make the test pass, and finally refactoring the code to make it neater and tidier. This process is commonly called *red-green-refactor*. The reasons for developing code this way are twofold. First, it makes you consider how the code should be running before it's used by anybody. Second, it gives you an automated test you can run as often as you like to ensure that your code is still working as you intended. This book uses the MiniTest tool for TDD.

BDD is a methodology based on TDD. You write an automated test to check the interaction between the different parts of the codebase rather than to test that each part works independently. Two tools used for BDD when building Rails applications are RSpec and Cucumber. This book relies heavily on RSpec and forgoes Cucumber.

> **CUCUMBER VS. OTHER TOOLS** Cucumber was used in earlier editions of this book, but the community has drifted away from using it, as there are other tools (like Capybara, mentioned later) that provide a very similar way to test, but in a much neater, pure-Ruby syntax.

Let's begin by looking at TDD and MiniTest.

2.2 *Test-driven development basics*

Automated testing is much, much easier than manual testing. Have you ever gone through a website and manually filled in a form with specific values to make sure it conforms to your expectations? Wouldn't it be faster and easier to have the computer do this work? Yes, it would, and that's the beauty of automated testing: you won't spend your time manually testing your code, because you'll have written test code to do that for you.

On the off chance that you break something, the tests are there to tell you the what, when, how, and why of the breakage. Although tests can never be 100% guaranteed, your chances of getting this information without first having written tests are 0%. Nothing is worse than finding out through an early morning phone call from an angry customer that something is broken. Tests help prevent such scenarios by giving you and your client peace of mind. If the tests aren't broken, chances are high (although not guaranteed) that the implementation isn't either.

Sooner or later, it's likely that something in your application will break when a user attempts to perform an action you didn't consider in your tests. With a base of tests, you can easily duplicate the scenario in which the user encountered the breakage, generate your own failed test, and use this information to fix the bug. This commonly used practice is called *regression testing*.

It's valuable to have a solid base of tests in the application so you can spend time developing new features *properly*, rather than fixing the old ones you didn't do quite right. An application without tests is most likely broken in one way or another.

2.2.1 *Writing your first test*

The first testing library for Ruby was Test::Unit, which was written by Nathaniel Talbott back in 2000 and is now part of the Ruby standard library. The documentation for this library gives a fantastic overview of its purpose, as summarized by the man himself:

> *The general idea behind unit testing is that you write a test method that makes certain assertions about your code, working against a test fixture. A bunch of these test methods are bundled up into a test suite and can be run any time the developer wants. The results of a run are gathered in a test result and displayed to the user through some UI.*
>
> —Nathaniel Talbott

The UI Talbott references could be a terminal, a web page, or even a light.[2]

In Rails 4, Test::Unit has been superseded by MiniTest, which is a library of a similar style but with a more modern heritage. MiniTest is also part of the Ruby standard library.

A common practice you'll hopefully have experienced by now in the Ruby world is to let the libraries do a lot of the hard work for you. Sure, you *could* write a file yourself that loads one of your other files and runs a method and makes sure it works, but why

---

[2] Such as the one GitHub has made: http://github.com/blog/653-our-new-build-status-indicator.

do that when MiniTest already provides that functionality for such little cost? Never reinvent the wheel when somebody's done it for you.

Now you'll write a test, and you'll write the code for it later. Welcome to TDD.

TRYING OUT MINITEST

To try out MiniTest, first create a new directory called chapter_2, and in that directory make a file called example_test.rb. It's good practice to suffix your filenames with _*test* so it's obvious from the filename that it's a test file. In this file, you'll define the most basic test possible, as shown in the following listing.

Listing 2.1   chapter_2/example_test.rb

```ruby
require "minitest/autorun"

class ExampleTest < Minitest::Test
  def test_truth
    assert true
  end
end
```

To make this a MiniTest test, you begin by requiring minitest/autorun, which is part of Ruby's standard library. This provides the `Minitest::Test` class inherited from on the next line. Inheriting from this class provides the functionality to run any method defined in this class whose name begins with `test`.

To run this file, you run `ruby example_test.rb` in the terminal, from inside the chapter_2 directory. When this code completes, you'll see some output, the most relevant being the last three lines:

```
.

Finished in 0.001245s, 803.2129 runs/s, 803.2129 assertions/s.

1 runs, 1 assertions, 0 failures, 0 errors, 0 skips
```

The first line is a singular period. This is MiniTest's way of indicating that it ran a test and the test passed. If the test had failed, it would show up as an F; if it had errored, an E. The second and third lines provide statistics on what happened—specifically that there was one test and one assertion, and that nothing failed, there were no errors, and nothing was skipped. Great success!

The `assert` method in your test makes an assertion that the argument passed to it evaluates to `true`. This test passes given anything that's not `nil` or `false`. When this method fails, it fails the test and raises an exception. Go ahead and try putting 1 there instead of `true`. It still works:

```
Finished tests in 0.001071s, 933.7068 tests/s, 933.7068 assertions/s.

1 runs, 1 assertions, 0 failures, 0 errors, 0 skips
```

In the following listing, you remove the `test_` from the beginning of your method and define it as a `truth` method.

Listing 2.2 chapter_2/example_test.rb, alternate truth test

```
def truth
  assert true
end
```

When you run the test again with `ruby example_test.rb`, MiniTest tells you there were no tests specified:

```
0 runs, 0 assertions, 0 failures, 0 errors, 0 skips
```

See, no tests! Remember to always prefix MiniTest methods with `test`!

2.2.2 *Saving bacon*

Let's make this a little more complex by creating a bacon_test.rb file in the same folder and writing the test shown next.

Listing 2.3 chapter_2/bacon_test.rb

```
require "minitest/autorun"

class BaconTest < Minitest::Test
  def test_saved
    assert Bacon.saved?
  end
end
```

Of course, you want to ensure that your bacon (both the metaphorical and the crispy kinds) is always saved, and this is how you do it. If you now run the code to run this file, `ruby bacon_test.rb`, you'll get an error:

```
1) Error:
BaconTest#test_saved:
NameError: uninitialized constant BaconTest::Bacon
    bacon_test.rb:5:in `test_saved'
```

Your test is looking for a constant called `Bacon` when you call `Bacon.saved?`, and it can't find it because you haven't yet defined the constant.

For this test, the constant you want to define is a `Bacon` class, and you can define this class before or after the test. Note that in Ruby you usually must define constants and variables before you use them, but in MiniTest tests, the code is only run when MiniTest finishes evaluating it, which means you can define the `Bacon` class after the test. In the next listing, you follow the more conventional method of defining the class above the test.

Listing 2.4 chapter_2/bacon_test.rb, now with Bacon class

```
require "minitest/autorun"

class Bacon
end
```

```
class BaconTest < Minitest::Test
  def test_saved
    assert Bacon.saved?
  end
end
```

Upon rerunning the test, you get a different error:

```
1) Error:
BaconTest#test_saved:
NoMethodError: undefined method `saved?' for Bacon:Class
    bacon_test.rb:8:in `test_saved'
```

Progress! It recognizes there's now a Bacon class. But there's no saved? method for this class, so you must define one.

Listing 2.5   Bacon class in chapter_2/bacon_test.rb

```
class Bacon
  def self.saved?
    true
  end
end
```

One more run of `ruby bacon_test.rb`, and you can see that the test is now passing:

```
.

Finished tests in 0.000596s, 1677.8523 tests/s, 1677.8523 assertions/s.

1 runs, 1 assertions, 0 failures, 0 errors, 0 skips
```

Your bacon is indeed saved! Now any time you want to check whether it's saved, you can run this file. If somebody else comes along and changes that `true` value to a `false`, the test will fail:

```
F

Finished in 0.001037s, 964.3825 runs/s, 964.3825 assertions/s.

  1) Failure:
BaconTest#test_saved [bacon_test.rb:11]:
Failed assertion, no message given.
```

MiniTest reports "Failed assertion, no message given" when an assertion fails. You should probably make that error message clearer! To do so, you can specify an additional argument to the `assert` method in your test, like this:

```
def test_saved
  assert Bacon.saved?, "Our bacon was not saved :("
end
```

Now when you run the test, you get a clearer error message:

```
1) Failure:
BaconTest#test_saved [bacon_test.rb:11]:
Our bacon was not saved :(
```

And that, our friend, is the basics of TDD using MiniTest. Although we won't use this method in the book, it's handy to know about, because it establishes the basis for TDD in Ruby, in case you wish to use it in the future. MiniTest is also the default testing framework for Rails, so you may see it around in your travels.

From this point on, we'll focus on pure RSpec, which you'll use to develop your next Rails application.

2.3 *Behavior-driven development basics*

BDD is similar to TDD, but the tests for BDD are written in an easier-to-understand language so that developers and clients alike can clearly understand what's being tested. The tool you'll use for all BDD examples in this book is RSpec.

RSpec tests are written in a Ruby domain-specific language (DSL), like this:

```
RSpec.describe Bacon do
  it "is edible" do
    expect(Bacon).to be_edible
  end
end
```

The benefits of writing tests like this are that clients can understand precisely what the test is testing and then use these steps in acceptance testing; a developer can read what the feature should do and then implement it; and finally, the test can be run as an automated test. With tests written in a DSL, you have the three important elements of your business (the clients, the developers, and the code) all operating in the same language.

ACCEPTANCE TESTING *Acceptance testing* is a process whereby people follow a set of instructions to ensure that a feature is performing as intended.

RSpec is an extension of the methods already provided by MiniTest. You can even use MiniTest methods in RSpec tests if you wish. But we'll use the simpler, easier-to-understand syntax that RSpec provides.

2.3.1 *Introducing RSpec*

RSpec is a BDD tool written by Steven R. Baker and now maintained by Myron Marston and Andy Lindeman as a cleaner alternative to MiniTest. With RSpec, you write code known as *specs* that contain *examples*, which are synonymous with the *tests* you know from MiniTest. In this example, you'll define the Bacon constant and then define the edible? method on it.

Let's jump right in and install RSpec. The latest version of the gem (at writing) is 3.2.0, and you can install it by running gem install rspec -v 3.2.0. You should see something like the following output:

```
Fetching: diff-lcs-1.2.5.gem (100%)
Successfully installed diff-lcs-1.2.5
Fetching: rspec-support-3.2.2.gem (100%)
```

```
Successfully installed rspec-support-3.2.2
Fetching: rspec-mocks-3.2.1.gem (100%)
Successfully installed rspec-mocks-3.2.1
Fetching: rspec-expectations-3.2.0.gem (100%)
Successfully installed rspec-expectations-3.2.0
Fetching: rspec-core-3.2.2.gem (100%)
Successfully installed rspec-core-3.2.2
Fetching: rspec-3.2.0.gem (100%)
Successfully installed rspec-3.2.0
6 gems installed
```

You can see that the final line says the rspec gem is installed, with the version number specified after the name.

2.3.2 *Writing your first spec*

When the gem is installed, you can create a new directory called *bacon* for your tests anywhere you like; in that directory, create another directory called *spec*. If you're running a UNIX-based operating system such as Linux or Mac OS X, you can run the command mkdir -p bacon/spec to create these two directories. This code will generate a bacon directory, if it doesn't already exist, and then generate a spec directory inside it.

   In the spec directory, create a file called bacon_spec.rb. This is the file you'll use to test your currently nonexistent Bacon class. Put the code from the following listing in spec/bacon_spec.rb.

> **Listing 2.6   bacon/spec/bacon_spec.rb**

```
RSpec.describe Bacon do
  it "is edible" do
    expect(Bacon.edible?).to be(true)
  end
end
```

You use RSpec.describe to describe the behavior of the (currently undefined) Bacon class and write an example for it, declaring that Bacon is edible. The describe block contains tests (examples) that describe the behavior of bacon. In this example, whenever you call edible? on Bacon, the result should be true. expect and to serve a purpose similar to that of assert, which is to assert that the object passed to expect matches the arguments passed to to. If the outcome isn't what you say it should be, then RSpec raises an error and goes no further with that spec.

THERE'S MORE THAN ONE WAY TO WRITE A SPEC

An alternative way to write the spec would be like in the following listing.

> **Listing 2.7   An alternate way to check if Bacon is edible**

```
RSpec.describe Bacon do
  it "is edible" do
    expect(Bacon).to be_edible
  end
end
```

RSpec will internally translate the be_edible method call into edible?, and call that on Bacon. If the overall result of the Bacon.edible? statement is *truthy* (anything other than nil or false), then the spec will pass. But for now, we'll stick with the first version—it's a little less magical, and it's easier to see what's going on.

2.3.3 Running the spec

To run the spec, you run rspec spec in a terminal inside your bacon directory. You specify the spec directory as the main argument to the rspec executable so RSpec will run all the tests in that directory. This code can also take files as its arguments if you want to run tests only from those files.

When you run this spec, you'll get an uninitialized constant Bacon (NameError) error, because you haven't yet defined your Bacon constant. To define it, create another directory in your Bacon project folder called *lib*, and in this directory, create a file called *bacon.rb*. This is the file where you define the Bacon constant, a class.

Listing 2.8 bacon/lib/bacon.rb

```
class Bacon
end
```

You can now require this file in spec/bacon_spec.rb by placing the following line at the top of the file:

```
require "bacon"
```

When you run your spec again, because you told it to load bacon, RSpec will have added the lib directory to Ruby's load path on the same level as the spec directory, so it will find lib/bacon.rb for your require. By requiring the lib/bacon.rb file, you ensure that the Bacon constant is defined. The next time you run the spec, you'll get an undefined method for your new constant:

```
1) Bacon is edible
   Failure/Error: expect(Bacon.new.edible?).to be(true)
   NoMethodError:
     undefined method `edible?' for #<Bacon:0x007f2530184988>
   # ./spec/bacon_spec.rb:5:in `block (2 levels) in <top (required)>'
```

This means you need to define the edible? method on your Bacon class. Reopen lib/bacon.rb, and add this method definition to the class:

```
def self.edible?
  true
end
```

Now the entire file looks like the following listing.

Listing 2.9 bacon/lib/bacon.rb

```
class Bacon
  def self.edible?
```

```
      true
   end
end
```

By defining the method as `self.edible?`, you define it for the class. If you didn't prefix the method with `self.`, it would define the method for an instance of the class rather than for the class itself.

Running `rspec spec` now outputs a period, which indicates the test has passed. That's the first test—done.

2.3.4 *Much more bacon*

For the next test, you want to create many instances of the `Bacon` class and have the `edible?` method defined on them. To do this, open lib/bacon.rb and change the `edible?` class method to an instance method by removing the `self.` from before the method, as shown next.

> **Listing 2.10 bacon/lib/bacon.rb**

```
class Bacon
  def edible?
    true
  end
end
```

When you run `rspec spec` again, you'll get the familiar error:

```
1) Bacon is edible
   Failure/Error: expect(Bacon.edible?).to be(true)
   NoMethodError:
     undefined method `edible?' for Bacon:Class
   # ./spec/bacon_spec.rb:5:in `block (2 levels) in <top (required)>'
```

Oops! You broke a test! You should be changing the spec to suit your new ideas before changing the code! Let's reverse the changes made in lib/bacon.rb.

> **Listing 2.11 bacon/lib/bacon.rb**

```
class Bacon
  def self.edible?
    true
  end
end
```

When you run `rspec spec` again, it passes. Now let's change the spec first.

> **Listing 2.12 bacon/spec/bacon_spec.rb**

```
RSpec.describe Bacon do
  it "is edible" do
    expect(Bacon.new.edible?).to be(true)
  end
end
```

In this code, you instantiate a new object of the class rather than use the Bacon class. When you run rspec spec, it breaks once again:

```
NoMethodError:
  undefined method `edible?' for #<Bacon:0x101deff38>
```

If you remove the self. from the edible? method, your test will now pass:

```
.

Finished in 0.00167 seconds
1 example, 0 failures
```

2.3.5 Expiring bacon

You can go about breaking your test once more by adding functionality: an expired! method, which will make your bacon inedible. This method sets an instance variable on the Bacon object called @expired to true, and you can use it in your edible? method to check the bacon's status.

First you must test that this expired! method will do what you think it should do. Create another example in spec/bacon_spec.rb so that the whole file looks like the following listing.

Listing 2.13 bacon/spec/bacon_spec.rb

```ruby
require "bacon"

RSpec.describe Bacon do
  it "is edible" do
    expect(Bacon.new.edible?).to be(true)
  end

  it "can expire" do
    bacon = Bacon.new
    bacon.expired!
    expect(bacon).to_not be_edible
  end
end
```

This uses the second format of the assertion—RSpec again translates be_edible to edible? and calls bacon.edible?. But this time it's expected to return something *falsey* (either nil or false), due to the negative to_not (instead of to).

If you run rspec again, your first spec still passes, but your second one fails because you have yet to define your expired! method. Let's do that now in lib/bacon.rb.

Listing 2.14 bacon/lib/bacon.rb

```ruby
class Bacon
  def edible?
    true
  end
```

```
  def expired!
    self.expired = true
  end
end
```

By running rspec spec again, you get an undefined method error:

```
1) Bacon can expire
   Failure/Error: bacon.expired!
   NoMethodError:
     undefined method `expired=' for #<Bacon:0x007ff116460c58>
   # ./lib/bacon.rb:7:in `expired!'
```

This method is called by this line in the previous listing:

```
self.expired = true
```

To define this method, you can use the attr_accessor method provided by Ruby, as shown in listing 2.15; the attr prefix of the method means *attribute*. If you pass a Symbol (or collection of symbols) to this method, it defines methods for setting (expired=) and retrieving the attribute's expired values, referred to as a *setter* and a *getter*, respectively. It also defines an instance variable called @expired on every object of this class to store the value that was specified by the expired= method calls.

> **THE SELF. METHOD PREFIX** In Ruby you can call methods without the self. prefix. In this case, though, when calling the expired= method, you need to specify the prefix or the interpreter will think that you're defining a local variable called expired, rather than calling the method. For setter methods, you should always use the prefix.

> **Listing 2.15   attr_accessor method for Bacon in bacon/lib/bacon.rb**

```
class Bacon
  attr_accessor :expired
  ...
end
```

With this in place, if you run rspec spec again, your example fails on the line following your previous failure:

```
1) Bacon can expire
   Failure/Error: expect(bacon).to_not be_edible
     expected `#<Bacon:0x007f0fa5f56cc8 @expired=true>.edible?` to
     return false, got true
   # ./spec/bacon_spec.rb:11:in `block (2 levels) in <top (required)>'
```

Even though this sets the expired attribute on the Bacon object, you've still hard-coded true in your edible? method. Now change the method to use the attribute method, as in the following listing.

Listing 2.16 `Bacon#edible?` **method**

```
def edible?
  !expired
end
```

When you run `rspec spec` again, both your specs will pass:

```
..

Finished in 0.00191 seconds
2 examples, 0 failures
```

Let's go back into lib/bacon.rb and remove the `self.` from the `expired!` method, just to see what happens:

```
def expired!
  expired = true
end
```

If you run `rspec spec` again, you'll see that your second spec is now broken:

```
1) Bacon can expire
   Failure/Error: expect(bacon).to_not be_edible
     expected `#<Bacon:0x007fbc555d0930>.edible?` to return false,
     got true
   # ./spec/bacon_spec.rb:11:in `block (2 levels) in <top (required)>'
```

You can see that your Bacon instance (#<Bacon:0x007fbc555d0930>) no longer has an @expired attribute set to `true`, like you had in the previous failure, because you're not calling the `expired=` method anymore.

Tests save you from making mistakes such as this. If you write the test first and then write the code to make the test pass, you have a solid base and can refactor the code to be clearer or smaller, and finally you can ensure that it's still working with the test you wrote in the first place. If the test still passes, then you're probably doing it right.

If you change this method back now,

```
def expired!
  self.expired = true
end
```

and then run your specs using `rspec spec`, you'll see that they once again pass:

```
..

2 examples, 0 failures
```

Everything's normal and working, which is great!

That ends our little foray into RSpec for now. You'll use it again later when you develop your application. If you'd like to know more about RSpec, Noel Rappin's *Rails 4 Test Prescriptions* (https://pragprog.com/book/nrtest2/rails-4-test-prescriptions) is recommended reading.

2.4   *Summary*

This chapter demonstrated how to apply TDD and BDD principles to test some rudimentary code. You can (and should!) apply these principles to all the code you write, because testing the code ensures that it's maintainable from now into the future. You don't have to use the gems shown in this chapter to test your Rails application; they're just preferred by a large portion of the community.

You'll apply what you learned in this chapter to build a Rails application from scratch in upcoming chapters. You'll use RSpec and another tool called Capybara to build out acceptance tests that will describe the behavior of your application. Then you'll implement the behavior of the application to make these tests pass, and you'll know you're doing it right when the tests are all green.

Let's get into it!

Developing
a real Rails application

## 3

This chapter covers

- Using a Git client and GitHub for Version control
- Setting up and configuring a Rails application
- Writing our first application feature
- Creating a Project model
- Creating an interface for saving new projects

This chapter will get you started on building a Ruby on Rails application from scratch using the techniques covered in the previous chapter, plus a couple of new ones. With the techniques you learned in chapter 2, you can write features describing the behavior of the specific actions in your application and then implement the code you need to get the features passing.

For the remainder of the book, this application will be the main focus. We'll guide you through it in an agile-like fashion. Agile focuses largely on iterative development: developing one feature at a time from start to finish, and then refining the feature until it's viewed as complete before moving on to the next one.

> **AGILE** You can find more information about agile on Wikipedia: http://en.wikipedia.org/wiki/Agile_software_development.

For this example application, your imaginary client, who has limitless time and budget (unlike clients in the real world), wants you to develop a ticket-tracking application to track the company's numerous projects. You'll develop this application using the methodologies outlined in chapter 2: you'll work iteratively, delivering small working pieces of the software to the client and then gathering the client's feedback to improve the application as necessary. If no improvement is needed, you can move on to the next prioritized chunk of work.

The first couple of features you'll develop for this application will lay down the foundation for the application, enabling people to create projects and tickets. Later, in chapters 6 through 8, you'll implement authentication and authorization so that people can sign in to the application and only have access to certain projects. Other chapters cover things like adding comments to tickets, notifying users by email, and file uploading.

BDD and RSpec (the testing framework you saw in the previous chapter) are used all the way through the development process. They provide the client with a stable application, and when (not if) a bug crops up, you have a nice test base you can use to determine what's broken. Then you can fix the bug so it doesn't happen again, a process called *regression testing* (mentioned in chapter 2).

As you work with your client to build the features of the application using this BDD technique, the client may ask why all this prework is necessary. This can be a tricky question to answer. Explain that writing the tests before the code and then implementing the code to make the tests pass creates a safety net to ensure that the code is always working. (Note that tests will make your code more maintainable, but they won't make your code bug-proof.)

The tests also give you a clearer picture of what your client *really* wants. Having it all written down in code gives you a solid reference of point if clients say they suggested something different. *Story-driven development* is BDD with an emphasis on things a user can do with the system.

By using story-driven development, you know what clients want, clients know you know what they want, you have something you can run automated tests with to ensure that all the pieces are working, and, finally, if something *does* break, you have the test suite in place to catch it. It's a win-win-win situation.

Some of the concepts covered in this chapter were explained in chapter 1. But rather than using scaffolding, as you did previously, you'll write this application from the ground up using the BDD process and other generators provided by Rails. The `scaffold` generator is great for prototyping, but it's less than ideal for delivering simple, well-tested code that works precisely the way you want it to work. The code provided by the scaffold generator often may differ from the code you want. In this case, you can turn to Rails for lightweight alternatives to the scaffold code options, and you'll likely end up with cleaner, better code.

First, you need to set up your application!

3.1 *First steps*

Chapter 1 explained how to quickly start a Rails application. This chapter explains a couple of additional processes that improve the flow of your application development. One process uses BDD to create the features of the application; the other process uses version control. Both will make your life easier.

3.1.1 *The application story*

Your client may have a good idea of the application they want you to develop. How can you transform the idea that's in your client's brain into beautifully formed code? First, you sit down with your client and talk through the parts of the application. In the programming business, we call these parts *user stories*, and you'll use RSpec and Capybara to develop them.

> **WHAT IS CAPYBARA?** Capybara is a testing tool that allows you to simulate the steps of a user of your application. You can tell it to visit pages, fill in fields, click buttons (and links), and assert that pages have certain content. And there's a lot more that it can do, which you'll see throughout this book. It's used quite extensively throughout.

Start with the most basic story, and ask your client how they want it to behave. Then sketch out a basic flow of how the feature would work by building an acceptance test using RSpec and Capybara. If this feature was a login form, the test for it would look something like this:

```
RSpec.feature "Users can log in to the site" do
  scenario "as a user with a valid account" do
    visit "/login"
    fill_in "Email", with: "user@ticketee.com"
    fill_in "Password", with: "password"
    click_button "Login"
    expect(page).to have_content("You have been successfully logged in.")
  end
end
```

The form of this test is simple enough that even people who don't understand Ruby should be able to understand the flow of it. With the function and form laid out, you have a pretty good idea of what the client wants.

3.1.2 *Laying the foundations*

To start building the application you'll develop throughout this book, run the good old `rails` command, preferably outside the directory of the previous application. Call this app *Ticketee*, the Australian slang for a person who validates tickets on trains in an attempt to catch fare evaders. It also has to do with this project being a ticket-tracking application, and a Rails application, at that.[1] To generate this application, run this command:

```
$ rails new ticketee
```

---

[1] Hey, at least *we* thought it was funny!

> **Help!**
>
> If you want to see what else you can do with this `new` command (hint: there's a lot!), you can use the `--help` option:
>
> ```
> $ rails new --help
> ```
>
> The `--help` option shows you the options you can pass to the `new` command to modify the output of your application.

Presto! It's done. From this bare-bones application, you'll build an application that does the following:

- Tracks tickets (of course) and groups them into projects
- Provides a way to restrict users to certain projects
- Allows users to upload files to tickets
- Lets users tag tickets so they're easy to find
- Provides an API on which users can base development of their own applications

You can't do all this with a command as simple as `rails new [application_name]`, but you can do it step by step and test it along the way so you develop a stable and worthwhile application.

Throughout the development of the application, we advise you to use a version-control system. The next section covers that topic using Git. You're welcome to use a different version-control system, but this book uses Git exclusively.

3.2   *Version control*

It's wise during development to use version-control software to provide checkpoints in your code. When the code is working, you can make a commit; and if anything goes wrong later in development, you can revert back to that known-working commit. Additionally, you can create branches for experimental features and work on those independent of the main codebase, without damaging working code.

This book doesn't go into detail on how to use a version-control system, but it does recommend using Git. Git is a distributed version-control system that's easy to use and extremely powerful. If you wish to learn about Git, we recommend reading *Pro Git*, a free online book by Scott Chacon and Ben Straub (Apress, 2014, http://git-scm.com/book/en/v2).

Git is used by most developers in the Rails community and by tools such as Bundler, discussed shortly. Learning Git along with Rails is advantageous when you come across a gem or plug-in that you have to install using Git. Because most of the Rails community uses Git, you can find a lot of information about how to use it with Rails (even in this book!), should you ever get stuck.

If you don't have Git already installed, GitHub's help site offers installation guides for Mac, Linux, and Windows at https://help.github.com/articles/set-up-git.

The precompiled installer should work well for Macs, and the package-distributed versions (via apt, yum, emerge, and so on) work well for Linux machines. For Windows, the GitHub for Windows program does just fine.

3.2.1 Getting started with GitHub

For an online place to put your Git repository, we recommend GitHub (http://github.com), which offers free accounts. If you set up an account now, you can upload your code to GitHub as you progress, ensuring that you won't lose it if anything happens to your computer.

> **BITBUCKET** Bitbucket (http://bitbucket.org) is a popular alternative to GitHub, and it also allows you to have free private repositories.

To get started with GitHub, you first need to generate a secure shell (SSH) key, which is used to authenticate you with GitHub when you do a `git push` to GitHub's servers.[2] After you sign up at GitHub, click the Settings link (see figure 3.1) in the menu at the top, select SSH Keys, and then click Add SSH Key (see figure 3.2). You can then copy your public key's content (usually found at ~/.ssh/id_rsa.pub) into the key field.

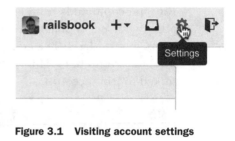

Figure 3.1 Visiting account settings

Now that you're set up with GitHub, click New Repository on the dashboard (see figure 3.3) to begin creating a new repository. Enter the Project Name as `Ticketee`, and click Create Repository to create the repository on GitHub.

Now you're on your project's page. It has some basic instructions on how to set up your code in your new repository, but first you need to configure Git on your own

Figure 3.2 Adding an SSH key

[2] You can find a guide for this process at https://help.github.com/articles/generating-ssh-keys.

Figure 3.3   Creating a new repository

machine. Git needs to know a bit about you for identification purposes—so you can properly be credited (or blamed) for any code that you write.

3.2.2   *Configuring your Git client*

Run the commands from listing 3.1 in your terminal or command prompt to tell Git about yourself, replacing `Your Name` with your real name and `you@example.com` with your email address. The email address you provide should be the same as the one you used to sign up to GitHub, so that when you push your code to GitHub, it will also be linked to your account.

Listing 3.1   Configuring your identity in Git

```
$ git config --global user.name "Your Name"
$ git config --global user.email you@example.com
```

You already have a ticketee directory, created when you generated your Rails app, and you're probably already in it. If not, you should be. To make this directory a Git repository, run this easy command:

```
$ git init
```

Your ticketee directory now contains a .git directory, which is your Git repository. It's all kept in one neat little package.

To add all the files for your application to this repository's *staging area*, run this command:

```
$ git add .
```

The staging area for the repository is the location where all the changes for the next commit are kept. A commit can be considered a checkpoint for your code. If you make a change, you must *stage* that change before you can create a commit for it.

To create a commit with a message, run the following command:

```
$ git commit -m "Generate the Rails 4 application"
```

This command generates quite a bit of output, but the most important lines are the first two:

```
[master (root-commit) d825bbc] Generate the Rails 4 application
 57 files changed, 984 insertions(+)
```

d825bbc is the *short commit ID*, a unique identifier for the commit, so it changes with each commit you make. (The number of files and insertions may also be different.) In Git, commits are tracked against *branches*, and the default branch for a Git repository is the *master* branch, which you just committed to.

The second line lists the number of files changed, insertions (new lines added), and deletions. If you modify a line, it's counted as both an insertion and a deletion, because, according to Git, you've removed the line and replaced it with the modified version.

To view a list of commits for the current branch, type git log. You should see output similar to the following listing.

> **Listing 3.2 Viewing the commit log**

```
commit d825bbc23854cc256d5829a06516ceb19d148131
Author: Your Name <you@example.com>
Date:   [date stamp]

    Generate the Rails 4 application
```

The hash after the word commit is the *long commit ID*; it's the longer version of the previous short commit ID. A commit can be referenced by either the long or the short commit ID in Git, providing no two commits begin with the same short ID.[3] With that commit in your repository, you have something to push to GitHub, which you can do by running the following commands, making sure you substitute your GitHub username for [your username]:

```
$ git remote add origin git@github.com:[your username]/ticketee.git
$ git push origin master -u
```

The first command tells Git that you have a remote server called *origin* for this repository. To access it, you use the git@github.com:[your username]/ticketee.git path, which connects via SSH to the repository you created on GitHub. The second command pushes the named branch to that remote server, and the -u option tells Git to always pull from this remote server for this branch unless told differently.

The output from this command is similar to the following.

> **Listing 3.3 git push output**

```
Counting objects: 73, done.
Compressing objects: 100% (58/58), done.
Writing objects: 100% (73/73), 86.50 KiB, done.
Total 73 (delta 2), reused 0 (delta 0)
To git@github.com:rubysherpas/r4ia_examples.git
* [new branch]   master -> master
Branch master set up to track remote branch master from origin.
```

---

[3] The chances of this happening are 1 in 268,435,456.

The second-to-last line in this output indicates that your push to GitHub succeeded, because it shows that a new branch called master was created on GitHub.

As we go through the book, we'll also git push just like you. You can compare your code to ours by checking out our repository on GitHub: https://github.com/rubysherpas/r4ia_examples.

To roll back the code to a given point in time, check out git log:

```
commit d1e9b6f398748d3ca8583727c1f86496465ba298
Author: Rebecca Skinner <[email redacted]>
Date:   Sat Apr 4 00:00:33 2015 +0800

    Protect state_id from users who do not have permission
       to change it

commit ceb67d45cfcddbb8439da7b126802e6a48b1b9ea
Author: Rebecca Skinner <[email redacted]>
Date:   Fri Apr 3 23:27:20 2015 +0800

    Only admins and managers can change states of a ticket

commit ef5ec0f15e7add662852d6634de50648373f6116
Author: Rebecca Skinner <[email redacted]>
Date:   Fri Apr 3 23:01:48 2015 +0800

    Auto-assign the default state to newly-created tickets
```

Each of these lines represents a commit, and the commits will line up with when we tell you to commit in the book. You can also check out the commit list on GitHub, if you find that easier: https://github.com/rubysherpas/r4ia_examples/commits.

Once you've found the commit with the right message, make note of the long commit ID associated with it. Use this value with git checkout to roll the code back in time:

```
$ git checkout 23729a
```

You only need to know enough of the hash for it to be unique: six characters is usually enough. When you're done poking around, go forward in time to the most recent commit with git checkout again:

```
$ git checkout master
```

This is a tiny, tiny taste of the power of Git. Time travel at will! You just have to learn the commands.

Next, you must set up your application to use RSpec.

3.3 Application configuration

Even though Rails passionately promotes the *convention over configuration* line, some parts of the application will need configuration. It's impossible to avoid *all* configuration. The main parts are gem dependency configuration, database settings, and styling. Let's look at these parts now.

3.3.1 *The Gemfile and generators*

The Gemfile is used for tracking which gems are used in your application. *Gem* is the Ruby word for a library of code, all packaged up to be included into your app—Rails is a gem, and it in turn depends on many other gems.

Bundler is a gem, and Bundler is also responsible for everything to do with the Gemfile. It's Bundler's job to ensure that all the gems listed inside the Gemfile are installed when your application is initialized. The following listing shows how it looks inside.

Listing 3.4　Default Gemfile in a new Rails app

```
source 'https://rubygems.org'

# Bundle edge Rails instead: gem 'rails', github: 'rails/rails'
gem 'rails', '4.2.1'
# Use sqlite3 as the database for Active Record
gem 'sqlite3'
# Use SCSS for stylesheets
gem 'sass-rails', '~> 5.0'
# Use Uglifier as compressor for JavaScript assets
gem 'uglifier', '>= 1.3.0'
# Use CoffeeScript for .coffee assets and views
gem 'coffee-rails', '~> 4.1.0'
# See https://github.com/sstephenson/execjs#readme for more supported...
# gem 'therubyracer', platforms: :ruby

# Use jquery as the JavaScript library
gem 'jquery-rails'
# Turbolinks makes following links in your web application faster...
gem 'turbolinks'
# Build JSON APIs with ease. Read more: https://github.com/rails/jbu...
gem 'jbuilder', '~> 2.0'
# bundle exec rake doc:rails generates the API under doc/api.
gem 'sdoc', '~> 0.4.0', group: :doc

# Use ActiveModel has_secure_password
# gem 'bcrypt', '~> 3.1.7'

# Use Unicorn as the app server
# gem 'unicorn'

# Use Capistrano for deployment
# gem 'capistrano-rails', group: :development

group :development, :test do
  # Call 'byebug' anywhere in the code to stop execution and get a...
  gem 'byebug'

  # Access an IRB console on exception pages or by using <%= console...
  gem 'web-console', '~> 2.0'

  # Spring speeds up development by keeping your application running in the
```

```
background. Read more: https://github.com/rails/spring
  gem 'spring'
end
```

In this file, Rails sets a source to be https://rubygems.org (the canonical repository for Ruby gems). All gems you specify for your application are gathered from the source. Next, it tells Bundler it requires version 4.2.1 of the rails gem. Bundler inspects the dependencies of the requested gem, as well as all gem dependencies of those dependencies (and so on), and then does what it needs to do to make them all available to your application.

This file also requires the sqlite3 gem, which is used for interacting with SQLite3 databases, the default when working with Rails. If you were to use another database system, you'd need to take out this line and replace it with the relevant gem, such as mysql2 for MySQL or pg for PostgreSQL.

Groups in the Gemfile are used to define gems that should be loaded in specific scenarios. When using Bundler with Rails, you can specify a gem group for each Rails *environment*, and by doing so, you specify which gems should be required by that environment. A default Rails application has three standard environments: development, test, and production.

> ### Rails application environments
>
> The *development* environment is used for your local application, such as when you're playing with it in the browser on your local machine. In development mode, page and class caching are turned off, so requests may take a little longer than they do in production mode. (Don't worry—this is only the case for larger applications.) Things like more detailed error messages are also turned on, for easier debugging.
>
> The *test* environment is used when you run the automated test suite for the application. This environment is kept separate from the development environment so your tests start with a clean database to ensure predictability, and so you can include extra gems specifically to aid in testing.
>
> The *production* environment is used when you finally deploy your application out into the world for others to use. This mode is designed for speed, and any changes you make to your application's classes aren't effective until the server is restarted.

This automatic requiring of gems in the Rails environment groups is done by the following line in config/application.rb:

```
Bundler.require(*Rails.groups)
```

The `Rails.groups` line provides two groups for Bundler to require: `default` and `development`. The latter will change depending on the environment that you're running. This code will tell Bundler to load only the gems in the `default` group (which is all gems not in any specific group), as well as any gems in a group that has the same name as the environment.

GETTING STARTED WITH BDD

Chapter 2 focused on behavior-driven development (BDD), and, as was more than hinted at, you'll use it to develop this application. To get started, you need to alter the Gemfile to ensure that you have the correct gem for RSpec for your application.

To add the rspec-rails gem, add this line to the bottom of the :development, :test group in your Gemfile:

```
gem "rspec-rails", "~> 3.2.1"
```

This group in your Gemfile lists all the gems that will be loaded in the development and test environments of your application. These gems won't be available in a production environment. You add rspec-rails to this group because you're going to need a generator from it to be available in development. Additionally, when you run a generator for a controller or model, it'll use RSpec, rather than the default Test::Unit, to generate the tests for that class.

You've specified a version number with ~> 3.2.1,[4] which tells RubyGems you want rspec-rails 3.2.1 *or higher*, but less than rspec-rails 3.3. This means when RSpec releases 3.2.2 and you go to install your gems, RubyGems will install the latest version it can find, rather than only 3.2.1.

Next, you'll need to add Capybara to the Gemfile, in a new group specifically for the test environment. You don't put Capybara in the same group as the rspec-rails gem because it doesn't offer any generators that you need, so you only need this gem loaded in the test environment.

```
group :test do
  gem "capybara", "~> 2.4"
end
```

Capybara is a browser simulator in Ruby that's used for *integration testing*, which you'll be doing shortly. This kind of testing ensures that when a link is clicked in your application, it goes to the correct page; or that when you fill in a form and click Submit, an onscreen message tells you that the form's operation was successful.

Capybara also supports real browser testing. If you tell RSpec that your test is a *JavaScript* test, it will open a new Firefox window and run the test there—you'll be able to see your tests as they occur, and your application will behave exactly the same as it does when you view it yourself. You'll use this extensively when we start writing JavaScript in chapter 9.

To install these gems on your system, run `bundle update` at the root of your application. This command tells Bundler to ignore your Gemfile.lock file and use your Gemfile to install all the gems specified in it. Bundler then updates Gemfile.lock with the list of gems that were installed, as well as their versions. The next time `bundle` is

---

[4] The ~> operator is called the *approximate version constraint.*

run, the gems will be read from the Gemfile.lock file, rather than the Gemfile. You should commit this file to your repository so that when other people work on your project and run `bundle install`, they'll get exactly the same versions that you have.

With the necessary gems for the application installed, you can run the `rspec:install` generator, a generator provided by RSpec to set your Rails application up for testing:

```
$ rails g rspec:install
```

REMINDER   Remember, `rails g` is a shortcut for running `rails generate`!

You can also remove the automatically generated `test` application in the root folder of your application—you won't be using it.

With this generated code in place, you should make a commit so you have another base to roll back to if anything goes wrong:

```
$ git add .
$ git commit -m "Set up gem dependencies and run RSpec generator"
$ git push
```

3.3.2 Database configuration

By default, Rails uses a database system called SQLite3, which stores each environment's database in separate files in the db directory. SQLite3 is the default database system because it's the easiest to set up. Out of the box, Rails also supports the MySQL and PostgreSQL databases, and gems are available that can provide functionality for connecting to other database systems such as Oracle.

If you want to change which database your application connects to, you can open config/database.yml (whose development configuration is shown in the following listing) and alter the settings to the new database system.

> **Listing 3.5 config/database.yml, SQLite3 example**

```
development:
  adapter: sqlite3
  database: db/development.sqlite3
  pool: 5
  timeout: 5000
```

For example, if you want to use PostgreSQL, change the settings to match those in the following listing. It's common convention, but not mandatory, to call the environment's database [app_name]_[environment].

> **Listing 3.6 config/database.yml, PostgreSQL example**

```
development:
  adapter: postgresql
  database: ticketee_development
  username: root
  password: t0ps3cr3t
```

You're welcome to change the database if you wish. Rails will go about its business. But it's good practice to develop and deploy on the same database system to avoid strange behavior between two different systems. Systems such as PostgreSQL perform faster than SQLite, so switching to it may increase your application's performance. Be mindful, however, that switching database systems doesn't automatically move your existing data over for you.

It's generally wise to use different names for the different database environments: if you use the same database in development and test modes, the database would be emptied of all data when the tests were run, eliminating anything you might have set up in development mode. You should never work on the live production database directly unless you're absolutely sure of what you're doing, and even then extreme care should be taken.

Finally, if you're using MySQL, it's wise to set the encoding to utf-8 for the database, using the following setup in the config/database.yml file.

Listing 3.7 config/database.yml, MySQL example

```
development:
  adapter: mysql2
  database: ticketee_development
  username: root
  password: t0ps3cr3t
  encoding: utf8
```

This way, the database is set up automatically to work with UTF-8, eliminating any potential encoding issues that may be encountered otherwise.

That's database configuration in a nutshell. For this book and for the Ticketee application, we'll use the default of SQLite3, but it's good to know about the alternatives and how to configure them.

3.4 *Beginning your first feature*

You now have version control for your application, and you're hosting it on GitHub. It's time to write your first Capybara-based test, which isn't nearly as daunting as it sounds. We'll explore things such as models and RESTful routing while you do it. It'll be simple, promise!

The CRUD (create, read, update, delete) acronym is something you'll see all the time in the Rails world. It represents the creation, reading, updating, and deleting of something, but it doesn't say what that something is.

In the Rails world, CRUD is usually referred to when talking about *resources*. Resources are the representation of the information throughout your application—the things that your application is designed to manage. The following section goes through the beginnings of generating a CRUD interface for a *project* resource by applying the BDD practices you learned in chapter 2 to the application you just bootstrapped. What comes next is a sampler of how to apply these practices when developing a Rails application.

Throughout the remainder of the book, you'll continue to apply these practices to ensure that you have a stable and maintainable application.

Let's get into it!

3.4.1 Creating projects

The first story for your application is the creation (the *C* in CRUD). You'll create a resource representing projects in your application by first writing a test for the process by which a user will create projects, then creating a controller and model, and then creating a route. Then you'll add a validation to ensure that no project can be created without a name. When you're done with this feature, you'll have a form that looks like figure 3.4.

First, create a new directory at spec/features—all of the specs covering your features will go there. Then, in a file called spec/features/creating_projects_spec.rb, you'll put the test that will make sure this feature works correctly when it's fully implemented. The test code is shown in the following listing.

New Project

Name

Description

Create Project

Figure 3.4 Form to create projects

Listing 3.8 spec/features/creating_projects_spec.rb

```
require "rails_helper"

RSpec.feature "Users can create new projects" do
  scenario "with valid attributes" do
    visit "/"

    click_link "New Project"

    fill_in "Name", with: "Sublime Text 3"
    fill_in "Description", with: "A text editor for everyone"
    click_button "Create Project"

    expect(page).to have_content "Project has been created."
  end
end
```

To run this test, run `bundle exec rspec` from inside your ticketee folder. This command will run all of your specs and display the first failure of your application's first test:

```
1) Users can create new projects with valid attributes
   Failure/Error: visit "/"
   ActionController::RoutingError:
     No route matches [GET] "/"
```

THE SCHEMA.RB FILE Before the test failure, you'll also get a warning that your schema.rb file doesn't exist yet. This schema.rb file represents Rails' knowledge about the application's database. You haven't created a database yet, so it's safe to ignore this warning for now. It will get resolved when you create your first database table shortly.

It falls on the application's *router* to figure out where the request should go. Typically, the request would be routed to an action in a controller, but at the moment there are no routes at all for the application. With no routes, the Rails router can't find the route for "/" and so gives you the error shown.

You have to tell Rails what to do with a request for "/". You can do this easily in config/routes.rb. At the moment, this file has the following content (comments removed).

Listing 3.9   config/routes.rb

```
Rails.application.routes.draw do
end
```

The comments are good for a read if you're interested in the other routing syntax, but they're not necessary at the moment. (We've removed them from the code displayed here, but you can keep them if you like.) To define a root route, you use the root method like this in the block for the draw method:

```
Rails.application.routes.draw do
  root "projects#index"
end
```

This defines a route for requests to "/" (the root route) to point at the index action of the ProjectsController. This controller doesn't exist yet, and so the test should probably complain about that if you got the route right. Run bundle exec rspec to find out:

```
1) Users can create new projects with valid attributes
   Failure/Error: visit "/"
   ActionController::RoutingError:
     uninitialized constant ProjectsController
```

This error is happening because the route is pointing at a controller that doesn't exist. When the request is made, the router attempts to load the controller, and because it can't find it, you'll get this error.

To define this ProjectsController constant, you must generate a *controller*. The controller is the first port of call for your routes (as you can see now!), and it's responsible for querying the model for information in an action and then doing something with that information (such as rendering a template). (Lots of new terms are explained later. Patience, grasshopper.) To generate the controller, run this command:

```
$ rails g controller projects
```

You may be wondering why we use a pluralized name for the controller. Well, the controller is going to be dealing with a plural number of projects during its lifetime, so it makes sense to name it like this. The models are singular because their names refer to their types. Another way to put it: you're a human, not a humans. But a controller that dealt with multiple humans would be called HumansController.

The controller generator produces output similar to that produced when you ran rails new earlier, but this time it creates files just for the controller you've asked Rails to generate. The most important of these is the controller itself, which is housed in app/controllers/projects_controller.rb and defines the `ProjectsController` constant that your test needs. This controller is where all the actions will live, just like app/controllers/purchases_controller.rb back in chapter 1. Here's what this command outputs:

```
create  app/controllers/projects_controller.rb
invoke  erb
create     app/views/projects
invoke  rspec
create     spec/controllers/projects_controller_spec.rb
invoke  helper
create     app/helpers/projects_helper.rb
invoke     rspec
create        spec/helpers/projects_helper_spec.rb
invoke  assets
invoke     coffee
create        app/assets/javascripts/projects.coffee
invoke     scss
create        app/assets/stylesheets/projects.scss
```

A few notes about the output:

- app/views/projects contains the views relating to your actions (more on this shortly).

- invoke helper shows that the `helper` generator was called here, generating a file at app/helpers/projects_helper.rb. This file defines a `ProjectsHelper` module. Helpers generally contain custom methods to be used in your view to help with the rendering of content, and they come as blank slates when they're first created.

- invoke erb signifies that the Embedded Ruby (ERB) generator was invoked. Actions to be generated for this controller have corresponding ERB views located in app/views/projects. For instance, the index action's default view is located at app/views/projects/index.html.erb.

- invoke rspec shows that the RSpec generator was also invoked during the generation. This means RSpec has generated a new file at spec/controllers/projects_controller_spec.rb, which you can use to test your controller—but not right now.[5]

- Finally, the assets for the controller are generated. Two files are generated here: app/assets/javascripts/projects.coffee and app/assets/stylesheets/projects.scss. The first file should contain any JavaScript related to the controller, written as CoffeeScript (http://coffeescript.org). The second file should contain any CSS related to the controller, written using SCSS (http://sass-lang.com). In the development environment, these files are automatically parsed into JavaScript and CSS, respectively.

---

[5] By generating RSpec tests rather than Test::Unit tests, a longstanding issue in Rails has been fixed. In previous versions of Rails, even if you specified the RSpec gem, all the default generators still generated Test::Unit tests. With Rails, the testing framework you use is just one of a large number of configurable things in your application.

You've just run the generator to generate a new `ProjectsController` class and all its goodies. This should fix the "uninitialized constant" error message. If you run `bundle exec rspec` again, it declares that the `index` action is missing:

```
1) Users can create new projects with valid attributes
   Failure/Error: visit "/"
   AbstractController::ActionNotFound:
     The action 'index' could not be found for ProjectsController
```

3.4.2 Defining a controller action

To define the `index` action in your controller, you must define a method in the `ProjectsController` class, just as you did when you generated your first application.

> **Listing 3.10 app/controllers/projects_controller.rb**

```ruby
class ProjectsController < ApplicationController
  def index
  end
end
```

If you run `bundle exec rspec` again, this time Rails complains of a missing projects/index template:

```
1) Users can create new projects with valid attributes
   Failure/Error: visit "/"
   ActionView::MissingTemplate:
     Missing template projects/index, application/index with
     {
      :locale => [:en],
      :formats => [:html],
      :variants => [],
      :handlers => [:erb, :builder, :raw, :ruby, :coffee, :jbuilder]
     }.

     Searched in:
     * ".../ticketee/app/views"
```

We've reformatted the error message to make it a little easier on the untrained eye. It doesn't look very helpful, but if you know how to put the pieces together, you can determine that it's trying to look for a template called projects/index or application/index, but it's not finding it. These templates are primarily kept at app/views, so it's fair to guess that it's expecting something like app/views/projects/index.

The extension of the file will be composed of two parts: the format followed by the handler. The error output lists `:html` as an available format, which is good, because we want to render an HTML page. But what's a handler?

A *handler* is a preprocessor for the template, or a templating language. There are a number of handlers built in (as the error output lists), and many more can be added by using extra gems, but the default for Rails views is `:erb`. Putting it all together, the view that your `index` action will render belongs in app/views/projects/index.html.erb.

Rails view `variants`

We haven't discussed the `variants` option in the output at all. View variants are a relatively new feature within Rails, and they allow you to provide different views based on certain criteria, such as what device a user is accessing the site through.

The Rails 4.1 release notes have the best information about variants, so if you're interested in what they can do, check them out here: http://guides.rubyonrails.org/ 4_1_release_notes.html#action-pack-variants.

You could also create a file at app/views/application/index.html.erb to provide the view for the index action from the `ProjectsController`. This would work because `ProjectsController` inherits from `ApplicationController`. If you had another controller inherit from `ProjectsController`, you could put an action's template at app/ views/application, app/views/projects, or app/views/that_controller, and Rails would still pick up on it. This allows different controllers to share views in a simple fashion. Creating a view at app/views/application/index.html.erb would make this view available for all controllers that inherit from `ApplicationController`, but that's not what we want to do in this case.

To generate this view, create the app/views/projects/index.html.erb file and leave it blank for now. You can run just the single spec for creating projects with `bundle exec rspec`:

```
1) Users can create new projects with valid attributes
   Failure/Error: click_link "New Project"
   Capybara::ElementNotFound:
     Unable to find link "New Project"
```

You've defined a homepage for your application by defining a root route, generating a controller, putting an action in it, and creating a view for that action. Now Capybara is successfully navigating to it and rendering it. That's the first step in the first test passing for your first application, and it's a great first step!

The second line in your spec is now failing, and it's up to you to fix it. You need a link on the root page of your application that reads "New Project." That link should go in the view of the controller that's serving the root route request: app/views/projects/ index.html.erb. Open app/views/projects/index.html.erb and put the link in by using the `link_to` method:

```
<%= link_to "New Project", new_project_path %>
```

This single line re-introduces two old concepts and a new one: ERB output tags, the `link_to` method (both of which you saw in chapter 1), and the mysterious `new_project_path` method.

As a refresher, in ERB, when you use `<%=` (known as an ERB output tag), you're telling ERB that whatever the output of this Ruby is, put it on the page. If you only want to evaluate (and not output) Ruby, you use an ERB evaluation tag <%, which doesn't output content to the page but only evaluates it. Both of these tags end in %>.

The link_to method in Rails generates an <a> tag with the text of the first argument and the href of the second argument. This method can also be used in block format if you have a lot of text you want to link to:

```
<%= link_to new_project_path do %>
  bunch
  of
  text
<% end %>
```

Where new_project_path comes from deserves its own section. It's the very next one.

3.4.3 RESTful routing

The new_project_path method is as yet undefined. If you ran the test again, it would complain of an "undefined local variable or method, 'new_project_path'." You can define this method by defining a route to what's known as a *resource* in Rails. Resources are collections of objects that all belong in a common location, such as projects, users, or tickets.

You can add the projects resource in config/routes.rb by using the resources method, putting it directly under the root method in this file.

Listing 3.11 resources :projects **line in config/routes.rb**

```
Rails.application.routes.draw do
  root "projects#index"

  resources :projects
end
```

This is called a *resource* route, and it defines the routes to the seven *RESTful* actions in your projects controller. When something is said to be RESTful, it means it conforms to Rails' interpretation of the Representational State Transfer (REST) architectural style. (See Wikipedia for more information on REST: http://en.wikipedia.org/wiki/Representational_state_transfer.)

Rails can't get you all the way there, but it can help. With Rails, this means the related controller has seven potential actions:

- index
- show
- new
- create
- edit
- update
- destroy

These seven actions match up with just four request paths:

- /projects
- /projects/new
- /projects/:id
- /projects/:id/edit

How can four be equal to seven? It can't! Not in this world, anyway. Rails will determine what action to route to on the basis of the HTTP method of the requests to these paths. Table 3.1 lists the routes, HTTP methods, and corresponding actions to make it clearer.

Table 3.1   RESTful routing match-up

HTTP method	Route	Action
GET	/projects	index
POST	/projects	create
GET	/projects/new	new
GET	/projects/:id	show
PATCH/PUT	/projects/:id	update
DELETE	/projects/:id	destroy
GET	/projects/:id/edit	edit

The routes listed in the table are provided when you use `resources :projects`. This is yet another great example of how Rails takes care of the configuration so you can take care of the coding.

To review the routes you've defined, you can run the `bundle exec rake routes` command and get output similar to that in table 3.1:

```
Prefix Verb    URI Pattern                    Controller#Action
        root GET    /                             projects#index
    projects GET    /projects(.:format)           projects#index
             POST   /projects(.:format)           projects#create
 new_project GET    /projects/new(.:format)       projects#new
edit_project GET    /projects/:id/edit(.:format)  projects#edit
     project GET    /projects/:id(.:format)       projects#show
             PATCH  /projects/:id(.:format)        projects#update
             PUT    /projects/:id(.:format)        projects#update
             DELETE /projects/:id(.:format)        projects#destroy
```

The words in the leftmost column of this output are the beginnings of the method names you can use in your controllers or views to access them. If you want just the path to a route, such as /projects, then use `projects_path`. If you want the full URL, such as http://yoursite.com/projects, use `projects_url`. It's best to use these helpers rather than hardcoding the URLs; doing so makes your application consistent across the board.

For example, to generate the route to a single project, you'd use either `project_path` or `project_url`:

```
project_path(@project)
```

This method takes one argument, shown in the URI pattern with the :id notation, and generates the path according to this object. The four paths mentioned earlier match up to the helpers in table 3.2.

Table 3.2   RESTful routing match-up for GET routes

URL	Helper
GET /projects	projects_path
GET /projects/new	new_project_path
GET /projects/:id	project_path
GET /projects/:id/edit	edit_project_path

Running `bundle exec rspec` now produces a complaint about a missing new action:

```
1) Users can create new projects with valid attributes
   Failure/Error: click_link "New Project"
   AbstractController::ActionNotFound:
     The action 'new' could not be found for ProjectsController
```

As shown in the following listing, you define the new action in your controller by defining a new method directly underneath the index method.

Listing 3.12   app/controllers/projects_controller.rb

```ruby
class ProjectsController < ApplicationController
  def index
  end

  def new
  end
end
```

Running `bundle exec rspec` now results in a complaint about a missing new template, just as it did with the index action:

```
1) Users can create new projects with valid attributes
   Failure/Error: click_link "New Project"
   ActionView::MissingTemplate:
     Missing template projects/new, application/new with
     {
       :locale => [:en],
       :formats => [:html],
       :variants => [],
       :handlers => [:erb, :builder, :raw, :ruby, :coffee, :jbuilder]
     }.

     Searched in:
     * ".../ticketee/app/views"
```

You can create the file at app/views/projects/new.html.erb to make this test go one step further, although this is a temporary solution. You'll come back to this file later to add content to it.

When you run the spec again, the line that should be failing is the one regarding filling in the Name field. Find out if this is the case by running bundle exec rspec:

```
1) Users can create new projects with valid attributes
   Failure/Error: fill_in "Name", with: "Sublime Text 3"
   Capybara::ElementNotFound:
     Unable to find field "Name"
```

Now Capybara is complaining about a missing Name field on the page it's currently on: the new page. You must add this field so that Capybara can fill it in. Before you do that, however, fill out the new action in the ProjectsController as follows:

```
def new
  @project = Project.new
end
```

When you fill out the view with the fields you need to create a new project, you'll need something to base the fields on—an instance of the class you want to create. This Project constant will be a class located at app/models/project.rb, thereby making it a *model*.

OF MODELS AND MIGRATIONS

A model is used to retrieve information from the database. Because models by default inherit from Active Record, you don't have to set up anything extra. Run the following command to generate your first model:

```
$ rails g model project name description
```

This syntax is similar to the controller generator's syntax, except that you specify that you want a model, not a controller.

When the generator runs, it generates not only the model file but also a *migration* containing the code to create the table (containing the specified fields) for the model. You can specify as many fields as you like after the model's name. They default to string type, so you don't need to specify them. If you wanted to be explicit, you could use a colon followed by the field type, like this:

```
$ rails g model project name:string description:string
```

A model provides a place for any business logic that your application performs—one common bit of logic is the way your application interacts with a database. A model is also the place where you define *validations* (seen later in this chapter), *associations* (discussed in chapter 5), and *scopes* (easy-to-use filters for database calls, discussed in chapter 7), among other things. To perform any interaction with data in your database, you go through a model.[6]

---

[6] Although it's possible to perform database operations without a model in Rails, 99% of the time you'll want to use a model.

Migrations are effectively version control for the database. They're defined as Ruby classes, which allows them to apply to multiple database schemas without having to be altered. All migrations have a change method in them when they're first defined. For example, the code shown in the following listing comes from the migration that was just generated.

Listing 3.13 db/migrate/[date]_create_projects.rb

```ruby
class CreateProjects < ActiveRecord::Migration
  def change
    create_table :projects do |t|
      t.string :name
      t.string :description

      t.timestamps null: false
    end
  end
end
```

When you run the migration forward (using bundle exec rake db:migrate), it creates the table in the database. When you roll the migration back (with bundle exec rake db:rollback), it deletes (or *drops*) the table from the database.

If you need to do something different on the up and down parts, you can use those methods instead.

Listing 3.14 Explicitly using up and down methods to define a migration

```ruby
class CreateProjects < ActiveRecord::Migration
  def up
    create_table :projects do |t|
      t.string :name
      t.string :description

      t.timestamps null: false
    end
  end

  def down
    drop_table :projects
  end
end
```

Here, the up method would be called if you ran the migration forward, and the down method would be run if you ran it backward.

This syntax is especially helpful if the migration does something that has a reverse function that isn't clear, such as removing a column:[7]

---

[7] Rails actually does know how to reverse the removal of a column if you provide an extra field type argument to remove_column; for example, remove_column :projects, :name, :string. We'll leave this here for demonstration purposes, though.

```
class CreateProjects < ActiveRecord::Migration
  def up
    remove_column :projects, :name
  end

  def down
    add_column :projects, :name, :string
  end
end
```

In this case, Active Record wouldn't know what type of field to re-add this column as, so you must tell it what to do in the case of this migration being rolled back.

In the projects migration, the first line of the `change` method tells Active Record that you want to create a table called `projects`. You call this method in the block format, which returns an object that defines the table. To add fields to this table, you call methods on the block's object (called `t` in this example and in all model migrations), the name of which usually reflects the type of column it is; the first argument is the name of that field. The `timestamps` method is special: it creates two fields, `created_at` and `updated_at`, which are by default set to the current time in coordinated universal time (UTC)[8] by Rails when a record is created and updated, respectively.

A migration doesn't automatically run when you create it—you must run it yourself using this command:

```
$ bundle exec rake db:migrate
```

This command migrates the database up to the latest migration, which for now is your only migration. If you create a whole slew of migrations at once, then invoking `bundle exec rake db:migrate` will migrate them in the order in which they were created. This is the purpose of the timestamp in the migration filename—to keep the migrations in chronological order.

The end of `rake db:test:prepare`

In older versions of Rails (before 4.1), whenever you ran a migration in the development environment with `rake db:migrate`, you also had to manually keep your test database in sync with `rake db:test:prepare`. This led to much confusion. Your tests could raise errors about missing database fields, but they were there—you'd run migrations to create them but not run `rake db:test:prepare` to sync those changes to the test database.

Now the two databases are kept in sync automatically, with this line in your spec/rails_helper.rb file:

`ActiveRecord::Migration.maintain_test_schema!`

No more need to call `rake db:test:prepare`!

---

[8] Yes, coordinated universal time has an initialism of *UTC*. This is what happens when you name things by committee (http://en.wikipedia.org/wiki/Coordinated_Universal_Time#Etymology).

With this model created and its related migration run, your test won't get any further, but you can start building out the form to create a new project.

FORM BUILDING

To add the fields for creating a new project to the new action's view, you can put them in a form, but not just any form: a form_for.

Listing 3.15 app/views/projects/new.html.erb

```erb
<h1>New Project</h1>
<%= form_for(@project) do |f| %>
  <p>
    <%= f.label :name %><br>
    <%= f.text_field :name %>
  </p>

  <p>
    <%= f.label :description %><br>
    <%= f.text_field :description %>
  </p>

  <%= f.submit %>
<% end %>
```

So many new things!

Starting at the top, the form_for method is Rails' way of building forms for Active Record objects. You pass it the @project object you defined in your controller as the first argument, and with this, the helper does much more than simply place a form tag on the page. form_for inspects the @project object and creates a form builder specifically for that object. The two main things it inspects are whether it's a new record and what the class name is.

What action attribute the form has (the URL the form submits its data to) depends on whether or not the object is a new record. A record is classified as new when it hasn't been saved to the database. This check is performed internally to Rails using the persisted? method, which returns true if the record is stored in the database and false if it's not.

The class of the object also plays a pivotal role in where the form is sent—Rails inspects this class and, from it, determines what the route should be. Because @project is new and is an object of class Project, Rails determines that the submit URL is /projects and the method for the form is POST. Therefore, a request is sent to the create action in ProjectsController.

After that part of form_for is complete, you use the block syntax to receive an f variable, which is a FormBuilder object. You can use this object to define your form's fields. The first element you define is a label. label tags directly relate to the input fields on the page and serve two purposes. First, they give users a larger area to click, rather than just the field, radio button, or check box. Second, you can reference the label's text in the test, and Capybara will know what field to fill in.

> ### Alternative label naming
> By default, the label's text value will be the "humanized" value of the field name; for example, :name becomes "Name." If you want to customize the text, you can pass the label method a second argument:
>
> ```
> <%= f.label :name, "Your name" %>
> ```

After the label, you add the `text_field`, which renders an `<input>` tag corresponding to the label and the field. The output tag looks like this:

```
<input type="text" name="project[name]" id="project_name" />
```

Then you use the `submit` method to provide users with a Submit button for your form. Because you call this method on the `f` object, Rails checks whether the record is new and sets the text to read "Create Project" if the record is new or "Update Project" if it isn't. You'll see this in use a little later when you build the `edit` action. For now, we'll focus on the `new` action!

Run `bundle exec rspec spec/features/creating_projects_spec.rb` once more, and you can see that your spec is one step closer to finishing—the field fill-in steps have passed:

```
1) Users can create new projects with valid attributes
   Failure/Error: click_button "Create Project"
   AbstractController::ActionNotFound:
     The action 'create' could not be found for ProjectsController
```

Capybara finds the label containing the `Name` text you ask for in your scenario, and fills out the corresponding field with the value you specify. Capybara has a number of ways to locate a field, such as by the name of the corresponding label, the `id` attribute of the field, or the `name` attribute. The last two look like these:

```
fill_in "project_name", with: "Sublime Text 3"
# or
fill_in "project[name]", with: "Sublime Text 3"
```

> **SHOULD YOU USE THE ID OR THE LABEL?** Some argue that using the field's ID or name is a better approach, because these attributes don't change as often as labels may. But your tests should aim to be as human-readable as possible— when you write them, you don't want to be thinking of field IDs; you're describing the behavior at a higher level than that. To keep things simple, you should continue using the label name.

Capybara does the same thing for the Description field and then clicks the button you told it to click. The spec is now complaining about a missing action called `create`. Let's fix that.

CREATING THE CREATE ACTION

To define this action, you define the `create` method underneath the `new` method in the `ProjectsController`.

> **Listing 3.16 The `create` action of `ProjectsController`**

```
def create
  @project = Project.new(project_params)

  if @project.save
    flash[:notice] = "Project has been created."
    redirect_to @project
  else
    # nothing, yet
  end
end
```

The `Project.new` method takes one argument, which is a list of attributes that will be assigned to this new `Project` object. For now, we'll just call that list `project_params`.

After you build your new `@project` instance, you call `@project.save` to save it to the `projects` table in your database. Before that happens, though, Rails will run all the data validations on the model, ensuring that it's valid. At the moment, you have no validations on the model, so it will save just fine.

The `flash` method in your `create` action is a way of passing messages to the next request, and it takes the form of a hash. These messages are stored in the session and are cleared at the completion of the next request. Here you set the `:notice` key of the flash hash to be "Project has been created" to inform the user what has happened. This message is displayed later, as is required by the final step in your feature.

The `redirect_to` method can take several different arguments—an object, or the name of a route. If an object is given, Rails inspects it to determine what route it should go to; in this case, it goes to `project_path(@project)` because the object has now been saved to the database. This method generates a path in the form of /projects/:id, where :id is the record's `id` attribute assigned by your database system. The `redirect_to` method tells the browser to begin making a new request to that path and sends back an empty response body; the HTTP status code will be a "302 Redirect," and the URL to redirect to will match the URL of the currently nonexistent `show` action.

If you run `bundle exec rspec` now, you'll get an error about an undefined local variable or method "project_params":

```
1) Users can create new projects with valid attributes
   Failure/Error: click_button "Create Project"
   NameError:
     undefined local variable or method `project_params' for
     #<ProjectsController:0x007fe704e31848>
```

Where does the data you want to make a new project from, come from? It comes from the params provided to the controller, available to all Rails controller actions.

> **Combining `redirect_to` and `flash`**
>
> You can combine `flash` and `redirect_to` by passing the `flash` as an option to the `redirect_to`. If you want to pass a success message, use the `notice` flash key; otherwise use the `alert` key.
>
> To use either of these two keys, you can use this syntax:
>
> ```
> redirect_to @project, notice: "Project has been created."
> # or
> redirect_to @project, alert: "Project has not been created."
> ```
>
> If you don't wish to use either `notice` or `alert`, you must specify `flash` as a hash:
>
> ```
> redirect_to @project, flash: { success: "Project has been created."}
> ```

The `params` method returns the parameters passed to the action, such as those from the form or query parameters from a URL, as a `HashWithIndifferentAccess` object. This is different from a normal `Hash` object, because you can reference a `String` key by using a matching `Symbol`, and vice versa.

In this case, the `params` hash looks like this:

```
{
  "utf8" => "?",
  "authenticity_token" => "WRHnKqU...",
  "project" => {
    "name" => "Sublime Text 3",
    "description" => "A text editor for everyone"
  },
  "commit" => "Create Project",
  "controller" => "projects",
  "action" => "create"
}
```

You can easily see what parameters your controller is receiving by looking at the server logs in your terminal console. If you run your `rails server`, visit http://local-host:3000/projects/new, and submit the data that your test is trying to submit, you'll see the following in the terminal:

```
Started POST "/projects" for 127.0.0.1 at [timestamp]
Processing by ProjectsController#create as HTML
  Parameters: {"utf8"=>"?", "authenticity_token"=>"WRHnKqU...",
  "project"=>{"name"=>"Sublime Text 3", "description"=>"A text editor
  for everyone"}, "commit"=>"Create Project"}
```

The parameters are all listed right there.

All the hashes nested inside the `params` hash are also `HashWithIndifferentAccess` hashes. If you want to get the name key from the `project` hash here, you can use either `{ :name => "Sublime Text 3" }[:name]`, as in a normal `Hash` object, or `{ :name => "Sublime Text 3" }['name']`; you may use either the `String` or the `Symbol` version—it doesn't matter.

The `utf8` and `authenticity_token` params

There are two special parameters in the `params` hash: `utf8` and `authenticity_token`.

The `utf8` parameter is a hack for older browsers (read: old versions of Internet Explorer) to force them into UTF-8 compatibility. You can safely ignore this one.

The `authenticity_token` parameter is used by Rails to validate that the request is authentic. Rails generates this in the `<meta>` tag on the page (using `<%= csrf_meta_tags %>` in app/views/layouts/application.html.erb) and also stores it in the user's session. Upon the submission of the form, it compares the value in the form with the one in the session, and if they match the request is deemed authentic. Using `authenticity_token` mitigates cross-site request forgery (CSRF) attacks and so is a recommended best practice.

The first key in the `params` hash, `commit`, comes from the submit button of the form, which has the value `"Create Project"`. This is accessible as `params[:commit]`. The second key, `action`, is one of two parameters always available; the other is `controller`. These represent exactly what their names imply: the controller and action of the request, accessible as `params[:controller]` and `params[:action]`, respectively. The final key, `project`, is, as mentioned before, a `HashWithIndifferentAccess`. It contains the fields from your form and is accessible via `params[:project]`. To access the name key in the `params[:project]` object, use `params[:project][:name]`, which calls the `[]` method on `params` to get the value of the `:project` key and then, on the resulting hash, calls `[]` again, this time with the `:name` key to get the name of the project passed in.

    `params[:project]` has all the data you need to pass to `Project.new`, but you can't just pass it directly in. If you try to substitute `project_params` with `params[:project]` in your controller, and then run `bundle exec rspec` again, you'll get the following error:

```
Failure/Error: click_button "Create Project"
ActiveModel::ForbiddenAttributesError:
  ActiveModel::ForbiddenAttributesError
```

STRONG PARAMETERS

Oooh, forbidden attributes. Sounds scary. But this is important: it's one form of security help that Rails gives you via a feature called *strong parameters,* new as of Rails 4.

    You don't want to accept just any submitted parameters; you want to accept the ones that you want and expect, and no more. That way, someone can't mess around with your application by doing things like tampering with the form and adding new fields before submitting it.

Strong parameters vs. `attr_accessible`

Before Rails 4.0, Rails supported a feature called `attr_accessible` for protecting your models from unexpected attributes. You may see this used in older Rails projects—it involves listing out every field in the model that should be mass-assignable via user-submitted data.

The `attr_accessible` approach caused problems because different controllers might want to make available different sets of parameters for the same model, depending on the context. For instance, an admin area of the site may want to permit different fields than the user-facing area of the site—admins might have more fields, such as the ability to set the owner of a project.

The advantage of strong parameters is that the permitted parameters are now listed on a controller level, rather than at the model level. This allows for a higher degree of flexibility.

Change the `ProjectsController` code to add a new definition for the `project_params` method:

```ruby
def create
  @project = Project.new(project_params)

  if @project.save
    flash[:notice] = "Project has been created."
    redirect_to @project
  else
    # nothing, yet
  end
end

private

def project_params
  params.require(:project).permit(:name, :description)
end
```

You now call the `require` method on your params, and you require that the `:project` key exists. You also allow it to have `:name` and `:description` entries—any other fields submitted will be discarded. Finally, you wrap up that logic into a method so you can use it in other actions, and you make it private so you don't expose it as some kind of weird action! You'll use this method in one other action in this controller later on—the `update` action.

With that done, run `bundle exec rspec` again, and you'll get a new error:

```
1) Users can create new projects with valid attributes
   Failure/Error: click_button "Create Project"
   AbstractController::ActionNotFound:
     The action 'show' could not be found for ProjectsController
```

The test has made it through the `create` action, followed the redirect you issued, and now it's stuck on the next request—the page you redirected to, the `show` action.

The `show` action is responsible for displaying a single record's information. Retrieving a record to display is done by default using the record's ID. You know the URL for this page will be something like /projects/1, but how do you get the *1* from that URL? Well, when you use resource routing, as you've done already, the *1* part of this URL is available as `params[:id]`, just as `params[:controller]` and `params[:action]` are also automatically made available by Rails. You can then use this `params[:id]` parameter in your `show` action to find a specific `Project` object. In this case, the `show` action should be showing the newly created project.

Put the code from the following listing into app/controllers/projects_controller .rb to set up the `show` action. Make sure it comes above the `private` declaration, or you won't be able to use it as an action!

Listing 3.17 The `show` action of `ProjectsController`

```
def show
  @project = Project.find(params[:id])
end
```

You pass the `params[:id]` object to `Project.find`. This gives you a single `Project` object that relates to a record in the database, which has its `id` field set to whatever `params[:id]` is. If Active Record can't find a record matching that ID, it raises an `ActiveRecord::RecordNotFound` exception.

When you rerun `bundle exec rspec spec/features/creating_projects _spec.rb`, you'll get an error telling you that the `show` action's template is missing:

```
1) Users can create new projects with valid attributes
   Failure/Error: click_button "Create Project"
   ActionView::MissingTemplate:
     Missing template projects/show, application/show with
     {
      :locale => [:en],
      :formats => [:html],
      :variants => [],
      :handlers => [:erb, :builder, :raw, :ruby, :coffee, :jbuilder]
     }.

     Searched in:
     * ".../ticketee/app/views"
```

You can create the file app/views/projects/show.html.erb, with the following content for now, to display the project's name and description:

```
<h1><%= @project.name %></h1>
<p><%= @project.description %></p>
```

It's a pretty plain page for a project, but it'll serve our purpose.

When you run the test again with `bundle exec rspec spec/features/creating _projects_spec.rb`, you'll see this message:

```
1) Users can create new projects with valid attributes
     Failure/Error: expect(page).to have_content "Project has been
     created."
       expected to find text "Project has been created." in "Sublime
       Text 3 A text editor for everyone"
     # ./spec/features/creating_projects_spec.rb:13:in ...
```

This error message shows that the "Project has been created" text isn't being displayed on the page. You must put it somewhere, but where?

THE APPLICATION LAYOUT

The best location for this text is in the application layout, located at app/views/ layouts/application.html.erb. This file provides the layout for all templates in your application, so it's a great spot to output a flash message—no matter what controller you set it in, it will be rendered on the page.

The application layout is quite the interesting file.

> **Listing 3.18 app/views/layouts/application.html.erb**

```
<!DOCTYPE html>
<html>
<head>
  <title>Ticketee</title>
  <%= stylesheet_link_tag    'application', media: 'all',
    'data-turbolinks-track' => true %>
  <%= javascript_include_tag 'application',
    'data-turbolinks-track' => true %>
  <%= csrf_meta_tags %>
</head>
<body>

<%= yield %>

</body>
</html>
```

The first line sets up the doctype to be HTML for the layout, and three new methods are used: `stylesheet_link_tag`, `javascript_include_tag`, and `csrf_meta_tags`.

`stylesheet_link_tag` is for including CSS stylesheets from the app/assets/ stylesheets directory. Using this tag results in the following output, where `[digest]` represents an MD5 hash of the contents of the file:

```
<link rel="stylesheet" href="/assets/projects-[digest].css?body=1"
media="all" data-turbolinks-track="true" />
<link rel="stylesheet" href="/assets/application-[digest].css?body=1"
media="all" data-turbolinks-track="true" />
```

The /assets path is served by a gem called Sprockets. In this case, the tag specifies the /assets/application-[digest].css path, and any route prefixed with /assets is served by

Sprockets. Sprockets provides a feature commonly referred to as the *asset pipeline*. When files are requested through the asset pipeline, they're preprocessed and then served out to the browser.

> **ASSET PIPELINE GUIDE** If you want to know about the ins and outs of the asset pipeline, read the official Ruby on Rails guide: http://guides.rubyonrails.org/ asset_pipeline.html. It covers far more functionality than we'll touch on in this entire book!

There's also a second tag for the projects-[digest].css file. In development mode, Rails generates tags for all of your stylesheets and JavaScript separately, for ease of debugging. If you were to run the application in production mode, you'd get something very different:

```
<link data-turbolinks-track="true" href="/assets/application-[digest].css"
media="all" rel="stylesheet" />
```

This single stylesheet is all of your stylesheets, concatenated together and minified. That way, your users will load up all of your styles on their first visit, and the styles will be cached for the rest of their stay, increasing overall performance.

When the /assets/application-[digest].css asset is requested, Sprockets looks for a file named application.css in the asset paths for your application. The three asset paths it searches by default are app/assets, lib/assets, and vendor/assets, in that order. Some gems add extra paths to this list, so you're able to use assets from within those gems as well.

If the file has any additional extensions on it, such as a file called application.css.scss, Sprockets will look up a preprocessor for the .scss extension and run the file through that before serving it as CSS. You can chain together any number of extensions, and Sprockets will parse the file for each one, working right to left.

The application.css file that's searched for in this example lives at app/assets/ application.css.scss. This has an additional .scss extension on it, so it'll be preprocessed by the Sass preprocessor before being served as CSS by the `stylesheet_link_tag` call in the application layout.

Using Sass or SCSS

For your CSS files, you can use the Sass or SCSS language to produce more powerful stylesheets. Your application depends on the sass-rails gem, which itself depends on sass, the gem for these stylesheets. We won't go into detail here because the Sass site covers most of that ground: http://sass-lang.com/.

Rails automatically generates stylesheets for each controller that uses Sass, as indicated by the .scss extensions.

The `javascript_include_tag` is for including JavaScript files from the JavaScript directories of the asset pipeline. When the `application` string is specified here, Rails loads the app/assets/javascripts/application.js file, which looks like this:

```
//= require jquery
//= require jquery_ujs
//= require turbolinks
//= require_tree .
```

This file includes some Sprockets-specific code that includes the jquery.js and jquery_ujs.js files, located in the jquery-rails gem. (The jquery-rails gem is listed in your Gemfile as a dependency of your application.) It also includes the JavaScript file for Turbolinks, which is a feature we'll discuss later. It compiles these three files, plus all the files in the app/assets/javascripts directory, with the `//= require_tree .` into one superfile called application.js.

In development mode, these JavaScript files all get included into your page separately, just like stylesheets, for ease of debugging. In the output of your page, you'll have the following:

```
<script src="/assets/jquery-[digest].js?body=1"
  data-turbolinks-track="true"></script>
<script src="/assets/jquery_ujs-[digest].js?body=1"
  data-turbolinks-track="true"></script>
<script src="/assets/turbolinks-[digest].js?body=1"
  data-turbolinks-track="true"></script>
<script src="/assets/projects-[digest].js?body=1"
  data-turbolinks-track="true"></script>
<script src="/assets/application-[digest].js?body=1"
  data-turbolinks-track="true"></script>
```

These files are also served through the Sprockets gem. As with your stylesheets, you can use an alternative syntax called CoffeeScript (http://coffeescript.org), which provides a simpler JavaScript syntax that compiles into proper JavaScript. Just as with the Sass stylesheets, Rails generates CoffeeScript files in app/assets/javascripts with the extension .coffee, indicating to Sprockets that they're to be parsed by a CoffeeScript interpreter before serving. You'll use CoffeeScript a little later, in chapter 9.

(If this is all going a bit over your head for now, don't worry. We'll come back to it later when we need to modify assets and add a design to the application.)

`csrf_meta_tags` is for protecting your forms from CSRF (http://en.wikipedia.org/wiki/CSRF) attacks. These types of attacks were mentioned a short while ago when we looked at the parameters for the `create` action. The `csrf_meta_tags` helper creates two `meta` tags, one called `csrf-param` and the other `csrf-token`. This unique token works by setting a specific key on forms that is then sent back to the server. The server checks this key, and if the key is valid, the form is deemed valid. If the key is invalid, an `ActionController::InvalidAuthenticityToken` exception occurs and the user's session is reset as a precaution.

Later in app/views/layouts/application.html.erb is this single line:

```
<%= yield %>
```

This line indicates to the layout where the current action's template is to be rendered. Create a new line just before `<%= yield %>`, and place the following code there:

```
<% flash.each do |key, message| %>
  <div><%= message %></div>
<% end %>
```

This code renders all the `flash` messages that are defined, regardless of their name and the controller they come from. These lines will display the `flash[:notice]` that you set up in the `create` action of the `ProjectsController`.

Run `bundle exec rspec` again, and you'll see that the test is now fully passing:

```
3 examples, 0 failures, 2 pending
```

Why do you have two pending tests? If you examine the output more closely, you'll see this:

```
.**

Pending: (Failures listed here are expected and do not affect your
suite's status)

  1) ProjectsHelper add some examples to (or delete)
     .../ticketee/spec/helpers/projects_helper_spec.rb
     # Not yet implemented
     # ./spec/helpers/projects_helper_spec.rb:14

  2) Project add some examples to (or delete)
     .../ticketee/spec/models/project_spec.rb
     # Not yet implemented
     # ./spec/models/project_spec.rb:4

Finished in 0.07268 seconds (files took 1.26 seconds to load)
3 examples, 0 failures, 2 pending
```

The key part is "or delete." Let's delete those two files, because you're not using them yet:

```
$ rm spec/models/project_spec.rb
$ rm spec/helpers/projects_helper_spec.rb
```

Afterward, run `bundle exec rspec` one more time:

```
.

Finished in 0.07521 seconds (files took 1.25 seconds to load)
1 example, 0 failures
```

Yippee! You've just written your first BDD test for this application! That's all there is to it.

If this process feels slow, that's how it's supposed to feel when you're new to anything. Remember when you were learning to drive a car? You didn't drive like Michael Schumacher as soon as you got behind the wheel. You learned by doing it slowly and methodically. As you progressed, you were able to do it more quickly, as you can all things with practice.

3.4.4   Committing changes

Now you're at a point where all your specs are running (just the one, for now). Points like this are great times to make a commit:

```
$ git add .
$ git commit -m "'Create a new project' feature complete."
```

Committing with older Git versions

If you're using a version of Git older than 2.0, running `git add .` when you want to stage the deletion of files will raise an error. You'll see something like the following:

```
warning: You ran 'git add' with neither '-A (--all)' or '--ignore-removal',
whose behaviour will change in Git 2.0 with respect to paths you removed.
Paths like '[filename]' that are
removed from your working tree are ignored with this version of Git.
```

If this happens, you can add the `-A` option to `git add`, which will stage *all* file changes, including file deletions:

```
$ git add -A .
```

You should commit often, because commits provide checkpoints you can revert back to if anything goes wrong. If you're going down a path where things aren't working, and you want to get back to the last commit, you can revert all your changes by using

```
$ git checkout .
```

> **USE GIT CHECKOUT . CAREFULLY!** This command doesn't prompt you to ask whether you're sure you want to take this action. You should be incredibly sure that you want to destroy your changes. If you're not sure and want to keep your changes while reverting back to the previous revision, it's best to use the `git stash` command. This command stashes your unstaged changes to allow you to work on a clean directory and lets you restore the changes using `git stash pop`.

With the changes committed to your local repository, you can push them off to the GitHub servers. If for some reason the code on your local machine goes missing, you have GitHub as a backup.

Run this command to push the code up to GitHub's servers:

```
$ git push
```

Commit early. Commit often.

3.4.5   Setting a page title

Before you completely finish working with this story, there's one more thing to point out: the templates (such as show.html.erb) are rendered *before* the layout. You can use this to your benefit by setting an instance variable such as @title in the show action's template; then you can reference it in your application's layout to show a title for your page at the top of the tab or window.

To test that the page title is correctly implemented, add a little bit extra to your scenario for it. At the bottom of the test in spec/features/creating_projects_spec.rb, add the four lines shown in the following listing.

Listing 3.19 spec/features/creating_projects_spec.rb

```
project = Project.find_by(name: "Sublime Text 3")
expect(page.current_url).to eq project_url(project)

title = "Sublime Text 3 - Projects - Ticketee"
expect(page).to have_title title
```

The first line here uses the find_by method to find a project by its name. This finds the project that has just been created by the code directly above it. The second line ensures that you're on what should be the show action in the ProjectsController. The third and fourth lines find the title element on the page by using Capybara's find method and check using have_title that this element contains the page title of "Sublime Text 3 - Projects - Ticketee."

If you run bundle exec rspec spec/features/creating_projects_spec.rb now, you'll see this error:

```
1) Users can create new projects with valid attributes
   Failure/Error: expect(page).to have_title title
     expected "Ticketee" to include "Sublime Text 3 - Projects -
     Ticketee"
```

This error is happening because the title element doesn't contain all the right parts, but this is fixable! Write this code into the top of app/views/projects/show.html.erb:

```
<% @title = "Sublime Text 3 - Projects - Ticketee" %>
```

This sets up a @title instance variable in the template. Because the template is rendered before the layout, you're able to then use this variable in the layout.

But if a page doesn't have a @title variable set, there should be a default title of "Ticketee." To set this up, enter the following code in app/views/layouts/application.html.erb where the title tag currently is:

```
<title><%= @title || "Ticketee" %></title>
```

In Ruby, instance variables that aren't set return nil as their value. If you try to access an instance variable that returns a nil value, you can use || to return a different value, as in this example.

With this in place, the test should pass when you run bundle exec rspec:

```
1 example, 0 failures
```

Now that this test passes, you can change your code and have a solid base to ensure that whatever you change works as you expect. To demonstrate this point, let's change the code in show to use a *helper* instead of setting a variable.

Helpers are methods you can define in the files in app/helpers, and they're made available in your views. Helpers are for extracting the logic from the views; views should just be about displaying information. Every controller that comes from the controller generator has a corresponding helper, and another helper module exists for the entire application: the `ApplicationHelper` module, which lives at app/helpers/application_helper.rb.

Open app/helpers/application_helper.rb and insert the code from the following listing.

Listing 3.20   app/helpers/application_helper.rb

```
module ApplicationHelper
  def title(*parts)
    unless parts.empty?
      content_for :title do
        (parts << "Ticketee").join(" - ")
      end
    end
  end
end
```

When you specify an argument in a method beginning with the splat operator (`*`), any arguments passed from this point will be available in the method as an array. Here that array can be referenced as `parts`. Inside the method, you check to see if `parts` is `empty?` by using a keyword that's the opposite of `if`: `unless`. If no arguments are passed to the `title` method, `parts` will be empty and `empty?` will return `true`.

If parts are specified for the `title` method, then you use the `content_for` method to define a named block of content, giving it the name `title`. Inside this content block, you join the parts together using a hyphen (-), meaning that this helper will output something like `"Sublime Text 3 - Projects - Ticketee"`.

This helper method will build up a text string that you can use as the title of any page, including the default value of `"Ticketee"`, and all you need to do is call it from the view with the right arguments—an array of the parts that will make up the title of the page. Neat.

Now you can replace the title line in app/views/projects/show.html.erb with this:

```
<% title(@project.name, "Projects") %>
```

Let's replace the `title` tag line in app/views/layouts/application.html.erb with this code:

```
<title>
  <% if content_for?(:title) %>
    <%= yield(:title) %>
  <% else %>
    Ticketee
  <% end %>
</title>
```

This code uses a new method called `content_for?`, which checks that the specified content block is defined. It's defined only if `content_for(:title)` is called somewhere, such as in the template. If it is, you use `yield` and pass it the name of the content block, which causes the content for that block to be rendered. If it isn't, then you output the word *Ticketee*, and that becomes the title.

When you run this test again with `bundle exec rspec`, it will still pass:

```
1 example, 0 failures
```

That's a lot neater, isn't it? Create a commit for that functionality and push your changes:

```
$ git add .
$ git commit -m "Add title functionality for project show page"
$ git push
```

Next up, we'll look at how you can stop users from entering invalid data into your forms.

3.4.6 Validations

The next problem to solve is preventing users from leaving a required field blank. A project with no name isn't useful to anybody. Thankfully, Active Record provides *validations* for this purpose. Validations are run just before an object is saved to the database, and if the validations fail, the object isn't saved. Ideally, in this situation, you want to tell the user what went wrong so they can fix it and attempt to create the project again.

With this in mind, you can add another test to ensure that this happens. Add it to spec/features/creating_projects_spec.rb using the code from the following listing.

Listing 3.21 spec/features/creating_projects_spec.rb

```
scenario "when providing invalid attributes" do
  visit "/"

  click_link "New Project"
  click_button "Create Project"

  expect(page).to have content "Project has not been created."
  expect(page).to have_content "Name can't be blank"
end
```

The first two lines are identical to the ones you placed in the other scenario. You should eliminate this duplication by making your code DRY (Don't Repeat Yourself!). This is another term you'll hear a lot in the Ruby world.[9] It's easy to extract common code from where it's being duplicated and move it into a method or module that you

---

[9] Some people like to use "DRY" like an adjective, and also refer to code that isn't DRY as WET (which doesn't actually stand for anything). We think those people are a bit weird.

can use instead of the duplication. One line of code is 100 times better than 100 lines of duplicated code.

To DRY up your code, define a `before` block before the first scenario. For RSpec, before blocks are run before *every* test in the file. Change spec/features/ creating_projects_spec.rb to look like this.

Listing 3.22   spec/features/creating_projects_spec.rb

```ruby
require "rails_helper"

RSpec.feature "Users can create new projects" do
  before do
    visit "/"

    click_link "New Project"
  end

  scenario "with valid attributes" do
    fill_in "Name", with: "Sublime Text 3"
    fill_in "Description", with: "A text editor for everyone"
    click_button "Create Project"

    expect(page).to have_content "Project has been created."

    project = Project.find_by(name: "Sublime Text 3")
    expect(page.current_url).to eq project_url(project)

    title = "Sublime Text 3 - Projects - Ticketee"
    expect(page).to have_title title
  end

  scenario "when providing invalid attributes" do
    click_button "Create Project"

    expect(page).to have_content "Project has not been created."
    expect(page).to have_content "Name can't be blank"
  end
end
```

There! That looks a lot better!

Now when you run `bundle exec rspec`, it will fail because it can't see the error message that it's expecting to see on the page:

```
1) Users can create new projects when providing invalid attributes
   Failure/Error: expect(page).to have_content "Project has not been
   created."
     expected to find text "Project has not been created." in "Project
     has been created."
```

ADDING VALIDATIONS

To get this test to do what you want it to do, you'll need to add a validation. Validations are defined on the model and are run before the data is saved to the database.

To define a validation to ensure that the name attribute is provided when a project is created, open the app/models/project.rb file and make it look like the following listing.

Listing 3.23   app/models/project.rb

```
class Project < ActiveRecord::Base
  validates :name, presence: true
end
```

The validates method's usage is the same as how you used it in chapter 1. It tells the model that you want to validate the name field, and that you want to validate its presence. There are other kinds of validations as well; for example, the :uniqueness key, when passed true as the value, validates the uniqueness of this field as well, ensuring that only one record in the table has that specific value.

UNIQUENESS VALIDATION   There are potential gotchas with the Active Record uniqueness validation that may allow duplicate data to be saved to the database. We're intentionally ignoring them for now, but we'll cover them, and how to resolve the issues they raise, in section 6.1.

With the presence validation in place, you can experiment with the validation by using the Rails console, which allows you to have all the classes and the environment from your application loaded in a sandbox environment. You can launch the console with this command,

```
$ rails console
```

or with its shorter alternative:

```
$ rails c
```

If you're familiar with Ruby, you may realize that this is effectively IRB with some Rails sugar on top. If you're new to both, IRB stands for Interactive Ruby, and it provides an environment for you to experiment with Ruby without having to create new files. The console prompt looks like this:[10]

```
Loading development environment (Rails 4.2.1)
irb(main):001:0>
```

At this prompt, you can enter any valid Ruby, and it'll be evaluated.

For now, the purpose of opening this console is to test the newly appointed validation. To do this, try to create a new project record by calling the create method. The create method is similar to the new method, but it attempts to create an object and then a database record for it rather than just the object. You use it identically to the new method:

```
irb(main):001:0> Project.create
=> #<Project id: nil, name: nil, description: nil, created_at: nil,
    updated_at: nil>
```

---

[10] Alternatively, you may see something similar to ruby-2.2.1:001 >, which is fine.

Here you get a new `Project` object with the `name` and `description` attributes set to nil, as you should expect, because you didn't specify it. The `id` attribute is `nil` too, which indicates that this object isn't persisted (saved) in the database.

If you comment out or remove the validation from the `Project` class and type `reload!` in your console, the changes you just made to the model are reloaded. When the validation is removed, you have a slightly different outcome when you call `Project.create`:

```
irb(main):001:0> Project.create
=> #<Project id: 1, name: nil, description: nil,
    created_at: [timestamp], updated_at: [timestamp]>
```

Here, the `name` field is still expectedly `nil`, but the other three attributes have values. Why? When you call `create` on the `Project` model, Rails builds a new `Project` object with any attributes you pass it and checks to see if that object is valid.[11] If it is, Rails sets the `created_at` and `updated_at` attributes to the current time and then saves the object to the database. After it's saved, the `id` is returned from the database and set on your object. This object is valid, according to Rails, because you removed the validation, so Rails goes through the entire process of saving.

The `create` method has a bigger, meaner brother called `create!` (pronounced *create BANG!*). Re-add or uncomment the validation from the model, and type `reload!` in the console, and you'll see what this mean variant does with this line:

```
irb(main):001:0> Project.create!
ActiveRecord::RecordInvalid: Validation failed: Name can't be blank
```

The `create!` method, instead of nonchalantly handing back a `Project` object regardless of any validations, raises an `ActiveRecord::RecordInvalid` exception if any of the validations fail; it shows the exception followed by a large stack trace, which you can safely ignore for now. You're notified which validation failed.

To stop it from failing, you must pass in a `name` attribute, and `create!` will happily return a saved `Project` object:

```
irb(main):002:0> Project.create!(name: "Sublime Text 3")
=> #<Project id: 2, name: "Sublime Text 3", description: nil,
    created_at: [timestamp], updated_at: [timestamp]>
```

That's how to use `create!` to test your validations in the console.

You've created some bad data in your database during this experimentation, so you should clean that up before you continue:

```
irb(main):003:0> Project.delete_all
=> 2
```

Back in your `ProjectsController`, you use the method shown in the following listing instead.

---

[11] The first argument for this method is the attributes. If no argument is passed, then all attributes default to their default values.

Listing 3.24 Part of the `create` action of `ProjectsController`

```
def create
  @project = Project.new(project_params)

  if @project.save
    ...
```

The `save` method doesn't raise an exception if validations fail, as `create!` does; instead it returns `false`. If the validations pass, `save` returns `true`.

You can use this to your advantage to show the user an error message when `save` returns `false` by using it in an `if` statement. Make the `create` action in the `Projects-Controller` look like the following listing.

Listing 3.25 The new `create` action from `ProjectsController`

```
def create
  @project = Project.new(project_params)

  if @project.save
    flash[:notice] = "Project has been created."
    redirect_to @project
  else
    flash.now[:alert] = "Project has not been created."
    render "new"
  end
end
```

---

flash vs. flash.now

The controller action in listing 3.25 uses two different methods to access the array of flash messages for your page—flash and flash.now. What's the difference?

flash is the standard way of setting flash messages, and it will store the message to display on the very *next* page load. You do this immediately before issuing redirects—in this case you redirect immediately to the show page in the ProjectsController, and that page is the next page load, meaning that the flash message displays on the show view.

flash.now is an alternative way of setting flash messages, and it will store the message to display on the *current* page load. In this case, you don't redirect anywhere, you simply render a view out from the same action, so you need to use flash.now to make sure the user sees the error message when you render the new view.

There's also a third method—flash.keep—but this is used very rarely. If you want to keep an existing flash message around for another request, you can call flash.keep in your controller, and the flash message will hang around for a little while longer.

If you were to use flash instead of flash.now in this case, the user would see the message twice—once on the current page and once on the next page.

If the `@project` object has a `name` attribute—meaning it's valid—`save` returns `true` and executes everything between `if` and `else`. If it isn't valid, then everything between `else` and the following `end` is executed. In the `else`, you specify a different key for the flash message because you'll want to style alert messages differently from notices later in the application's lifecycle. When good things happen, the messages for them will be colored with a green background; when bad things happen, red.

When you run `bundle exec rspec spec/features/creating_projects_spec.rb` now, the line in the spec that checks for the "Project has not been created" message doesn't fail, so it goes to the next line, which checks for the "Name can't be blank" message. You haven't done anything to make this message appear on the page yet, which is why the test is failing again:

```
1) Users can create new projects when providing invalid attributes
   Failure/Error: expect(page).to have_content "Name can't be blank"
      expected to find text "Name can't be blank" in "Project has not
      been created. New Project Name Description"
```

The validation errors for the project aren't being displayed on this page, which is causing the test to fail. To display validation errors in the view, you need to code something up yourself.

When an object fails validation, Rails will populate the `errors` of the object with any validation errors. You can test this back in your Rails console:

```
irb(main):001:0> project = Project.create
=> #<Project id: nil, name: nil, description: nil, created_at: nil,
      updated_at: nil>
rb(main):002:0> project.errors
=> #<ActiveModel::Errors:0x007fd5938197f8 @base=#<Project id: nil,
      name: nil, description: nil, created_at: nil, updated_at: nil>,
      @messages={:name=>["can't be blank"]}>
```

`ActiveModel::Errors` provides some nice helper methods for working with validation errors that you can use in your views to display the errors to the user. In the app/views/projects/new.html.erb file, directly under the `form_for` line, on a new line, insert the following into app/views/projects/new.html.erb to display the error messages in the form:

```erb
<% if @project.errors.any? %>
 <div id="error_explanation">
   <h2><%= pluralize(@project.errors.count, "error") %>
   prohibited this project from being saved:</h2>

   <ul>
     <% @project.errors.full_messages.each do |msg| %>
      <li><%= msg %></li>
     <% end %>
   </ul>
 </div>
<% end %>
```

Error messages for the object represented by your form, the @project object, will now be displayed by each.

When you run bundle exec rspec, you'll now get this output:

```
2 examples, 0 failures
```

Commit and push, and then you're done with this story!

```
$ git add .
$ git commit -m "Add validation to ensure names are specified when
  creating projects"
$ git push
```

3.5 *Summary*

We first covered how to version-control an application, which is a critical part of the application development cycle. Without proper version control, you're liable to lose valuable work or be unable to roll back to a known working stage. We used Git and GitHub as examples, but you may use an alternative, such as SVN or Mercurial, if you prefer. This book covers only Git, because covering everything would result in a multi-volume series, which is difficult to transport.

Next we covered the basic setup of a Rails application, which started with the rails new command that initializes an application. Then we segued into setting up the Gemfile to require certain gems for certain environments, such as RSpec in the test environment. You learned about the beautiful Bundler gem in the process, and then you ran the installers for these gems so your application was fully configured to use them. For instance, after running rails g rspec:install, your application was set up to use RSpec and so will generate RSpec specs rather than the default Test::Unit tests for your models and controllers.

Finally, you wrote the first story for your application, which involved generating a controller and a model as well as getting an introduction to RESTful routing and validations. With this feature of your application covered by RSpec, you can be notified if it's broken by running bundle exec rspec. This command runs all the tests of the application and lets you know if everything is working or if anything is broken. If something is broken, the spec will fail, and then it's up to you to fix it. Without this automated testing, you'd have to do it all manually, and that isn't any fun.

Now that you've got a first feature under your belt, let's get into writing the next one!

Oh, CRUD!

This chapter covers

- Building read, update, and delete functionality for projects
- Creating test data with Factory Girl
- Handling errors and rescuing exceptions
- Working with Sass and the asset pipeline
- Styling the application using Bootstrap
- Simplifying form markup with Simple Form

In chapter 3 you began writing stories for a CRUD (create, read, update, delete) interface for your Project model. Here you'll continue in that vein, beginning with writing a story for the *R* part of CRUD: reading. We often refer to reading as *viewing* in this and future chapters—we mean the same thing, but sometimes viewing is a better word.

In the remainder of the chapter, you'll round out the CRUD interface for projects, providing your users with ways to edit, update, and delete projects too. Best of all, you'll do this using behavior-driven development (BDD) the whole way through, continuing your use of the RSpec and Capybara gems that you saw in the last chapter.

This chapter's length is a testament to exactly how quickly you can get some CRUD actions up and running on a resource with Ruby on Rails.

Also in this chapter, you'll see a way to create test data extremely easily for your tests using a gem called factory_girl, as well as a way to make standard controllers a lot neater.

4.1 Viewing projects

The show action generated for the story in chapter 3 was only half of the viewing part of CRUD. The other part is the index action, which is responsible for showing a list of all of the projects. From this list, you can navigate to the show action for a particular project. The next story is about adding functionality that allows you to do that.

Create a new file in the features directory called spec/features/ viewing_projects_spec.rb.

> **Listing 4.1 spec/features/viewing_projects_spec.rb**

```
require "rails_helper"

RSpec.feature "Users can view projects" do
  scenario "with the project details" do
    project = FactoryGirl.create(:project, name: "Sublime Text 3")

    visit "/"
    click_link "Sublime Text 3"
    expect(page.current_url).to eq project_url(project)
  end
end
```

To run this single test, you can use `bundle exec rspec spec/features/ viewing_projects_spec.rb`. When you do, you'll see the following failure:

```
1) Users can view projects with the project details
   Failure/Error: project = FactoryGirl.create(:project,
   name: "Sublime Text 3")
   NameError:
     uninitialized constant FactoryGirl
```

The FactoryGirl constant is defined by another gem: the factory_girl gem.

4.1.1 Introducing Factory Girl

The factory_girl gem, created by thoughtbot (http://thoughtbot.com), provides an easy way to use *factories* to create new objects for your tests. Factories define a bunch of default values for an object, allowing you to easily craft example objects you can use in your tests.

Before you can use this gem, you need to add it to the :test group in your Gemfile. Now the entire group looks like this:

```
group :test do
  gem "capybara", "~> 2.4"
  gem "factory_girl_rails", "~> 4.5"
end
```

To install the gem, run `bundle`. With the factory_girl_rails gem installed, the Factory-Girl constant is now defined.

Run `bundle exec rspec spec/features/viewing_projects_spec.rb` again, and you'll see a new error:

```
1) Users can view projects with the project details
   Failure/Error: project = FactoryGirl.create(:project,
   name: "Sublime Text 3")
   ArgumentError:
     Factory not registered: project
```

When using Factory Girl, you must create a *factory* for each model you wish to use the gem with. If a factory isn't registered with Factory Girl, you'll get the previous error.

To register/create a factory, create a new directory in the spec directory called *factories*, and then in that directory create a new file called project_factory.rb. Fill that file with the content from the following listing.

Listing 4.2   spec/factories/project_factory.rb

```
FactoryGirl.define do
  factory :project do
    name "Example project"
  end
end
```

When you define the factory in this file, you give it a name attribute so that every new project generated by the factory via `FactoryGirl.create :project` will have the name "Example project." The `name: "Sublime Text 3"` part of this method call in spec/features/viewing_projects_spec.rb changes the name for that instance to the one passed in.

You use factories here because you don't need to be concerned about any other attribute on the Project object. If you weren't using factories, you'd just create the project the way you would anywhere else, like in the console:

```
Project.create(name: "Sublime Text 3")
```

Although this code is about the same length as its `FactoryGirl.create` variant, it isn't future-proof. If you were to add another field to the projects table and add a validation (say, a presence one) for that field, you'd have to change all occurrences of the `create` method in your tests to contain this new field. Over time, as your Project model got more and more attributes, the actual information that you cared about—in this case, the name—would get lost in all the unrelated data. In contrast, when you use a factory, you just need to change it in one place—where the factory is defined. If you cared about what that field was set to, you could modify it by passing it as one of the key/value pairs in the Factory call.

That's a lot of theory—how about some practice? Let's see what happens when you run `bundle exec rspec spec/features/viewing_projects_spec.rb` again:

```
1) Users can view projects with the project details
   Failure/Error: click_link "Sublime Text 3"
   Capybara::ElementNotFound:
     Unable to find link "Sublime Text 3"
```

A link appears to be missing. You'll add that next.

4.1.2 Adding a link to a project

Capybara is expecting a link on the page with the words "Sublime Text 3" but can't find it. The page in question is the homepage, which is the index action from your `ProjectsController`. Capybara can't find it because you haven't yet put it there, which is what you'll do now.

Open app/views/projects/index.html.erb and change the contents to the following.

Listing 4.3 app/views/projects/index.html.erb

```
<h1>Projects</h1>

<%= link_to "New Project", new_project_path %>

<div id="projects">
  <% @projects.each do |project| %>
    <h2><%= link_to project.name, project %></h2>
    <p><%= project.description %></p>
  <% end %>
</div>
```

This code adds a heading and some details on each of the projects. If you run the spec again, you'll get this error, which isn't helpful at first glance:

```
1) Users can view projects with the project details
   Failure/Error: visit "/"
   ActionView::Template::Error:
     undefined method `each' for nil:NilClass
   # ./app/views/projects/index.html.erb:6:in ...
```

This error points at line 6 of your app/views/projects/index.html.erb file, which reads `<% @projects.each do |project| %>`. From this you can determine that the error must have something to do with the `@projects` variable. This variable hasn't yet been defined, and as mentioned in chapter 3, instance variables in Ruby return `nil` rather than raise an exception. So because `@projects` is nil, and there's no each method on nil, you get this error, `undefined method 'each' for nil:NilClass`. Watch out for this in Ruby—as you can see here, it can sting you hard.

You need to define this variable in the index action of your controller. Open `ProjectsController` at app/controllers/projects_controller.rb, and change the index method definition to look like this.

Listing 4.4 index action of `ProjectsController`

```
def index
  @projects = Project.all
end
```

By calling `all` on the `Project` model, you retrieve all the records from the database as `Project` objects, and they're available as an enumerable `Array`-like object.

Now that you've put all the pieces in place, you can run the feature with `bundle exec rspec spec/features/viewing_projects_spec.rb`, and it should pass:

```
1 example, 0 failures
```

The spec now passes. Is everything else still working, though? You can check by running `bundle exec rspec`. Rather than just running the one test, this code runs all the tests in the spec directory. When you run the code, you should see this:

```
3 examples, 0 failures
```

All the specs are passing, meaning all the functionality you've written so far is working as it should. Commit and push them to GitHub using these commands:

```
$ git add .
$ git commit -m "Add the ability to view a list of all projects"
$ git push
```

The reading part of this CRUD resource is done! You've got the `index` and `show` actions for the `ProjectsController` behaving as they should. Now you can move on to *updating*.

4.2   *Editing projects*

With the first two parts of CRUD (creating and reading) done, you're ready for the third part: updating. Updating is similar to creating and reading in that it has two actions for each part (creation has `new` and `create`; reading has `index` and `show`). The two actions for updating are `edit` and `update`.

Let's begin by writing a feature and creating the `edit` action.

4.2.1   *The edit action*

As with the form used for creating new projects, you want a form that allows users to edit the information of a project that already exists. You first put an "Edit Project" link on the `show` page that takes users to the `edit` action, where they can edit the project. Put the code from the following listing into spec/features/editing_projects_spec.rb.

> **Listing 4.5   spec/features/editing_projects_spec.rb**

```
require "rails_helper"

RSpec.feature "Users can edit existing projects" do
  scenario "with valid attributes" do
    FactoryGirl.create(:project, name: "Sublime Text 3")

    visit "/"
    click_link "Sublime Text 3"
    click_link "Edit Project"
    fill_in "Name", with: "Sublime Text 4 beta"
    click_button "Update Project"
```

```
    expect(page).to have_content "Project has been updated."
    expect(page).to have_content "Sublime Text 4 beta"
  end
end
```

If you remember, FactoryGirl#create builds you an entire object and lets you tweak the defaults. In this case, you're changing the name.

Also, it's common for tests to take this overall form: *arrange, act, assert*. (This is also referred to as *given, when, then*, to describe the actions that take place in each section.) That's why the whitespace is there: it clearly splits the test. Your tests won't always look like this, but it's good form.

After writing this story, again use the rspec command to run just this one feature: bundle exec rspec spec/features/editing_projects_spec.rb. The first couple of lines for this scenario pass because of the work you've already done, but it fails on the line that attempts to find the "Edit Project" link:

```
1) Users can edit existing projects with valid attributes
   Failure/Error: click_link "Edit Project"
   Capybara::ElementNotFound:
     Unable to find link "Edit Project"
```

To add this link, open app/views/projects/show.html.erb and add the link under the heading for the project name:

```
<%= link_to "Edit Project", edit_project_path(@project) %>
```

The edit_project_path method generates a link pointing to the edit action of the ProjectsController. This method is provided to you because of the resources :projects line in config/routes.rb.

If you run bundle exec rspec spec/features/editing_projects_spec.rb again, it now complains about the missing edit action:

```
1) Users can edit existing projects with valid attributes
   Failure/Error: click_link "Edit Project"
   AbstractController::ActionNotFound:
     The action 'edit' could not be found for ProjectsController
```

Define this action in your ProjectsController, under the show action (but above the private line), as in the following listing.

Listing 4.6 app/controllers/projects_controller.rb

```
def edit
  @project = Project.find(params[:id])
end
```

As you can see, this action works in a fashion identical to the show action, where the ID for the resource is automatically passed as params[:id]. After we've finished building the functionality in this controller, we'll look at DRYing it up to remove the duplicated code.[1]

---

[1] As a reminder: DRY = Don't Repeat Yourself!

When you run the spec again, you're told that the edit view is missing:

```
1) Users can edit existing projects with valid attributes
   Failure/Error: click_link "Edit Project"
   ActionView::MissingTemplate:
     Missing template projects/edit, application/edit with
       {
       :locale => [:en],
       :formats => [:html],
       :variants => [],
       :handlers => [:erb, :builder, :raw, :ruby, :coffee, :jbuilder]
       }.

     Searched in:
     * ".../ticketee/app/views"
```

It looks like you need to create this template. The edit action's form is similar to the form in the new action—if only there were a way to extract out just the form into its own template. Well, in Rails, there is! You can extract out the form from app/views/projects/new.html.erb into what's called a *partial*. You saw partials briefly in chapter 1.

A *partial* is a template that contains code that can be shared between other templates. To extract the form from the new template into a new partial, take the following code out of app/views/projects/new.html.erb.

Listing 4.7   app/views/projects/new.html.erb

```erb
<%= form_for(@project) do |f| %>
  <% if @project.errors.any? %>
   <div id="error_explanation">
     <h2><%= pluralize(@project.errors.count, "error") %>
     prohibited this project from being saved:</h2>

     <ul>
       <% @project.errors.full_messages.each do |msg| %>
        <li><%= msg %></li>
       <% end %>
     </ul>
   </div>
  <% end %>

  <p>
   <%= f.label :name %><br>
   <%= f.text_field :name %>
  </p>

  <p>
   <%= f.label :description %><br>
   <%= f.text_field :description %>
  </p>

  <%= f.submit %>
<% end %>
```

This will leave the new template looking pretty bare, with just the heading.

Then create a new file called app/views/projects/_form.html.erb and put the code you just extracted from the new template into it. While moving it, you should also change all instances of @project to project.

```erb
<%= form_for(project) do |f| %>
  <% if project.errors.any? %>
   <div id="error_explanation">
     <h2><%= pluralize(project.errors.count, "error") %>
     prohibited this project from being saved:</h2>

     <ul>
       <% project.errors.full_messages.each do |msg| %>
        <li><%= msg %></li>
       <% end %>
     </ul>
   </div>
  <% end %>

  <p>
    <%= f.label :name %><br>
    <%= f.text_field :name %>
  </p>

  <p>
    <%= f.label :description %><br>
    <%= f.text_field :description %>
  </p>

  <%= f.submit %>
<% end %>
```

FILE-NAMING CONVENTIONS FOR PARTIALS   The filenames of partials must always start with an underscore, which is why we've written _form instead of form.

Why do this variable renaming? Because to be reusable, partial views shouldn't rely on instance variables—they should be totally self-sufficient. When you render the partial from your main view, you can *pass in* the data that the partial needs to render—in this case, you'll pass in the @project variable from the new template, which means it will be accessible as a local variable from within the partial.

To render the partial and pass in the @project instance, modify your new template in app/views/projects/new.html.erb and add this line where the form previously was:

```erb
<%= render "form", project: @project %>
```

This will leave your new template very slim indeed.

```erb
<h1>New Project</h1>
<%= render "form", project: @project %>
```

REFACTORING Extracting the form code and creating the partial is an example of *refactoring*—changing the internals of the code without affecting functionality. You can confirm that this refactoring hasn't affected your ability to create projects by running the test for it—bundle exec rspec spec/ features/creating_projects_spec.rb. It will still pass, so you can be very confident that everything still works.

Now you need to create the edit action's template. Create a new file at app/views/ projects/edit.html.erb with the following content.

Listing 4.10 app/views/projects/edit.html.erb

```
<h1>Edit Project</h1>
<%= render "form", project: @project %>
```

When you pass a string to the render method, Rails looks up a partial in the same directory as the current template matching the string, and renders that instead.

Using the partial, the next line passes without any further intervention from you when you run bundle exec rspec spec/features/editing_projects_spec.rb:

```
1) Users can edit existing projects with valid attributes
   Failure/Error: click_button "Update Project"
   AbstractController::ActionNotFound:
     The action 'update' could not be found for ProjectsController
```

The test has filled in the Name field successfully; but it fails when Update Project is clicked, because it can't find the update action in the ProjectsController. To make this work, you'll need to create that update action.

4.2.2 *The update action*

As the following listing shows, you can now define update under the edit action in your controller.

Listing 4.11 app/controllers/projects_controller.rb

```
def update
  @project = Project.find(params[:id])
  @project.update(project_params)

  flash[:notice] = "Project has been updated."
  redirect_to @project
end
```

Notice the new method on @project here: update. It takes a hash of attributes identical to the ones passed to new or create, updates those specified attributes on the object, and then saves them to the database if they're valid. This method, like save, returns true if the update is valid or false if it isn't.

Now that you've implemented the update action, let's see how the test is going by running bundle exec rspec spec/features/editing_projects_spec.rb:

```
1 example, 0 failures
```

That was easy! But what happens if somebody fills in the Name field with a blank value? The user should receive an error, just as in the create action, due to the validation in the Project model. You should write a test to verify this behavior.

Move the first four steps from the first scenario in spec/features/editing_projects_spec.rb into a before block, because when a user is editing a project, the first four steps will always be the same: a project needs to exist, and then a user goes to the homepage, finds a project, and clicks Edit Project. Change spec/features/editing_projects_spec.rb so it looks like this.

Listing 4.12   After introducing a before block to simplify test setup

```
require "rails_helper"

RSpec.feature "Users can edit existing projects" do
  before do
    FactoryGirl.create(:project, name: "Sublime Text 3")

    visit "/"
    click_link "Sublime Text 3"
    click_link "Edit Project"
  end

  scenario "with valid attributes" do
    fill_in "Name", with: "Sublime Text 4 beta"
    click_button "Update Project"

    expect(page).to have_content "Project has been updated."
    expect(page).to have_content "Sublime Text 4 beta"
  end
end
```

A before block can help set up state for multiple tests; the block runs before each test executes. Sometimes, setting up is more than just creating objects; interacting with an application is totally legitimate as part of the setup.

DEFINING BEHAVIOR FOR WHEN AN UPDATE FAILS

Now you can add a new scenario, as shown in the following listing, to test that the user is shown an error message when the validations fail during the update action. Add this new scenario directly under the one currently in this file.

Listing 4.13   Specifying expected behavior when a project fails validation

```
scenario "when providing invalid attributes" do
  fill_in "Name", with: ""
  click_button "Update Project"

  expect(page).to have_content "Project has not been updated."
end
```

When you run `bundle exec rspec spec/features/editing_projects_spec.rb`, filling in the Name field works, but when the form is submitted, the test doesn't see the "Project has not been updated" message:

```
1) Users can edit existing projects when providing invalid attributes
   Failure/Error: expect(page).to have_content "Project has not been
   updated."
      expected to find text "Project has not been updated." in "Project
      has been updated. Sublime Text 3 Edit Project"
```

The test can't find the message on the page because you haven't written any code to test for what to do if the project being updated is now invalid. In your controller, use the code in the following listing for the `update` action so that it shows the error message if the `update` method returns `false`.

Listing 4.14   The `update` action of `ProjectsController`

```
def update
  @project = Project.find(params[:id])

  if @project.update(project_params)
    flash[:notice] = "Project has been updated."
    redirect_to @project
  else
    flash.now[:alert] = "Project has not been updated."
    render "edit"
  end
end
```

Now you can see that the feature passes when you rerun `bundle exec rspec spec/features/editing_projects_spec.rb`:

```
2 examples, 0 failures
```

Again, you should ensure that everything else is still working by running `bundle exec rspec`. You should see this summary:

```
5 examples, 0 failures
```

Looks like a great spot to make a commit and push:

```
$ git add .
$ git commit -m "Projects can now be updated"
$ git push
```

The third part of CRUD, updating, is done now. The fourth and final part is *deleting*.

4.3   Deleting projects

We've reached the final stage of CRUD: deletion. This involves implementing the final action of your controller: the `destroy` action, which allows you to delete projects.

Of course, you'll need a feature to get going: a "Delete Project" link on the `show` page that, when clicked, prompts the user for confirmation that they really want to delete the project.[2] Put the feature at spec/features/deleting_projects_spec.rb using the code in the following listing.

Listing 4.15   spec/features/deleting_projects_spec.rb

```
require "rails_helper"

RSpec.feature "Users can delete projects" do
  scenario "successfully" do
    FactoryGirl.create(:project, name: "Sublime Text 3")

    visit "/"
    click_link "Sublime Text 3"
    click_link "Delete Project"

    expect(page).to have_content "Project has been deleted."
    expect(page.current_url).to eq projects_url
    expect(page).to have_no_content "Sublime Text 3"
  end
end
```

When you run this test using `bundle exec rspec spec/features/deleting_projects _spec.rb`, the first couple of lines pass because they're just creating a project using Factory Girl, visiting the homepage, and then clicking the link to go to the project page. The fourth line in this scenario fails, however, with this message:

```
1) Users can delete projects successfully
   Failure/Error: click_link "Delete Project"
   Capybara::ElementNotFound:
     Unable to find link "Delete Project"
```

To get this to work, you need to add a "Delete Project" link to the `show` action's template, app/views/projects/show.html.erb. Put it on the line after the "Edit Project" link using this code:

```
<%= link_to "Delete Project",
    project_path(@project),
    method: :delete,
    data: { confirm: "Are you sure you want to delete this project?" }
%>
```

Here you pass two new options to the `link_to` method—`:method` and `:data`. The `:method` option tells Rails what HTTP method this link should be using, and here's where you specify the `:delete` method. In the previous chapter, the four HTTP methods were mentioned; the final one is `DELETE`. When you developed your first application, chapter 1 explained why you use the `DELETE` method, but let's review the reasons.

If all actions are available by `GET` requests, then anybody can create a URL that directly corresponds to the `destroy` action of your controller. If they send you the link, and you click it, then it's bye-bye precious data. Using `DELETE`, you protect an

---

[2] The test won't check for this prompt, due to the difficulty in testing JS confirmation boxes in tests.

important route for your controller by ensuring that a user has to follow the correct link from your site to make the proper request to delete this resource.

The :data option containing a :confirm key brings up a prompt, using JavaScript, that asks users if they're sure that's what they want to do. If you launch a browser and follow the steps in the feature to get to this "Delete Project" link, and then you click the link, you'll see the confirmation prompt. This prompt is exceptionally helpful for preventing accidental deletions.

Both this prompt and the DELETE request are created by jquery_ujs—part of the jquery-rails gem, which is listed in your Gemfile.

Troubleshooting deletion

If you ever create delete functionality and clicking the link goes to the show action instead of the destroy action, you might not be loading the jquery_ujs file correctly. You should check your app/assets/javascripts/application.js file and make sure it's loading the file:

```
//= require jquery_ujs
```

Because Capybara doesn't support JavaScript by default, the prompt is ignored. You don't have to tell Capybara to click OK in response to the prompt—there is no prompt, because Rails has a built-in fallback for users without JavaScript enabled.

When you run the spec again with bundle exec rspec spec/features/deleting_projects_spec.rb, it complains of a missing destroy action:

```
1) Users can delete projects successfully
   Failure/Error: click_link "Delete Project"
   AbstractController::ActionNotFound:
     The action 'destroy' could not be found for ProjectsController
```

This is the final action you need to implement in your controller; it goes under the update action. The action is shown in the following listing.

Listing 4.16   The destroy action from ProjectsController

```ruby
def destroy
  @project = Project.find(params[:id])
  @project.destroy

  flash[:notice] = "Project has been deleted."
  redirect_to projects_path
end
```

Here you call the destroy method on the @project object that you get back from your find call. No validations are run, so no conditional setup is needed. Once you call destroy on that object, the relevant database record is gone for good; but the Ruby object representation of this record still exists until the end of the request.

After the record has been deleted from the database, you set the flash[:notice] to indicate to the user that their action was successful, and redirect back to the project's index page by using the projects_path routing helper in combination with redirect_to.

With this last action in place, your newest feature should pass when you run bundle exec rspec spec/features/deleting_projects_spec.rb:

```
1 example, 0 failures
```

Let's see if everything else is running with bundle exec rspec:

```
6 examples, 0 failures
```

Great! Commit that:

```
$ git add .
$ git commit -m "Projects can now be deleted"
$ git push
```

Done! Now you have full support for CRUD operations in your ProjectsController. You've coded support for all of the cases you can think of, that you expect to see during the day-to-day running of the web application, but what about the ones you don't expect? You can make a few small adjustments to your work so far, making for a nicer experience when these edge cases occur. As an added bonus, you'll refactor your controller to get rid of some of the duplicated code, and make it simpler overall.

4.4 What happens when things can't be found

People sometimes poke around an application looking for things that are no longer there, or they muck about with the URL. As an example, launch your application's server by using rails server, and try to navigate to http://localhost:3000/projects/not-here. You'll see the exception shown in figure 4.1.

This is Rails' way of displaying exceptions in development mode. Under this error, more information is displayed, such as the backtrace of the error. Rails will only do this in the development environment because of the consider_all_requests_local

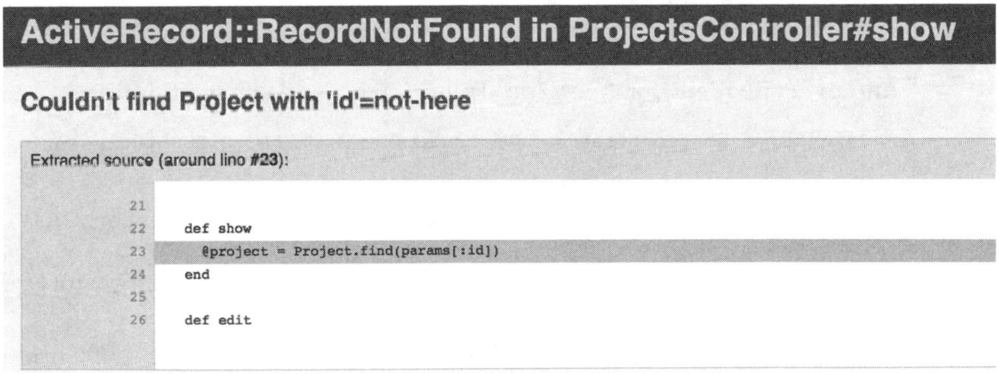

ActiveRecord::RecordNotFound in ProjectsController#show

Couldn't find Project with 'id'=not-here

Extracted source (around line #23):

```
21
22      def show
23        @project = Project.find(params[:id])
24      end
25
26      def edit
```

Figure 4.1 ActiveRecord::RecordNotFound **exception**

configuration setting in config/environments/development.rb. This file contains all the custom settings for your development environment, and the `consider_all _requests_local` setting is `true` by default. This means Rails will show the complete exception information when it runs in the development environment.

If you were running in the *production* environment, you'd see a different error because `consider_all_requests_local` in config/environments/production.rb is set to `false`.

Let's try to reproduce this production error now.

4.4.1   *Visualizing the error*

Stop any Rails server that's currently running, and run these commands to start preparing to run a new one in production mode:

```
$ bundle exec rake assets:precompile
$ bundle exec rake db:migrate RAILS_ENV=production
```

In order for the Rails production environment to work correctly, you must first compile the assets for the project using the `assets:precompile` rake task. This goes through all the assets of the application, compiles them into their CSS and JS counterparts, and then places these new files into public/assets so they can be served by the web server that's running Rails. This isn't too relevant to what you're doing now, but it's necessary so that you can see what the production environment will do.

On the second line, you must specify the `RAILS_ENV` environment variable to tell Rails that you want to run the migrations on your production database. By default in Rails, the development and production databases are kept separate so you don't make the mistake of working with production data and deleting something you shouldn't when you're working in the development environment. This problem is also typically solved by placing the production version of the code on a different server from the one you're developing on—usually you'd have your production server out in the cloud, serving your app to the world.

In the production environment, the Rails server is configured to not serve static assets (such as JavaScript and images) itself. Instead, it relies on the host web server to serve the assets out of the public directory. In order for assets to be served correctly in the production environment while running a `rails server` session, you need to go into the config/environments/production.rb file and change this line,

```
config.serve_static_files = ENV['RAILS_SERVE_STATIC_FILES'].present?
```

to this:

```
config.serve_static_files = true
```

This tells Rails that you want to serve static assets from the public directory using Rails itself.

Next, start the server running in the production environment by using this command:

```
$ SECRET_KEY_BASE=`rake secret` rails s -e production
```

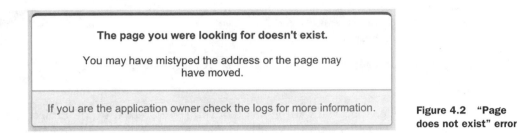

Figure 4.2 "Page
does not exist" error

You pass the -e production option to the rails server command, which tells Rails to boot the server using the production environment. The SECRET_KEY_BASE at the start is used to provide an environment variable of the same name that's used in config/secrets.yml. This key is used to encrypt sessions in a production environment.

Next, navigate to http://localhost:3000/projects/not-here. When you do this, you'll get the standard Rails 404 page (see figure 4.2), which, to your users, is unhelpful.

It's not the page that's gone missing; rather, the *resource* you're looking for isn't found. If users see this error, they'll probably have to click the Back button and then refresh the page. You could give users a much better experience by dealing with the error message yourself and redirecting them back to the homepage.

Before we move on, let's undo the stuff you just did: it's not a good idea to have Rails serve assets in production, and it's also not good to check compiled assets into source control. Stop the server you just started, and to undo your code changes, do this:

```
$ git add .
$ git reset --hard
```

Yay for Git! This adds all of your changes to the repository index, including the pre-compiled assets, and then resets that index to the last commit (effectively deleting all of the changes you just added). Easy!

4.4.2 Handling the ActiveRecord::RecordNotFound exception

To handle the ActiveRecord::RecordNotFound exception, you can *rescue* it and, rather than letting Rails render a 404 page, redirect the user to the index action with an error message. To test that users are shown an error message rather than a "Page does not exist" error, you'll write an RSpec controller test instead of a feature test, because viewing projects that aren't there is something a user *can* do, but not something that *should* happen over the course of a normal browsing session. Plus, it's easier.

The file for this controller test, spec/controllers/projects_controller_spec.rb, was automatically generated when you ran the controller generator, because you have the rspec-rails gem in your Gemfile.[3] Open this controller spec file. It should look like the following listing.

---

[3] The rspec-rails gem automatically generates the file using a Railtie, the code for which can be found at http://mng.bz/7X4i.

Listing 4.17   spec/controllers/projects_controller_spec.rb

```
require 'rails_helper'

RSpec.describe ProjectsController, type: :controller do

end
```

In this controller spec, you want to test that you're redirected to the Projects page if you attempt to access a resource that no longer exists. You also want to ensure that a flash[:alert] is set.

To do all this, put the following code in the RSpec.describe block:

```
it "handles a missing project correctly" do
  get :show, id: "not-here"

  expect(response).to redirect_to(projects_path)

  message = "The project you were looking for could not be found."
  expect(flash[:alert]).to eq message
end
```

The first line in this RSpec test—more commonly called an *example*—tells RSpec to make a GET request to the show action of the ProjectsController. How does it know which controller should receive the GET request? RSpec infers it from the class used for the describe block.

In the next line, you tell RSpec that you expect the response to take you back to the projects_path through a redirect_to call. If it doesn't, the test fails, and nothing more in this test is executed: RSpec stops in its tracks.

The final line tells RSpec that you expect flash[:alert] to contain a useful message explaining the redirection to the index action.

To run this spec, use the bundle exec rspec spec/controllers/ projects_controller_spec.rb command. When this runs, you'll see this error:

```
1) ProjectsController handles a missing project correctly
   Failure/Error: get :show, id: "not-here"
   ActiveRecord::RecordNotFound:
     Couldn't find Project with 'id'=not-here
```

This is the same failure you saw when you tried running the application using the development environment with rails server. Now that you have a failing test, you can fix it.

Open the app/controllers/projects_controller.rb file, and put the code from the following listing under the private line in the controller.

Listing 4.18   set_project method in ProjectsController

```
def set_project
  @project = Project.find(params[:id])
rescue ActiveRecord::RecordNotFound
```

```
    flash[:alert] = "The project you were looking for could not be found."
    redirect_to projects_path
end
```

Because it's under the `private` line, the controller doesn't respond to this method as an action. To call this method before every action that looks up a project, use the `before_action` method. Place this line directly under the `class ProjectsController` definition:

```
before_action :set_project, only: [:show, :edit, :update, :destroy]
```

What does all this mean? Methods referenced by `before_action` are run before all the actions in your controller, unless you specify either the `:except` or `:only` option. Here you have the `:only` option, defining actions for which you want `before_action` to run. The `:except` option is the opposite of the `:only` option, specifying the actions for which you *don't* want `before_action` to run. `before_action` calls the `set_project` method before the specified actions, setting up the `@project` variable for you. This means you can remove the following line from your `show`, `edit`, `update`, and `destroy` actions:

```
@project = Project.find(params[:id])
```

This makes the `show` and `edit` actions empty. If you remove these actions from your controller and run `bundle exec rspec` again, all the scenarios will still pass:

```
7 examples, 0 failures
```

Controller actions don't need to exist in the controllers if there are templates corresponding to those actions, which you have for these actions. For readability's sake though, it's best to leave these in the controller so anyone who reads the code knows that the controller can respond to these actions, so put the empty `show` and `edit` actions back in. Future-you will thank you.

Back to the spec now. If you run `bundle exec rspec spec/controllers/projects_controller_spec.rb` once more, the test now passes:

```
1 example, 0 failures
```

Let's check to see if everything else is still working by running `bundle exec rspec`. You should see this:

```
7 examples, 0 failures
```

Red-green-refactor! With that out of the way, you can commit and push:

```
$ git add .
$ git commit -m "Redirect the users back to the projects page if they
  try going to a project that does not exist"
$ git push
```

This completes the basic CRUD implementation for your `Project` resource. Now you can create, read, update, and delete projects to your heart's content.

4.5 *Styling the application*

The application is currently looking a bit plain, as you can see in figure 4.3.

You can change this by using Bootstrap, which is a front-end CSS and JavaScript framework that comes with a collection of styles that you can apply to your application.

> **BOOTSTRAP ALTERNATIVES** Instead of Bootstrap, you could use Zurb Foundation (http://foundation.zurb.com) or any one of the other CSS frameworks out there. We recommend Bootstrap out of preference.

New Project

Name

Description

Create Project

Figure 4.3 A plain form

As part of your application styling you'll also add a gem called Simple Form, which in conjunction with Bootstrap will turn the previous form into what you see in figure 4.4.

You'll notice the asterisk next to the Name field here. This is because the Name field is a required field, required because you have a validation on your `Project` model for the presence of this field. Simple Form detects this and displays the field as a required field.

Simple Form not only makes the form neater, but also makes the code for generating a form much simpler. You have now this:

```
<p>
  <%= f.label :name %><br>
  <%= f.text_field :name %>
</p>

<p>
  <%= f.label :description %><br>
  <%= f.text_field :description %>
</p>
```

Simple Form allows you to write this instead:

```
<%= f.input :name %>
<%= f.input :description %>
```

New Project

* Name

Description

Create Project

Figure 4.4 A neater form

Bootstrap also lends itself to more than just forms. You'll use it in this section to style the flash messages from your application, as well as add a navbar to the top of the screen. Let's get started!

4.5.1 Installing Bootstrap

The first thing you need to do is install the bootstrap-sass gem, which comes with Sass versions of the Bootstrap assets. This gem is the recommended way to install Bootstrap into a Rails application, because Rails includes the sass-rails gem in its Gemfile by default.

Install this gem now by adding the following line outside of any groups inside your Gemfile:

```
gem "bootstrap-sass", "~> 3.3"
```

Next, you'll need to run bundle to install the gem, and restart the Rails server if it's running already.

To add Bootstrap's styles to your application, you make your main application stylesheet a Sass file by renaming app/assets/stylesheets/application.css to application.css.scss, adding the .scss extension to the end of the filename. This extension tells the asset pipeline that this file should be processed using the Sass preprocessor before it's presented as a CSS file. This preprocessing will parse the @import directives that you're about to use.

Replace the entire contents of that application.css.scss file with the following listing.

> **Listing 4.19 app/assets/stylesheets/application.css.scss, with Bootstrap imported**

```
@import "bootstrap-sprockets";
@import "bootstrap";
```

These two lines import all of Bootstrap's CSS components.

> **LIMITING BOOTSTRAP IMPORTS** The preceding import includes *a lot* of CSS and probably includes pieces that you won't ever use. If you're concerned about how much this includes, you can pick and choose @import lines from bootstrap-sass (http://git.io/YgGoCw) to only include the parts you want.

With these assets now imported, you can restart your server and go to http://localhost:3000 to see some changes immediately (see figure 4.5).

The styling of your homepage has changed to reflect Bootstrap's default styling. That was easy! It's all flush against the left side of the page, though. You can fix this by wrapping all of the content in a container in app/views/layouts/application.html.erb:

Figure 4.5   Projects page, Bootstrapified

```
<body>

  <div class="container">
  <% flash.each do |key, message| %>
    <div><%= message %></div>
  <% end %>

  <%= yield %>
</div>

</body>
```

Figure 4.6   Now with padding!

This element will shift the content away from the left side of the page, as shown in figure 4.6.

4.5.2   *Improving the page's header*

Next up, let's make the header section of the page look a little bit nicer, starting with the main heading. Bootstrap provides a nice `page-header` class you can use to give a bit of style, so you can wrap that around the h1 in app/views/projects/index.html.erb:

```
<div class="page-header">
  <h1>Projects</h1>
</div>
```

It adds some nice spacing around the important header, and an underline. So far so good.

   Now let's look at the actions you can take on this page—the most obvious action is to create a new project, so let's make the "New Project" link stand out. You can also make the button be part of the page header and put it on the right side to give the page a bit of balance.

   In app/views/projects/index.html.erb, change the code from this,

```
<div class="page-header">
  <h1>Projects</h1>
</div>

<%= link_to "New Project", new_project_path %>
```

to this:

```
<div class="page-header">
  <h1>Projects</h1>

  <ul class="actions">
    <li><%= link_to "New Project", new_project_path,
      class: "btn btn-success" %></li>
  </ul>
</div>
```

The relevant page actions are now part of the header, in a list (some pages will have multiple actions to take, such as edit and delete). Adding the two `btn btn-success` classes to any HTML element will change its appearance into a button, as shown in figure 4.7.

Figure 4.7   The new New Project button

The `btn-success` turns it into a specific *type* of button.[4] You can add a little more flair to this button by adding an icon from the Font Awesome project (http://fontawesome.github.io/Font-Awesome/), turning it into this:

To get to that newest, best-looking version of the form, add  the font-awesome-rails gem to your Gemfile, underneath the bootstrap-sass gem:

```
gem "font-awesome-rails", "~> 4.3"
```

Just like the bootstrap-sass gem, the font-awesome-rails gem also comes with some assets. The assets from the font-awesome-rails gem give you a whole range of icons, shown on the Font Awesome icons page: http://fontawesome.github.io/Font-Awesome/icons/.

To use these icons, you must first run `bundle` and restart the Rails server. Then you'll need to add another `@import` line to app/assets/stylesheets/application.css.scss, after the ones that you have already.

Listing 4.20   Adding font-awesome to your application.css.scss

```
@import "font-awesome";
```

To add the icon to the button, you can use the `fa_icon` helper as part of the link in app/views/projects/index.html.erb, like this:

```
<li><%= link_to fa_icon("plus") + " New Project", new_project_path,
  class: "btn btn-success" %></li>
```

It will now look like figure 4.8.

As for positioning it where you want, you can do so with a couple of lines of CSS, to be placed at the bottom of your app/assets/stylesheets/application .css.scss file:

Figure 4.8   The new new New Project button

```
.page-header {
  position: relative;
  padding-bottom: 0px;

  &:first-child {
    margin-top: 20px;
  }

  h1, h2, h3, h4, h5, h6 {
    max-width: 55%;
  }
}

ul.actions {
  @extend .list-unstyled;
  @extend .list-inline;
  position: absolute;
  bottom: -2px;
```

---

[4]   The other button types can be found here: http://getbootstrap.com/css/#buttons.

```
  right: 2px;
  max-width: 45%;
  text-align: right;
}
```

This does several things:

- It reduces the spacing between the heading and the underline with padding-bottom: 0px, and makes the header *relatively positioned* so you can move the list of actions around in it at will.
- It changes the top margin on the first .page-header on the page to 20 px.
- It makes the list of actions *absolutely positioned* and declares that you want it to be near the bottom right of the parent .page-header element.
- It uses some of Bootstrap's classes to remove the bullet points that normally denote lists and make the list items sit side by side instead of below each other.
- It sets maximum widths on the two elements in the .page-header div, to prevent any possible overlap.

If that's a lot to take in and it doesn't really make sense, that's okay—this isn't meant to be a CSS tutorial. But it will make your headers look nice, as shown in figure 4.9.

Figure 4.9   The final page header on the Projects index view

You can apply similar styling to the views for the new, edit, and show actions. The new and edit views have no action menus, so their page headers can simply be tweaked to add the .page-header wrapper element.

Listing 4.21   The new header on app/views/projects/new.html.erb

```
<div class="page-header">
  <h1>New Project</h1>
</div>
```

Listing 4.22   The new header on app/views/projects/edit.html.erb

```
<div class="page-header">
  <h1>Edit Project</h1>
</div>
```

4.5.3   *Improving the show view*

The show view is a little more work, because it has links of different types. One link edits; the other deletes. The header section of the page currently looks like figure 4.10.

Figure 4.10   The unstyled page header on app/views/projects/show.html.erb

Let's change that header to look like this:

```
<div class="page-header">
  <h1><%= @project.name %></h1>

  <ul class="actions">
    <li><%= link_to fa_icon("pencil") + " Edit Project",
      edit_project_path(@project), class: "btn btn-primary" %></li>
    <li><%= link_to fa_icon("trash") + " Delete Project",
      project_path(@project),
      method: :delete,
      data: { confirm: "Are you sure you want to delete this project?" },
      class: "btn btn-danger" %></li>
  </ul>
</div>
```

Like before, there's a `<div class="page-header">` around the header, and the links are now in a list of action links. We've chosen different button styles for this page—btn-primary for editing and btn-danger for deleting. btn-danger links are bright red, indicating a dangerous action. There are also some appropriate icons for the links.

These links will now be styled nicely, as shown in figure 4.11. That's all looking better, but you can do a lot better in the code!

Figure 4.11 The improved show view

4.5.4 Semantic styling

As it stands at the moment, whenever you have a link in your application to create, edit or delete an object, you'll have to add all this markup around it with the fa_icon and the class attribute. Rather than repeating all that markup, you can use *semantic styling*. All the creation links will look the same way, all the editing links will look the same way, and all the deletion links will look the same way; so why not style them all in an easier fashion? Plus, if you decide later that all creation links should be styled differently, you'll only have to update the code in one place—in the stylesheet. Very DRY.

STYLING BUTTONS

To make your buttons semantic, you can go back to app/views/projects/index.html.erb and change the "New Project" link to the following.

Listing 4.23 Less presentational markup in the HTML

```
<%= link_to "New Project", new_project_path, class: "new" %>
```

The new class will contain *all* the stylings for any "New" link in your application, including the icon.

To make this new button look just like your old unsemantic button, you'll need to write some new Sass in application.css.scss.

> **Listing 4.24 More presentational styling in the CSS, where it belongs**

```
a.new {
  @extend .btn;
  @extend .btn-success;

  &:before {
    font-family: "FontAwesome";
    @extend .fa-plus;
    padding-right: 0.5em;
  }
}
```

This new code first adds the styles from Bootstrap's btn and btn-success classes to any a element with the new class, using the @extend directive from Sass. This directive allows you to extend any element's styling with any other element's styles.

Next, you use the &:before rule, which allows you to place content *before* the content within an element. In this case, you set the font-family to "FontAwesome" so that it uses the icon font. Then you use @extend again to add the same plus icon that you had earlier. The fa_icon helper method that we used previously in our view generated an i element with the class fa-plus—we can replicate the styles from that element by extending that same fa-plus class here. The final line, padding-right, adds padding to the right side of this element so that the icon and the "New Project" text have space between them.

If you look at the "New Project" link again, you'll see it still has the same styles.

All of this has been accomplished with less styling in the view, and more in the CSS file where it belongs. You can use these same techniques for the "Edit" and "Delete" links inside of app/views/projects/show.html.erb, converting them to just this:

```
<ul class="actions">
  <li><%= link_to "Edit Project", edit_project_path(@project),
    class: "edit" %></li>

  <li><%= link_to "Delete Project", project_path(@project),
    method: :delete,
    data: { confirm: "Are you sure you want to delete this project?" },
    class: "delete" %></li>
</ul>
```

Next, you can add styles for edit and delete classes to app/assets/stylesheets/application.css.scss, in much the same way as you added styles for the new class:

```
a.edit {
  @extend .btn;
  @extend .btn-primary;
```

```
  &:before {
    font-family: "FontAwesome";
    @extend .fa-pencil;
    padding-right: 0.5em;
  }
}

a.delete {
  @extend .btn;
  @extend .btn-danger;

  &:before {
    font-family: "FontAwesome";
    @extend .fa-trash;
    padding-right: 0.5em;
  }
}
```

If you go to your project's page once again, shown in figure 4.12, you'll see the "Edit Project" and "Delete Project" links have stayed the same.

Figure 4.12   The refactored page looks unchanged

You're not done, though. There's a bit of duplication happening in this file, which you can clean up to just the following.

Listing 4.25   Removing duplication from the `new`, `edit`, and `delete` styles

```
a.new, a.edit, a.delete {
  @extend .btn;

  &:before {
    font-family: "FontAwesome";
    padding-right: 0.5em;
  }
}

a.new {
  @extend .btn-success;

  &:before {
    @extend .fa-plus;
  }
}

a.edit {
  @extend .btn-primary;

  &:before {
    @extend .fa-pencil;
  }
}
```

```
a.delete {
  @extend .btn-danger;

  &:before {
    @extend .fa-trash;
  }
}
```

The links with `new`, `edit`, and `delete` classes will now be styled identically as buttons that use Font Awesome. From there, each different class has its button type and icon specified in different rules.

Where else can you apply this semantic styling? Well, you could replace the `<div class="page-header">` tags with something more meaningful, like a `<header>` tag. After all, if you want to use more than one of the page headers on a single page, it's not really a *page* header, is it?

You can make those changes to your views that use `<div class="page-header">`, as in listings 4.26 through 4.29.

Listing 4.26   app/views/projects/index.html.erb

```
<header>
  <h1>Projects</h1>
  ...
</header>
```

Listing 4.27   app/views/projects/new.html.erb

```
<header>
  <h1>New Project</h1>
</header>
```

Listing 4.28   app/views/projects/edit.html.erb

```
<header>
  <h1>Edit Project</h1>
</header>
```

Listing 4.29   app/views/projects/show.html.erb

```
<header>
  <h1><%= @project.name %></h1>
  ...
</header>
```

Now you can style your new `header` tags by using the `@extend` directive again, this time to extend the `.page-header` class you were using before. You can do this in your stylesheet, replacing the old `.page-header` selector you were using.

Listing 4.30　app/assets/stylesheets/application.css.scss

```
header {
  @extend .page-header;
  position: relative;
  padding-bottom: 0px;

  &:first-child {
    margin-top: 20px;
  }
}
```

If you refresh all your pages, they should look exactly the same as they did before—you haven't changed any styles with your `header` tag, you've just made them more semantic.

Back on the homepage, you can now tackle the overly large headings for the names of projects. It's easy to do with CSS. Because this CSS is specific to projects of your site, you can put it in the stylesheet that was generated when you generated the `ProjectsController` in app/assets/stylesheets/projects.scss.

Listing 4.31　Specific styling for projects

```
#projects h2 {
  font-size: 16px;
  font-weight: bold;
  margin: 20px 0px 0px;
}
```

You can then load this stylesheet into your application.css.scss with another `@import` rule, below the rule that loads font-awesome.

Listing 4.32　Importing the projects.scss stylesheet

```
@import "projects";
```

If you refresh your browser now, you can see that the headings are a bit larger than the descriptions of the projects, they're bold, and they're nicely spaced (see figure 4.13).

STYLING FLASH MESSAGES

The next thing that you can style is the flash messages that appear. If you create another project in the Ticketee application, you can see how plain they are:

Project has been created.

Projects

Sublime Text 3
The newest hotness around.

Test Project
Test Project Description

Figure 4.13　A projects listing that doesn't look ugly!

To make flash messages stand out more, you can apply Bootstrap's alert styling to them. Open app/views/layouts/application.html.erb and change the code in listing 4.33 to match that in listing 4.34.

Listing 4.33   Unstyled flash message output

```
<% flash.each do |key, message| %>
  <div><%= message %></div>
<% end %>
```

Listing 4.34   Styled flash message output

```
<% flash.each do |key, message| %>
  <div class="alert alert-<%= key %>">
    <%= message %>
  </div>
<% end %>
```

The alert class for each piece of the flash will make this object stand out more, and the alert-<%= key %> will use another class called alert-notice or alert-alert to color the flash message box a different color. If you look at Bootstrap's documentation for its alerts (http://getbootstrap.com/components/#alerts), you can see that alert-notice and alert-alert aren't available, as shown in figure 4.14.

In the alerts figure, you can see two that look like the kind of thing you want: alert-success and alert-danger. You can make your alert-notice and alert-alert classes

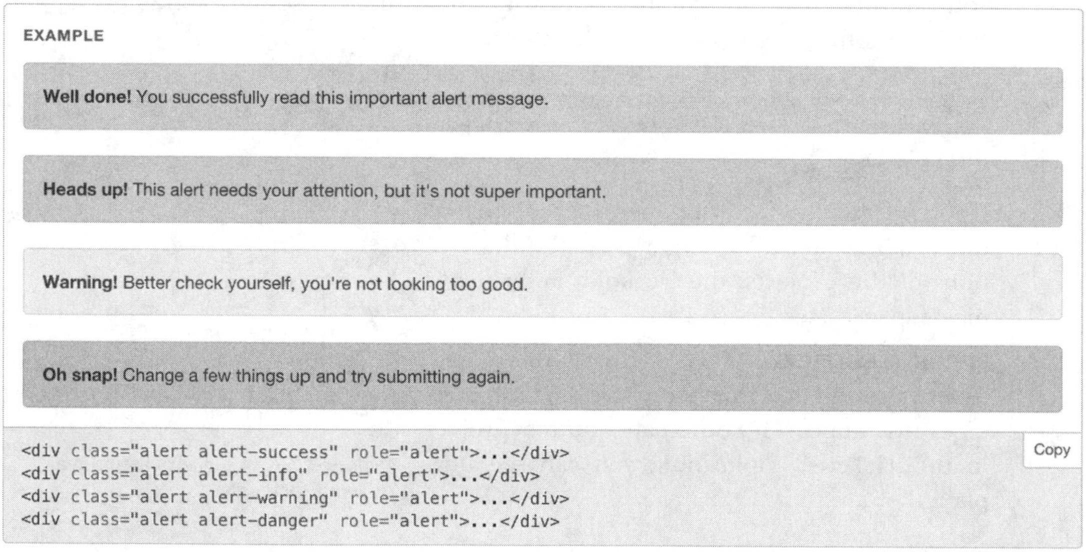

EXAMPLE

Well done! You successfully read this important alert message.

Heads up! This alert needs your attention, but it's not super important.

Warning! Better check yourself, you're not looking too good.

Oh snap! Change a few things up and try submitting again.

```
<div class="alert alert-success" role="alert">...</div>
<div class="alert alert-info" role="alert">...</div>
<div class="alert alert-warning" role="alert">...</div>
<div class="alert alert-danger" role="alert">...</div>
```

Copy

Figure 4.14   Bootstrap alerts

use the stylings of these two other classes by adding the following code to app/assets/
stylesheets/application.css.scss:

```
.alert-notice {
  @extend .alert-success;
}

.alert-alert {
  @extend .alert-danger;
}
```

When an alert with the `class` attribute of `alert-notice` is displayed, it will be styled as
if it had a `class` attribute of `alert-success`. This is thanks to the `@extend` directive in
Sass, which you used earlier with the "New," "Edit," and "Delete" links. When you create a project again, you should see a much nicer
styled flash message.

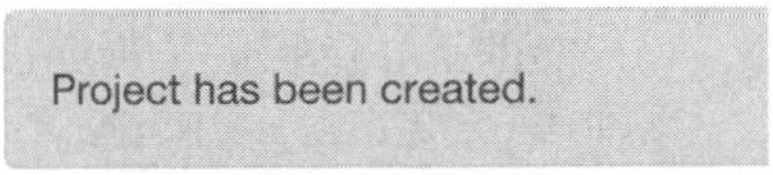

> Project has been created.

That's much nicer! Let's see what it looks like
when you force a validation error by not entering
a name for a new project.

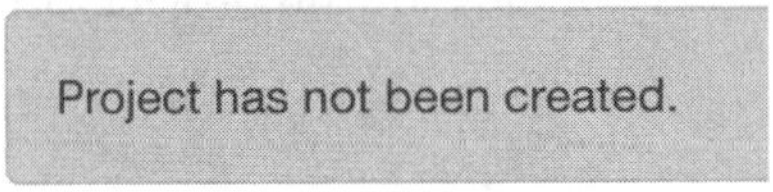

> Project has not been created.

That's looking good too! That's all for the
flash stylings. The next thing to do is restyle your
project form to take it from its appearance in figure 4.15 to what is shown in figure 4.16.

4.5.5 Using Simple Form

To change the form to its new styling, we'll enlist the help of another gem called Simple
Form, which provides not only a shorter syntax for rendering forms, but also has Bootstrap integration. Add this gem under the font-awesome-rails gem in your Gemfile:

```
gem "simple_form", "~> 3.1.0"
```

Run `bundle` to install the gem.

New Project

Name

[   ]

Description

[   ]

[Create Project]

**Figure 4.15   The current "New
Project" form**

New Project

* Name

[   ]

Description

[   ]

[Create Project]

Figure 4.16   The restyled "New Project" form

Next, run this command to set up the gem for the application:

```
$ rails g simple_form:install --bootstrap
```

This command will install the things that Simple Form needs, as well as two config files—simple_form.rb and simple_form_bootstrap.rb. Files such as these in the config/ initializers directory are run when a Rails server boots. After installing this gem, restart your server once again.

To use Simple Form for your projects form, you'll need to make a few changes. First, change the first line in app/views/projects/_form.html.erb from this,

```
<%= form_for(project) do |f| %>
```

to this:

```
<%= simple_form_for(project) do |f| %>
```

This will tell the view to use the form builder from Simple Form rather than the one that's built into Rails.

Next, you can simplify the code used for rendering the `name` and `description` fields for the project form, turning it from this,

```
<p>
  <%= f.label :name %><br>
  <%= f.text_field :name %>
</p>

<p>
  <%= f.label :description %><br>
  <%= f.text_field :description %>
</p>

<%= f.submit %>
```

into this:

```
<%= f.input :name %>
<%= f.input :description %>

<%= f.button :submit, class: "btn-primary" %>
```

You don't need to use the surrounding `<p>` tags any more, or even describe what types of fields these are. The Simple Form gem takes care of all of that for you with the `input` helper. It also generates a button for you, using its `button` helper, which operates similarly to the old `f.submit` method, but styles it using Bootstrap's default styles. You add the `btn-primary` class here to make the button blue.

> **WHY NOT USE SEMANTIC STYLING FOR THE BUTTON?**   We could use semantic styling for the form's Submit button and have it automatically take the `btn-primary` class, because it's simply a Submit button for a form. But some forms in the application may do dangerous things, and we may want those buttons styled differently. Therefore, we'll explicitly style each button as we go along.

New Project

* Name

Description

Create Project

Figure 4.17   The revised "New Project" form

If you refresh the form page now, you'll see the form shown in figure 4.17.

It's looking good. But if you submit the form with some validation errors, you'll get a nasty shock (see figure 4.18).

You now have two sets of error messages, one styled, and one not! You only put one set of errors on the page—the top "1 error prohibited this project from being saved" set. The second set of errors, next to the fields they relate to, are provided by Simple Form. They're easier for users to understand—if you had a long form and you wanted to know which fields you have errors for, it might require scrolling up and down. So you can just use the Simple Form errors, and delete the error messages you added.

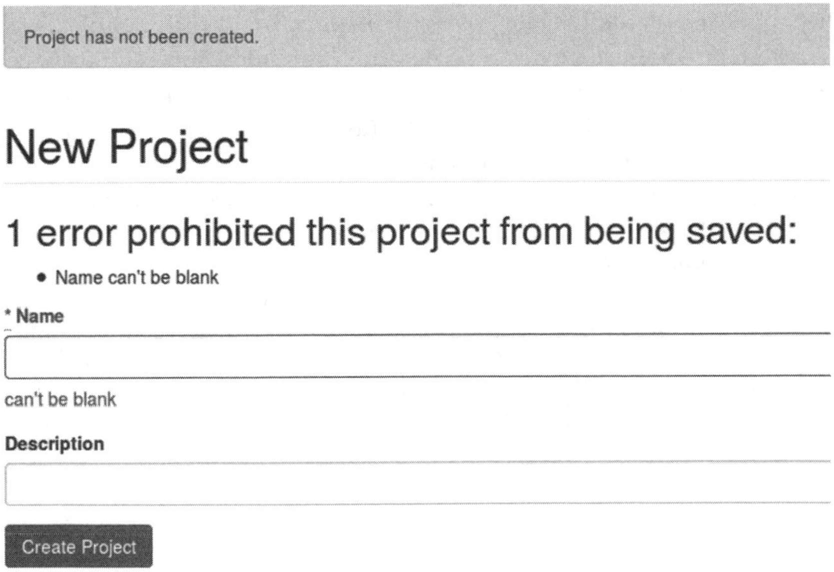

Project has not been created.

New Project

1 error prohibited this project from being saved:

- Name can't be blank

* Name

can't be blank

Description

Create Project

Figure 4.18   The "New Project" form with validation errors

Open up app/views/projects/_form.html.erb and delete the whole errors block so that it looks like the following listing.

Listing 4.35   The new _form.html.erb partial, without duplicate error messages

```
<%= simple_form_for(project) do |f| %>
  <%= f.input :name %>
  <%= f.input :description %>

  <%= f.button :submit, class: 'btn-primary' %>
<% end %>
```

The code is much simpler than the original form partial you started off with, and the unsightly double errors are now gone!

This has an unfortunate side effect though, as you'll see if you run the spec for creating projects, with bundle exec rspec spec/features/creating_projects_spec.rb:

```
1) Users can create new projects when providing invalid attributes
   Failure/Error: expect(page).to have_content "Name can't be blank"
     expected to find text "Name can't be blank" in "Project has not
     been created. New Project * Name can't be blank Description"
```

Oops. You were checking for the presence of an error message that you just deleted, and by default Simple Form displays shortened error messages, such as "can't be blank." Luckily, it's easy to configure Simple Form to use full error messages that include the name of the field. Because you're using Simple Form with Bootstrap, the configuration you want is in config/initializers/simple_form_bootstrap.rb.

The initializer file defines lots of *wrappers*—instructions to Simple Form on the HTML to generate for given types of forms and form fields. You can nearly completely customize the HTML output, including the error messages. The default wrapper that Simple Form uses is called :vertical_form (as specified at the bottom of the config file), so that's the wrapper you need to modify.

Inside the config.wrappers :vertical_form, tag: 'div', class: 'form-group' block, you need to modify the line that references using the :error component, shown in the following listing.

Listing 4.36   Using the default error component of Simple Form and Bootstrap

```
config.wrappers :vertical_form, tag: 'div', class: 'form-group',
error_class: 'has-error' do |b|
  ...
  b.use :error, wrap_with: { tag: 'span', class: 'help-block' }
  ...
end
```

Simple Form also provides a :full_error component that will include the name of the field in the error message, giving you friendlier messages like "Name can't be blank." Change this line to use the :full_error component instead.

Listing 4.37 Using the :`full_error` component

```
b.use :full_error, wrap_with: { tag: 'span', class: 'help-block' }
```

After changing the initializer file, restart your Rails server. Refresh the form, and the error messages will now be in the correct format.

This will also fix the broken spec—you can verify this by running `bundle exec rspec spec/features/creating_projects_spec.rb`:

```
2 examples, 0 failures
```

Perfect.

The fields on this form are quite long. In fact, they stretch all the way across the page. This is unnecessary, so you can shorten them by applying a `max-width` to all basic form elements in your application.css.scss file. The form now looks like what you see in figure 4.19.

```
form {
  max-width: 500px;
}
```

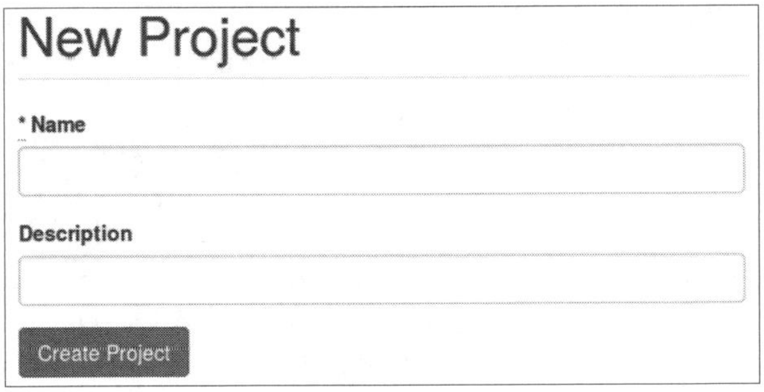

Figure 4.19   The "New Project" form with shorter fields

Great! Now all of the project pages in your application are looking good.

4.5.6   Adding a navigation bar

We'll do one more thing and then wrap up here: add a navigation bar to the top of the application's layout. It will look like figure 4.20.

Figure 4.20   Adding a navigation bar

This is by far easier than the Bootstrap work that you've done so far; all you need to do is add this content above the flash messages (above the `<div class="container">` in your application's layout).

Listing 4.38   app/views/layouts/application.html.erb

```erb
<nav class="navbar navbar-default navbar-fixed-top" role="navigation">
  <div class="container">
    <div class="navbar-header">
      <%= link_to "Ticketee", root_path, class: "navbar-brand" %>
      <button type="button" class="navbar-toggle collapsed"
        data-toggle="collapse" data-target="#collapse">
        <span class="sr-only">Toggle navigation</span>
        <span class="icon-bar"></span>
        <span class="icon-bar"></span>
        <span class="icon-bar"></span>
      </button>
    </div>

    <div class="collapse navbar-collapse" id="collapse">
      <ul class="nav navbar-nav">
        <li class="<%= "active" if current_page?("/") %>">
          <%= link_to "Home", root_path %>
        </li>
      </ul>
    </div>
  </div>
</nav>
```

The `navbar` contains two different parts: a header and the navigation itself. The header contains a link that shows the "Ticketee" text, and when that link is clicked it will take the user back to the homepage. In the navigation, you add a "Home" link, in case people don't realize that clicking Ticketee will take them back to the root path. If the user is currently at the / path, then an extra class called `active` is added to the `li` for that link, turning it a different color.

If you go to the application's homepage, you'll now see the navbar, as in figure 4.21.

Figure 4.21   Home-page with navbar

Oops, you've got a fixed navbar that sits at the top of the page, but now it overlaps the content that was previously sitting at the top of the page. You can fix that by adding some padding to the top of the body, which will push all of the content down (but won't affect the navbar, because it's *absolutely positioned* just like your action links are).

Listing 4.39   The bottom of app/assets/stylesheets/application.css.scss

```scss
body {
  padding-top: 70px;
}
```

Ticketee | Home

Projects

Figure 4.22 Home-page with navbar and padding

Now things are much better spaced, as you can see in figure 4.22.

You're also using the *responsive* navbar, meaning that it will display nicely on both large and small screens. You can test this out by resizing your browser wider and smaller. When the window gets below 768 px wide, the navbar will automatically switch to its "small" display (see figure 4.23).

Ticketee ≡

Figure 4.23 The Ticketee header, optimized for small screens

It looks good! But the button at the top right, which is supposed to cause the menu to expand, doesn't work yet—it uses JavaScript to show and hide the menu contents, and you haven't included Bootstrap's JavaScript into your application yet.

Like you included Bootstrap's CSS into your application.css.scss file, you also need to include its JavaScript. Open up app/assets/javascripts/application.js and check out what it looks like. You haven't modified it yet, so at the bottom it will have four important lines.

Listing 4.40 The important parts of the default application.js file

```
//= require jquery
//= require jquery_ujs
//= require turbolinks
//= require_tree .
```

They look like JavaScript comments, but they're actually instructions for Sprockets, which powers the asset pipeline, to include the named files. You can add Bootstrap's JavaScript file in here with the following line placed before the require_tree . line:

```
//= require bootstrap-sprockets
```

Now when you refresh your browser and click the little three-bar icon,[5] the menu should expand and contract, like in figure 4.24.

Ticketee ≡

Home

Figure 4.24 The optimized Ticketee header, now with added navigation

The is a little bare at the moment, but you'll fill it out in future chapters.

---

[5] Or "hamburger icon," as it's often called.

4.5.7   *Responsive styling*

You've fixed the top navigation bar to be fully responsive, but it would be great if your whole app looked good on the go, whether on a mobile phone, tablet, or any other device. Let's look at implementing that now.

First, you need to include a special `meta` tag in your document to ensure that responsive styles get picked up by mobile devices. Without this tag, you'd see the same layout as you do on a desktop, just very, very small to fit on the smaller screens.

Add the following line of code just inside the <head> section of the page, in app/views/layouts/application.html.erb:

```
<meta name="viewport" content="width=device-width, initial-scale=1">
```

> **THE META TAG**   Some background information on this `meta` tag can be found on the Mozilla Developer Network (https://developer.mozilla.org/en/docs/Mozilla/Mobile/Viewport_meta_tag).

For now, you don't have to know exactly how it works, but you know that it does work—your mobile browser won't artificially pretend it has more pixels than it has, to render larger layouts in smaller spaces.

Now your pages will use properly responsive styles on mobile. What else can you improve? You can use similar responsive styling for tweaking the `header` sections of your pages.

At the moment, if the text gets long and the window gets small, you'll end up with some very squashed text and a lot of whitespace around the buttons (see figure 4.25). On such a small screen, the buttons visually take precedence over the heading. The heading should come first, and then the actions below it, in a neater fashion.

You can do this by introducing *media queries* for your styles. These involve wrapping `media` method calls around your styles, as in the following listing.

Figure 4.25   I'm not a designer but … I can make this look better!

Listing 4.41   A media query example

```
@media(max-width: 500px) {
  p { color: red }
}
```

This sample rule states that if the width of the screen is less than 500 px, then all paragraphs should be red. You could add this rule to your stylesheet, try resizing your browser, and watch your text change colors on the fly. Cool, huh?

Bootstrap uses media queries internally for lots of things, like the navbar styles you saw earlier. If the screen is larger, the links in the bar appear in a line; if its smaller, they're hidden, but then appear on their own line when revealed. You can do a similar sort of thing using Bootstrap's own defined styles.

Bootstrap defines several screen sizes, as detailed in its CSS documentation: http://getbootstrap.com/css/#responsive-utilities. Each of these sizes has two Sass variables relating to the minimum and maximum screen widths the styles apply to; for example, the sm small screen size has $screen-sm-min and $screen-sm-max definitions. You can use these variables in your own media queries so your rules line up with Bootstrap's styles.

xs (extra-small) screens are the ones you want to change your styles for—this is the typical phone size. On xs screens, you want to do a couple of things:

- Undo the max-width setting for headings inside header blocks, since it's far too narrow.
- Undo the max-width and position styles for ul.actions link blocks.

But instead of this approach, it would be better to change those styles so that they only apply to styles that are bigger than xs. Is that possible? It sure is.

Make a new stylesheet in your app/assets/stylesheets folder and call it responsive.scss. This is where all your responsive styles will go. As you did earlier with projects.scss, you can include this new stylesheet in your main application.css.scss by using the @import rule.

Listing 4.42   After including the responsive.scss file

```
@import "bootstrap-sprockets";
@import "bootstrap";
@import "font-awesome";
@import "projects";
@import "responsive";
```

Inside this responsive.scss file, you can write a media query to target all browsers that are wider than the xs screen size.

Listing 4.43   Targeting bigger-than-xs screen sizes

```
@media(min-width. $screen-sm-min) {
}
```

You can also move some of your existing styles into your new media query. In particular, you can move the header { h1, h2, h3, h4, h5, h6 {} } rule and most of the ul.actions styles. In the end, you should have the two blocks in the following two listings.

Listing 4.44   In the main application.css.scss

```scss
header {
  @extend .page-header;
  position: relative;
  padding-bottom: 0px;

  &:first-child {
    margin-top: 20px;
  }
}

ul.actions {
  @extend .list-unstyled;
  @extend .list-inline;
}
```

Listing 4.45   In responsive.scss

```scss
@media(min-width: $screen-sm-min) {
  header {
    h1, h2, h3, h4, h5, h6 {
      max-width: 55%;
    }
  }

  ul.actions {
    position: absolute;
    bottom: -2px;
    right: 2px;
    max-width: 45%;
    text-align: right;
  }
}
```

Now let's see what happens when you resize the browser, smaller and larger. When you get to the xs screen size, when the top navigation changes styles, your main heading goes to full width and the buttons slide to sit underneath it. It's not super-beautiful, but it's much more usable on smaller screens, including on phones, as seen in figure 4.26.

Whew, that was a lot of styling work! That completes all of the Bootstrap additions for the time being. Throughout the remainder of the book, we'll use features of Bootstrap as they're needed to improve the design of the application, but you've got the basic foundation in place.

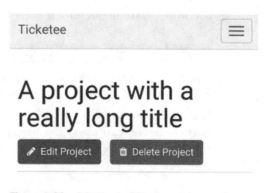

Figure 4.26   A better-looking layout for small screens

Commit and push your recent changes now:

```
$ git add .
$ git commit -m "Added Bootstrap for styling"
$ git push
```

4.6   *Summary*

This chapter continued developing the first part of your application using test-first practices with RSpec and Capybara, building it one step at a time. Now you have an application that's truly maintainable. If you want to know if these specs are working later in the project, you can run `bundle exec rspec`; if something is broken that you've written a test for, you'll know about it. Doesn't that beat manual testing? Just think of all the time you'll save in the long run.

You learned firsthand how rapidly you can develop the CRUD interface for a resource in Rails. There are even faster ways to do it (such as by using *scaffolding*, discussed in chapter 1); but to absorb how this process works, it's best to go through it yourself, step by step, as you did in these last two chapters.

So far, you've been developing your application using test-first techniques, and as your application grows, it will become more evident how useful these techniques are. The main thing they'll provide is assurance that what you've coded so far still works exactly as it did when you first wrote it. Without these tests, you may accidentally break functionality and not know about it until a user—or worse, a client—reports it. It's best that you spend some time implementing tests for this functionality now so you don't spend even more time later apologizing for whatever's broken and fixing it.

With the basic projects functionality for creating and managing projects done, you're ready for the next step. Because you're building a ticket-tracking application, it makes sense to implement functionality that lets you track tickets, right? That's precisely what you'll do in the next chapter. We'll also cover nested routing and association methods for models. Let's go!

Nested resources 5

This chapter covers

- Nested routing helpers and named routes
- Creating associations to link models together
- Making tests more expressive using let and let!

The project resource CRUD was completed in chapter 4, so the next step is to set up the ability to create tickets within the scope of a given project. This chapter explores how to set up a nested resource in Rails, by defining routes for `Ticket` resources and creating a CRUD interface for them, all scoped under the project resource that you just created.

In this chapter, you'll see how easy it is to retrieve all ticket records for a specific project and perform CRUD operations on them, mainly with the powerful associations interface that Rails provides through its Active Record component.

5.1 Creating tickets

To add the functionality to create tickets under projects, you'll first develop the Capybara features, and then implement the code required to make them pass. Nesting one resource under another involves additional routing, working with associations in Active Record, and using more calls to `before_action`. Let's get into this.

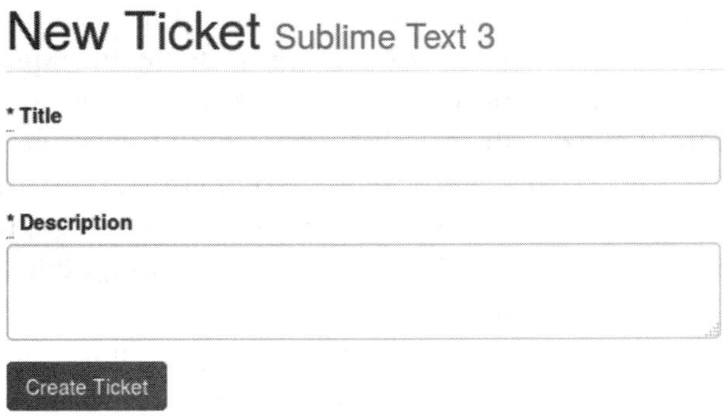

New Ticket Sublime Text 3

* Title

* Description

Create Ticket

**Figure 5.1   Form for
creating new tickets**

**Figure 5.1   Form for
creating new tickets**

To create tickets for your application, you need an idea of what you're going to implement. You want to create tickets only for particular projects, so you need a "New Ticket" link on a project's show page. The link must lead to a form where a name and a description for your ticket can be entered, and the form needs a button that submits it to a create action in your controller. You also want to ensure that the data entered is valid, as you did with the Project model. This new form will look like figure 5.1.

Start by putting the code from the following listing in a new file.

Listing 5.1   spec/features/creating_tickets_spec.rb

```
require "rails_helper"

RSpec.feature "Users can create new tickets" do
  before do
    project = FactoryGirl.create(:project, name: "Internet Explorer")

    visit project_path(project)
    click_link "New Ticket"
  end

  scenario "with valid attributes" do
    fill_in "Name", with: "Non-standards compliance"
    fill_in "Description", with: "My pages are ugly!"
    click_button "Create Ticket"

    expect(page).to have_content "Ticket has been created."
  end

  scenario "when providing invalid attributes" do
    click_button "Create Ticket"

    expect(page).to have_content "Ticket has not been created."
    expect(page).to have_content "Name can't be blank"
    expect(page).to have_content "Description can't be blank"
  end
end
```

You've seen the `before` method before, in section 4.2, when you were setting up the project data you needed for the "Users can edit existing projects" feature spec to run. Here you do a similar thing—set up the project that your tickets will be attached to. Your ticket objects need a parent project object to belong to (in this example system, a ticket can't exist outside of a project), so it makes sense to build one before every test.

You want to make sure you test the basic functionality of creating a ticket. It's pretty straightforward: start on the project page, click the "New Ticket" link, fill in the attributes, click the Submit button, and make sure it works!

You should also test the failure case. Because you need to have a name and description, a failing case is easy: click the Create Ticket button prematurely, before filling out all of the required information.

When you run this new feature using the `bundle exec rspec spec/features/ creating_tickets_spec.rb` command, both of your tests will fail due to your `before` block:

```
1) Users can create new tickets with valid attributes
   Failure/Error: click_link "New Ticket"
   Capybara::ElementNotFound:
     Unable to find link "New Ticket"

# and the second error is identical
```

You need to add the "New Ticket" link to the bottom of the app/views/projects/ show.html.erb template so that this line in the test will work. You can copy the format you used for the projects `index` view, and build a `header` with the action link in it.

Listing 5.2   A new section for tickets

```
<header>
  <h2>Tickets</h2>

  <ul class="actions">
    <li><%= link_to "New Ticket", new_project_ticket_path(@project),
      class: "new" %></li>
  </ul>
</header>
```

This `new_project_ticket_path` named route is a _nested route_, created via nested routing definitions. It's like the standard routing helper—the similarities and differences between the two are explained in the next section.

5.1.1   *Nested routing helpers*

When defining the "New Ticket" link, you used a nested routing helper— `new_project_ticket_path`—rather than a standard routing helper such as `new_ticket_path`, because you want to create a new ticket for a given project. Both helpers work in a similar fashion, except the nested routing helper always takes at least one argument: the `Project` object that the ticket belongs to. This is the parent resource that your ticket resource will be nested inside. The route to any ticket URL is always scoped by /projects/:id in your application.

This helper and its brethren are defined by changing this line in config/routes.rb,

```
resources :projects
```

to these lines:

```
resources :projects do
  resources :tickets
end
```

This code tells the routing for Rails that you have a `tickets` resource nested inside the `projects` resource. Effectively, any time you access a ticket resource, you access it within the scope of a project. Just as the `resources :projects` method gave you helpers to use in controllers and views, this nested resource of tickets within projects gives you the helpers shown in table 5.1. In the table's left column are the routes that can be accessed, and in the right are the routing helper methods you can use to access them.

Table 5.1 Nested RESTful routing match-up

Route	Helper
/projects/:project_id/tickets	project_tickets_path
/projects/:project_id/tickets/new	new_project_ticket_path
/projects/:project_id/tickets/:id/edit	edit_project_ticket_path
/projects/:project_id/tickets/:id	project_ticket_path

The routes belonging to a specific `Ticket` instance will now take two parameters—the project that the ticket belongs to, and the ticket itself—to generate URLs like http://localhost:3000/projects/1/tickets/2/edit.

As before, you can use the `*_url` or `*_path` alternatives to these helpers, such as `project_tickets_url`, to get the full URL if you so desire.

Let's use these routing helper methods by first creating your `TicketsController`.

5.1.2 *Creating a tickets controller*

Because you defined this route in your routes.rb file, Capybara can now click the "New Ticket" link in your feature and proceed before complaining about the missing `TicketsController`. If you rerun your spec with `bundle exec rspec spec/features/creating_tickets_spec.rb`, it spits out an error followed by a stack trace:

```
1) Users can create new tickets with valid attributes
   Failure/Error: click_link "New Ticket"
   ActionController::RoutingError:
     uninitialized constant TicketsController

# and the second error is identical
```

Some guides may have you generate the model before you generate the controller, but the order in which you create them isn't important. When writing tests, you follow the bouncing ball, and if the test tells you it can't find a controller, then the next thing you do is generate the controller it's looking for. Later, when you inevitably receive an error that it can't find the `Ticket` model, as you did for the `Project` model, you generate that too. This is often referred to as *top-down design*.[1]

To generate this controller and fix the `uninitialized constant` error, use this command:

```
$ rails g controller tickets
```

You may be able to preempt what's going to happen next if you run the test— it'll complain of a missing `new` action that it's trying to get to by clicking the "New Ticket" link. Let's just rerun the test to make sure:

```
1) Users can create new tickets with valid attributes
     Failure/Error: click_link "New Ticket"
     AbstractController::ActionNotFound:
        The action 'new' could not be found for TicketsController
```

Your next step is to define the `new` action. Open app/controllers/tickets _controller.rb, and add the `new` action inside the `TicketsController` definition.

Listing 5.3   The `new` action for `TicketsController`

```
def new
  @ticket = @project.tickets.build
end
```

There's a lot of magic in this one line. You're referring to `@project` but you haven't defined it, you're referring to a `tickets` method on a `Project` instance but you haven't defined one, and you're calling a method named `build` on whatever `tickets` returns. Whew! One step at a time.

5.1.3   *Demystifying the new action*

We'll start with the `@project` instance variable. As you declared in your routes, the `tickets` resource is nested under a `projects` resource, giving you URLs like those listed in table 5.1.

The *placeholders* in the URLs (`:project_id` and `:id`) are what you get as part of your params when you request these URLs. When you request http://localhost:3000/projects/1/tickets/2, your placeholders have the values of 1 and 2, so params will include the following:

```
{ project_id: 1, id: 2 }
```

---

[1] Top-down and bottom-up design are explained on this Wikipedia page: http://en.wikipedia.org/wiki/Top-down_and_bottom-up_design.

You can use the provided :project_id value to load up the right Project instance in a before_action, like you did for certain actions in your ProjectsController. Unlike the ProjectsController, though, this before_action will be run before *every* action, because the project will *always* be present; and it will use params[:project_id], instead of params[:id].

Add the following line under the class definition in app/controllers/tickets_controller.rb:

```
before_action :set_project
```

And now, under the new action, you can define this set_project method that will use the params[:project_id] variable to load the @project variable:

```
private

  def set_project
    @project = Project.find(params[:project_id])
  end
```

Now your @project variable is defined. What about a tickets method? Is that the next thing you need to define? Rerun the test with bundle exec rspec spec/features/creating_tickets_spec.rb to see:

```
1) Users can create new tickets with valid attributes
   Failure/Error: click_link "New Ticket"
   NoMethodError:
     undefined method `tickets' for #<Project:0x007f26fa162628>
```

It's the next thing you need to define. You'll define tickets to be an *association* on your Project model—a link between the two models, so you can call @project.tickets and get an array of all of the Ticket instances that are part of the @project. Seems magical. Let's look at how it works.

5.1.4 Defining a has_many association

The tickets method on Project objects is defined by calling an association method in the Project class called has_many, which you can use as follows in app/models/project.rb:

```
class Project < ActiveRecord::Base
  has_many :tickets

  ...
```

As mentioned before, this defines the tickets method you need, as well as the association. With the has_many method called in the Project model, you can now get to all the tickets for any given project by calling the tickets method on any Project object.

Defining a has_many association in the model also gives you a whole slew of other useful methods, such as the build method, which you're currently calling in the new action of TicketsController. The build method is equivalent to new for the Ticket class (which you'll create in a moment), but it associates the new object instantly with the @project object by setting a foreign key called project_id automatically.

> **BENEFITS OF HAS_MANY**   For a complete list of what you get with a simple call to has_many, see the Active Record Associations guide: http://guides.rubyonrails .org/association_basics.html#has-many-association-reference.

Upon rerunning bundle exec rspec spec/features/creating_tickets_spec.rb, you'll get this:

```
1) Users can create new tickets with valid attributes
   Failure/Error: click_link "New Ticket"
   NameError:
     uninitialized constant Project::Ticket
```

You can determine from this output that the method is looking for the Ticket class, but why? The tickets method on Project objects is defined by the has_many call in the Project model. This method assumes that when you want to get the tickets, you actually want instances of the Ticket model. This model is currently missing; hence, the error.

You can add this model now with the following command:

```
$ rails g model ticket name:string description:text project:references
```

The project:references part defines an integer column for the tickets table called project_id. It also defines an index on this column so that lookups for the tickets for a specific project will be faster. The new migration for this model looks like the following listing.

Listing 5.4   db/migrate/[timestamp]_create_tickets.rb

```
class CreateTickets < ActiveRecord::Migration
  def change
    create_table :tickets do |t|
      t.string :name
      t.text :description
      t.references :project, index: true, foreign_key: true

      t.timestamps null: false
    end
  end
end
```

The project_id column represents the project to which this ticket links and is called a *foreign key*. The purpose of this field is to store the primary key of the project the ticket relates to. When you create a ticket on the project with the id field of 1, the project_id field in the tickets table will also be set to 1.

The foreign_key: true part of the command enforces database-level foreign key restrictions for those platforms that support it, such as PostgreSQL. (You can read more about the specifics of Rails foreign key support in the Ruby on Rails 4.2 release notes at http://guides.rubyonrails.org/4_2_release_notes.html#foreign-key-support.) The SQLite driver you're using doesn't support foreign keys like this, so you don't get any benefit from specifying them, but neither does it do any harm. We'll look at using Post-greSQL when we cover deployment in chapter 13.

Run the migration with `bundle exec rake db:migrate`. The `db:migrate` task runs the migrations and then dumps the structure of the database to a file called db/schema.rb. This structure allows you to restore your database using the `bundle exec rake db:schema:load` task if you wish, which is better than running all the migrations on a large project again!

> **RESTORING WITH RAKE** Large projects can have hundreds of migrations, which may not run due to changes in the system over time. It's best to use `bundle exec rake db:schema:load`.

Now when you run `bundle exec rspec spec/features/creating_tickets_spec.rb`, you're told the new template is missing:

```
1) Users can create new tickets with valid attributes
   Failure/Error: click_link "New Ticket"
   ActionView::MissingTemplate:
     Missing template tickets/new, application/new with
     {
      :locale => [:en],
      :formats => [:html],
      :variants => [],
      :handlers => [:erb, :builder, :raw, :ruby, :coffee, :jbuilder]
     }.

     Searched in:
     * ".../ticketee/app/views"
```

You must create this missing template, `tickets/new`, in order to continue.

5.1.5 Creating tickets in a project

Create the file at app/views/tickets/new.html.erb, and put the following in it:

```erb
<header>
  <h1>
    New Ticket
    <small><%= @project.name %></small>
  </h1>
</header>

<%= render "form", project: @project, ticket: @ticket %>
```

We're continuing the Bootstrap styles that we started using in the previous chapter, and to make it easier for users, you display in the main heading the project that the ticket is going to be for.

Like you did for projects, this template will render a `form` partial (so you can reuse it for the `edit` page when you get to it). The partial also goes in the app/views/tickets folder. Create a new file called _form.html.erb, using the code in the following listing.

Listing 5.5   app/views/tickets/_form.html.erb

```
<%= simple_form_for([project, ticket]) do |f| %>
  <%= f.input :name %>
  <%= f.input :description %>

  <%= f.button :submit, class: "btn-primary" %>
<% end %>
```

Note that `simple_form_for` is passed an array of objects rather than

```
<%= simple_form_for ticket do |f| %>
```

This version of `simple_form_for`, with an array argument, indicates that you want the form to post to a nested route. For the `new` action, this generates a route like /projects/1/tickets, and for the `edit` action, it generates a route like /projects/1/tickets/2. This type of routing is known as *polymorphic routing*.

> **POLYMORPHIC ROUTING**   A great description of polymorphic routing can be found on blog, "The Life of a Radar," at http://ryanbigg.com/2012/03/polymorphic-routes.

When you run `bundle exec rspec spec/features/creating_tickets_spec.rb` again, you're told the `create` action is missing:

```
1) Users can create new tickets with valid attributes
   Failure/Error: click_button "Create Ticket"
   AbstractController::ActionNotFound:
     The action 'create' could not be found for TicketsController
```

To define this action, put it directly under the `new` action in `TicketsController` but before the `private` method. Also add the appropriate strong parameters helper method right below `private`, as shown in the following listing.

Listing 5.6   The `create` action from `TicketsController`

```
def create
  @ticket = @project.tickets.build(ticket_params)

  if @ticket.save
    flash[:notice] = "Ticket has been created."
    redirect_to [@project, @ticket]
  else
    flash.now[:alert] = "Ticket has not been created."
    render "new"
  end
end

private

def ticket_params
  params.require(:ticket).permit(:name, :description)
end
```

In this action, you use `redirect_to` and specify an `Array`—the same array you used in `form_for` earlier—containing a `Project` object and a `Ticket` object. Rails inspects any array passed to helpers, such as `redirect_to` and `link_to`, and determines what you mean from the values. For this particular case, Rails figures out that you want this helper:

```
project_ticket_path(@project, @ticket)
```

Rails determines this helper because, at this stage, `@project` and `@ticket` are both objects that exist in the database, and you can therefore route to them. The route generated would be /projects/1/tickets/2 or something similar. Back in the `form_for`, `@ticket` was new, so the route happened to be /projects/1/tickets. You could have been explicit and specifically used `project_ticket_path` in the action, but using an array is less repetitive.

When you run `bundle exec rspec spec/features/creating_tickets_spec.rb`, both scenarios continue to report the same error:

```
1) Users can create new tickets with valid attributes
   Failure/Error: click_button "Create Ticket"
   AbstractController::ActionNotFound:
     The action 'show' could not be found for TicketsController
```

Therefore, you must create a `show` action for the `TicketsController`. But when you do so, you'll need to find tickets only for the given project.

5.1.6 *Finding tickets scoped by project*

Currently, both of your scenarios are failing due to a missing action. The next logical step is to define the `show` action for your controller, which will look up a given ticket by ID. But, being quick to learn and spot trends, you can anticipate that you'll also need to find a ticket by ID for the `edit`, `update`, and `destroy` actions, and preempt similar errors when it comes to building those actions. You can make this a `before_action`, as you did in the `ProjectsController` with the `set_project` method.

You define this finder under the `set_project` method in the `TicketsController`:

```
def set_ticket
  @ticket = @project.tickets.find(params[:id])
end
```

`find` is yet another association method provided by Rails when you declared that your `Project` model has_many `:tickets`. This code attempts to find tickets only within the collection of tickets owned by the specified project.

Put your new `before_action` at the top of your class, under the action to find the project:

```
before_action :set_project
before_action :set_ticket, only: [:show, :edit, :update, :destroy]
```

The sequence here is important, because you want to find the `@project` before you go looking for tickets for it.

Then you can create the action that your test is asking for, below the `create` method (but above `private`) in your `TicketsController`.

Listing 5.7   show action in app/controllers/tickets_controller.rb

```ruby
def show
end
```

Again, it doesn't need to have anything in it—you've already loaded all of the content the action needs in your `before_action` calls. But it's good to know it's there.

Then create the view template for this action at app/views/tickets/show.html.erb, using this code:

```erb
<div id="ticket">
  <header>
    <h1><%= @project.name %></h1>
  </header>

  <header>
    <h2><%= @ticket.name %></h2>
  </header>

  <%= simple_format(@ticket.description) %>
</div>
```

The new method, `simple_format`, converts the line breaks entered into the description field into HTML break tags (`<br>`) so that the description renders exactly how the user intends it to.

LINE BREAKS IN RUBY   Line breaks are represented as \n and \r\n in strings in Ruby rather than as visible line breaks.

Based solely on the changes you've made so far, your first scenario should be passing. Let's check with a quick run of `bundle exec rspec spec/features/creating_tickets _spec.rb`:

```
1) Users can create new tickets when providing invalid attributes
   Failure/Error: expect(page).to have_content "Ticket has not been
   created."
     expected to find text "Ticket has not been created." in "Ticketee Toggle
     navigation Home Ticket has been created. Internet Explorer"

...
2 examples, 1 failure
```

This means you've got the first scenario under control, and users of your application can create tickets within a project. Next, you need to add validations to the `Ticket` model to get the second scenario of the ticket-creation feature spec to pass.

5.1.7 Ticket validations

The second scenario fails because the `@ticket` that it saves isn't valid, at least according to your tests in their current state:

```
expected to find text "Ticket has not been created." in "Ticketee ...
```

You need to ensure that when somebody enters a ticket into the application, the `title` and `description` attributes are filled in. To do this, define the following validations in the `Ticket` model.

Listing 5.8 app/models/ticket.rb

```ruby
validates :name, presence: true
validates :description, presence: true
```

> ### Validating two fields using one line
> You could also validate the presence of both of these fields using a single line:
>
> ```ruby
> validates :name, :description, presence: true
> ```
>
> But it's easier to see the associations for a given field if they're all in one place. If you were to add, for example, an extra length validation to the description field, it might look like this:
>
> ```ruby
> validates :name, :description, presence: true
> validates :description, length: { maximum: 1000 }
> ```
>
> And it would not be immediately obvious that both validations apply to one field (the `description` field). As more and more fields get added (you might validate the presence of over a dozen fields!), the problem would get worse and worse as the details get spread further and further apart.
>
> Our preference is to have validations for different fields on individual lines. But you don't have to use two lines to do it; we can still be friends.

Now when you run `bundle exec spec/features/creating_tickets_spec.rb`, the entire feature passes:

```
2 examples, 0 failures
```

Before we wrap up here, let's add one more scenario to ensure that what is entered into the Description field is longer than 10 characters. You want the descriptions to be useful! Add this scenario to the spec/features/creating_tickets_spec.rb file:

```ruby
scenario "with an invalid description" do
  fill_in "Name", with: "Non-standards compliance"
  fill_in "Description", with: "It sucks"
  click_button "Create Ticket"

  expect(page).to have_content "Ticket has not been created."
  expect(page).to have_content "Description is too short"
end
```

To implement the code needed to make this scenario pass, add another option to the end of the validation for the `description` in your `Ticket` model, like this:

```
validates :description, presence: true, length: { minimum: 10 }
```

By default, this will generate a message identical to the one you used in your test. You can verify this with the console—if you run `rails console` and try to create a new `Ticket` object by using `create!`, you can get the full text for your error:

```
irb(main):001:0> Ticket.create!
ActiveRecord::RecordInvalid: ... Description is too short
(minimum is 10 characters)
```

If you're getting that error message on the console, that means it will appear like that in the app too. Find out by running `bundle exec rspec spec/features/ creating_tickets_spec.rb` again:

```
3 examples, 0 failures
```

That one's passing now. Excellent! You should ensure that the rest of the project still works by running `bundle exec rspec` again. You'll see this output:

```
12 examples, 0 failures, 2 pending
```

There are two pending specs here: one located in spec/helpers/tickets_helper_spec.rb and the other in spec/models/ticket_spec.rb. These were automatically generated when you ran the commands to generate your `TicketsController` and `Ticket` model, but you don't need them right now, so you can just delete these two files. When you've done that, rerunning `bundle exec rspec` outputs a lovely green result:

```
10 examples, 0 failures
```

Great! Everything's still working. Commit and push the changes!

```
$ git add .
$ git commit -m "Implement creating tickets for a project"
$ git push
```

This section covered how to create tickets and link them to a specific project through the foreign key called `project_id` on records in the `tickets` table. The next section shows how easily you can list tickets for individual projects.

5.2 *Viewing tickets*

Now that you have the ability to create tickets, you'll use the `show` action of the `TicketsController` to view them individually. When displaying a list of projects, you use the `index` action of the `ProjectsController`. For tickets, however, you'll list them as part of showing the details of a project, on the `show` action of the `ProjectsController`. This page currently isn't being used for anything else in particular, but also it just makes sense to see the project's tickets when you view the project.

To test it, put a new feature at spec/features/viewing_tickets_spec.rb using the code from the following listing.

> **Listing 5.9 spec/features/viewing_tickets_spec.rb**

```ruby
require "rails_helper"

RSpec.feature "Users can view tickets" do
  before do
    sublime = FactoryGirl.create(:project, name: "Sublime Text 3")
    FactoryGirl.create(:ticket, project: sublime,
      name: "Make it shiny!",
      description: "Gradients! Starbursts! Oh my!")

    ie = FactoryGirl.create(:project, name: "Internet Explorer")
    FactoryGirl.create(:ticket, project: ie,
      name: "Standards compliance", description: "Isn't a joke.")

    visit "/"
  end

  scenario "for a given project" do
    click_link "Sublime Text 3"

    expect(page).to have_content "Make it shiny!"
    expect(page).to_not have_content "Standards compliance"

    click_link "Make it shiny!"
    within("#ticket h2") do
      expect(page).to have_content "Make it shiny!"
    end

    expect(page).to have_content "Gradients! Starbursts! Oh my!"
  end
end
```

Quite the long feature! It covers a couple of things—both viewing the list of tickets for a project, and then viewing the details for a specific ticket. We'll go through it piece by piece in a moment.

> **ONE FEATURE, TWO FEATURES** Purists would probably split this out into two separate features, but the second feature would depend on the first—if you can't see a list of tickets (feature 1), it would be impossible to click the link to see a ticket's details (feature 2). So we've included them both as parts of one feature.

First, let's examine the `within` usage in the scenario. Rather than checking the entire page for content, this step checks the specific element using CSS selectors. The `#ticket` `h2` selector finds all `h2` elements within a div with the ID of `ticket`, and then you make sure the content is visible within one of those elements.[2] This content should appear in the specified tag only when you're on the ticket page, so this is a great way to make sure you're on the right page and that the page is displaying relevant information.

---

[2] We'll revisit this in chapter 10—hardcoding CSS selectors in a test isn't a great idea because you're testing what the user can see, and they don't care about selectors and tags; they just care about content.

When you run this spec with `bundle exec rspec spec/features/viewing_tickets` `_spec.rb`, you'll see that it can't find the ticket factory:

```
1) Users can view tickets for a given project
   Failure/Error: FactoryGirl.create(:ticket, project: sublime,
   ArgumentError:
     Factory not registered: ticket
```

You need to create the ticket factory now. It should create an example ticket with a valid name and description. To do this, create a new file called spec/factories/ticket_factory.rb with the following content.

Listing 5.10 spec/factories/ticket_factory.rb

```
FactoryGirl.define do
  factory :ticket do
    name "Example ticket"
    description "An example ticket, nothing more"
  end
end
```

With the ticket factory defined, the `before` block of this spec should now run all the way through when you run `bundle exec rspec spec/features/` `viewing_tickets_spec.rb`. You'll see this error:

```
1) Users can view tickets for a given project
   Failure/Error: expect(page).to have_content "Make it shiny!"
     expected to find text "Make it shiny!" in "Ticketee Toggle ..."
```

The spec is attempting to see the ticket's name on the page. But it can't see it at the moment, because you're not displaying a list of tickets on the project `show` template yet.

5.2.1 *Listing tickets*

To display a ticket on the `show` template, you can iterate through the project's tickets by using the `tickets` method on a `Project` object, made available by the `has_many` `:tickets` call in your model. Put this code at the bottom of app/views/projects/show.html.erb.

Listing 5.11 app/views/projects/show.html.erb

```
<ul id="tickets">
  <% @project.tickets.each do |ticket| %>
    <li>
      #<%= ticket.id %> -
      <%= link_to ticket.name, [@project, ticket] %>
    </li>
  <% end %>
</ul>
```

BE CAREFUL WHEN USING LINK_TO. If you use a @ticket variable in place of the ticket variable as the second argument to link_to, it will be nil. You haven't initialized the @ticket variable, and uninitialized instance variables are nil by default. If @ticket rather than the correct ticket is passed in, the URL generated will be a projects URL, such as /projects/1, rather than the correct /projects/1/tickets/2.

Here you iterate over the items in @project.tickets using the each method, which does the iterating for you, assigning each item to a ticket variable used in the block. The code in this block runs for every ticket.

If you run bundle exec rspec spec/features/viewing_tickets_spec.rb, it passes because the app now has the means to go to a specific ticket from the project's page:

```
1 example, 0 failures
```

Time to make sure everything else is still working by running bundle exec rspec. You should see all green:

```
11 examples, 0 failures
```

Fantastic! Push!

```
$ git add .
$ git commit -m "Implement tickets display"
$ git push
```

You can now see tickets for a particular project, but what happens when a project is deleted? The tickets for that project aren't magically deleted. To implement this behavior, you can pass options to the has_many association, which will delete the tickets when a project is deleted.

5.2.2 Culling tickets

When a project is deleted, its tickets become useless: they're inaccessible because of how you defined their routes. Therefore, when you delete a project, you should also delete the tickets for that project. You can do that by using the :dependent option on the has_many association for tickets defined in your Project model.

This option has five choices that all act slightly differently. The first one is the :destroy value:

```
has_many :tickets, dependent: :destroy
```

If you put this in your Project model, any time you call destroy on a Project object, Rails will iterate through the tickets for this project, and call destroy on each of them in turn (as well as any other destroy-related callbacks on the project itself). In turn, each ticket object will have any destroy-related callbacks called on it, and if it has any has_many associations with the dependent: :destroy option set, then those objects will be destroyed, and so on. The problem is that if you have a large number of tickets, destroy is called on each one, which will be slow.

The solution is the second value for this option:

```
has_many :tickets, dependent: :delete_all
```

This deletes all the tickets using a SQL delete, like this:

```
DELETE FROM tickets WHERE project_id = :project_id
```

This operation is quick and is exceptionally useful if you have a large number of tickets that *don't* have callbacks or that have callbacks you don't necessarily care about when deleting a project. If you *do* have callbacks on `Ticket` for a destroy operation, then you should use the first option, `dependent: :destroy`.

Thirdly, if you want to disassociate tickets from a project and unset the `project_id` field, you can use this option:

```
has_many :tickets, dependent: :nullify
```

When a project is deleted with this type of `:dependent` option defined, it will execute a SQL query such as this:

```
UPDATE tickets SET project_id = NULL WHERE project_id = :project_id
```

Rather than deleting the tickets, this option keeps them around, but their `project_id` fields are unset, leaving them orphaned, which isn't suitable for this system.

This option would be useful if you were building a task-tracking application, for example, and instead of projects and tickets, you had users and tasks. If you deleted a user, you might want to unassign rather than delete the tasks associated with that user, in which case you'd use the `dependent: :nullify` option.

Finally, there are two options that work similarly—`:restrict_with_error` and `:restrict_with_exception`. Both options will prevent records from being deleted if the association isn't empty; for example, in your projects and tickets scenario, you wouldn't be able to delete projects if they had any tickets in them.

If you were using `:restrict_with_error`, then calling `@project.destroy` on a project with tickets would add a validation error to the `@project` instance, as well as return `false`. Using `:restrict_with_exception` in this case would raise an exception that your application would have to manually catch and handle, or else the user would receive an HTTP response of 500—Internal Server Error.

An example of where this could be useful is in a billing scenario; it wouldn't be good for business if users were able to cancel/delete their own accounts in your system if they had associated bills that still required payment.

In the projects and tickets scenario, though, you'd use `dependent: :destroy` if you had callbacks to run on tickets when they're destroyed, or `dependent: :delete_all` if you had no callbacks on tickets. To ensure that all tickets are deleted on a project when the project is deleted, change the `has_many` association in your `Project` model to the following.

Listing 5.12   app/models/project.rb

```
has_many :tickets, dependent: :delete_all
```

With this new :dependent option in the Project model, all tickets for the project will be deleted when the project is deleted.

You aren't writing any tests for this behavior because it's simple and you'd basically be testing that you changed one tiny option. This is more of an internal implementation detail than it is customer-facing, and you're writing feature tests right now, not model tests.

Let's check that you didn't break existing tests by running bundle exec rspec:

```
11 examples, 0 failures
```

Good! Commit:

```
$ git add .
$ git commit -m "Cull tickets when project gets destroyed"
$ git push
```

Next, let's look at how to edit the tickets in your application.

5.3 Editing tickets

You want users to be able to edit tickets—that's the *updating* part of this CRUD interface for tickets. This section covers creating the edit and update actions for the TicketsController. This functionality follows a thread similar to the project-editing feature, where you follow an "Edit" link in the show template, change a field, and then click an Update button and expect to see two things: a message indicating that the ticket was updated successfully, and the modified data for that ticket.

As always, we'll start with a test that covers the functionality you wish you had and will soon be building.

5.3.1 The ticket-editing spec

Just as you made a spec for creating a ticket, you need one for editing and updating existing tickets. Specs for testing update functionality are always a little more complex than specs for testing create functionality, because you need to have an existing object that's built properly before the test, and then you can change it during the test.

With that in mind, you can write this feature using the code in the following listing. Put the code in a file at spec/features/editing_tickets_spec.rb.

Listing 5.13 spec/features/editing_tickets_spec.rb

```
require "rails_helper"

RSpec.feature "Users can edit existing tickets" do
  let(:project) { FactoryGirl.create(:project) }
  let(:ticket)  { FactoryGirl.create(:ticket, project: project) }

  before do
    visit project_ticket_path(project, ticket)
    click_link "Edit Ticket"
  end
```

```
  scenario "with valid attributes" do
    fill_in "Name", with: "Make it really shiny!"
    click_button "Update Ticket"

    expect(page).to have_content "Ticket has been updated."

    within("#ticket h2") do
      expect(page).to have_content "Make it really shiny!"
      expect(page).not_to have_content ticket.name
    end
  end

  scenario "with invalid attributes" do
    fill_in "Name", with: ""
    click_button "Update Ticket"

    expect(page).to have_content "Ticket has not been updated."
  end
end
```

At the top of this feature, you use a new RSpec method called `let`. In fact, you use it twice. It defines a new method with the same name as the symbol passed in, and that new method then evaluates (and caches) the content of the block whenever that method is called. It's also *lazy-loaded*—the block won't be evaluated until the first time you call the method denoted by the symbol (`project` or `ticket`, in this case).

It also has a bigger brother, called `let!` (with a bang!). `let!` isn't lazy-loaded—when you define a method with `let!`, it will be evaluated immediately, before your tests start running.

For a concrete example, suppose you had a test that looked like the following.

Listing 5.14 Testing `let` and `let!`

```
RSpec.describe "A sample test" do
  let!(:project) { FactoryGirl.create(:project) }
  let(:ticket)   { FactoryGirl.create(:ticket) }

  it "lazily loads `let` methods" do
    puts Project.count
    puts Ticket.count

    puts ticket.name
    puts Ticket.count
  end
end
```

If you were to run it, what do you think it might output? If you guessed the following, you get a gold star!

- `Project.count` outputs 1 (because `project` is already evaluated).
- `Ticket.count` outputs 0 (`ticket` has not been evaluated yet).

- `ticket.name` outputs Example ticket (from your factory).
- `Ticket.count` outputs 1 (ticket has now been evaluated and exists in the database).

In this case, it makes no difference if you use `let` or `let!`. The first thing you do in the before block is instantiate both `project` and `ticket` by visiting the ticket's `show` page. If, however, you were visiting the homepage and then navigating to the ticket's page, it wouldn't work—the ticket would never be created.

After you visit the ticket's `show` page, you click the "Edit" link, make some changes, and verify that those changes get persisted. You're also testing the failure case—what happens if you can't update a ticket for some reason. It looks pretty similar to the update case, but rather than try to factor out all the commonalities, you repeat yourself. Some duplication in tests is OK; if it makes the test easier to follow, it's worth a little repetition.

When you run this feature using `bundle exec rspec spec/features/editing _tickets_spec.rb`, the first three lines in the before run fine, but the fourth fails:

```
1) Users can edit existing tickets with valid attributes
   Failure/Error: click_link "Edit Ticket"
   Capybara::ElementNotFound:
     Unable to find link "Edit Ticket"
```

To fix this, add the "Edit Ticket" link to the `show` template of the `TicketsController`, because that's the page you've visited in the feature. It sounds like an action link for the ticket, so you can add a list of action links into the `header` that specifies the ticket's name:

```
<header>
  <h2><%= @ticket.name %></h2>

  <ul class="actions">
    <li><%= link_to "Edit Ticket", [:edit, @project, @ticket],
      class: "edit" %></li>
  </ul>
</header>
```

Here's yet another use of the `Array` argument passed to the `link_to` method, but rather than passing only Active Record objects, you pass a `Symbol` first. Rails, yet again, works out from the `Array` what route you wish to follow. Rails interprets this array to mean the `edit_project_ticket_path` method, which is called like this:

```
edit_project_ticket_path(@project, @ticket)
```

Now that you have an "Edit Ticket" link, you need to add the `edit` action to the `TicketsController`, because that will be the next thing to error when you run `bundle exec rspec spec/features/editing_tickets_spec.rb`:

```
1) Users can edit existing tickets with valid attributes
   Failure/Error: click_link "Edit Ticket"
   AbstractController::ActionNotFound:
     The action 'edit' could not be found for TicketsController
```

5.3.2 Adding the edit action

The next logical step is to define the edit action in your TicketsController. Like the edit action in ProjectsController, technically it doesn't need to exist because it will be empty—all it needs to do is load the @project and @ticket variables, which are already done via set_project and set_ticket. But it's good practice to define it, so add it in under the show action in TicketsController, but before the private call.

Listing 5.15   app/controllers/tickets_controller.rb

```
def edit
end
```

The next logical step is to create the view for this action. Put it at app/views/tickets/edit.html.erb, and fill it with this content:

```
<header>
  <h1>
    Edit Ticket
    <small><%= @project.name %></small>
  </h1>
</header>

<%= render "form", project: @project, ticket: @ticket %>
```

Here you reuse the form partial you created for the new action, which is handy. The form_for knows which action to go to.

If you run the feature spec again with bundle exec rspec spec/features/editing_tickets_spec.rb, you're told the update action is missing:

```
1) Users can edit existing tickets with valid attributes
   Failure/Error: click_button "Update Ticket"
   AbstractController::ActionNotFound:
     The action 'update' could not be found for TicketsController
```

5.3.3 Adding the update action

You should now define the update action in your TicketsController.

Listing 5.16   The update action of TicketsController

```
def update
  if @ticket.update(ticket_params)
    flash[:notice] = "Ticket has been updated."
    redirect_to [@project, @ticket]
  else
    flash.now[:alert] = "Ticket has not been updated."
    render "edit"
  end
end
```

Remember that in this action you don't have to find the @ticket or @project objects because a before_action does it for the show, edit, update, and destroy actions.

With this single action implemented, both scenarios in the ticket-editing feature will now pass when you run bundle exec rspec spec/features/editing_tickets _spec.rb:

```
2 examples, 0 failures
```

Check to see if everything works with a quick run of bundle exec rspec:

```
13 examples, 0 failures
```

Great! Commit and push that:

```
$ git add .
$ git commit -m "Tickets can now be edited"
$ git push
```

In this section, you implemented edit and update for the TicketsController by using the scoped finders and some familiar methods, such as update. You've got one more part to go: deletion.

5.4 Deleting tickets

We now reach the final story for this nested resource: deleting tickets. As with some of the other actions in this chapter, this story doesn't differ from what you used in the ProjectsController, except you'll change the name *project* to *ticket* for your variables and flash[:notice]. It's good to have the reinforcement of the techniques previously used: practice makes perfect.

Use the code from the next listing to write a new feature in spec/features/ deleting_tickets_spec.rb.

> **Listing 5.17 spec/features/deleting_tickets_spec.rb**

```
require "rails_helper"

RSpec.feature "Users can delete tickets" do
  let(:project) { FactoryGirl.create(:project) }
  let(:ticket)  { FactoryGirl.create(:ticket, project: project) }

  before do
    visit project_ticket_path(project, ticket)
  end

  scenario "successfully" do
    click_link "Delete Ticket"

    expect(page).to have_content "Ticket has been deleted."
    expect(page.current_url).to eq project_url(project)
  end
end
```

When you run this spec using `bundle exec rspec spec/features/deleting_tickets _spec.rb`, it will fail because you don't yet have a "Delete Ticket" link on the show template for tickets:

```
1) Users can delete tickets successfully
   Failure/Error: click_link "Delete Ticket"
   Capybara::ElementNotFound:
     Unable to find link "Delete Ticket"
```

You can add the "Delete Ticket" link to the list of actions on app/views/tickets/ show.html.erb, right after the "Edit Ticket" link:

```
<li><%= link_to "Delete Ticket", [@project, @ticket], method: :delete,
  data: { confirm: "Are you sure you want to delete this ticket?"},
  class: "delete" %></li>
```

The `method: :delete` is specified again, turning the request into one headed for the destroy action in the controller. Without this `:method` option, you'd be off to the show action because the `link_to` method defaults to the GET method.

Upon running `bundle exec rspec spec/features/deleting_tickets_spec.rb` again, you're told a destroy action is missing:

```
1) Users can delete tickets successfully
   Failure/Error: click_link "Delete Ticket"
   AbstractController::ActionNotFound:
     The action 'destroy' could not be found for TicketsController
```

The next step must be to define this action, right? Open app/controllers/ tickets_controller.rb, and define it directly under the update action.

Listing 5.18   The `destroy` action from `TicketsController`

```
def destroy
  @ticket.destroy
  flash[:notice] = "Ticket has been deleted."

  redirect_to @project
end
```

After you delete the ticket, you redirect the user back to the show page for the project the ticket belonged to. With that done, your feature should now pass when you run `bundle exec rspec spec/features/deleting_tickets_spec.rb` again:

```
1 example, 0 failures
```

Yet again, check to see that everything is still going as well as it should be by using `bundle exec rspec`. You haven't changed much, so it's likely that things are still working. You should see this output:

```
14 examples, 0 failures
```

Commit and push!

```
$ git add .
$ git commit -m "Implement deleting tickets feature"
$ git push
```

You've now created another CRUD interface, this time for the `tickets` resource, which is only accessible within the scope of a project. This means you must request it using a URL such as /projects/1/tickets/2 rather than /tickets/2.

5.5   *Summary*

In this chapter, you generated another controller, the `TicketsController`, which allows you to create records for your `Ticket` model that will end up in your `tickets` table. The difference between this controller and the `ProjectsController` is that the `TicketsController` is accessible only within the scope of an existing project because you used nested routing.

In this controller, you scoped the finds for the `Ticket` model by using the `tickets` association method provided by the association helper method `has_many` call in your `Project` model. `has_many` also provides the `build` method, which you used to begin creating new `Ticket` records that are scoped to a project.

In the next chapter, you'll learn how to let users sign up and sign in to your application. You'll also implement a basic authorization for actions such as creating a project.

Authentication 6

This chapter covers

- Adding authentication to an application
- Using the Devise gem
- More associations, linking tickets to users

You've created two resources for your Ticketee application: projects and tickets. Now you'll add authentication to let users sign in to your application. With this feature, you can track which tickets were created by which users. A little later, you'll use these user records to allow and deny access to certain parts of the application. To round out the chapter, you'll create another CRUD interface, this time for the users resource, but with a twist.

The general idea behind having users for this application is that some users are in charge of creating projects (project owners), and others use whatever the projects provide. If they find something wrong with a project or wish to suggest an improvement, filing a ticket is a great way to inform the project owner about their request. To round out the chapter, we'll link tickets to the users who created them. This way, anyone viewing a ticket can know exactly who created it, rather than it just being yet another ticket in the application.

In this chapter, you'll add authentication to your application using a gem called Devise (https://github.com/plataformatec/devise/). Devise is maintained by Plataformatec (http://plataformatec.com.br/), a web development company run by some prominent Rails developers. Devise has been proven time and time again to be a capable gem for authentication, so that's what we'll use here. Most of the functionality for this chapter comes from within Devise itself.

6.1 Using Devise

Devise is a gem that provides the authentication features that nearly every Rails application needs, such as user registration, sign-in, password reset emails, and confirmation emails. We'll cover the first two of those in this chapter.

When a user signs up with Devise, their credentials are stored securely in a database using industry-standard cryptography. If you were to build authentication yourself, the cryptography methods you'd choose might not be as strong. Devise saves you from having to worry about these things.

You can install the Devise gem now by adding this line to your Gemfile.

Listing 6.1 Adding Devise to the application Gemfile

```
gem "devise", "~> 3.4.1"
```

Then run `bundle` to install it.

Next, run the generator, which will install Devise:

```
$ rails g devise:install
```

This generator will create an *initializer* at config/initializers/devise.rb, which contains the configuration for Devise. As you saw earlier with the Simple Form gem, files in config/initializers are run during the process of booting a Rails application and are used to set up anything that's necessary for the application to run. In this case, Devise's configuration sets the scene for using Devise later in your application.

The `devise:install` generator gets your application ready for Devise by setting up some default configuration, but it's the `devise` generator that does the hard work of adding the major pieces. Run this command now:

```
$ rails g devise user
```

This generator generates a `User` model, which you'll use to keep track of users within the application. Along with this comes a migration to generate a `users` table, so you can now run the following command to apply this new migration to your database:

```
$ bundle exec rake db:migrate
```

The following model contains configuration specific to Devise.

```
class User < ActiveRecord::Base
  # Include default devise modules. Others available are:
  # :confirmable, :lockable, :timeoutable and :omniauthable
  devise :database_authenticatable, :registerable,
         :recoverable, :rememberable, :trackable, :validatable
end
```

The devise method in this model sets up the model to use the specified Devise modules. By default, Devise provides the following modules and features with this default config:

- database_authenticatable—Allows the user to sign in to your app using credentials stored in the database, such as an email address and password.
- registerable—Allows users to register or sign up with your application.
- recoverable—Allows a user who forgets their password to reset it via email.
- rememberable—Remembers a user's session in your application. This means users won't have to sign in every time they restart their browser.
- trackable—Tracks information such as last sign-in time and IP for each user.
- validatable—Validates the user's email address and password length. By default, passwords are expected to be between 8 and 128 characters. This setting can be changed in config/initializers/devise.rb by altering the config.password_length value.

As you can see from this list, Devise offers quite a lot! It has even more, as listed in the comment above the devise method:

- confirmable—Requires a user to confirm their email address by clicking a link in a confirmation email before they can sign in.
- lockable—Provides extra security by automatically locking accounts after a given number of failed sign-in attempts.
- timeoutable—Provides extra security by automatically logging out users who haven't been active for a given amount of time.
- omniauthable—Adds support for OmniAuth (https://github.com/intridea/omniauth), which will allow users to authenticate with your app via an external service, such as Facebook or Twitter.

We won't be using any of these advanced modules, but it's good to know they're there, and that they're built in and well supported.

Beware race conditions with a uniqueness validator

One of the validations that Devise's validatable module adds is a uniqueness rule for email addresses, so two people can't sign up with the same email address, or an existing user can't change their email address to be the same as another user's. The code for that validation looks like this:

```
validates_uniqueness_of :email, allow_blank: true, if: :email_changed?
```

This uniqueness validator works by checking to see whether any records matching the validation criteria exist in the database already. In our case, the validator checks if there are any `User` records with the same email address as this user. If no such records exist, the validation passes.

A problem arises if two connections to the database both make this check at almost exactly the same time. Both connections will claim that no such records exist, so each will pass validation and allow the record to be saved, resulting in non-unique records.

A way to prevent this is to use a database uniqueness index so that the database, not Rails, does the uniqueness validation. For information on how to do this, consult your database's manual.

Although this problem doesn't happen often, it *can* happen, especially on larger and more popular sites, so it's something to watch out for.

The `devise` generator also adds a line to config/routes.rb:

```
devise_for :users
```

This one little line generates a bunch of routes for your application, which you can see when you run `bundle exec rake routes` (controller column omitted for brevity):

```
Prefix Verb    URI Pattern
         new_user_session GET    /users/sign_in(.:format)
             user_session POST   /users/sign_in(.:format)
     destroy_user_session DELETE /users/sign_out(.:format)
            user_password POST   /users/password(.:format)
        new_user_password GET    /users/password/new(.:format)
       edit_user_password GET    /users/password/edit(.:format)
                          PATCH  /users/password(.:format)
                          PUT    /users/password(.:format)
    cancel_user_registration GET    /users/cancel(.:format)
         user_registration POST   /users(.:format)
     new_user_registration GET    /users/sign_up(.:format)
    edit_user_registration GET    /users/edit(.:format)
                          PATCH  /users(.:format)
                          PUT    /users(.:format)
                          DELETE /users(.:format)
```

These routes are all for controllers within Devise. Devise is not only a gem, but also a Rails engine.[1] This means that it contains its own set of controllers and views, which exist outside of the application. This keeps your application's code separate from Devise, giving you less code to manage overall.

With Devise installed and configured, you can now go about adding the ability for users to sign up in your application with Devise.

---

[1] For more information about engines, read the official Engines Guide: http://guides.rubyonrails.org/engines.html.

6.2   *Adding sign-up*

Users will be able to sign up in your application by click-ing a link in Ticketee's navigation bar labeled "Sign up." When they click that link, they'll see the page in figure 6.1.

From here, they'll be able to enter their email address and password and sign up with the application. From then on, they can come back to the application, sign in, and use the application to their heart's content.

To make sure that this feature works, you'll write a test for it in spec/features/signing_up_spec.rb, using the code in the following listing.

Sign up

Email

Password *(8 characters minimum)*

Password confirmation

Sign up

Log in

Figure 6.1   The "Sign up" form

Listing 6.3   spec/features/signing_up_spec.rb

```ruby
require "rails_helper"

RSpec.feature "Users can sign up" do
  scenario "when providing valid details" do
    visit "/"
    click_link "Sign up"
    fill_in "Email", with: "test@example.com"
    fill_in "user_password", with: "password"
    fill_in "Password confirmation", with: "password"
    click_button "Sign up"
    expect(page).to have_content("You have signed up successfully.")
  end
end
```

While this might seem silly—after all, Devise provides all of this functionality, and Devise already has its own tests—this can prevent very silly mistakes, such as changing the view and accidentally introducing a bug that prevents people from signing up.[2] Besides, the test is very straightforward—it just walks through the process we just described. It nav-igates to the homepage, clicks a "Sign up" link, and then proceeds to sign up.

> **Password vs. `user_password`**
>
> You might wonder why we're using `user_password` here to select the Password field, rather than simply "Password."
>
> To start with, there are two fields with the label "Password" on the page: Password and Password Confirmation. Capybara has a setting called `exact`, which will specify what to do in this situation—by default, `exact` defaults to a value of `:smart`, which means it looks for an exact string match first, and uses that field if it exists. This will work for now, as you have a field specifically labeled "Password."

---

[2] You may scoff, but we've seen this happen, in front of paying clients. They were not amused.

> But later on, you'll be tweaking and customizing views to fit the theme on your site, which will unfortunately change the label so it's no longer an exact match. Simple Form prefixes required fields with an asterisk (*) to indicate that status to the user, and this will unfortunately confuse Capybara.
>
> If you left it as `fill_in "Password", with: "password"`, then later on you'd get an error like the following:
>
> ```
> 1) Users can sign up when providing valid details
>    Failure/Error: fill_in "Password", with: "password"
>    Capybara::Ambiguous:
>      Ambiguous match, found 2 elements matching field "Password"
> ```
>
> Luckily, Capybara also lets you select fields by either the HTML `id` or `name` attributes. In this case, `user_password` is the generated *ID* of the field, so you can use it to select the field to fill it in.

Now when you run your test with `bundle exec rspec spec/features/signing_up _spec.rb`, you'll see this error:

```
1) Users can sign up when providing valid details
   Failure/Error: click_link "Sign up"
   Capybara::ElementNotFound:
     Unable to find link "Sign up"
```

This one is easy enough to fix. You're just missing a link to "Sign up" in your application. You can add this to the navigation bar in app/views/layouts/application .html.erb, underneath the "Home" link you already have there:

```erb
<li class="<%= "active" if current_page?("/users/sign_up") %>">
  <%= link_to "Sign up", new_user_registration_path %>
</li>
```

The `new_user_registration_path` helper is provided by Devise, and you can see it and its brethren by running `bundle exec rake routes`. You're not just pulling these out of the air here!

With that link in place, your test should run a little further:

```
1 example, 0 failures
```

Oh, that's surprising! It all passed. The only thing that you needed to do was add the sign-up link. Devise provides you with the rest.

Run all of your tests now to ensure that you haven't broken anything. Run `bundle exec rspec` to see this:

```
16 examples, 0 failures, 1 pending
```

You have one pending spec at spec/models/user_spec.rb, which came from the devise generator. Remove this and rerun `bundle exec rspec`:

```
15 examples, 0 failures
```

That's better! With that all done, make a commit:

```
$ git add .
$ git commit -m "Added Devise + sign up feature"
$ git push
```

Now that users can sign up in your application, the next thing that you need is the ability for them to sign in.

6.3   *Adding sign-in and sign-out*

Devise allowed you to easily add a sign-up feature to your application. Now let's see about adding a way for users to sign in and out of the application.

6.3.1   *Adding sign-in*

To add sign-in, first you need to add a feature spec at spec/features/signing_in _spec.rb using the code from the following listing.

Listing 6.4   spec/features/signing_in_spec.rb

```
require "rails_helper"

RSpec.feature "Users can sign in" do
  let!(:user) { FactoryGirl.create(:user) }

  scenario "with valid credentials" do
    visit "/"
    click_link "Sign in"
    fill_in "Email", with: user.email
    fill_in "Password", with: "password"
    click_button "Log in"

    expect(page).to have_content "Signed in successfully."
    expect(page).to have_content "Signed in as #{user.email}"
  end
end
```

If this test looks very similar to the sign-up feature, that's because it is! The two flows are very similar. In this test, the difference is that you're creating a user using a `FactoryGirl` factory, and then signing in as that user.

When you run the test with `bundle exec rspec spec/features/signing_in _spec.rb`, you'll see that the user factory is missing:

```
1) Users can sign in with valid credentials
   Failure/Error: let!(:user) { FactoryGirl.create(:user) }
   ArgumentError:
     Factory not registered: user
```

You can create this new factory file at spec/factories/user_factory.rb.

Listing 6.5   spec/factories/user_factory.rb

```
FactoryGirl.define do
  factory :user do
    sequence(:email) { |n| "test#{n}@example.com" }
    password "password"
  end
end
```

This factory can be used to create new users in your tests. The sequence method will generate sequential email addresses for your users, such as test1@example.com and test2@example.com. You do this so that each user has a unique email address, and that will keep Devise's unique email validation happy.

When you run your test again, you'll see that it can't find the "Sign in" link:

```
1) Users can sign in with valid credentials
   Failure/Error: click_link "Sign in"
   Capybara::ElementNotFound:
     Unable to find link "Sign in"
```

Add the following code underneath the "Sign up" link in app/views/layouts/application.html.erb.

Listing 6.6   app/views/layouts/application.html.erb

```
<li class="<%= "active" if current_page?("/users/sign_in") %>">
  <%= link_to "Sign in", new_user_session_path %>
</li>
```

The new_user_session_path is another routing helper provided by Devise, this time to a SessionsController.

When you run your test again, it will go all the way up to the last step:

```
1) Users can sign in with valid credentials
   Failure/Error: expect(page).to have_content "Signed in as
   #{user.email}"
     expected to find text "Signed in as test1@example.com" in "Ticketee
     Toggle navigation Home Sign up Sign in Signed in successfully..."
```

This final line of the feature, seen in the error message, is checking that a message on the page indicates to the user which email address they've used to sign in. This can be useful in situations where a computer may be shared.

You'll put this line in app/views/layouts/application.html.erb, but you don't want it to show all the time. Conversely, it's not useful for the sign-in or sign-up links to appear when the user has already signed in. You can hide those links when the user is signed in, and replace them with the "Signed in as..." message.

You can do that by changing the content in app/views/layouts/application .html.erb shown in listing 6.7 to what's shown in listing 6.8.

Listing 6.7 Showing the "Sign up" and "Sign in" links to all users

```
<li class="<%= "active" if current_page?("/users/sign_up") %>">
  <%= link_to "Sign up", new_user_registration_path %>
</li>
<li class="<%= "active" if current_page?("/users/sign_in") %>">
  <%= link_to "Sign in", new_user_session_path %>
</li>
```

Listing 6.8 Showing the "Sign up" and "Sign in" links to only non-signed-in users

```
<% unless user_signed_in? %>
  <li class="<%= "active" if current_page?("/users/sign_up") %>">
    <%= link_to "Sign up", new_user_registration_path %>
  </li>
  <li class="<%= "active" if current_page?("/users/sign_in") %>">
    <%= link_to "Sign in", new_user_session_path %>
  </li>
<% end %>
```

Then immediately after the `ul.nav.navbar-nav` tag that those `li` tags are contained within, add the following code.

Listing 6.9 Showing the currently signed-in user's email address

```
<% if user_signed_in? %>
  <div class="navbar-right">
    <p class="navbar-text">
      Signed in as <%= current_user.email %>
    </p>
  </div>
<% end %>
```

These new pieces of code use two new methods: `user_signed_in?` and `current_user`. Both methods are provided by Devise, and both methods do exactly as they say. The `user_signed_in?` method returns `true` if the user is signed in; otherwise it returns `false`. The `current_user` method will return either a `User` instance that represents the current user, or `nil` if the user isn't signed in. With these two methods, you can hide the "Sign up" and "Sign in" links *and* you can show the "Signed in as…" message on the right side of the navbar when the user is signed in.

The navbar will now look like figure 6.2 when a user is signed in.

Run your test again with `bundle exec rspec spec/features/signing_in_spec.rb`. This time it will pass:

```
1 example, 0 failures
```

| Ticketee | Home | | Signed in as admin@example.com |

Figure 6.2 "Signed in as…" message in the navbar

Excellent! The sign-in part of this section is done. Now let's add the sign-out part of this task.

6.3.2   *Adding sign-out*

Before you write any code to build this sign-out functionality, you need to write a test using the code from the following listing.

Listing 6.10   spec/features/signing_out_spec.rb

```
require "rails_helper"

RSpec.feature "Signed-in users can sign out" do
  let!(:user) { FactoryGirl.create(:user) }

  before do
    login_as(user)
  end

  scenario do
    visit "/"
    click_link "Sign out"
    expect(page).to have_content "Signed out successfully."
  end
end
```

This test is a fairly simple one that reuses a bit of code from the sign-in feature, but with a subtle twist. There's now a `login_as` call in the `before` block. This `login_as` method doesn't come from Devise, but rather a gem Devise uses called Warden. Warden provides the user session management, whereas Devise provides the pretty face for it all. The `login_as` method will log in a user without having to walk through the whole sign-in process—visit the sign-in page, fill in a username and password, and so on.

When you're done with this feature, you'll have a "Sign out" link in your application that looks like figure 6.3.

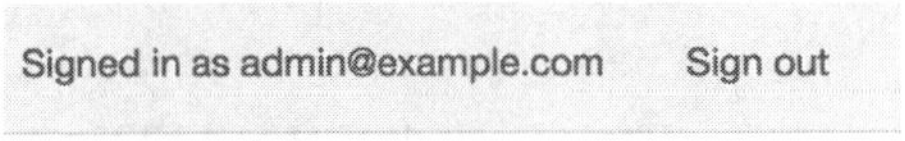

The `login_as` method isn't defined for your tests yet, though, as you'll see if you try to run this test with `bin/rspec spec/features/signing_out_spec.rb`:

Signed in as admin@example.com   Sign out

Figure 6.3   The "Sign out" link

```
1) Signed-in users can sign out
   Failure/Error: login_as(user)
   NoMethodError:
     undefined method `login_as' for #<RSpec::ExampleGroups::SignedIn...
```

This method isn't included automatically by Warden, so you'll need to manually include the module that defines it. You can do this in spec/rails helper.rb, the file that defines all of the configuration for your Rails tests, by putting the following code at the bottom of the `RSpec.configure` block.

Listing 6.11   Configuring Warden for use in feature specs

```
config.include Warden::Test::Helpers, type: :feature
config.after(type: :feature) { Warden.test_reset! }
```

The include method will include the specified module into your tests, and the type option passed to it will make it so that this module is only included in tests that reside in spec/features. You also need to tell Warden to reset itself after each test, which is done with the second line.

With those lines now in place, when you run your test it will complain that it can't find the "Sign out" link:

```
1) Signed-in users can sign out
   Failure/Error: click_link "Sign out"
   Capybara::ElementNotFound:
     Unable to find link "Sign out"
```

You can add this link next to the "Signed in as..." message in app/views/layouts/application.html.erb.

Listing 6.12   Adding the "Sign out" link after the "Signed in as..." text

```
<% if user_signed_in? %>
  <div class="navbar-right">
    <p class="navbar-text">
      Signed in as <%= current_user.email %>
    </p>
    <ul class="nav navbar-nav">
      <li><%= link_to "Sign out", destroy_user_session_path,
        method: :delete %>
      </li>
    </ul>
  </div>
<% end %>
```

When you run the test again with bundle exec rspec spec/features/signing_out _spec.rb, you can see that Devise has—for the third time in a row—taken care of the hard work. All you needed to provide was the link, and now your test passes:

```
1 example, 0 failures
```

That's great to see. Run all of your tests now with bundle exec rspec and see if they're all working:

```
17 examples, 0 failures
```

Yes, good! They are all indeed working. Commit this:

```
$ git add .
$ git commit -m "Add sign in and sign out"
$ git push
```

In this section, you've implemented sign-in and sign-out for your application to complement the sign-up feature that you added earlier in the chapter. You now have a

Sign up

Email

Password *(8 characters minimum)*

Password confirmation

Sign up

Log in

Figure 6.4   The unstyled "Sign up" form

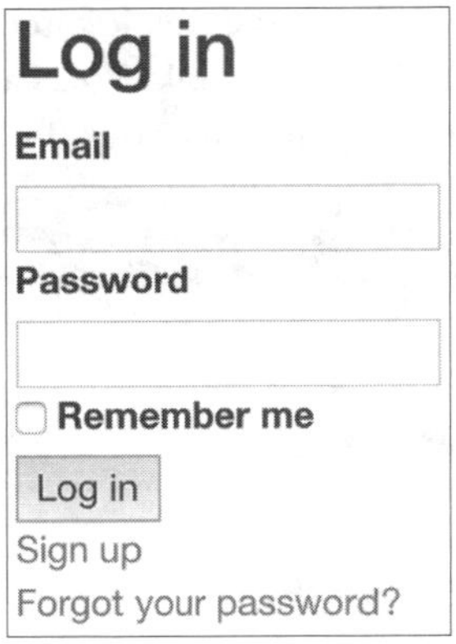

Log in

Email

Password

☐ Remember me

Log in

Sign up

Forgot your password?

Figure 6.5   The unstyled "Log in" form

taste of what Devise can do for you. Go and play around with the application now. Try signing up, signing in, and signing out.

You may notice during these experiments that the sign-up and sign-in forms aren't styled as neatly as the project and ticket forms (see figures 6.4 and 6.5).

This is because Devise provides basic views that don't use Bootstrap styling. Your next task will be to fix up these views.

6.3.3   Styling the Devise views

Devise is an *engine*, and this means that its controllers and views live inside the gem, rather than inside your application. In order to customize these views, you'll need to copy them into your application. Devise provides a method for you to do this by way of its `devise:views` generator. Run this in your application now:

```
$ rails g devise:views
```

This command copies over all of Devise's views to your application's app/views directory, inside another directory called app/ views/devise. If you navigate to the sign-up page now, you'll be pleasantly surprised to see that this page has already been styled using Bootstrap (see figure 6.6).

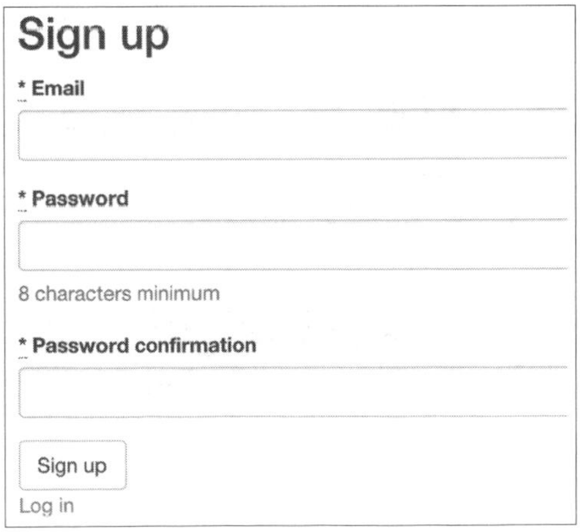

There are only a couple of small changes to make:

- Add the `header` wrapper tag to make the heading consistent.
- Remove the block error messages.
- Make the "Sign up" button blue to match the styling for the rest of the application.

Sign up

* Email

* Password

8 characters minimum

* Password confirmation

Sign up

Log in

Figure 6.6   The automatically styled "Sign up" form

The view for this page is located at app/views/devise/registrations/new.html.erb, so open it and have a look. You can replace the old heading in this view (listing 6.13) with a new one that matches the style of your application (listing 6.14).

Listing 6.13   The old Devise-generated heading

```
<h2>Sign up</h2>
```

Listing 6.14   The new Bootstrap-styled heading

```
<header>
  <h1>Sign Up</h1>
</header>
```

You can remove the following line.

Listing 6.15   The old-style block errors—yuck

```
<%= f.error_notification %>
```

And you can add the btn btn-primary Bootstrap classes to the button.

Listing 6.16   A shiny blue Submit button

```
<div class="form-actions">
  <%= f.button :submit, "Sign up", class: "btn btn-primary" %>
</div>
```

Now this button will be the standard blue color that you've been using for Submit buttons across the application.

You'll also need to make these same changes to the view for the sign-in page, which is in app/views/devise/sessions/new.html.erb. While you're here, it would be nice to change the words "Log in" to "Sign in" as well, to keep it consistent with the link you put in the top navigation.

Listing 6.17   The new heading on the sign-in page

```
<header>
  <h1>Sign In</h1>
</header>
```

Listing 6.18   The new submit button on the sign-in page

```
<div class="form-actions">
  <%= f.button :submit, "Sign in", class: "btn btn-primary" %>
</div>
```

And that's it.

Run your tests with `bundle exec rspec` to make sure you haven't broken anything ...

```
Failures:

  1) Users can sign in with valid credentials
     Failure/Error: click_button "Log in"
     Capybara::ElementNotFound:
       Unable to find button "Log in"

...
17 examples, 1 failure
```

And you have. Your sign-in test is looking for a button named "Log in," and you renamed it "Sign in." It's a quick fix—you just need to update the test to use the right value for the button. Inside spec/features/signing_in_spec.rb, update the step that clicks the sign-in button so that it's looking for the right text.

Listing 6.19   Part of spec/features/signing_in_spec.rb

```
...
click_button "Sign in"
...
```

We've renamed the button because the action users are taking is "signing in," since they click the "Sign in" link in the navbar to do so. The button's name should match.

If you rerun your specs with `bundle exec rspec` after making this change, you'll see that everything is now passing again:

```
17 examples, 0 failures
```

Now the design for your "Sign up" and "Sign in" forms is more consistent with the rest of the application. Make a commit for this change:

```
$ git add .
$ git commit -m "Styled sign up and sign in forms"
$ git push
```

You can go through and similarly style the other views that Devise provides, if you feel like it. We won't go through that whole process in order to keep this section short.

Now that you have users in your application, let's put them to use.

6.4   *Linking tickets to users*

Currently, when a user creates a ticket in the application, there's no way to tell after the fact which user created that ticket. As the last part of this chapter, let's fix up this little problem with your application.

When you're done, a ticket will clearly indicate who created it, as shown in figure 6.7.

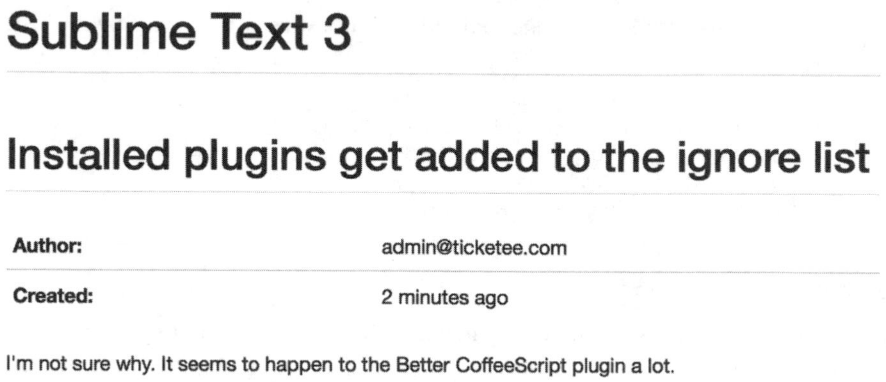

Sublime Text 3

Installed plugins get added to the ignore list

Author: admin@ticketee.com

Created: 2 minutes ago

I'm not sure why. It seems to happen to the Better CoffeeScript plugin a lot.

Figure 6.7   Ticket authorship in full view

Rather than creating a new feature, you'll add to a previous feature: spec/features/creating_tickets_spec.rb. In the very first scenario for that feature, you'll add a few lines to assert that you can see that the current user is the author of the ticket.

Listing 6.20   Verifying that you display which user created a ticket

```
scenario "with valid attributes" do
  fill_in "Name", with: "Non-standards compliance"
  fill_in "Description", with: "My pages are ugly!"
  click_button "Create Ticket"

  expect(page).to have_content "Ticket has been created."
  within("#ticket") do
    expect(page).to have_content "Author: #{user.email}"
  end
end
```

The user variable that you use in this new code doesn't exist yet, so you can add a `let` at the top of this feature. You'll also need to sign in as this user using the `login_as` helper from Warden, which you can do by adding the following code to the top of the before block in this feature.

Listing 6.21   Defining the user that will author the new ticket, and signing them in

```
RSpec.feature "Users can create new tickets" do
      let(:user) { FactoryGirl.create(:user) }
before do
  login_as(user)
  ...
```

Now your new code is set up and ready to go. Give it a whirl by running `bundle exec rspec spec/features/creating_tickets_spec.rb`. The first thing you'll notice is that the content you expect to be present on the page isn't there:

```
1) Users can create new tickets with valid attributes
   Failure/Error: expect(page).to have_content "Author: #{user.email}"
   expected to find text "Author: test1@example.com" in "Internet
   Explorer Non-standards compliance Edit Ticket Delete Ticket My ..."
```

To fix this error, add the code in the following listing to the code within app/views/tickets/show.html.erb, underneath the header with the ticket title.

Listing 6.22   Displaying attributes in app/views/tickets/show.html.erb

```
<table id="attributes">
  <tr>
    <th>Author:</th>
    <td><%= @ticket.author.email %></td>
  </tr>
  <tr>
    <th>Created:</th>
    <td><%= time_ago_in_words(@ticket.created_at) %> ago</td>
  </tr>
</table>
```

The Ticket object is likely to have many attributes added to it over the course of the book, so we're leaving room for expansion by creating a table that you can add extra rows to.

With this code, you call an author method on the @ticket object. The author method will return the user who created the ticket, and email will show you the email address for that user.

THE TIME_AGO_IN_WORDS VIEW HELPER You're using a *view helper* called time_ago_in_words here. It will present the timestamp for when the ticket was created in a nice readable format, such as "about 3 minutes" or "about 2 hours." Just a little nicety. You can find time_ago_in_words at http://api.rubyonrails.org/classes/ActionView/Helpers/DateHelper.html#method-i-time_ago_in_words.

The author association isn't defined on your Ticket model yet, but you can add that with a single line of code after the belongs_to :project line in app/models/ticket.rb:

```
class Ticket < ActiveRecord::Base
  belongs_to :project
  belongs_to :author, class_name: "User"
...
```

Here you define a new association called author on your Ticket instances. By default, the association name of :author assumes that your class is named Author, but because you don't have a model called Author and the model is instead called User, you need to tell the association that. You do that with the class_name option.

With a new belongs_to association comes the need to add a new field to your tickets table to track the IDs of the authors of your tickets. You can do that now by running this command:

```
$ rails g migration add_author_to_tickets author:references
```

This migration will add the `author_id` to your `tickets` table by using the following code.

Listing 6.23   db/migrate/[timestamp]_add_author_to_tickets.rb

```
class AddAuthorToTickets < ActiveRecord::Migration
  def change
    add_reference :tickets, :author, index: true, foreign_key: true
  end
end
```

There's just one small change you have to make to this code before you can run it. Rails assumes that you want to add a foreign key constraint to your association, which you do—but you don't want it the way it will behave out of the box.

You need to remove the `foreign_key: true` part of the `add_reference` line and add a foreign key constraint separately, so your migration should look like the following.

Listing 6.24   After fixing the foreign key that Rails generated

```
class AddAuthorToTickets < ActiveRecord::Migration
  def change
    add_reference :tickets, :author, index: true
    add_foreign_key :tickets, :users, column: :author_id
  end
end
```

Why do you need to do this? Because Rails' automatic inference will try to apply a foreign key on your `tickets` table, pointing to an `authors` table—and you don't have a `ticket` table. The author will be a `User`, living in the `users` table, so you need to specifically tell Rails that the foreign key should point to the `users` table instead (but still use the `author_id` field to do so.)

> **FOREIGN KEY SUPPORT ACROSS DIFFERENT DATABASE ADAPTERS** If you left the line about foreign keys as it was, it would still work in this scenario, as long as you're using SQLite. Rails doesn't support foreign keys natively in SQLite, only in PostgreSQL and MySQL, so this would work just fine. It just wouldn't do anything. You would, however, run into big problems down the road when it comes to using alternative database systems, as you will in chapter 13 when we look at using PostgreSQL on Heroku. So it's best to fix it up now to prevent problems later on.

You can now run the migration to add the `author_id` field to the `tickets` table:

```
$ bundle exec rake db:migrate
```

With that element now within app/views/tickets/show.html.erb, you can see if your feature has gotten any further by running it again with `bundle exec rspec spec/features/creating_tickets_spec.rb`:

```
1) Users can create new tickets with valid attributes
   Failure/Error: click_button "Create Ticket"
   ActionView::Template::Error:
    undefined method `email' for nil:NilClass
    # ./app/views/tickets/show.html.erb:21:in ...
```

This error is happening on the line that you just added to app/views/tickets/show.html.erb that references @ticket.author.email, and it's happening because you're not yet linking users to the tickets that they create. In order to remedy this, you'll need to do the actual linking, and the best place for that linking is in the controller action where tickets are created: the create action of TicketsController.

After you build a ticket in this action, you need to also set the ticket's author. You can do this by adding the author assignment to the create action for TicketsController.

> **Listing 6.25 Setting the current user as the ticket's author**

```
def create
  @ticket = @project.tickets.build(ticket_params)
  @ticket.author = current_user

  if @ticket.save
  ...
```

By associating an author with the @ticket object here, directly before the save, you link the current_user to the ticket. Once the ticket has been saved, that Ticket instance and that User instance will be tied together forever in a ticket-author relationship.

> **SETTING TICKET AUTHORS SECURELY** A naive, but unfortunately common, way to associate tickets to users would be to create a hidden field for author_id in the "New Ticket" form and populate it with the current user's ID. This is a big security hole—a malicious user could simply edit the HTML and change the user ID to be something else, thus creating tickets on another user's behalf. Manually setting the author in the controller is much safer—there's no way for the user to fake this data if they're logged in. They can only assign tickets to themselves.

Check now if your test gets any further by running it again with bundle exec rspec spec/features/creating _tickets_spec.rb. It should pass:

```
3 examples, 0 failures
```

Great! You're showing a ticket's author on the ticket page itself.

You can now add a couple of quick styles to app/assets/stylesheets/application .css.scss to make it look a bit prettier. It currently looks like figure 6.8.

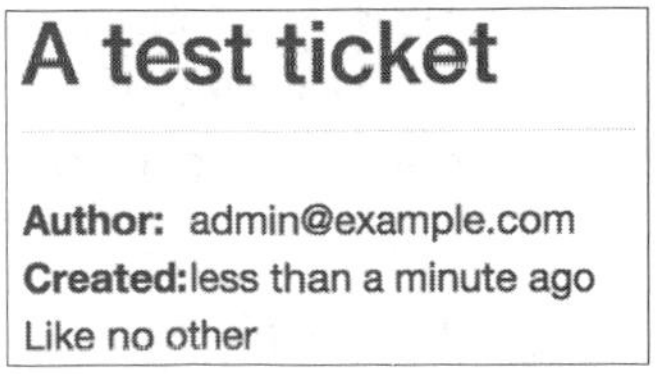

A test ticket

Author: admin@example.com
Created: less than a minute ago
Like no other

Figure 6.8 An unstyled version of the ticket attributes display

You can make it a little better by adding the following set of styles to your stylesheet specifically for tickets, located in app/assets/stylesheets/tickets.scss. This was generated when you generated a controller for your tickets, back in chapter 5.

Listing 6.26   app/assets/stylesheets/tickets.scss

```scss
#attributes {
  @extend .table;
  @extend .table-condensed;
  width: 65%;

  th {
   width: 35%;
  }

  tr:first-child {
   td, th {
     border-top: 0px;
   }
  }

  td, th {
   line-height: 24px !important;
  }
}
```

You extend Bootstrap's table styles again and tweak some of the margins and line heights for spacing reasons. You'll have to include this stylesheet into your application .css.scss with the following import line.

Listing 6.27   Importing tickets.scss

```scss
...
@import "projects";
@import "tickets";
@import "responsive";
...
```

Your attributes table now looks a lot better, as you can see in figure 6.9.

Now run all your tests with bundle exec rspec and confirm that you haven't broken anything:

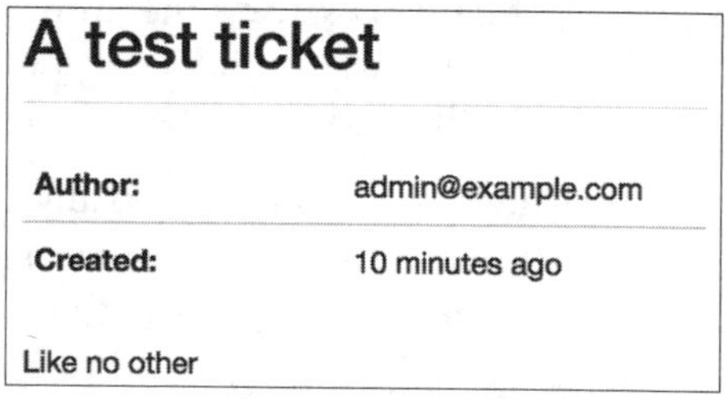

```
17 examples, 4 failures
```

A test ticket

Author:	admin@example.com
Created:	10 minutes ago

Like no other

Figure 6.9 A styled version of the ticket attributes display

```
Failed examples:

rspec ./spec/features/deleting_tickets_spec.rb:11
rspec ./spec/features/editing_tickets_spec.rb:12
rspec ./spec/features/editing_tickets_spec.rb:24
rspec ./spec/features/viewing_tickets_spec.rb:17
```

Oops, it appears you've broken some of your features! Fortunately, they all fail for the same reason:

```
1) Users can delete tickets successfully
   Failure/Error: visit project_ticket_path(project, ticket)
   ActionView::Template::Error:
    undefined method `email' for nil:NilClass
   # ./app/views/tickets/show.html.erb:21:in ...
```

They're all failing because the tickets created by Factory Girl in the features don't link to an author. When the app/views/tickets/show.html.erb page attempts to show the author's email address, it can't find the author, so it raises this error.

Let's see about fixing up those features, one at a time.

6.4.1 *Fixing the failing four features*

The first of these is the deleting-tickets feature. The issue here is that the ticket created in this feature isn't linked to any particular author. You can fix that up by changing the series of the `let` blocks at the top of spec/features/deleting_tickets_spec.rb to the following.

Listing 6.28 Assigning test tickets to an author for deleting tickets

```
let(:author)  { FactoryGirl.create(:user) }
let(:project) { FactoryGirl.create(:project) }
let(:ticket) do
  FactoryGirl.create(:ticket, project: project, author: author)
end
```

You create an author and assign the ticket to the user. When you run this test with `bundle exec rspec spec/features/deleting_tickets_spec.rb`, it will now pass:

```
1 example, 0 failures
```

Now apply the same fix to the remaining tests. The next batch is in spec/features/editing_tickets_spec.rb, and both scenarios from this file are currently failing. Again, you can fix this up by using the same `let` blocks as before.

Listing 6.29 Assigning test tickets to an author for editing tickets

```
let(:author)  { FactoryGirl.create(:user) }
let(:project) { FactoryGirl.create(:project) }
let(:ticket) do
  FactoryGirl.create(:ticket, project: project, author: author)
end
```

When you run this feature file with `bundle exec spec/features/editing_tickets_spec.rb`, it will now pass:

```
2 examples, 0 failures
```

The final feature file that you need to fix up is spec/features/viewing_tickets_spec.rb. This one's a little more complicated. In this file, you need to change the `before` block to create a user, and link that user to the tickets, which you can do with the following code.

Listing 6.30   Assigning test tickets to an author for viewing tickets

```ruby
before do
  author = FactoryGirl.create(:user)

  sublime = FactoryGirl.create(:project, name: "Sublime Text 3")
  FactoryGirl.create(:ticket, project: sublime,
   author: author, name: "Make it shiny!",
   description: "Gradients! Starbursts! Oh my!")

  ie = FactoryGirl.create(:project, name: "Internet Explorer")
  FactoryGirl.create(:ticket, project: ie, author: author,
   name: "Standards compliance", description: "Isn't a joke.")

  visit "/"
end
```

In this new version of the `before` block, you create a user and then link that user to both tickets that are created. When you run `bundle exec rspec spec/features/ viewing_tickets_spec.rb`, you can see that your changes have fixed this feature also:

```
1 example, 0 failures
```

That should be the last of your features to fix. You can confirm that by running `bundle exec rspec` again. This time you'll see all of your tests are passing:

```
17 examples, 0 failures
```

Excellent. Go ahead and make a commit for all this now:

```
$ git add .
$ git commit -m "Link tickets and users upon ticket creation"
$ git push
```

That wraps up the last section of this chapter.

6.5   *Summary*

This chapter covered how to set up authentication so that users can sign up and sign in to your application to accomplish certain tasks. You learned about a very popular gem used to handle authentication, Devise, and you also verified the functionality it provides by writing Capybara features to go with it.

Then came linking tickets to users, so you can track which user created which ticket. You did this by using the setter method provided by the `belongs_to` method's presence on the `Ticket` class.

We encourage you to start up the application with `rails server`, visit http://local-host:3000, and play around to get an idea of how it's looking right now. The application is taking shape and currently offers a lot of functionality for the minimal work you've put into it so far.

In the next chapter, we'll look at restricting certain actions to only users who are signed in or who have a special attribute set on them.

Basic access control

7

This chapter covers

- Authorizing administrative users
- Organizing code in namespaces
- Seeding the database with sample data
- Adding an admin-only interface to edit user records

As your application now stands, anybody, whether they're signed in or not, can create new projects. In this chapter, you'll restrict access to certain actions in the Projects-Controller, allowing only a certain subset of users—users with one particular attribute that's set in one particular way—to access the actions.

You'll track which users are administrators by putting a Boolean field called admin in the users table. This is the most basic form of user *authorization*, not to be confused with authentication, which you implemented in chapter 6. *Authentication* is the process users go through to confirm their identity, whereas *authorization* is the process used by the system to determine which users should have access to certain things. (More simply, authentication is "Who are you?" and authorization is "Now that I know who you are, what are you allowed to do?")

You'll see how you can organize code into *namespaces* so that you can easily restrict access to all subcontrollers to only admin users. If you didn't do this, you'd need to restrict access on a per-controller basis, which is prone to errors—it's easy to miss one and accidentally leave a part of your app wide open for the world to use and abuse.

Some people may suggest using gems such as rails_admin or activeadmin for this type of feature. Although these gems can provide you with an easier way of creating admin interfaces, they obfuscate the underlying code that's required to get this type of feature to work, and can often be very hard to customize. It's for these reasons we recommend staying away from these gems, and learning to build your own admin interface.

7.1 *Turning users into admins*

To start the process of restricting the creation of projects to admins, you need to add an `admin` attribute to `User` objects. Only users who have this `admin` attribute set to `true` will be able to create projects. You can start enforcing this first via your existing tests—you have a feature spec for creating projects, and you can make sure the user creating the projects is an admin.

Alter the existing `before` in spec/features/creating_projects_spec.rb and insert a line to log in as an admin user at the beginning of the `before` block.

Listing 7.1 Logging in as an admin before creating a project

```
before do
  login_as(FactoryGirl.create(:user, :admin))
  ...
```

This line uses the `user` factory you defined in chapter 6, and adds what's known as a Factory Girl *trait*. Traits can describe a certain type of a model, or they can group together similar and related attributes under a meaningful name. In this example, any user with this admin trait will be able to perform special actions within your application.

FACTORY GIRL TRAITS For the details on traits, see the Factory Girl documentation: https://github.com/thoughtbot/factory_girl/blob/master/GETTING _STARTED.md#traits.

To add this trait to your `user` factory, all you need to do is call the `trait` method inside the factory, as in the following listing.

Listing 7.2 Defining an `admin` trait

```
FactoryGirl.define do
  factory :user do
    sequence(:email) { |n| "test#{n}@example.com" }
    password "password"

    trait :admin do
      admin true
    end
  end
end
```

A trait can add or modify any attributes set in the factory it's defined in. This new addition to your code means that any user created with `FactoryGirl.create(:user, :admin)` will have their `admin` attribute set to `true`.

When you run `bundle exec rspec spec/features/creating_projects_spec.rb`, you'll see that no `admin=` method is defined for a `User` object:

```
1) Users can create new projects with valid attributes
   Failure/Error: login_as(FactoryGirl.create(:user, :admin))
   NoMethodError:
     undefined method `admin=' for #<User:0x007f4138da7688>
```

Therefore, the next logical step is to define a field in the database so the attribute-setter method is available.

7.1.1 *Adding the admin field to the users table*

You can generate a migration to add the `admin` field by running this command:

```
$ rails g migration add_admin_to_users admin:boolean
```

Rails does a pretty good job of inferring what you want the migration to do, just from the name you specified. From `add_admin_to_users` it presumes you want to add a field named `admin` to the table called `users`, which is exactly what you want. The extra `admin:boolean` tells Rails that the `admin` field should be a Boolean field.

But you'll want to modify this migration so that when users are created, the `admin` field is set to `false` rather than defaulting to `nil`. Even though `nil` is "falsey" in Ruby, it's clearer to make it explicitly `false`. `nil` means users have no admin information, but they do: they're not an admin. It's better to be explicit about things.

> **Falsey and truthy in Ruby**
>
> In Ruby, `nil` and `false` are both considered to be "falsey" and won't pass a conditional test, such as `puts "foo" if false`. Everything else is considered "truthy," including things like `0`, `[]`, `""`, and `{}`. This can confuse people coming from other languages!
>
> Changing the default value from `nil` to `false` makes even more sense if you consider it from a database SQL perspective. We traditionally treat `nil` in Ruby (meaning *no value*) as equivalent to `null` in SQL, but `null` in SQL means *an unknown value*. In this case, `null` in the database isn't an appropriate default value because you'll always know whether or not the user is an admin.

To change the default, open the freshly generated migration (which will be in db/migrate/<timestamp>_add_admin_to_users.rb) and change this line,

```
add_column :users, :admin, :boolean
```

to this:

```
add_column :users, :admin, :boolean, default: false
```

When you pass in the `:default` option, the `admin` field defaults to `false`, ensuring that users aren't accidentally created as admins.

> **YOU CAN ROLL BACK CHANGES IF YOU WISH** If you jumped the gun and ran `bundle exec rake db:migrate` before modifying the migration, the `admin` field will default to `null`, which is no good. It may seem like you're screwed at this point, but you're not. Run `bundle exec rake db:rollback` to undo this latest migration so that you can modify it and get back on track. Once the modification is done correctly, don't forget to run `bundle exec rake db:migrate` again!

Run `bundle exec rake db:migrate` so that the migration adds the `admin` field to the users table in both the development and test databases. When you run `bundle exec rspec spec/features/creating_projects_spec.rb` now, it will run fully:

```
2 examples, 0 failures
```

Great! With the new `admin` trait on the `user` factory defined, you can use it to test restricting the acts of creating, updating, and destroying projects to only those users who are admins.

7.1.2 Creating the first admin user

Now that you have the ability to distinguish normal users from admin users, it would be great if you actually had an admin user to use your development app. You've got one in your tests, but not one in the development environment.

Data like this—data that you really need to have created in your database before the application can be used—is called *seed data*. Rails has a defined place to put your seed data—in db/seeds.rb.

Open db/seeds.rb. It's empty at the moment, but contains instructions for how it can be used. You can put commands to create the relevant data in the file, and then run it with `bundle exec rake db:seed`.

You can put the code needed to create a new admin user at the bottom of the file shown next.

Listing 7.3 Seeding Ticketee with an admin user

```
unless User.exists?(email: "admin@ticketee.com")
  User.create!(email: "admin@ticketee.com", password: "password", admin: true
    )
end
```

While you're here, you can also add some other sample data to play with when you use the application.

Listing 7.4 Seeding Ticketee with a non-admin user and some sample projects

```
unless User.exists?(email: "viewer@ticketee.com")
  User.create!(email: "viewer@ticketee.com", password: "password")
end
```

```
["Sublime Text 3", "Internet Explorer"].each do |name|
  unless Project.exists?(name: name)
    Project.create!(name: name, description: "A sample project about #{name}"
      )
  end
end
```

Run the following command to load the seeds into your application:

```
$ bundle exec rake db:seed
```

Now you have an admin user that can sign in to Ticketee, and can see and test all of the admin functionality you'll build from here on out.

Before you do that, it's time to commit everything:

```
$ git add .
$ git commit -m "Added admin flag to User model, and seeded the first
  ➥ admin user"
$ git push
```

7.2   *Controller namespacing*

It's all well and good having an `admin` flag on a user record, but at the moment it doesn't actually do anything. We'll fix that now.

You already have some functionality that you want only admins to be able to access—the ability to create and delete projects—and later on you'll build more. An easy way to restrict access to all of this functionality at once is to move it into its own controller *namespace*.

You've already seen an example of namespaces for controllers, though you might not realize it—your `ApplicationController` (in app/controllers/application _controller.rb) that was created when you generated the initial Rails app inherits from `ActionController::Base`. In this case, `ActionController` is the namespace, and `Base` is the name of the class inside the namespace.

You can define your own namespace, which we'll imaginatively call `Admin` in this example. Inside this namespace, you can define all of the controllers you like, and they'll all inherit from a base controller also inside the namespace. And inside that base controller, you can implement a `before_action` that will run before every action and check if the user is an admin—if they're not, you can simply turn them away.

7.2.1   *Generating a namespaced controller*

The first thing you'll need is the base controller in the new namespace that all of the other admin controllers will inherit from. You can generate it by running this command:

```
$ rails g controller admin/application index
```

When you use the / separator between parts of the controller, Rails knows that you want a namespace. In this case, it will generate a namespaced controller called `Admin::ApplicationController` at app/controllers/admin/application_controller.rb. The views for this controller are at app/views/admin/application, and the spec is at spec/controllers/admin/application_controller_spec.rb. Because you passed in the word index at the end, this controller will contain an index action, and there will also be a view at app/views/admin/application/index.html.erb for this action, as well as a route defined in config/routes.rb, like this:

```
namespace :admin do
  get 'application/index'
end
```

> **NAMING APPLICATIONCONTROLLER** Why use the name Admin::Application-Controller over something that might be more explicit, like Admin::Base-Controller? The main controller of your app, in the *root* namespace, is called ApplicationController, so it makes sense that any other main controllers in namespaces should also be called ApplicationController.

What URLs and named routes does this generate? You can run bundle exec rake routes and see (controller column omitted for brevity):

```
Prefix  Verb  URI Pattern
 admin_application_index  GET   /admin/application/index(.:format)
```

The namespace block in your routing has directly translated to a folder name in the generated URL structure, which is nice. The application/index part is ugly, though—it would make more sense for your action to be the root route of the namespace, like you defined projects#index to be the root route of the root namespace.

Replace the entire namespace block in config/routes.rb with the following.

Listing 7.5 Defining a root route for the admin namespace

```
namespace :admin do
  root "application#index"
end
```

And now bundle exec rake routes gives you some nicer URLs:

```
Prefix  Verb  URI Pattern          Controller#Action
admin_root  GET    /admin(.:format)    admin/application#index
```

This root admin page is the first page your admins will see in the admin area, so you may as well make it a bit pretty. Open the generated view for it, app/views/admin/application/index.html.erb, and replace its contents with the following.

Listing 7.6 Default content for the admin homepage

```
<div class="row" id="admin">
  <div class="col-md-9">
    <header>
      <h1>Admin Lounge</h1>
    </header>
```

```
      <p>Welcome to Ticketee's Admin Lounge. Please enjoy your stay.</p>
    </div>

    <div class="col-md-3">
      <h2>Admin Links</h2>
      <ul class="nav nav-stacked">
        <li>Links will go here. Soon.</li>
      </ul>
    </div>
  </div>
```

You've used a few more of Bootstrap's styles here, for adding a grid layout (so you can have a sidebar defining admin links). The only styles you need to add are for the h2 in the sidebar, so it doesn't look large and overwhelming.

When you generated Admin::ApplicationController, you also got a new empty stylesheet in app/assets/stylesheets/admin/application.scss. You can add your styles for the h2 there.

Listing 7.7   app/assets/stylesheets/admin/application.scss

```
#admin .col-md-3 h2 {
  font-size: 13px;
  letter-spacing: 1px;
  text-transform: uppercase;
  font-weight: bold;
  color: #959595;
  padding-left: 15px;
}
```

You'll also need to import this stylesheet into your main application.css.scss file.

Listing 7.8   app/assets/stylesheets/application.css.scss

```
...
@import "tickets";
@import "admin/application";
@import "responsive";
...
```

Once you've done that, you can refresh the admin homepage and see a page that looks like figure 7.1.

But anyone can access this page at the moment. You don't even need to be logged in. The next step is to make sure this page is only accessible to admin users, and you'll do that with a before_action that checks not only whether a user is signed in, but also whether the user is an admin. We'll start (as always) with a test.

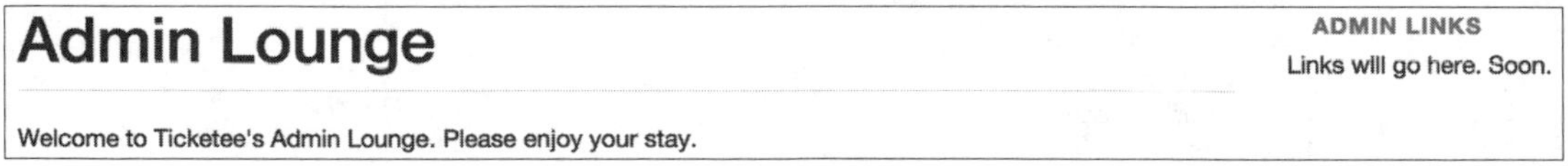

Admin Lounge

ADMIN LINKS
Links will go here. Soon.

Welcome to Ticketee's Admin Lounge. Please enjoy your stay.

Figure 7.1   The styled admin page

7.2.2 *Testing a namespaced controller*

A controller spec is much better suited to testing this functionality than the feature specs we've been using heavily up to this point. Feature specs are great for defining and testing a series of actions that a user can perform in your application, but controller specs are much better for quickly testing singular points, such as whether a user can go to a specific action in a controller. You used this same reasoning back in chapter 4 to test what happens when a user attempts to go to a project that doesn't exist.

Open spec/controllers/admin/application_controller_spec.rb, and write the following example to ensure that non-signed-in and non-admin users can't access the index action. You can replace the current contents of the file.

Listing 7.9   spec/controllers/admin/application_controller_spec.rb

```ruby
require "rails_helper"

RSpec.describe Admin::ApplicationController, type: :controller do
  let(:user) { FactoryGirl.create(:user) }

  before do
    allow(controller).to receive(:current_user).and_return(user)
  end

  context "non-admin users" do
    it "are not able to access the index action" do
      get :index

      expect(response).to redirect_to "/"
      expect(flash[:alert]).to eq "You must be an admin to do that."
    end
  end
end
```

Here you set up a user by using the `user` factory, and then you use not one but two new methods. The `controller` method returns the instance of the controller that will be used during this test. The `allow` method allows you to fake method responses on that object. In this case, you're *stubbing* the `current_user` method. If you were to call `current_user` in the controller, you wouldn't actually call the `current_user` method defined in the controller; the test would intercept the call and simply return `user` instead. By doing this, you don't have to actually sign in as the user at all. The controller will think that the user has already signed in.

There are a couple of good reasons to do this. Primarily, the whole authentication process is not what you're testing in this test; you're testing what happens when an already-signed-in user accesses a specific controller action. If there's a bug in the sign-in process, every test that requires a signed-in user shouldn't fail—only ones that specifically test the sign-in process. This helps reduce false failures—tests that fail, even though the logic they're testing works perfectly. As a bonus side effect, your tests will be faster. You're not repeating the sign-in process over and over again, maybe hundreds of times for the entire test suite.

> ### Stubbing in feature tests
>
> You can't stub like this in feature tests because you don't have direct access to the controller instances that you're using. If you did, then you wouldn't use Warden's own `login_as` helper to sign in. You also couldn't use `login_as` in a controller spec, because Warden's proxy object isn't available in controller tests at all. This is because the Warden middleware doesn't come into play at all during controller tests; the tests hit the controllers themselves without going through the layers of middleware.
>
> Ideally, you should be doing very little stubbing in feature tests—they're designed to test your entire app, and how all the pieces fit together, like they do when your user is viewing them in a browser.[1] This is why you don't stub out authentication in feature tests, but you can stub it out here in a controller test.

With this test, you're testing that when a non-admin user makes a GET request to the index action of the `Admin::ApplicationController`, the response redirects them to the root path of the application and also sets a `flash[:alert]` message to "You must be an admin to do that."

When you run this test using `bundle exec rspec spec/controllers/admin/application_controller_spec.rb`, it fails like this:

```
1) Admin::ApplicationController non-admin users are not able to access
   the index action
   Failure/Error: expect(response).to redirect_to "/"
     Expected response to be a <redirect>, but was <200>
```

This error message tells you that although you expected to be redirected, the response was actually 200, indicating a successful response. This isn't what you want; you want a redirect! Now let's get it to pass.

The first step is to define a new method to be used as the `before_action` admin check on the `Admin::ApplicationController`. This method will check whether a user is an admin, and, if not, will set the "You must be an admin to do that" message and redirect the user back to the root path.

Define this new method in app/controllers/admin/application_controller.rb by placing the code from the following listing at the end of the class.

Listing 7.10 app/controllers/admin/application_controller.rb

```
class Admin::ApplicationController < ApplicationController
  ...

  private
```

---

[1] There are exceptions to every rule. Interactions with external services, such as logging in via Facebook, should always have their responses stubbed out. Imagine if your test suite was actually visiting Facebook every time you ran a test. It would be *so* slow!

```
def authorize_admin!
  authenticate_user!

  unless current_user.admin?
    redirect_to root_path, alert: "You must be an admin to do that."
  end
end
end
```

This method uses the `authenticate_user!` method provided by Devise to ensure that the user is signed in. If the user isn't signed in, they will be redirected to the sign-in page. If you didn't use this method here, you'd get an error when you call `admin?` on `current_user`, because the `current_user` method would return `nil`.

To call the `authorize_admin!` method, call `before_action` at the top of your `Admin::ApplicationController`:

```
class Admin::ApplicationController < ApplicationController
  before_action :authorize_admin!
  ...
```

With that in place, you can rerun the spec. When you do, you'll see this error:

```
1) Admin::ApplicationController non-admin users are not able to access
   the index action
   Failure/Error: get :index
   NoMethodError:
     undefined method `authenticate!' for nil:NilClass
   # .../lib/devise/controllers/helpers.rb:112:in `authenticate_user!'
   # .../admin/application_controller.rb:10:in `authorize_admin!'
```

Your application isn't too happy with the `authenticate_user!` call that you have inside the `authorize_admin!` method inside the controller. It's complaining that it can't find an `authenticate!` method on `nil`. This is happening because `authenticate_user!` attempts to call this method on a thing called the *Warden proxy object*, which isn't available in controller tests.

To work around this problem, you can stub out the `authenticate_user!` method to do nothing in your controller spec. Do this by using the `allow` method once more in the `before` block at the top of your test:

```
RSpec.describe Admin::ApplicationController, type: :controller do
  let(:user) { FactoryGirl.create(:user) }

  before do
    allow(controller).to receive(:authenticate_user!)
    allow(controller).to receive(:current_user).and_return(user)
  end
  ...
```

When using `allow` in this fashion (without an `and_return` call), the `authenticate_user!` method is stubbed to return nil, and the real `authenticate_user!` method doesn't get called. You put this at the top of this test because the `show` action test at the bottom of this file will also need this.

Ultimately, that all means that you should now have worked around the error that you saw in the last test. Run the test again and see what happens:

```
1 example, 0 failures
```

Excellent! You have a controller that's only accessible by admin users of your application. With that done, you can ensure that everything is working as expected by running `bundle exec rspec`:

```
20 examples, 0 failures, 2 pending
```

Everything is still passing, but there are two pending tests:

```
# ./spec/helpers/admin/application_helper_spec.rb:14
# ./spec/views/admin/application/index.html.erb_spec.rb:4
```

These two tests were added when you ran `rails g controller admin/controller`. The first is a simple helper test, and the second is a *view spec*, which can be used to ensure that rendering a particular view works as intended.[2] You don't need these two tests, so you can delete both files. When you rerun `bundle exec rspec`, you should see this output:

```
18 examples, 0 failures
```

You can commit this now:

```
$ git add .
$ git commit -m "Add admin namespace with application controller"
$ git push
```

7.2.3   *Moving functionality into the admin namespace*

Now that you have a working admin namespace that only admin users can access, you can start moving functionality into it. Normal users shouldn't have the ability to create and delete projects—only admins should—so that functionality sounds like a good candidate for moving. You have tests that cover that functionality, so if you accidentally break it in the process of moving it, you'll know it straight away.

To start with, those tests (spec/features/creating_projects_spec.rb and spec/features/deleting_projects_spec.rb) should be moved into spec/features/admin, to reflect where the functionality will be placed. Rerun them, and they will still pass:

```
$ bundle exec rspec spec/features/admin
...

3 examples, 0 failures
```

You can make another `ProjectsController` inside the `Admin` namespace, which is where the moved controller actions will go. You can generate another namespaced controller for the projects resource.

```
$ rails g controller admin/projects
```

---

[2]   Read more about view spec testing at https://www.relishapp.com/rspec/rspec-rails/v/3-2/docs/view-specs/view-spec.

The only change that you'll need to make to this generated controller is to change what it inherits from—a default controller inherits from `ApplicationController`, but you want your admin controllers to inherit from `Admin::ApplicationController`. Inside the new controller, app/controllers/admin/projects_controller.rb, change the first line from this,

```
class Admin::ProjectsController < ApplicationController
```

to this:

```
class Admin::ProjectsController < Admin::ApplicationController
```

The actions that you'll move to this new controller are the `new`, `create`, and `destroy` actions of the existing `ProjectsController`. You can cut and paste those actions from the old controller to the new one, so that your `ProjectsController` looks like the following listing.

Listing 7.11 The new `ProjectsController`

```ruby
class ProjectsController < ApplicationController
  before_action :set_project, only: [:show, :edit, :update, :destroy]

  def index
    @projects = Project.all
  end

  def show
  end

  def edit
  end

  def update
    if @project.update(project_params)
      flash[:notice] = "Project has been updated."
      redirect_to @project
    else
      flash.now[:alert] = "Project has not been updated."
      render "edit"
    end
  end

  private

  def set_project
    @project = Project.find(params[:id])
  rescue ActiveRecord::RecordNotFound
    flash[:alert] = "The project you were looking for could not be found."
    redirect_to projects_path
  end

  def project_params
    params.require(:project).permit(:name, :description)
  end
end
```

The `Admin::ProjectsController` will look like the next listing.

Listing 7.12   The new `Admin::ProjectsController`

```
class Admin::ProjectsController < Admin::ApplicationController
  def new
    @project = Project.new
  end

  def create
    @project = Project.new(project_params)

    if @project.save
      flash[:notice] = "Project has been created."
      redirect_to @project
    else
      flash.now[:alert] = "Project has not been created."
      render "new"
    end
  end

  def destroy
    @project.destroy

    flash[:notice] = "Project has been deleted."
    redirect_to projects_path
  end
end
```

The `project_params` method will have to be duplicated into the `Admin::Projects-Controller`, since it's used in both the `create` action of the `Admin::ProjectsCon-troller` as well as in the `update` action of the `ProjectsController`. You also need to load the `@project` variable in the `destroy` action of the `Admin::ProjectsController`, because you no longer have the `before_action` that sets the `@project` variable. You can also remove `:destroy` from the list of actions the `before_action` does run, in the `ProjectsController`.

Listing 7.13   The final `Admin::ProjectsController`

```
class Admin::ProjectsController < Admin::ApplicationController
  def new
    @project = Project.new
  end

  def create
    @project = Project.new(project_params)

    if @project.save
      flash[:notice] = "Project has been created."
      redirect_to @project
    else
      flash.now[:alert] = "Project has not been created."
```

```
      render "new"
    end
  end

  def destroy
    @project = Project.find(params[:id])
    @project.destroy

    flash[:notice] = "Project has been deleted."
    redirect_to projects_path
  end

  private

  def project_params
    params.require(:project).permit(:name, :description)
  end
end
```

What else do you need to do? You still need the views that these actions were render-ing! Do the following:

- Move the new view in app/views/projects/new.html.erb to app/views/admin/ projects/new.html.erb so that the new action you moved can still use it.
- The new view uses the _form partial back in the app/views/projects folder. For now you can duplicate this _form partial into the app/views/admin/projects folder.

You can rerun the admin specs with bundle exec rspec spec/features/admin now to see what has been broken:

```
FFF

Failures:

  1) Users can create new projects with valid attributes
     Failure/Error: click_link "New Project"
     AbstractController::ActionNotFound:
       The action 'new' could not be found for ProjectsController

  2) Users can create new projects when providing invalid attributes
     Failure/Error: click_link "New Project"
     AbstractController::ActionNotFound:
       The action 'new' could not be found for ProjectsController

  3) Users can delete projects successfully
     Failure/Error: click_link "Delete Project"
     AbstractController::ActionNotFound:
       The action 'destroy' could not be found for ProjectsController

3 examples, 3 failures
```

You haven't updated the links in your views—the "New Project" and "Delete Project" links are still pointing at routes that reference actions that no longer exist.

You'll need to update your routes to point to the new actions, and you can also remove the routes for the old actions, to keep things tidy. Your old routes for projects looked like the following listing.

Listing 7.14 Non-admin route definition for projects

```
resources :projects do
  resources :tickets
end
```

This defines the seven default RESTful routes for a `projects` resource: `index`, `new`, `create`, `show`, `edit`, `update`, and `destroy`. If you want to remove some of those (because you've removed the actions), you can use the `only` option when defining the routes.

Listing 7.15 Non-admin route definition for projects

```
resources :projects, only: [:index, :show, :edit, :update] do
  resources :tickets
end
```

> **THE ONLY OPTION** only works as a whitelist, listing the routes that *should* be generated. There's also a blacklist version, called `except`, to list the routes that *should not* be generated. See the Rails Routing from the Outside In guide: http://guides.rubyonrails.org/routing.html#restricting-the-routes-created.

You can add the new routes inside the admin namespace, as shown in the following listing.

Listing 7.16 Admin route definition for projects

```
namespace :admin do
  root "application#index"

  resources :projects, only: [:new, :create, :destroy]
end
```

This generates the following named routes:

```
Prefix Verb    URI Pattern                      Controller#Action
      admin_root GET     /admin(.:format)                 admin/
    application#index
   admin_projects POST    /admin/projects(.:format)       admin/projects#create
new_admin_project GET     /admin/projects/new(.:format) admin/projects#new
    admin_project DELETE /admin/projects/:id(.:format) admin/
    projects#destroy
```

Now you can edit the links to "New Project" and "Delete Project" in the `index` and `show` views, to point to the new named routes.

Listing 7.17   The new link to create a project in app/views/projects/index.html.erb

```
<li>
  <%= link_to "New Project", new_admin_project_path, class: "new" %>
</li>
```

Listing 7.18   The new link to delete a project in app/views/projects/show.html.erb

```
<li><%= link_to "Delete Project",
  admin_project_path(@project),
  method: :delete,
  data: { confirm: "Are you sure you want to delete this project?" },
  class: "delete" %></li>
```

Even though the "Delete Project" link is only accessible to admins in your application, it will still show up for non-admins. This is a problem you'll fix a little later in this chapter.

Rerunning the project-creating spec with `bundle exec rspec spec/features/admin/creating_projects_spec.rb` gives you a different error:

```
1) Users can create new projects with valid attributes
   Failure/Error: click_button "Create Project"
   ActionController::RoutingError:
     No route matches [POST] "/projects"
```

The test is trying to click the button on the form to create a project, but the route that the form is submitting to no longer exists. This is because you just copied the old form partial—you should edit that form to submit to the new `create` action in the admin namespace instead. Open the admin project form in app/views/admin/projects/_form.html.erb, and modify the first line as in the next listing.

Listing 7.19   The start of the updated _form.html.erb partial

```
<%= simple_form_for([:admin, project]) do |f| %>
```

For this `simple_form_for`, you use the array form you saw earlier with `[@project, @ticket]`, but this time you pass in a symbol rather than a model object. Rails interprets the symbol literally, generating a route such as `admin_users_path` rather than `users_path`, which would be generated if you used `simple_form_for @user` instead. You can also use this array syntax with the `link_to` (shown earlier) and `redirect_to` helpers. Any symbol passed anywhere in the array for any of these methods is interpreted literally. The same goes for strings.

Now your spec for creating a project will pass:

```
2 examples, 0 failures
```

THE PROJECT-DELETION FEATURE

What about deleting projects? If you run `bundle exec rspec spec/features/admin/deleting_projects_spec.rb`, you'll get the following error:

```
1) Users can delete projects successfully
   Failure/Error: expect(page).to have_content "Project has been deleted."
     expected to find text "Project has been deleted." in "Ticketee
     Toggle navigation Home Sign up Sign in You need to sign in or sign
     up before continuing. Sign In Email Password Remember me Sign up..."
```

The test isn't logging in as an admin user (or as any user), before attempting to delete a project—that's why the text on the page includes "You need to sign in or sign up before continuing." You can sign in as an admin the same way you did in the creating projects spec, in the before block, putting it directly before the scenario block in spec/features/admin/deleting_projects_spec.rb.

Listing 7.20   spec/features/admin/deleting_projects_spec.rb

```
RSpec.feature "Users can delete projects" do
  before do
    login_as(FactoryGirl.create(:user, :admin))
  end

  ...
```

Now the project-deletion spec will pass as well:

```
1 example, 0 failures
```

As always, run `bundle exec rspec` to make sure that nothing else is broken:

```
19 examples, 0 failures, 1 pending
```

Everything is passing, but you have another pending spec, coming from autogenerated code:

```
# ./spec/helpers/admin/projects_helper_spec.rb:14
```

You can delete this file because you're not using it at all. Then rerun the specs to verify that everything is all green:

```
18 examples, 0 failures
```

Great! You've moved this admin-only functionality into the `admin` namespace, which restricts it so that non-admin users can't access it. It's a good time to stop and commit your changes:

```
$ git add .
$ git commit -m "Only admins can create or delete projects"
$ git push
```

You've restricted the controller actions by putting them into the namespace, but the links to perform these actions, such as "New Project" and "Delete Project," are still visible to users. You should hide (or protect) these links from users who aren't admins, because it's useless to show actions to people who can't perform them. Let's look at how to do that.

7.3 *Hiding links*

In this section, you'll learn how to hide certain links such as "New Project" and "Delete Project" from users who have no authorization to perform those actions in your application.

If these links were available for users to follow, they'd be told "You must be an admin to do that," thanks to the `before_action` that you set up in `Admin::Application-Controller`. This happens because these links link to `Admin::ProjectsController`, which inherits from `Admin::ApplicationController`.

It's pointless to display these links to people who shouldn't be able to click them, so let's look at hiding them.

7.3.1 *Hiding the "New Project" link*

To begin, open a new file called spec/features/hidden_links_spec.rb. In this file, you'll write scenarios to ensure that the right links are shown to the right people.

Let's start with the code for checking that the "New Project" link is hidden from regular users who are either signed out or signed in, and that it is shown to admins.

Listing 7.21   spec/features/hidden_links_spec.rb

```ruby
require "rails_helper"

RSpec.feature "Users can only see the appropriate links" do
  let(:user) { FactoryGirl.create(:user) }
  let(:admin) { FactoryGirl.create(:user, :admin) }

  context "anonymous users" do
    scenario "cannot see the New Project link" do
      visit "/"
      expect(page).not_to have_link "New Project"
    end
  end

  context "regular users" do
    before { login_as(user) }

    scenario "cannot see the New Project link" do
      visit "/"
      expect(page).not_to have_link "New Project"
    end
  end

  context "admin users" do
    before { login_as(admin) }

    scenario "can see the New Project link" do
      visit "/"
      expect(page).to have_link "New Project"
    end
  end
end
```

In this spec, you first define two `let` blocks: one for user and one for admin. These create a non-admin user and an admin user, respectively, when they're called.

You have three `context` blocks—one for each permutation of the scenario. In the first, you act as an anonymous user and check that there is indeed no "New Project" link on the page. In the second, you act as a regular user and again check that there's no "New Project" link on the page. In the third, however, you sign in as an admin, and when *that* happens, the "New Project" link should appear on the page.

When you run this feature using `bundle exec rspec spec/features/hidden_links_spec.rb`, you'll get some expected failure messages:

```
1) Users can only see the appropriate links anonymous users cannot see
   the New Project link
   Failure/Error: expect(page).not_to have_link "New Project"
     expected not to find link "New Project", found 1 match: "New
     Project"
   # ./spec/features/hidden_links_spec.rb:10:in `block (3 levels) in...

2) Users can only see the appropriate links regular users cannot see
   the New Project link
   Failure/Error: expect(page).not_to have_link "New Project"
     expected not to find link "New Project", found 1 match: "New
     Project"
   # ./spec/features/hidden_links_spec.rb:19:in `block (3 levels) in...
```

The first two scenarios from your new feature fail, of course, because you've done nothing yet to hide the link they're checking for.

Open app/views/projects/index.html.erb, and change the "New Project" link to the following to start the process of hiding it.

Listing 7.22 Only showing the "New Project" link to admins

```
<% admins_only do %>
  <ul class="actions">
    <li>
      <%= link_to "New Project", new_admin_project_path, class: "new" %>
    </li>
  </ul>
<% end %>
```

The `admins_only` method won't magically be there, so you'll need to define it. The method needs to take a block. If `current_user` is an admin, the method should run the code in the block; if they're not, it should show nothing.

You'll want this helper to be available everywhere in your application's views, so the best place to define it is in `ApplicationHelper`. If you wanted it to be available only to a specific controller's views, you'd place it in the helper that shares the name with the controller.

To define the `admins_only` helper, open app/helpers/application_helper.rb and define the method in the module using the following code.

Listing 7.23   app/helpers/application_helper.rb

```
def admins_only(&block)
  block.call if current_user.try(:admin?)
end
```

The `admins_only` method takes a block (as promised), which is the code between the `admins_only do` and `end` in your view. To run this code in the block, you call `block.call`, which only runs it if `current_user.try(:admin?)` returns `true`. This `try` method tries a method on an object; if the object is `nil` (as it would be if no user is currently logged in), `try` gives up and returns `nil`, rather than raising a `NoMethodError` exception.

When you run this feature using `bundle exec rspec spec/features/ hidden_links_spec.rb`, it passes because the links are being hidden and shown as required:

```
3 examples, 0 failures
```

Now that the "New Project" link hides if the user isn't an admin, let's do the same thing for the "Delete Project" link.

7.3.2   *Hiding the delete link*

You need to add this `admins_only` helper to the "Delete Project" links on the project's show view, to hide this link from people who shouldn't see it. (Later on you'll hide the "Edit Project" link too, but a little differently.) Before you do this, though, you should add further scenarios to spec/features/hidden_links_spec.rb to cover the change to the "Delete Project" link.

In order to test that the link works, you need to create a project during these tests. To do so, define a `let` block with the two for users and admins in this file, as follows.

Listing 7.24   spec/features/hidden_links_spec.rb, when creating a project to test against

```
RSpec.feature "Users can only see the appropriate links" do
  let(:project) { FactoryGirl.create(:project) }
  ...
```

Now you can use this `project` method to define scenarios in the anonymous users context block, to ensure that anonymous users can't see the "Delete Project" link. Use the code from the following listing.

Listing 7.25   spec/features/hidden_links_spec.rb

```
context "anonymous users" do
  ...
  scenario "cannot see the Delete Project link" do
    visit project_path(project)
    expect(page).not_to have_link "Delete Project"
  end
end
```

Next, copy the scenario into the "regular users" context block.

Listing 7.26   spec/features/hidden_links_spec.rb

```
context "regular users" do
  ...
  scenario "cannot see the Delete Project link" do
    visit project_path(project)
    expect(page).not_to have_link "Delete Project"
  end
end
```

Finally, ensure that admin users can see the link by placing the code from this listing in the "admin users" context.

Listing 7.27   spec/features/hidden_links_spec.rb

```
context "admin users" do
  ...

  scenario "can see the Delete Project link" do
    visit project_path(project)
    expect(page).to have_link "Delete Project"
  end
end
```

With these latest changes, you should now have three new scenarios in the hidden-links feature:

- One checks the links for anonymous users
- One checks for regular users
- One checks for admins

Run this feature now with `bundle exec rspec spec/features/hidden_links_spec.rb` to see the new failures:

```
1) Users can only see the appropriate links anonymous users cannot see
   the Delete Project link
   Failure/Error: expect(page).not_to have_link "Delete Project"
     expected not to find link "Delete Project", found 1 match: "Delete
     Project"
   # ./spec/features/hidden_links_spec.rb:16:in `block (3 levels) in...

2) Users can only see the appropriate links regular users cannot see the
   Delete Project link
   Failure/Error: expect(page).not_to have_link "Delete Project"
     expected not to find link "Delete Project", found 1 match: "Delete
     Project"
   # ./spec/features/hidden_links_spec.rb:30:in `block (3 levels) in...
```

Again, you haven't done anything to hide the link, so the two tests that expect the link not to be there are failing. To make these tests pass, change the link in app/views/

projects/show.html.erb and wrap it in the admins_only helper, as shown in the following listing.

Listing 7.28   app/views/projects/show.html.erb

```
<ul class="actions">
  <li><%= link_to "Edit Project", edit_project_path(@project),
    class: "edit" %></li>
  <% admins_only do %>
    <li><%= link_to "Delete Project", admin_project_path(@project),
      method: :delete,
      data: { confirm: "Are you sure you want to delete this project?" },
      class: "delete" %></li>
  <% end %>
</ul>
```

You keep the "Edit Project" link public (for now), but you hide the "Delete Project" link so it's only visible to admins.

A great way to check if your code is working as intended is to run the test using bundle exec rspec spec/features/hidden_links_spec.rb. When you do, you should see this:

```
6 examples, 0 failures
```

That was a little too easy, but that's Rails.

This is a great point to ensure that everything is still working by running all the tests with bundle exec rspec. According to the following output, everything's in working order:

```
24 examples, 0 failures
```

Commit and push that:

```
$ git add .
$ git commit -m "Only admins can see the links to create and
                 delete projects"
$ git push
```

In this section, you defined a namespace and ensured that only users with the admin attribute set to true were able to access actions inside it. This is a great example of authorization.

Now that you have the namespace set up, you can start building new functionality inside it. You only have one admin user, which you created in your seed data—it would be nice if your admin user had an interface for creating new users, or for making existing users into admins as well.

7.4   *Namespace-based CRUD*

Now that only admins can access the admin namespace, you can create the CRUD actions for Admin::UsersController too, as you did for the TicketsController and ProjectsController controllers. This will allow admin users to create new users in the application, without them needing to sign up first.

The first part of creating CRUD actions is creating a resource, so it would be a great idea to start with that. Begin by creating a new feature in a new file called spec/ features/admin/creating_users_spec.rb. Use the code from the following listing for this new feature.

Listing 7.29 spec/features/admin/creating_users_spec.rb

```
require "rails_helper"

RSpec.feature "Admins can create new users" do
  let(:admin) { FactoryGirl.create(:user, :admin) }

  before do
    login_as(admin)
    visit "/"
    click_link "Admin"
    click_link "Users"
    click_link "New User"
  end

  scenario "with valid credentials" do
    fill_in "Email", with: "newbie@example.com"
    fill_in "Password", with: "password"
    click_button "Create User"
    expect(page).to have_content "User has been created."
  end
end
```

When you run this feature using `bundle exec rspec spec/features/admin/ creating_users_spec.rb`, the first couple of lines in the `before` block pass, but it fails due to a missing "Admin" link:

```
1) Admins can create new users with valid credentials
   Failure/Error: click_link "Admin"
   Capybara::ElementNotFound:
     Unable to find link "Admin"
```

This is a link that you'll have in the top navigation, linking to your admin area. You need this link for the feature to pass, but you want to show it only for admins. You can use the `admins_only` helper you defined earlier and put the link in app/views/ layouts/application.html.erb, after the "Home" link.

Listing 7.30 The new "Admin" link in the top navigation

```
<ul class="nav navbar-nav">
  <li class="<%= "active" if current_page?("/") %>">
    <%= link_to "Home", root_path %>
  </li>
  <% admins_only do %>
    <li>
      <%= link_to "Admin", admin_root_path %>
    </li>
```

```
<% end %>
<% unless user_signed_in? %>
  ...
```

This way, the link will only be shown to users who are admins.

Now when you run the feature again using `bundle exec rspec spec/features/admin/creating_users_spec.rb`, you should get a little bit further:

```
1) Admins can create new users with valid credentials
   Failure/Error: click_link "Users"
   Capybara::ElementNotFound:
     Unable to find link "Users"
```

The admin homepage you created earlier doesn't have a link to "Users." It sounds like a good candidate for the Admin Links menu that you have on the page!

Edit the app/views/admin/application/index.html.erb view and add a link to "Users" in the Admin Links menu.

> **Listing 7.31 Adding a link to manage users in the Admin Links menu**

```
<h2>Admin Links</h2>
<ul class="nav nav-stacked">
  <li><%= link_to "Users", admin_users_path %></li>
</ul>
```

What exactly did you just link to?

7.4.1   *The index action*

You don't yet have an index page for users, and it would make sense to have the link to create a new user in the header section on a users page, like you did for projects and tickets.

So let's create a `UsersController` in the `Admin` namespace, and use it for the rest of this section. Run the following command to generate a new `Admin::UsersController`, with an `index` action prepopulated:

```
$ rails g controller admin/users index
```

This generates some odd output:

```
$ rails g controller admin/users index
      create  app/controllers/admin/users_controller.rb
       route  namespace :admin do
  get 'users/index'
end
      invoke  erb
        ...
```

It generated another admin namespace in your config/routes.rb file, with `get 'users/index'` inside it. But you already have an admin namespace, and you'll want to put a users resource in it so you can add the rest of the CRUD actions.

Replace the two `namespace :admin` declarations in config/routes.rb with the following.

Listing 7.32   Creating a single admin namespace from the generated routes

```
namespace :admin do
  root "application#index"

  resources :projects, only: [:new, :create, :destroy]
  resources :users
end
```

You'll also have to tweak the controller that got generated, to make sure it extends from the `Admin::ApplicationController` you created earlier. Open app/controllers/admin/users_controller.rb and replace the first line with the following code.

Listing 7.33   app/controllers/admin/users_controller.rb

```
class Admin::UsersController < Admin::ApplicationController
```

Now, because the generator also generated a skeleton view, your test will get a bit further:

```
1) Admins can create new users with valid credentials
   Failure/Error: click_link "New User"
   Capybara::ElementNotFound:
     Unable to find link "New User"
```

LISTING USERS

What content should be in the admin user index? A list of all the users in the system might be a great start. Edit the `Admin::UsersController` again, and load a list of users to display, in the `index` action.

Listing 7.34   Looking up users to render in the index action

```
class Admin::UsersController < Admin::ApplicationController
  def index
    @users = User.order(:email)
  end
end
```

Next, you need to rewrite the template for this action, which lives at app/views/admin/users/index.html.erb, so it contains the "New User" link and lists all the users loaded by the controller. Use the code in the following listing.

Listing 7.35   app/views/admin/users/index.html.erb

```
<header>
  <h1>Users</h1>

  <ul class="actions">
```

```
    <li>
      <%= link_to "New User", new_admin_user_path, class: "new" %>
    </li>
  </ul>
</header>

<ul>
  <% @users.each do |user| %>
    <li><%= link_to user.email, [:admin, user] %></li>
  <% end %>
</ul>
```

In this example, when you specify a `Symbol` as an element in the route for the `link_to`, Rails uses that element as a literal part of the route generation, making it use `admin_user_path` rather than `user_path`. You saw this in chapter 5 when you used it with `[:edit, project, ticket]`, but it bears repeating here.

When you run `bundle exec rspec spec/features/admin/creating_users_spec.rb` again, you're told the new action is missing:

```
1) Admins can create new users with valid credentials
   Failure/Error: click_link "New User"
   AbstractController::ActionNotFound:
      The action 'new' could not be found for Admin::UsersController
```

Great! This means that the test is able to navigate to the admin area, then to the `index` page for `UsersController`, and then it's able to click the "New User" link. We're getting through this feature pretty quickly.

7.4.2   *The new action*

Add the `new` action to `Admin::UsersController` now by using the following code.

> **Listing 7.36   The new action in `Admin::UsersController`**

```
def new
  @user = User.new
end
```

And create the view for this action at app/views/admin/users/new.html.erb:

> **Listing 7.37   The new view for `Admin::UsersController`**

```
<header>
  <h1>New User</h1>
</header>

<%= render "form", user: @user %>
```

Next, you need to create the form partial that's used in the `new` template, which you can do by using the following code. It must contain the `email` and `password` fields, which are the bare essentials for creating a user.

Listing 7.38 app/views/admin/users/_form.html.erb

```
<%= simple_form_for [:admin, user] do |f| %>
  <%= f.input :email %>
  <%= f.input :password %>

  <%= f.button :submit, class: "btn btn-primary" %>
<% end %>
```

For this `simple_form_for`, you use the array form you saw earlier with [project, ticket], but this time you pass in a symbol rather than a model object. Rails interprets the symbol literally, generating a route such as `admin_users_path` rather than `users_path`, which would be generated if you used `simple_form_for user` instead. You can also use this array syntax with `link_to` (shown earlier) and `redirect_to` helpers. Any symbol passed anywhere in the array for any of these methods is interpreted literally. The same goes for strings.

When you run the feature again with `bundle exec rspec spec/features/admin/creating_users_spec.rb`, you're told there's no action called `create`:

```
1) Admins can create new users with valid credentials
     Failure/Error: click_button "Create User"
     AbstractController::ActionNotFound:
       The action 'create' could not be found for Admin::UsersController
```

7.4.3 *The create action*

You can create that action now by using the following code.

Listing 7.39 The create action of `Admin::UsersController`

```
def create
  @user = User.new(user_params)

  if @user.save
    flash[:notice] = "User has been created."
    redirect_to admin_users_path
  else
    flash.now[:alert] = "User has not been created."
    render "new"
  end
end

private
  def user_params
    params.require(:user).permit(:email, :password)
  end
```

You've used this same pattern in a few controllers, so it should be old hat by now.

You now have an "Admin" link in the top navigation menu that an admin can click, which takes them to the `index` action in `Admin::ApplicationController`. On the template rendered for this action (app/views/admin/application/index.html.erb) is a "Users" link that goes to the `index` action in `Admin::UsersController`. On the template for *this* action is a "New User" link that presents the user with a form to create a user. When the user fills in this form and clicks the Create User button, it goes to the `create` action in `Admin::UsersController`.

With all these steps implemented, your feature should now pass. Find out with a final run of `bundle exec rspec spec/features/admin/creating_users_spec.rb`:

```
1 examples, 0 failures
```

Great! Run `bundle exec rspec` to make sure everything's still working:

```
28 examples, 1 failure, 2 pending
```

What have you broken *this* time??

It turns out it isn't anything that you've broken—again it's autogenerated tests that you don't even want, located in three files:

- spec/helpers/admin/users_helper_spec.rb
- spec/views/admin/users/index.html.erb_spec.rb
- spec/controllers/admin/users_controller_spec.rb

You can delete all three of those files. Run `bundle exec rspec` again just to make sure:

```
25 examples, 0 failures
```

This is another great middle point for a commit, so do that now:

```
$ git add .
$ git commit -m "Add the ability to create users
                 through the admin backend"
$ git push
```

Although this functionality allows you to create new users through the admin back end, it doesn't let you create *admin* users. That's up next.

7.4.4 Creating admin users

To create admin users, you can add a check box on the form you use to create a new user. When this check box is selected and the `User` record is saved, that user will be an admin.

To get started, add another scenario to spec/features/admin/creating_users_spec.rb using the code in the following listing.

Listing 7.40 Testing that you can create admins via our admin interface

```
scenario "when the new user is an admin" do
  fill_in "Email", with: "admin@example.com"
  fill_in "Password", with: "password"
  check "Is an admin?"
  click_button "Create User"
  expect(page).to have_content "User has been created."
  expect(page).to have_content "admin@example.com (Admin)"
end
```

When you run `bundle exec rspec spec/features/admin/creating_users_spec.rb`, it fails when it attempts to select the "Is an admin?" check box:

```
1) Admins can create new users when the new user is an admin
   Failure/Error: check "Is an admin?"
    Capybara::ElementNotFound:
      Unable to find checkbox "Is an admin?"
```

You need to add this check box to the form for creating users, which you can do by adding the following code to the `simple_form_for` block in app/views/admin/users/_form.html.erb.

Listing 7.41   Adding a form field for setting the `admin` attribute

```
...
<%= f.input :password %>
<%= f.input :admin, label: "Is an admin?" %>
...
```

Simple Form is smart enough to know that it should generate a check box, because the admin field is a Boolean field in the database. Awesome!

Because you've added a new field to this form, you'll need to add it to the list of permitted parameters in `Admin::UsersController` by changing the `user_params` method to the following.

Listing 7.42   Permitting the `admin` attribute in `Admin::UsersController`

```
def user_params
  params.require(:user).permit(:email, :password, :admin)
end
```

With this check box in place, when you rerun `bin/rspec spec/features/admin/creating_users_spec.rb`, it can't find "admin@example.com (Admin)" on the page:

```
1) Admins can create new users when the new user is an admin
   Failure/Error: expect(page).to have_content "admin@example.com
   (Admin)"
     expected to find text "admin@example.com (Admin)" in "Ticketee
     Toggle navigation Home Admin Signed in as test2@example.com Sign
     out User has been created. Users New User admin@example.com..."
```

The problem is that only the user's email address is displayed; no text appears to indicate that the person is an admin. To get this text to appear, change the display of the user in app/views/admin/users/index.html.erb from this,

```
<li><%= link_to user.email, [:admin, user] %></li>
```

to this:

```
<li><%= link_to user, [:admin, user] %></li>
```

By not calling any methods on the `user` object and attempting to write it out of the view, you cause Ruby to call `to_s` on this method, which by default outputs something similar to the following listing (which isn't human-friendly).

Listing 7.43 Default `to_s` output on an Active Record model

```
#<User:0xb6fd6054>
```

You can override the `to_s` method on the `User` model to provide the string containing the email and admin status of the user by putting the following code in the class definition in app/models/user.rb, underneath the `devise` call.

Listing 7.44 Overriding `to_s` on an ActiveRecord model

```
def to_s
  "#{email} (#{admin? ? "Admin" : "User"})"
end
```

The `to_s` method will now output something like "user@example.com (User)" if the user isn't an admin, or "admin@example.com (Admin)" if the user is an admin. With the `admin` field set and an indication displayed on the page regarding whether the user is an admin, the feature should pass when you run `bundle exec rspec spec/features/admin/creating_users_spec.rb`:

```
2 examples, 0 failures
```

Again, run `bundle exec rspec` to make sure everything works:

```
26 examples, 0 failures
```

This is another great time to commit. Push it:

```
$ git add .
$ git commit -m "Add the ability to create admin
            users through the admin backend"
$ git push
```

Now you can create normal and admin users through the back end. In the future, you may need to modify an existing user's details or delete a user, so we'll examine the *updating* and *deleting* parts of CRUD next.

7.4.5 Editing users

This section focuses on adding updating capabilities for `Admin::UsersController`. As usual, you start by writing a feature to cover this functionality. Place the file at spec/features/admin/editing_users_spec.rb, and fill it with the content from the following listing.

Listing 7.45   spec/features/admin/editing_users_spec.rb

```
require "rails_helper"

RSpec.feature "Admins can change a user's details" do
  let(:admin_user) { FactoryGirl.create(:user, :admin) }
  let(:user) { FactoryGirl.create(:user) }

  before do
    login_as(admin_user)
    visit admin_user_path(user)
    click_link "Edit User"
  end

  scenario "with valid details" do
    fill_in "Email", with: "newguy@example.com"
    click_button "Update User"

    expect(page).to have_content "User has been updated."
    expect(page).to have_content "newguy@example.com"
    expect(page).to_not have_content user.email
  end

  scenario "when toggling a user's admin ability" do
    check "Is an admin?"
    click_button "Update User"

    expect(page).to have_content "User has been updated."
    expect(page).to have_content "#{user.email} (Admin)"
  end
end
```

When you run the feature with `bundle exec rspec spec/features/admin/editing _users_spec.rb`, you'll see both of the scenarios fail this way:

```
1) Admins can change a user's details with valid details
   Failure/Error: visit admin_user_path(user)
   AbstractController::ActionNotFound:
     The action 'show' could not be found for Admin::UsersController
```

This failure is at the very start of the test, when visiting a user's details page in the admin area. You've got a link to the `show` action of `Admin::UsersController`, but the action isn't defined. Define the `show` action in `Admin::UsersController`, directly under the `index` action.

> **ORDERING CRUD COMPONENTS** Grouping the different parts of CRUD is conventionally done in this order: index, show, new, create, edit, update, destroy. It's not a hard-and-fast rule, but consistency makes controllers easier to read and follow.

The `show` action can just be a blank action.

Listing 7.46   Adding the `show` action to `Admin::UsersController`

```
def show
end
```

The show action template requires a @user variable, so you should create a set_user method that you can call as a before_action in Admin::UsersController. This is just like the set_project and set_ticket methods defined in ProjectsController and TicketsController, respectively. Define this new set_user method under all the other methods already in the controller, because it will be a private method:

```
def set_user
  @user = User.find(params[:id])
end
```

You then need to call this method using a before_action, which should run before the show, edit, update, and destroy actions. Put this call to before_action at the top of your class definition for Admin::UsersController.

Listing 7.47 Defining the `before_action` in `Admin::UsersController`

```
class Admin::UsersController < Admin::ApplicationController
  before_action :set_user, only: [:show, :edit, :update, :destroy]
  ...
```

With the set_user and show methods in place in the controller, what's the next step? Find out by running bundle exec rspec spec/features/admin/editing_users _spec.rb again. You'll see this error:

```
1) Admins can change a user's details with valid details
   Failure/Error: visit admin_user_path(user)
   ActionView::MissingTemplate:
     Missing template admin/users/show, admin/application/show,
     application/show with
     {
       :locale => [:en],
       :formats => [:html],
       :variants => [],
       :handlers => [:erb, :builder, :raw, :ruby, :coffee, :jbuilder]
     }.

     Searched in:
     * ".../ticketee/app/views"
     * ".../devise-3.4.1/app/views"
```

Template inheritance

When you get a MissingTemplate error from an action inside a namespaced controller, such as when you render the show action of Admin::UsersController, three different templates are listed: admin/users/show, admin/application/show, and application/show. Rails is attempting to look for these three templates in exactly that order, but it can't find any of them.

Why this happens was explained earlier, but it's good to review it. The reason is that Admin::UsersController inherits from Admin::ApplicationController and therefore inherits the templates in app/views/admin/application as well.

(continued)

`Admin ::ApplicationController` inherits from `ApplicationController`, and so by inheritance both `Admin::ApplicationController` and `Admin::Users-Controller` also have the templates from the (imaginary) app/views/application directory.

An example of where this might be useful is if you're rendering different partials depending on the namespace; for example, if you had something like the following in app/views/layout/application.html.erb:

`render "sidebar"`

This could render different partials. In the base root namespace, it could render app/views/sidebar.html.erb, but in the admin namespace you could override that partial by creating a file named app/views/admin/sidebar.html.erb. This lets you have different context-aware content, without changing your code.

You can write the template for the `show` action to make this step pass. This file goes at app/views/admin/users/show.html.erb and should use the following code.

Listing 7.48   app/views/admin/users/show.html.erb

```
<header>
  <h1><%= @user %></h1>

  <ul class="actions">
    <li>
      <%= link_to "Edit User", [:edit, :admin, @user], class: "edit" %>
    </li>
  </ul>
</header>
```

The `<h1>` at the top of this view will display the "user@example.com (User)" or "user@example.com (Admin)" text, and the "Edit User" link will allow you to navigate to the action where you can edit this user's details. This is a pretty boring view for now, but later on you might want to add details to it, like the list of projects a user belongs to, or their activity history on the site, or something like that.

When you run bundle exec rspec spec/features/admin/editing_users_spec.rb now, the line that visits the user's details page passes, and you're on to the next step:

```
1) Admins can change a user's details with valid details
   Failure/Error: click_link "Edit User"
   AbstractController::ActionNotFound:
     The action 'edit' could not be found for Admin::UsersController
```

Good; you're progressing nicely. You created the `show` action for `Admin::Users-Controller`, which displays information about a user to a signed-in admin user. Now you need to create the `edit` action so admin users can edit a user's details.

7.4.6   *The edit and update actions*

Add the `edit` action directly under the `create` action in your controller. It should be another blank method like `show`.

> **Listing 7.49   Defining an `edit` action in `Admin::UsersController`**

```
def edit
end
```

With this action defined and the `@user` variable used in its view already set by the `before_action`, you can now create the template for this action at app/views/admin/users/edit.html.erb. This template renders the same form partial as the new template:

```
<header>
  <h1>Edit User</h1>
</header>

<%= render "form", user: @user %>
```

OK, you've dealt with the current failure for the feature. Find out what's next with another run of `bundle exec rspec spec/features/admin/editing_users_spec.rb`. You should be told the update action doesn't exist:

```
1) Admins can change a user's details with valid details
   Failure/Error: click_button "Update User"
   AbstractController::ActionNotFound:
     The action 'update' could not be found for Admin::UsersController
```

Indeed it doesn't, so let's create it. Add the `update` action to `Admin::Users-Controller`, as shown in the following listing. You don't need to set up the `@user` variable here because the `set_user` `before_action` does it for you.

> **Listing 7.50   Defining an `update` action in `Admin::UsersController`**

```
def update
  if @user.update(user_params)
    flash[:notice] = "User has been updated."
    redirect_to admin_users_path
  else
    flash.now[:alert] = "User has not been updated."
    render "edit"
  end
end
```

Looks like a standard update action. Rerun the test and see what happens now:

```
1) Admins can change a user's details with valid details
   Failure/Error: expect(page).to have_content "User has been updated."
     expected to find text "User has been updated." in "Ticketee Toggle
     navigation Home Admin Signed in as test1@example.com Sign out User
     has not been updated. Edit User Email PasswordPassword can't be
     blank Is an admin?"
```

You expected the user to be updated, but it wasn't. Why not? The error message shows the actual content on the page, which gives you the answer (although it's a little hidden)—the user's password can't be blank.

The application has naively tried to take the data you submitted, which included an empty password field, and update the user with those details, which is triggering your validations that require a user to have a password. But why is the password blank? Because you don't store user passwords directly in the database—you only store hashed versions of them.

> **HASHING PASSWORDS** For an explanation of why password hashing is so important, see "Why passwords should be hashed" on the IT Security Community Blog: http://security.blogoverflow.com/2011/11/why-passwords-should-be-hashed/.

In this case, if you submit a blank password, it should mean "don't change the user's current password." So you can remove the field if it's blank, before you update the user. Above the if @user.update(user_params) line, insert this code:

```
if params[:user][:password].blank?
  params[:user].delete(:password)
end
```

Now the entire action looks like the following listing.

Listing 7.51 app/controllers/admin/users_controller.rb, with blank password removal

```
def update
  if params[:user][:password].blank?
    params[:user].delete(:password)
  end

  if @user.update(user_params)
    flash[:notice] = "User has been updated."
    redirect_to admin_users_path
  else
    flash.now[:alert] = "User has not been updated."
    render "edit"
  end
end
```

When you run bundle exec rspec spec/features/admin/editing_users_spec.rb again, all the scenarios should pass:

```
2 examples, 0 failures
```

In this section, you added two more actions to Admin::UsersController: edit and update. Admin users can now update users' details as they please.

As always, run bundle exec rspec to make sure you didn't break anything. Just one quick run will show this:

```
28 examples, 0 failures
```

Done! Make a commit for this new feature:

```
$ git add .
$ git commit -m "Add ability for admins to edit and update users"
$ git push
```

With the updating done, there's only one more part to go for your admin CRUD interface: deleting users.

7.4.7 Archiving users

There comes a time in an application's life when you need to remove users from your app. Maybe they asked for their account to be closed. Maybe they were being pesky and you wanted to kick them out. Or maybe you have another reason to remove them. Whatever the case, having the functionality to remove users is helpful.

But in Ticketee, users have a trail of activity behind them—they can create tickets on projects. In the future, they'll also be able to take other actions in the system that you'll want to keep for posterity. Deleting users isn't the right action to take, but you can *archive* them instead so you can still see everything they've done, but they can take no further part in the system. They can't even sign in anymore.

Keeping with the theme so far, you'll first write a feature for archiving users (using the following listing) and put it at spec/features/admin/archiving_users_spec.rb.

> **Listing 7.52 spec/features/admin/archiving_users_spec.rb**

```
require "rails_helper"

RSpec.feature "An admin can archive users" do
  let(:admin_user) { FactoryGirl.create(:user, :admin) }
  let(:user) { FactoryGirl.create(:user) }

  before do
    login_as(admin_user)
  end

  scenario "successfully" do
    visit admin_user_path(user)
    click_link "Archive User"

    expect(page).to have_content "User has been archived"
    expect(page).not_to have_content user.email
  end
end
```

When you run this feature using bundle exec rspec spec/features/admin/ archiving_users_spec.rb, you'll get right up to the first line in the scenario with no issue. Then it complains:

```
1) An admin can archive users successfully
   Failure/Error: click_link "Archive User"
   Capybara::ElementNotFound:
     Unable to find link "Archive User"
```

Of course, you need the "Archive User" link. Add it to app/views/admin/users/show.html.erb right under the "Edit User" link.

Listing 7.53   Adding an "Archive User" link to app/views/admin/users/show.html.erb

```
<li>
  <%= link_to "Archive User", [:archive, :admin, @user], method: :patch,
    data: { confirm: "Are you sure you want to archive this user?"},
    class: "delete" %>
</li>
```

This is the first time you stray away from Rails' default RESTful resources and the seven default routes. Archiving doesn't fit in with the list of index, show, new, create, edit, update, or destroy, so you'll need to make a new route for it, called archive. This is why you needed to specify the symbol archive in the URL for the link—[:archive, :admin, @user]. It's another example of the polymorphic routing that you saw earlier in section 5.1.5.

The HTTP method you'll use for the link is patch, the same HTTP method that the update action uses. You are, in effect, updating a user—but it's a very specific kind of update.

When you rerun the spec, you'll get a different error:

```
1) An admin can archive users successfully
   Failure/Error: visit admin_user_path(user)
   ActionView::Template::Error:
     undefined method `archive_admin_user_path' for ...
```

You can define this method as a *member* route on your users resource. A member route provides the routing helpers and, more importantly, the route itself to a custom controller action for a single instance of a resource.

Member routes vs. collection routes

When you're looking at defining custom routes outside the normal seven RESTful routes, you'll come across these terms: *member routes* and *collection routes*. The difference can often be confusing for people learning Rails—which type do you use, and when?

Collection routes are typically used when you want to perform an action on a group of model instances. index is an example of a collection route—other examples might be search, or autocomplete, or export. These routes will generate URLs like /projects/search or /projects/export.

Member routes are typically used when you want to perform an action on a single model instance. edit, update, and destroy are all examples of member routes—they first find an instance of a model, and then take some action on it. Other examples might be archive, or approve, or preview. These routes will generate URLs like /projects/1/archive or /projects/3/approve.

To define the new member route, change the resources :users line in the admin namespace inside config/routes.rb to the following.

Listing 7.54 Defining the archive member route for a User resource

```
namespace :admin do
  ...
  resources :users do
    member do
      patch :archive
    end
  end
end
```

Inside the member block here, you specify that each user resource has a new action called archive that can be accessed through a PATCH request. As stated previously, by defining the route in this fashion, you also get the archive_admin_user_path helper, which is what you've used in app/views/admin/users/show.html.erb.

You need to add the archive action next, directly under the update action in Admin::UsersController.

Listing 7.55 Defining an archive action in Admin::UsersController

```
def archive
  @user.archive

  flash[:notice] = "User has been archived."
  redirect_to admin_users_path
end
```

You don't need to think about what it means to actually archive a user yet—you just want to call the archive method on the user and be done with it. You'll also need to modify the call to before_action in your Admin::UsersController to add this new archive action to the list of actions it will run before. If you don't do this, the @user variable won't be instantiated correctly.

Listing 7.56 Running set_user before the archive action

```
class Admin::UsersController < Admin::ApplicationController
  before_action :set_user, only: [:show, :edit, :update, :archive]

  ...
```

When you run bundle exec rspec spec/features/admin/deleting_users_spec.rb, the error you get now is different:

```
1) An admin can archive users successfully
   Failure/Error: click_link "Archive User"
   NoMethodError:
     undefined method `archive' for #<User:0x007f8b2fbec8c0>
```

What does it mean to actually *archive* a user? You could have a simple Boolean field on your User model called archived that you could set to true if the user is archived or false if not. Alternatively, you could keep with the chronological tracking of events—you record and display when tickets are created, so perhaps you should record *when* users are archived.

In keeping with Rails' convention for naming timestamp fields, let's add a new field called archived_at to the User model that will store a timestamp indicating when a user was archived. Run the following command in your terminal:

```
$ rails g migration add_archived_at_to_users archived_at:timestamp
```

Again, Rails is smart enough to infer what you want to do and will generate a migration that looks like the following listing.

Listing 7.57   db/migrate/[timestamp]_add_archived_at_to_users.rb

```
class AddArchivedAtToUsers < ActiveRecord::Migration
  def change
    add_column :users, :archived_at, :timestamp
  end
end
```

You don't need to modify this migration. It's good to run as is. Run it with bundle exec rake db:migrate.

Now you can look at filling in the missing method in your model. Remember, your last test failure was about a missing archive method on the User model. To mark a user as archived, what you need to do is set the archived_at timestamp on the user, and then save it. You can do that by adding the following method to the User model located in app/models/user.rb.

Listing 7.58   Archiving a user

```
class User < ActiveRecord::Base
  ...

  def archive
    self.update(archived_at: Time.now)
  end
end
```

Archiving is a very specific form of updating a user, so you can use the same update method, which will update the attributes and then save the changes.

When you rerun your archiving spec with bundle exec spec features/admin/archiving_users_spec.rb, it's nearly complete:

```
1) An admin can archive users successfully
   Failure/Error: expect(page).not_to have_content user.email
     expected not to find text "test2@example.com" in "Ticketee Toggle
     navigation Home Admin Signed in as test1@example.com Sign out User
     has been archived. Users New User test1@example.com (Admin)
     test2@example.com (User)"
```

You've archived the user, but they still appear in the list of users—you're not doing anything in your index action to hide archived users. Your index action in Admin::UsersController just looks like the following.

Listing 7.59 Loading all users in the index action of Admin::UsersController

```
class Admin::UsersController < Admin::ApplicationController
  ...
  def index
    @users = User.order(:email)
  end
  ...
```

You can use a feature called *scoping* to limit the list of users that you show. Scopes are methods that you can define on your Active Record models, very similar to class methods—methods you call on the class itself, not an instance of the class. order in listing 7.59. is an example of a class method.

Inside the User model, you can define a scope to find only users that aren't archived. Define it between the devise and to_s methods.

Listing 7.60 app/models/user.rb

```
class User < ActiveRecord::Base
  ...
  scope :excluding_archived, lambda { where(archived_at: nil) }
  ...
```

Users that don't have an archived_at date must, by definition, be not archived. You can then alter the index action of your controller, to call this scope as in the following listing.

Listing 7.61 Using the excluding_archived scope in the index action

```
class Admin::UsersController < Admin::ApplicationController
  ...
  def index
    @users = User.excluding_archived.order(:email)
  end
  ...
```

The reason you write these scopes in your model is because the controller isn't responsible for knowing things like what defines an archived user—only the User model cares about the difference between archived and not archived.

You can write scopes for all kinds of things. For example, you could write scopes to find all users who have created more than one ticket, or to find users who have created tickets for a specific project. The scope you've written here is a very simple scope, as a demonstration.

Now when you run your archiving spec with `bundle exec rspec spec/features/admin/archiving_users_spec.rb`, it will pass happily:

```
1 example, 0 failures
```

There's one small problem with this feature, though: it doesn't stop you from archiving yourself!

7.4.8   *Ensuring that you can't archive yourself*

To make it impossible to archive yourself, you can add another scenario to spec/features/admin/archiving_users_spec.rb, as shown in the following listing.

Listing 7.62   A test to ensure that users can't archive themselves

```
scenario "but cannot archive themselves" do
  visit admin_user_path(admin_user)
  click_link "Archive User"

  expect(page).to have_content "You cannot archive yourself!"
end
```

When you run this feature with `bundle exec rspec spec/features/admin/archiving_users_spec.rb`, the first two lines of the scenario pass, but the third one fails—as you might expect, because you haven't added the message. Change the archive action in `Admin::UsersController` as follows.

Listing 7.63   Updating the `archive` action to prevent archiving yourself

```
def archive
  if @user == current_user
    flash[:alert] = "You cannot archive yourself!"
  else
    @user.archive
    flash[:notice] = "User has been archived."
  end

  redirect_to admin_users_path
end
```

Now, before the `archive` method does anything, it checks to see if the user attempting deletion is the current user, and, if so, stops the process with the message "You cannot archive yourself!"

When you run `bundle exec rspec spec/features/admin/archiving_users_spec.rb` this time, the scenario passes:

```
2 examples, 0 failures
```

Great! Having implemented the ability to delete users, you've completed the CRUD for `Admin::UsersController` and for the entire users resource. Make sure you haven't broken anything by running `bundle exec rspec`. You should see this output:

```
30 examples, 0 failures
```

Fantastic! Commit and push that:

```
$ git add .
$ git commit -m "Add feature for archiving users, including protection
  against self-archiving"
$ git push
```

7.4.9 *Preventing archived users from signing in*

There's just one last feature you need to build as part of archiving users, and we alluded to it earlier—archived users should no longer be able to sign in to Ticketee.

To verify that this is the case, you can add another scenario to the sign-in feature you created in chapter 6, in spec/features/signing_in_spec.rb.

Listing 7.64 Testing that archived users can't sign in

```
RSpec.feature "Users can sign in" do
  ...

  scenario "unless they are archived" do
    user.archive

    visit "/"
    click_link "Sign in"
    fill_in "Email", with: user.email
    fill_in "Password", with: "password"
    click_button "Sign in"

    expect(page).to have_content "Your account has been archived."
  end
end
```

This looks very similar to the previous scenario for successful sign-in, except you call `user.archive` before filling in the "Sign in" form. When an archived user tries to sign in, you should show them a nice "Your account has been archived" message.

If you run this feature with `bundle exec rspec spec/features/signing_in _spec.rb`, your new scenario will fail:

```
1) Users can sign in unless they are archived
   Failure/Error: expect(page).to have_content "Your account has been
   archived."
     expected to find text "Your account has been archived." in
     "Ticketee Toggle navigation Home Signed in as test2@example.com
     Sign out Signed in successfully. Projects"
```

This is expected—you haven't yet configured your app to not allow archived users to sign in.

Devise determines if a user can sign in to your app with a method called `active_for_authentication?`. Each of the Devise strategies we listed in chapter 6 (`lockable`, `confirmable`, and so on) can add conditions to determine whether or not a user is able to sign in—for example, the `lockable` strategy will overwrite this active_for_authentication? method to return `false` if the user's record is locked. If the method returns `false`, then the user is not allowed to sign in.

You can write your own active_for_authentication? method in your User model to disallow authentication if a user is archived. You can do that with the following method, defined at the bottom of your User model.

Listing 7.65   Determining which users are allowed to sign in to Ticketee

```
class User < ActiveRecord::Base
  ...
  def active_for_authentication?
    super && archived_at.nil?
  end
end
```

The call to `super` in this method will allow all of the other checks to take place, to make sure the user's account is unlocked, and confirmed, and so on. If you left that out, you'd stop archived users from signing in, but you'd also allow locked users or unconfirmed users to sign in, as long as they weren't archived. Not good.

This looks like it's been way too easy, but that's the power of leveraging well-written gems. If you rerun your sign-in spec, you'll see the following:

```
1) Users can sign in unless they are archived
   Failure/Error: expect(page).to have_content "Your account has been
   archived."
     expected to find text "Your account has been archived." in
     "Ticketee Toggle navigation Home Sign up Sign in Your account is
     not activated yet. Sign In Email Password Remember me Sign up..."
```

You've stopped the user from signing in! But you're not showing the right message back to the user, as to why their sign-in failed.

To do this, you can overwrite another method provided by Devise, called inactive_message. This method will get called by Devise when active_for_authentication? returns `false`, and it should return the *translation key* of the message that should be displayed to the user.

We haven't looked at translations and internationalization (i18n) yet in Rails, but the framework has a great system built in to allow your apps to be fully multilingual, and Devise has complete support for it. Define the inactive_message method below active_for_authentication? in your User model to look like the following.

Listing 7.66   Defining the message that gets displayed back to the user

```
def inactive_message
  archived_at.nil? ? super : :archived
end
```

If the user isn't archived (archived_at is `nil`), then there was some other reason why they couldn't log in, so you call `super` again. If the user's account is locked, or unconfirmed, this allows those strategies to supply the correct message to let the user know why they couldn't log in.

But if `archived_at` isn't `nil`, you return this `:archived` symbol. What does this symbol mean? If you rerun your specs after defining this method, you'll see what it does:

```
1) Users can sign in unless they are archived
   Failure/Error: expect(page).to have_content "Your account has been
   archived."
     expected to find text "Your account has been archived." in
     "Ticketee Toggle navigation Home Sign up Sign in
     translation missing: en.devise.failure.user.archived ..."
```

It uses the symbol to look up a *translation*, which you haven't defined. Devise provides a lot of its own translations, generated when you ran `rails g devise:install`—these translations are located in config/locales/devise.en.yml. If you look inside that file, you'll see a tree structure of YAML data.

Listing 7.67   The start of config/locals/devise.en.yml

```
en:
  devise:
    confirmations:
      confirmed: "Your email address has been successfully confirmed."
      ...
```

The keys on each level of the tree are added together to define the final translation key—the key shown in the preceding listing would be `en.devise.confirmations` `.confirmed`. Knowing this, you can define your missing `en.devise.failure` `.user.archived` key. There's already a section below `confirmations` in the file called `failure`, so inside that you can define new levels for `user` and `archived`, as in the following listing.

Listing 7.68   Defining a custom translation

```
en:
  devise:
    confirmations:
      ...
    failure:
      ...
      user:
        archived: "Your account has been archived."
    mailer:
      ...
```

Once you've defined this custom translation, you can rerun your spec with `bundle exec rspec spec/features/signing_in_spec.rb`:

```
2 examples, 0 failures
```

Fantastic! You've customized some of Devise's functionality to prevent archived users from signing in to Ticketee, and you've backed it up with tests. You've also learned a little bit about how i18n works in Rails.

Run `bundle exec rspec` to make sure your changes haven't broken anything else:

```
31 examples, 0 failures
```

Now commit and push these changes:

```
$ git add .
$ git commit -m "Archived users cannot sign in to the app"
$ git push
```

With this final commit, you've created your admin section. It provides a great CRUD interface for users in this system so that admins can modify their details when necessary.

7.5 Summary

In this chapter, you dove into basic access control and added a field called `admin` to the users table. You used this `admin` field to allow and restrict access to a namespaced controller, as well as to show and hide links.

Then you wrote the CRUD interface for the `users` resource under the `admin` namespace, including archiving users and then forbidding those archived users from signing in. This interface is used in the next chapter to expand on the authorization you've implemented so far: restricting users, whether admin users or not, to certain actions on certain projects. You rounded out the chapter by not allowing users to delete themselves.

The next chapter focuses on enhancing the basic permission system you've implemented so far, introducing a gem called Pundit. With this permission system, you'll have more fine-grained control over what users of your application can and can't do to projects and tickets.

Fine-grained access control 8

This chapter covers

- Implementing authorization using the Pundit gem
- Writing a custom RSpec matcher
- Enforcing authorization for future-proofing your code
- Building a completely custom form for managing a user's roles

At the end of chapter 7, you learned a basic form of authorization based on a Boolean field called `admin` on the users table. If this field is set to `true`, the user is an admin user, and can therefore access the create/destroy functions of the `Project` resource, as well as an admin namespace where they can perform CRUD on the `User` resource.

In this chapter, you'll expand on authorization options by implementing a broader authorization system using a `Role` model. The records for this model's table define the roles that specified users will have on specific projects in your system. Each record tracks a user who has a specific role, the project to which the role applies, and the type of role granted. You'll create three types of roles in your system:

- *Viewer*—For people who will be able to read everything on the project but not edit anything.
- *Editor*—For people who will be able to read everything and also create and update tickets on the project.
- *Manager*—For people who will be able to read everything, manage tickets, and also administrate some facets of the project itself, including editing the project's details. They won't be able to delete the project, though—that's reserved for admins of the site.

These Role objects will then be used to determine exactly what actions a user can take on an object like a project or a ticket. You'll also build the authorization system so that it will be easy to extend later on, if you need to add more roles.

The authorization implemented in this chapter is *whitelist authorization*. Under whitelist authorization, all users are denied access to everything by default, and you must specify what the user is allowed to do. The opposite is *blacklist authorization*, under which all users are allowed access to everything by default, and you must block what they may not access. There are many reasons to prefer whitelist authorization, such as these:

- You may have many projects and want to assign a user to only one of them. It's easier to add a user to one project than to remove them from every project except the one you want.
- If you add a new project, everyone will by default have access to it. To be safe, you'll need to remove everyone except the people you want to have access to it.

A good way to think about whitelist authorization is as the kind of list a security guard would have at an event. If you're not on the list, you don't get in. In comparison, a blacklist would be if the security guard had a list of people who *weren't* allowed in.

This chapter guides you through restricting access to the CRUD operations of ProjectsController and TicketsController one by one, starting with reading and then moving on to creating, updating, and deleting. Any time a user wants to perform one of these actions, you'll check if they have any roles that give them permission to do so (meaning whether or not they're on the whitelist). During this process, you'll become familiar with another gem called Pundit, which provides methods for your controllers and views that will help you check the current user's ability to perform a specific action.

You'll write extensive tests to cover both the enforcement of permission checking and the permissions granted by the roles themselves. Once you're finished with restricting the actions in your controller, you'll generate functionality in the back end to allow administrators of the application to assign roles to users.

8.1   *Project-viewing permission*

A time comes in every ticket-tracking application's life when it's necessary to restrict which users can see which projects. For example, you could be operating in a consultancy where some people are working on one application and others are working on another. You want the admins of the application to be able to customize permissions, controlling which projects each user can see.

In this section, you'll begin building the broad authorization system by first creating a model called `Role` that tracks which users have which roles for which projects. As usual, you'll start with a test that tests exactly what you want to happen, even if you don't know exactly how it's going to work yet. You'll update one of your existing features to make sure only users who have permission to read a project are able to do so.

8.1.1 Assigning Roles in specs

You'll be working with your spec/features/viewing_projects_spec.rb feature here. You'll update this spec to accommodate a user signing in and also add the *viewer* role. Update the code in this file to what's shown in the following listing.

Listing 8.1   spec/features/viewing_projects_spec.rb

```
require "rails_helper"

RSpec.feature "Users can view projects" do
  let(:user) { FactoryGirl.create(:user) }
  let(:project) { FactoryGirl.create(:project, name: "Sublime Text 3") }

  before do
    login_as(user)
    assign_role!(user, :viewer, project)
  end

  scenario "with the project details" do
    visit "/"
    click_link "Sublime Text 3"
    expect(page.current_url).to eq project_url(project)
  end
end
```

You've effectively rewritten a large portion of this feature, which is common practice when implementing such large changes. The `assign_role!` method will create a new `Role` record and will be responsible for giving the specified user a role on the specified project. This method is currently undefined, so when you run `bundle exec rspec spec/features/viewing_projects_spec.rb`, it complains about that:

```
1) Users can view projects with the project details
   Failure/Error: assign_role!(user, :viewer, project)
   NoMethodError:
     undefined method `assign_role!' for #<RSpec::ExampleGroups::...
```

Common helper methods that will be reused across specs typically belong in a spec/support folder, which doesn't yet exist in your application, so you can create it now. Create a new file at spec/support/authorization_helpers.rb, and put the following content in it.

Listing 8.2 spec/support/authorization_helpers.rb

```
module AuthorizationHelpers
  def assign_role!(user, role, project)
    Role.where(user: user, project: project).delete_all
    Role.create!(user: user, role: role, project: project)
  end
end

RSpec.configure do |c|
  c.include AuthorizationHelpers
end
```

The assign_role! method creates a new instance of a Role model to link together the user, a name of a role, and a project. (You'll define what actual permissions this named role will give the user starting in section 8.1.3, when you meet the Pundit gem.) Once you've defined your module of methods, you need to tell RSpec to make it available to your specs with the RSpec.configure block.

Lastly, you need to tell RSpec to actually include files in the spec/support folder. Prior to RSpec 3.0 this was done automatically, but it does have some overhead— larger projects can have many helper files that will be loaded for every running of a test, including tests that don't need any of the support methods. Inside spec/ rails_helper.rb, you'll find a section like the following.

Listing 8.3 spec/rails_helper.rb

```
# The following line is provided for convenience purposes. It has the
# downside of increasing the boot-up time by auto-requiring all files in
# the support directory. Alternatively, in the individual `*_spec.rb`
# files, manually require only the support files necessary.
#
# Dir[Rails.root.join("spec/support/**/*.rb")].each { |f| require f }
```

You've read and accepted the terms and condit… er, rather, the downsides of using such a helper line, but you want to use it anyway. Uncomment the Dir[] line by removing the leading #.

The alternative to spec/support

If you don't want to enable this functionality, you could do what the comment suggests and edit your projects-viewing spec to start with the following:

```
require "rails_helper"
require "support/authorization_helpers"

RSpec.feature "Users can view projects" do
  ...
```

The downside of this approach is that you'd have to include every support file in every test you want to use them in. Your spec files become longer, and updates become very tedious. Enabling the global support loading is quicker and easier.

With the `assign_role!` method defined, rerunning this spec with `bundle exec rspec spec/features/viewing_projects_spec.rb` results in a complaint about the missing `Role` class:

```
1) Users can view projects with the project details
   Failure/Error: assign_role!(user, :viewer, project)
   NameError:
      uninitialized constant AuthorizationHelpers::Role
```

We'll address this in the next section.

8.1.2 Creating the Role model

The last failure in the previous section indicated that you need to create a new `Role` model to track which users have which kind of role on a project. This model needs three things: a reference to a `user` to track the association with the user, a `role` field to track what kind of role the user has, and a reference to a `project` to track which project the role applies to.

Create the `Role` model by generating it using the following command:

```
$ rails g model role user:references role:string project:references
```

This generates a migration that looks like the following code.

> **Listing 8.4 db/migrate/<timestamp>_create_roles.rb**

```
class CreateRoles < ActiveRecord::Migration
  def change
    create_table :roles do |t|
      t.references :user, index: true, foreign_key: true
      t.string :role
      t.references :project, index: true, foreign_key: true

      t.timestamps null: false
    end
  end
end
```

But what does this actually *mean?*

The `user:references` is a shortcut for doing several things:

- Adding a `user_id` integer field to the `roles` table
- Adding an index to the `roles` table on the `user_id` field (seen in the migration as `index: true`)
- Adding a foreign key between the `user_id` field on the `roles` table and the `id` field on the `roles` table (seen in the migration as `foreign_key: true`)
- Adding a `belongs_to :user` association to the generated `Role` model

If you didn't want to use this shortcut, you could have made the association manually by doing the following:

- Specifying `user_id:integer` when generating the migration
- Adding the index in the migration with `add_index :roles, :user_id`
- Adding the foreign key in the migration with `add_foreign_key :roles, :users`
- Editing the generated `Role` model and adding the required association

But using the functionality that Rails provides is so much easier. It *is* extra magic, though, so it's good to know what this `references` method does under the hood.

The generated `Role` model ends up looking like the following listing.

Listing 8.5 app/models/role.rb

```
class Role < ActiveRecord::Base
  belongs_to :user
  belongs_to :project
end
```

Not bad for a single command in your terminal.

With this model and its related migration, you can run `bundle exec rake db:migrate` to set up the development and test databases. When you run your feature again with `bundle exec rspec spec/features/viewing_projects_spec.rb`, you might get a bit of a surprise:

```
1 example, 0 failures
```

But there's a catch. The feature will pass with or without the new `assign_role!` step, because, at the moment, the roles we assign to users in specs have no bearing on what projects a user can actually see. Enter Pundit.

8.1.3 *Setting up Pundit*

Pundit is a gem that helps define what permissions users have on resources and actions through what are known as *policies*. Policies are checked on a resource-by-resource basis. Pundit is maintained by Jonas Nicklas (of Capybara fame) and his coworkers at Elabs.

We'll use the Pundit gem to do a couple of things:

- Translate roles into permissions (for example, `:viewer` of Project A means that the user can access the `show` action of the `ProjectsController` for Project A)
- Enforce those permissions by automatically checking if a user has permissions for the current action, and if not, redirecting them

To install Pundit, first add this line to your Gemfile:

```
gem "pundit", "~> 0.3.0"
```

Then run `bundle` to install the Pundit gem.

Next, you'll need to set up Pundit, which can be done by running this command:

```
$ rails g pundit:install
```

This will create an `ApplicationPolicy` class, which will be the base class for all policies throughout the application. You'll create a specific policy class to define permissions for each of the classes in your system, and they'll all inherit basic rules from this `ApplicationPolicy` class.

ADDING PUNDIT'S SPEC HELPERS

Next, add Pundit's helpers to your tests, which will be useful when you test the policy classes you'll create. Add the second line in the following listing to load Pundit's test helpers into your specs in spec/rails_helper.rb, below the line that indicates that this is where your `require` should go.

Listing 8.6 spec/rails_helper.rb, after loading Pundit's test helpers

```
# Add additional requires below this line. Rails is not loaded until this point!
require "pundit/rspec"
```

The final piece of setup is in app/controllers/application_controller.rb, and it involves including the `Pundit` module in your application. You can do this by adding the following line right underneath the `class` definition in that file.

Listing 8.7 Including Pundit in the `ApplicationController`

```
class ApplicationController < ActionController::Base
  include Pundit
  ...
```

Including the `Pundit` module will include Pundit's helper methods in your controller, and one of those is the `authorize` method.

You can use that method in the `show` action of your `ProjectsController`, after loading the `@project` instance. Update the `show` action of the `ProjectsController`.

Listing 8.8 The new `show` action of `ProjectsController`, Punditified

```
def show
  authorize @project, :show?
end
```

This uses Pundit to make sure that the current user is allowed to *show* the current project. If they are, the view will render as normal. If they aren't, then a `Pundit::NotAuthorizedError` exception will be raised, which you can rescue and handle however you want. More on that soon.

Now that you've installed Pundit and have attempted to use it, you can try rerunning bundle exec rspec spec/features/viewing_projects_spec.rb:

```
1) Users can view projects with the project details
   Failure/Error: click_link "Sublime Text 3"
   Pundit::NotDefinedError:
     unable to find policy ProjectPolicy for #<Project:0x007fea5995b230>
   # ...
   # ./app/controllers/projects_controller.rb:9:in `show'
```

You've called `authorize` with an instance of a `Project`, so Pundit has determined that it should use a `ProjectPolicy` class to check permissions for it. (If you had tried to authorize a `Ticket` instance, it would look for a `TicketPolicy` class instead. This is another example of *convention over configuration*.)

You haven't yet defined the `ProjectPolicy` class, but Pundit comes with a Rails generator to do it for you. You can easily generate a `ProjectPolicy` with the following command.

Listing 8.9   Generating a `ProjectPolicy` class

```
$ rails g pundit:policy project
```

Take a look at this new file, which has been created at app/policies/project_policy.rb.

Listing 8.10   app/policies/project_policy.rb

```
class ProjectPolicy < ApplicationPolicy
  class Scope < Scope
    def resolve
      scope
    end
  end
end
```

This file defines the `ProjectPolicy` class, and a `Scope` class inside of that. The `Scope` class can be used to filter out resources, depending on what permissions people have. For example, you could limit which objects are returned to display in an `index` action.

With your new policy class defined, what happens when you run your test?

```
1 examples, 0 failures
```

Seems like magic. You didn't actually *do* anything, but your test passes. How?

When you ran the Rails generator for Pundit, it generated a default `Application-Policy` class that your `ProjectPolicy` inherits from. Calling `authorize @project, :show?` will do a few things:

- Initialize a new `ProjectPolicy` instance with the current user and the record in question; in this case, your `@project` variable.
- Call the `show?` method on the policy.
- If a truthy value (something other than `nil` or `false`) is returned from the `show?` action, it will continue as normal (the user is allowed to access the action).
- If a falsey value (`nil` or `false`) is returned, it will raise a `Pundit::NotAuthorized-Error`. By default, this will show the big red error screen that you've probably seen a lot of in development, looking like figure 8.1.

Pundit::NotAuthorizedError in ProjectsController#show

not allowed to show? this #<Project:0x007ffe52a22c60>

Figure 8.1   The unhandled `Pundit::NotAuthorizedError` exception, as seen in a development environment

The show? method is where you can write custom logic to determine who can access the show action of your controller. By default, the ApplicationPolicy states that if the project exists in the database, then permission is granted.

Listing 8.11 Part of the default `ApplicationPolicy`

```
def show?
  scope.where(:id => record.id).exists?
end
```

You can overwrite that method in the ProjectPolicy class to state that anyone who has an assigned role on the project should be able to read the project. All of your roles will have read permission, but only some will have write permission. But before that, you need to write some tests!

8.1.4   *Testing the ProjectPolicy*

The Pundit policy generator also generates some specs, located in spec/policies/ project_policy_spec.rb. That file is pretty empty at the moment, but you can fill up the permissions :show? block with examples.

Listing 8.12 Testing the `show?` permission on `ProjectPolicy`

```
permissions :show? do
  let(:user) { FactoryGirl.create :user }
  let(:project) { FactoryGirl.create :project }

  it "blocks anonymous users" do
    expect(subject).not_to permit(nil, project)
  end

  it "allows viewers of the project" do
    assign_role!(user, :viewer, project)
    expect(subject).to permit(user, project)
  end

  it "allows editors of the project" do
    assign_role!(user, :editor, project)
    expect(subject).to permit(user, project)
  end

  it "allows managers of the project" do
    assign_role!(user, :manager, project)
    expect(subject).to permit(user, project)
  end

  it "allows administrators" do
    admin = FactoryGirl.create :user, :admin
    expect(subject).to permit(admin, project)
  end

  it "doesn't allow users assigned to other projects" do
```

```
      other_project = FactoryGirl.create :project
      assign_role!(user, :manager, other_project)
      expect(subject).not_to permit(user, project)
    end
end
```

The preceding examples are very explicit—for each of the role types in your system, and some extra edge case scenarios, you assign the right role and then check whether the user is permitted to perform the action defined by the `permission` block, in this case `show?`. Permissions are something you really don't want to get wrong, and they deserve to be tested thoroughly.

Before you run the specs, there's just one last thing you need to do—change the line at the top of the file from `require "spec_helper"` to `require "rails_helper"`, to set up Rails. This way, Rails will be loaded, Factory Girl will be loaded, and then Rails can autoload the `ProjectPolicy` class correctly.

The `subject` syntax

You'll also notice that we've introduced new syntax in the tests: `subject`. The `subject` method is used to denote the main purpose of the test—the method you want to test.

The autogenerated spec file defines `subject` at the very top of the spec with a block, and sets it to be the described class itself: `ProjectPolicy`. If you were testing a specific method on the `ProjectPolicy` class, you might set the `subject` with `subject { ProjectPolicy.my_awesome_method(and_its_argument) }`, inside the `describe` block for that method.

It's a great way to make your tests more DRY: defining an unchanging method call in one place, and then simply referring to it when you need it.

Once you've done that, you can run the spec with `bundle exec rspec spec/policies/project_policy_spec.rb`. You'll get a bunch of pending specs, and two failures:

```
1) ProjectPolicy show? blocks anonymous users
   Failure/Error: expect(subject).not_to permit(nil, project)
     Expected ProjectPolicy not to grant show? on
     #<Project:0x007f4fa8eddbc8> but it did
   # ./spec/policies/project_policy_spec.rb:22:in ...

2) ProjectPolicy show? doesn't allow users assigned to other projects
   Failure/Error: expect(subject).not_to permit(user, project)
     Expected ProjectPolicy not to grant show? on
     #<Project:0x007f4faae95a88> but it did
   # ./spec/policies/project_policy_spec.rb:48:in ...
```

USING EXISTS? TO CHECK USER ROLES

As expected, your policy is giving everyone access, even though it shouldn't be. Now you can define a new `show?` method in `ProjectPolicy` to allow anyone that has any role on the project. This should be defined just underneath the end of the Scope class inside your ProjectPolicy.

Listing 8.13 Part of `ProjectPolicy`, with the new `show?` method added

```ruby
class ProjectPolicy < ApplicationPolicy
  class Scope < Scope
    def resolve
      scope
    end
  end

  def show?
    record.roles.exists?(user_id: user)
  end
end
```

This is where you get to the meaty part of this whole thing. This code calls the exists? method on record.roles, which will be an association that returns all the users' roles on this project. (This association doesn't exist yet; you'll set it up in just a moment.) The exists? method is from Active Record, and it checks to see if any matching records exist in the collection. If they do, the method will return true.

In this example, you check if there are any roles on the project for the currently logged-in user. If there are records to the affirmative, then the user will be permitted to show the project. Otherwise, they'll get an error.

Now running the ProjectPolicy spec gives many errors, all the same:

```
1) ProjectPolicy show? blocks anonymous users
   Failure/Error: expect(subject).not_to permit(nil, project)
   NoMethodError:
     undefined method `roles' for #<Project:0x007fa12c854510>
   # ...
   # ./app/policies/project_policy.rb:9:in `show?'
```

Your Role model has an association to projects and users, but the Project model has no association with roles. You can fill in the missing has_many association in app/models/project.rb.

Listing 8.14 app/models/project.rb

```ruby
class Project < ActiveRecord::Base
  ...
  has_many :roles, dependent: :delete_all
end
```

Again, you specify delete_all on the association. When a project is deleted, all of the associated roles should be deleted—they're meaningless without it.

Now running the specs gives you only one error:

```
1) ProjectPolicy show? allows administrators
   Failure/Error: expect(subject).to permit(admin, project)
     Expected ProjectPolicy to grant show? on
     #<Project:0x007f8557ddcd48> but it didn't
```

The site administrators don't have a specific role on the project, but they should be able to do everything. You can modify the `show?` method in `ProjectPolicy` to allow administrators as well:

```
def show?
  user.try(:admin?) || record.roles.exists?(user_id: user)
end
```

`try` is a clever little method, and it works as an extra layer of defense against unexpected `nil` objects. In this scenario, if `user` is `nil`, and you call `user.admin?`, you'll get a nasty `NoMethodError` because `nil` has no `admin?` method. `try` will protect you against this—if `user` is `nil`, it won't even try to call `admin?` on it; it will just return `nil`.

`try` in real-world apps

`try` can be seen as a code smell.[1] If you don't know whether or not your `user` variable has a `nil` value, it doesn't look like you have confidence in your code. But in this case, you know exactly when you have `nil` and exactly when you don't—if no user is currently logged in, then `user` will be `nil`.

If this book were much longer and you were building a real-world production app, you could look at implementing a "guest" user record that would always return `false` to the question of `admin?`. But we'll leave that for you to explore. (Hint: this is called the Null Object Pattern.)

Now running `bundle exec rspec spec/policies/project_policy_spec.rb` is mostly happy:

```
10 examples, 0 failures, 4 pending
```

The four pending specs are for other blocks in the spec—`scope`, `create?`, `update?`, and `destroy?`. For now you're not using those `permissions` blocks, so you can delete them.

Rerun the specs to verify that everything is now all green:

```
6 examples, 0 failures
```

The actual feature that covers viewing projects (spec/features/viewing_projects _spec.rb) still passes:

```
1 example, 0 failures
```

Fantastic! Now that you've implemented that little chunk of functionality and everything seems to be going smoothly, you can make sure the entire application is going the same way by running `bundle exec rspec`:

---

[1] See http://en.wikipedia.org/wiki/Code_smell.

```
Failed examples:

rspec ./spec/features/creating_tickets_spec.rb:14
rspec ./spec/features/creating_tickets_spec.rb:25
rspec ./spec/features/creating_tickets_spec.rb:33
rspec ./spec/features/deleting_tickets_spec.rb:14
rspec ./spec/features/editing_projects_spec.rb:12
rspec ./spec/features/editing_projects_spec.rb:20
rspec ./spec/features/hidden_links_spec.rb:14
rspec ./spec/features/hidden_links_spec.rb:28
rspec ./spec/features/viewing_tickets_spec.rb:19
```

Oh dear—you broke just about every other feature! These features are all broken because they involve visiting a project's page, and you've just restricted who can access that show action. Let's fix them, from the top, one at a time.

8.1.5 *Fixing what you broke*

Currently, you have a whole bundle of features that are failing. When this happens, it may look like everything's broken (and maybe some things are on fire), but the reality isn't as bad as it seems. The best way to fix a mess like this is to break it into smaller chunks and tackle it one chunk at a time.

The output from `bundle exec rspec` provided a list of the broken features: they're your chunks. Let's go through them and fix them, starting with the ticket-creation feature.

FIXING TICKET CREATION

When you run `bundle exec rspec spec/features/creating_tickets_spec.rb`, all of the tests fail because they can't get to the project page:

```
1) Users can create new tickets with valid attributes
   Failure/Error: visit project_path(project)
   Pundit::NotAuthorizedError:
     not allowed to show? this #<Project:0x007f17919b4fd8>
```

To fix this issue, you should assign the user in the test to the project, with a role that has permission to view the project. Alter the beginning of the `before` block in spec/features/creating_tickets_spec.rb so that the role is given to the user. After the line to create a project, use `assign_role!` to define a new Role record for this user.

Listing 8.15 After assigning the user as a viewer of the project

```
before do
  login_as(user)
  project = FactoryGirl.create(:project, name: "Internet Explorer")
  assign_role!(user, :viewer, project)

  visit project_path(project)
  click_link "New Ticket"
end
```

You're just giving them the lowest possible permissions to make this spec pass for now.

All the pieces are now in place for this feature to work. When you run it again with `bundle exec rspec spec/features/creating_tickets_spec.rb`, all the scenarios should pass:

```
3 examples, 0 failures
```

One down, several to go. The next failing feature is ticket deletion.

FIXING TICKET DELETION AND TICKET VIEWING

This feature fails for the same reason as the ticket-creation feature: the user doesn't have access to view the project and then delete a ticket. You can fix this now by putting the following lines at the top of the `before` block in spec/features/deleting_tickets_spec.rb.

> **Listing 8.16   After assigning the ticket author as a viewer on the project**

```
before do
  login_as(author)
  assign_role!(author, :viewer, project)
  visit project_ticket_path(project, ticket)
end
```

That's a little too easy! When you run `bundle exec rspec spec/features/deleting_tickets_spec.rb`, this feature passes once again:

```
1 example, 0 failures
```

Great! Next up is ticket viewing, which you fix in a way similar to the previous features. Inside the spec/features/viewing_tickets_spec.rb file, the `before` block currently looks like the following listing.

> **Listing 8.17   The `before` block, before making changes**

```
before do
  author = FactoryGirl.create(:user)

  sublime = FactoryGirl.create(:project, name: "Sublime Text 3")
  FactoryGirl.create(:ticket, project: sublime,
    author: author, name: "Make it shiny!",
    description: "Gradients! Starbursts! Oh my!")

  ie = FactoryGirl.create(:project, name: "Internet Explorer")
  FactoryGirl.create(:ticket, project: ie, author: author,
    name: "Standards compliance", description: "Isn't a joke.")

  visit "/"
end
```

You need to assign the `author` to the two projects you've created in the block, both `sublime` and `ie`, and you also need to make the author sign in before they try to visit the ticket page.

Adjust the before block so that it now looks like the following.

Listing 8.18 The before block, after making changes

```
before do
  author = FactoryGirl.create(:user)

  sublime = FactoryGirl.create(:project, name: "Sublime Text 3")
  assign_role!(author, :viewer, sublime)
  FactoryGirl.create(:ticket, project: sublime,
    author: author, name: "Make it shiny!",
    description: "Gradients! Starbursts! Oh my!")

  ie = FactoryGirl.create(:project, name: "Internet Explorer")
  assign_role!(author, :viewer, ie)
  FactoryGirl.create(:ticket, project: ie, author: author,
    name: "Standards compliance", description: "Isn't a joke.")

  login_as(author)
  visit "/"
end
```

That should be enough to make the feature pass. Running `bundle exec rspec spec/features/viewing_tickets_spec.rb` will verify:

```
1 example, 0 failures
```

FIXING PROJECT EDITING AND HIDDEN LINKS

Next up is project editing, which needs the same kind of treatment in the before block inside spec/features/editing_projects_spec.rb:

```
RSpec.feature "Users can edit existing projects" do
  let(:user) { FactoryGirl.create(:user) }
  let(:project) { FactoryGirl.create(:project, name: "Sublime Text 3") }

  before do
    login_as(user)
    assign_role!(user, :viewer, project)
    ...
```

Last is the hidden-links spec, which needs two changes:

- You have a test verifying that an anonymous user can't visit the project page and see the "Delete Project" link. Now anonymous users can't even visit the project page, so this test can be safely deleted.
- You have a test verifying that regular users can't see the "Delete Project" link. You originally wrote "regular users" to mean "non-administrator users," so they could have any other role in the system—you'll now make them viewers of the project, and update the context to reflect this change. Now it should look like the following listing.

Listing 8.19   Clarifying "regular user" to mean a viewer of the project

```
context "non-admin users (project viewers)" do
  before do
    login_as(user)
    assign_role!(user, :viewer, project)
  end

  ...
```

Now that spec file should pass, too. Double-check with `bundle exec spec/features/hidden_links_spec.rb`:

```
5 examples, 0 failures
```

That was fast! All of the failing features are fixed. Well, so you hope. You've independently verified them, but run `bundle exec rspec` to make sure nothing else is broken:

```
37 examples, 0 failures, 1 pending
```

There's one pending spec from spec/models/role_spec.rb. You can delete this file now, and then when you rerun `bundle exec rspec`, you'll see this output:

```
36 examples, 0 failures
```

Great! Everything's working again! You can commit that:

```
$ git add .
$ git commit -m "Make projects only visible to users with
                 permission to see them"
$ git push
```

8.1.6   *Handling authorization errors*

But what happens if the user *doesn't* have permission to read a project? Nasty red error screens are no fun in development, and users in production would get an unhelpful page (see figure 8.2), much like the 404 page you saw earlier in section 4.4.1.

You can do much better than that. In the same way that you rescued the exception that Rails throws when records aren't found, you can rescue the exception that Pundit throws when the user doesn't have permission to do something, and redirect them back to a safe place.

You'll start with a controller test, just like you tested the 404 error handling. Inside spec/controllers/projects_controller_spec.rb, you can add a new scenario to cover

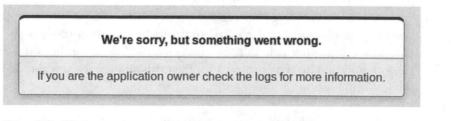

We're sorry, but something went wrong.

If you are the application owner check the logs for more information.

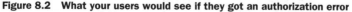

Figure 8.2   What your users would see if they got an authorization error

the case where a user is attempting to view a project they don't have permission to view.

Listing 8.20 Testing what happens when a user views a project they don't have access to

```ruby
RSpec.describe ProjectsController, type: :controller do
  ...

  it "handles permission errors by redirecting to a safe place" do
    allow(controller).to receive(:current_user)

    project = FactoryGirl.create(:project)
    get :show, id: project

    expect(response).to redirect_to(root_path)
    message = "You aren't allowed to do that."
    expect(flash[:alert]).to eq message
  end
end
```

It's a simple test and very similar to the scenario above it. You don't even log in, you just create a project and then try to view it. A safe course of action would be to redirect them to the homepage, displaying an appropriate message. You do have an extra safeguard in there to stub out the current_user method on the controller—otherwise you'd get Devise errors, similar to those you saw when testing your Admin::ApplicationController.

When you run this spec with bundle exec rspec spec/controllers/projects_controller_spec.rb, you'll get the expected error message:

```
1) ProjectsController handles permission errors by redirecting to a safe
   place
   Failure/Error: get :show, id: project
   Pundit::NotAuthorizedError:
     not allowed to show? this #<Project:0x007fc191e224d0>
```

Now how to implement it?

You can implement it with a global rescue_from in your base Application-Controller that all your controllers inherit from. It will rescue the exception you specify, no matter where it happens in your application. This is different from the rescue you specified in ProjectsController earlier—that was protecting a single call to Project.find, whereas this will protect the entire application.

Inside app/controllers/application_controller.rb, add the following code right at the end of the class definition.

Listing 8.21 Part of ApplicationController

```ruby
class ApplicationController < ActionController::Base
  ...

  rescue_from Pundit::NotAuthorizedError, with: :not_authorized
```

```
    private

    def not_authorized
      redirect_to root_path, alert: "You aren't allowed to do that."
    end
end
```

Now whenever a `Pundit::NotAuthorizedError` is raised anywhere in your app, the `:not_authorized` symbol you provided means the `not_authorized` method should be run, which does appropriate things. You redirect back to the homepage and display a nice message.

And your tests in spec/controllers/projects_controller_spec.rb will pass:

```
2 examples, 0 failures
```

There are two final notes on this `rescue_from` functionality:

- It covers the entire application, but you only wrote one test for a single action in a child controller. If you were being very thorough, you could write a test for a dummy controller that extends `ApplicationController` to be sure that the functionality was defined in the top-level `ApplicationController` and would therefore cover the entire application. We'll leave that for you to explore on your own.
- It can make some things harder to test in the future. If any of your tests fail in the future due to permission errors, you won't get the same "not allowed to <action> on <object>" error that you did earlier, because you're rescuing and recovering from it. Instead, the errors will be harder to diagnose—they might result in missing content on the page, or not being on the right page—but with practice (and our hand to guide you) you'll learn to spot these errors. And of course, testing the policies is a must as well.

While these may seem like big downsides for developers, the better user interface for users is worth the trade-off. No one likes ugly error pages, and if you're running a public-facing website, you'll get sick of users reporting them—we like to minimize them where we can.

You can commit this new functionality:

```
$ git add .
$ git commit -m "Handle authorization errors gracefully"
$ git push
```

8.1.7 One more thing

You've protected the `show` action of the `ProjectsController` from unauthorized access, but the links to all projects are still visible to all users in the `index` action. This is definitely something you should look at fixing.

You can add another scenario to an existing feature to make sure that when you fix this behavior, it stays fixed. You can use the feature in spec/features/viewing _projects_spec.rb.

To test that certain links are hidden on the index action, add a new scenario under the existing one that looks like the following listing.

Listing 8.22 Testing that only viewable projects are listed on the index page

```
RSpec.feature "Users can view projects" do
  ...

  scenario "unless they do not have permission" do
    FactoryGirl.create(:project, name: "Hidden")
    visit "/"
    expect(page).not_to have_content "Hidden"
  end
end
```

This feature will now ensure that users who don't have permission to view the new "Hidden" project will no longer see a link to it. When you run this feature using bundle exec rspec spec/features/viewing_projects_spec.rb, it fails as expected:

```
1) Users can view projects unless they do not have permission
   Failure/Error: expect(page).not_to have_content "Hidden"
     expected not to find text "Hidden" in "Ticketee Toggle navigation
     Home Signed in as test2@example.com Sign out Projects Sublime
     Text 3 Hidden"
   # ./spec/features/viewing_projects_spec.rb:21:in ...
```

To fix it, you need to modify the index action of app/controllers/ projects_controller.rb. To filter the list of projects loaded, you could manually write a scope in your Project model like you did (in the previous chapter) in the User model to filter out archived users, or you could use Pundit again—it provides a policy _scope method to scope objects based on permissions.

Listing 8.23 The new index action in ProjectsController

```
class ProjectsController < ApplicationController
  ...

  def index
    @projects = policy_scope(Project)
  end
```

Pundit will then call the resolve method in the Scope class of your ProjectPolicy. At the moment this is pretty basic, looking like the following listing.

Listing 8.24   The `resolve` method of `ProjectPolicy`

```
class Scope < Scope
  def resolve
    scope
  end
end
```

Here, `scope` is the argument you passed to `policy_scope`, which in this case is just
`Project`.

Just as you tested the `show?` method of the `ProjectPolicy`, you can test the scope
as well, by adding the following code above the `permissions :show?` block in spec/
policies/project_policy_spec.rb.

Listing 8.25   spec/policies/project_policy_spec.rb

```
context "policy_scope" do
  subject { Pundit.policy_scope(user, Project) }

  let!(:project) { FactoryGirl.create :project }
  let(:user) { FactoryGirl.create :user }

  it "is empty for anonymous users" do
    expect(Pundit.policy_scope(nil, Project)).to be_empty
  end

  it "includes projects a user is allowed to view" do
    assign_role!(user, :viewer, project)
    expect(subject).to include(project)
  end

  it "doesn't include projects a user is not allowed to view" do
    expect(subject).to be_empty
  end

  it "returns all projects for admins" do
    user.admin = true
    expect(subject).to include(project)
  end
end
```

These are similar to the `show?` specs—you test every possible combination for the type
of user being logged in and permission. Admins should see all projects listed, because
they can see everything; anonymous users don't have permission to see anything; and
other users can see different data depending on their assigned roles. You've defined a
new subject for your `context` of specs—the `policy_scope` method you want to test.
And you don't have access to the controller helpers in your specs, so you have to manually specify `Pundit.policy_scope` instead.

Naturally, all of your new specs will now fail when you run them with `bundle exec
rspec spec/policies/project_policy_spec.rb`:

```
1) ProjectPolicy policy_scope is empty for anonymous users
   Failure/Error: expect(Pundit.policy_scope(nil, Project)).to be_empty
     expected Project to respond to `empty?`
   # ./spec/policies/project_policy_spec.rb:16:in ...

2) ProjectPolicy policy_scope includes projects a user is allowed to
   view
   Failure/Error: expect(subject).to include(project)
   TypeError:
     wrong argument type Project (expected Module)
   # ./spec/policies/project_policy_spec.rb:21:in ...
```

. . .

This is because `Project` is being returned from your scope, instead of a list of projects. You can make these specs pass by rewriting the `resolve` method in your `Project-Policy::Scope` class.

Listing 8.26 The new `resolve` method

```
class ProjectPolicy < ApplicationPolicy
  def resolve
    return scope.none if user.nil?
    return scope.all if user.admin?

    scope.joins(:roles).where(roles: {user_id: user})
  end
```

    . . .

You deal with the two edge case scenarios first: no user, and an admin user. If there's no user signed in, then `user` will be `nil`—in this case you can return `scope.none`. Remember that `scope` is the argument to `policy_scope`, in this case the `Project` model. `none` is a convenience method provided by Active Record to automatically return no records, no matter what other conditions may be added later—it sounds like a perfect fit for your scenario.

Admin users can see everything, so you return `scope.all`; as the name implies, this will return all records.

The last line is the meat of the method and may be a little confusing. The `joins` method joins the `roles` table using a SQL `INNER JOIN`, allowing you to perform queries using columns from the `roles` table as well as the base `projects` table. You do that with the `where` method, specifying a hash that contains the `roles` key, which points to another hash containing the fields you want to search on and their expected values. This scope then returns all the `Project` objects containing a related record in the `roles` table that has the user ID equal to that of the passed-in user, which is your signed-in user. All of your roles have read access to projects, so if there are any roles joining the user and the project, then the project is readable by the user.

With these couple of short lines, the specs for `ProjectPolicy` will now pass:

```
10 examples, 0 failures
```

What about your original spec/features/viewing_projects_spec.rb?

```
2 example, 0 failures
```

What about the entire test suite?

```
42 examples, 0 failures
```

Success! Commit your changes:

```
$ git add .
$ git commit -m "Don't list projects that a user doesn't have
    permission to see"
$ git push
```

Now unauthorized users can't see any evidence of projects, either via the `index` or `show` actions, but there's nothing stopping a crafty user from *editing* projects. You haven't placed any authorization restrictions on the `edit` and `update` actions, so a user could go straight to the form if they knew (or guessed) the URL, and still edit anything they wished. We'll look at fixing this next.

8.2 *Project-updating permission*

As discussed at the beginning of the chapter, you have three roles in your system—viewers, editors, and managers. Only one of those roles should be allowed to edit the details of the project itself—the managers. You should restrict access to the `edit` and `update` actions of the `ProjectsController` to allow managers of the project to access them, but not cditors, viewers, or users who aren't logged in.

You'll start with writing tests for your new permissions, in spec/policies/project_policy_spec.rb.

8.2.1 *Testing the ProjectPolicy again*

For now you'll test in a very naive way, by copying and pasting all of the existing tests and code you wrote for the `show?` action, and then you'll do some refactoring—the code will be nearly identical, and a lot of the permission stuff you'll do in the future will be very similar as well.

To test the `update?` permission, insert the following code in a block below the `permissions :show?` do block.

> **Listing 8.27 Specs for testing whether a user can edit a project**

```
permissions :update? do
  let(:user) { FactoryGirl.create :user }
  let(:project) { FactoryGirl.create :project }

  it "blocks anonymous users" do
    expect(subject).not_to permit(nil, project)
  end

  it "doesn't allow viewers of the project" do
```

```
    assign_role!(user, :viewer, project)
    expect(subject).not_to permit(user, project)
  end

  it "doesn't allows editors of the project" do
    assign_role!(user, :editor, project)
    expect(subject).not_to permit(user, project)
  end

  it "allows managers of the project" do
    assign_role!(user, :manager, project)
    expect(subject).to permit(user, project)
  end

  it "allows administrators" do
    admin = FactoryGirl.create :user, :admin
    expect(subject).to permit(admin, project)
  end

  it "doesn't allow users assigned to other projects" do
    other_project = FactoryGirl.create :project
    assign_role!(user, :manager, other_project)
    expect(subject).not_to permit(user, project)
  end
end
```

The only differences between these specs and the show? specs are that you've flipped a few of the expect(subject).to to expect(subject).not_to.

Not surprisingly, if you run the specs with bundle exec rspec spec/policies/ project_policy_spec.rb, you'll get a few failures:

```
1) ProjectPolicy update? allows managers of the project
   Failure/Error: expect(subject).to permit(user, project)
     Expected ProjectPolicy to grant update? on
     #<Project:0x007f2c45b270c8> but it didn't
   # ./spec/policies/project_policy_spec.rb:89:in ...

2) ProjectPolicy update? allows administrators
   Failure/Error: expect(subject).to permit(admin, project)
     Expected ProjectPolicy to grant update? on
     #<Project:0x007f2c490922f8> but it didn't
   # ./spec/policies/project_policy_spec.rb:94:in ...
```

Why does this happen? Well, according to ApplicationPolicy, all users are blocked from updating records by default; see the following listing.

> **Listing 8.28 The default update? method in ApplicationPolicy**

```
class ApplicationPolicy
  ...

  def update?
    false
  end
```

Like with show?, you can overwrite this method by defining an update? method in ProjectPolicy. The contents will be very similar to show?, only differing in making sure that the role filter also only selects Role records with the role name "manager."

> **Listing 8.29 The new update? method in ProjectPolicy**

```
class ProjectPolicy < ApplicationPolicy
  ...

  def update?
    user.try(:admin?) || record.roles.exists?(user_id: user,
      role: 'manager')
  end
```

If the user is an admin or they're a manager for this specific project, they'll be authorized to update it.

Now you can rerun your ProjectPolicy specs with bundle exec rspec spec/policies/project_policy_spec.rb:

```
16 examples, 0 failures
```

8.2.2 *Applying the authorization*

Now that you have specs to make sure that only managers can edit projects, you can apply that authorization in your ProjectsController, using the authorize method just like you did for the show action. Edit the edit and update actions to use the update? permission you just wrote.

> **Listing 8.30 The edit and update actions of ProjectsController**

```
class ProjectsController < ApplicationController
  ...

  def edit
    authorize @project, :update?
  end

  def update
    authorize @project, :update?
    if @project.update(project_params)
      flash[:notice] = "Project has been updated."
      redirect_to @project
    else
      flash.now[:alert] = "Project has not been updated."
      render "edit"
    end
  end
```

Now you're cooking. But this might have broken something in the rest of your tests—likely the features you wrote that make sure users can edit projects. If you run bundle exec rspec now, you'll get a couple of failures:

```
1) Users can edit existing projects with valid attributes
   Failure/Error: fill_in "Name", with: "Sublime Text 4 beta"
   Capybara::ElementNotFound:
     Unable to find field "Name"

2) Users can edit existing projects when providing invalid attributes
   Failure/Error: fill_in "Name", with: ""
   Capybara::ElementNotFound:
     Unable to find field "Name"
```

It's exactly as expected. The start of spec/features/editing_projects_spec.rb looks like the following.

Listing 8.31   The start of spec/features/editing_projects_spec.rb

```
require "rails_helper"

RSpec.feature "Users can edit existing projects" do
  let(:user) { FactoryGirl.create(:user) }
  let(:project) { FactoryGirl.create(:project, name: "Sublime Text 3") }

  before do
    login_as(user)
    assign_role!(user, :viewer, project)
    ...
```

In your test, you're logging in as a *viewer* of the project, but you've just written code to make sure that only *managers* can edit projects. Update the line that assigns the role to assign the `manager` role instead of the `viewer` role.

Listing 8.32   Assigning the `manager` role

```
before do
  login_as(user)
  assign_role!(user, :manager, project)
  ...
```

Let's also rename the test in the top-level `RSpec.feature` description—it's not "_Users_ can edit existing projects," but rather "_Project managers_ can edit existing projects."

Now if you rerun `bundle exec rspec`, all of the tests will pass again:

```
48 examples, 0 failures
```

This looks like a good time to commit your changes:

```
$ git add .
$ git commit -m "Only admins and managers of a project can edit
                 the project's details"
$ git push
```

8.2.3   *Hiding the "Edit Project" link*

Like you did in chapter 7, you should also be hiding the "Edit Project" link from those users who don't have permission to update the project. If you don't, any user who has permission to view the project could click the link, and they'd just get a "You aren't allowed to do that" message. Not very friendly.

Add another two scenarios to spec/features/hidden_links_spec.rb to cover this.

Listing 8.33   New scenarios in spec/features/hidden_links_spec.rb

```
context "non-admin users (project viewers)" do
  ...

  scenario "cannot see the Edit Project link" do
    visit project_path(project)
    expect(page).not_to have_link "Edit Project"
  end
end

context "admin users" do
  ...

  scenario "can see the Edit Project link" do
    visit project_path(project)
    expect(page).to have_link "Edit Project"
  end
end
```

The viewers of a project don't have permission to see the link, so it shouldn't appear when they visit the project page. The admins do have permission, so they should see the link.

When you run `bundle exec rspec spec/features/hidden_links_spec.rb`, one of the two new specs you wrote should fail:

```
1) Users can only see the appropriate links non-admin users (project
   viewers) cannot see the Edit Project link
   Failure/Error: expect(page).not_to have_link "Edit Project"
     expected not to find link "Edit Project", found 1 match:
     "Edit Project"
   # ./spec/features/hidden_links_spec.rb:28:in ...
```

This makes sense, because you haven't yet hidden the link for anyone.

Pundit also provides a helper for your views, to show or hide specific content if the user is or isn't authorized to do something. It's appropriately called `policy` and can be used as in the next listing.

Listing 8.34   An example of using Pundit's `policy` helper in views

```
<% if policy(@project).update? %>
  <p>This displays if the user has the "update" permission
  on the @project.</p>
```

```
<% else %>
  <p>This displays if the user doesn't have the "update" permission on
  the @project. No soup for you!</p>
<% end %>
```

You can use this helper in your app/views/projects/show.html.erb, around the action link in the top header.

Listing 8.35 Only display Edit Project button if the user is authorized
---

```
<ul class="actions">
  <% if policy(@project).update? %>
    <li><%= link_to "Edit Project", edit_project_path(@project),
      class: "edit" %></li>
  <% end %>
  ...
```

Now `bundle exec rspec spec/features/hidden_links_spec.rb` will be a lot happier:

```
7 examples, 0 failures
```

And nothing else should fail when you run `bundle exec rspec`:

```
50 examples, 0 failures
```

You're accomplishing a lot of functionality with very little code! Commit these changes as well:

```
$ git add .
$ git commit -m "Only show the 'Edit Project' button if the user
                 can update the project"
$ git push
```

Everything in the `ProjectsController` is now protected by Pundit's authorization helpers—the `index` action by `policy_scope`, and the `show`, `edit`, and `update` actions by `authorize`.

For the seven default CRUD actions for a Rails model, you've implemented the following authorizations:

- Anyone can view the `index` action, but they will only see projects they are a member of.
- Only admins can see the `new` and `create` actions.
- Only members of a project can see the `show` action.
- Only admins, or managers of a project, can see the `edit` and `update` actions.
- Only admins can see the `destroy` action.

So far so good. But you haven't yet looked at `TicketsController`. This is a problem, because users can still create, view, and delete tickets for a project, even if they don't have access to the project itself. We'll look at addressing these problems next.

8.3   *Ticket-viewing permission*

If you had a project that had a lot of tickets in it, the URLs would start looking fairly predictable. They might look like this:

- /projects/1/tickets/2
- /projects/1/tickets/4
- /projects/1/tickets/5

And so on. A user could start constructing other URLs in the same format, such as /projects/2/tickets/7. If that corresponds to a valid ticket, they'd be able to view the details of it, even if they don't belong to the project. This sounds like a Bad Thing.

The way your role structure is designed (with viewers, editors, and managers), viewing tickets will have the same permissions as viewing projects—anyone who belongs to the project (with any role) should be able to see the details of any ticket in the project.

You already have a spec that covers viewing the details of a ticket—spec/features/viewing_tickets_spec.rb. If you run it now, it should pass happily:

```
1 example, 0 failures
```

This will be your litmus test—what you run to make sure you haven't broken anything while adding authorizations.

Open the `TicketsController` in app/controllers/tickets_controller.rb, and modify the `show` action to add an authorization check using `authorize`.

Listing 8.36   The `show` action of `TicketsController`, now with added authorization

```
class TicketsController < ApplicationController
  ...

  def show
    authorize @ticket, :show?
  end

  ...
end
```

You already have `@ticket` loaded due to `before_action :set_ticket`, so this should just work. But run `bundle exec rspec spec/features/viewing_tickets_spec.rb` again, and you'll see it's already broken:

```
1) Users can view tickets for a given project
   Failure/Error: click_link "Make it shiny!"
   Pundit::NotDefinedError:
     unable to find policy TicketPolicy for #<Ticket:0x007f13e0d92bc8>
   # ...
   # ./app/controllers/tickets_controller.rb:23:in `show'
```

Because you're now doing authorization against a `Ticket` object, instead of a `Project` object, you need a `TicketPolicy` class. Run the Rails generator provided by Pundit again to generate a new policy:

```
$ rails g pundit:policy ticket
```

Now you have a `TicketPolicy` class, defined in app/policies/ticket_policy.rb, and the ticket-viewing spec is happy again:

```
1 example, 0 failures
```

You can now start writing specs in spec/policies/ticket_policy_spec.rb to ensure that only the right people can view ticket details.

8.3.1 *Refactoring policy specs*

Since the `show?` specs for your `TicketPolicy` will be exactly the same as the `show?` specs for your `ProjectPolicy`, it might be tempting to just copy and paste them and keep on going. But this will be the second time you've copied and pasted them—you did the same for the `update?` permissions block in `ProjectPolicy`. Duplicating code once is okay, but if you're doing it multiple times, it might be time for some refactoring.

One way of solving all of this duplication is to write a *custom RSpec matcher*. This will make the code easier to read, and also rearrange the way the tests are laid out. At the moment, you go through each permission type (such as `update?`) and for each type check each role (such as `viewer`)—the code to create a role is repeated for each permission type. If instead you created the roles first, then ran the permission checks, the code might be a lot shorter.

In the quest to always stay DRY, we'll introduce a new flavor of the `it` RSpec syntax, affectionately called the "one-liner `should` syntax." More on this follows, so for now, replace both the `permissions :show?` and `permissions :update?` blocks in spec/policies/project_policy_spec.rb with the following code.

Listing 8.37 A shorter and more concise way of writing policy specs

```ruby
context "permissions" do
  subject { ProjectPolicy.new(user, project) }

  let(:user) { FactoryGirl.create(:user) }
  let(:project) { FactoryGirl.create(:project) }

  context "for anonymous users" do
    let(:user) { nil }

    it { should_not permit_action :show }
    it { should_not permit_action :update }
  end

  context "for viewers of the project" do
    before { assign_role!(user, :viewer, project) }
```

```
    it { should permit_action :show }
    it { should_not permit_action :update }
  end

  context "for editors of the project" do
    before { assign_role!(user, :editor, project) }

    it { should permit_action :show }
    it { should_not permit_action :update }
  end

  context "for managers of the project" do
    before { assign_role!(user, :manager, project) }

    it { should permit_action :show }
    it { should permit_action :update }
  end

  context "for managers of other projects" do
    before do
      assign_role!(user, :manager, FactoryGirl.create(:project))
    end

    it { should_not permit_action :show }
    it { should_not permit_action :update }
  end

  context "for administrators" do
    let(:user) { FactoryGirl.create :user, :admin }

    it { should permit_action :show }
    it { should permit_action :update }
  end
end
```

This is 20 lines shorter than the code you replaced, but what does it do?

You have a new context block for each type of user (anonymous, viewer, admin, and so on), and in each block you set up the user with the right role before running your specs. Then you introduce your custom permit_action RSpec method—which isn't defined yet, so all of the specs will fail.

it { should permit_action :show } is a shortcut for writing something like the following code.

Listing 8.38   The long form of the one-liner should syntax

```
it "should permit the show action" do
  expect(subject).to permit_action :show
end
```

That, as you can agree, is nowhere near as pretty. It can also be written like the following.

Listing 8.39   The non-should version of the one-liner syntax

```
it { is_expected.to permit_action :show }
```

Which of the two one-liner syntaxes you choose is up to you—we personally find the should form more aesthetically pleasing, so that's what we'll go with.

Now that you've dealt with the different syntaxes, how do you define permit_action? You can do it with a custom RSpec matcher—this includes the check that you should perform and some error messages for both the positive and negative cases. Create a new file called spec/support/pundit_matcher.rb, and put the following code in it.

Listing 8.40 spec/support/pundit_matcher.rb

```ruby
RSpec::Matchers.define :permit_action do |action|
  match do |policy|
    policy.public_send("#{action}?")
  end

  failure_message do |policy|
    "#{policy.class} does not allow #{policy.user || "nil"} to " +
      "perform :#{action}? on #{policy.record}."
  end

  failure_message_when_negated do |policy|
    "#{policy.class} does not forbid #{policy.user || "nil"} from " +
      "performing :#{action}? on #{policy.record}."
  end
end
```

You can chain this permit_action method after should, should_not, expect().to, or expect().to_not because it's been defined as a matcher. The action argument is what you pass in when you call the method—such as :show in it { should permit _action :show }—and the policy argument is the subject of the test itself, in this case the ProjectPolicy instance.

The public_send("#{action}?") method might look a little bit odd—it's part of Ruby's metaprogramming magic. public_send (and its more dangerous brother, send) allow you to pass in a method name as a string, and then that method will be called. This is great here, because you have the name of the permission you want to check already stored in the action variable.

In this case, a line like it { should permit_action :update } will call policy .public_send("update?"), which translates to policy.update?. That might look familiar—it's very similar to how you called authorization methods in your view, and they returned true or false depending on whether or not the action could be performed. You leverage that here—if the method returns true, the matcher succeeds, and the test passes if the assertion was positive (that is, should instead of should_not.)

This might be a lot to take in, but that's okay. If you're interested in further reading on custom RSpec matchers, the official documentation is a great resource: www .relishapp.com/rspec/rspec-expectations/v/3-2/docs/custom-matchers/define-matcher.

With this matcher defined, you can now run your `ProjectPolicy` spec file with `bundle exec rspec spec/policies/project_policy_spec.rb`. If you've done everything correctly, you should get the following:

```
16 examples, 0 failures
```

Happy dance time!

This shorter style of specs is also much easier to extend. If you had to authorize another action, such as `destroy?`, instead of copying the entire long `permissions` block, you could just define an extra `it { should permit_action :destroy }` line for each role in your system. And if you added a new role such as `client`, you'd only have to add one new context block and check each permission inside it.

8.3.2   *Testing the TicketPolicy*

You can adopt your new testing style when you write your new `TicketPolicy` specs. Open spec/policies/ticket_policy_spec.rb and replace the contents of the file with the following listing.

Listing 8.41   spec/policies/ticket_policy_spec.rb

```ruby
require "rails_helper"

RSpec.describe TicketPolicy do
  context "permissions" do
    subject { TicketPolicy.new(user, ticket) }

    let(:user) { FactoryGirl.create(:user) }
    let(:project) { FactoryGirl.create(:project) }
    let(:ticket) { FactoryGirl.create(:ticket, project: project) }

    context "for anonymous users" do
      let(:user) { nil }

      it { should_not permit_action :show }
    end

    context "for viewers of the project" do
      before { assign_role!(user, :viewer, project) }

      it { should permit_action :show }
    end

    context "for editors of the project" do
      before { assign_role!(user, :editor, project) }

      it { should permit_action :show }
    end

    context "for managers of the project" do
```

```
      before { assign_role!(user, :manager, project) }

      it { should permit_action :show }
    end

    context "for managers of other projects" do
      before do
        assign_role!(user, :manager, FactoryGirl.create(:project))
      end

      it { should_not permit_action :show }
    end

    context "for administrators" do
      let(:user) { FactoryGirl.create :user, :admin }

      it { should permit_action :show }
    end
  end
end
```

DON'T FORGET! Don't forget to make sure that `require 'spec_helper'` at the top is changed to `require "rails_helper"`! If you don't do this, the test won't be able to find the `TicketPolicy` class.

It looks long, but it's fundamentally similar to the `ProjectPolicy` permission specs you just refactored. In each `context` block, you create a different type of user, and then check whether or not the `show` action is permitted for each. In this case, you don't permit anonymous users or users that only belong to other projects, but you allow anyone that belongs to the project that the ticket belongs to, to view it.

When you run this spec with `bundle exec rspec spec/policies/ticket_policy _spec.rb`, you'll get a couple of failures:

```
1) TicketPolicy permissions for anonymous users should not permit action
   :show
   Failure/Error: it { should_not permit_action :show }
     TicketPolicy does not forbid nil from performing :show? on
     #<Ticket:0x007fbf69644030>.

2) TicketPolicy permissions for managers of other projects should not
   permit action :show
   Failure/Error: it { should_not permit_action :show }
     TicketPolicy does not forbid test4@example.com (User) from
     performing :show? on #<Ticket:0x007fbf6b5d3a40>.
```

This is because, by default, `show` is permitted as long as the ticket exists in the database. You saw the same thing when you wrote custom rules for `ProjectPolicy`.

You can fix those two failures by adding the following custom `show?` method to the `TicketPolicy` class in app/policies/ticket_policy.rb.

Listing 8.42   app/policies/ticket_policy.rb

```
class TicketPolicy < ApplicationPolicy
  ...

  def show?
    user.try(:admin?) || record.project.roles.exists?(user_id: user)
  end
```

With this code, you check that a user is authorized to see a ticket by checking if that user has any role for the project that the ticket belongs to. If a user is a viewer or a manager or an admin, they should be able to access a ticket.

Now, running `bundle exec rspec spec/policies/ticket_policy_spec.rb` will be all green:

```
6 examples, 0 failures
```

Make sure you haven't broken anything by running the entire test suite:

```
1) Users can edit existing tickets with valid attributes
   Failure/Error: click_link "Edit Ticket"
   Capybara::ElementNotFound:
     Unable to find link "Edit Ticket"
   # ...
   # ./spec/features/editing_tickets_spec.rb:12:in ...

2) Users can edit existing tickets with invalid attributes
   Failure/Error: click_link "Edit Ticket"
   Capybara::ElementNotFound:
     Unable to find link "Edit Ticket"
   # ...
   # ./spec/features/editing_tickets_spec.rb:12:in ...
```

```
56 examples, 2 failures
```

You've changed the rules on who can view tickets—you no longer allow anonymous users to view them. But in your ticket-editing spec, you're not signing in before you try to view the ticket page, and hence the test fails.

You need to update that spec to assign a valid role to a user, and then log that user in. Open spec/features/editing_tickets_spec.rb, and update the beginning of the before block in much the same way that you fixed your other specs earlier.

Listing 8.43   spec/features/editing_tickets_spec.rb

```
RSpec.feature "Users can edit existing tickets" do
  ...

  before do
    assign_role!(author, :viewer, project)
    login_as(author)
    ...
```

Now that the signed-in user is a member of the project, viewing the ticket should be successful. Rerun that spec with `bundle exec rspec spec/features/editing_tickets _spec.rb` to verify:

```
2 examples, 0 failures
```

And also rerun `bundle exec rspec` to make sure everything is all green:

```
56 examples, 0 failures
```

Great! Check in your changes and push:

```
$ git add .
$ git commit -m "Only members of a project can view tickets in it"
$ git push
```

8.3.3 Refactoring policies

Some of the code in your policies is starting to get a bit repetitive—the constant checks like `record.roles.where(user_id: user, role: "manager")` and `record .project.roles.where(user_id: user)`. Wouldn't it be great if you could write things like `record.has_manager?(user)` or `record.project.has_member?(user)`? You can do that by writing some nice helper methods on your `Project` model.

This is another example of that red-green-refactor style of workflow you saw earlier in chapters 2 and 4. It's a great workflow, as it enables you to tidy up your codebase while working on a stable base of tests.

To add your new helper methods, open app/models/project.rb and add the following at the bottom of the class.

> **Listing 8.44 Metaprogramming magic to add more-expressive method names**

```ruby
class Project < ActiveRecord::Base
  ...

  def has_member?(user)
    roles.exists?(user_id: user)
  end

  [:manager, :editor, :viewer].each do |role|
    define_method "has_#{role}?" do |user|
      roles.exists?(user_id: user, role: role)
    end
  end
end
```

This is a little bit of Ruby metaprogramming magic. Instead of manually defining `has_manager?`, `has_editor?`, and `has_viewer?`—which would all have identical code, just with a different role name—you dynamically create methods in a loop using `define_method`. `define_method` takes the name of the method to define as the first argument, the arguments to the method as the block arguments (`|user|`), and the content of the method as the content of the block. These methods work identically to those you'd write normally, just with less code.

Now you can edit your `ProjectPolicy` and `TicketPolicy` classes to substitute in the new methods you just defined.

Listing 8.45 Updated version of `ProjectPolicy` with `has_*?` helpers

```
class ProjectPolicy < ApplicationPolicy
  ...

  def show?
    user.try(:admin?) || record.has_member?(user)
  end

  def update?
    user.try(:admin?) || record.has_manager?(user)
  end
end
```

Listing 8.46 Updated version of `TicketPolicy` with `has_*?` helpers

```
class TicketPolicy < ApplicationPolicy
  ...

  def show?
    user.try(:admin?) || record.project.has_member?(user)
  end
end
```

All of your specs will still pass when you run `bundle exec rspec`:

```
56 examples, 0 failures
```

This is an example of a tiny refactoring that can make your code so much nicer to read. And later on, if your definition of what it means for a user to be a member of a project changes, you don't have to change all your policies. You only need to change your code in one place—in the `has_member?` method.

Let's move on!

8.4   Ticket-creation permission

We're moving through each of the actions in your controllers, applying valid authorization to them one by one. Next, you also need to lock down the `new` and `create` actions of `TicketsController`, so people can't just go to /projects/2/tickets/new and create tickets, even if they don't have access to the project. You should look at fixing that now.

8.4.1   Testing the TicketPolicy ... again

In your system, viewers of a project won't have the access necessary to create tickets for the project, but editors and managers will. And, of course, admins can do anything they like. You can expand the specs you wrote earlier in spec/policies/

ticket_policy_spec.rb to add these new requirements. Add the new specs to the existing context blocks.

Listing 8.47 The new `create?` permission specs for `TicketPolicy`

```
context "for anonymous users" do
  ...
  it { should_not permit_action :create }
end

context "for viewers of the project" do
  ...
  it { should_not permit_action :create }
end

context "for editors of the project" do
  ...
  it { should permit_action :create }
end

context "for managers of the project" do
  ...
  it { should permit_action :create }
end

context "for managers of other projects" do
  ...
  it { should_not permit_action :create }
end

context "for administrators" do
  ...
  it { should permit_action :create }
end
```

See how much easier adding new permissions is, with this new spec format?

When you run these specs with `bundle exec rspec spec/policies/ticket_policy _spec.rb`, you'll get a few expected failures:

```
1) TicketPolicy permissions for editors of the project should permit
   action :create
   Failure/Error: it { should permit action :create }
     TicketPolicy does not allow test4@example.com (User) to perform
     :create? on #<Ticket:0x007f70d64b2848>.
   # ./spec/policies/ticket_policy_spec.rb:29:in ...

2) TicketPolicy permissions for managers of the project should permit
   action :create
   Failure/Error: it { should permit_action :create }
     TicketPolicy does not allow test6@example.com (User) to perform
     :create? on #<Ticket:0x007f70d8924438>.
   # ./spec/policies/ticket_policy_spec.rb:36:in ...

3) TicketPolicy permissions for administrators should permit action
```

```
:create
Failure/Error: it { should permit_action :create }
  TicketPolicy does not allow test10@example.com (Admin) to perform
  :create? on #<Ticket:0x007f70d54b3aa0>.
# ./spec/policies/ticket_policy_spec.rb:52:in ...
```

This is the same as you saw earlier with ApplicationPolicy—by default, create? is forbidden to all. You can fix this by adding a new create? method to your TicketPolicy that encapsulates the logic you want.

Listing 8.48   Defining who can create tickets

```
class TicketPolicy < ApplicationPolicy
  ...

  def create?
    user.try(:admin?) || record.project.has_manager?(user) ||
      record.project.has_editor?(user)
  end
end
```

That should make all of your TicketPolicy specs pass. Check with bundle exec rspec spec/policies/ticket_policy_spec.rb:

```
12 examples, 0 failures
```

Now that you know the policy works the way you want, you can look at using it in your TicketsController. If this is starting to get very quick and formulaic, it's because you've done all the heavy lifting to get an authorization scheme in place, and now you're just making sure the rest of your code uses it!

8.4.2   *Applying the authorization*

Open app/controllers/tickets_controller.rb, and you can add your new authorization steps to the new and create actions.

Listing 8.49   new and create actions in TicketsController

```
class TicketsController < ApplicationController
  ...

  def new
    @ticket = @project.tickets.build
    authorize @ticket, :create?
  end

  def create
    @ticket = @project.tickets.build(ticket_params)
    @ticket.author = current_user
    authorize @ticket, :create?

    if @ticket.save
      ...
```

AUTHORIZE BEFORE SAVING Remember, you need to perform your authorization checks *before* you save any data to the database, meaning before you call `@ticket.save` or `@ticket.create`. If you don't, the object will be persisted, even if the authorization check then fails!

You should expect some of your existing specs to fail now, because you aren't making sure your users in your specs have the right permissions again. Running `bundle exec rspec` will confirm this:

```
1) Users can create new tickets with valid attributes
   Failure/Error: fill_in "Name", with: "Non-standards compliance"
   Capybara::ElementNotFound:
     Unable to find field "Name"
   # ...
   # ./spec/features/creating_tickets_spec.rb:16:in ...

2) Users can create new tickets when providing invalid attributes
   Failure/Error: click_button "Create Ticket"
   Capybara::ElementNotFound:
     Unable to find button "Create Ticket"
   # ...
   # ./spec/features/creating_tickets_spec.rb:27:in ...

3) Users can create new tickets with an invalid description
   Failure/Error: fill_in "Name", with: "Non-standards compliance"
   Capybara::ElementNotFound:
     Unable to find field "Name"
   # ...
   # ./spec/features/creating_tickets_spec.rb:35:in ...
```

It isn't immediately obvious from the test failures what the problem is. We mentioned earlier that handling permission errors by redirecting users to a safe place may make broken tests harder to debug; this is a great example of that. It's only because you've been doing lots of the same steps here that you might immediately know what the problem is; otherwise you might have to debug the contents of the page in the spec, which would lead to debugging the controller and seeing that it gets caught on the authorization step. Debugging is a tricky process—luckily there are books[2] and gems[3] out there to teach you how to do it effectively.

Now that you know you have a permissions problem, open spec/features/creating _tickets_spec.rb and see what permissions you've assigned to your user in the spec.

Listing 8.50 The offending permission

```
before do
  ...
  assign_role!(user, :viewer, project)
  ...
end
```

---

[2] Such as *Debugging Ruby* by Ryan Bigg (http://leanpub.com/debuggingruby).
[3] Such as Pry (https://github.com/pry/pry).

Given you just wrote all this code to make sure that regular viewers can't create tickets, you should change the user's role in the spec, to a role that can create tickets.

Listing 8.51   Making it all better!

```
before do
  ...
  assign_role!(user, :editor, project)
  ...
end
```

Now all of your specs will be back to passing again, if you check with `bundle exec rspec`:

```
62 examples, 0 failures
```

Check in the changes you just made:

```
$ git add .
$ git commit -m "Only editors, managers and admins can create tickets"
$ git push
```

There's just one thing left to do before this ticket-creation authorization feature can be considered to be complete—hiding the link to create a new ticket.

HIDING THE "NEW TICKET" LINK

Only some of your users viewing a project's details will have permission to create a new ticket, so you should hide the "New Ticket" link for those users.

You can do this the same way you hid the "Edit Project" link, and it's even in the same view. But you'll start with tests again, adding some more specs to the hidden-links feature.

Open spec/features/hidden_links_spec.rb and add some more scenarios for the "New Ticket" link:

```
RSpec.feature "Users can only see the appropriate links" do
  ...
  context "non-admin users (project viewers)" do
    ...

    scenario "cannot see the New Ticket link" do
      visit project_path(project)
      expect(page).not_to have_link "New Ticket"
    end
  end

  context "admin users" do
    ...

    scenario "can see the New Ticket link" do
      visit project_path(project)
      expect(page).to have_link "New Ticket"
    end
  end
  ...
end
```

The first spec will fail when you run `bundle exec rspec spec/features/hidden_links` `_spec.rb` because all users viewing the page can see the "New Ticket" link:

```
1) Users can only see the appropriate links non-admin users (project
   viewers) cannot see the New Ticket link
   Failure/Error: expect(page).not_to have_link "New Ticket"
     expected not to find link "New Ticket", found 1 match: "New Ticket"
   # ./spec/features/hidden_links_spec.rb:38:in ...
```

Now you can use Pundit's `policy` helper to hide the link when it needs to be hidden. Open app/views/projects/show.html.erb, which is where the "New Ticket" link lives.

Listing 8.52 `Tickets` header on the projects show view

```
<header>
  <h2>Tickets</h2>

  <ul class="actions">
    <li><%= link_to "New Ticket", new_project_ticket_path(@project),
      class: "new" %></li>
  </ul>
</header>
```

You can wrap the `policy` method around the list item that displays the "New Ticket" link, to only show the link if the user has permission to create the ticket.

Listing 8.53 `Tickets` header projects viewing with added policy checking

```
<header>
  <h2>Tickets</h2>

  <ul class="actions">
    <% if policy(Ticket.new(project: @project)).create? %>
      <li><%= link_to "New Ticket", new_project_ticket_path(@project),
        class: "new" %></li>
    <% end %>
  </ul>
</header>
```

This is a little different than the last time you used `policy`. Because you want to only show the link if the user can create a ticket on the current project, you have to build a new (unsaved) ticket on the current project to check against. So you instantiate a new ticket manually with `Ticket.new(project: @project)` and pass it to the `policy` method. If the user can `create?` it, then you display the link.

> **SPECIAL SYNTAX? WHY?** Why use `Ticket.new(project: @project)` here instead of `@project.tickets.new`? If you were to use the latter, Rails would add the ticket you built into the list of tickets you get when you call `@project` `.tickets`. Further down the page, you iterate over `@project.tickets` and display links to each of them. You don't want the new ticket you've just built to appear in that list!

If you rerun your hidden_links_spec.rb specs with bundle exec rspec spec/features/hidden_links_spec.rb, the tests are now passing:

```
8 examples, 0 failures
```

This one's a wrap! Commit your changes. It's starting to take shape.

```
$ git add .
$ git commit -m "Hide the New Ticket link when the user can't create
                  tickets on the project"
$ git push
```

8.5   *Ticket-updating permission*

Implementing the permissions for updating tickets will follow a series of steps very similar to implementing them for creating tickets:

1 Write tests for the update? method on TicketPolicy.
2 Implement authorization in your TicketsController.
3 Fix any failing features due to the new permissions.
4 Hide the "Edit Ticket" link in your view.

There's just one catch—in your app, editors only have a low-level write access to projects, so they should only be able to edit tickets if they created them. Managers and admins have a high-level write access, so they should be able to edit any ticket on the project.

Let's start with the writing of specs.

8.5.1   *Testing the TicketPolicy ... turbocharged*

Based on the preceding description of your requirements, you can add a new set of specs to your TicketPolicy spec in spec/policies/ticket_policy_spec.rb.

> **Listing 8.54   Defining update permissions in TicketPolicy**

```
RSpec.describe TicketPolicy do
  context "permissions" do
    ...
    context "for anonymous users" do
      ...
      it { should_not permit_action :update }
    end

    context "for viewers of the project" do
      ...
      it { should_not permit_action :update }
    end

    context "for editors of the project" do
      ...
      it { should_not permit_action :update }
```

```
      context "when the editor created the ticket" do
        before { ticket.author = user }

        it { should permit_action :update }
      end
    end

    context "for managers of the project" do
      ...
      it { should permit_action :update }
    end

    context "for managers of other projects" do
      ...
      it { should_not permit_action :update }
    end

    context "for administrators" do
      ...
      it { should permit_action :update }
    end
  end
end
```

The catch we mentioned has been added as nested context, within the editors context. In the outer block, the user is just a normal editor on the project; in the inner block, they're also the owner of the ticket.

When you run the spec with bundle exec rspec spec/policies/ticket_policy _spec.rb, you'll get a few expected failures:

```
1) TicketPolicy permissions for editors of the project when the editor
   created the ticket should permit action :update
   Failure/Error: it { should permit_action :update }
     TicketPolicy does not allow test7@example.com (User) to perform
     :update? on #<Ticket:0x007f5146022d28>.
   # ./spec/policies/ticket_policy_spec.rb:37:in ...

2) TicketPolicy permissions for managers of the project should permit
   action :update
   Failure/Error: it { should permit_action :update }
     TicketPolicy does not allow test10@example.com (User) to perform
     :update? on #<Ticket:0x007f51445d1a00>.
   # ./spec/policies/ticket_policy_spec.rb:46:in ...

3) TicketPolicy permissions for administrators should permit action
   :update
   Failure/Error: it { should permit_action :update }
     TicketPolicy does not allow test16@example.com (Admin) to perform
     :update? on #<Ticket:0x007f514433dd48>.
   # ./spec/policies/ticket_policy_spec.rb:64:in ...
```

Fixing this should be old hat now. Open your TicketPolicy class in app/policies/ ticket_policy.rb, and define a new update? method. It looks like the following listing.

Listing 8.55 The new `update?` method in `TicketPolicy`

```
class TicketPolicy < ApplicationPolicy
  ...

  def update?
    user.try(:admin?) || record.project.has_manager?(user) ||
      (record.project.has_editor?(user) && record.author == user)
  end
end
```

It's a little bit cumbersome, but it neatly includes all of your requirements, all joined together with logical ORs, meaning any of these conditions can be true for the user to be granted access:

- The user is an admin.
- The user is a manager of the project.
- The user is an editor of the project, and the user is also the author of the ticket.

Rerunning with `bundle exec rspec spec/policies/ticket_policy_spec.rb`, your specs will be all green:

```
19 examples, 0 failures
```

The next step is implementing the authorization in your controller.

8.5.2 *Implementing controller authorization*

By themselves, the rules you've defined in your `TicketPolicy` class don't mean anything unless you actually enforce them. So open your `TicketsController` class in app/controllers/tickets_controller.rb and add the necessary `authorize` calls to both the `edit` and `update` actions.

Listing 8.56 `TicketsController` with added authorization in `edit` and `update`

```
class TicketsController < ApplicationController
  ...

  def edit
    authorize @ticket, :update?
  end

  def update
    authorize @ticket, :update?

    if @ticket.update(ticket_params)
    ...
```

It's important to call `authorize` *before* any of the methods that change data. This is *really* important—check out the following code example.

Listing 8.57 Don't do this. Ever.

```
if @ticket.update(ticket_params) && authorize(@ticket, :update?)
```

If you were to do something like that and the authorization check failed, the ticket would still be updated anyway, because the update method is called first! Bad idea. Big security hole. Make sure you always authorize as early as possible, to limit the chance of making mistakes.

Now that you have that in place, you need to fix the feature specs you just broke, which weren't expecting this authorization check. Running bundle exec rspec gives just two failures:

```
1) Users can edit existing tickets with valid attributes
   Failure/Error: fill_in "Name", with: "Make it really shiny!"
   Capybara::ElementNotFound:
     Unable to find field "Name"
   # ...
   # ./spec/features/editing_tickets_spec.rb:19:in ...

2) Users can edit existing tickets with invalid attributes
   Failure/Error: fill_in "Name", with: ""
   Capybara::ElementNotFound:
     Unable to find field "Name"
   # ...
   # ./spec/features/editing_tickets_spec.rb:31:in ...
```

The tests can no longer find the fields on the ticket-editing form, because they aren't on the expected page. They're not on the ticket-editing page—they've been redirected back to the homepage because "You don't have permission to do that."

Open spec/features/editing_tickets_spec.rb, and make sure the user in the spec has a role that will allow them to edit the tickets.

Listing 8.58   The new "editor" role in editing_tickets_spec.rb

```
RSpec.feature "Users can edit existing tickets" do
  ...

  before do
    assign_role!(author, :editor, project)
    login_as(author)
    ...
```

And presto! All of the specs pass again:

```
71 examples, 0 failures
```

That was pretty simple! You're really getting the hang of this!

8.5.3   *Hiding the "Edit Ticket" link*

Lastly, you shouldn't be teasing users with the "Edit Ticket" link if they can't do anything with it. That's just mean.

You need to write some tests to make sure the link is hidden and shown when appropriate in spec/features/hidden_links_spec.rb.

Just how exhaustive should your specs be, anyway?

You might have wondered why the tests in hidden_links_spec.rb are very simplistic—they don't cover all the scenarios in which the link is shown and hidden. Should you be writing tests to ensure that editors don't see the link, but editors that created the ticket do see it?

The short answer is no. You've already tested the logic of who can edit tickets and who can't in your `TicketPolicy` spec. Repeating the testing of all of the nuances of that logic here would be code duplication and massive wastage. If you changed the logic of who could update a project, you'd have to update it here as well, even though this is just looking for content on a given page.

You also test for these links in your feature specs, like the ticket-creation and ticket-editing features. With these features, you're asserting that people who are authorized to perform these actions can find these links and click on them.

Your hidden-links feature test is really only a smoke test—a really quick way of making sure that the link is sometimes shown and sometimes hidden. You test that it shows in one scenario and doesn't show in another.

If you really wanted to make sure that you only display the link if the user is allowed to update the ticket, a better fit would be a *view test*. We don't cover view testing in this book, but the idea is that you write two specs that manually render the ticket's show.html.erb view, which holds the "Edit Ticket" link. In one spec, `policy(@ticket).update?` would be stubbed out to return `true`, and you'd verify that the link is shown. In the other, `policy(@ticket).update?` would be stubbed out to return `false`, and you'd verify that the link is not shown.

More on view specs can be found in the Rails documentation: www.relishapp.com/rspec/rspec-rails/v/3-2/docs/view-specs/view-spec.

Open spec/features/hidden_links_spec.rb and add some new scenarios for testing the presence of the "Edit Ticket" link.

Listing 8.59 Testing the presence or absence of the "Edit Ticket" link

```
RSpec.feature "Users can only see the appropriate links" do
  ...
  let(:ticket) do
    FactoryGirl.create(:ticket, project: project, author: user)
  end

  context "non-admin users (project viewers)" do
    ...

    scenario "cannot see the Edit Ticket link" do
      visit project_ticket_path(project, ticket)
      expect(page).not_to have_link "Edit Ticket"
    end
  end
end
```

```
context "admin users" do
  ...

  scenario "can see the Edit Ticket link" do
    visit project_ticket_path(project, ticket)
    expect(page).to have_link "Edit Ticket"
  end
end
end
```

You've had to create and assign a new ticket to the project, with a valid user (or the ticket's show view will explode due to a missing email). Then you test that normal users can't see the link and admin users do.

When you run the spec with bundle exec rspec spec/features/hidden_links _spec.rb, you get one failure because all users can still see the link:

```
1) Users can only see the appropriate links non-admin users (project
   viewers) cannot see the Edit Ticket link
   Failure/Error: expect(page).not_to have_link "Edit Ticket"
     expected not to find link "Edit Ticket", found 1 match: "Edit
     Ticket"
   # ./spec/features/hidden_links_spec.rb:46:in ...
```

Now you can open the view and add the code to conditionally display the link.

Open app/views/tickets/show.html.erb and find the code for the link. It looks like the following listing.

Listing 8.60 Action links for the ticket, in app/views/tickets/show.html.erb

```
<ul class="actions">
  <li><%= link_to "Edit Ticket", [:edit, @project, @ticket],
    class: "edit" %></li>
  <li><%= link_to "Delete Ticket", [@project, @ticket], method: :delete,
    data: { confirm: "Are you sure you want to delete this ticket?"},
    class: "delete" %></li>
</ul>
```

Like before, you can wrap the list item and the link in a call to policy. You include the list item as well, so that if the permissions check fails, you don't render an empty list item—that might wreck the styling on the page.

Listing 8.61 Action links for the ticket, with added policy checking

```
<ul class="actions">
  <% if policy(@ticket).update? %>
    <li><%= link_to "Edit Ticket", [:edit, @project, @ticket],
      class: "edit" %></li>
  <% end %>
  <li><%= link_to "Delete Ticket", [@project, @ticket], method: :delete,
    data: { confirm: "Are you sure you want to delete this ticket?"},
    class: "delete" %></li>
</ul>
```

Now your hidden_links_spec.rb tests will pass:

```
11 examples, 0 failures
```

Will all of the specs pass? You betcha.

```
73 examples, 0 failures
```

Commit and push the changes you've made:

```
$ git add .
$ git commit -m "Added permissions for editing tickets"
$ git push
```

Now you only have one more set of permission checking to go.

8.6 Ticket-destroying permission

We'll try to push through this section a bit more quickly, because the more interesting stuff is coming up in the next section. In Ticketee, editors won't have the ability to destroy tickets—only managers and admins will. Later, you'll add the ability for tickets to have a status, so editors will be able to mark tickets as closed, but not destroy them entirely. That's a super-special thing to do.

You'll start, as always, with writing some policy specs to codify those requirements.

8.6.1 Testing the TicketPolicy ... for the final time

Open spec/policies/ticket_policy_spec.rb, and add some more scenarios for the new destroy? permission you'll be implementing. It might look like the following listing.

> **Listing 8.62 New `destroy` specs in the `TicketPolicy` spec**

```
RSpec.describe TicketPolicy do
  context "permissions" do
    ...
    context "for anonymous users" do
      ...
      it { should_not permit_action :destroy }
    end

    context "for viewers of the project" do
      ...
      it { should_not permit_action :destroy }
    end

    context "for editors of the project" do
      ...
      it { should_not permit_action :destroy }
      ...
    end

    context "for managers of the project" do
      ...
```

```
      it { should permit_action :destroy }
    end

    context "for managers of other projects" do
      ...
      it { should_not permit_action :destroy }
    end

    context "for administrators" do
      ...
      it { should permit_action :destroy }
    end
  end
end
```

When you run the specs with bundle exec rspec spec/policies/ticket_policy
_spec.rb, you get the expected failures, because no one is allowed to destroy tickets at
present:

```
1) TicketPolicy permissions for managers of the project should permit
   action :destroy
   Failure/Error: it { should permit_action :destroy }
     TicketPolicy does not allow test13@example.com (User) to perform
     :destroy? on #<Ticket:0x007f1c10f60a80>.
   # ./spec/policies/ticket_policy_spec.rb:50:in ...

2) TicketPolicy permissions for administrators should permit action
   :destroy
   Failure/Error: it { should permit_action :destroy }
     TicketPolicy does not allow test21@example.com (Admin) to perform
     :destroy? on #<Ticket:0x007f1c111613e8>.
   # ./spec/policies/ticket_policy_spec.rb:70:in ...
```

You can fix this by defining a new destroy? method in your TicketPolicy class, overwriting the default one in ApplicationPolicy. Open app/policies/ticket_policy.rb
and add the destroy? method definition.

Listing 8.63 The new `destroy?` method in `TicketPolicy`

```
class TicketPolicy < ApplicationPolicy
  ...

  def destroy?
    user.try(:admin?) || record.project.has_manager?(user)
  end
end
```

Admins can destroy tickets, and so can managers of the project. Easy as pie.

Rerun bundle exec rspec spec/policies/ticket_policy_spec.rb, and they will
all now pass:

```
25 examples, 0 failures
```

8.6.2 *Implementing controller authorization*

Now you can make sure your `TicketsController` uses the permission rules you just implemented and tested. Open app/controllers/tickets_controller.rb and add the requisite `authorize` check to the `destroy` action.

Listing 8.64   Authorization checking in the `destroy` action

```
class TicketsController < ApplicationController
  ...

  def destroy
    authorize @ticket, :destroy?

    @ticket.destroy
    ...
```

Again, you need to call the `authorize` method here *before* `@ticket.destroy`; otherwise the ticket will be destroyed even if the user isn't authorized to do that!

Did adding that new authorization step break any of your existing specs? Running `bundle exec rspec` will show you that it did because your spec user is only a viewer of the project, not a manager:

```
1) Users can delete tickets successfully
   Failure/Error: expect(page).to have_content "Ticket has been
   deleted."
     expected to find text "Ticket has been deleted." in "Ticketee
     Toggle navigation Home Signed in as test17@example.com Sign out
     You aren't allowed to do that. Projects Example project"
   # ./spec/features/deleting_tickets_spec.rb:19:in ...
```

You can change that by changing the role assigned to the user in spec/features/deleting_tickets_spec.rb.

Listing 8.65   The new and improved user role

```
RSpec.feature "Users can delete tickets" do
  ...

  before do
    login_as(author)
    assign_role!(author, :manager, project)
    ...
```

Now all of your specs pass!

```
79 examples, 0 failures
```

HIDING THE "DELETE TICKET" LINK

Finally, you need to hide the "Delete Ticket" link from users who can see the ticket page but aren't allowed to destroy the ticket.

Start by adding some trusty specs in spec/features/hidden_links_spec.rb to make sure that some users don't see the link, and some users do.

Listing 8.66 Hiding the "Delete Ticket" link under specific conditions

```
RSpec.feature "Users can only see the appropriate links" do
  context "non-admin users (project viewers)" do
    ...

    scenario "cannot see the Delete Ticket link" do
      visit project_ticket_path(project, ticket)
      expect(page).not_to have_link "Delete Ticket"
    end
  end

  context "admin users" do
    ...

    scenario "can see the Delete Ticket link" do
      visit project_ticket_path(project, ticket)
      expect(page).to have_link "Delete Ticket"
    end
  end
end
```

When you run these specs with `bundle exec rspec spec/features/hidden_links _spec.rb`, you get just one failure:

```
1) Users can only see the appropriate links non-admin users (project
   viewers) cannot see the Delete Ticket link
   Failure/Error: expect(page).not_to have_link "Delete Ticket"
     expected not to find link "Delete Ticket", found 1 match: "Delete
     Ticket"
   # ./spec/features/hidden_links_spec.rb:51:in ...
```

All users can see the link, even if they shouldn't. Now you can hide it.

Open the ticket's show view, in app/views/tickets/show.html.erb, and check out the ticket header.

Listing 8.67 Actions on a ticket in app/views/tickets/show.html.erb

```
<ul class="actions">
  <% if policy(@ticket).update? %>
    <li><%= link_to "Edit Ticket", [:edit, @project, @ticket],
      class: "edit" %></li>
  <% end %>
  <li><%= link_to "Delete Ticket", [@project, @ticket], method: :delete,
    data: { confirm: "Are you sure you want to delete this ticket?"},
    class: "delete" %></li>
</ul>
```

You were just here in the previous section, adding authorization around the "Edit Ticket" link. You can repeat the process for the "Delete Ticket" link.

Listing 8.68 Actions on a ticket, now with extra authorization

```
<ul class="actions">
  <% if policy(@ticket).update? %>
    <li><%= link_to "Edit Ticket", [:edit, @project, @ticket],
      class: "edit" %></li>
  <% end %>
  <% if policy(@ticket).destroy? %>
    <li><%= link_to "Delete Ticket", [@project, @ticket],
      method: :delete,
      data: { confirm: "Are you sure you want to delete this ticket?" },
      class: "delete" %></li>
  <% end %>
</ul>
```

Now all of your hidden_links_spec.rb specs will pass again:

```
13 examples, 0 failures
```

Double-check to make sure nothing else has broken by running the entire test suite with `bundle exec rspec`:

```
81 examples, 0 failures
```

Great! Commit and push this final authorization check:

```
$ git add .
$ git commit -m "Only managers and admins can delete tickets"
$ git push
```

8.7 *Ensuring authorization for all actions*

You've manually fixed all of your existing controller actions to add authorization checking to them using Pundit's magical helpers. But what's to stop you from simply adding a new controller at some point down the track, and forgetting to authorize it? You're potentially leaving yourself open for some big problems, if future-you isn't as conscientious as current-you.

You can add a little bit more checking, to force your actions to call `authorize`. Pundit provides more controller helpers, called `verify_authorized` and `verify_policy_scoped`, that are designed to be run as `after_action` methods in your controllers. If `verify_authorized` is set as an `after_action`, and the action doesn't call `authorize`, you'll get a nasty surprise, as shown in figure 8.3. This is a good failsafe, to protect you against future mistakes and carelessness.

You can add these `after_action` calls to your `ApplicationController`, to ensure that all actions in your entire app are protected.

Listing 8.69 Require authorization on all of the things!

```
class ApplicationController < ActionController::Base
  include Pundit

  after_action :verify_authorized, except: [:index]
  after_action :verify_policy_scoped, only: [:index]

  ...
```

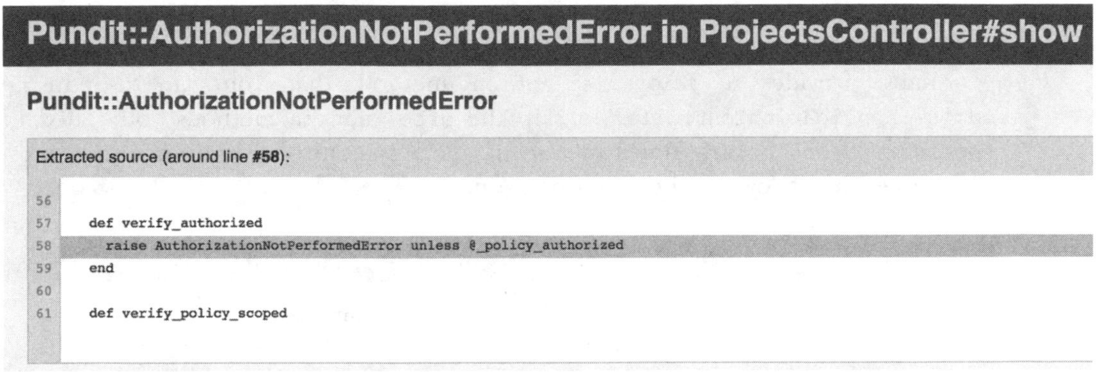

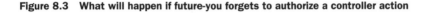

Pundit::AuthorizationNotPerformedError in ProjectsController#show

Pundit::AuthorizationNotPerformedError

Extracted source (around line **#58**):

```
56
57    def verify_authorized
58      raise AuthorizationNotPerformedError unless @_policy_authorized
59    end
60
61    def verify_policy_scoped
```

Figure 8.3 What will happen if future-you forgets to authorize a controller action

verify_authorized will ensure that authorize is called in a controller action, and verify_policy_scoped will ensure that policy_scope is called, which you did way back when you filtered projects to be displayed on the index action of ProjectController.

So far so good. Now, after you add that, have you actually remembered to call authorize and policy_scope everywhere you needed to? Running your test suite with bundle exec rspec will tell you if you have:

```
81 examples, 13 failures

Failed examples:

rspec ./spec/features/admin/archiving_users_spec.rb:11
rspec ./spec/features/admin/archiving_users_spec.rb:19
rspec ./spec/features/admin/creating_projects_spec.rb:12
rspec ./spec/features/admin/creating_projects_spec.rb:26
rspec ./spec/features/admin/creating_users_spec.rb:14
rspec ./spec/features/admin/creating_users_spec.rb:21
rspec ./spec/features/admin/deleting_projects_spec.rb:8
rspec ./spec/features/admin/editing_users_spec.rb:13
rspec ./spec/features/admin/editing_users_spec.rb:22
rspec ./spec/features/signing_in_spec.rb:6
rspec ./spec/features/signing_in_spec.rb:17
rspec ./spec/features/signing_out_spec.rb:10
rspec ./spec/features/signing_up_spec.rb:4
```

That's … a lot of errors. Where did you go wrong?

Well, you've made two mistakes:

- You haven't called authorize in any actions in your admin area, within the admin namespace. You have a global before_action defined in that namespace that will reject all non-admins, but that isn't an authorize call. That's why all of the features in the admin folder are failing.
- You aren't calling authorize in any of the controllers that Devise provides. That's why your authentication-related specs are failing.

You really don't need to call `authorize` in those places, so you can safely skip doing so. But how do you skip an `after_action`?

Rails provides a `skip_after_action` method that you can use inside `Admin::ApplicationController` to skip the `after_action` methods you called in `ApplicationController`. You can use it in app/controllers/admin/application _controller.rb as shown in the following listing.

Listing 8.70   Skipping an `after_action` in `Admin::ApplicationController`

```
class Admin::ApplicationController < ApplicationController
  skip_after_action :verify_authorized, :verify_policy_scoped
  ...
```

Running `bundle exec rspec` will show you that this has cleared up all of the errors in admin-related specs:

```
81 examples, 4 failures

Failed examples:

rspec ./spec/features/signing_in_spec.rb:6
rspec ./spec/features/signing_in_spec.rb:17
rspec ./spec/features/signing_out_spec.rb:10
rspec ./spec/features/signing_up_spec.rb:4
```

You can skip the `after_action` in all Devise controllers by only applying the `after_action` in non-Devise controllers. You can use the `devise_controller?` helper method that Devise provides to achieve that. Edit the `after_action` calls that you just added to `ApplicationController` to add this new condition.

Listing 8.71   Skipping the `after_action` for Devise controllers

```
class ApplicationController < ActionController::Base
  include Pundit

  after_action :verify_authorized, except: [:index],
    unless: :devise_controller?
  after_action :verify_policy_scoped, only: [:index],
    unless: :devise_controller?

  ...
```

Doing this will clear up all of your specs. Run them again with `bundle exec rspec`:

```
81 examples, 0 failures
```

Not sure that this is working as intended? Try commenting out one of the `authorize` lines in a controller, such as the `show` action in `ProjectsController`, and running your specs with `bundle exec rspec`:[4]

---

[4] You can use the # character to mark everything after it on that line of code as a comment.

```
1) ProjectsController handles permission errors by redirecting to a safe
   place
   Failure/Error: get :show, id: project
   Pundit::AuthorizationNotPerformedError:
     Pundit::AuthorizationNotPerformedError
```

(and 16 more just like it)

Yep, it's working. Undo the change you just made to `ProjectsController`, and make sure all of your specs are passing again:

```
81 examples, 0 failures
```

You've just done some great future-proofing against other people's (or your own) silliness. Now if anyone creates a controller outside the `admin` namespace that isn't a Devise controller, and that doesn't perform proper authorization checks, they'll get big red error messages and angry explosions. Pat on the back.

Commit all of your changes, and push:

```
$ git add .
$ git commit -m "Verify that we use authorization in all controllers"
$ git push
```

You're done with adding authorization! You've got a solid system in place, so that all of your users and visitors to the site can only access the things you want them to. It'll be easy to extend, when you add new controllers, or new roles, or new business logic that determines what each role can do. It's grand!

But you're missing one tiny thing—the ability to give users these roles, so that they can use the site properly. We'll look at that next. It'll be fun. We promise.

8.8 Assigning roles to users

In chapter 7 you added an `admin` field to your `User` model and then set it through the admin back end by checking or unchecking a check box. You'll do something similar for roles for users on projects. When you're finished, you'll have a permissions section when you edit a user in the admin area—it'll list all of the projects in the system, and allow you to set a role for the user on each project. It'll look something like figure 8.4 when it's all said and done.

Figure 8.4   The permissions screen you're striving to implement

8.8.1 *Planning the permission screen with a feature spec*

In this section, you'll implement the foundations for assigning roles through the admin back end. You might not be too clear yet on how it will work internally, but you have a good idea of what it should look like, based on figure 8.4. Using that, you can write a feature spec that describes how an admin will be able to assign new roles to users.

Create a new spec at spec/features/admin/managing_roles_spec.rb, and begin with the code from the following listing.

Listing 8.72 spec/features/admin/managing_roles_spec.rb

```ruby
require "rails_helper"

RSpec.feature "Admins can manage a user's roles" do
  let(:admin) { FactoryGirl.create(:user, :admin) }
  let(:user) { FactoryGirl.create(:user) }

  let!(:ie) { FactoryGirl.create(:project, name: "Internet Explorer") }
  let!(:st3) { FactoryGirl.create(:project, name: "Sublime Text 3") }

  before do
    login_as(admin)
  end

  scenario "when assigning roles to an existing user" do
    visit admin_user_path(user)
    click_link "Edit User"

    select "Viewer", from: "Internet Explorer"
    select "Manager", from: "Sublime Text 3"

    click_button "Update User"
    expect(page).to have_content "User has been updated"

    click_link user.email
    expect(page).to have_content "Internet Explorer: Viewer"
    expect(page).to have_content "Sublime Text 3: Manager"
  end
end
```

This scenario has two users: an admin user and a normal user. You sign in as the admin user, edit the user's details in the admin area, and assign some roles to the normal user on two projects that you also set up earlier.

Then you click the Update button and ensure that the roles you just set are displayed on the page. You don't need to go as far as testing that a normal user can now log in and use their roles successfully—that's duplicating logic you tested earlier.

When you run `bundle exec rspec spec/features/admin/managing_roles _spec.rb`, it fails when it tries to select roles:

```
1) Admins can manage a user's roles when assigning roles to an
   existing user
```

```
Failure/Error: select "Viewer", from: "Internet Explorer"
Capybara::ElementNotFound:
  Unable to find select box "Internet Explorer"
```

That makes sense, as you haven't done anything on the user management form to display available projects and roles for them. We'll look at fixing that now.

8.8.2 The roles screen

You'll build on the existing admin user form, which is located in app/views/admin/users/_form.html.erb. Open it, and above the Submit button, add a section for managing roles.

Listing 8.73 The roles section of the user edit form

```erb
<%= simple_form_for [:admin, user] do |f| %>
  ...

  <header>
    <h2>Roles</h2>
  </header>

  <!-- what will go here...? -->

  <%= f.button :submit, class: "btn btn-primary" %>
<% end %>
```

Now you just need to work out what will go in the "what will go here...?" section. If this were a normal form, you'd likely iterate over an association, such as @user.roles, and display some form fields for each role that the user has. But this will be slightly different—you'll want to display a list of all the projects in the system and a select box with all of the available roles that a user can take on the project. Some of the select boxes might already have values if the user already has a role on the project, but the rest should start off blank.

8.8.3 Building a list of projects in a select box

You can start filling in some of the blanks in your form.

Listing 8.74 Now with a list of projects

```erb
<%= simple_form_for [:admin, user] do |f| %>
  ...

  <header>
    <h2>Roles</h2>
  </header>

  <table class="roles">
    <% projects.each do |project| %>
      <tr>
        <th><%= label_tag dom_id(project), project.name %></th>
```

```
    <td>
      <%= select_tag dom_id(project), options_for_select(roles,
        user.role_on(project)), name: "roles[#{project.id}]",
        include_blank: true %>
    </td>
  </tr>
<% end %>
</table>

  <%= f.button :submit, class: "btn btn-primary" %>
<% end %>
```

Looks a bit intimidating—it's some of the most complex view logic you've seen so far. You load up a list of projects in `projects`, and then iterate over them, building up rows in a table. In each of the rows, you create an HTML `label` element using Rails' `label_tag` view helper, and you use `dom_id` to generate a name for the label. `dom_id` will generate something like `project_2` for the project record with ID 2. This way, you can guarantee that all of your names are unique.

Then you use Rails' `select_tag` helper to build a select box, which will eventually be populated with a list of all the roles in the system. The `role_on` method also doesn't exist yet, but wouldn't it be nice if it returned the role name that the user has on the project? You'll write it to do just that, and then use that value to determine which option in the select box should be selected.

It looks like some nifty code, but it doesn't do what you want just yet. If you start up a Rails server and visit the admin user edit page in your browser (a novel concept that we haven't done in a while!), you'll see the error in figure 8.5. You haven't defined a list of projects to display on the form.

ADMIN LOGIN CREDENTIALS If you've forgotten the default admin login credentials, check db/seeds.rb.

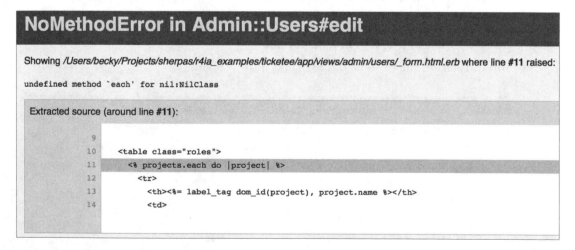

Figure 8.5   You want to iterate over the projects, but you haven't yet loaded them.

DEFINING PROJECTS TO BE DISPLAYED ON THE FORM

You can set up the list of projects to be displayed on the form by defining the `@projects` variable in your `Admin::UsersController` and then passing that variable into your form partial. Open up the controller, in app/controllers/admin/users _controller.rb, and add the following code.

Listing 8.75 Loading role-related data in `Admin::UsersController`

```
class Admin::UsersController < Admin::ApplicationController
  before_action :set_projects, only: [:new, :create, :edit, :update]

  ...

  private

  def set_projects
    @projects = Project.order(:name)
  end

  ...
```

Why do it in a `before_action`? Because this `User` management form is used in multiple places: when creating a new user (`new` action), when re-rendering the form if creating a user fails (`create` action), when editing a user (`edit` action), and when re-rendering the form if editing a user fails (`update` action). You'll need the same data loaded for all four of those actions to render the view successfully, and instead of repeating the same code four times, you can just put it in a `before_action` to define it once. So far so good.

You can then edit the `new` and `edit` templates in app/views/admin/users/ new.html.erb and app/views/admin/users/edit.html.erb to pass that `@projects` variable into your form partial for use. Those two renderings of the form partial should now look like the following.

Listing 8.76 Adding the list of projects to the admin user form partial

```
<%= render "form", user: @user, projects: @projects %>
```

If you refresh the page now, you'll get a different error:

```
ActionView::Template::Error (undefined local variable or method `roles'
for #<#<Class:0x007ff501b56a78>:0x007ff501b55e98>):
    12:    <tr>
    13:      <th><%= label_tag dom_id(project), project.name %></th>
    14:      <td>
    15:        <%= select_tag dom_id(project), options_for_select(roles,
    16:          user.role_on(project)), name: "roles[#{project.id}]",
    17:          include_blank: true %>
    18:      </td>
app/views/admin/users/_form.html.erb:15:in ...
```

You haven't yet defined the `roles` variable or method. What should it be? Rails expects it to be a hash, with the keys matching the display value, and the values matching the value that will be submitted to the server if that option is selected; something like the following:

```
{ 'Manager' => 'manager', 'Editor' => 'editor', 'Viewer' => 'viewer' }
```

You can define a *view helper* method to give you this data. You've written a few view helpers before, for things like page titles and outputting certain HTML for admins only—now you'll write one to generate a list of roles.

Open app/helpers/admin/application_helper.rb, and add a new method definition for `roles` inside the module.

> **Listing 8.77 A naive `roles` definition in `Admin::ApplicationHelper`**

```
module Admin::ApplicationHelper
  def roles
    {
      'Manager' => 'manager',
      'Editor' => 'editor',
      'Viewer' => 'viewer'
    }
  end
end
```

You can do a bit better, though. What if you add new roles? Plus, the display names just look like the name of the role, with a capital letter. What about this instead?

> **Listing 8.78 An improved `roles` definition**

```
module Admin::ApplicationHelper
  def roles
    hash = {}
    %w(manager editor viewer).each do |role|
      hash[role.titleize] = role
    end
    hash
  end
end
```

Now you only list the names of the roles once, using Ruby's special `%w()` notation, which is a shortcut for generating an array of strings. Then you build up a hash in the right format by calling Rails' `titleize` helper[5] on each role name. But you're still listing out role names manually, when that information really belongs somewhere else—like in the `Role` model.

You can move that to a method in app/models/role.rb:

---

5 See http://api.rubyonrails.org/classes/ActiveSupport/Inflector.html#method-i-titleize.

```
class Role < ActiveRecord::Base
  ...

  def self.available_roles
    %w(manager editor viewer)
  end
end
```

And now you can call that method in your view helper.

Listing 8.79 The final version of `roles`

```
module Admin::ApplicationHelper
  def roles
    hash = {}

    Role.available_roles.each do |role|
      hash[role.titleize] = role
    end

    hash
  end
end
```

What error do you get when refreshing your user-edit form now?

```
ActionView::Template::Error (undefined method `role_on' for
#<User:0x007ff501cfb338>):
    13:        <th><%= label_tag dom_id(project), project.name %></th>
    14:        <td>
    15:          <%= select_tag dom_id(project), options_for_select(roles,
    16:            user.role_on(project)), name: "roles[#{project.id}]",
    17:            include_blank: true %>
    18:        </td>
    19:      </tr>
  app/views/admin/users/_form.html.erb:16:in ...
```

The nifty helper you were going to write to get the name of the role a user has in a project still needs to be defined. It's looking for the `role_on` method on an instance of the `User` model, so open app/models/user.rb and define the new method at the bottom.

Listing 8.80 An easy way of getting a user's role on a project

```
class User < ActiveRecord::Base
  has_many :roles

  ...

  def role_on(project)
    roles.find_by(project_id: project).try(:name)
  end
end
```

You've added a missing association between the User and Role models, so @user.roles will now give you a list of all of the user's roles across various projects. One of the methods this association provides is find_by—you can find the right Role record that belongs to both the user and project in question.

If the user isn't a member of the project, the find_by(project_id: project) will return nil, so again you use try to prevent errors caused by calling name on nil. If the user is a member of the project, you'll get a Role record from find_by, and then you can call name on it to get a string like "manager" or "editor."

Now, if you refresh your admin-user form, you might see something a bit amazing. As you can see in figure 8.6, it looks like … an unstyled version of your finished product.

Next you can put some nice Bootstrap styling in there.

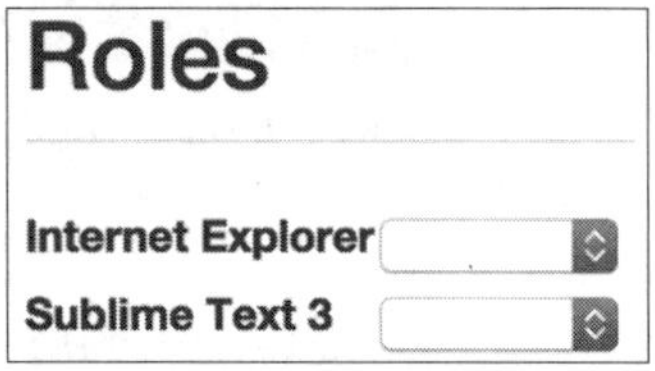

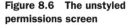

Figure 8.6   The unstyled permissions screen

ADDING BOOTSTRAP STYLING

Because you're not using Simple Form to generate the form, you don't get any of the Bootstrap styles applied for free. You'll need to mix them manually into the HTML structure you've created. Plus, you can make the table a bit cleaner.

Because this code is specific to the users part of the admin area, add the following code to the bottom of app/assets/stylesheets/admin/users.scss.

Listing 8.81   Styles for the `roles` table

```scss
.roles {
  @extend .table;
  @extend .form-horizontal;

  tr:first-child {
    td, th {
      border-top: 0px;
    }
  }

  label {
    @extend .control-label;
  }

  select {
    @extend .form-control;
  }
}
```

Then, like all your other custom Sass files, you'll need to include it into your main application.css.scss file. Open up app/assets/stylesheets/application.css.scss and add an import line for the admin/users.scss file:

```
...
@import "admin/application";
@import "admin/users";
@import "responsive";
...
```

Refresh the edit form, and now you'll see something really amazing (figure 8.7)!

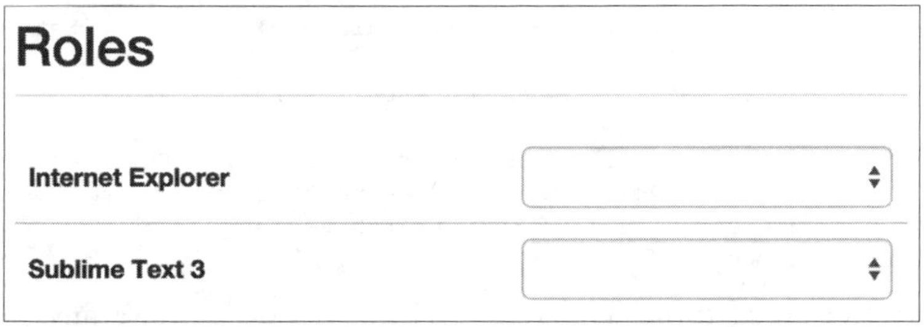

Figure 8.7   The styled permissions screen

It looks really good! You display a list of all the projects in your system, with a select box to select a role for the user on the project.

Have you really finished with this task already? Run `bundle exec rspec spec/ features/admin/managing_roles_spec.rb` to see:

```
1) Admins can manage a user's roles when assigning roles to an existing
   user
   Failure/Error: expect(page).to have_content "Internet Explorer:
   Viewer"
     expected to find text "Internet Explorer: Viewer" in "Ticketee
     Toggle navigation Home Admin Signed in as test1@example.com Sign
     out test2@example.com (User) Edit User Archive User"
```

Not yet, unfortunately. There's nothing role-related on the user details page in the admin area. If you fix that, will you really be finished with the task?

DISPLAYING A USER'S ROLES

Open the show view, in app/views/admin/users/show.html.erb. Add a section for displaying a user's roles at the bottom of the page, as follows.

Listing 8.82   The roles section in app/views/admin/users/show.html.erb

```
<header>
  <h2>Roles</h2>
</header>

<% if @user.roles.any? %>
  <ul>
    <% @user.roles.each do |role| %>
      <li><%= role.project.name %>: <%= role.role.titleize %></li>
    <% end %>
  </ul>
```

```
<% else %>
  <p>This user has no roles.</p>
<% end %>
```

You list the project names with the role name, and if the user doesn't have any roles, you print that out nicely. Great!

Rerun the test and see if it worked:

```
1) Admins can manage a user's roles when assigning roles to an existing
   user
   Failure/Error: expect(page).to have_content "Internet Explorer:
   Viewer"
     expected to find text "Internet Explorer: Viewer" in "Ticketee
     Toggle navigation Home Admin Signed in as test1@example.com Sign
     out test2@example.com (User) Edit User Archive User Roles
     This user has no roles."
```

Of course it wasn't going to be that simple. The user doesn't have any roles—you haven't yet written any code to save the roles you assign in the form. You'll have to fix that next.

8.8.4 Processing the submitted role data

This is a normal user-edit form, so when it gets submitted, it submits to the `update` action of `Admin::UsersController`. You'll need to add some code to that action to process all of the extra role data that you're submitting.

What exactly is the format of the data you're submitting? If you visit the admin user page in your browser and submit some roles for the user, you'll see something like the following in your server logs, in your terminal (formatting added to make it easier to read):

```
Started PATCH "/admin/users/2" for 127.0.0.1 at 2015-03-30 18:14:42 +0800
Processing by Admin::UsersController#update as HTML
  Parameters:
  {
    "utf8" => "?",
    "authenticity_token" => "9lj9dM...",
    "user" =>
    {
      "email" => "admin@ticketee.com",
      "password" => "[FILTERED]",
      "admin" => "1"
    },
    "roles" =>
    {
      "2" => "editor",
      "1" => "manager"
    },
    "commit" => "Update User",
    "id" => "2"
  }
```

Inside the params hash, you have a nested user hash—that's what you're currently using to update the user's details. But you also have a roles hash—this has the IDs of the projects as keys, and the roles you want to assign as values. You can pull out this data in the update action, and update the user's Role records from those.

Open Admin::UsersController and edit the code of the update action with the following.

> **Listing 8.83   The new update action**

```
def update
  if params[:user][:password].blank?
    params[:user].delete(:password)
  end

  User.transaction do
    @user.roles.clear
    role_data = params.fetch(:roles, [])
    role_data.each do |project_id, role_name|
      if role_name.present?
        @user.roles.build(project_id: project_id, role: role_name)
      end
    end

    if @user.update(user_params)
      flash[:notice] = "User has been updated."
      redirect_to admin_users_path
    else
      flash.now[:alert] = "User has not been updated."
      render "edit"
      raise ActiveRecord::Rollback
    end
  end
end
```

The start of the method is the same, but after that you introduce a *database transaction* with User.transaction. You wrap this block around both the code that deals with updating a user's roles—it deletes all of their existing roles and then makes new ones based on the data you submitted—and the code that updates their basic details as before.

The beauty of a database transaction is that either all of the database operations in the transaction block will take place, or none of them will. In this case, if you've changed all the roles, but then you can't update the user because you submitted invalid details (such as if there's a missing email address), the roles shouldn't be changed either. In that scenario, you raise an ActiveRecord::Rollback exception, which will revert, or *roll back*, all of the changes you made to the roles.

At the end of the transaction block, if it hasn't been rolled back, it will be *committed*, or saved, to the database. Perfect.

With this done, everything should work exactly as you expect: you're saving the roles that you assign when you edit a user. Rerun `bundle exec rspec spec/features/ admin/managing_roles_spec.rb` and see if it now passes:

```
1 example, 0 failures
```

Excellent! Do all of the specs still pass? Check with `bundle exec rspec`:

```
82 examples, 0 failures
```

Great! Commit your changes:

```
$ git add .
$ git commit -m "Admins can edit project roles of existing users"
$ git push
```

8.8.5 *Saving roles of new users*

But what about *new* users? This roles section will appear on the new-user form too, but you haven't written any code to save roles that you assign when you create a new user. You can add a spec for that to managing_roles_spec.rb, and see if it passes.

> **Listing 8.84 Another scenario, for assigning roles when creating a new user**

```
scenario "when assigning roles to a new user" do
  visit new_admin_user_path

  fill_in "Email", with: "newuser@ticketee.com"
  fill_in "Password", with: "password"

  select "Editor", from: "Internet Explorer"
  click_button "Create User"

  click_link "newuser@ticketee.com"
  expect(page).to have_content "Internet Explorer: Editor"
  expect(page).not_to have_content "Sublime Text 3"
end
```

If you run that spec with `bundle exec rspec spec/features/admin/managing_roles _spec.rb`, you'll find that it doesn't pass:

```
1) Admins can manage a user's roles when assigning roles to a new user
   Failure/Error: expect(page).to have_content "Internet Explorer:
   Editor"
     expected to find text "Internet Explorer: Editor" in "Ticketee
     Toggle navigation Home Admin Signed in as test3@example.com Sign
     out newuser@ticketee.com (User) Edit User Archive User Roles
     This user has no roles."
```

Nope, no assigned roles. You'll need to include the logic for creating roles to the create action of `Admin::UsersController`, but it can be simpler than in the update action—you don't need to worry about transactions, or anything like that. You can just build the roles for the user, and then save them all in one hit.

Listing 8.85 The new `create` action in `Admin::UsersController`

```
class Admin::UsersController < Admin::ApplicationController
  ...

  def create
    @user = User.new(user_params)
    build_roles_for(@user)
    if @user.save
      ...
```

Because part of the code for the create action is going to be exactly the same as in the update, you should pull it out into a shared method, which we've called build _roles_for.

You can use that same build_roles_for method in the update action.

Listing 8.86 The new `update` action, with common code extracted

```
class Admin::UsersController < Admin::ApplicationController
  ...

  def update
    if params[:user][:password].blank?
      params[:user].delete(:password)
    end

    User.transaction do
      @user.roles.clear
      build_roles_for(@user)

      if @user.update(user_params)
        ...
```

Then you can build the build_roles_for method at the bottom of the controller, underneath the set_projects method, with the code you just removed from the update action.

Listing 8.87 The new `build_roles_for` method

```
def build_roles_for(user)
  role_data = params.fetch(:roles, [])
  role_data.each do |project_id, role_name|
    if role_name.present?
      user.roles.build(project_id: project_id, role: role_name)
    end
  end
end
```

Now does your managing_roles_spec.rb pass?

```
2 examples, 0 failures
```

Run `bundle exec rspec` to make sure nothing else is broken:

```
83 examples, 0 failures
```

Fantastic! You can commit your fixes so that admins can now create new users and assign roles to them at the same time:

```
$ git add .
$ git commit -m "Roles can also be assigned when admins create new users"
$ git push
```

Now there's a way for admin users of your application to assign roles to all kinds of users, so that they're able to view projects as well as create, edit, and update tickets for those projects. While implementing this, you've learned how you can update multiple records at the same time.

8.9   Summary

This chapter covered implementing authorization for your application and setting up a permissions-based system for both `ProjectsController` and `TicketsController`.

You started with a `Role` model, which defined named roles for a user on any specific project.

Then you used the Pundit gem to translate those named roles into actual permissions—a user with a role of *viewer* on a project has read-only access to the entire project. You used Pundit in your controllers to ensure that users were allowed to access the actions they accessed, as well as only showing links in views if the user had permission to carry out the task that the link performed.

You also implemented a way for admins to change a user's roles through the admin back end of the system by displaying a list of all projects, and the available roles for each project. You tweaked the existing `create` and `update` actions in your `Admin::UsersController` to also update multiple roles, and you learned a little bit about using transactions as well.

In chapter 9, you'll learn how to attach files to tickets. File uploading is an essential part of any ticket-tracking application, because files can provide that additional piece of context required for a ticket, such as a screenshot, a patch, or any type of file. You'll also learn some CoffeeScript to make it easy to upload any number of files, and some strategies for testing JavaScript.

File uploading

9

This chapter covers

- Attaching files to Active Record models using the CarrierWave gem
- Securing file uploads by serving them via a controller
- An introduction to writing JavaScript using CoffeeScript
- Listening and responding to Rails' JavaScript events

In chapter 8, you learned how to restrict access to specific actions in your application, such as viewing projects and creating tickets, by defining a Role model that keeps track of which users have which roles on which projects. Ticketee's getting pretty useful now. This chapter focuses on file uploading, the next logical step in a ticket tracking application.

Sometimes, when people file a ticket on an application such as Ticketee, they want to attach a file to provide more information for that ticket, because words alone can only describe so much. For example, a ticket description saying "This button should move up a bit" could be better explained with a picture showing where the button is now and where it should be. Users may want to attach any kind of file: a picture, a crash log, a text file, you name it. Currently, Ticketee has no way to attach files to the ticket; people would have to upload them elsewhere and then include a link with their ticket description.

By providing Ticketee with the functionality to attach files to the ticket, you give the project owners a useful context that will help them more easily understand what the ticket creator means. Luckily, a gem called CarrierWave allows you to implement this feature easily.

Once you're familiar with CarrierWave, you'll change your application to accept multiple files attached to the same ticket using a JavaScript library called jQuery (which comes with Rails by default, through the jquery-rails gem) and some custom JavaScript code of your own. Because you'll use JavaScript, you'll have to alter the way you test parts of your application. To test JavaScript functionality, you'll use Web-Driver, which is a framework built for automatic control of web browsers. WebDriver is especially handy because you can follow the same steps you use for standard Capybara tests, and Capybara will take care of driving the browser. By running the tests in the browser, you ensure that the JavaScript on the page will be executed, and then you can run the tests on the results. Pretty handy!

WEBDRIVER   There's a great post explaining WebDriver on the Google Open Source blog: http://mng.bz/2Y3k.

Finally, you'll see how you can restrict access to the files contained in your application's projects so that confidential information isn't shared with people who don't have access to a particular project.

File uploading is also useful in other types of applications. Suppose you wrote a Rails application for a book. You could upload the chapters to this application, and then people could provide notes on those chapters. Another example is a photo gallery application that allows you to upload images of your favorite cars for people to vote on. File uploading has many different uses and is a cornerstone of many Rails applications.

9.1   *Attaching a file*

The first step in enabling users to upload files is to let them attach files when they begin creating a ticket. As explained before, files attached to tickets can provide useful context about what feature a user is requesting or can point out a specific bug. A picture is worth a thousand words, as they say. It doesn't have to be an image; it can be any type of file. This kind of context is key to solving tickets.

To provide this functionality, you must add a file-upload box to the new ticket page, which allows users to select a file to upload. When the form is submitted, the file is submitted along with it. You'll use the CarrierWave gem to store the file in your application's directory.

9.1.1 A feature featuring files

You first need to write a scenario to make sure the functionality works. This scenario will show you how to deal with file uploads when creating a ticket. Users should be able to create a ticket, and then select a file and upload it. Then they should be able to see this file, along with the other ticket details, on the ticket's page. They may choose to click the filename, which would download the file.

You can test all this by adding a scenario at the bottom of spec/features/creating_tickets_spec.rb that creates a ticket with an attachment, as shown in the following listing.

> **BLINK, BLINK, BLINK** This attachment references the blink tag. Note that although the blink tag was once a part of HTML, you should never use it. The same goes for the marquee tag. We reference them in our text files to add some light humor to the scenario, not because documentation for these tags is a good idea.

Listing 9.1 spec/features/creating_tickets_spec.rb

```
RSpec.feature "Users can create new tickets" do
  ...

  scenario "with an attachment" do
    fill_in "Name", with: "Add documentation for blink tag"
    fill_in "Description", with: "The blink tag has a speed attribute"
    attach_file "File", "spec/fixtures/speed.txt"
    click_button "Create Ticket"

    expect(page).to have_content "Ticket has been created."

    within("#ticket .attachment") do
      expect(page).to have_content "speed.txt"
    end
  end
end
```

This feature introduces a new concept: the attach_file method of this scenario, which attaches the file found at the specified path to the specified field. The path here is deliberately set in the spec/fixtures directory because you may use this file for functional tests later. This directory would usually be used for test fixtures, but at the moment you don't have any.[1] Create the spec/fixtures/speed.txt file, and fill it with some random filler text like this:

```
The blink tag can blink faster if you use the speed="hyper" attribute.
```

---

[1] Nor will you ever, because factories replace them in your application.

Try running this feature using `bundle exec rspec spec/features/creating_tickets _spec.rb` and see how far you get. It fails on the `attach_file` line because the `File` field isn't available yet:

```
1) Users can create new tickets with an attachment
   Failure/Error: attach_file "File", "spec/fixtures/speed.txt"
   Capybara::ElementNotFound:
     Unable to find file field "File"
```

Add the `File` field to the ticket form partial directly under the `<%= f.input :description %>` field, using the code in the following listing.

Listing 9.2   app/views/tickets/_form.html.erb

```
<%= f.input :attachment, as: :file, label: "File" %>
```

You call this field `attachment` internally, but the user will see "File." We've used *attachment* rather than *file* for naming because there's already a `File` class in Ruby. `Attachment` is a good alternative, and it describes well what you're doing—adding attachments to a ticket.

If you run `bundle exec rspec spec/features/creating_tickets_spec.rb` again, it fails with this error:

```
1) Users can create new tickets with an attachment
   Failure/Error: within("#ticket .attachment") do
   Capybara::ElementNotFound:
     Unable to find css "#ticket .attachment"
```

Wow, it looks like you're nearly the whole way there already! You've uploaded a file, submitted the form, and you're just missing the display of the file on the ticket page! Well… not so fast. You're uploading a file, that's true, but you're not yet saving it with the ticket file or processing it in any way, so there's not anything yet to display on the ticket page. You'll fix that now, using CarrierWave.

9.1.2   *Enter, stage right: CarrierWave*

Uploading files is something many web applications need to allow, which makes this functionality perfect to put into a gem. The current best-of-breed gem in this area is CarrierWave. CarrierWave makes uploading files easy. When you need more advanced features, such as processing uploaded files or storing them in something like Amazon S3 rather than on your web server, CarrierWave is there to help you, too.

To install CarrierWave, you need to add a line to the Gemfile to tell Bundler that you want to use this gem. Put this under the line specifying the Pundit gem, separated by a line because it's a different type of gem (Pundit has to do with users, and CarrierWave has to do with files).

Listing 9.3   Adding CarrierWave to your Gemfile

```
gem "carrierwave", "~> 0.10.0"
```

Next, run `bundle` to install this gem.

With CarrierWave installed, you can work on defining the `attachment` attribute that your model wants. It's not really an attribute; the error message is misleading in that respect. All it needs is a setter method (`attachment=`), and it would be happy. But you need this method to do more than set an attribute on this object; you need it to accept the uploaded file and store it locally.

CarrierWave lets you define this fairly easily with its `mount_uploader` method. This method goes in the `Ticket` model, it defines the setter method you need, and it gives your application the ability to accept and process this file. Add it to your `Ticket` model with the `mount_uploader` line in the next listing.

Listing 9.4   Adding a file uploader to your `Ticket` model

```
class Ticket < ActiveRecord::Base
  ...
  mount_uploader :attachment, AttachmentUploader
end
```

This `attachment=` method is defined, but you're not done yet.

9.1.3   Using CarrierWave

You've told your `Ticket` model to mount an uploader. Now you just need an actual uploader.

CarrierWave wraps all of the functionality for uploading files into classes called uploaders. You can generate one with a generator provided by CarrierWave.

Listing 9.5   Generating an `AttachmentUploader`

```
$ rails g uploader Attachment
```

This will generate a new file in app/uploaders/attachment_uploader.rb.

To connect the uploader to your `Ticket` model, you also need to add an `attachment` field to the model, so you need a new migration to add the new field. Generate the new migration with the following line:

```
$ rails g migration add_attachment_to_tickets attachment:string
```

> **HOW CARRIERWAVE RECORDS FILES IN YOUR DATABASE** CarrierWave only requires a string field in the database to use with an uploader—it saves the filename of the file in the field. Internally, it has a few methods to generate a full path and URL from that filename—these methods are completely customizable for each uploader.

To run the migration and add the new column to your development environment's database, run `bundle exec rake db:migrate`.

You have one last thing to do: update your controller to allow you to pass in the uploaded attachment when creating or editing a ticket. Change the `ticket_params` method in app/controllers/tickets_controller.rb to look like this:

```
class TicketsController < ApplicationController
  ...
  def ticket_params
    params.require(:ticket).permit(:name, :description, :attachment)
  end
  ...
end
```

Everything should be hooked up correctly now for your file uploading to work. But if you rerun your spec, you'll still get the same error:

```
1) Users can create new tickets with an attachment
   Failure/Error: within("#ticket .attachment") do
   Capybara::ElementNotFound:
     Unable to find css "#ticket .attachment"
```

But now you have the correct data structures in place, so you can look at actually resolving the error.

You can see that the scenario failed because Capybara can't find the text in this element on the show view of `TicketsController`; neither text nor element exists. So let's add some output in the view, to show the details of any file that's been uploaded to the ticket. Spice it up by adding the file size there, too, as shown in the following listing.

Listing 9.6 app/views/tickets/show.html.erb

```erb
<%= simple_format(@ticket.description) %>

<% if @ticket.attachment.present? %>
  <h4>Attachment</h4>
  <div class="attachment">
    <p>
      <%= link_to File.basename(@ticket.attachment.url),
        @ticket.attachment.url %>
      (<%= number_to_human_size(@ticket.attachment.size) %>)
    </p>
  </div>
<% end %>
```

You use the `url` method from the ticket's `attachment` here, with `link_to` to provide the user with a link to download the file.[2] In this case, the URL for this file would be something like http://localhost:3000/uploads/ticket/attachment/1/file.txt.

You've only defined the `attachment` field as a string, but CarrierWave has turned that string into an entire object you can call methods on, simply by mounting an uploader to the field. Magic!

---

[2] Some browsers open certain files as pages rather than downloading them. Modern browsers do so for .txt files and the like.

Where is the route for these uploaded files defined? Well, it's not defined any-where—it's not a route. It's a directory in the public folder of your application, where CarrierWave saves your files by default.

Requests to files from the public directory are handled by the server rather than by Rails, and anybody who enters the URL in their browser can access them. This is bad because the files in a project should be visible only to authorized users. You'll handle that problem later in the chapter.

Under the filename, you display the size of the file, which is stored in the database as the number of bytes. To convert it to a human-readable output, (such as "71 Bytes," which will be displayed for your file), you use the `number_to_human_size` view helper.

With the uploaded file's information now being output in app/views/tickets/show.html.erb, this feature passes when you run `bundle exec rspec spec/features/creating_tickets_spec.rb`:

```
4 examples, 0 failures
```

Awesome! Your files are being uploaded and taken care of by CarrierWave, which stores them at public/uploads. Let's see if your changes have brought destruction or salvation by running `bundle exec rspec`:

```
84 examples, 0 failures
```

Sweet salvation! Commit this but don't push it yet:

```
$ git add .
$ git commit -m "Add the ability to attach a file to a ticket"
```

Have a look at the commit output. It contains this line:

```
create mode 100644 public/uploads/ticket/attachment/1/speed.txt
```

This line is a leftover file from your test, and it shouldn't be committed to the repository because you could be testing using files much larger than this. You can tell Git to ignore the entire public/uploads directory by adding it to the .gitignore file. Open that file, and add the line in the following listing to the bottom.

Listing 9.7 Don't commit uploaded files into your repository!

```
public/uploads
```

This file tells Git which files you don't want versioned. The entire file should look like the following (minus all the comments).

Listing 9.8 .gitignore after adding public/uploads

```
/.bundle
/db/*.sqlite3
/db/*.sqlite3-journal
/log/*
!/log/.keep
/tmp
public/uploads
```

By default, the .bundle directory (for Bundler's configuration), the SQLite3 databases, the logs for the application, and any files in tmp are ignored. With public/uploads added, this directory is now ignored by Git too.

You should also remove this directory from your latest commit, and thankfully Git provides a way to do so by using the three following commands.

> **Listing 9.9   Redoing your last commit without the uploaded `attachment` files**

```
$ git add .gitignore
$ git rm -r public/uploads/ticket/attachment/
$ git commit --amend --reuse-message HEAD
```

The first command will add the updates you made to your .gitignore file to your repository's staging area. The second command will remove any accidentally committed files from your filesystem, and also tell Git to remove them from the repository. The final command will *amend* your latest commit with your newly staged changes, and it will be as if your first commit with this message never existed. The `--reuse-message` `HEAD` option uses the commit message of your latest commit.

You can push this change now:

```
$ git push
```

Great! Now you can attach a file to a ticket. There's a tiny issue, though, that will pop up in the following scenario:

1 A user visits the "Create Ticket" form.
2 They upload a file to the ticket.
3 They submit the form with invalid details, such as a missing title.

The form will be rerendered with the validation error, as you expect, but the uploaded file is now gone. If you then submit the form with valid details, the ticket is created, but with no attached file. We'll fix that minor issue next.

9.1.4   *Persisting uploads when redisplaying a form*

If you submit the new-ticket form but get validation errors, the form should remember that you uploaded a file and repopulate it on the form. This is easy to do with Carrier-Wave—it requires adding another field to the ticket form, called a *cache field*.

You should cover this functionality with a test, so that you know when you've got it working. Inside spec/features/creating_tickets_spec.rb, add another scenario with the following content:

```
scenario "persisting file uploads across form displays" do
  attach_file "File", "spec/fixtures/speed.txt"
  click_button "Create Ticket"

  fill_in "Name", with: "Add documentation for blink tag"
  fill_in "Description", with: "The blink tag has a speed attribute"
  click_button "Create Ticket"
```

```
  within("#ticket .attachment") do
    expect(page).to have_content "speed.txt"
  end
end
```

This nicely encapsulates the steps to re-create the problem. If you run this new spec with `bundle exec rspec spec/features/creating_tickets_spec.rb`, your new scenario will fail:

```
1) Users can create new tickets persisting file uploads across form
   displays
   Failure/Error: within("#ticket .attachment") do
   Capybara::ElementNotFound:
     Unable to find css "#ticket .attachment"
```

The attachment section only gets displayed when you have an attachment to display, so the file upload isn't being saved properly when the form is rerendering.

You can add a cache field to the ticket form in app/views/tickets/_form.html.erb after the `attachment` file field, as in the following listing.

Listing 9.10   The `attachment` cache field, which will cache file uploads

```
<%= simple_form_for([project, ticket]) do |f| %>
  ...
  <%= f.input :attachment, as: :file, label: "File" %>
  <%= f.input :attachment_cache %>
  ...
```

CarrierWave will *cache* any uploaded file into this secondary field when rerendering the form. When rendering with data on an invalid form, it looks like figure 9.1.

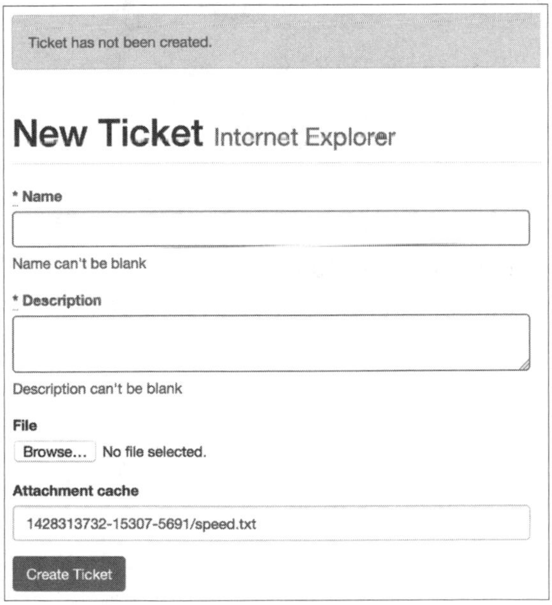

Figure 9.1   New Ticket screen with asset cache

But you don't need to *see* it rendering; you just want it to work seamlessly in the background. You can turn the `attachment_cache` field into a hidden field, which will hide it from view. You can do this with the `:as` option to the input.

Listing 9.11   Making the attachment cache field hidden

```
<%= simple_form_for([project, ticket]) do |f| %>
  ...
  <%= f.input :attachment, as: :file, label: "File" %>
  <%= f.input :attachment_cache, as: :hidden %>
  ...
```

Refresh the page, and the attachment cache field is now hidden. But will your test pass? Check with `bundle exec rspec spec/features/creating_tickets_spec.rb`:

```
1) Users can create new tickets persisting file uploads across form
   displays
   Failure/Error: within("#ticket .attachment") do
   Capybara::ElementNotFound:
     Unable to find css "#ticket .attachment"
```

Your new spec still isn't passing! Why not?

You missed one important step with your `attachment_cache` field when adding the attachment field—you didn't permit it in your `TicketsController`. The field is getting submitted correctly, but then you're discarding it before you pass the data to the `Ticket` model.

You can fix this by updating the definition of `ticket_params` in `TicketsController`, adding the `attachment_cache` field to the list of permitted parameters.

Listing 9.12   Permitting the `attachment_cache` field in `TicketsController`

```
class TicketsController < ApplicationController
  ...
  def ticket_params
    params.require(:ticket).permit(:name, :description, :attachment,
      :attachment_cache)
  end
  ...
```

Now if you rerun your test, it should pass successfully:

```
5 examples, 0 failures
```

Success. Commit and push your changes:

```
$ git add .
$ git commit -m "File uploads are persisted across form re-displays"
$ git push
```

There's still some work to do, though. What would happen if somebody wanted to add more than one file to a ticket? Let's look at how to do that next.

9.2   *Attaching many files*

You have an interface for attaching a single file to a ticket, but no way for a user to attach more than one. Let's imagine your pretend client asked you to boost the number of file-input fields on this page from one to three.

If you're going to add these three file-input fields to your view, you need more fields in your database to handle them. You could define a new field for each file-upload field, but a much better way to handle this is to add another model.

Creating another model gives you the advantage of being able to scale it to not just three file-input fields, but more if you ever need them. You'll call this model `Attachment`, after the name you gave to `mount _uploader` in the `Ticket` model. When you're done with this feature, you'll see three file-upload fields, as shown in figure 9.2.

You can create new instances of this model through the ticket form by using *nested attributes*. Nested attributes have been a feature of Rails since version 2.3, and they allow the attributes of any kind of association to be passed from the creation or update of a particular resource. In this case, you'll pass nested attributes for a collection of new `Attachment` objects while creating a new `Ticket` model. The best part is that the code to do all this remains the same in the controller.

Figure 9.2   File-upload input fields

9.2.1   *Testing multiple-file upload*

Let's take the scenario for creating a ticket with an attachment from spec/features/ creating_tickets_spec.rb, and update it by adding two file-upload fields. You can also update the name of the scenario, so the entire scenario looks like the following listing.

Listing 9.13   File attachment scenario, spec/features/creating_tickets_spec.rb

```
scenario "with multiple attachments" do
  fill_in "Name", with: "Add documentation for blink tag"
  fill_in "Description", with: "The blink tag has a speed attribute"

  attach_file "File #1", Rails.root.join("spec/fixtures/speed.txt")
  attach_file "File #2", Rails.root.join("spec/fixtures/spin.txt")
  attach_file "File #3", Rails.root.join("spec/fixtures/gradient.txt")

  click_button "Create Ticket"

  expect(page).to have_content "Ticket has been created."

  within("#ticket .attachments") do
    expect(page).to have_content "speed.txt"
    expect(page).to have_content "spin.txt"
    expect(page).to have_content "gradient.txt"
  end
end
```

In this scenario, you attach three files to your ticket and assert that you see them within the `attachments` element, which was previously called `#ticket .attachment` but now has the pluralized name of `#ticket .attachments`.

This version also introduces `Rails.root`, which is a handy shortcut used to refer to the root directory of your Rails application. The `.join` will append the text in parentheses—in this case, the directory and file path.

Now run this single scenario using `bundle exec rspec spec/features/creating_tickets_spec.rb`. It should fail on the first `attach_file` step, because you renamed the label of this field:

```
1) Users can create new tickets with multiple attachments
   Failure/Error: attach_file "File #1",
   Rails.root.join("spec/fixtures/speed.txt")
   Capybara::ElementNotFound:
     Unable to find file field "File #1"
```

9.2.2　Implementing multiple-file upload

To get this step to pass, you can change the label on the field in app/views/tickets/_form.html.erb to "File #1."

Listing 9.14　Renaming the `attachment` field to make the test proceed

```erb
<%= simple_form_for([project, ticket]) do |f| %>
  ...
  <%= f.input :attachment, as: :file, label: "File #1" %>
  ...
```

While you're changing things, you may as well update app/views/tickets/show.html.erb to reflect what you plan to do with your attachments. Instead of a ticket having a single attachment accessible via `@ticket.attachment`, it will have multiple attachments accessible via `@ticket.attachments`. You can then iterate over the attachments and print out the details of each.

Replace the attachment display in app/views/tickets/show.html.erb with the following code.

Listing 9.15　Displaying all the attachments of a ticket, not just one

```erb
<% if @ticket.attachments.any? %>
  <h4>Attachments</h4>
  <div class="attachments">
    <% @ticket.attachments.each do |attachment| %>
      <p>
        <%= link_to File.basename(attachment.file.url),
          attachment.file.url %>
        (<%= number_to_human_size(attachment.file.size) %>)
      </p>
    <% end %>
  </div>
<% end %>
```

When you call any?, it calls the `ActiveRecord::Base` association method, which checks whether there are any attachments on a ticket and returns `true` if there are. Although `attachments` isn't yet defined, you can probably guess what you're about to do.

All these changes combined will help to get your scenario closer to passing, which is a great thing. It won't look like it, though, when you run the entire feature again. Run `bundle exec rspec spec/features/creating_tickets_spec.rb` and several of the scenarios will now fail:

```
1) Users can create new tickets with valid attributes
   Failure/Error: click_button "Create Ticket"
   ActionView::Template::Error:
     undefined method `attachments' for #<Ticket:0x007fd709871af8>
   # ...
   # ./app/views/tickets/show.html.erb:36:in ...

2) Users can create new tickets with multiple attachments
   Failure/Error: attach_file "File #2", Rails.root.join...
   Capybara::FileNotFound:
     cannot attach file, .../spec/fixtures/spin.txt does not exist
     # ...
     # ./spec/features/creating_tickets_spec.rb:48:in ...

3) Users can create new tickets persisting file uploads across form
   displays
   Failure/Error: click_button "Create Ticket"
   ActionView::Template::Error:
     undefined method `attachments' for #<Ticket:0x007fd70a0db180>
   # ...
   # ./app/views/tickets/show.html.erb:36:in ...
```

For now we'll just worry about the multiple-attachments scenario—the rest will fall into place. You can run just one scenario from a file by adding a line number to the end of the command—the multiple-attachments scenario covers lines 43-60 in spec/features/creating_tickets_spec.rb, so you could run just the one scenario with the following command:

```
$ bundle exec rspec spec/features/creating_tickets_spec.rb:43
```

Now you'll just get the one failure to deal with, which is a bit less overwhelming. It's failing because you're now trying to attach three different files to three different file fields, but you have only one file, named speed.txt.

You can fix the error by creating the other files that the spec is asking for—spin.txt and gradient.txt—within the same spec/fixtures folder. Populate them with some goofy content, for the fun of it, as well.

Listing 9.16 spec/fixtures/spin.txt

```
Spinning blink tags have a 200% higher click rate!
```

Listing 9.17   spec/fixtures/gradient.txt

```
Everything looks better with a gradient!
```

This is random filler meant only to provide some easily distinguishable text if you ever need to reference it.

On the next run of `bundle exec rspec spec/features/creating_tickets _spec.rb:43`, the error is now replaced with a new one:

```
1) Users can create new tickets with multiple attachments
   Failure/Error: attach_file "File #2", Rails.root.join...
   Capybara::ElementNotFound:
     Unable to find file field "File #2"
```

You *could* just add another field to the form.

Listing 9.18   One way you could achieve it ...

```
<%= f.input :attachment_2, as: :file, label: "File #2" %>
```

But that's a messy way of going about it. The best way to handle this problem is to have some code automatically present a number of fields—say, three—on the page to the user, with an option to add more if they like. This is possible by using a `has_many` association for attachments on the `Ticket` class, and by using nested attributes with Rails' `fields_for` helper.

This helper defines as many fields as you'd like for an association's records. Remove the two lines from app/views/tickets/_form.html.erb that only allow one file upload (shown in listing 9.19) and replace them with the code in listing 9.20.

Listing 9.19   app/views/tickets/_form.html.erb, showing one `attachment` field

```
<%= f.input :attachment, as: :file, label: "File #1" %>
<%= f.input :attachment_cache, as: :hidden %>
```

Listing 9.20   app/views/tickets/_form.html.erb, with dynamic `attachments` fields

```
<h3>Attachments</h3>
<%= f.simple_fields_for :attachments do |ff| %>
  <%= ff.input :file, as: :file, label: "File ##{ff.index + 1}" %>
  <%= ff.input :file_cache, as: :hidden %>
<% end %>
```

You use `fields_for` (and its Simple Form equivalent, `simple_fields_for`) much in the same way you use `form_for`. You call `simple_fields_for` on the `f` block variable from `form_for`, which tells it you want to define a set of nested fields within the original form. The argument to `simple_fields_for`—`:attachments`—tells Rails the name of the association that should be used for the nested fields. The fields within the `simple_fields_for` block will render once for each element in the association.

When the parent form is submitted, the attributes for each of the `attachment` instances will be nested inside the parent `ticket` hash—you'd expect to have something like the following.

Listing 9.21   The format of the data submitted from the `Ticket` form

```
ticket: {
  name: "Test Ticket",
  description: "Test Ticket's Description",
  attachments_attributes: [
    0: { file: ..., file_cache: ... }
    1: { file: ..., file_cache: ... }
    ...
```

When you run this scenario again with `bundle exec rspec spec/features/ creating_tickets_spec.rb:43`, you get a bit of an unusual error, from earlier in the spec.

```
1) Users can create new tickets with multiple attachments
   Failure/Error: click_link "New Ticket"
   ActionView::Template::Error:
     undefined method `+' for nil:NilClass
   # ./app/views/tickets/_form.html.erb:7:in ...
```

The spec can't render the new-ticket form at all! It's complaining about `undefined method '+' for nil:NilClass`, and the only place you're now calling + is when you call `ff.index + 1`. Why is `ff.index` nil? What is it supposed to be?

From the bottom of the documentation of `fields_for`,[3] `ff.index` should be the index of each object in the array of attachments—the first attachment in the array should give 1, the second attachment should be 2, and so on.

There's one special case, however, which is what you've hit. In order for `fields_for` to work correctly, you need to first configure your parent model—the `Ticket` model—to accept the nested attributes for `attachments` that you'll be submitting. Before you can do that, you need to define the `attachments` association in your `Ticket` model. Defining this association will also stop the other scenarios that are currently failing in the ticket-creation feature from complaining about the missing `attachments` method.

If this `attachments` association is defined on the `Ticket` model and you've declared that your model accepts nested attributes for the association, `fields_for` iterates through the output from this method and renders the fields from `fields_for` for each element. This means a file field will be rendered for every `Attachment` object in the `@ticket.attachments` collection.

You can define this `attachments` method by defining a `has_many` association in your `Ticket` model.

---

[3] See http://api.rubyonrails.org/classes/ActionView/Helpers/FormHelper.html#method-i-fields_for.

Listing 9.22　Adding a new association for attachments

```
class Ticket < ActiveRecord::Base
  belongs_to :project
  belongs_to :author, class_name: "User"
  has_many :attachments, dependent: :destroy
  ...
```

You add `dependent: :destroy` to the association as well, so that if the ticket gets deleted, all of its uploaded files get deleted as well.

Under this `has_many`, you also define that a `Ticket` model needs to accept nested attributes for attachments by using `accepts_nested_attributes_for`.

Listing 9.23　Forms for tickets will now also accept attributes for attachments

```
class Ticket < ActiveRecord::Base
  ...
  accepts_nested_attributes_for :attachments, reject_if: :all_blank
  ...
```

This little helper tells your model to accept attachment attributes along with ticket attributes whenever you call methods like `new`, `build`, and `update`. It will also change how `fields_for` performs in your form, making it reference the `attachments` association, and calling the parameters that get generated in the form `attachments _attributes` rather than `attachments`.

The `reject_if: :all_blank` option/value pair means that if blank values (such as when the user hasn't uploaded a file into the field) are submitted, the data should be ignored. Each file field on the page will be submitted, whether or not the user has uploaded a file into it—and if you're going to display three file fields by default, and the user only uploads one file, then you should ignore the other two fields.

When you run your scenario again with `bundle exec rspec spec/features/ creating_tickets_spec.rb:43`, you'll see that Rails is basically *demanding* that there be an `Attachments` class. So needy!

```
1) Users can create new tickets with multiple attachments
   Failure/Error: click_link "New Ticket"
   ActionView::Template::Error:
     uninitialized constant Ticket::Attachment
```

You'd best get onto that then!

9.2.3　*Using nested attributes*

Your `Attachment` model[4] will have two things—the attachment itself in a string field like you added to the `Ticket` model before, and a reference to the ticket object that the attachment has been added to. To generate this new `Attachment` model in your application, run the model generator:

```
$ rails g model attachment file:string ticket:references
```

---

[4]　Remember that you can't use `File` for a name because it's the name of an existing class in Ruby.

This will generate a migration for your new `Attachment` model, with the two fields you've specified.

There's one other migration you can generate—because you have a whole separate model for attachments now, you can remove the `attachment` field you previously added to your `Ticket` model. You can use the `migration` generator to automatically do this, like so:

```
$ rails g migration remove_attachment_from_tickets attachment:string
```

This will generate a migration that looks like the following.

Listing 9.24   db/migrate/[timestamp]_remove_attachment_from_tickets.rb

```
class RemoveAttachmentFromTickets < ActiveRecord::Migration
  def change
    remove_column :tickets, :attachment, :string
  end
end
```

Making migrations revertible

This might look a little odd—why do you need to know the type of column when you're deleting it? Strictly speaking, you don't—`remove_column :tickets, :attachment` would work just fine when removing the column, but a migration written with the column type can be easily *reverted*, which is the opposite of *running* a migration.

Rails automatically knows how to revert lots of common tasks—for example, the opposite of `create_table` would be `drop_table` to delete the table from the database. In this case, the opposite of `remove_column` would be `add_column`, but in order to add a column to the database, Rails needs to know what type the column is, so you tell Rails that the `attachment` column was of `string` type.

Now the migration can be run both ways—up and down—and the column can easily be both removed and added again.

Now that you have both of your migrations, run them with `bundle exec rake db:migrate`.

When you run the feature spec again with `bundle exec rspec spec/features/creating_tickets_spec.rb:43`, your "File #1" field is now missing:

```
1) Users can create new tickets with multiple attachments
   Failure/Error: attach_file "File #1", Rails.root.join...
   Capybara::ElementNotFound:
     Unable to find file field "File #1"
```

You've gone backward! Or so it seems.

As mentioned earlier, `fields_for` detects that the `attachments` method is defined on your `Ticket` object, and then iterates through each object in this collection, rendering the fields in `fields_for` for each object. When the collection in

@ticket.attachments is empty, the fields_for block won't print anything at all—hence no "File #1" field.

To get this action to render three file-input fields, you must initialize three new Attachment objects, associated to the Ticket object the form uses. You can do this as part of the new action in TicketsController.

Listing 9.25   Adding some attachments to render on the form

```
class TicketsController < ApplicationController
  ...
  def new
    @ticket = @project.tickets.build
    authorize @ticket, :create?
    3.times { @ticket.attachments.build }
  end
  ...
```

The final line of this action calls @ticket.attachments.build three times, which creates the three Attachment objects you need for fields_for. Doing this means that @ticket.attachments will have three new attachments in it, and the fields_for block will display those three objects as three empty file-upload fields, just like you want.

When you run your scenario again, the three fields are available, but the scenario now fails due to an unknown field called file_cache:

```
) Users can create new tickets with multiple attachments
    Failure/Error: click_link "New Ticket"
    ActionView::Template::Error:
      undefined method `file_cache' for #<Attachment:0x007f85152eafd0>
```

file_cache is a method provided by the CarrierWave uploader that you generated earlier and attached to the Ticket model to assist with file uploading. Now you've moved the file uploading to the Attachment model, so you should move the mount_uploader line too, from the Ticket model to the Attachment model.

Listing 9.26   Move this uploader line from the Ticket model...

```
class Ticket < ActiveRecord::Base
  ...
  mount_uploader :attachment, AttachmentUploader
  ...
```

Listing 9.27   ...to the Attachment model where it belongs!

```
class Attachment < ActiveRecord::Base
  ...
  mount_uploader :file, AttachmentUploader
end
```

Once the line has been moved, running the spec again will give a different error:

```
1) Users can create new tickets with multiple attachments
   Failure/Error: within("#ticket .attachments") do
   Capybara::ElementNotFound:
     Unable to find css "#ticket .attachments"
```

Remember this from earlier, when you added the first `attachment` file to the form? It means you need to modify your `ticket_params` method, in your `TicketsController`, to permit the nested attributes you're now submitting from the form. Here's the revised `ticket_params` method inside app/controllers/tickets_controller.rb:

Listing 9.28 Permitting file-related attributes for the nested `Attachment` model

```
class TicketsController < ApplicationController
  ...

  def ticket_params
    params.require(:ticket).permit(:name, :description,
      attachments_attributes: [:file, :file_cache])
  end
  ...
```

Tricky! `:attachment` becomes `:attachments_attributes`, and you also need to say that `attachments_attributes` is an array, and that each element of the array contains inner `file` and `file_cache` fields. This mirrors the structure of your models: a `Ticket` `has_many` attachments, and each `Attachment` has an uploaded file, named `file`. Whew!

This should be all that's required to get the multiple-asset uploading working. Find out by running `bundle exec rspec spec/features/creating_tickets_spec.rb`:

```
1) Users can create new tickets persisting file uploads across form
   displays
   Failure/Error: attach_file "File", "spec/fixtures/speed.txt"
   Capybara::Ambiguous:
     Ambiguous match, found 3 elements matching file field "File"
```

Your second test, to make sure that the file upload is persisted across form redisplays, is now broken—you don't have a "File" field anymore, you have a "File #1" field.

That's a quick fix to make—inside spec/features/creating_tickets_spec.rb, update the "persisting file uploads across form displays" scenario to start off with the following:

```
RSpec.feature "Users can create new tickets" do
  ...

  scenario "persisting file uploads across form displays" do
    attach_file "File #1", "spec/fixtures/speed.txt"
  ...
```

The end of the spec will have to be updated as well—from this,

```
within("#ticket .attachment") do
```

to this:

```
within("#ticket .attachments") do
```

Now when you rerun the specs in spec/features/creating_tickets_spec.rb, you should see this output:

```
5 examples, 0 failures
```

You can rerun all of your specs with `bundle exec rspec` to make sure nothing else is broken:

```
86 examples, 0 failures, 1 pending
```

Nothing's broken, but there's one pending spec that lives in spec/models/attachment_spec.rb. Delete this file now. If you rerun `bundle exec rspec`, you should see no more pending specs:

```
85 examples, 0 failures
```

Awesome—commit and push this:

```
$ git add .
$ git commit -m "Users can now upload 3 files at a time when creating a
  ticket"
$ git push
```

In this section, you set up the form that creates new `Ticket` objects to also upload files and create associated `Attachment` objects, by using nested attributes. This process was made possible by moving the responsibility of handling file uploads out of the `Ticket` model and into the associated `Attachment` model. The `accepts_nested_attributes` call in the `Ticket` model, as well as the `simple_fields_for` call in app/views/tickets/ _form.html.erb, also played vital roles in getting this to work.

You're done with nested attributes! Earlier we mentioned that the files uploaded to your application are publicly available for anybody to access because these files are uploaded to the public directory. Any file in the public directory is served up automatically by any web server, bypassing all the authentication and authorization in your Rails application. This is a bad thing. What if one of the projects in your application has files that should be accessed only by authorized users?

9.3 *Serving files through a controller*

You can solve the issue of unauthorized file access by serving the uploaded files through a controller for your application. Using authorization similar to what you used previously in `ProjectsController` and `TicketsController`, this controller will check that the user attempting to access a file has permission to do so before serving the file.

You're not adding any new functionality for a user to see here; you're just changing how some existing functionality (a user viewing uploaded files) works. Regardless, you should write a feature spec to cover it, with some extra checking in there to make sure it's working via your new controller.

9.3.1 *Testing existing functionality*

Create a new file in spec/features/viewing_attachments_spec.rb, and fill it with the following content.

> **Listing 9.29   spec/features/viewing_attachments_spec.rb**

```
require "rails_helper"

RSpec.feature "Users can view a ticket's attached files" do
  let(:user) { FactoryGirl.create :user }
  let(:project) { FactoryGirl.create :project }
  let(:ticket) { FactoryGirl.create :ticket, project: project,
    author: user }
  let!(:attachment) { FactoryGirl.create :attachment, ticket: ticket,
    file_to_attach: "spec/fixtures/speed.txt" }

  before do
    assign_role!(user, :viewer, project)
    login_as(user)
  end

  scenario "successfully" do
    visit project_ticket_path(project, ticket)
    click_link "speed.txt"

    expect(current_path).to eq attachment_path(attachment)
    expect(page).to have_content "The blink tag can blink faster"
  end
end
```

In this setup, you create a project, a ticket for the project, and an attachment for the ticket; then you test that when you click to view the attachment, you can actually see the content of the attachment. You use known files—the speed.txt file you created in a previous section—so you can match directly on the content of the file.

  If you run this spec with bundle exec rspec spec/features/viewing_attachments _spec.rb, you'll get an error early on:

```
1) Users can view a ticket's attached files successfully
   Failure/Error: let!(:attachment) { FactoryGirl.create :attachment,
   ticket: ticket,
   ArgumentError:
     Factory not registered: attachment
```

You can fix this by defining a new Factory Girl factory for your Attachment model in spec/factories/attachment_factory.rb. You can define it like the following.

> **Listing 9.30   Defining an attachment factory**

```
FactoryGirl.define do
  factory :attachment do
    transient do
```

```
        file_to_attach "spec/fixtures/speed.txt"
      end

      file { File.open file_to_attach }
    end
end
```

You're making the factory a little more complex, so you can make the test a little simpler. To create a new `Attachment` object, you need to open and read the file you want to upload to it—but you don't want to have to write that in every test you build an attachment in. So you use a *transient* attribute[5] for the file—your `Attachment` model doesn't actually have a `file_to_attach` attribute, but you can use the `file_to_attach` attribute you pass to the factory to generate the `file` attribute that you *do* have on the model.

Once the factory is defined, rerunning the spec will give a different error:

```
1) Users can view a ticket's attached files successfully
   Failure/Error: expect(current_path).to eq attachment_path(attachment)
   NoMethodError:
     undefined method `attachment_path' for ...
```

Because you'll be using a controller to serve the files, it makes sense that your controller will have an associated named route—we've called it `attachment_path`.

Now you can move into building your controller with its associated permission checking.

9.3.2 *Protecting attachments*

Like you did earlier when starting to build the authorization system, you'll start with your policy and its permissions. Generate a new Pundit policy for protecting your `Attachment` model:

```
$ rails g pundit:policy attachment
```

This will generate a new policy file in app/policies/attachment_policy.rb and a template spec file in spec/policies/attachment_policy_spec.rb.

Who should have permission to view an attachment? A reasonable assumption might be to allow anyone who has permission to view the ticket that the attachment belongs to.

You can write some tests for that in your spec/policies/attachment_policy_spec.rb file, copying the same format you used for the `TicketPolicy` and `ProjectPolicy` specs.

> **Listing 9.31   Specs for the new `AttachmentPolicy` class**

```
require "rails_helper"

RSpec.describe AttachmentPolicy do
  context "permissions" do
```

---

[5] See the Factory Girl documentation: https://github.com/thoughtbot/factory_girl/blob/master/GETTING_STARTED.md#transient-attributes.

```
      subject { AttachmentPolicy.new(user, attachment) }

      let(:user) { FactoryGirl.create(:user) }
      let(:project) { FactoryGirl.create(:project) }
      let(:ticket) { FactoryGirl.create(:ticket, project: project) }
      let(:attachment) { FactoryGirl.create(:attachment, ticket: ticket) }

      context "for anonymous users" do
        let(:user) { nil }
        it { should_not permit_action :show }
      end

      context "for viewers of the project" do
        before { assign_role!(user, :viewer, project) }
        it { should permit_action :show }
      end

      context "for editors of the project" do
        before { assign_role!(user, :editor, project) }
        it { should permit_action :show }
      end

      context "for managers of the project" do
        before { assign_role!(user, :manager, project) }
        it { should permit_action :show }
      end

      context "for managers of other projects" do
        before do
          assign_role!(user, :manager, FactoryGirl.create(:project))
        end
        it { should_not permit_action :show }
      end

      context "for administrators" do
        let(:user) { FactoryGirl.create :user, :admin }
        it { should permit_action :show }
      end
    end
  end
end
```

The format should look familiar to you—you create an attachment object with Factory Girl, and then cycle through all of the different types of roles that a user can have on the attachment's project, testing if they are allowed to show the attachment in question.

When you run your new specs with bundle exec rspec spec/policies/attachment_policy_spec.rb, you'll get a couple of failures:

```
1) AttachmentPolicy permissions for anonymous users should not permit
   action :show
   Failure/Error: it { should_not permit_action :show }
     AttachmentPolicy does not forbid nil from performing :show? on
     #<Attachment:0x007fa6ca838858>.
   # ./spec/policies/attachment_policy_spec.rb:14:in ...

2) AttachmentPolicy permissions for managers of other projects should
```

```
not permit action :show
Failure/Error: it { should_not permit_action :show }
  AttachmentPolicy does not forbid test4@example.com (User) from
  performing :show? on #<Attachment:0x007fa6c956fbe0>.
# ./spec/policies/attachment_policy_spec.rb:36:in ...
```

By default, the policy allows everyone to show the attachment—even the people that it shouldn't allow. You can fix this by defining a new show? method in the Attachment-Policy class in app/policies/attachment_policy.rb to say that only admins and people who can view the project can view the attachment.

Listing 9.32   A new `show?` method defining who can view an attachment

```
class AttachmentPolicy < ApplicationPolicy
  ...
  def show?
    user.try(:admin?) || record.ticket.project.has_member?(user)
  end
end
```

When you rerun bundle exec rspec spec/policies/attachment_policy_spec.rb, everything will pass:

```
6 examples, 0 failures
```

To protect the attachments with this new policy, you need to configure CarrierWave to not store them in the public directory. Instead, you'll store them outside the public directory and create a new controller that will perform the authorization checking. Once the authorization checks are satisfied, then the controller can serve the attachment to the browser. We'll look at doing that now.

9.3.3   *Showing your attachments*

You can start by generating a new controller to show the attachments to the users—we'll be very imaginative and call it AttachmentsController. It should only have one action—show—so you can generate it with the following command:

```
$ rails g controller attachments
```

This will generate a new empty controller in app/controllers/attachments _controller.rb. Inside it, you can define a new show action, look up the correct Attachment record, and then use send_file to send the attachment's file to the browser.

Listing 9.33   app/controllers/attachments_controller.rb

```
class AttachmentsController < ApplicationController
  def show
    attachment = Attachment.find(params[:id])
    authorize attachment, :show?
    send_file attachment.file.path, disposition: :inline
  end
end
```

The send_file method sends a file as the response from the action rather than rendering a template or redirecting. The first argument for send_file is the path to the file you're sending.[6] The next argument is an options hash—you'll only use one option, the disposition option. This is used to tell the browser whether to download the file or display it directly—the default value (attachment) will download it, so you need to change it to inline to display it instead.

To route requests to this controller, define a route in your config/routes.rb file, which you can do with the following resources line.

Listing 9.34   Defining the routes to serve attachments with

```
Rails.application.routes.draw do
  ...
  resources :attachments, only: [:show]
end
```

> **CUSTOMIZING WHICH ROUTES ARE GENERATED WITH RESOURCES**   You use only: [:show] because you only have the one show action in your controller, so you only need the one route instead of the full set of seven RESTful routes.

Great! You've begun to serve the files from AttachmentsController only to people who have access to the attachment's relative projects. Defining the route for the attachments resource will also generate the named attachment_path route, so your original test will get a little further.

You can rerun it to see what you need to do next, with bundle exec rspec spec/ features/viewing_attachments_spec.rb:

```
1) Users can view a ticket's attached files successfully
   Failure/Error: expect(current_path).to eq attachment_path(attachment)

      expected: "/attachments/1"
           got: "/uploads/attachment/file/1/speed.txt"
```

The link to an attachment in the view is still using the old route in public, and not the new route you defined. Also, all of the attachments are still located in public/uploads, so requests to them will be served by the web server, bypassing your controller. These files need to move.

9.3.4   *Public attachments*

People can still get to your files as long as they have the link provided to them, because the files are stored in the public folder.

Let's see how this is possible by starting up the server using rails server, signing in, and creating a ticket. Upload the spec/fixtures/spin.txt file as the only file attached to this ticket. You should see a ticket like the one in figure 9.3.

---

[6] See the Rails documentation for send_file: http://api.rubyonrails.org/classes/ActionController/ DataStreaming.html#method-i-send_file.

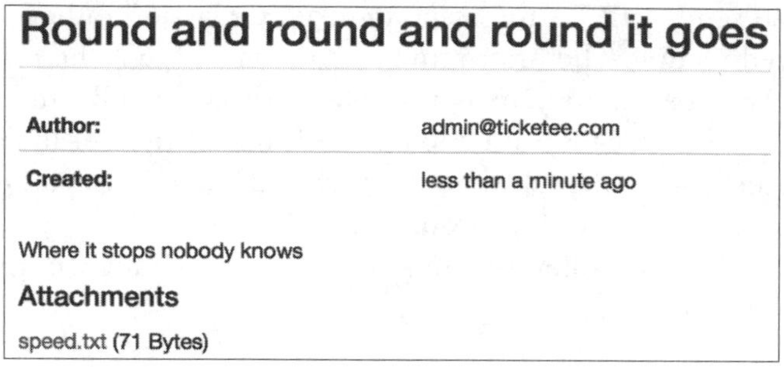

Round and round and round it goes

Author:	admin@ticketee.com
Created:	less than a minute ago

Where it stops nobody knows

Attachments

speed.txt (71 Bytes)

Figure 9.3   A ticket with spin!

Hover over the spin.txt link on this page and you'll see a link like this:

```
http://localhost:3000/uploads/attachment/file/1/spin.txt
```

As you saw earlier in this chapter, this link isn't a route to a controller in your application but to a file in the public directory. Any file in the public directory is accessible to the public. Sensible naming schemes rock!

If you copy the link to this file, sign out, and then paste the link into your browser window, you can still access it. These files need to be protected, and you can do that by moving them out of the public directory and into another directory at the root of your application called *uploads*. Create this directory now.

9.3.5   *Privatizing attachments*

You can make the uploaded files private by storing them in the uploads folder, outside of the public folder. You don't have to move them there manually; you can tell Carrier-Wave to put them there by default. There are a couple of ways you can do this.

If you want to configure a single uploader to store its files outside of the public folder, you can do this by changing the `store_dir` method in the uploader. In the `AttachmentUploader` example, you could change it to look like the following listing.

Listing 9.35   Changing where the `AttachmentUploader` will store its files

```
class AttachmentUploader < CarrierWave::Uploader::Base
  ...
  def store_dir
    Rails.root.join "uploads/#{model.class.to_s.underscore}/" + \
      "#{mounted_as}/#{model.id}"
  end
  ...
```

Alternatively, if you want to configure CarrierWave to store *all* files for *all* uploaders outside of the public folder, you can change the value of `CarrierWave.root`, which defaults to the public folder. You can do this by creating a new *initializer* file in config/initializers—files in this folder are run when you start up your server with `rails server`.

Listing 9.36 A new initializer in config/initializers/carrierwave.rb

```
CarrierWave.configure do |config|
  config.root = Rails.root
end
```

For this example, you can take the second approach, to secure all uploads in your app by default.

After creating the new initializer file, you'll need to stop and start your `rails server`, to make sure the new configuration is picked up by the server. Try creating another ticket and attaching the spec/fixtures/spin.txt file. This time, when you use the link to access the file, you're told there's no route. This is shown in figure 9.4.

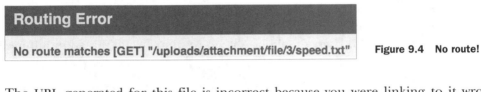

Routing Error

No route matches [GET] "/uploads/attachment/file/3/speed.txt"   Figure 9.4   No route!

The URL generated for this file is incorrect because you were linking to it wrong. You're relying on CarrierWave to generate a URL with `attachment.file.url`, but you want to use the new `attachment_path` route. Modify app/views/tickets/show.html.erb to use `attachment_path`.

Listing 9.37 Using `attachment_path` to link to your new `AttachmentsController`

```
<% @ticket.attachments.each do |attachment| %>
  <p>
    <%= link_to File.basename(attachment.file.url),
      attachment_path(attachment) %>
    (<%= number_to_human_size(attachment.file.size) %>)
  </p>
<% end %>
```

Now, if you refresh the browser, you should be able to see the spin.txt file you uploaded to your ticket. Success!

Run your tests now to see if they all pass, with `bundle exec rspec`:

```
93 examples, 0 failures, 1 pending
```

You have one pending test in spec/helpers/attachments_helper_spec.rb that was generated when you generated the controller, which you don't want, so you can just delete it. Once you do that, rerun your specs with `bundle exec rspec`:

```
92 examples, 0 failures
```

Great! With all of your specs passing, the files are being served through the `AttachmentsController` controller correctly. You're done with implementing the functionality to protect attachments from unauthorized access, so you should commit.

One last thing before you do commit all of this work: earlier, you set `.gitignore` to deal with uploads in the public directory, but you've moved them! Go ahead and take the public/ part off of that final line in .gitignore, so it just says uploads. Cool. Commit and push your changes:

```
$ git add .
$ git commit -m "Uploaded attachments are now served through the
  AttachmentsController for extra security"
$ git push
```

By serving these files through AttachmentsController, you can provide a level of control over who can see them and who can't by allowing only those who have access to the attachment's project to have access to the attachment.

Inevitably, somebody's going to want to attach more than three files to a ticket, and then what? Well, you could add more fields until people stop asking for them, or you could be lazy and code a solution to save time. This solution entails putting an "Add another file" link under the final file field in your form that, when clicked, adds another file field. Users should be able to continue to do this ad infinitum. How do you implement this?

You use JavaScript. That's how.

9.4   *Using JavaScript*

You started this chapter with only one file field, and then you moved to three after you realized users might want to upload more than one file to your application. Although having three fields suits the purposes of many users, others may wish to upload yet more files.

You could keep adding file fields until all the users are satisfied, or you could be sensible about it and switch back to using one field and, directly under it, providing a link that, when clicked, adds another file field. Using this solution, you can also clean up your UI a bit by removing extra file fields but allowing users to attach as many files as they like. This is where JavaScript comes in.

When you introduce JavaScript into your application, you have to run any scenarios that rely on it through another piece of software called WebDriver. WebDriver is a browser driver that was installed when the Capybara gem was installed, so you don't have to do anything to set it up. Capybara without WebDriver won't run JavaScript because Capybara doesn't support JavaScript by itself. By running these JavaScript-reliant scenarios through WebDriver, you ensure that the JavaScript will be executed.

One of the great things about this WebDriver and Capybara partnership is that you can use the same old, familiar Capybara steps to test JavaScript behavior.

9.4.1   *JavaScript testing*

Capybara provides an easy way to trigger WebDriver testing. You *tag* a scenario (or feature) with the js: true option, and it launches a new web browser window and tests your code by using the same steps as standard Capybara testing, but in a browser. Isn't that neat?

Let's replace the multiple-attachments scenario in spec/features/creating_tickets _spec.rb with the one in the following listing, to cover what you want to build next.

Listing 9.38 spec/features/creating_tickets_spec.rb

```ruby
RSpec.feature "Users can create new tickets" do
  ...
  scenario "with multiple attachments", js: true do
    fill_in "Name", with: "Add documentation for blink tag"
    fill_in "Description", with: "Blink tag's speed attribute"

    attach_file "File #1", Rails.root.join("spec/fixtures/speed.txt")
    click_link "Add another file"

    attach_file "File #2", Rails.root.join("spec/fixtures/spin.txt")
    click_button "Create Ticket"

    expect(page).to have_content "Ticket has been created."

    within("#ticket .attachments") do
      expect(page).to have_content "speed.txt"
      expect(page).to have_content "spin.txt"
    end
  end
  ...
```

The `js: true` option at the top of this scenario tells Capybara that the scenario should use JavaScript, so it should be run in a browser using WebDriver. Also in this scenario, you've filled in only one file field because, as stated before, you're going to reduce the number of initial file fields to one. After filling in this field, you click an "Add another file" link that triggers a JavaScript event, which renders the second file field that you can then fill in. The rest of this scenario remains the same, ensuring that the ticket is created and that you can see the files in the element with the class `attachments`.

If you run this scenario with `bundle exec rspec spec/features/creating_tickets_spec.rb`, you'll see that the test can't even get started:

```
1) Users can create new tickets with multiple attachments
   Failure/Error: visit project_path(project)
   LoadError:
     Capybara's selenium driver is unable to load `selenium-webdriver`,
     please install the gem and add `gem 'selenium-webdriver'` to your
     Gemfile if you are using bundler.
```

The default WebDriver that Capybara uses is called Selenium, and it's located in the selenium-webdriver gem.

This is easy enough to fix—add the `selenium-webdrive` line in the following listing to the section of your Gemfile dealing with test gems.

Listing 9.39 Adding selenium-webdriver to your Gemfile

```ruby
group :test do
  gem "capybara", "~> 2.4"
  gem "factory_girl_rails", "~> 4.5"
  gem "selenium-webdriver", "~> 2.45"
end
```

Now run `bundle` to get the selenium-webdriver gem installed. Once that's done, run the tests again with `bundle exec rspec spec/features/creating_tickets_spec.rb`.

Don't be startled when a new empty browser window pops up on your screen—that's the window being controlled by Selenium. But the window won't do anything, and you'll get an error for your specs:

```
1) Users can create new tickets with multiple attachments
   Failure/Error: Unable to find matching line from backtrace
   ActiveRecord::StatementInvalid:
     SQLite3::BusyException: database is locked: UPDATE "users" SET ...
```

That's strange. Why isn't this scenario working, but the others still are? The only thing that changed was the addition of the `js: true` option to the end of the scenario.

Well, that's exactly the problem. When you pass this option to a scenario, it runs the test using a real browser, and the real browser is running in a different process than the one that's running the tests in your terminal.

9.4.2 *Cleaning the database*

By itself, this isn't a big problem. But in combination with the following line in the spec/rails_helper.rb configuration, a perfect storm is created:

```
config.use_transactional_fixtures = true
```

This line tells RSpec to run all of its tests in individual database transactions. This means a new database transaction is begun at the same time as a test, and then a ROLL-BACK command is issued to revert the database back to a clean state. This is why you can always test using the same database without having to clean out the data after the test run.

Due to this transaction, the data created by the test set up in spec/features/creating _tickets_spec.rb will exist purely in this transaction. It's never committed to the database. When the other thread is spawned for the JavaScript testing and it tries to access the same database, it gets stalled due to the open transaction, and it times out.

There are multiple solutions to this problem (aren't there always!):

- You can disable transactions for JavaScript tests, and use *data truncation* instead. Rather than running each test in a transaction block that's then rolled back at the end of the test, data truncation involves an automatic wipe of the database at the end of each test. To achieve this, you can use a gem called database_cleaner (https://github.com/DatabaseCleaner/database_cleaner).
- You can patch Active Record to allow multiple threads to share the same database connection. This was a solution proposed by José Valim, of the Rails core team, back in 2010.[7] It means you can still use transactions for your tests, so you have to change very little of your code.

---

[7] Bragged about on Twitter—https://twitter.com/josevalim/status/18195382848—and then backed up with code—https://gist.github.com/josevalim/470808.

Each approach has pros and cons—DatabaseCleaner will slow down your tests dramatically, whereas sharing a connection can cause odd, nondeterministic problems if your code is sufficiently complex with threads. We'll opt for the more stable approach, with DatabaseCleaner, but it's good to know what other options are out there.

The database_cleaner gem can be installed into your application by adding this line in the test group of your Gemfile:

```
gem "database_cleaner", "~> 1.4"
```

Run bundle to install this gem now.

To configure the gem, create a new file at spec/support/database_cleaning.rb and put the following content into it.

Listing 9.40 Configuring DatabaseCleaner for test awesomeness

```
RSpec.configure do |config|
  config.before(:suite) do
    DatabaseCleaner.strategy = :deletion
    DatabaseCleaner.clean_with(:deletion)
  end

  config.before(:each) do
    DatabaseCleaner.start
  end

  config.after(:each) do
    DatabaseCleaner.clean
  end
end
```

You also need to change the use_transactional_fixtures line in spec/rails_helper.rb to set this option to false.

Listing 9.41 Disabling database transactions for tests

```
config.use_transactional_fixtures = false
```

With these changes, the database will be truncated after every test run. It's significantly slower than using database transactions, but it will allow data to be shared between your tests and your Selenium thread safely and securely. If you wanted to get fancy, you could configure different strategies for different types of tests—you only need to use truncation for feature specs that are tagged with js: true, and you could use transaction for everything else. If you get too annoyed with the speed of your specs, look at doing that for a bit of homework.

When you run bundle exec rspec spec/features/creating_tickets_spec.rb now, the spec fails because the "Add another file" link doesn't yet exist:

```
1) Users can create new tickets with multiple attachments
   Failure/Error: click_link "Add another file"
   Capybara::ElementNotFound:
     Unable to find link "Add another file"
```

Before you fix it, however, you can make the form render only a single `attachment` field again. You can do this by changing the `3.times { @ticket.attachments.build }` line in the new action in `TicketsController` to be just `@ticket.attachments.build`.

Listing 9.42   Rendering three `attachment` fields on the new-ticket form

```
class TicketsController < ApplicationController
  ...
  def new
    ...
    3.times { @ticket.attachments.build }
```

By building only one asset to begin with, you show users that they may upload a file. By providing the link to "Add another file," you show them that they may upload more than one if they please. This is the best UI solution because you're not presenting the user with fields they can't use.

It's time to make the "Add another file" link exist and do something useful!

9.4.3   *Introducing jQuery*

The "Add another file" link, when clicked, will trigger an asynchronous call back to the server, which will return the HTML for another file field to be added to the page. Every time this link is clicked, another file field will be added.

For the "Add another file" link to perform the request when it's clicked, you can use the JavaScript framework called jQuery. This is already in use in your application; your application's Gemfile references the jquery-rails gem, which provides the correct jQuery files. It's the task of your app/assets/javascripts/application.js file to include the two jQuery files Rails needs, which it does by using these two lines:

```
//= require jquery
//= require jquery_ujs
```

What is jquery_ujs?

The jquery_ujs asset here includes some Rails-specific code for unobtrusive JavaScript in your application. This provides many helpful features that you've already used, like confirmation dialog boxes that appear when you click a Delete link in your application.

Derek Prior from Thoughtbot did a great write-up on the features of the jquery_ujs file: "A Tour of Rails' jQuery UJS" (http://robots.thoughtbot.com/a-tour-of-rails-jquery-ujs). We recommend having a read.

If you were to remove these two lines from application.js, or if you were to remove the line that includes application.js in the application layout, things such as confirmation boxes on delete requests and asynchronous links would stop working. So please don't remove these lines! The following line in app/views/layouts/application.html.erb are what loads your application.js

Listing 9.43   Loading JavaScript into the application.html.erb layout file

```
<%= javascript_include_tag 'application', 'data-turbolinks-track' =>
  true %>
```

It generates HTML like this:

```
<script src="/assets/jquery-[digest].js?body=1"
  data-turbolinks-track="true"></script>
<script src="/assets/jquery_ujs-[digest].js?body=1"
  data-turbolinks-track="true"></script>
... many more files ...
<script src="/assets/application-[digest].js?body=1"
  data-turbolinks-track="true"></script>
```

The /assets path here is handled by the Sprockets gem, which comes standard with Rails. When this route is requested, the Sprockets gem takes care of serving it. It begins by reading the app/assets/javascripts/application.js file, which by default specifies the following things:

```
//= require jquery
//= require jquery_ujs
//= require turbolinks
//= require_tree .
```

Yours will look a little different, because you've also required bootstrap-sprockets.

Lines in the file prefixed with //= are *directives* that tell Sprockets what to do. The first two directives *require* the jquery and jquery_ujs files from the jquery-rails gem. The jquery file is the jQuery framework itself, and jquery-ujs contains Rails-provided *unobtrusive JavaScript* helpers. As an example, jquery-ujs provides the confirmation box that pops up when you define a :confirm attribute on a link_to helper.

> **DON'T REMOVE JQUERY_UJS!**   You've been warned twice already, but here we go again: be mindful of accidentally removing the jquery_ujs file—it catches a lot of people out. You'll know, because your confirmation boxes will disappear and your delete links won't work in your views either.

The call to require_tree . tells Sprockets to recursively include all JavaScript files for the current directory and those underneath it. This just leaves you with the //= require turbolinks line, which we'll address next.

TO TURBOLINK OR NOT TO TURBOLINK?

By default, Rails 4 ships with a gem called Turbolinks. Turbolinks attempts to speed up your site by overriding the links in your application with JavaScript. Although this is a great thing for mostly server-side sites, it's our opinion that as soon as you start writing some JavaScript, it causes more problems than it's worth.

Fortunately, removing Turbolinks is quite trivial—just follow these three steps:

1 Remove the `gem 'turbolinks'` line from your Gemfile, and then run `bundle` `update` to update your `Gemfile.lock`, so it's truly gone.

2 Remove the `//= require turbolinks` line from app/assets/javascripts/ application.js.

3 Change the stylesheet and JavaScript loading lines near the top of app/views/ layouts/application.html.erb. Afterward, they should look like this:

```
<%= stylesheet_link_tag    'application', media: 'all' %>
<%= javascript_include_tag 'application' %>
```

That was pretty painless, huh? Now your setup is done, so let's define the "Add another file" link.

9.4.4 *Adding more files with JavaScript*

You must add the "Add another file" link to your tickets form at app/views/tickets/ _form.html.erb. Put it under the `end` for `simple_fields_for`, so it's displayed below existing file fields:

```
<h3>Attachments</h3>
...
<p>
  <%= link_to "Add another file", new_attachment_path, remote: true,
    id: "add_file" %>
</p>
```

Here you use the `link_to` method to define a link, and you pass it the `remote: true` option, which tells Rails that you want to generate a link that uses JavaScript to make a background request, called an *asynchronous request,* to the server. More precisely, the request uses the JavaScript provided by the jquery-ujs.js file that comes with the jquery-rails gem. You've also given the link an HTML ID—this is so you can easily find it from JavaScript later.

Eventually, you'll want this link to return some HTML for the new-form field that you can then insert into the right part of the page. But at the moment there's no clear place to insert it. If you wrap all of the file fields into a new `div` element, it will be easier to do—you can just say "insert it at the end of this `div`."

Listing 9.44   app/views/tickets/_form.html.erb with an added wrapper `div`

```
<div id="attachments">
  <h3>Attachments</h3>
  <% index = 0 %>
  <%= f.simple_fields_for :attachments, child_index: index do |ff| %>
    <%= ff.input :file, as: :file, label: "File ##{index += 1}" %>
    <%= ff.input :file_cache, as: :hidden %>
  <% end %>
</div>
```

This code also changes `ff.index` to be just `index`, a variable you define specially before you start looping over the attachments, and set it as the `child_index` for `simple_fields_for`. This will manually set the index of each of the child attachment objects. If you were to initially set `index` to 3, then your assets would be submitted with indexes 3, 4, 5, like in the next listing.

> **Listing 9.45 Changing the `index` value changes the data submitted**

```
ticket: {
  name: "Test Ticket",
  description: "Test Ticket's Description",
  attachments_attributes: [
    3: { file: ..., file_cache: ... }
    4: { file: ..., file_cache: ... }
    5: { file: ..., file_cache: ... }
    ...
```

You'll use this to manually set the index shortly, when you generate new fields for the form.

Now when you rerun your spec with `bundle exec rspec spec/features/creating _tickets_spec.rb`, all of the scenarios in the feature will fail for the same reason:

```
1) Users can create new tickets with valid attributes
   Failure/Error: click_link "New Ticket"
   ActionView::Template::Error:
     undefined local variable or method `new_attachment_path' for ...
```

The "Add another file" link uses the `new_attachment_path` route, but the route doesn't yet exist. It should point to the `new` action of the `AttachmentsController`, so you can edit the routes you wrote in the previous section to add the `new` action.

> **Listing 9.46   config/routes.rb with the added new route**

```
Rails.application.routes.draw do
  ...
  resources :attachments, only: [:show, :new]
end
```

This action isn't defined at the moment, so the feature still won't work. Therefore, the next step is to define the action you need.

9.5   *Responding to an asynchronous request*

The job of the `new` action in `AttachmentsController` is to render a single file field for the ticket form, so users can upload another file. This action needs to render the fields for an attachment, which you already do in app/views/tickets/_form.html.erb by using the following lines.

> **Listing 9.47   Rendering out file fields for all of the ticket's attachments**

```
<%= f.simple_fields_for :attachments, child_index: index do |ff| %>
  <%= ff.input :file, as: :file, label: "File ##{index += 1}" %>
  <%= ff.input :file_cache, as: :hidden %>
<% end %>
```

You can reuse this code for the new action in the `AttachmentsController`. The first step in doing that is to move that code into a new partial file, located at app/views/attachments/_form.html.erb.

Back in app/views/tickets/_form.html.erb, you can then replace the lines, and the `index` definition above them, with a call to the partial so that it looks like this:

```
<div id="attachments">
  <h3>Attachments</h3>
  <%= render partial: "attachments/form", locals: { f: f, index: 0 } %>
</div>
```

When you pass the `locals` option to `render`, you can set local variables that can be used in the partial. Local variables in views are usable only in the views or partials in which they're defined, unless you pass them through by using `locals`. You pass through the starting number of your file field and the form builder object for your ticket form.

Now you can start building the `new` action of `AttachmentsController`, which will be rendered when you click the "Add another file" link. Start by defining an empty `new` action in the controller:

```
class AttachmentsController < ApplicationController
  ...

  def new
  end
end
```

This will render the view in app/views/attachments/new.html.erb by default. You can call the `form` partial you just created from this view in nearly the same way that you called it in the tickets/_form partial—you've just removed the "attachments" prefix because it's not needed here.

Listing 9.48   app/views/attachments/new.html.erb

```
<%= render partial: "form", locals: { f: f, index: 0 } %>
```

Now when you rerun the feature with `bundle exec rspec spec/features/creating_tickets_spec.rb`, you'll get a new error:

```
1) Users can create new tickets with multiple attachments
   Failure/Error: Unable to find matching line from backtrace
   ActionView::Template::Error:
     undefined local variable or method `f' for #<#<Class:...
   # ./app/views/attachments/new.html.erb:1:in ...
```

Of course, you haven't defined the `f` variable in your new view. You can do this by wrapping some more form setup around the partial call in app/views/attachments/new.html.erb:

```
<%= fields_for @ticket do |f| %>
  <%= render partial: "form", locals: { f: f, index: 0 } %>
<% end %>
```

This will define the f variable, but it should raise alarm bells in your head, because you haven't defined @ticket yet. Rerunning the spec will verify that this is a problem:

```
1) Users can create new tickets with multiple attachments
   Failure/Error: Unable to find matching line from backtrace
   ActionView::Template::Error:
     undefined method `model_name' for nil:NilClass
   # ...
   # ./app/views/attachments/new.html.erb:1:in ...
```

So @ticket is set to nil. You can define @ticket in the new action of Attachments-Controller to be a new ticket, and then build an attachment for the ticket so that the form renders a form field, as you did in the new action of the TicketsController.

Listing 9.49   The new action of AttachmentsController

```
class AttachmentsController < ApplicationController
  ...
  def new
    @ticket = Ticket.new
    @ticket.attachments.build
    render layout: false
  end
end
```

Here you add the layout option because you don't want to render the layout of the page when making this request—the navigation and header and anything else on the page. You just want to render the new view with none of the wrappers around it. And because the Ticket object for your form is only a new record, it isn't important precisely what object it is; all new Ticket objects are the same until they're saved to the database and given a unique identifier.

If you run the ticket-creation feature now using bundle exec rspec spec/features/ creating_tickets_spec.rb, you'll see this error come up:

```
1) Users can create new tickets with multiple attachments
   Failure/Error: Unable to find matching line from backtrace
   Pundit::AuthorizationNotPerformedError:
     Pundit::AuthorizationNotPerformedError
```

How should you authorize this action? You don't have any kind of identifying information about the ticket, or the project, so you can't make sure that the user has access to the project. Should you just skip authorization? Are any kittens going to be harmed if some user accidentally gets access to this action and sees a couple of empty form fields? No, not really. So let's skip authorization for this action by adding a skip_after _action at the top of the controller.

Listing 9.50   Skipping authorization for the new action—it won't hurt anyone

```
class AttachmentsController < ApplicationController
  skip_after_action :verify_authorized, only: [:new]

  ...
```

When you rerun bundle exec rspec spec/features/creating_tickets_spec.rb, you now see that it's unable to see the second file field on this page:

```
1) Users can create new tickets with multiple attachments
   Failure/Error: attach_file "File #2", Rails.root.join...
   Capybara::ElementNotFound:
     Unable to find file field "File #2"
```

Clicking the link to "Add another file" is working without raising any errors, but it's not actually adding the new form fields to the page. You need to fix this by writing some code to handle the response.

9.5.1 *Appending new content to the form*

You've configured your "Add another file" link to perform a JavaScript request for the HTML, by providing the remote: true option. This request is performed by the jquery-ujs helper, and it provides a lot of *events* that you can hook into with your own JavaScript. For example, you can intercept the request before it's made by listening for the ajax:before event, or deal with any error that gets raised by the request by listening for the ajax:error event.

Let's look at some CoffeeScript, which you can use to start listening for these special events.

LEARNING COFFEESCRIPT

CoffeeScript is, in the words of its website, "a little language that compiles into JavaScript." It's written in a simple syntax, like this:

```
square = (x) -> x * x
```

This code compiles into the following JavaScript code:

```
var square;
square = function(x) {
  return x * x;
};
```

In the CoffeeScript version, you define a variable called square. Because this isn't yet initialized, it's set up using var square; in the JavaScript output. You assign a function to this variable, specifying the arguments using parentheses (x) and then specifying the code of the function after ->. The code in the function in this case is converted into literal JavaScript, making this function take an argument, multiply it by itself, and return the result.

Although this is a pretty basic example of CoffeeScript, it shows off the language's power. What you'd write with four lines of JavaScript requires just one line of extremely easy-to-understand CoffeeScript.

Each time you generate a controller using Rails, a new file called app/assets/javascripts/[controller_name].coffee is created (as long as you have the coffee-rails gem in your Gemfile). This file is created so you have a location to put CoffeeScript code that's specific to views for the relevant controller. This is helpful in your situation, because you're going to use CoffeeScript to handle the response from the "Add another file" link.

Open app/assets/javascripts/tickets.coffee, and let's build up the function line by line so you can understand what you're doing. Put this line first:

```
$ ->
```

It seems like a random amalgamation of characters, but this line is helpful. It calls the jQuery $ function[8] and passes it a function as an argument. This line runs the function only when the page has fully loaded.[9] You need this because otherwise the JavaScript would be executed before the link you're going to reference is loaded.

Now add a second line:

```
$ ->
  $("#add_file").on "ajax:success", (event, data) ->
```

This line uses jQuery's $ function to select an element on the page with the ID of add_file, which just happens to correspond to your "Add another file" link. It will *listen* to this link, waiting for it to raise the ajax:success event. When the link raises the event, then the anonymous method defined with the -> at the end of the line will be called with the response from the request in the data parameter.

If this were to be written in plain JavaScript, it would look like this:

```
$(document).ready(function() {
  $("#add_file").on("ajax:success", function(event, data) {
  });
});
```

The CoffeeScript version is a lot less noisy, and much easier to read.

Now add a third line:

```
$ ->
  $("#add_file").on "ajax:success", (event, data) ->
    $("#attachments").append data
```

Here you take the data that gets returned from the request, and you use jQuery's append method to append it to the element with the ID attachments. You used that ID earlier, on the section of the form that wrapped up all of the file fields.

Figure 9.5 shows what happens in the browser when you visit the new-ticket form and click the "Add another file" link a couple of times. You're actually getting the form fields appended on the page!

All that, with just three lines of CoffeeScript. It's a powerful little language. But it's not perfect—you might have noticed that all of your new fields say "File #1," instead of using the next

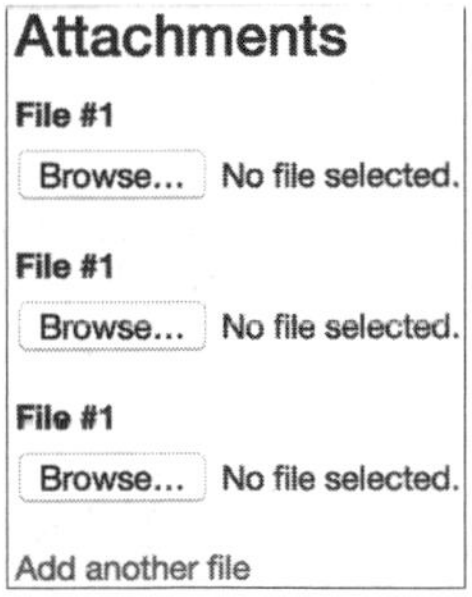

Attachments

File #1
[Browse...] No file selected.

File #1
[Browse...] No file selected.

File #1
[Browse...] No file selected.

Add another file

Figure 9.5   New form fields

---

[8] Aliased from the jQuery function: http://api.jquery.com/jquery/.

[9] For the meaning of *loaded*, see the documentation of the .ready() method: http://api.jquery.com/ready.

number. You can fix that by intercepting the request before it's made, and adding the number that should be shown for the new field.

9.5.2 *Sending parameters for an asynchronous request*

In your `AttachmentsController` new view, you're still just saying that `index` should always be 0 when you pass `index: 0` to the `_form` partial.

Instead of hardcoding 0 in the new view, you can change it to be a variable that you'll assign from the controller.

Listing 9.51   Without hardcoding the `index` to be 0

```
<%= render partial: "form", locals: { f: f, index: @index } %>
```

By default, `@index` will be `nil`. In the new action of `AttachmentsController`, set `@index` to be read from the params that you'll pass in when you make the request:

```
class AttachmentsController < ApplicationController
  ...
  def new
    @index = params[:index].to_i
  ...
```

You've converted `params[:index]` to an integer, because all params are strings by default. Now you just need to submit an `index` variable when you make the request to the `new` action.

What should the variable be? It should be the number of file fields currently on the page. If you have two fields, and you submit `index` as 2, then you increment it by 1 and you'll get back "File #3" for the new third field.

You can take advantage of another feature of jquery-ujs—if you set the `params` data attribute on the link being submitted remotely, then that data will automatically be submitted with the JavaScript request when you click the link.

You can default this data attribute to the number of attachments associated with the ticket, and then increment it every time the link is clicked. In the app/views/tickets/ _form.html.erb view, setting it to 0 can be done like the following.

Listing 9.52   Setting the `params` data attribute in the ticket form

```
<%= link_to "Add another file", new_attachment_path, remote: true,
  id: "add_file", data: { params: {index: ticket.attachments.size} } %>
```

This will generate an HTML link on a new-ticket form that looks like the following:

```
<a id="add_file" data-params="{&quot;index&quot;:1}" data-remote="true"
  href="/attachments/new">Add another file</a>
```

The hash of `{index: 1}` has been encoded and placed inside the `data-params` attribute. If you now click the link with that data attribute set, it will submit the `index` value of 1 to the controller:

```
Started GET "/attachments/new?index=1" for ::1 at [timestamp]
Processing by AttachmentsController#new as JS
  Parameters: {"index"=>"1"}
  ...
```

Now you just need to update it when the link is clicked. You can add a fourth line to the CoffeeScript you wrote earlier, to make it look like this:

```
$ ->
  $("#add_file").on "ajax:success", (event, data) ->
    $("#attachments").append data
    $(this).data "params", { index: $("#attachments div.file").length }
```

This will set the `index` part of the `params` attribute to the number of `#attachment div.file` elements on the page, which is the number of file fields. Every time you click, a new field is added, the length will increase, and the data attribute will be updated and incremented.

That's all there is to it! When your server receives a request at /assets/application.js, the request is handled by the Sprockets gem. The Sprockets gem then combines jquery, jquery_ujs, and app/assets/javascripts/tickets.coffee into one JavaScript file, parsing the CoffeeScript into the following JavaScript:

```
(function() {
  $(function() {
    return $("#add_file").on("ajax:success", function(event, data) {
      $("#attachments").append(data);
      return $(this).data("params", {
        index: $("#attachments div.file").length
      });
    });
  });

}).call(this);
```

This JavaScript is a little more verbose than the CoffeeScript, and it's another great demonstration of how CoffeeScript allows you to write more with less. For more information about and usage examples of CoffeeScript, see the CoffeeScript site: http://coffeescript.org.

Now if you refresh this page and attempt to upload two files, you should see that it works. Does your scenario agree? Find out by running `bundle exec rspec spec/features/creating_tickets_spec.rb`:

```
5 examples, 0 failures
```

Yup, all working! You've switched the ticket form back to providing only one file field, but you've provided a link called "Add another file" that adds another file field on the page every time it's clicked. You originally implemented this link using the `:remote` option for `link_to`, and you added some CoffeeScript magic to work with jquery-ujs to submit an `index` data attribute. A couple of other small changes, and you got it all working neatly again!

This is a great time to see how the application is faring before committing. Run the tests with `bundle exec rspec`. You should see the following:

```
92 examples, 0 failures
```

Awesome! Commit it:

```
$ git add .
$ git commit -m "Provide an 'Add another file' link that uses JavaScript
  so that users can upload more than one file"
$ git push
```

This section showed how you can use JavaScript and CoffeeScript to provide the user with another file field on the page using some basic helpers. JavaScript is a powerful language and is a mainstay of web development that has gained a lot of traction in recent years, thanks to libraries such as the two you saw here, jQuery and CoffeeScript, as well as larger frameworks such as Ember.js and AngularJS.

By using JavaScript, you can provide some great functionality to your users. The best part? Just as you can test your Rails code, you can make sure JavaScript is working by writing tests that use WebDriver.

9.6   *Summary*

This chapter covered two flavors of file uploading: single-file and multiple-file. You first saw how to upload a single file by using the CarrierWave gem to handle the file when it arrives in your application.

After you conquered single-file uploading, you tackled multiple-file uploading. You offloaded the file handling to another model called `Attachment`, which kept a record of each file you uploaded. You passed the files from your form by using nested attributes, which allowed you to create `Attachment` objects related to the ticket being created through the form.

After multiple-file uploading, you learned how to restrict which files are served through your application by serving them through a controller. By using a controller, you could use Pundit's `authorize` helper to determine whether the currently signed-in user has access to the requested attachment's project. If so, you give the user the requested attachment using the `send_file` controller method. If not, you deny all knowledge of the attachment ever having existed.

Finally, you used a JavaScript library called jQuery, in combination with a simpler way of writing JavaScript called CoffeeScript, to provide users with an "Add another file" link that they can click every time they want to add another file to the form. jQuery does more than simple asynchronous requests, though, and if you're interested, the documentation is definitely worth exploring (http://api.jquery.com).

In the next chapter, you'll look at giving tickets a concept of state, which enables users to see which tickets need to be worked on and which are closed. Tickets will also have a default state so they can be easily identified when they're created.

Tracking state

10

This chapter covers

- Adding state to tickets and comments
- Using Active Record callbacks to trigger state changes
- Recording and displaying state transitions
- Securing specific model attributes elements against unauthorized modification

In a ticket-tracking application such as Ticketee, tickets aren't there to provide information about specific problems or suggestions; rather, they're there to provide the workflow for them.

The general workflow of a ticket starts when a user files the ticket; the ticket will be classified as a "New" ticket. When the developers of the project look at this ticket and decide to work on it, they'll switch the state on the ticket to "open," and once they're done they'll mark it as "resolved." If a ticket needs more information, they'll add another state, such as "needs more info." A ticket could also be a duplicate of another ticket, or it could be something that the developers determine isn't worth working on. In cases such as these, the ticket may be marked as "duplicate" or "invalid."

The point is that tickets have a workflow, and that workflow revolves around state changes. In this chapter, you'll allow the admin users to add states, but not to delete them. If an admin were to delete a state that was used, you'd have no record of that state ever existing. It's best that states not be deleted once they've been created and used on a ticket.

Alternatively, states you want to delete could be moved into an "archived" state so they couldn't be assigned to new tickets but still would be visible on older tickets.

To track the states, you'll let users leave a comment. Users will be able to leave a text comment about the ticket and may also elect to change the state of the ticket by selecting another state from a drop-down list. But not all users will be able to leave a comment and change the state—you'll protect both creating a comment and changing the state from unauthorized access. By the time you're done with all of this, the users of your application will have the ability to add comments to tickets. Some users, depending on their permissions, will be able to change the state of a ticket through the comment interface.

You'll begin by creating the interface through which a user will create a comment, and then you'll build the ability for the user to change the state of a ticket. Let's get into it.

10.1   Leaving a comment

The first step is to add the ability to leave a comment. Once you've done so, you'll have a simple form that looks like figure 10.1.

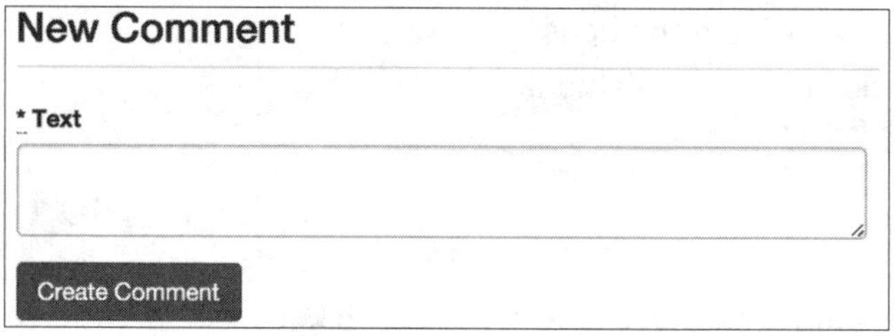

Figure 10.1   The "New Comment" form

To get started, you need to write a Capybara feature that goes through the process of creating a comment. When you're done with this feature, you'll have a comment form at the bottom of the `show` view for the `TicketsController`, which you'll then use as a base for adding a `State` select box later on.

Put this feature in a new file at spec/features/creating_comments_spec.rb and make it look like the following listing.

Listing 10.1   spec/features/creating_comments_spec.rb

```
require "rails_helper"

RSpec.feature "Users can comment on tickets" do
  let(:user) { FactoryGirl.create(:user) }
```

```
let(:project) { FactoryGirl.create(:project) }
let(:ticket) { FactoryGirl.create(:ticket,
  project: project, author: user) }

before do
  login_as(user)
  assign_role!(user, :manager, project)
end

scenario "with valid attributes" do
  visit project_ticket_path(project, ticket)
  fill_in "Text", with: "Added a comment!"
  click_button "Create Comment"

  expect(page).to have_content "Comment has been created."
  within("#comments") do
    expect(page).to have_content "Added a comment!"
  end
end

scenario "with invalid attributes" do
  visit project_ticket_path(project, ticket)
  click_button "Create Comment"

  expect(page).to have_content "Comment has not been created."
  end
end
```

Here you jump straight to the ticket's details page, fill in the comment box with some text, and create your comment. The visiting of the ticket is inside the scenarios rather than in the before block, because you'll use this same feature for permission-checking later on.

Try running this feature now by running bundle exec rspec spec/features/ creating_comments_spec.rb. You'll see this output:

```
1) Users can comment on tickets with valid attributes
   Failure/Error: fill_in "Text", with: "Added a comment!"
   Capybara::ElementNotFound:
     Unable to find field "Text"
   # ...
   # ./spec/features/creating_comments_spec.rb:17:in ...

2) Users can comment on tickets with invalid attributes
   Failure/Error: click_button "Create Comment"
   Capybara::ElementNotFound:
     Unable to find button "Create Comment"
   # ...
   # ./spec/features/creating_comments_spec.rb:27:in ...
```

The failing specs mean that you've got work to do! Start with the first scenario, the "happy" path. The label the spec is looking for is going to belong to the comment box underneath your ticket's information. Neither the label nor the field are there, and that's what the scenario requires, so now's a great time to add them.

10.1.1   *The comment form*

Let's begin to build the comment form for the application. This comment form will initially consist of a single text field into which the user can insert their comment.

Add a single line to the bottom of app/views/tickets/show.html.erb to render a comment form partial:

```
<div id="ticket">
  ...
</div>

<%= render "comments/form", ticket: @ticket, comment: @comment %>
```

This line renders the partial from app/views/comments/_form.html.erb, which you can now create and fill with the content in the following listing.

Listing 10.2   app/views/comments/_form.html.erb

```
<header>
  <h3>New Comment</h3>
</header>

<%= simple_form_for [ticket, comment] do |f| %>
  <%= f.input :text %>
  <%= f.submit class: "btn btn-primary" %>
<% end %>
```

This is pretty much the standard `simple_form_for`, except you use the `Array` argument syntax again, which will generate a nested route.

You need to do four things before this form will work:

1. Define the `@comment` variable in the `show` action of your `TicketsController`. This will reference a new `Comment` instance and give this `simple_form_for` something to work with.

2. Create the `Comment` model and associate it with your `Ticket` model. This is so you can create new comment records from the form and associate them with the right ticket.

3. Define the nested resource in your routes, so that the `simple_form_for` can make a `POST` request to the correct URL—one similar to /tickets/1/comments. The `simple_form_for` will generate the URL by combining the classes of the objects in the array; without this it'll give you an undefined method of `ticket_comments_path`.

4. Generate the `CommentsController` and the `create` action along with it, so that your form has somewhere to go when a user submits it.

Let's look at each of these in turn. First, you need to set up your `TicketsController` to use the `Comment` model for creating new comments. But to do this, you need to first build a new `Comment` object using the `comments` association on your `@ticket` object.

THE COMMENT MODEL

The first step to getting this comment-creation feature working is to define a @comment variable for the form in the show action of your TicketsController. Open up app/controllers/tickets_controller.rb and add the line to define the @comment instance.

Listing 10.3   app/controllers/tickets_controller.rb

```
class TicketsController < ApplicationController
  ...
  def show
    authorize @ticket, :show?
    @comment = @ticket.comments.build
  end
  ...
```

This action will use the build method on the comments association for your @ticket object (which is set up by before_action :set_ticket) to create a new Comment object for the view's form_for.

Next, you need to generate the Comment model, so that you can define the comments association on your Ticket model. This model will need to have an attribute called text for the text from the form, a foreign key to link it to a ticket, and another foreign key to link it to a user record so you know who wrote the comment. You can generate this model using the following command:

```
$ rails g model comment text:text ticket:references author:references
```

This will generate a migration that looks like the following listing.

Listing 10.4   db/migrate/[timestamp]_create_comments.rb

```
class CreateComments < ActiveRecord::Migration
  def change
    create_table .comments do |t|
      t.text :text
      t.references :ticket, index: true, foreign_key: true
      t.references :author, index: true, foreign_key: true

      t.timestamps null: false
    end
  end
end
```

There's just one tiny change you need to make to this file before you can run it, and it's the same change you made to the migration for adding authors to tickets. By default, using foreign_key: true on t.references :author will mean that it tries to make a link to an authors table, which you don't have—an author is actually a user. So you need to remove the foreign_key: true from that line, and manually add another foreign key below. It should look like the following.

Listing 10.5 db/migrate/[timestamp]_create_comments.rb, with fixed foreign keys

```ruby
class CreateComments < ActiveRecord::Migration
  def change
    create_table :comments do |t|
      t.text :text
      t.references :ticket, index: true, foreign_key: true
      t.references :author, index: true

      t.timestamps null: false
    end

    add_foreign_key :comments, :users, column: :author_id
  end
end
```

Once that change is made, you can run the migration for this model on your development database by running this familiar command:

```
$ bundle exec rake db:migrate
```

With that done, your next step is to add the `comments` association to the `Ticket` model. Add this line to app/models/ticket.rb, below the `has_many :attachments` line.

Listing 10.6 Defining the `comments` association for tickets

```ruby
class Ticket < ActiveRecord::Base
  ...
  has_many :comments, dependent: :destroy
  ...
```

You don't need to add any associations to the `Comment` model—the model generator did that automatically when you said that `ticket` and `author` were *references*. But you should add a validation for the `text` field, to make sure the user actually enters some text for the comment. You can do this by adding a validation to app/models/comment.rb. It should now look like the following listing.

Listing 10.7 The complete `Comment` model

```ruby
class Comment < ActiveRecord::Base
  belongs_to :ticket
  belongs_to :author

  validates :text, presence: true
end
```

This will help your second scenario pass, because it requires that an error message be displayed when you don't enter any text.

When you run your feature with `bundle exec rspec spec/features/ creating_comments_spec.rb` at this midpoint, both specs will fail for the same reason—the `simple_form_for` can't find the routing helper it's trying to use:

```
1) Users can comment on tickets with valid attributes
   Failure/Error: visit project_ticket_path(project, ticket)
   ActionView::Template::Error:
     undefined method `ticket_comments_path' for ...

2) Users can comment on tickets with invalid attributes
   Failure/Error: visit project_ticket_path(project, ticket)
   ActionView::Template::Error:
     undefined method `ticket_comments_path' for ...
```

This is because you don't have a nested route for comments inside your `tickets` resource yet. To define one, you'll need to add it to config/routes.rb. Currently in your config/routes.rb you've got the `tickets` resource nested inside the `projects` resource with these lines:

```
resources :projects, only: [:index, :show, :edit, :update] do
  resources :tickets
end
```

This generates helpers such as `project_tickets_path`. But for your form, it's not important what comment the project is being created for; you only care about the ticket, so you can use `ticket_comments_path` instead.

This means you'll need to define a separate non-nested resource for your tickets, and then a nested resource under that for your comments, as shown in the following listing.

> **Listing 10.8   config/routes.rb, now with nested `comments` resources**

```
resources :projects, only: [:index, :show, :edit, :update] do
  resources :tickets
end

resources :tickets, only: [] do
  resources :comments, only: [:create]
end
```

Defining the new tickets resource with `only: []` is a little bit odd, but it works for this scenario. You don't actually want to generate any non-nested ticket routes, like /tickets/2. You're only using this route in conjunction with the nested comments to generate URLs like /tickets/2/comments.

The last three lines in the listing are the lines that define `ticket_comments_path`, which will make your form work. In general, it's a good idea to only go one level deep with the nesting of your resources. It's very rare that you'll need two levels of scoping information—one will usually do just fine.

With a route now defined, that error in your spec will be resolved. If you rerun your specs with `bundle exec rspec spec/features/creating_comments_spec.rb`, you'll get a different error:

```
1) Users can comment on tickets with valid attributes
   Failure/Error: click_button "Create Comment"
   ActionController::RoutingError:
     uninitialized constant CommentsController
```

Creating a `CommentsController` will be your next step.

10.1.2   *The comments controller*

The comments form you created is submitting a POST request to the `create` action of `CommentsController`, so now you need to make it. You can do this by running the following command:

```
$ rails g controller comments
```

A `create` action in this controller will provide the receiving end for the comment form, so you can add this now. You'll need to define a `before_action` in this controller as well, to load the `Ticket` object you'll be creating a comment for. Update your controller to what's shown in the following listing.

> **Listing 10.9   app/controllers/comments_controller.rb**

```ruby
class CommentsController < ApplicationController
  before_action :set_ticket

  def create
    @comment = @ticket.comments.build(comment_params)
    @comment.author = current_user
    authorize @comment, :create?

    if @comment.save
      flash[:notice] = "Comment has been created."
      redirect_to [@ticket.project, @ticket]
    else
      flash.now[:alert] = "Comment has not been created."
      @project = @ticket.project
      render "tickets/show"
    end
  end

private

  def set_ticket
    @ticket = Ticket.find(params[:ticket_id])
  end

  def comment_params
    params.require(:comment).permit(:text)
  end
end
```

Most of this controller should look familiar by now. It's long, but there are no new concepts in it.

In the `create` action, first note the `comment_params`. You only allow the `:text` key to make it through, and neither of the two associations: the author nor the ticket. This is because the author should always be the `current_user`, and you can get the ID of the ticket from the URL, rather than trust some sort of input from the user.

Next, note that if the `@comment` saves successfully, you redirect back to the ticket's page by passing an `Array` argument to `redirect_to`, which compiles the path from the arguments passed in. This is like what `form_for` does to a nested route such as /projects/1/tickets/2.

But if your `@comment.save` returns `false`, you'll actually render the tickets/show view again, which belongs to an entirely different controller. That's okay, you're allowed to do that, but note that you're just rendering the specified view, not running the entire action, so you'll need to set up all the right variables that the view needs to render. That's why you define `@project` to be the ticket's project—you don't need it in this action, but tickets/show needs it to render correctly.

Now when you rerun your spec with `bundle exec rspec spec/features/creating_comments_spec.rb`, the failure message has mutated again:

```
1) Users can comment on tickets with valid attributes
   Failure/Error: click_button "Create Comment"
   NameError:
     uninitialized constant Comment::Author
```

You defined that your comment's association to a user is called `author`, but the class for your author isn't `Author`, it's `User`. You can fix this by specifying the `class_name` option on the `author` association in the `Comment` model. Open up app/models/comment.rb and add the right `class_name` option:

```
class Comment < ActiveRecord::Base
  ...
  belongs_to :author, class_name: "User"
  ...
```

If you have a sharp memory, you might remember that you also had to do this when you added an `author` reference to the `Ticket` model. Your associations don't have to strictly map to your class names, and in some cases they can't. What if, for example, you had some approval process for comments, and you wanted to record who had approved a comment for publishing on the website. That would be a second reference from the `Comment` model to the `User` model—and they couldn't both be called `:user`! Using domain language is much more appropriate. In this hypothetical scenario, you could have both an `author` and an `approver` association, both mapping to the `User` model.

Great. What's failing next? Run your spec with `bundle exec rspec spec/features/creating_comments_spec.rb` again and see:

```
1) Users can comment on tickets with valid attributes
   Failure/Error: click_button "Create Comment"
   Pundit::NotDefinedError:
     unable to find policy CommentPolicy for #<Comment:0x007ff740362880>
```

Ah, that pesky authorization has tripped you up. You'll need to get used to authorizing every action by default and setting up the required policies as you create new models. You're authorizing a new `Comment` model, so Pundit has inferred that you need a new `CommentPolicy` class. You'll create that next.

AUTHORIZING THE COMMENTS CONTROLLER

The permissions for creating comments on tickets in Ticketee will be identical to those for creating a ticket on a project, so we'll go through this section quickly.

You can create the CommentPolicy class with the following command:

```
$ rails g pundit:policy comment
```

You now need to write a set of specs in the generated spec/policies/comment_policy _spec.rb file, very similar to those you wrote earlier in ticket_policy_spec.rb.

Listing 10.10   spec/policies/comment_policy_spec.rb

```ruby
require "rails_helper"

RSpec.describe CommentPolicy do
  context "permissions" do
    subject { CommentPolicy.new(user, comment) }

    let(:user) { FactoryGirl.create(:user) }
    let(:project) { FactoryGirl.create(:project) }
    let(:ticket) { FactoryGirl.create(:ticket, project: project) }
    let(:comment) { FactoryGirl.create(:comment, ticket: ticket) }

    context "for anonymous users" do
      let(:user) { nil }
      it { should_not permit_action :create }
    end

    context "for viewers of the project" do
      before { assign_role!(user, :viewer, project) }
      it { should_not permit_action :create }
    end

    context "for editors of the project" do
      before { assign_role!(user, :editor, project) }
      it { should permit_action :create }
    end

    context "for managers of the project" do
      before { assign_role!(user, :manager, project) }
      it { should permit_action :create }
    end

    context "for managers of other projects" do
      before do
        assign_role!(user, :manager, FactoryGirl.create(:project))
      end
      it { should_not permit_action :create }
    end

    context "for administrators" do
      let(:user) { FactoryGirl.create :user, :admin }
      it { should permit_action :create }
    end
  end
end
```

To get these specs running, you'll need to define a `Comment` factory. You can do so with the code from the following listing, in spec/factories/comment_factory.rb.

Listing 10.11 A new shiny `Comment` factory

```
FactoryGirl.define do
  factory :comment do
    text { "A comment describing some changes that should be made
      to this ticket." }
  end
end
```

Now when you run the new policy specs with `bundle exec rspec spec/policies/comment_policy_spec.rb`, you'll get several failures:

```
1) CommentPolicy permissions for editors of the project should permit
   action :create
   Failure/Error: it { should permit_action :create }
     CommentPolicy does not allow test2@example.com (User) to perform
     :create? on #<Comment:0x007fc4e14e5d10>.
   # ./spec/policies/comment_policy_spec.rb:24:in ...

2) CommentPolicy permissions for managers of the project should permit
   action :create
   Failure/Error: it { should permit_action :create }
     CommentPolicy does not allow test3@example.com (User) to perform
     :create? on #<Comment:0x007fc4dc36ab48>.
   # ./spec/policies/comment_policy_spec.rb:29:in ...

3) CommentPolicy permissions for administrators should permit action
   :create
   Failure/Error: it { should permit_action :create }
     CommentPolicy does not allow test5@example.com (Admin) to perform
     :create? on #<Comment:0x007fc4e2a3a828>.
   # ./spec/policies/comment_policy_spec.rb:41:in ...
```

Like before, creating new objects is denied to all users by default, so you need to manually add rules to allow the users who can create tickets through. You can be a little bit clever about it, however, because the rules for comments will be identical to those for tickets.

You can change your `CommentPolicy` class to *inherit* from your `TicketPolicy` class, as in the following listing.

Listing 10.12 The much shorter `CommentPolicy` class

```
class CommentPolicy < TicketPolicy
end
```

No rules? It can just inherit everything from the parent `TicketPolicy`? Surely it can't be that easy...

```
1) CommentPolicy permissions for anonymous users should not permit
   action :create
   Failure/Error: it { should_not permit_action :create }
   NoMethodError:
     undefined method `project' for #<Comment:0x007fc68ed46b40>
...
```

Unfortunately it's not that easy. The create? method in TicketPolicy looks like the following listing.

```
class TicketPolicy < ApplicationPolicy
  ...
  def create?
    user.try(:admin?) || record.project.has_manager?(user) ||
      record.project.has_editor?(user)
  end
```

record is now going to be the Comment instance you pass to the policy. You don't have any link between the Comment and Project models yet, so calling record.project is raising an error. The Ticket model does have a link to the Project model though. Can you use that instead?

You can add a link (of sorts) to the Comment model by *delegating* any calls to project to the comment's ticket. Do this by adding the following to app/models/comment.rb.

```
class Comment < ActiveRecord::Base
  ...
  delegate :project, to: :ticket
end
```

This is kind of like a Comment instance saying "if you call project on me, I'm just going to pass the message on to my ticket, and call ticket.project instead." That's all you need to make this work, amazingly! You can verify it with bundle exec rspec spec/policies/comment_policy_spec.rb:

```
6 examples, 0 failures
```

Now that your CommentPolicy specs are passing and you're satisfied that you're correctly authorizing the create action of your CommentsController, you can return to the previously failing comment-creation spec. Run that again with bundle exec rspec spec/features/creating_comments_spec.rb and see what failures shake out:

```
1) Users can comment on tickets with valid attributes
   Failure/Error: within("#comments") do
   Capybara::ElementNotFound:
     Unable to find css "#comments"
```

> ### Shouldn't we just use delegation and inheritance all the time?
>
> Inheritance works really well here because the permission rules for comments and tickets are identical. If the rules for either model were to change significantly, it would be better to change the `CommentPolicy` to extend from `ApplicationPolicy` instead, and define new separate rules inside `CommentPolicy`.
>
> We've also very deliberately left the tests as uncomplicated as possible, while making the code a bit smarter. You can get away with this because you've got the tests to verify the behavior of your code, but if you accidentally introduce a bug into the tests by being too clever, you don't have any more safety nets to catch it.
>
> Your tests should also be a little dumb, and not know the inner workings of the class they're testing. All they care about is input and output.

You're making a lot of progress! You're now able to create a comment in your application, and the "Comment has been created" text displays on the page too. All that's left to do is to show the comment itself.

You made the executive decision to display previous comments on the ticket inside an HTML element with the `id` of `comments`, but you haven't added that element to the `show` template yet.

Add this element to the app/views/tickets/show.html.erb template by adding the following code above the spot where you render the `comment` form partial.

Listing 10.15   app/views/tickets/show.html.erb

```
<header>
  <h3>Comments</h3>
</header>

<div id="comments">
  <% if @ticket.comments.persisted.any? %>
    <%= render @ticket.comments.persisted %>
  <% else %>
    <p>There are no comments for this ticket.</p>
  <% end %>
</div>

<%= render "comments/form", ticket: @ticket, comment: @comment %>
```

Here you create the element that the scenario requires: one with an `id` attribute of `comments`.

You also use a new method here, called `persisted`, on your relation of comments. You need to do this because you've added an *unpersisted* (not saved in the database) comment to the list when you did `@ticket.comments.new`, to render with the comment form. You don't want to display that new comment in your list of all the posted comments, so you'll filter it out.

To do this, you can define a new scope in the `Comment` model. We first looked at scopes in chapter 7 when we looked at filtering out archived users, and you can write another here to filter out unpersisted comments.

Inside the `Comment` model in app/models/comment.rb, add the following scope.

Listing 10.16   Defining a `persisted` scope

```
class Comment < ActiveRecord::Base
  ...
  scope :persisted, lambda { where.not(id: nil) }
  ...
```

It's another very simple scope that simply selects all comments where the `id` field is not `nil`. Any persisted object will have a numerical ID, so this filters out non-persisted ones. Easy.

You also check if there are no comments by using the `any?` method from Active Record and displaying an appropriate no-comments message if this is the case. This will do a light query, similar to the following, to check if there are any comments:

```
SELECT 1 AS one FROM "comments" WHERE "comments"."ticket_id" = 1 LIMIT 1
```

If there are any records in the `comments` table with a `ticket_id` of 1, this just returns the number 1 to Active Record. It also limits the result set to 1, which will stop looking after it finds the first comment on the ticket, resulting in a super-fast query. (You also used `any?` back in chapter 9, when you checked if a ticket had any attachments.)

You could use `empty?` here instead, but that would load the `comments` association in its entirety and then check to see if the array was empty. If there were a lot of comments, this approach would be slow. By using `any?`, you stop this potential performance issue from cropping up.

Inside this `div`, if there are comments, you call `render` and pass it the argument of `@ticket.comments.persisted`.

The use of `render` in this form will cause Rails to render a partial for every single element in this collection and to try to locate the partial using the first object's class name.

Objects in this particular collection are of the `Comment` class, so the partial Rails will try to find will be at app/views/comments/_comment.html.erb. This file doesn't exist yet, but you can create it and fill it with the content from the following listing.

Listing 10.17   app/views/comments/_comment.html.erb

```
<blockquote class="comment">
  <%= simple_format(comment.text) %>
  <footer>
    <%= time_ago_in_words(comment.created_at) %> ago
    by <cite><%= comment.author %></cite>
  </footer>
</blockquote>
```

The class method from this tag is used to style your comments so that they'll look like figure 10.2.

Whoa, the text in those comments is a little big! You can tweak the size of the font with the following style. Place it in app/assets/stylesheets/tickets.scss:

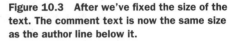

Figure 10.2   A comment, in its natural habitat

```
blockquote.comment p {
  font-size: 14px;
}
```

The new comment style is shown in figure 10.3. Much better.

With the code in place not only to create comments but also to display them, your feature should pass when you run it with bundle exec rspec spec/features/creating_comments_spec.rb:

```
2 examples, 0 failures
```

Figure 10.3   After we've fixed the size of the text. The comment text is now the same size as the author line below it.

With this form added to the ticket's page, users are now able to leave comments on tickets. You've done some authorization in your CommentsController too—viewers of a project can't leave comments, but editors and managers can.

However, you haven't done anything to hide the "New Comment" form on the ticket page. Viewers of a project will still be able to see the form, fill it out, and submit it—and then they'll be told that they're not allowed to do that. It's not a great user experience. You should hide the form if the user doesn't have permission to submit a comment.

You should start by adding some tests to make sure that the form is hidden under some circumstances. In the past you've done this by adding new scenarios to your hidden-links scenario—you can do that again here.

Open spec/features/hidden_links_spec.rb, and add some more scenarios for the "New Comment" form:

```
RSpec.feature "Users can only see the appropriate links" do
  ...

  context "non-admin users (project viewers)" do
    ...

    scenario "cannot see the New Comment form" do
      visit project_ticket_path(project, ticket)
      expect(page).not_to have_heading "New Comment"
    end
  end

  context "admin users" do
    ...
```

```
   scenario "can see the New Comment form" do
     visit project_ticket_path(project, ticket)
     expect(page).to have_heading "New Comment"
   end
 end
```

If you run these specs now with `bundle exec rspec spec/features/hidden_links _spec.rb`, you'll get some failures, but they don't fail for the reasons you might expect:

```
1) Users can only see the appropriate links non-admin users (project
   viewers) cannot see the New Comment form
   Failure/Error: expect(page).not_to have_heading "New Comment"
      expected #<Capybara::Session:0x007fa10e49c918> to respond to
      `has_heading?`
   # ./spec/features/hidden_links_spec.rb:56:in ...

2) Users can only see the appropriate links admin users can see the New
   Comment form
   Failure/Error: expect(page).to have_heading "New Comment"
      expected #<Capybara::Session:0x007fa10e49c918> to respond to
      `has_heading?`
   # ./spec/features/hidden_links_spec.rb:95:in ...
```

You've used a method called `have_heading` in your spec, but that method doesn't exist. In the past you've used methods like `have_content` that haven't existed either, so what's going on? This is a little bit of RSpec magic—internally it will make this translation:

```
# You write this...
expect(page).to have_heading("New Comment")

# and RSpec converts it to this!
expect(page.has_heading?("New Comment")).to be_true
```

The `have_heading` assertion gets converted into the `has_heading?` question. The same thing happens with `have_content`—it gets converted to `has_content?`, which is a method defined in Capybara.[1] You can define your own methods like this—in this case, a `has_heading?` method that will test what you want to test.

This will be another support method that you can use in multiple specs, and as such you should define it in a new file inside the spec/support folder. Call it capybara_matchers.rb.

Listing 10.18   spec/support/capybara_matchers.rb

```
module CapybaraMatchers
  def has_heading?(text)
    has_css?("h1, h2, h3, h4, h5, h6", text: text)
```

---

[1] www.rubydoc.info/github/jnicklas/capybara/master/Capybara/Node/Matchers#has_text%3F-instance_method

```
    end
end

Capybara::Session.include(CapybaraMatchers)
```

You've defined a custom has_heading? method, and then included it in Capybara's Capybara::Session module so that you can use it on any page references, which are instances of Capybara::Session.

Alternate methods of implementing has_heading

The has_heading method we define here could also be written as another custom RSpec matcher, like the following:

```
RSpec::Matchers.define :have_heading do |text|
  match do |page|
    page.has_css?("h1, h2, h3, h4, h5, h6", text: text)
  end

  failure_message do
    "Expected page to have heading '#{text}'"
  end

  failure_message_when_negated do |policy|
    "Expected page not to have heading '#{text}'"
  end
end
```

We think adding the method directly to Capybara::Session is more idiomatic, as it more closely matches how Capybara's other matchers are implemented. You can also use both has_heading? and have_heading and get the same result.

Now when you run bundle exec rspec, you get just one failure:

```
1) Users can only see the appropriate links non-admin users (project
   viewers) cannot see the New Comment form
   Failure/Error: expect(page).not_to have_heading "New Comment"
     expected #has_heading?("New Comment") to return false, got true
   # ./spec/features/hidden_links_spec.rb:56:in ...
```

And now you can make it pass!

As you've done in the past, you can use Pundit's policy view helper to hide the form from users who shouldn't see it. You can wrap the comment form partial in app/views/tickets/show.html.erb in this helper like so:

```
<% if policy(@comment).create? %>
  <%= render "comments/form", ticket: @ticket, comment: @comment %>
<% end %>
```

Now if you were to log in as a viewer of a project, you'd be able to see all of the existing comments, but not leave a new one. That's good to see. Your tests will verify this—running bundle exec rspec will give you this output:

```
104 examples, 0 failures, 2 pending
```

The two pending tests in this output are from spec/helpers/comments_helper _spec.rb and spec/models/comment_spec.rb. You can delete those two files, as they don't contain any useful tests.

If you rerun `bundle exec rspec`, you'll see this:

```
102 examples, 0 failures
```

Good stuff! Now commit and push this:

```
$ git add .
$ git commit -m "Authorized users can now leave comments on tickets"
$ git push
```

This feature of your application is useful because it provides a way for users of a project to have a discussion about a ticket and keep track of it. Next up, you'll add a way to provide additional context to this ticket by changing states.

10.2 *Changing a ticket's state*

States help standardize the way a ticket's progress is tracked. By glancing at the state of a ticket, a user can determine if that ticket needs more work or if it's complete, as shown in figure 10.4.

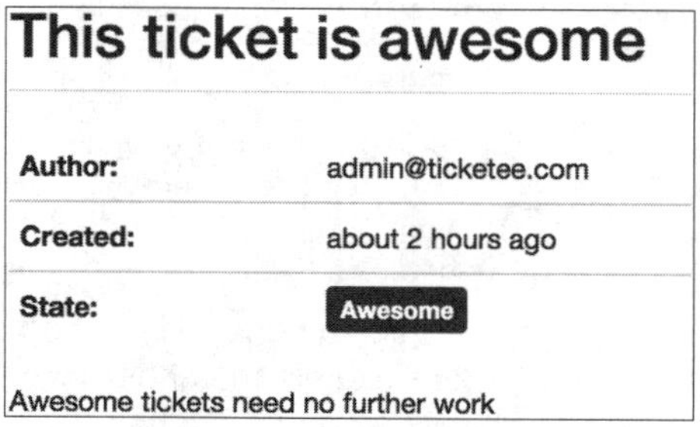

To allow users to change a ticket's state, you'll add a select box on the comment form, from which a state can be selected. These states will be stored in another table called `states`, and they'll be accessed through a `State` model.

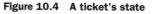

This ticket is awesome

Author:	admin@ticketee.com
Created:	about 2 hours ago
State:	Awesome

Awesome tickets need no further work

Figure 10.4   A ticket's state

Later on, you'll give some users the ability to add states for the select box, and make one of them the default. First, though, you need to create the select box so that states can be selected.

As usual, you'll start creating a comment that changes a ticket's state by writing another scenario. This scenario will go at the bottom of spec/features/ creating_comments_spec.rb, and it's shown in the following listing.

Listing 10.19   Testing that users can change the state of a comment

```
RSpec.feature "Users can comment on tickets" do
  ...
  scenario "when changing a ticket's state" do
    visit project_ticket_path(project, ticket)
    fill_in "Text", with: "This is a real issue"
    select "Open", from: "State"
    click_button "Create Comment"

    expect(page).to have_content "Comment has been created."
    within("#ticket .state") do
```

```
        expect(page).to have_content "Open"
      end
    end
end
```

In this scenario, you go through the process of creating a comment, much like in the previous scenario in this file, but this time you select a state. This is the first part of the scenario, and you can expect it to fail because you don't have a `State` select box yet.

After the comment is created, you should see the state appearing in the `#ticket` `.state` area. This is the second part of the scenario that will fail.

When you run this scenario with `bundle exec rspec spec/features/creating _comments_spec.rb`, it will fail like this:

```
1) Users can comment on tickets when changing a ticket's state
   Failure/Error: select "Open", from: "State"
   Capybara::ElementNotFound:
     Unable to find select box "State"
```

As you can see from this output, the line that attempts to select "Open" from "State" can't find the select box because you haven't added it yet. With this select box, users of your application should be able to change the ticket's state by selecting a value from it, entering some comment text, and clicking the Create Comment button. Before you do all that, however, you need to create the `State` model and its related table, which is used to store the states.

10.2.1 Creating the State model

Right now you need to add a select box. When you're done, you should have one that looks like figure 10.5.

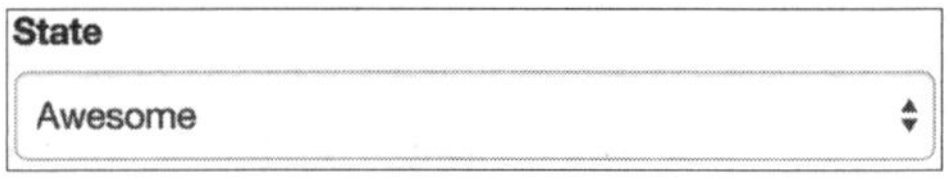

The states in the select box will be populated from the database, because you

State

Awesome

Figure 10.5 The `State` select box

want users to eventually be able to create their own states. For now, you'll define this `State` model to have a name field as well as a color[9] field, which will define the colors of the label for each state.

Create this `State` model and its associated migration by running this command:

```
$ rails g model state name:string color:string
```

But don't run the migration just yet!

Before running the migration you just created, you'll need to define a way for states to link to comments and to tickets, but there are a few things worth mentioning beforehand. For comments you'll want to track that a comment has changed the ticket's state, and for tickets you'll want to track the current state of the ticket. You'll use references on the `Ticket` and `Comment` models for this, and, as a bonus, you can

---

[2] This is *not* our preferred way of spelling "colour," but we're trying to please our audience.

add these fields to the migration. You can also remove the `timestamps` call from within `create_table`, as it's not important when states were created or updated.

When you're done, the whole migration should look like the following listing.

Listing 10.20   db/migrate/[date]_create_states.rb

```ruby
class CreateStates < ActiveRecord::Migration
  def change
    create_table :states do |t|
      t.string :name
      t.string :color
    end

    add_reference :tickets,  :state, index: true, foreign_key: true
    add_reference :comments, :state, foreign_key: true
  end
end
```

In this migration, you use the `index: true` option on the reference to add a database index on the `tickets` table's `state_id` field. By adding an index on this field, you can speed up queries that search for tickets that have a particular value in this field.

The downsides of indexing are that it will result in slower writes and use more disk space, but the benefits far outweigh these. It's always important to have indexes on non-primary-key fields that you do lookups on because of the great read-speed increase.[3] Applications generally read from the database more often than write to it.

Run this migration now by running this command:

```
$ bundle exec rake db:migrate
```

There you have it! The `State` model is up and running. You can now associate this class with the `Comment` class by adding the following line to the top of the `Comment` model's definition:

```ruby
class Comment < ActiveRecord::Base
  belongs_to :state
  ...
```

The `state` method provided by this `belongs_to` will be used shortly to display the state on the ticket page, as shown in figure 10.6.

Before doing that, however, you'll need to add the select box for the state to the comment form.

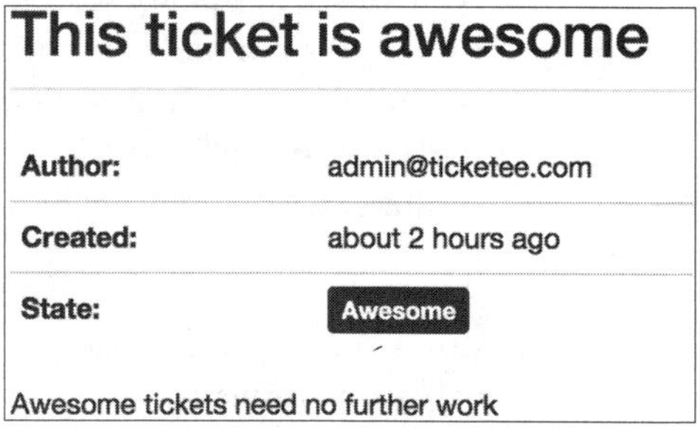

This ticket is awesome

Author:	admin@ticketee.com
Created:	about 2 hours ago
State:	Awesome

Awesome tickets need no further work

Figure 10.6   How we'll display the current state on a ticket's page

---

[3] The primary key, in this case, is the `id` field, which is automatically created for each model by `create_table`. Primary key fields are, by default, indexed.

10.2.2 *Selecting states*

In your comment form partial, you can add the select box underneath the text box.

```
<%= simple_form_for [ticket, comment] do |f| %>
  <%= f.input :text %>
  <%= f.association :state %>
  <%= f.submit class: "btn btn-primary" %>
<% end %>
```

What … that's it? Yes, that's really all you need to do. Simple Form is very, very clever—if you tell your form that :state is an association like this, it will inspect your model to learn that the state field is a reference to the State class, and it will create a select box on your form, prepopulated with all of the states from the states table. Wow.

> #### Using normal Rails form helpers instead
> If you were using the normal Rails form helpers instead of Simple Form, the code would be significantly more complicated here. You'd have to manually load a list of State instances in your controller to display on the form, and your form code would look something like the following:
>
> ```
> <%= f.label :state_id %>
> <%= f.select :state_id, @states.map { |s| [s.name, s.id] } %>
> ```
>
> Simple Form really does make your forms so much simpler, and it's a gem we love using!

For a ticket that has its state set to "New," the select box generated by f.association :state could look like this:

```
<select class="select optional form-control" name="comment[state_id]"
  id="comment_state_id">
  <option value="1" selected="selected">New</option>
  <option value="2">Open</option>
  <option value="3">Closed</option>
</select>
```

The first option tag in the select tag has an additional attribute: selected. When this attribute is set, that option will be the one selected as the default for the select.

Which option tag gets the selected attribute is determined by the :selected option for f.association. The value for this option is the corresponding value attribute for the option tag. By default, Simple Form will use the state_id value of the comment object, because you're in a form for a comment. For example, if this comment object had a state_id of 2, and the state with the ID 2 had the name "Rejected," then "Rejected" would automatically be selected in the state select box for the comment. Nifty!

With the select box in place, you're almost at the point where this scenario will pass. You can see how far you've gotten by running `bundle exec rspec spec/features/ creating_comments_spec.rb`:

```
1) Users can comment on tickets when changing a ticket's state
   Failure/Error: select "Open", from: "State"
   Capybara::ElementNotFound:
     Unable to find option "Open"
```

The `state` field is rendering correctly, but it's empty—there's no "Open" option to select. You don't have any states in the database, so you have to add one.

To do this, add a line in your state-changing scenario to create a new `State` object:

```
RSpec.feature "Users can comment on tickets" do
  ...

  scenario "when changing a ticket's state" do
    FactoryGirl.create(:state, name: "Open")
    ...
```

For this to work, you'll need to define a `state` factory. Do that in a new file called spec/factories/state_factory.rb using the content from the following listing.

Listing 10.22 spec/factories/state_factory.rb

```
FactoryGirl.define do
  factory :state do
    name "A state"
  end
end
```

Now that the `state` factory is defined, when you rerun `bundle exec rspec spec/ features/creating_comments_spec.rb`, the final scenario will fail with this error:

```
1) Users can comment on tickets when changing a ticket's state
   Failure/Error: within("#ticket .state") do
   Capybara::ElementNotFound:
     Unable to find css "#ticket .state"
```

This output means it's looking for any element with the `id` attribute of `ticket` that contains any type of element with the `class` of `state`, but it can't find it. This should be easy to fix; you just need to display the state you're saving on the page.

Rather than putting the state inside the `show` view of `TicketsController`, let's try putting it in a partial. This will allow you to reuse this code to display a state wherever you need it in the future. Additionally, you can apply a dynamic class around the state so you can style it later.

Create the new partial at app/views/states/_state.html.erb and fill it with the following content.

Listing 10.23   Defining what a state looks like

```
<span class="state state-<%= state.name.parameterize %>">
  <%= state -%>
</span>
```

To style the element, you need a valid CSS class name, which you can get by using the `parameterize` method. If, for example, you had a state called "Drop bears strike without warning!" and you used `parameterize` on it, all the spaces and characters that aren't valid in URLs would be stripped, leaving you with "drop-bears-strike-without-warning," which is a perfectly valid CSS class name. You'll use this generated class name later on to style the state using the `color` attribute of the state.

You'll now render this partial as part of the table displaying a ticket's attributes. Add another row at the bottom of the table in app/views/tickets/show.html.erb, using the following line.

Listing 10.24   Displaying the current state of a ticket

```
<table id="attributes">
  ...

  <% if @ticket.state.present? %>
    <tr>
      <th>State:</th>
      <td><%= render @ticket.state %></td>
    </tr>
  <% end %>
</table>
```

You use the short form of rendering a partial here again, and you conditionally render it if the ticket has a state. If you didn't have the `if` around the state, and the state was `nil`, this would raise an exception—the partial would try to call `nil.name .parameterize` when generating a class name for the state.

Now that you have the name of the state on the page, rerun the spec. Have you missed anything?

```
1) Users can comment on tickets with valid attributes
   Failure/Error: visit project_ticket_path(project, ticket)
   ActionView::Template::Error:
     undefined method `state' for #<Ticket:0x007fa9c1dc6cd0>
```

All three of the specs are failing! Huh? Didn't you add a `state` association to the `Ticket` model? You added the right `state_id` field to the `tickets` table of the database when you created the states table…but you didn't add the `state` association to the `Ticket` model.

Only comments have a state at the moment, not tickets. So you'll need to add the association between `Ticket` and `State` in your `Ticket` model. This method should go directly below the `belongs_to :author` line in app/models/ticket.rb.

Listing 10.25   A ticket has a state too!

```
class Ticket < ActiveRecord::Base
  ...
  belongs_to :state
  ...
```

If you run the feature again with `bundle exec rspec spec/features/creating
_comments_spec.rb`, it will still fail. Aww.

```
1) Users can comment on tickets when changing a ticket's state
   Failure/Error: within("#ticket .state") do
   Capybara::ElementNotFound:
     Unable to find css "#ticket .state"
```

All these failures are tiring, but at least you're running out of things that can go wrong
as you fix them one at a time. The `#ticket .state` element still isn't displaying on the
ticket's show view, which only happens if `@ticket.state` isn't present, meaning it's `nil`.

In your controller you're creating a new `Comment` object, and you may think you're
saving the `state` you select, inside it. But in the view, you're displaying the `state` of
the ticket object, *not* the comment you just created! How can you get the `state` saved
on the ticket instance as well?

You can do this with a *callback*, defined as part of your `Comment` model, to set the
ticket's status when a user changes it through the comment form.

A callback is a method that's automatically called either before or after a certain
event occurs. You've seen and used controller callbacks before, when you wrote the
`before_action` and `after_action` methods. For models, there are before and after
callbacks defined for the following events (where * represents either `before` or
`after`):

- Validating (`*_validation`)
- Creating (`*_create`)
- Updating (`*_update`)
- Saving (`*_save`)
- Destroying (`*_destroy`)

You can trigger a specific piece of code or method to run before or after any of these
events.

If you define a callback that occurs after a comment is *created*, you can then copy
the state from the comment to the ticket itself. You can use the `after_create` method
in your `Comment` model to do this.

Listing 10.26   app/models/comment.rb

```
class Comment < ActiveRecord::Base
  ...
  after_create :set_ticket_state
end
```

The symbol passed to the `after_create` method in listing 10.26 is the name of the method this callback will call. You can define this method at the bottom of your `Comment` model using the code from the following listing.

> **Listing 10.27 app/models/comment.rb with the callback fully defined**

```
class Comment < ActiveRecord::Base
  ...
  after_create :set_ticket_state

  private

  def set_ticket_state
    ticket.state = state
    ticket.save!
  end
end
```

With this callback and the associated method now in place, the ticket's state will be set to the comment's state after the comment is created. Great! But when you run your feature again with `bundle exec rspec spec/features/creating_comments_spec.rb`, it still fails:

```
1) Users can comment on tickets when changing a ticket's state
   Failure/Error: within("#ticket .state") do
   Capybara::ElementNotFound:
     Unable to find css "#ticket .state"
```

Wait, the same error? Even though you're displaying the ticket state on the page (if the ticket has one), you're not seeing it displayed? So the ticket doesn't have a state... what did you miss? This shouldn't be difficult to figure out, but you're probably sitting there thinking someone somewhere has made a terrible mistake.

The subtle bug is one that's caught us a couple of times in the past—you added a state field to your form, but you forgot to add it to the list of parameters you're permitting and whitelisting in your controller. That's really annoying. Luckily, Rails lets you configure how you want your app to respond when you have unpermitted parameters. By default, you'll get a little message in your log files like the following:

```
...
Started POST "/tickets/1/comments" for ::1 at [timestamp]
Processing by CommentsController#create as HTML
  Parameters: {"utf8"=>"?", "authenticity_token"=>"VEsOog...",
  "comment"=>{"text"=>"This is a test", "state_id"=>"2"}...
  Ticket Load (0.1ms)  SELECT "tickets".* FROM "tickets" WHERE ...
Unpermitted parameter: state_id
  User Load (0.4ms)  SELECT "users".* FROM "users" WHERE "users"....
  (0.1ms)  begin transaction
  SQL (0.4ms)  INSERT INTO "comments" ("text", "ticket_id", "author_...
  ...
```

It's really easy to miss, even if you're looking for it. You can make it much, much more obvious by changing a configuration option for your test environment. Open the environment file that controls your test environment, in config/environments/test.rb, and add the following line at the bottom of the block.

Listing 10.28   Configuring the behavior on unpermitted params

```
Rails.application.configure do
  ...

  config.action_controller.action_on_unpermitted_parameters = :raise
end
```

Rails will now throw a big nasty exception if you pass unpermitted params to your params.permit method, which you're doing right now. You can see what this looks like by rerunning the comment-creation spec, with bundle exec rspec spec/features/creating_comments_spec.rb:

```
1) Users can comment on tickets with valid attributes
   Failure/Error: click_button "Create Comment"
   ActionController::UnpermittedParameters:
     found unpermitted parameter: state_id
```

Ka-booooom!

This sounds like a good setting to leave on in test mode, so leave that setting in your test.rb. Now you know what you need to do—permit the state_id parameter. Inside your CommentsController in app/controllers/comments_controller.rb, permit the state_id parameter in your comment_params method so it looks like the following.

Listing 10.29   Now with bonus state_id

```
class CommentsController < ApplicationController
  ...
  def comment_params
    params.require(:comment).permit(:text, :state_id)
  end
end
```

That will clear up that unpermitted parameter error. It might clear up more errors too. Rerun the spec and see:

```
1) Users can comment on tickets when changing a ticket's state
   Failure/Error: expect(page).to have_content "Open"
     expected to find text "Open" in "#<State:0x007feddd3b3670>"
```

You now show *something* that looks like it might be a state with a lot of added junk. By default, objects in Ruby have a to_s method that will output the ugly, inspected version of this object. By overriding this method in the model to call the name method, you can get it to display the state's name rather than its object output. You did this earlier on the User class as well.

Open your `State` model in app/models/state.rb and define a new `to_s` model that looks like this:

```
class State < ActiveRecord::Base
  ...
  def to_s
    name
  end
end
```

Great! This should mean that the last scenario in your comment-creation feature will pass. Run it with `bundle exec rspec spec/features/creating_comments_spec.rb` and find out:

```
3 examples, 0 failures
```

It's passing! This is a good time to ensure that everything's working by running `bundle exec rspec`:

```
104 examples, 0 failures, 1 pending
```

The one pending spec that's cramping your style is located in spec/models/state_spec.rb. You can delete this file, as it doesn't contain any useful specs.

When you rerun `bundle exec rspec`, you'll see it's now lovely and green:

```
103 examples, 0 failures
```

Excellent, everything's fixed. Commit these changes now:

```
$ git add .
$ git commit -m "Tickets can have a state assigned when comments are
  created"
$ git push
```

You can now change a ticket's state by adding a new comment with a state, but then if you load the comment form again, the state form will be a little misleading, as you can see in figure 10.7.

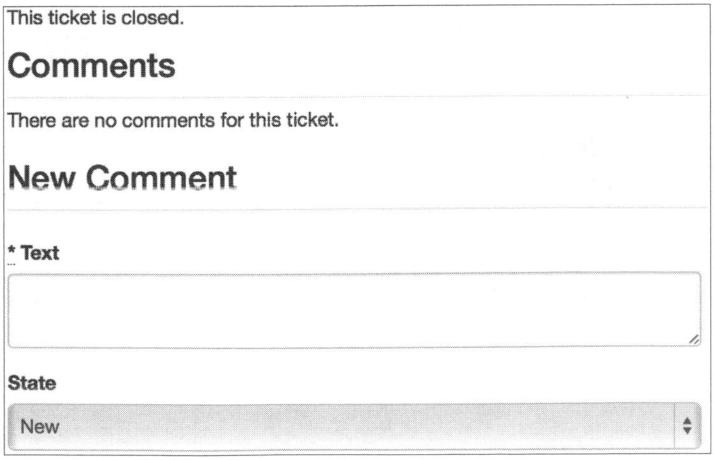

Figure 10.7 The `state` field has been reset!

You've marked the ticket as "Closed," but if you add a new comment just by typing some text and submitting it, then the state will be reset to "New"! It would be great if the default value of the state field were the current state of the ticket, to prevent accidental changing of state. We'll look at fixing that next.

10.2.3   *Setting a default state for a comment*

At the moment, you're not specifying which state should be set as the default value of the select box. You only have the following code in your comment form:

```
<%= f.association :state %>
```

Simple Form will automagically set the selected value of the state box to be whatever the state_id property of the comment is. By default, the state_id of a comment is nil, which you can verify by instantiating a new Comment instance in a Rails console.

> **Listing 10.30   Testing out code in `rails console`**

```
irb(main):001:0> Comment.new
=> #<Comment id: nil, text: nil, ticket_id: nil, author_id: nil,
   created_at: nil, updated_at: nil, state_id: nil>
```

You can fix this by setting the state_id of the newly built Comment object when you build it in the show action of TicketsController. Open the controller in app/controllers/tickets_controller.rb, and change the show action to set the state_id.

> **Listing 10.31   Setting the `state_id` of the comment on the "New Comment" form**

```
def show
  authorize @ticket, :show?
  @comment = @ticket.comments.build(state_id: @ticket.state_id)
end
```

This will change the default value that gets selected in the "New Comment" form to be whatever the current state of the @ticket is. Great!

You've now got the ticket status updating along with the comment status. It's time to add some *seed* states to the application, so you can see this functionality working in your browsers.

10.2.4   *Seeding your app with states*

Seeds can be added to db/seeds.rb. Add some to the bottom of the file like so:

```
unless State.exists?
  State.create(name: "New", color: "#0066CC")
  State.create(name: "Open", color: "#008000")
  State.create(name: "Closed", color: "#990000")
  State.create(name: "Awesome", color: "#663399")
end
```

This will load four states into your system—"New," "Open," "Closed," and "Awesome."[4] Load these seed states into your database by running the following:

```
$ bundle exec rake db:seed
```

Now when you load up your Ticketee application in your browser, you'll be able to set states on your comments, making working with the next section a lot easier.

Now that you have statuses in the system, it would be handy to know what the timeline of status changes looks like. You can display this on the comment by showing a little indication of whether the state has changed during that comment. Let's work on adding this little tidbit of information to the comments right now.

10.3 *Tracking changes*

When a person posts a comment that changes the state of a ticket, you'd like this information to be displayed on the page next to the comment, as shown in figure 10.8.

Figure 10.8   State transitions

By visually tracking this state change, along with the text of the comment, you can provide context as to why the state was changed. At the moment, you only track the state of the comment and don't even display it alongside the comment's text; you only use it to update the ticket's status.

10.3.1 *Ch-ch-changes*

What you'll need now is some way of making sure that, when changing a ticket's state by way of a comment, a record of that change appears in the comments area. A scenario would fit this bill, and luckily you wrote one that fits almost perfectly. This would be the final scenario ("Changing a ticket's state") in spec/features/creating _comments_spec.rb.

To check for the state-change text in your "When changing a ticket's state" scenario, you can add these lines to the bottom of the scenario:

```
scenario "when changing a ticket's state" do
  ...
  within("#comments") do
    expect(page).to have_content "state changed to Open"
  end
end
```

If the ticket was assigned the "New" state, this text would say "state changed from New to Open," but because your tickets don't have default states assigned to them yet, the previous state for the first comment will be `nil`. We wouldn't want to display the text "state changed from nil to Open," so we'll shortcut it to just "state changed to Open."

---

[4] The hexadecimal color #663399 is also known as "rebeccapurple," in memory of Rebecca Meyer, beloved daughter of CSS guru Eric Meyer.

When you run this scenario using `bundle exec rspec spec/features/ creating_comments_spec.rb`, it will fail:

```
1) Users can comment on tickets when changing a ticket's state
     Failure/Error: expect(page).to have_content "state changed to Open"
       expected to find text "state changed to Open" in "This is a real
       issue less than a minute ago by test3@example.com (User)"
```

Good. You've got a way to test the state message that should appear when a comment changes the state of the ticket. Now you'd like to track the state that the ticket had *before* the comment, as well as the state of the comment itself.

To track this extra attribute, you'll need to create another field on your `comments` table, called `previous_state_id`. Before you save a comment, you'll update this field to the current state of the ticket. You can then use this field to show a state transition on a comment, as pictured in figure 10.9.

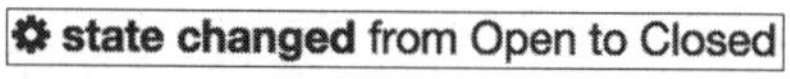

✿ state changed from Open to Closed

Figure 10.9   A state transition

With this little bit of information, users can see which comments changed the ticket's state. This can be helpful for determining what steps the ticket has gone through.

You can create a new migration to add the `previous_state_id` field to your `comments` table by running the following command:

```
$ rails g migration add_previous_state_to_comments \
  previous_state:references
```

Rails is pretty smart here and would typically use the name of the migration to infer that you want to add a column called `previous_state` to a table called `comments`. You only have to tell it what the type of this field is, and you do that by passing `previous_state:references` to the migration—now Rails knows that it will be adding a foreign key, so it expands `previous_state` to add a field called `previous_state_id`.

If you open this migration now, you'll see that it defines a `change` method that calls the `add_reference` method inside it. You can see the entire migration in the following listing.

Listing 10.32   db/migrate/[timestamp]_add_previous_state_to_comments.rb

```ruby
class AddPreviousStateToComments < ActiveRecord::Migration
  def change
    add_reference :comments, :previous_state, index: true,
      foreign_key: true
  end
end
```

Like you did with your migration to create comments, you'll need to fix the usage of `foreign_key: true`. You don't have a previous_states table; a previous state is just an instance of a state. So update the migration to match the following listing.

Listing 10.33 After fixing the foreign key reference

```
class AddPreviousStateToComments < ActiveRecord::Migration
  def change
    add_reference :comments, :previous_state, index: true
    add_foreign_key :comments, :states, column: :previous_state_id
  end
end
```

Now you can run the migration by running `bundle exec rake db:migrate`.

To use the `previous_state_id` field properly, you're going to need to add another callback to save it.

10.3.2 *Another c-c-callback*

To set the `previous_state_id` field before a comment is created, you'll use a `before_create` callback on the `Comment` model. A `before_create` callback is triggered—as the name suggests—before a record is created, but after the validations have been run. This means that this callback will only be triggered for valid objects that are about to be saved to the database for the first time. This sounds like the right time to set the previous state of the ticket to your new comment.

Put this new callback on a line directly above the `after_create` inside the `Comment` model, because it makes sense to group all your callbacks together and in the order that they're called:

```
class Comment < ActiveRecord::Base
  ...
  before_create :set_previous_state
  after_create :set_ticket_state
  ...
```

Call the `set_previous_state` method for this callback, which you'll define at the bottom of your `Comment` model, just before the `set_ticket_state` method, like this:

```
class Comment < ActiveRecord::Base
  ...
  private

  def set_previous_state
    self.previous_state = ticket.state
  end
  ...
```

The `previous_state=` method you call here isn't yet defined. You can define this method by declaring that a `Comment` object `belongs_to` a `previous_state`, which is a `State` object. Put this line with the `belongs_to` in your `Comment` model:

```
class Comment < ActiveRecord::Base
  belongs_to :previous_state, class_name: "State"
  ...
```

Again you have to specify the class that the `previous_state` field refers to—by default Rails would try to use a `PreviousState` class, due to the name, but you don't have one of those—the previous state of a comment is just a normal `State`.

With this `belongs_to` defined, you get the `previous_state=` method for free, so your callback should work alright. There's one way to make sure of this, and that's to attempt to display these transitions between states in your view, so that your feature will potentially pass. You'll now work on displaying these transitions.

10.3.3 *Displaying changes*

When you display a comment that changes a ticket's state, you want to display this state transition along with the comment. To get this text to show up, start by adding the following lines to app/views/comments/_comment.html.erb underneath the `blockquote` tag.

Listing 10.34   First version of displaying a comment transition

```
<p>
  <strong><i class="fa fa-gear"></i> state changed</strong> from
  <%= render comment.previous_state %> to <%= render comment.state %>
</p>
```

You've used the idea of calling `render` on an object before, knowing that Rails will look up a partial based on the class of the object. You pass a `State` object here, in both `comment.previous_state` and `comment.state`, so Rails will load the app/views/state/_state.html.erb partial you defined earlier.

There are a couple of hiccups with this though, and a few things you could do better. What happens if this is the first comment, and the `previous_state` is `nil`? This won't work. You'll be calling `render nil`, which will blow up with an error:

```
ActionView::Template::Error ('nil' is not an ActiveModel-compatible
object. It must implement :to_partial_path.):
    8:
    9: <p>
   10:   <strong><i class="fa fa-gear"></i> state changed</strong> from
   11:   <%= render comment.previous_state %> to <%= render comment...
   12: </p>
app/views/comments/_comment.html.erb:11:in ...
```

You can add another conditional to your view, to only display the previous state if it exists.

Listing 10.35   Second version of displaying a comment transition

```
<p>
  <strong><i class="fa fa-gear"></i> state changed</strong>
  <% if comment.previous_state.present? %>
    from <%= render comment.previous_state %>
  <% end %>
  to <%= render comment.state %>
</p>
```

This is almost correct, but there's a slight problem. Your callback will set the `previous_state` regardless of what the current state is, and you could end up with something like figure 10.10.

☼ **state changed** from Open to Open

Figure 10.10   State transition from itself to itself

To stop this from happening, you can wrap the whole lot in an `if` statement.

Listing 10.36   Third version of displaying a comment transition

```
<% if comment.previous_state != comment.state %>
  <p>
    <strong><i class="fa fa-gear"></i> state changed</strong>
    <% if comment.previous_state.present? %>
      from <%= render comment.previous_state %>
    <% end %>
    to <%= render comment.state %>
  </p>
<% end %>
```

Now this text will only show up when the previous state isn't the same as the current state.

You can go one step further and move this code into a helper. You can tell that this code belongs in a helper because it has more ERB tags than actual HTML code. Views are more for displaying information; deciding how it should be output should be left to the helpers and controllers. Move this code into the app/helpers/tickets_helper.rb file, because this partial is displayed from the `show` view of the `TicketsController`. You'll have to rewrite it from HTML and ERB to Ruby, but it will be worth it.

The entire `TicketsHelper` should now look like the following listing.

Listing 10.37   app/helpers/tickets_helper.rb

```
module TicketsHelper
  def state_transition_for(comment)
    if comment.previous_state != comment.state
      content_tag(:p) do
        value = "<strong><i class='fa fa-gear'></i> state changed</strong>"
        if comment.previous_state.present?
          value += " from #{render comment.previous_state}"
        end
        value += " to #{render comment.state}"
        value.html_safe
      end
    end
  end
end
```

It's a little bit longer than the HTML+ERB version of the code, but it's easier to read—no `<% %> <% %> <% %>` obscuring the meaning of the code. It works identically to the previous version—it checks if the states have changed, and builds up and returns an HTML string that will conditionally include a record of the previous state as well, if present.

THE NEW `CONTENT_TAG` There's also a new `content_tag` in this code. `content_tag` is a view helper that wraps the content in the block in the tag specified. In this case, you've passed `:p`, which will wrap the block's return value in a paragraph (`<p></p>`) tag.

You can now replace the whole `if` statement in app/views/comments/_comment.html.erb with a single call to your new helper method.

Listing 10.38 Using the `state_transition_for` helper you defined

```
<blockquote class="comment">
...
</blockquote>

<%= state_transition_for(comment) %>
```

Much neater!

Next, you can check to see if this is working by running your scenario with `bundle exec rspec spec/features/creating_comments_spec.rb`. It will pass:

```
3 examples, 0 failures
```

Excellent! You've got your application showing users what state a comment has switched the ticket to. This is a good time to check that you haven't broken anything. When you run `bundle exec rspec`, you should see that everything is A-OK:

```
103 examples, 0 failures
```

You have state transitions showing in your application, which is great to see. Commit and push this to GitHub:

```
$ git add .
$ git commit -m "Display a comment's state transition"
$ git push
```

Looking good, right? Wrong. Time to add some styles to your states.

10.3.4 Styling states

Ticketee's state styles could use a little work—at the moment you can't distinguish one state from another. Look at figure 10.11 and gaze upon their

| ✿ **state changed** from Open to Closed |

Figure 10.11 Ugly, ugly states

ugliness. You could distinguish them by using the colors you've specified in the attributes.

Earlier, you wrapped the state name in a special `span` that will allow you to style these elements based on the class. For the "New" state, the HTML for the span looks like this:

```
<span class="state state-new">
  New
</span>
```

You can use the `state` class to add generic styles that will apply to all states, and the `state-new` class to apply the colors from that specific `State` record to this element. To do so, you'll need to dynamically define some CSS that will apply the colors.

The states in your system can change at any time in the future, so you can't just put styles in app/assets/stylesheets/application.css for them. To get around this, you can do two things:

- Add generic styles for the `state` class in app/assets/stylesheets/tickets.scss
- Add specific styles for your individual states in a `<style>` block in your application layout, so you can use the styles for states in every page

---

Wait ... styles in your HTML?!

"But wait," we hear you crying, "why can't I just make a new stylesheet like states.css.erb, load the states in it, and generate a stylesheet like that? Dirtying up the application layout is soooo ugly!"

Well, it is ugly, you're right, but without a lot of Sprockets hackery, you don't really have a choice. You could create a stylesheet called something like states.css.erb, and fill it with the following code:

```
<% State.all.each do |state| %>
  .state-<%= state.name.parameterize %> {
    background-color: <%= state.color %>;
  }
<% end %>
```

If you included this file into your application.css.scss, it would work great...in development. You could even change the `State` instances in your database, or add new ones, and the stylesheet would be updated with the updated `State` styles.

But when it comes to deployment, you'll be using Sprockets to compile stylesheets just once, at deploy time, so any changes you made to states after deployment would not be reflected on your site. That would be awful!

Although putting styles in your HTML is ugly, for now it's a necessary evil. We'll talk more about precompilation of stylesheets and other assets when we cover deployment in chapter 13.

The first step is easy—adding styles for the base `state` class. You'll base them on Bootstrap's label styles, so you can write some CSS that _extends_ those label styles, and then tweaks them to make them a little bigger and add some extra padding. Place the following styles at the bottom of app/assets/stylesheets/tickets.scss.

Listing 10.39 Basic styles for your displayed states

```
.state {
  @extend .label;
  font-size: 12px;
  padding: 0.3em 0.6em;
}
```

The second step is a bit trickier—you'll have to iterate over your styles in your layout file in app/views/layouts/application.html.erb, and print out some CSS to apply to your individual styles. Add them at the bottom of the <head> tag, as follows:

```
...
  <%= javascript_include_tag 'application' %>
  <%= csrf_meta_tags %>
  <style>
    <% State.all.each do |state| %>
      .state-<%= state.name.parameterize %> {
        background-color: <%= state.color %>;
      }
    <% end %>
  </style>
</head>
```

With these few lines of code, your states should now be styled. If you visit a ticket page that has comments that have changed the state, you should see the state styled, as shown in figure 10.12.

Figure 10.12   **States, now with 100% more style**

While you're in the business of prettying things up, you can also add the state of your ticket to the listing on app/views/projects/show.html.erb so that users can easily glance at the list of tickets and see a state next to each of them. Add this to the right of the ticket name, so that the li element is as follows.

Listing 10.40   Displaying the state of tickets on the project page

```
<li>
  #<%= ticket.id %> -
  <%= link_to ticket.name, [@project, ticket] %>
  <%= render ticket.state if ticket.state %>
</li>
```

You can also add an extra margin to stop the ticket states pressing right up against each other, in app/assets/stylesheets/tickets.scss.

Listing 10.41   Separating out the ticket listing

```
#tickets li {
  padding-bottom: 10px;
}
```

See figure 10.13. That's looking a lot better!

You've completed all that you need to do to let users change the state of a ticket. They can select a state from the State select box on the comment form, and when they create a comment, that

Tickets

- #1 - Round and round and round it goes New
- #2 - This ticket is awesome Awesome

Figure 10.13   **Tickets and their states at a glance**

ticket will be updated to the new state. Right after the comment's text on the ticket page, the state transition is shown and (ideally) the comment's text will provide context for that change.

Commit this before you go any further:

```
$ git add .
$ git commit -m "Prettify states."
$ git push
```

Why did you add states in the first place? Because they provide a great way of standardizing the lifecycle of a ticket. When a ticket is assigned a "New" state, it means that the ticket is up for grabs. The next phase of a ticket's life is the "Open" state, which means that the ticket is being looked into or cared for by somebody. When the ticket is fixed, it should be marked as "Closed," perhaps with some information in the related comment about where the fix is located.

If you want to add more states than these three, you can't at the moment. But that would be a useful feature. Tickets could be marked as "Closed" for a few different reasons: one could be "Yes, this is now fixed" and another could be "No, I don't believe this is a problem." A third type could be "I couldn't reproduce the problem described."

It would be great if you could add more states to the application without having to add them to the state list in db/seeds.rb, wouldn't it? Well, that's easy enough. You can create an interface for the admin users of your application to allow them to add additional states.

10.4 Managing states

Currently your application has only four states: "New," "Open," "Closed," and "Awesome." If you wanted to add more, you'd have to go into the console and add them there. Admins of this application should be able to add more states through the application itself, without using the console. They should also be able to rename states and delete them, but only if they don't have any tickets assigned to them. Finally, the admins should also be able to set a default state for the application, because no ticket should be without a state.

In this section, you'll start out by writing a feature to create new states, which will involve creating a new controller called `Admin::StatesController`. This controller will provide the admins of your application with the basic CRUD functionality for states, as well as the ability to mark a state as the default, which all new tickets will then be associated with.

We won't look at adding an `edit`, `update`, or `destroy` action to this controller because we've covered that previously. You can add them yourself if you'd like some practice.

10.4.1 Adding additional states

You currently have the four default states that come from the db/seeds.rb file in your application. If the admin users of your application wish to add more, they can't—not until you've created the `Admin::StatesController` controller and the new and create actions inside it. These will allow admin users to create additional states, which then can be assigned to a ticket.

But before you write any real code, you need to write a feature that describes the process of creating a state. Put it in a new file called spec/features/admin/ creating_states_spec.rb.

Listing 10.42   spec/features/admin/creating_states_spec.rb

```
require "rails_helper"

RSpec.feature "Admins can create new states for tickets" do
  before do
    login_as(FactoryGirl.create(:user, :admin))
  end

  scenario "with valid details" do
    visit admin_root_path
    click_link "States"
    click_link "New State"

    fill_in "Name", with: "Won't Fix"
    fill_in "Color", with: "orange"
    click_button "Create State"

    expect(page).to have_content "State has been created."
  end
end
```

Here you sign in as an admin user and go through the motions of creating a new state. If you run this new feature using the command `bundle exec rspec spec/features/ admin/creating_states_spec.rb`, it will fail because it can't find the "States" link:

```
1) Admins can create new states for tickets with valid details
   Failure/Error: click_link "States"
   Capybara::ElementNotFound:
     Unable to find link "States"
```

The "States" link should take you to the `index` action of the `Admin::StatesController`, but it doesn't. That's because this link is missing from the admin homepage, located at app/views/admin/application/index.html.erb. You can add this link now in the Admin Links list at the bottom of the file.

Listing 10.43   Admin links with the "States" link added

```
<div class="col-md-3">
  <h2>Admin Links</h2>
  <ul class="nav nav-stacked">
    <li><%= link_to "Users", admin_users_path %></li>
    <li><%= link_to "States", admin_states_path %></li>
  </ul>
</div>
```

The `admin_states_path` method won't be defined yet, but you can fix this by adding another `resources` line inside the `admin` namespace in config/routes.rb, as follows.

Listing 10.44 config/routes.rb

```
namespace :admin do
  ...
  resources :states, only: [:index, :new, :create]
end
```

> **DON'T GO CREATING UNUSED URLS!** Remember, it's good practice to only define the routes you'll be using. You're only dealing with listing states and creating new ones, so you only need the index, new, and create actions.

With this line inside the `admin` namespace, the `admin_states_path` method (and its siblings) will be defined. Run the feature again with `bundle exec rspec spec/features/admin/creating_states_spec.rb` to see what you have to do next:

```
1) Admins can create new states for tickets with valid details
   Failure/Error: click_link "States"
   ActionController::RoutingError:
     uninitialized constant Admin::StatesController
```

Ah, that's right! You need to generate your controller. You can do this by running the controller generator:

```
$ rails g controller admin/states
```

This will generate an empty `Admin::StatesController` in app/controllers/admin/states_controller.rb—enough to make that error go away. When you run the feature again, you'll be told that you're missing the `index` action from this controller:

```
1) Admins can create new states for tickets with valid details
   Failure/Error: click_link "States"
   AbstractController::ActionNotFound:
     The action 'index' could not be found for Admin::StatesController
```

Add this action to the app/controllers/admin/states_controller.rb file now, and make this controller inherit from `Admin::ApplicationController`. You know you'll be listing out all of the currently available states in the system in the view for this action, so you may as well load them up now. After you're done, the whole controller class will appear as shown in the following listing.

Listing 10.45 app/controllers/admin/states_controller.rb

```
class Admin::StatesController < Admin::ApplicationController
  def index
    @states = State.all
  end
end
```

Next on the menu is defining the view for this action in a brand-new file to be located at app/views/admin/states/index.html.erb. This view must contain the "New State" link your feature will go looking for, and it should also include a list of states so that anyone looking at the page knows which states already exist. The code to do all this is shown in the following listing.

Listing 10.46   app/views/admin/states/index.html.erb

```erb
<header>
  <h1>States</h1>

  <ul class="actions">
    <li><%= link_to "New State", new_admin_state_path, class: "new" %></li>
  </ul>
</header>

<ul id="states">
  <% @states.each do |state| %>
    <li><%= render "states/state", state: state %></li>
  <% end %>
</ul>
```

This is the same format you've used for all of your previous views—the header section at the top, with the "New State" link, and a list of all the existing states. You're reusing the state partial that you used to display the states with colors on the ticket page—but you have to tell Rails manually which partial to use, because now you're in the admin namespace (so Rails will only look for the partial in the app/views/admin folder).

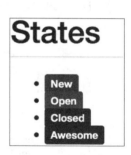

Figure 10.14   Smushed-up states

You can also add a little bit of CSS to make the states stand out from each other—at the moment they look like figure 10.14, which isn't very easy to read (or otherwise aesthetically pleasing).

To separate them a little bit, you can modify the selector at the bottom of app/assets/stylesheets/application.css.scss to add this new states list:

```scss
#tickets li, #states li {
  padding-bottom: 10px;
}
```

Now you'll have a pretty list of states displaying in your admin area. Nice.

With this view now written, your feature will progress a little further but whinge about the new action when you run bundle exec rspec spec/features/admin/ creating_states_spec.rb:

```
1) Admins can create new states for tickets with valid details
   Failure/Error: click_link "New State"
   AbstractController::ActionNotFound:
     The action 'new' could not be found for Admin::StatesController
```

You should add the `new` action to `Admin::StatesController` if you want to continue any further. It should be defined as follows inside that controller:

```
class Admin::StatesController < Admin::ApplicationController
  ...
  def new
    @state = State.new
  end
end
```

You now need to create the view for this action at app/views/admin/states/ new.html.erb and fill it in with the following content:

```
<header>
  <h1>New State</h1>
</header>

<%= render "form", state: @state %>
```

You use a form partial here again, because it's a best practice and also in case you ever want to use it for an `edit` action.

You can put the form that will be used to create new states in a new file for your partial, at app/views/admin/states/_form.html.erb. This form is pretty simple—it only needs a couple of text fields for the name and color, and a Submit button to submit the form.

```
<%= simple_form_for [:admin, state] do |f| %>
  <%= f.input :name %>
  <%= f.input :color %>

  <%= f.submit class: 'btn btn-primary' %>
<% end %>
```

Because the `state` variable rendered in the form is a new instance of the `State` model, the `submit` method will display a Submit button with the text "Create State." That's just what your feature needs.

With this form partial done, your feature should run a little further. You can check this now by running `bundle exec rspec spec/features/admin/creating_states _spec.rb`:

```
1) Admins can create new states for tickets with valid details
   Failure/Error: click_button "Create State"
   AbstractController::ActionNotFound:
     The action 'create' could not be found for Admin::StatesController
```

Right. You'll need to create the `create` action too, which you'll define inside `Admin::StatesController`.

Listing 10.48   The create action in `Admin::StatesController`

```ruby
class Admin::StatesController < Admin::ApplicationController
  ...
  def create
    @state = State.new(state_params)
    if @state.save
      flash[:notice] = "State has been created."
      redirect_to admin_states_path
    else
      flash.now[:alert] = "State has not been created."
      render "new"
    end
  end

  private

  def state_params
    params.require(:state).permit(:name, :color)
  end
end
```

There's nothing here that you haven't seen many times over by now. With the `create` action defined in your `Admin::StatesController`, you can now run `bundle exec rspec spec/features/admin/creating_states_spec.rb` and have it pass:

```
1 example, 0 failures
```

Very good! By implementing a feature that lets the admin users of your site create states, you've provided a base on which you can build the other state-related features.

You shouldn't have broken anything by making these changes, but it won't hurt to run `bundle exec rspec` to make sure. You should see the following:

```
105 examples, 0 failures, 1 pending
```

There's one pending spec inside spec/helpers/admin/states_helper_spec.rb. You can delete this file now. When you rerun `bundle exec rspec`, there should be this great green output:

```
104 examples, 0 failures
```

Celebrate with a glass of ice-cold refreshing Diet Coke,[5] and commit these changes now:

```
$ git add .
$ git commit -m "Admins can create new states for tickets"
$ git push
```

With this base defined, you can move on to more exciting things than CRUD, such as defining a default state for your tickets. You'll do a lot of CRUD-building in Rails apps, so hopefully it's becoming very natural to you by now.

---

[5] Or your preferred beverage of choice.

10.4.2 *Defining a default state*

Adding a default state for the tickets in your application will provide a sensible way of grouping tickets that haven't yet been actioned in the system, making it easier for them to be found. The easiest way to track which state is the default is to add a Boolean column called `default` to your `states` table; the column will be set to `true` if the state is the default, and `false` if not.

To get started, you need to write a feature that covers changing the default status. At the end of this feature, you'll end up with the `default` field in the `states` table, and then you can move on to making the tickets default to this state.

Create a new feature called spec/features/admin/managing_states_spec.rb and fill it with the content from the following listing.

Listing 10.49 spec/features/admin/managing_states_spec.rb

```
require "rails_helper"

RSpec.feature "Admins can manage states" do
  let!(:state) { FactoryGirl.create :state, name: "New" }

  before do
    login_as(FactoryGirl.create(:user, :admin))
    visit admin_states_path
  end

  scenario "and mark a state as default" do
    within list_item("New") do
      click_link "Make Default"
    end

    expect(page).to have_content "'New' is now the default state."
  end
end
```

In this scenario, you've got one new method call, which you'll need to define for this feature to run. This new `list_item` method will need to return a selector for the list item with the specified content.

This method is assisting the Capybara test in its job and will be reusable across many tests, so you should define it in a new file called spec/support/capybara _finders.rb. Define it using the code from the following listing.

Listing 10.50 spec/support/capybara_finders.rb

```
module CapybaraFinders
  def list_item(content)
    find("ul:not(.actions) li", text: content)
  end
end

RSpec.configure do |c|
  c.include CapybaraFinders, type: :feature
end
```

This method simply takes some text, finds a list item on the page (that isn't an action link) with the specified content, and then returns it. Capybara will then use that element as the basis for all actions inside the block. It's great to write these little helper methods that make your tests more readable, and it's so easy to do!

Now that this method is defined, see what the test says when it's run using `bundle exec rspec spec/features/admin/managing_states_spec.rb`:

```
1) Admins can manage states and mark a state as default
   Failure/Error: click_link "Make Default"
   Capybara::ElementNotFound:
     Unable to find link "Make Default"
```

The feature is failing now because it's found the right list item on the page, but there's no "Make Default" link in it. You can fix that now—open the app/views/admin/states/index.html.erb view and add a new "Make Default" link for each list item.

Listing 10.51   Now with added "Make Default" links

```erb
<% @states.each do |state| %>
<li>
  <%= render "states/state", state: state %>
  <% if state.default? %>
    (Default)
  <% else %>
    <%= link_to "Make Default", make_default_admin_state_path(state) %>
  <% end %>
</li>
<% end %>
```

In this view, you have the states being displayed with a "(Default)" label next to them if they're indeed the default state. If the state isn't the default, there's an option there to make it the default with the "Make Default" link.

When you run your feature again with `bundle exec rspec spec/features/admin/managing_states_spec.rb`, you'll find out that you haven't yet defined the `default?` method on your `State` instances:

```
1) Admins can manage states and mark a state as default
   Failure/Error: visit admin_states_path
   ActionView::Template::Error:
     undefined method `default?' for #<State id: 9, name: "New"...
```

We said earlier that you'd do this with a Boolean field on the `State` model—you need to set that up now. Generate a migration to create the new field with the following code:

```
$ rails g migration add_default_to_states default:boolean
```

Don't run this migration just yet. With the default column being a Boolean field, it's going to need to know what its default value should be: either `true` or `false`. Edit the migration and define that the default value of the `default` attribute should be `false`.

Listing 10.52   db/migrate/[timestamp]_add_default_to_states.rb

```
class AddDefaultToStates < ActiveRecord::Migration
  def change
    add_column :states, :default, :boolean, default: false
  end
end
```

With this small change, every `State` object that's created will have the `default` attribute set to `false` by default. Now run the migration using `bundle exec rake db:migrate`.

Having a field named `default` will generate getter and setter methods, called `default` and `default=`, on your model for you. But Rails will also create a convenience method called `default?` for you, because the field is a Boolean. Your test will get a little further now that this method is defined, so run it again with `bundle exec rspec spec/features/admin/managing_states_spec.rb`:

```
1) Admins can manage states and mark a state as default
   Failure/Error: visit admin_states_path
   ActionView::Template::Error:
     undefined method `make_default_admin_state_path' for #<#< Class:...
```

You don't yet have this method defined. It should take you to a new `make_default` action in `Admin::StatesController`, much like `edit_admin_state_path` takes you to the `edit` action.

To define the new member route, change the `resources :states` line in the `admin` namespace inside config/routes.rb to the following.

Listing 10.53   Adding a new non-resourceful `make_default` route

```
Rails.application.routes.draw do
  namespace :admin do
    ...
    resources :states, only: [:index, :new, :create] do
      member do
        get :make_default
      end
    end
    ...
```

With this member route now defined, your feature will complain that it's missing the `make_default` action when you rerun it with `bundle exec rspec spec/features/admin/managing_states_spec.rb`:

```
1) Admins can manage states and mark a state as default
   Failure/Error: click_link "Make Default"
   AbstractController::ActionNotFound:
     The action 'make_default' could not be found for
     Admin::StatesController
```

The `make_default` action will be responsible for making the state you've selected the new default state, as well as for setting the old default state to not be the default anymore. You can define this action inside app/controllers/admin/states_controller.rb.

Listing 10.54   The `make_default` action in `Admin::StatesController`

```
class Admin::StatesController < Admin::ApplicationController
  ...
  def make_default
    @state = State.find(params[:id])
    @state.make_default!

    flash[:notice] = "'#{@state.name}' is now the default state."
    redirect_to admin_states_path
  end
  ...
end
```

Rather than putting the logic that changes the selected state to the new default inside the controller, you should place it in the model. To trigger a state to become the new default state, you'll call the `make_default!` method on it. It's a best practice to put code that performs functionality like this inside the model, so that it can be in any place that uses an instance of this model.

This `make_default!` method can be defined in the `State` model.

Listing 10.55   app/models/state.rb

```
class State < ActiveRecord::Base
  def make_default!
    State.update_all(default: false)
    update!(default: true)
  end
  ...
```

There are two parts to this method—first you call `update_all` to make sure that all states in the system have their `default` value set to `false` (there should be only one, but it never hurts to make sure); and then you update the current state instance to have a `default` value of `true`.

When you run your feature again with `bundle exec rspec spec/features/admin/managing_states_spec.rb`, you'll get a happy ending to this feature:

```
1 example, 0 failures
```

Great to see! Make sure you haven't broken anything else in your specs by running `bundle exec rspec`:

```
105 examples, 0 failures
```

Now that you know you haven't broken anything, you can commit and push your changes:

```
$ git add .
$ git commit -m "Admins can now set a default state for tickets"
$ git push
```

You now have a concept of having a default state, but at the moment you're not actually *using* the default state for anything. It would be great if your app automatically assigned this new state to newly created tickets—we'll look at implementing that next.

10.4.3 *Applying the default state*

When a ticket is created now, the state of that ticket will be `nil`—you're not assigning a state anywhere. A state will only be assigned when a comment is created, which isn't great. You have a method of setting a default state in our system now—that state should be automatically assigned to newly created tickets. Because this should be automatic functionality every time anyone creates a ticket, you can implement it with another callback, this time in your `Ticket` model.

You can start by modifying your existing ticket-creation spec to make sure the default state gets assigned. Add a new definition of a default state to the top of the spec, as follows.

Listing 10.56   spec/features/creating_tickets_spec.rb

```
require "rails_helper"

RSpec.feature "Users can create new tickets" do
  let!(:state) { FactoryGirl.create :state, name: "New", default: true }
  ...
```

You can verify that the state is assigned to the ticket after you create it:

```
...
scenario "with valid attributes" do
  ...
  expect(page).to have_content "Ticket has been created."
  expect(page).to have_content "State: New"
  ...
```

If you run this spec now with `bundle exec rspec spec/features/creating_tickets_spec.rb`, it will fail:

```
1) Users can create new tickets with valid attributes
   Failure/Error: expect(page).to have_content "State: New"
     expected to find text "State: New" in "Ticketee Toggle navigation..
```

The state isn't getting assigned correctly. Now you can implement the functionality and *know* that it works, as long as your tests pass.

You can start by implementing a new callback at the bottom of your `Ticket` model, to be run *before* a ticket is *created*.

Listing 10.57   A new `before_create` callback in app/models/ticket.rb

```
class Ticket < ActiveRecord::Base
  ...
  before_create :assign_default_state
```

```
  private

  def assign_default_state
    self.state ||= State.default
  end
end
```

Is it really that simple? Well, no. If you run the specs again, you'll see that you haven't defined the `State.default` method anywhere:

```
1) Users can create new tickets with valid attributes
   Failure/Error: click_button "Create Ticket"
   NoMethodError:
     undefined method `default' for State(id: integer, name: string,
     color: string, default: boolean):Class
```

`default` needs to be a new class method on the `State` model in order to return the state with the field `default` set to `true`. You could have done this query directly in the callback, but that would be exposing the internals of the `State` model to the `Ticket` model. The `Ticket` model doesn't care that the default value of a `State` is decided by a Boolean value—it just cares that it can ask the `State` model what the default state is, and then use it.

You can define this new `default` method at the top of the `State` model.

Listing 10.58   Looking up the default state in a class method

```
class State < ActiveRecord::Base
  def self.default
    find_by(default: true)
  end

  ...
```

Is it really *that* simple? Well...yes. Run your spec with `bundle exec rspec spec/features/creating_tickets_spec.rb` again to make sure:

```
5 examples, 0 failures
```

Perfect! You're creating a new ticket, and the state that you designated as the default state is automatically being assigned to the ticket. Make sure you haven't broken anything else by running `bundle exec rspec`:

```
105 examples, 0 failures
```

Awesome. Commit and push your new changes:

```
$ git add .
$ git commit -m "Auto-assign the default state to newly-created tickets"
$ git push
```

10.4.4 Setting a default state in seed states

There's just one last thing that you need to do with default states—you need to set one of the states you've defined in your seeds as the default state.

In db/seeds.rb you earlier defined four states:

```
unless State.exists?
  State.create(name: "New", color: "#0066CC")
  State.create(name: "Open", color: "#008000")
  State.create(name: "Closed", color: "#990000")
  State.create(name: "Awesome", color: "#663399")
end
```

Logically, "New" should be the default state for all newly created tickets, so you can update that line to also set that state as the default.

Listing 10.59 Marking one of the seed states as the default state

```
State.create(name: "New", color: "#0066CC", default: true)
```

Easy, done! Now if you were to re-create your database from scratch, you'd have a correctly set default state, and all tickets you created from then on would have their state set correctly.

You're now very close to being done with states. So far you've added the functionality for users to change the state through the comment form and to display the state transition on a comment, and (just recently) you added the ability for admins to create new states and toggle which state is the default.

At the moment, though, any user is able to change the state of a ticket, which isn't a good thing. You'd like some users to have the ability to leave a comment but not to change the state, so let's look at creating this feature. This is the final feature you'll implement for states.

10.5 Locking down states

Locking down the ability of users to change states is going to take a little more than hiding the State select box from the form; you also need to tell the application to ignore the state_id parameter if the user doesn't have permission to change the state. You'll implement this one piece at a time, beginning with ensuring that the State select box is hidden from those who should be unable to change the state.

10.5.1 Hiding a select box

Earlier on in the chapter, you saw how you can hide the entire form from certain users by using the Pundit-provided policy view helper. You can also use this helper to hide *parts* of the form, like the state field, from users without permission to change the state. But first, you need to write a spec to ensure that the state box is always hidden from these users.

You can add this particular scenario to the bottom of the spec/features/ creating_comments_spec.rb file, because its operation is based on creating a comment. The scenario to ensure that you don't see this `state` field is short and simple:

```
RSpec.feature "Users can comment on tickets" do
  ...
  scenario "but cannot change the state without permission" do
    assign_role!(user, :editor, project)
    visit project_ticket_path(project, ticket)

    expect(page).not_to have_select "State"
  end
end
```

In the requirements for Ticketee, you've decided that editors of a project should be able to leave comments but not change a ticket's state; only managers of a project (and admins) can change the state. The scenario is pretty simple—you change the user's role on the project to be `editor` instead of `manager` and ensure that when the user views the form, there's no State select box present.

When you run this scenario by running `bundle exec rspec spec/features/ creating_comments_spec.rb`, you'll see it fail like this:

```
1) Users can comment on tickets but cannot change the state without permission
   Failure/Error: expect(page).not_to have_select "State"
     expected not to find select box "State", found 1 match: ""
   # ./spec/features/creating_comments_spec.rb:54:in
```

This test is correctly failing because the element is found on the page when it shouldn't be. Now it's time to make this test pass.

To do this, you can use the `policy` method to check that the user has permission to change states on this ticket. If the user doesn't have this permission, you hide the state field. With this change, your State select box code in app/views/comments/ _form.html.erb will look like the following listing.

Listing 10.60   Only show the State select box if the user is allowed to change the state

```
<% if policy(ticket).change_state? %>
  <%= f.association :state %>
<% end %>
```

Unfortunately, this little change will make *all* of the scenarios in your comment-creation scenario fail:

```
1) Users can comment on tickets with valid attributes
   Failure/Error: visit project_ticket_path(project, ticket)
   ActionView::Template::Error:
     undefined method `change_state?' for #<TicketPolicy:...
```

You've created a new permission here, the `change_state` permission, but you haven't defined that permission in your `TicketPolicy` class, so Rails doesn't know what to do with it. We'll address that now.

10.5.2 *Defining the change_state permission*

Before you look at implementing the permission in your `TicketPolicy` class, add some specs for it. You know which roles should be allowed to change state (manager and admin) and which roles shouldn't (viewer and editor), so add those tests to your `TicketPolicy` specs in spec/policies/ticket_policy_spec.rb.

Listing 10.61 Adding specs for the new `change_state` permission

```
context "for anonymous users" do
  ...
  it { should_not permit_action :change_state }
end

context "for viewers of the project" do
  ...
  it { should_not permit_action :change_state }
end

context "for editors of the project" do
  ...
  it { should_not permit_action :change_state }
  ...
end

context "for managers of the project" do
  ...
  it { should permit_action :change_state }
end

context "for managers of other projects" do
  ...
  it { should_not permit_action :change_state }
end

context "for administrators" do
  ...
  it { should permit_action :change_state }
end
```

If you run these new specs with `bundle exec rspec spec/policies/ticket_policy_spec.rb`, you expect all of them to fail, and they all do:

```
31 examples, 6 failures
```

Now you can look at implementing the permission in your `TicketPolicy` class.

Open up the class in app/policies/ticket_policy.rb, and look at the methods that are already defined. You want to allow admins and managers to change the states, which matches the rule defined in `destroy?`. You can define a `change_state?` method that just calls the `destroy?` method.

> **Listing 10.62   Reusing permissions in `TicketPolicy`**

```
class TicketPolicy < ApplicationPolicy
  ...
  def change_state?
    destroy?
  end
end
```

This looks a little odd, but don't worry. It's not going to start destroying your tickets when you're just trying to change the state of them. It's just saying, "If the user can destroy tickets, then they're allowed to change the ticket state as well."

Now if you rerun your `TicketPolicy` specs with `bundle exec rspec spec/policies/ticket_policy_spec.rb`, all will be happy and green:

```
31 examples, 0 failures
```

That will resolve the error you saw in the comment-creation spec. Rerun that spec now with `bundle exec rspec spec/features/creating_comments_spec.rb` and see what shakes out:

```
4 examples, 0 failures
```

Good! All the scenarios in this feature should now be passing, and all your existing specs should still be passing too. Make sure by running `bundle exec rspec`:

```
112 examples, 0 failures
```

Commit and push these changes now:

```
$ git add .
$ git commit -m "Only admins and managers can change states of a ticket"
$ git push
```

The final piece of the states puzzle is to stop the `state` parameter from being set in your `CommentsController` if a user passes it through and doesn't have permission to set states. First, you'll investigate how a user can fake this request. Then you'll write a controller spec that duplicates this and ensures that the state isn't set.

10.5.3   *Hacking a form*

Even if your `state` field is hidden from view, users are still able to submit a form containing this parameter, and your application will accept it. Let's see this in practice.

The first things you need to do are create a user and give them read access to a project, which you can do by starting `rails console` (or `rails c`) and running these commands:

```
user = User.create!(email: "hacker@ticketee.com", password: "password")
user.roles.create(project: Project.first, role: :editor)
```

This will create a new user with the email address hacker@ticketee.com, and give them editor access to the first project in the system, which should be the Sublime Text 3 project. (Remember, editors can create tickets and comments, but not change the state of

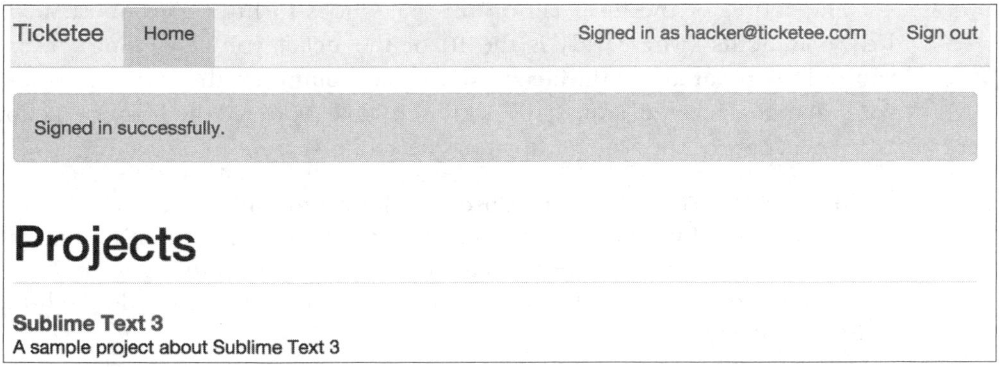

Figure 10.15   What the user sees

tickets.) Quit the console by typing `exit`, and then start up the application with `rails server`. Now you can sign in with this new account, using the password *password*. Once you're in, you should see the page shown in figure 10.15.

Go into this project and pick any ticket in the list, or create your own. It doesn't matter—you just need a ticket. When you're on the ticket page, save this page by going to your browser menu and selecting File > Save or File > Save Page As, and save this file in a memorable location. You'll be editing this saved file and adding in a State select box of your own.

Open the saved file in a text editor, and look for the following line.

Listing 10.63   The end of the form you're going to hack

```
<input name="commit" value="Create Comment" class="btn btn-primary"
  type="submit">
```

This is the Submit button for the form to create a new comment. You can add the `state` field just above it by adding this code to the page, assuming you know—or can at least guess—the IDs of the states.

Listing 10.64   The HTML you can use to hack the form

```
<select id="comment_state_id" name="comment[state_id]">
  <option value="1" selected="selected">New</option>
  <option value="2">Open</option>
  <option value="3">Closed</option>
  <option value="4">Awesome</option>
</select>
```

Save this page in your editor, and then open it up in a browser. You'll now be able to choose a state from the select box—it won't look as pretty as the select box that's actually on the site, but it will be perfectly functional.

The action of the form tag on this page goes to http://localhost:3000/tickets/ [id]/comments (where [id] is the ID of the ticket you're viewing). Even though you're looking at an HTML file saved on your computer, the form will still submit to your actual Ticketee app. This URL will take you to the `create` action inside `CommentsController`, which will—you guessed it—create a comment.

> **BROWSER DIFFERENCES** Only Chrome will save the fully qualified URL as the `action` of the form tag—Firefox and Safari will save the URL without the host-name (for example, /tickets/2/comments). If you want to replicate this trick in Firefox or Safari, you'll also need to modify the form tag to add the http:// localhost:3000/ part.

Open this saved page in a browser now, fill in some text for the comment, and select a value for the state. When you submit this form, it will create a comment and set the state. You should see your comment showing the state transition, as shown in figure 10.16.

Obviously, hiding the `state` field isn't a foolproof way to protect it. A better way to protect this attribute would be to delete it from the parameters before it gets to the method that creates a new comment.

10.5.4 *Ignoring a parameter*

If you removed the `state_id` key from the comment parameters before they're passed to the `build` method

Figure 10.16 Hacked state transition

in the `create` action for `CommentsController`, this problem wouldn't happen. Hackers could try to tamper with the form and submit the data, and you'd just silently delete it before creating the comment.

You can write a controller test to ensure that this security loophole is forever closed in your app. To do so, open spec/controllers/comments_controller_spec.rb and set up a project, ticket, state, and user for the spec you're about to write by putting the code from the following listing inside the `RSpec.describe CommentsController` block.

> **Listing 10.65 spec/controllers/comments_controller_spec.rb**

```
RSpec.describe CommentsController, type: :controller do
  let(:user) { FactoryGirl.create(:user) }
  let(:project) { Project.create!(name: "Ticketee") }
  let(:state) { State.create!(name: "Hacked") }
```

```
let(:ticket) do
  project.tickets.create(name: "State transitions",
    description: "Can't be hacked.", author: user)
end
```

The state you create will be the one you'll attempt to transition to in your spec, with the ticket's default state being not set, and therefore nil. The user you set up will be the user you use to sign in and change the state with. You need to set the user attribute separately from the other ticket attributes because it's protected from being mass-assigned. This user has no permissions at the moment, so it won't be able to change the states.

Your spec needs to make sure that a change doesn't take place when a user who doesn't have permission to change the status of a ticket for that ticket's project submits a state_id parameter. Put the code in the following listing directly underneath the setup you just wrote.

Listing 10.66 spec/controllers/comments_controller_spec.rb

```
context "a user without permission to set state" do
  before :each do
    assign_role!(user, :editor, project)
    sign_in user
  end

  it "cannot transition a state by passing through state_id" do
    post :create, { comment: { text: "Did I hack it??",
                                state_id: state.id },
                    ticket_id: ticket.id }
    ticket.reload
    expect(ticket.state).to be_nil
  end
end
```

To get access to the sign_in method, a helper provided by Devise, you'll need to include Devise's test helpers in your RSpec configuration. To do this, open your spec configuration in spec/rails_helper.rb, and add the following line at the bottom of your RSpec.configure block:

```
RSpec.configure do |config|
  ...
  config.include Devise::TestHelpers, type: :controller
end
```

Inside the example, you use the post method to make a POST request to the create action inside CommentsController, passing in the specified parameters. It's this state_id parameter that should be ignored in the action.

After the post method, you use a new method: reload. When you call reload on an Active Record object, it will fetch a fresh copy of the record from the database. You use this because the create action will load a fresh copy of the Ticket object from the database and update it, which won't affect the instance you've created in the test.

The final line here asserts that the `ticket.state` should be `nil`. When you run this spec by running `bundle exec rspec spec/controllers/comments_controller _spec.rb`, this final line will be the one to fail:

```
1) CommentsController a user without permission to set state cannot
   transition a state by passing through state_id
   Failure/Error: expect(ticket.state).to be_nil
     expected: nil
          got: #<State id: 42, name: "Hacked", color: nil...
```

The `ticket.state` is returning a `State` object because the user has been able to post it through in the parameter hash. With a failing spec now in place, you can stop this state parameter from going unchecked. To ignore this parameter, you can remove it from the `params` hash if the user doesn't have permission to change states.

At the top of the `create` action, inside of `CommentsController`, put the following lines:

```
class CommentsController < ApplicationController
  ...
  def create
    whitelisted_params = comment_params

    unless policy(@ticket).change_state?
      whitelisted_params.delete(:state_id)
    end

    @comment = @ticket.comments.build(whitelisted_params)
  ...
```

You call `comment_params` first now, to do all of the whitelisting of your params before you start modifying them. It makes sense to ensure that the params are there before you try to change them; otherwise you might be trying to delete `params[:comment][:state_id]`, when `params[:comment]` doesn't even exist!

If the user doesn't have permission to change the state on the ticket, then you simply delete that parameter, thereby preventing the user from being able to change the state. If you rerun your controller spec using `bundle exec rspec spec/controllers/ comments_controller_spec.rb`, you'll see that it now passes:

```
1 example, 0 failures
```

Great! Now nobody without permission will be able to download the ticket page, make modifications to it to add a `state` field, and then change the state.

You're done with this feature now, so it's time to make sure you didn't break anything with your changes by running `bundle exec rspec`. You should see that everything is squeaky clean:

```
113 examples, 0 failures
```

Great! Commit and push this to GitHub:

```
$ git add .
$ git commit -m "Protect state_id from users who do
              not have permission to change it"
$ git push
```

The `CommentsController` will now reject the `state_id` parameter if the user doesn't have permission to set it, thereby protecting the form from anybody hacking it to add a `state_id` field when they shouldn't.

The feature of protecting the `state_id` field from changes was the final piece of the state features puzzle. You've now learned how to stop a user from changing not only a particular record when they don't have permission to, but also a specific field on a record.

10.6 Summary

We began this chapter by writing the basis for the work later on in the chapter: comments. By letting users posts comments on a ticket, you can let them add further information to it and tell a story about it.

With the comment base laid down, you implemented the ability for users to change a ticket's state when they post a comment. You tracked the state of the ticket before the comment was saved and the state assigned to the comment so you could show transitions (as shown in figure 10.17).

Figure 10.17   Replay: state transitions

You finished up by limiting the ability to change states to only those who have permission to do so, much like how you previously limited the ability to read projects and create tickets in previous chapters. While doing this, you saw how easy it was for somebody to download the source of your form and alter it to do their bidding, and then how to protect against that.

In chapter 11, you'll add tags to your tickets. Tags are words or short phrases that provide categorization for tickets, making them easier for users to manage. Additionally, you'll implement a search interface that will allow users to find tickets with a given tag or state.

11 Tagging

This chapter covers

- Creating a `has_and_belongs_to_many` relationship between tickets and tags
- Restricting access to tag creation and tag editing
- Adding search functionality for tickets with a given tag or state

In chapter 10 you saw how to give your tickets states (such as "New" or "Open") so that their progress can be indicated. In this chapter, you'll see how to give your tickets tags. Tags are useful for grouping similar tickets together, whether by Agile iterations, feature sets, or any other method of grouping. Without tags, you could crudely group tickets together by setting a ticket's title to something such as "Tag - [name]." This method, however, is messy and difficult to sort through. Having a group of tickets with the same tag will make them much easier to find.

To manage tags, you'll set up a `Tag` model, which will have a `has_and _belongs_to_many` association to the `Ticket` model. You'll set up a *join table* for this association, which is a table that contains foreign key fields for each side of the association. A join table's sole purpose is to join together the two tables whose keys it

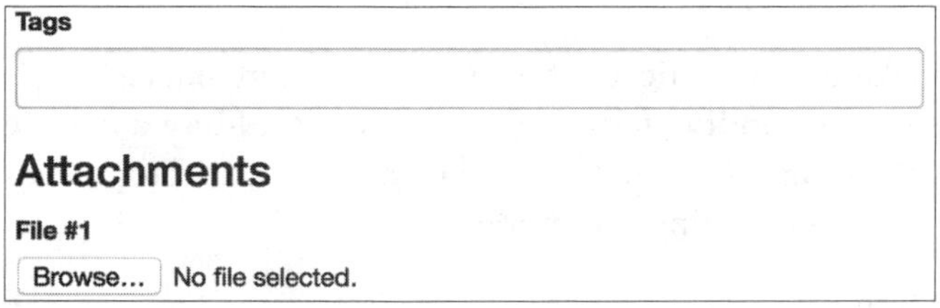

Figure 11.1   The tag box

has—in this case, the `tickets` and `tags` tables. As you move forward in developing this association, note that for all intents and purposes, `has_and_belongs _to_many` works like a two-way `has_many`.

You'll also create two ways to add tags to a ticket. On the new-ticket page, a text field beneath the form's description field will allow users to add multiple tags by using a comma to separate different tags, as shown in figure 11.1.

Additional tags can be added on a comment, with a text field providing the interface to add new tags. When a ticket is created, you'll show these tags underneath the tag description, as shown in figure 11.2.

When a user clicks on a tag, they'll be taken to a page where they can see all tickets with that particular tag. The actions of adding and removing a tag will both need to be added to your permission-checking.

Finally, you'll implement a way to search for tickets that match a state, a tag, or both, by using a gem called Searcher. The query will look like `tag:iteration_1 state:Open`.

That's all there is to this chapter! You'll add tags to Ticketee, which will allow you to easily group and sort tickets. Let's dig into the first feature: adding tags to a new ticket.

Figure 11.2   Tags for a ticket

11.1   *Creating tags*

Tags are useful for making similar tickets easy to find and manage. In this section, you'll create the interface for adding tags to a new ticket by adding a new field to the new-ticket page and defining a `has_and_belongs_to_many` association between the `Ticket` model and the not-yet-existing `Tag` model.

11.1.1   *The tag-creation feature*

First you'll add a text field beneath the description field on the new-ticket page for tags, like you saw in figure 11.1.

The words you enter into this field will become the tags for this ticket, and you should see them on the ticket page. To do this, add a scenario that creates a new ticket with tags at the bottom of spec/features/creating_tickets_spec.rb, as shown in the following listing.

Listing 11.1   spec/features/creating_tickets_spec.rb

```
RSpec.feature "Users can create new tickets" do
  ...
  scenario "with associated tags" do
    fill_in "Name", with: "Non-standards compliance"
    fill_in "Description", with: "My pages are ugly!"
    fill_in "Tags", with: "browser visual"
    click_button "Create Ticket"

    expect(page).to have_content "Ticket has been created."
    within("#ticket #tags") do
      expect(page).to have_content "browser"
      expect(page).to have_content "visual"
    end
  end
end
```

> **SMALL LIMITATION ON OUR IMPLEMENTATION**   For this app, tags can only be a single word, so a list of tags should be space-separated.

When you run the new spec using `bundle exec rspec spec/features/creating _tickets_spec.rb`, it will fail, declaring that it can't find the Tags field. Good! It's not there yet:

```
1) Users can create new tickets with associated tags
   Failure/Error: fill_in "Tags", with: "browser visual"
   Capybara::ElementNotFound:
     Unable to find field "Tags"
```

You'll take the data from this field, process each word into a new `Tag` object, and then link the tags to the ticket when the ticket is created. You'll use a `text_field` tag to render the Tags field this way, but unlike the `text_fields` that you've used previously, this one won't be tied to a database field.

To define this field, put the following code underneath the `description` field in app/views/tickets/_form.html.erb:

```
<%= simple_form_for([project, ticket]) do |f| %>
  ...
  <%= f.input :description %>
  <%= f.input :tag_names, label: "Tags" %>
  ...
```

When you rerun this scenario with `bundle exec rspec spec/features/creating _tickets_spec.rb:76`, it no longer complains about the missing Tags field, telling you instead that it can't find the `tag_names` method on `Ticket` objects:

```
1) Users can create new tickets with associated tags
   Failure/Error: click_link "New Ticket"
   ActionView::Template::Error:
     undefined method `tag_names' for #<Ticket:0x007ff02b1e4268>
   # ...
   # ./app/views/tickets/_form.html.erb:4:in ...
```

As mentioned previously, the `tag_names` attribute won't be tied to a database field, but instead will be a *virtual attribute*. A virtual attribute works just like a real attribute, except that it's not persisted to the database along with the normal attributes. Instead, it's constructed from other data within the model.

To define this virtual attribute in your `Ticket` model, put this line underneath the `has_many :comments` line in app/models/ticket.rb:

```
class Ticket < ActiveRecord::Base
  ...
  attr_accessor :tag_names
  ...
```

The `attr_accessor` call defines virtual attributes in classes for Ruby, so you can also use this feature in your Rails applications. The method will define setter and getter methods for the attribute name you specify, performing the equivalent of the following code.

Listing 11.2 What you get by defining `attr_accessor :tag_names`

```
def tag_names
  @tag_names
end

def tag_names=(names)
  @tag_names = names
end
```

The `attr_accessor` now will define the `tag_names` method that's sought after by the scenario. To make sure of this and to see what you need to do next, rerun the scenario with `bundle exec rspec spec/features/creating_tickets_spec.rb`:

```
1) Users can create new tickets with associated tags
   Failure/Error: click_button "Create Ticket"
   ActionController::UnpermittedParameters:
     found unpermitted parameter: tag_names
```

You need to add the `tag_names` field to the list of permitted parameters in your controller! Do so by opening your `TicketsController` in app/controllers/tickets_controller.rb, and adding the `tag_names` parameter inside the `ticket_params` method.

Listing 11.3   Now with permitted `tag_names`

```
class TicketsController < ApplicationController
  ...
  def ticket_params
    params.require(:ticket).permit(:name, :description, :tag_names,
      attachments_attributes: [:file, :file_cache])
  end
  ...
```

That error will now be resolved, so rerun the specs to see what issue appears next:

```
1) Users can create new tickets with associated tags
   Failure/Error: within("#ticket #tags") do
   Capybara::ElementNotFound:
     Unable to find css "#ticket #tags"
```

You now need to define this #tags element inside the #ticket element on the ticket's page, so that this part of the scenario will pass. This element will contain the tags for your ticket, which your scenario will assert are actually visible.

11.1.2 *Showing tags*

You can add this new #tags element, with its id attribute set to tags, to app/views/tickets/show.html.erb by adding these couple of simple lines as part of the table displaying properties of a ticket.

Listing 11.4   Displaying a ticket's tags

```
<table id="attributes">
  ...
  <% if @ticket.tags.any? %>
    <tr id="tags">
      <th>Tags:</th>
      <td><%= render @ticket.tags %></td>
    </tr>
  <% end %>
</table>
```

This creates the #ticket #tags element that your feature is looking for, and it will render the soon-to-be-created app/views/tags/_tag.html.erb partial for every element in the also-soon-to-be-created tags association on the @ticket object.

So which of these two do you create next? If you run your scenario again, you'll see that it can't find the `tags` method for a `Ticket` object:

```
1) Users can create new tickets with associated tags
   Failure/Error: click_button "Create Ticket"
   ActionView::Template::Error:
     undefined method `tags' for #<Ticket:0x007fb2b7f40f58>
```

You'll define this `tags` method with a `has_and_belongs_to_many` association between `Ticket` objects and `Tag` objects. This method will be responsible for returning a collection of all the tags associated with the given ticket, much like a `has_many` would. The difference is that this method works in the opposite direction as well, allowing you to find out what tickets have a specific tag.

11.1.3 *Defining the tags association*

You can define the `has_and_belongs_to_many` association on the `Ticket` model by placing this `has_and_belongs_to_many` line after the `has_many` definitions inside your `Ticket` model:

```
class Ticket < ActiveRecord::Base
  ...
  has_many :comments, dependent: :destroy
  has_and_belongs_to_many :tags, uniq: true
  ...
```

This association will rely on a join table that doesn't yet exist, called `tags_tickets`. By default, Rails will assume that the name of this join table is the combination, in alphabetical order, of the two tables you want to join. This table contains only two fields—one called `ticket_id` and one called `tag_id`—which are both foreign keys for tags and tickets. The join table will easily facilitate the union of these two tables, as it will have one record for each tag that links to a ticket, and vice versa.

> **UNIQUE BUGS** You're also passing the `uniq: true` option to your association, meaning that only *unique* tags will be retrieved for each ticket. You could list the "bug" tag twice when creating a ticket, like "bug bug," and two records would be created in the join table, but when you ask for a ticket's tags, you'd only get one "bug" tag back.

When you rerun your scenario, you'll be told that there's no constant called `Tag` yet:

```
1) Users can create new tickets with associated tags
   Failure/Error: click_button "Create Ticket"
   ActionView::Template::Error:
     uninitialized constant Ticket::Tag
```

In other words, there's no `Tag` model yet. You'll need to define this now if you want to go any further.

11.1.4 *The Tag model*

Your `Tag` model will have a single field called `name`, which should be unique. To generate this model and its related migration, run the `rails` command like this:

```
$ rails g model tag name:string --timestamps false
```

You don't want to track when tags were created or updated, so you pass the `timestamps` option to this migration with the value of `false`. This will skip adding the `t.timestamps null: false` line inside your migration.

Before you run that migration, generate another one for the join table for tags and tickets. The Rails migration generator can do this for you with the following command:

```
$ rails g migration create_join_table_tags_tickets tag ticket
```

The actual name you give the migration is irrelevant; it just has to have the words "join table" in it, like the preceding line does. You've specified the two models that should be joined together in this join table, and it will generate a migration with the following contents.

> **Listing 11.5   db/migrate/[timestamp]_create_join_table_tags_tickets.rb**

```ruby
class CreateJoinTableTagsTickets < ActiveRecord::Migration
  def change
    create_join_table :tags, :tickets do |t|
      # t.index [:tag_id, :ticket_id]
      # t.index [:ticket_id, :tag_id]
    end
  end
end
```

Uncomment the two commented-out lines, so that the two indexes will be created on the table. This will speed up lookups going both ways—looking up tags for a ticket, and looking up tickets for a tag. You can now run the two migrations:

```
$ bundle exec rake db:migrate
```

This will create the `tags` and `tags_tickets` tables specified in your two migrations.

When you run this scenario again with `bundle exec rspec spec/features/ creating_tickets_spec.rb:76`, it's now satisfied that the `tags` method is defined, and it has gone back to claiming it can't find the `#ticket #tags` element on the page:

```
1) Users can create new tickets with associated tags
   Failure/Error: within("#ticket #tags") do
   Capybara::ElementNotFound:
     Unable to find css "#ticket #tags"
```

This failure is because you haven't done anything to associate the text from the Tags field to the ticket you've created. This means that there are no tags to display, so this element isn't being displayed. The setter you defined with `attr_accessor` is being called, you're storing the tag names in an instance variable called `@tag_names`, but you're not saving those tag names to the database. You need to parse the content from this field into new `Tag` objects, and then associate them with the ticket you're creating, which you'll do right now.

11.1.5 *Displaying a ticket's tags*

You'll now take the names of the tags that are passed in to the `tag_names` attribute for `Ticket` objects, and turn them into objects of the `Tag` class. You'll do this by overwriting the `tag_names=` method provided by the `attr_accessor`, and use it to look up and add tags to the ticket.

To make this happen, go into your `Ticket` model and put these lines inside the class definition, just before the `private` line.

> **Listing 11.6   app/models/ticket.rb**

```
class Ticket < ActiveRecord::Base
  ...
  def tag_names=(names)
    @tag_names = names
    names.split.each do |name|
      self.tags << Tag.find_or_initialize_by(name: name)
    end
  end

  private
  ...
```

When you assign a string of tag names like "browser visual," the `tag_names=` method will split the string on spaces in the string, and find or build new `Tag` instances with each of the names you specified. This will reuse tags that already exist in the database, and initialize new ones that don't. Then when the ticket gets saved, all of the associated tags will be saved and all of the correct associations made.

You also leave the default `@tag_names = names` behavior that was in the autogenerated `tag_names` method before you overwrote it—you need that behavior when it comes to populating data back onto the "New Ticket" form in case of an invalid form submission.

The method you've just written will create the tags that you're displaying on the app/views/tickets/show.html.erb view by using the `render` method:

```
<%= render @ticket.tags %>
```

When you run this scenario again by running `bundle exec rspec spec/features/ creating_tickets_spec.rb:76`, you'll see this render is now failing with an error:

```
1) Users can create new tickets with associated tags
   Failure/Error: click_button "Create Ticket"
   ActionView::Template::Error:
     Missing partial tags/_tag with {:locale=>[:en], :formats=>...
```

This error happens now because `@ticket.tags` contains some tickets, and the `render` call attempts to render them. That's just like back in chapter 10 when you used this line:

```
<%= render @ticket.state %>
```

Rails will render a partial for the given objects based on the class name of the objects. In the case of `@ticket.state`, that class was `State`, so the app/views/states/_state partial was used.

When you iterate over a collection of objects, as you do with `@ticket.tags`, Rails will pick the first object from that collection and then render a partial for each of the

objects based on the class of that first element. This partial will live in app/views/tags/
_tag.html.erb, because the class for the first object is Tag.

The next step is to write the tag partial that your feature has complained about.
Put the following code in a new file called app/views/tags/_tag.html.erb.

Listing 11.7 Adding an HTML representation of a tag

```
<div class="tag">
  <%= link_to "<span></span>".html_safe, "#", class: "remove",
    title: "remove" %>
  <%= tag.name %>
</div>
```

By wrapping the tag name in a div element with the class of tag, you can easily add
some styles to it. You know the tags will also need a link in the future, from the
requirements stated earlier (being able to remove a tag from a ticket), so you include
a dummy link for now, with an href of #.

You can also add some styles for the new tags. You'll leverage some Bootstrap styles
by adding the following code to app/assets/stylesheets/tickets.scss.

Listing 11.8 Adding a CSS representation of a tag

```
.tag {
  @extend .state;
  @extend .label-info;
  margin-right: 10px;

  a {
    color: white;

    &.remove {
      font-family: "FontAwesome";
      @extend .fa-close;
      margin-right: 0.5em;
      text-decoration: none;
    }
  }
}
```

Defining this partial will stop the missing-template error from happening. When you
run your scenario again with bundle exec rspec spec/features/creating_tickets
_spec.rb, it should now pass:

```
7 examples, 0 failures
```

Great! This scenario is now complete. When a user creates a ticket, they can assign
tags to that ticket, and those tags will display along with the ticket's information on the
show action for TicketsController. The tag display was shown earlier in figure 11.2
and is shown again in figure 11.3.

IE6 has a lot of bugs in its CSS support

Author:	admin@ticketee.com
Created:	2 minutes ago
State:	New
Tags:	✖ IE6 ✖ browser ✖ bug

So do IE7 and IE8. Why do people still use this browser?

Figure 11.3 Look Ma, a tag!

You can now commit this change, but before you do, ensure that you haven't broken anything by running `bundle exec rspec`:

```
115 examples, 0 failures, 1 pending
```

Good to see that nothing's blown up this time. There's one pending spec located in spec/models/tag_spec.rb, and because there's nothing else in that file, it's safe to delete it. Go ahead and do that now. After you're done, a rerun of `bundle exec rspec` will produce this lovely green output:

```
114 examples, 0 failures
```

Yay! Commit your changes:

```
$ git add .
$ git commit -m "Users can tag tickets upon creation"
$ git push
```

Now that users can add a tag to a ticket when they create that ticket, you should also let them add tags to a ticket when they create a comment. When a ticket is being discussed, new information may arise that will require another tag to be added to the ticket to group it into a different set. A perfect way to let your users do this would be to let them add the tag when they comment.

11.2 Adding more tags

The tags for a ticket can change throughout the ticket's life; new tags can be added and old ones can be deleted. Let's look at how you can add more tags to a ticket through the comment form after the ticket has been created. Underneath the comment form on a ticket's page, you'll add the same Tags field that you previously used to add tags to your ticket on the new-ticket page.

We'll implement this function one scenario at a time. When you're done, you'll end up with the pretty picture in figure 11.4.

State

```
New                                                          ▲▼
```

Tags

```

```

Figure 11.4   Comment form with tags

11.2.1 *Adding tags through a comment*

To test that users can add tags when they create a comment, you need to add a new scenario to the spec/features/creating_comments_spec.rb feature.

> **Listing 11.9   spec/features/creating_comments_spec.rb**

```ruby
RSpec.feature "Users can comment on tickets" do
  ...
  scenario "when adding a new tag to a ticket" do
    visit project_ticket_path(project, ticket)
    expect(page).not_to have_content "bug"

    fill_in "Text", with: "Adding the bug tag"
    fill_in "Tags", with: "bug"
    click_button "Create Comment"

    expect(page).to have_content "Comment has been created."
    within("#ticket #tags") do
      expect(page).to have_content "bug"
    end
  end
end
```

First, you ensure that you don't see this tag on the page, to check that you don't have a false positive. Next, you fill in the text for the comment so it's valid, add the word "bug" to the Tags field, and click the Create Comment button. Finally, you ensure that the comment has been created and that the "bug" tag you entered into the comment form now appears in #ticket #tags.

When you run this scenario using bundle exec rspec spec/features/creating _comments_spec.rb, it will fail because there's no Tags field as part of the comments form yet:

```
1) Users can comment on tickets when adding a new tag to a ticket
   Failure/Error: fill_in "Tags", with: "bug"
   Capybara::ElementNotFound:
     Unable to find field "Tags"
```

You can reuse the code you put in the ticket form for entering tags, in case you want to add some magic around it later.[1] To do that, you can move the line rendering the Tags field from the ticket form, and place it in a partial that you can reuse.

---

[1] It would be cool if you had some kind of autocomplete for tag names. Just putting that out there.

Take the line that renders the Tags field and place it in a new partial, app/views/tags/_form.html.erb.

Listing 11.10   Your new tag/form partial

```
<%= f.input :tag_names, label: "Tags" %>
```

Then you can replace the Tags field with this form partial in your ticket form.

Listing 11.11   app/views/tickets/_form.html.erb

```
<%= simple_form_for([project, ticket]) do |f| %>
  ...
  <%= render "tags/form", f: f %>
  ...
```

This new line will render your new app/views/tags/_form.html.erb partial, passing in the form-building object, f, so that it's also available in that partial.

In order to make the failing step in your scenario now pass, you'll reuse this same line after the policy block in app/views/comments/_form.html.erb.

Listing 11.12   Adding tags to app/views/comments/_form.html.erb

```
<%= simple_form_for([ticket, comment]) do |f| %>
  ...
  <%= render "tags/form", f: f %>
  ...
```

When rendering the tags/form partial here, you'll pass in the form builder object for a Comment object, not a Ticket. Not that the partial will mind; all it really needs is some kind of object that has a tag_names method on it, and it's quite content.

When you rerun the scenario with bundle exec rspec spec/features/creating _comments_spec.rb, all of the scenarios in the feature will now fail:

```
1) Users can comment on tickets with valid attributes
   Failure/Error: visit project_ticket_path(project, ticket)
   ActionView::Template::Error:
     undefined method `tag_names' for #<Comment:0x007fdff9ae93a0>
```

When defining the tag fields inside the form for a Ticket, you came across this same problem. The problem back then happened because there was no attribute—real or virtual—defined for Ticket objects. The problem you face now is almost exactly the same, but this time it's for the Comment model.

Open app/models/comment.rb and make a call to attr_accessor to define a virtual attribute for tag_names:

```
class Comment < ActiveRecord::Base
  ...
  attr_accessor :tag_names
  ...
```

This new `attr_accessor` call in your `Comment` model will define the `tag_names` method that the scenario is looking for. To see what you need to do next, rerun the scenario. You'll see this:

```
1) Users can comment on tickets with valid attributes
   Failure/Error: click_button "Create Comment"
   ActionController::UnpermittedParameters:
     found unpermitted parameter: tag_names
```

You need to add the `tag_names` parameter to the whitelist of permitted parameters in your `CommentsController`. Open the controller in app/controllers/comments _controller.rb, and add the parameter to the `comment_params` method:

```ruby
class CommentsController < ApplicationController
  ...
  def comment_params
    params.require(:comment).permit(:text, :state_id, :tag_names)
  end
end
```

The next failure you'll get if you rerun your specs shows that you're getting closer to making this functionality work:

```
1) Users can comment on tickets when adding a new tag to a ticket
   Failure/Error: within("#ticket #tags") do
   Capybara::ElementNotFound:
     Unable to find css "#ticket #tags"
```

The scenario is not seeing the #ticket #tags element because the tags are not being assigned correctly. The code that should associate a tag with a ticket isn't in the `Comment` model—it's inside the `Ticket` model.

To fix this, you can use another `after_create` callback inside the `Comment` model to add all of the tags supplied in the comment to its parent ticket.

> **ORDER OF OPERATIONS MATTERS!** We'd love to just overwrite the `tag_names=` setter, like you did inside the `Ticket` model, and add the tags to the comment's ticket inside it, but in this case the ticket association isn't yet set when you assign the tag names. It's a little bit difficult to add tags to a ticket that doesn't exist!

You can define the `after_create` callback with your other callbacks in the `Comment` model like so:

```ruby
class Comment < ActiveRecord::Base
  ...
  after_create :set_ticket_state
  after_create :associate_tags_with_ticket
  ...
```

AFTER_CREATE VS. BEFORE_CREATE You want to use an `after_create` here so that the tags aren't associated prematurely with a ticket, which they would be if you used a `before_create`. When you add things to an association with methods like `ticket.tags << tag`, you don't have to save anything for that association to be created; it happens on the spot. So if the comment isn't valid and doesn't get saved, the tags would still be added—oops!

For this callback to work, you'll need to define the `associate_tags_with_ticket` method, too. Define this method at the bottom of the `Comment` model, like this:

```
class Comment < ActiveRecord::Base
  ...
  def associate_tags_with_ticket
    if tag_names
      tag_names.split.each do |name|
        ticket.tags << Tag.find_or_create_by(name: name)
      end
    end
  end
end
```

It's very similar to what you wrote in the `Ticket` model—you split the provided list of tags, and add a new tag to the association for each name. You don't need to save the ticket after you do this—as stated earlier, adding a tag to the association with `<<` will save the link automatically.

This should mean that now a comment's tags are associated with the ticket. Find out by running `bundle exec rspec spec/features/creating_comments_spec.rb`:

```
5 examples, 0 failures
```

Boom, that's passing! Good stuff. Now for the cleanup. Make sure you haven't broken anything else by running `bundle exec rspec`:

```
115 examples, 0 failures
```

With all the specs passing, it's commit time!

```
$ git add .
$ git commit -m "Users can add tags when adding a comment"
$ git push
```

In this section, you've created a way for your users to add more tags to a ticket when they add a comment, which allows your users to easily organize tickets into relevant groups after the tickets' creation. You now need to restrict this power to users with permission to manage tags. You don't want all users to create tags willy-nilly, since it's likely you'd end up with an overabundance of tags. For example, see the tags on the Rails Lighthouse account, at the bottom right of this page: https://rails.lighthouseapp.com/projects/8994-ruby-on-rails/overview. Too many tags makes it hard to identify which tags are useful and which are not. People with permission to tag things will know that with great power comes great responsibility.

11.3   *Tag restriction*

Using the roles system you built in chapter 8, you can easily integrate authorizations for managing tags for a ticket. In Ticketee, if a user is a manager or admin of a project, they're able to add and (later on) remove tags, much like they were allowed to change the state of a ticket in chapter 10.

11.3.1 *Testing tag restriction*

When a user without authorization attempts to submit a ticket or comment, the application shouldn't tag the ticket with the tags they've specified. You'll add this restriction to the `CommentsController`, but first you need to write a controller spec to cover this behavior.

Put the code from the following listing at the bottom of the block for `RSpec` `.describe CommentsController`, inside spec/controllers/comments_controller_spec.rb.

Listing 11.13   spec/controllers/comments_controller_spec.rb

```ruby
RSpec.describe CommentsController, type: :controller do
  ...
  context "a user without permission to tag a ticket" do
    before do
      assign_role!(user, :editor, project)
      sign_in user
    end

    it "cannot tag a ticket when creating a comment" do
      post :create, { comment: { text: "Tag!",
                                 tag_names: "one two" },
                      ticket_id: ticket.id }
      ticket.reload
      expect(ticket.tags).to be_empty
    end
  end
end
```

If you run this spec now with `bundle exec rspec spec/controllers/comments` `_controller_spec.rb`, it will produce this error:

```
1) CommentsController a user without permission to tag a ticket cannot
   tag a ticket when creating a comment
   Failure/Error: expect(ticket.tags).to be_empty
     expected `#<ActiveRecord::Associations::CollectionProxy [#<Tag id:
     15, name: "one">, #<Tag id: 16, name: "two">]>.empty?` to return
     true, got false
```

Good! A failing test is a good start to a new feature. To make this test pass, you should check that the user has the authorization to post tags in `CommentsController`. To remove the `tag_names` parameter from the comment's parameters if the user is unable to tag, you should do just what you did with the `state` parameter if the user wasn't able to change the state: just put these lines at the top of the create action, underneath the first unless statement.

Listing 11.14   Sanitizing parameters passed into the controller

```
class CommentsController < ApplicationController
  ...
  def create
    ...
    unless policy(@ticket).tag?
      whitelisted_params.delete(:tag_names)
    end
    ...
```

The create action now has a lot of logic at the top of the method to sanitize the parameters. It's getting quite crowded in there! To make it easier to follow, move the two unless statements checking for permissions out into a new private method for this class, like this:

```
class CommentsController < ApplicationController
  ...
  def sanitized_parameters
    whitelisted_params = comment_params

    unless policy(@ticket).change_state?
      whitelisted_params.delete(:state_id)
    end

    unless policy(@ticket).tag?
      whitelisted_params.delete(:tag_names)
    end

    whitelisted_params
  end
end
```

Now, rather than having two conditional statements at the top of the create action, you can call the sanitized_parameters method, so that the create action is a little neater:

```
class CommentsController < ApplicationController
  ...
  def create
    @comment = @ticket.comments.build(sanitized_parameters)
    @comment.author = current_user
    ...
```

If you wanted to add an update action to this controller later on, this action could also use the sanitized_parameters method. In fact, you *should* use the sanitized _parameters method.

When you rerun the spec with `bundle exec rspec spec/features/comments _controller_spec.rb`, both specs will fail because they can't find the `tag?` method for `TicketPolicy`:

```
1) CommentsController a user without permission to set state cannot
   transition a state by passing through state_id
   Failure/Error: post :create, { comment: { text: "Did I hack it??",
   NoMethodError:
     undefined method `tag?' for #<TicketPolicy:0x007fd65b4c0890>
```

Define this method in app/policies/ticket_policy.rb after the `change_state?` method. Like you did in chapter 10 for the `change_state` permission, you can write some specs for the new permission in app/policies/ticket_policy_spec.rb, using the same rules as you did for `change_state`.

Listing 11.15   Specs for the new-ticket `tag` permission

```ruby
RSpec.describe TicketPolicy do
  context "permissions" do
    ...
    context "for anonymous users" do
      ...
      it { should_not permit_action :tag }
    end

    context "for viewers of the project" do
      ...
      it { should_not permit_action :tag }
    end

    context "for editors of the project" do
      ...
      it { should_not permit_action :tag }
    end

    context "for managers of the project" do
      ...
      it { should permit_action :tag }
    end

    context "for managers of other projects" do
      ...
      it { should_not permit_action :tag }
    end

    context "for administrators" do
      ...
      it { should permit_action :tag }
    end
  end
end
```

You can then implement the `tag?` permission the same way you implemented the `change_state?` permission—by reusing the same rule as you did for the `destroy?` permission. Open app/policies/ticket_policy.rb and define a new `tag?` permission as follows.

Listing 11.16 Reusing policy definitions in `TicketPolicy`

```
class TicketPolicy < ApplicationPolicy
  ...
  def tag?
    destroy?
  end
end
```

In your test, the user is only an editor and therefore shouldn't be able to tag tickets by posting a comment. Run the policy specs you just wrote and make sure your logic is sound, with `bundle exec rspec spec/policies/ticket_policy_spec.rb`:

```
37 examples, 0 failures
```

Perfect. Everything should now be in place to make sure your controller specs pass. Verify this with `bundle exec rspec spec/controllers/comments_controller_spec.rb`:

```
2 examples, 0 failures
```

Good! You have something in place to block users from tagging tickets when they create a comment. Verify that nothing else has been broken by running `bundle exec rspec`:

```
122 examples, 0 failures
```

Great! Now you're only missing the blocking code for tagging a ticket when it's being created. You can create a spec test for this too, this time in spec/controllers/tickets_controller_spec.rb.

Listing 11.17 Testing that unauthorized users can't add tags when creating tickets

```
require "rails_helper"

RSpec.describe TicketsController, type: :controller do
  let(:project) { FactoryGirl.create(:project) }
  let(:user) { FactoryGirl.create(:user) }

  before :each do
    assign_role!(user, :editor, project)
    sign_in user
  end

  it "can create tickets, but not tag them" do
    post :create, ticket: { name: "New ticket!",
```

```
                        description: "Brand spankin' new",
                        tag_names: "these are tags" },
                  project_id: project.id
      expect(Ticket.last.tags).to be_empty
    end
end
```

In this spec, you create a project and a user that has an `editor` role on that project. You sign in as that user using the Devise test helper, `sign_in`, and then you attempt to create a ticket with tags. The `tag_names` parameter should be ignored by your controller, but if you run this spec with `bundle exec rspec spec/controllers/tickets _controller_spec.rb`, you'll see that the controller is not ignoring that parameter:

```
1) TicketsController can create tickets, but not tag them
   Failure/Error: expect(Ticket.last.tags).to be_empty
     expected `#<ActiveRecord::Associations::CollectionProxy [#<Tag
     id: 21, name: "these">, #<Tag id: 22, name: "are">, #<Tag id: 23,
     name: "tags">]>.empty?` to return true, got false
```

Because there's no restriction on tagging a ticket through the `create` action, there are tags for the ticket that was just created, and your example fails.

For your `create` action in the `TicketsController` action, you can do exactly what you did in the `create` action of the `CommentsController` action: sanitize the parameters before they're passed to where the object is created. To do this, make the beginning of the `create` action inside `TicketsController` look like this:

```
class TicketsController < ApplicationController
  ...

  def create
    @ticket = @project.tickets.new

    whitelisted_params = ticket_params
    unless policy(@ticket).tag?
      whitelisted_params.delete(:tag_names)
    end

    @ticket.attributes = whitelisted_params
    @ticket.author = current_user
    ...
```

This is a little more convoluted than the code in the `CommentsController`. First you need to build a new ticket to run your policy checks on. Then you can run your sanitizing checks, modifying the parameters if necessary. Then you can assign all of the sanitized attributes in one fell swoop.

When you rerun your spec with `bundle exec rspec spec/controllers/ tickets_controller_spec.rb`, it will pass:

```
1 example, 0 failures
```

Great, now you're protecting both of the ways a ticket can be tagged. You can also make the interface a little bit nicer, and not show the Tags field if the user doesn't have permission to add tags when creating a comment.

Open app/views/comments/_form.html.erb and wrap a conditional around the rendering of the tag form. You only want to show it if the current user can tag the ticket, like so:

```erb
<%= simple_form_for [ticket, comment] do |f| %>
  ...
  <% if policy(ticket).tag? %>
    <%= render "tags/form", f: f %>
  <% end %>
  ...
```

Because of this new restriction, the scenario that you created earlier to test that users can add tags when creating a comment will now be broken!

11.3.2 *Tags are allowed, for some*

When you run bundle exec rspec, you'll see one failing scenario:

```
Failures:

  1) Users can create new tickets with associated tags
     Failure/Error: within("#ticket #tags") do
     Capybara::ElementNotFound:
       Unable to find css "#ticket #tags"
     # ...
     # ./spec/features/creating_tickets_spec.rb:83:in ...

...

Failed examples:

rspec ./spec/features/creating_tickets_spec.rb:76
```

It looks like tags are not being assigned any more. How come? This might be happening if the logged-in user in this spec isn't authorized to do that. What role does the user have?

Look at the top of the creating_tickets_spec.rb, specifically at the before block:

```ruby
RSpec.feature "Users can create new tickets" do
  ...

  before do
    login_as(user)
    project = FactoryGirl.create(:project, name: "Internet Explorer")
    assign_role!(user, :editor, project)
    ...
```

In this code you're assigning the role of editor. Are editors allowed to tag tickets? Your `TicketPolicy` determines this:

```
class TicketPolicy < ApplicationPolicy
  ...

  def destroy?
    user.try(:admin?) || record.project.has_manager?(user)
  end

  ...

  def tag?
    destroy?
  end
end
```

The answer is no; editors are not allowed to tag tickets. To fix this test, you can change the role you assign at the top of this test to `manager`:

```
RSpec.feature "Users can create new tickets" do
  ...

  before do
    login_as(user)
    project = FactoryGirl.create(:project, name: "Internet Explorer")
    assign_role!(user, :manager, project)
    ...
```

Run all your tests again to make sure this is now fixed:

```
123 examples, 0 failures
```

In this section, you've restricted the ability to add tags to a ticket—whether through the new-ticket or comment forms—to only users who have the permission to tag a ticket. For the time being, you've defined this as admins or managers, but that may change over time. You've done this to restrict the flow of tags. Generally speaking, the people with the ability to tag should know to create only useful tags, so that the usefulness of the tags is not diluted.

You can now commit and push this:

```
$ git add .
$ git commit -m "Restrict tagging to only authorized users"
$ git push
```

In the next section, you'll use this same permission to determine which users are able to remove tags from tickets.

11.4 Deleting a tag

The ability to remove a tag from a ticket is helpful because a tag may become irrelevant over time. Say you tagged a ticket as "v0.1" for your project, but that milestone is complete and the ticket isn't, so it needs to be moved to "v0.2." You need a way to

IE6 has a lot of bugs in its CSS support

Author:	admin@ticketee.com
Created:	2 minutes ago
State:	`New`
Tags:	`✖ IE6` `✖ browser` `✖ bug`

So do IE7 and IE8. Why do people still use this browser?

Figure 11.5 X marks the spot

delete the old tag. With the ability to delete tags, you have some assurance that people will clean up tags when they need to.

To let users delete a tag, you added a placeholder cross (X) to the left of each of your tags, as shown in figure 11.5.

When this cross is clicked, the tag will disappear through the magic of JavaScript. Rather than making a request to the action to delete the tag and then redirecting back to the ticket page, the JavaScript will remove the tag's element from the page and make an asynchronous behind-the-scenes request to the controller action to delete the tag.

11.4.1 Testing tag deletion

As usual, you'll start by writing a feature to verify what should happen when you delete a tag from a ticket. Create a new file at spec/features/deleting_tags_spec.rb and put the following code in it.

Listing 11.18 spec/features/deleting_tags_spec.rb

```ruby
require "rails_helper"

RSpec.feature "Users can delete unwanted tags from a ticket" do
  let(:user) { FactoryGirl.create(:user) }
  let(:project) { FactoryGirl.create(:project) }
  let(:ticket) do
    FactoryGirl.create(:ticket, project: project,
      tag_names: "ThisTagMustDie", author: user)
  end

  before do
    login_as(user)
    assign_role!(user, :manager, project)
    visit project_ticket_path(project, ticket)
  end
```

```
    scenario "successfully", js: true do
      within tag("ThisTagMustDie") do
        click_link "remove"
      end
      expect(page).to_not have_content "ThisTagMustDie"
    end
  end
```

In this feature, you create a new user and sign in as that user. Then you create a new project and give the user the role of manager on it, which means the user can modify the tags of any of the project's tickets. A ticket has already been created with the tag "ThisTagMustDie," and the final couple of lines delete that tag and verify that it's gone.

When you run this feature using bundle exec rspec spec/features/deleting _tags_spec.rb, you'll get this error:

```
1) Users can delete unwanted tags from a ticket successfully
   Failure/Error: within tag("ThisTagMustDie") do
   NoMethodError:
     undefined method `tag' for #<RSpec::ExampleGroups::...
```

Alright. Time to implement this bad boy.

11.4.2 Adding a link to delete the tag

You've used a method called tag in your spec, but the method doesn't exist. This method should be a *finder*—you call it to find an element on the page, which you can then scope all of your future calls by. You want to use this method to find the particular HTML element for the tag in question; you can then click the X link to delete the tag inside that element.

You've written finders for Capybara before—inside the file spec/support/ capybara_finders.rb. There's one there called list_item. Underneath the list_item method, define another one to find tags.

> #### Listing 11.19 Adding another Capybara finder

```
module CapybaraFinders
  ...
  def tag(content)
    find("div.tag", text: content)
  end
end
```

This will find the div element with the class of tag, which you defined earlier to display your tags nicely. You also filter the list of tags by only selecting the one with the right text, which in this case is "ThisTagMustDie."

The "remove" link inside that tag needs to trigger an asynchronous request to an action that will remove a tag from a ticket. The perfect name for an action like this, if you were to put it in the TicketsController, would be remove_tag. But because it's acting on a tag, a better place for this action would be inside a new controller called TagsController.

Before you go and define this action, let's make sure that only people who can tag tickets can delete them by wrapping the "remove" link inside a policy check. Inside app/views/tags/_tag.html.erb, you can use the familiar `policy` method to do this.

Listing 11.20   app/views/tags/_tag.html.erb

```
<div class="tag">
  <% if policy(ticket).tag? %>
    <%= link_to "<span></span>".html_safe,
      remove_ticket_tag_path(ticket, tag), method: :delete, remote: true,
      class: "remove", title: "remove" %>
  <% end %>
  <%= tag.name %>
</div>
```

Here, you check that a user can tag the ticket—if they can't tag, then you won't show the X link to remove the tag. This is to prevent everyone from removing tags as they feel like it. Remember: with great power comes great responsibility.

You've also filled out the contents of the link, so it's no longer a dummy link to #. You use the `:remote` option for the `link_to` to indicate to Rails that you want this link to be an asynchronous request. This is similar to the "Add another file" link you provided in chapter 9, except this time you don't need any JavaScript to determine anything; you only need to make a request to a specific URL.

For the `:url` option, you pass through the `ticket` object to `remove_ticket_tag_path` so that your action knows which ticket to delete the tag from. Remember, your primary concern right now is disassociating a tag and a ticket, not completely deleting the tag.

Because this is a destructive action, you use the `:delete` method. You've used this previously to call destroy actions, but the `:delete` method is not exclusive to the destroy action, so you can use it here as well.

The final option, `:title`, lets you define the title for this link. You've set that to be "remove," and this is how Capybara will find the actual link to click it. Capybara supports following links by their internal text, or by their `name`, `id`, or `title` attributes.

When you run your feature with `bundle exec rspec spec/features/deleting _tags_spec.rb`, you'll see that it fails with this error:

```
1) Users can delete unwanted tags from a ticket successfully
   Failure/Error: Unable to find matching line from backtrace
   ActionView::Template::Error:
     undefined local variable or method `ticket' for ...
   # ./app/views/tags/_tag.html.erb:2:in ...
```

Line 2 in your _tag.html.erb partial refers to the `ticket` variable, which doesn't exist within your partial. You need to have a reference to the ticket for the link, or you won't know what ticket to remove the tag from!

In the parent app/views/tickets/show.html.erb view, you have a `@ticket` variable that's used to display the details of the current ticket—you should pass that variable into the partial as a local variable so you can use it for permission checking, and when generating the "remove" link.

Inside app/views/tickets/show.html.erb, modify the line that renders the tags for a ticket to also provide the @ticket variable to the partial.

Listing 11.21   Part of app/views/tickets/show.html.erb, for displaying tags

```
<table id="attributes">
  ...
  <% if @ticket.tags.any? %>
    <tr id="tags">
      <th>Tags:</th>
      <td><%= render @ticket.tags, ticket: @ticket %></td>
    </tr>
  <% end %>
</table>
```

The @ticket variable will now be available inside the tag partial as the local variable ticket. Now when you rerun your spec with bundle exec rspec spec/features/ deleting_tags_spec.rb, you'll get a different error:

```
1) Users can delete unwanted tags from a ticket successfully
   Failure/Error: Unable to find matching line from backtrace
   ActionView::Template::Error:
     undefined method `remove_ticket_tag_path' for ...
   # ./app/views/tags/_tag.html.erb:4:in ...
```

This error is coming up because you haven't defined the route to the remove action yet. You can define this route in config/routes.rb inside the resources :tickets block, morphing it into the following.

Listing 11.22   Defining a route for removing tags from tickets

```
Rails.application.routes.draw do
  ...
  resources :tickets, only: [] do
    resources :comments, only: [:create]
    resources :tags, only: [] do
      member do
        delete :remove
      end
    end
  end
  ...
end
```

By nesting the tags resource inside the ticket's resource, you're given routing helpers such as ticket_tag_path. With the member block inside that, you get the remove _ticket_tag_path helper, too.

Now you'll be able to render the page without error; the route you've provided will be recognized by Rails and will generate a URL that looks something like /tickets/1/ tags/2/remove. Now when you rerun the test, you'll get a different error:

```
1) Users can delete unwanted tags from a ticket successfully
   Failure/Error: Unable to find matching line from backtrace
   ActionController::RoutingError:
     uninitialized constant TagsController
```

The spec is loading the ticket page correctly, finding the "remove" link, and clicking it.

Now you need a controller to process the actual removal of the tag from the ticket, so generate a new controller called `TagsController`, as that's what the error message is looking for:

```
$ rails g controller tags
```

Now that you have a controller to define your action in, open app/controllers/tags _controller.rb and define the `remove` action in it.

Listing 11.23 Removing a tag from a ticket

```
class TagsController < ApplicationController
  def remove
    @ticket = Ticket.find(params[:ticket_id])
    @tag = Tag.find(params[:id])
    authorize @ticket, :tag?

    @ticket.tags.destroy(@tag)
    head :ok
  end
end
```

In this action, you find the ticket based on the ID passed through as params[:ticket_id], and the tag based on the ID passed through as params[:id]. You can then use `destroy`, which is a method provided by the tags association, to remove @tag from the list of tags in @ticket.tags.[2] Finally, you can send the simple header :ok, which will return a 200 OK status to your browser, signaling that everything went according to plan.

When you rerun your scenario with bundle exec rspec spec/features/ deleting_tags_spec.rb, it will successfully click the link, but the tag is still there:

```
1) Users can delete unwanted tags from a ticket successfully
   Failure/Error: expect(page).to_not have_content "ThisTagMustDie"
     expected not to find text "ThisTagMustDie" in "Ticketee Home ..."
```

---

[2] For a full list of all the methods that the tags association offers, check out the Active Record Associations Rails guide: http://guides.rubyonrails.org/association_basics.html#has-and-belongs-to-many-association-reference.

Your tag is unassociated from the ticket but not removed from the page, so your feature is still failing. The request is made to delete the ticket, but there's currently no code that removes the tag from the page. Let's add that code now.

11.4.3 *Removing a tag from the page*

You're removing a tag's association from a ticket, but you're not yet showing people that it has happened on the page. You're making the request to remove the tag *asynchronously* via JavaScript, so you can use JavaScript to hook into the lifecycle of that request and perform certain actions depending on the response.

You did this in chapter 9 when you added extra file upload fields to your "New Ticket" form from a JavaScript request. This will be a lot simpler.

You only want to remove the tag from the page if the request was a success, so you can use the `ajax:success` callback like you did before. Because this functionality relates to tags, you can add some code to app/assets/javascripts/tags.coffee:

```
$ ->
  $(".tag .remove").on "ajax:success", ->
    $(this).parent().fadeOut()
```

You target any "remove" links inside tags with the `$(".tag .remove")` selector, and then on a successful response from that link, you use jQuery's `parent()` and `fadeOut()` functions to find the link's parent `.tag` element, and fade it out of the page.[3] Easy!

When you run your feature using `bundle exec rspec spec/features/deleting _tags_spec.rb`, you'll see that it now passes:

```
1 example, 0 failures
```

Awesome! With this feature done, users with permission to tag tickets of a project will now be able to remove tags, too. Before you commit this feature, run `bundle exec rspec` to make sure everything is okay:

```
125 examples, 0 failures, 1 pending
```

That's awesome too! There's one pending spec inside spec/helpers/tags_helper _spec.rb. You can delete this file now, and if you rerun `bundle exec rspec`, you'll see this:

```
124 examples, 0 failures
```

Commit and push this:

```
$ git add .
$ git commit -m "Add the ability for users to remove tags from tickets"
$ git push
```

Now that you can add and remove tags, what's left to do? Find them! By implementing a way to find tickets with a given tag, you make it easier for users to see only the tickets

---

[3] See the jQuery API documentation for more info on the `parent()` (http://api.jquery.com/parent) and `fadeOut()` (http://api.jquery.com/fadeOut/) functions.

they want to see. As an added bonus, you'll also implement a way for users to find tickets for a given state, perhaps even at the same time as finding a tag.

When you're done with this next feature, you'll add some more functionality that will let users go to tickets for a tag by clicking on the tag name inside the ticket-show page.

11.5 Finding tags

At the beginning of this chapter, there was mention of searching for tickets using a query such as `tag:iteration_1 state:open`. This magical method would return all the tickets associated with the "iteration_1" tag that have the state of Open. This helps users scope down the list of tickets that appear on a project page so they can better focus on them.

There's a gem developed specifically for this purpose, called Searcher, which you can use. This gem is good for a lo-fi solution, but it shouldn't be used in a high-search-volume environment. For that, look into full-text-search support for your favorite database system (or an external system, like Elasticsearch).

The Searcher gem provides you with a search method on specific classes. It accepts a query like the one mentioned and returns the records that match it.

11.5.1 Testing search

As usual, you should (and will) test that searching for tickets with a given tag works. You'll do this by writing a new feature called spec/features/searching_spec.rb and filling it with the content from the following listing.

Listing 11.24 spec/features/searching_spec.rb

```
require "rails_helper"

RSpec.feature "Users can search for tickets matching specific criteria" do
  let(:user) { FactoryGirl.create(:user) }
  let(:project) { FactoryGirl.create(:project) }
  let!(:ticket_1) do
    FactoryGirl.create(:ticket, name: "Create projects",
      project: project, author: user, tag_names: "iteration_1")
  end

  let!(:ticket_2) do
    FactoryGirl.create(:ticket, name: "Create users",
      project: project, author: user, tag_names: "iteration_2")
  end

  before do
    assign_role!(user, :manager, project)
    login_as(user)
    visit project_path(project)
  end

  scenario "searching by tag" do
```

```
      fill_in "Search", with: "tag:iteration_1"
      click_button "Search"
      within("#tickets") do
        expect(page).to have_link "Create projects"
        expect(page).to_not have_link "Create users"
      end
    end
  end
end
```

In the setup for this feature, you create two tickets and give them two separate tags: "iteration_1" and "iteration_2." When you look for tickets tagged with "iteration_1," you shouldn't see tickets that don't have this tag, such as the one that's only tagged "iteration_2."

Run this feature using bundle exec rspec spec/features/searching_spec.rb, and it'll complain because there's no Search field on the page:

```
1) Users can search for tickets matching specific criteria searching by tag
   Failure/Error: fill_in "Search", with: "tag:iteration_1"
   Capybara::ElementNotFound:
     Unable to find field "Search"
```

In your feature, the last thing you do before attempting to fill in this Search field is go to the project page. This means that the Search field should be on that page, so that your feature, and more importantly your users, can fill it out.

Because you're searching tickets, you can place the search form inside the header section that lists out the tickets inside app/views/projects/show.html.erb.

Listing 11.25   Adding a ticket search form to the project details page

```
<h2>Tickets</h2>

<ul class="actions">
  <li>
    <%= form_tag search_project_tickets_path(@project), method: :get,
      class: "form-inline" do %>
      <%= label_tag "search", "Search", class: "sr-only" %>
      <%= text_field_tag "search", params[:search], class: "form-control" %>
      <%= submit_tag "Search", class: "btn btn-default" %>
    <% end %>
  </li>
  ...
```

You should also add some responsive styles for your search form, so that it looks okay on smaller screens. Inside app/assets/stylesheets/responsive.scss, add the following code.

Listing 11.26   Making sure your search form looks okay on small screens

```
@media(max-width: $screen-xs-max) {
  input#search {
    display: inline-block;
    vertical-align: middle;
    width: auto;
```

```
  }
}

@media(max-width: $screen-sm-max) {
  ul.actions .form-inline {
    padding-bottom: 5px;
  }
}
```

This will reuse the same search styles on smaller screens as larger ones, as well as put in some padding when the width of the form causes the New Ticket button to wrap to a second line.

This will give you a nice search form like the one in figure 11.6. (It won't look like that yet, because you haven't finished the feature. But it will when you're done.)

Figure 11.6   The search form

You've used form_tag before; this method generates a form that's not tied to any particular object but still gives you the style of form wrapper that form_for does. Inside the form_tag, you use the label tag and text_field_tag helpers to define a label and input field for the search terms, and you use submit_tag as a Submit button for the form. This example also uses a few of Bootstrap's classes, like sr-only, form-control, and btn btn-default, for a nice-looking form.

The search_project_tickets_path method is undefined at the moment, as you'll see when you run bundle exec rspec spec/features/searching_spec.rb:

```
1) Users can search for tickets matching specific criteria searching by
   tag
   Failure/Error: visit project_path(project)
   ActionView::Template::Error:
     undefined method `search_project_tickets_path' for ...
```

Notice the pluralized "tickets" in this method. To define nonstandard RESTful actions, you've previously used the member method inside of config/routes.rb. This has worked fine because you've always acted on a single resource, such as wanting to remove a single tag from a ticket. This time, however, you want to act on a *collection* of a resource—the entire set of tags assigned to a ticket—so you need to use the collection method in config/routes.rb.

To define this method, change the following lines in config/routes.rb to what's shown in listing 11.27:

```
Rails.application.routes.draw do
  ...
  resources :projects, only: [:index, :show, :edit, :update] do
    resources :tickets
  end
  ...
```

Listing 11.27   Adding our first `collection` route, for searching tickets

```
Rails.application.routes.draw do
  ...
  resources :projects, only: [:index, :show, :edit, :update] do
    resources :tickets do
      collection do
        get :search
      end
    end
  end
  ...
```

The `collection` block here defines that there's a `search` action that may act on a collection of tickets. This `search` action will receive the parameters passed through from the `simple_form_for` that you've set up.

When you run your feature again by using `bundle exec rspec spec/features/` `searching_spec.rb`, you'll see that it reports that the search action is missing:

```
1) Users can search for tickets matching specific criteria searching by
   tag
   Failure/Error: click_button "Search"
   AbstractController::ActionNotFound:
     The action 'search' could not be found for TicketsController
```

Good! The job of this action is to find all the tickets that match the criteria passed in from the form as `params[:search]`.

11.5.2 *Searching by tags*

You want to be able to parse labels in a query such as "tag:iteration_1" and find the records that match the query. Rather than working like Google, where you could enter "iteration_1" and Google would "know" what you mean, you have to tell your searching code what "iteration_1" means by prefixing it with "tag."

You'll use the following query with the search method on a model, and it will return only the records that match it.

Listing 11.28   The syntax you want to end up with

```
Ticket.search("tag:iteration_1")
```

Your form submits to a new search action that it expects to find in your Tickets-Controller. You can define that method in app/controllers/tickets_controller.rb like so:

```
class TicketsController < ApplicationController
  ...
  def search
    authorize @project, :show?
    if params[:search].present?
      @tickets = @project.tickets.search(params[:search])
    else
```

```
    @tickets = @project.tickets
  end
end
...
```

First, you need to authorize this action. If you don't do this, anyone could search for tickets in a project.

Secondly, you assign all the tickets retrieved by the search method to the `@tickets` variable, which you'd render in the search template if you didn't already have a template that was useful for rendering lists of tickets. That template is the one at app/ views/projects/show.html.erb, but to render it you'll make one small modification.

Currently this template renders all the tickets by using the following line.

Listing 11.29 Rendering all tickets on a project

```
...
<ul id="tickets">
  <% @project.tickets.each do |ticket| %>
    ...
```

This line will iterate through each of the tickets in the project and do whatever is inside the block for each of those tickets. If you were to render this template right now with the search action, it would return all tickets for the project, rather than just the ones returned by the search query. You can get around this by changing the line in the template to read as follows.

Listing 11.30 Rendering a selected collection of tickets on a project

```
...
<ul id="tickets">
  <% @tickets.each do |ticket| %>
    ...
```

With this change, you break the show action of the `ProjectsController`, because the `@tickets` variable is not defined there. You can see the error you'll get by running `bundle exec rspec spec/features/viewing_tickets_spec.rb`:

```
1) Users can view tickets for a given project
   Failure/Error: click_link "Sublime Text 3"
   ActionView::Template::Error:
     undefined method `each' for nil:NilClass
```

This is a great thing about the tests you've written—you immediately know if you've broken existing functionality.

To fix this error, you can define a `@tickets` variable inside the show action of `ProjectsController`, underneath the `authorize` call in that action:

```
class ProjectsController < ApplicationController
  ...
  def show
    authorize @project, :show?
```

```
    @tickets = @project.tickets
  end
  ...
```

When you rerun `bundle exec rspec spec/features/viewing_projects_spec.rb`, you'll see that it now passes:

```
1 example, 0 failures
```

Great! With the insurance that you're not going to break anything now, you can render that same app/views/projects/show.html.erb template in the `search` action of `TicketsController` by putting the `render` line at the bottom of that action, so that your controller action looks like this:

```
class TicketsController < ApplicationController
  ...
  def search
    authorize @project, :show?
    if params[:search].present?
      @tickets = @project.tickets.search(params[:search])
    else
      @tickets = @project.tickets
    end
    render "projects/show"
  end
  ...
```

By rendering this template, you'll show a page similar to `ProjectsController#show`, but this time it will only have the tickets for the given tag.

Now that you're rendering properly, you can run the main searching spec, `bundle exec rspec spec/features/searching_spec.rb`, again:

```
1) Users can search for tickets matching specific criteria searching by
   tag
   Failure/Error: click_button "Search"
   NoMethodError:
     undefined method `search' for #<Ticket::ActiveRecord_...
```

This error shows you that the test is getting to the `search` action of `TicketsController` and it's attempting to execute a search on the `Ticket` model using the `search` method. All of this is great!

Now that you have all the wiring set up, you just need to implement the actual functionality inside your `Ticket` model. You'll be using the Searcher gem to do this, so first you need to install it. Add the Searcher gem to your Gemfile.

Listing 11.31 Adding Searcher to your Gemfile

```
gem "searcher", github: "radar/searcher"
```

Rather than adding this as a normal gem to be sourced from RubyGems, the preceding code sources the Searcher gem from GitHub.[4] This syntax tells Bundler to clone the radar/searcher repo from GitHub and to use that as the source of your gem. After adding the gem to your Gemfile, run `bundle` to get the gem installed, and restart your Rails server if it's running.

To add this `search` method to `Ticket`, you can use the `searcher` class method that the Searcher gem provides, placing it underneath the `before_create` call in app/models/ticket.rb:

```
class Ticket < ActiveRecord::Base
  ...
  searcher do
    label :tag, from: :tags, field: "name"
  end
  ...
```

The `searcher` method takes a block in which you can specify the labels that you can use for searching. The `from` option tells Searcher that you want to look in the `tags` table, and the `field` option indicates that you want to pick the `name` field from that table. This will allow you to use search queries like `tags:TestTag`, which will search for tickets that are associated with a record in the `tags` table with the `name` field equal to `TestTag`—exactly what you're after.

When you run your search feature using `bundle exec rspec spec/features/searching_spec.rb`, it will now pass:

```
1 example, 0 failures
```

With this feature, users will be able to specify a search query, such as `tag:iteration_1`, to return all tickets that have that particular tag.

You prevented one breaking change by catching it as it was happening, but how about the rest of the test suite? Find out by running `bundle exec rspec`. You should see this result:

```
125 examples, 0 failures
```

Great! Commit this change now:

```
$ git add .
$ git commit -m "Add tag-based searching for tickets"
$ git push
```

Now that you have tag-based searching, why not spend a little bit of extra time letting your users search by state as well? This way, they'll be able to perform actions such as finding all remaining "Open" tickets in the tag "iteration_1" by using a search term of `state:Open tag:iteration_1`. It's easy to implement.

---

[4] The Searcher gem was written expressly for the purposes of this book, and as such isn't bulletproof enough for real-world apps. This is why we're not making it available on RubyGems for the whole world to use.

11.5.3 *Searching by state*

Implementing searching for a state is incredibly easy now that you have the Searcher gem set up and you have the search feature in place. As you did with searching for a tag, you'll test searching for a state in the search feature. But first, you need to set up your tickets to have states.

Change the code at the top of the feature in spec/features/searching_spec.rb so that states are specified for each of the tickets, replacing the two `let` blocks for the tickets with the code from the following listing.

Listing 11.32   Creating tickets with different states, for searching

```
RSpec.feature "Users can search for tickets matching specific criteria" do
  ...
  let(:open) { State.create(name: "Open", default: true) }
  let(:closed) { State.create(name: "Closed") }

  let!(:ticket_1) do
    FactoryGirl.create(:ticket, name: "Create projects",
      project: project, author: user, tag_names: "iteration_1",
      state: open)
  end

  let!(:ticket_2) do
    FactoryGirl.create(:ticket, name: "Create users",
      project: project, author: user, tag_names: "iteration_2",
      state: closed)
  end
  ...
```

When the two tickets in this feature are created, there will be two states associated with these tickets. Your next task is to write a scenario that will search for all tickets with a specific state. That scenario can be seen in the next listing.

Listing 11.33   Finding by state scenario, for the search feature

```
RSpec.feature "Users can search for tickets matching specific criteria" do
  ...

  scenario "searching by state" do
    fill_in "Search", with: "state:Open"
    click_button "Search"
    within("#tickets") do
      expect(page).to have_link "Create projects"
      expect(page).to_not have_link "Create users"
    end
  end
end
```

This should show any ticket with the "Open" state and hide all other tickets.

When you run this feature with `bundle exec rspec spec/features/searching_spec.rb`, you'll see that this is not the case. It can still see the "Create users" ticket.

```
1) Users can search for tickets matching specific criteria searching by
   state
   Failure/Error: expect(page).to_not have_link "Create users"
     expected not to find link "Create users", found 1 match:
     "Create users"
```

This test isn't working because you haven't enabled searching on states yet. You can fix this very easily by changing the `searcher` code in app/models/ticket.rb:

```
class Ticket < ActiveRecord::Base
  ...
  searcher do
    label :tag, from: :tags, field: "name"
    label :state, from: :state, field: "name"
  end
  ...
```

If you rerun the searching spec with `bundle exec rspec spec/features/searching _spec.rb`, you'll get a nice surprise:

```
2 examples, 0 failures
```

That's it for the search feature! In it, you've added the ability for users to find tickets with a given tag and/or state. It should be mentioned that these queries can be chained, so a user can enter a query such as `tag:iteration_1 state:Open`, and it will find all tickets with the "iteration_1" tag and the "Open" state.

As usual, commit your changes because you're done with this feature. But also as usual, check to make sure that everything is A-OK by running `bundle exec rspec`:

```
126 examples, 0 failures
```

Brilliant, you can commit:

```
$ git add .
$ git commit -m "Users may now search for tickets by state or tag"
$ git push
```

With searching in place and the ability to add and remove tags, you're almost done with this set of features.

11.5.4 Search, but without the search

The final feature for this chapter involves changing the tag name rendered in app/ views/tags/_tag.html.erb so that when a user clicks on it, they're shown all tickets for that specific tag.

To test this functionality, you can add another scenario to the bottom of spec/ features/searching_spec.rb. This will test that when a user clicks on a ticket's tag, they're only shown tickets for that tag. The new scenario looks pretty much identical to this:

```
RSpec.feature "Users can search for tickets matching specific criteria" do
  ...
  scenario "when clicking on a tag" do
    click_link "Create projects"
    click_link "iteration_1"
    within("#tickets") do
      expect(page).to have_content "Create projects"
      expect(page).to_not have_content "Create users"
    end
  end
end
```

When you run this last scenario using bundle exec rspec spec/features/searching
_spec.rb, you're told that it can't find the "iteration_1" link on the page:

```
1) Users can search for tickets matching specific criteria when clicking
   on a tag
   Failure/Error: click_link "iteration_1"
   Capybara::ElementNotFound:
     Unable to find link "iteration_1"
```

This scenario is successfully navigating to a ticket and then attempting to click a link
with the name of the tag, but it can't find any matching links. It's up to you to add this
functionality to your app.

Where you display the names of tags in your application, you need to change them
into links that go to pages displaying all tickets for that particular tag. You've isolated
the code to display tags in one place—app/views/tags/_tag.html.erb—so that's the
only place you need to change. Open the file, and change the output of the tag name
from what's in listing 11.34 to what's in listing 11.35.

Listing 11.34 Displaying the tag name

```
<%= tag.name %>
```

Listing 11.35 Displaying the tag name with a link to a prefilled search for tickets

```
<%= link_to tag.name, search_project_tickets_path(ticket.project,
  search: "tag:#{tag.name}") %>
```

For this link_to, you use the search_project_tickets_path helper. It generates a
route to the search action in TicketsController for the current ticket's project, but
then you do something different. After you specify which project to search with, using
ticket.project, you specify options. These options are passed in as additional
parameters to the route. Your search form passes through the params[:search] field,
and your link_to does the same thing.

When you run bundle exec rspec spec/features/searching_spec.rb, this new
scenario will now pass:

```
3 examples, 0 failures
```

This feature allows users to click a tag on a ticket's page, which then displays all tickets that have that tag.

Make sure you didn't break anything with this small change by running `bundle exec rspec`. You should see this output:

```
127 examples, 0 failures
```

Great, nothing broke! Commit this change:

```
$ git add .
$ git commit -m "Users can now click a tag's name to go to a page
  showing all tickets for it"
$ git push
```

Users are now able to search for tickets based on their state or tag, as well as go to a list of all tickets for a given tag by clicking on the tag name that appears on the ticket's page. This is the final feature you needed to implement in order to have a good tagging system for your application.

11.6 Summary

In this chapter, we covered how to use a `has_and_belongs_to_many` association to define a link between tickets and tags. Tickets are able to have more than one tag, but a tag is also able to have more than one ticket assigned to it, so you use this type of association. A `has_and_belongs_to_many` could also be used to associate people and the locations they've been to.[5]

You first wrote the functionality for tagging a ticket when it was created, and you continued by letting users tag a ticket through the comment form as well.

Next, we looked at how to remove a tag from the page using jQuery's `parent()` and `fadeOut()` functions, with the help of Rails' JavaScript callbacks. They allowed you to execute JavaScript code when an AJAX request completes, and you used them to remove the tag from the page.

You saw how to use the Searcher gem to implement label-based searching for not only tags, but states as well. Usually you'd implement some sort of help page that would demonstrate to users how to use the search box, but you can implement that on your own.

Your final feature, based on the previous feature, allowed users to click a tag name and view all the tickets for that tag, and it also showed how you can limit the scope of a resource without using nested resources.

In chapter 12, we'll look at how you can send emails to your users using Action Mailer. You'll use these emails to notify users about new tickets in their project, state transitions, and new comments.

---

[5] Foursquare does this.

Sending email

In the previous chapter, you implemented tagging for your application, which allows users to easily categorize and search for tickets. In this chapter, you'll begin to send emails to your users. When a user signs up to Ticketee, they use their email address as a way for the system to uniquely identify them. Once you have a user's validated email address, you can send them updates about important events in the system, such as a ticket being updated.

Before you go about configuring your application to send emails into the real world, you'll add two more features to Ticketee. The first feature automatically subscribes a user to a *watchers list* whenever that user creates a ticket. Every time this ticket is updated by another user, the creator of the ticket should receive an email. This is helpful, because it allows users to keep up to date with the tickets they've created. The second feature will allow users to add themselves to or remove themselves from the watchers list for a given ticket.

With these features in place, all users who are watching a ticket will be notified via email that a comment has been posted to that ticket, what the comment was, and about any state change that took place. If a user posts a comment to a ticket and they're not watching it, they'll automatically be added to its watchers list and receive notifications whenever anybody posts a comment on the ticket. They can unsubscribe later by visiting the ticket page and removing themselves from the watchers list. Email is a tried-and-true solution for receiving notifications of events such as this.

The first thing you'll do is set up a way for users to receive notifications when a comment is posted to a ticket they've created. Let's dive into creating the feature and code for this functionality now.

12.1 *Sending ticket notifications*

You want to provide users with the ability to watch a ticket. When watching a ticket, a user will be notified by email whenever a new comment is posted to the ticket. The email will contain the name of the user who updated the ticket, the comment text, and a URL to the ticket.

To test all this, you'll use the Email Spec gem (https://github.com/bmabey/email-spec/). This gem provides very useful RSpec helpers that allow you to easily verify that an email was sent during a test, and you'll take full advantage of the features that this gem provides in the feature that you'll write next.

12.1.1 *Automatically watching a ticket*

This feature will test that when a user creates a ticket, they're automatically added to the watchers list for that ticket. Whenever someone else updates this ticket, the user who created it (and later, anybody else watching the ticket) will receive an email notification.

Create a new file at spec/features/ticket_notifications_spec.rb, and fill it with the content from the following listing.

> **Listing 12.1 spec/features/ticket_notifications_spec.rb**

```
require "rails_helper"

RSpec.feature "Users can receive notifications about ticket updates" do
  let(:alice) { FactoryGirl.create(:user, email: "alice@example.com") }
  let(:bob) { FactoryGirl.create(:user, email: "bob@example.com") }
  let(:project) { FactoryGirl.create(:project) }
  let(:ticket) do
    FactoryGirl.create(:ticket, project: project, author: alice)
  end

  before do
    assign_role!(alice, :manager, project)
```

```
      assign_role!(bob, :manager, project)

      login_as(bob)
      visit project_ticket_path(project, ticket)
    end

    scenario "ticket authors automatically receive notifications" do
      fill_in "Text", with: "Is it out yet?"
      click_button "Create Comment"

      email = find_email!(alice.email)
      expected_subject = "[ticketee] #{project.name} - #{ticket.name}"
      expect(email.subject).to eq expected_subject

      click_first_link_in_email(email)
      expect(current_path).to eq project_ticket_path(project, ticket)
    end
  end
```

In this feature, you set up two users: Alice and Bob. When the feature signs in to Ticketee as Bob, and leaves a comment on the ticket that Alice has created, then Alice should receive an email.

The find_email! method here is from the Email Spec gem, and it will open the most recent email sent to the specified email address (or raise an exception if it can't find one). The next couple of lines in the scenario will check that email to see if it contains the correct subject, including the project and ticket names. The final trick in the scenario is to click the first link in the email (using click_first_link_in_email, surprise!), and then validate that the link goes to the ticket page for the correct ticket.

Speaking of Email Spec, you'll need to install it. Add an email_spec line to the test section of your Gemfile.

Listing 12.2 Adding Email Spec to your Gemfile

```
group :test do
  ...
  gem "email_spec", "~> 1.6.0"
end
```

And run bundle to install it.

You'll also need a tiny amount of configuration to include Email Spec's methods into your tests. Add this code to spec/support/email_spec.rb:

```
require "email_spec"

RSpec.configure do |config|
  config.include EmailSpec::Helpers
  config.include EmailSpec::Matchers
end
```

Without this, you couldn't use Email Spec and its helpers (such as `find_email!`) in your specs. This code also includes some RSpec matchers that we'll look at using later when you actually want to test your emails.

When you run the ticket-notifications feature using `bundle exec rspec spec/features/ticket_notifications_spec.rb`, you'll see that Alice isn't yet receiving an email:

```
1) Users can receive notifications about ticket updates ticket authors
   automatically receive notifications
   Failure/Error: email = find_email!(alice.email)
   EmailSpec::CouldNotFindEmailError:
     Could not find email  in the mailbox for alice@example.com.
      Found the following emails:

      []
```

When Bob updates the ticket, Alice doesn't receive an email yet. That's why you wrote the feature—so you can test the behavior that you're about to create!

YOU'RE NOT REALLY SENDING EMAILS

Before we carry on, we need to let you in on a little something: All of the emails you're about to create won't be sent to addresses in the real world, so you don't have to worry about using real email addresses in your tests. How is this? Well, there's a setting inside config/environments/test.rb that goes like this:

```
config.action_mailer.delivery_method = :test
```

This setting tells Action Mailer to intercept any emails that you try to send, and store them in the `ActionMailer::Base.deliveries` array.[1] You'll then read the emails out of this array using the helpers provided by Email Spec.

But for now, let's get Ticketee to send Alice an email. For this, you'll use what's known as a *service class*.

12.1.2 *Using service classes*

A service class provides a simple interface to a piece of business logic, and it's typically used to group together related actions and behavior that should always occur together. If this sounds generic, that's because it is—Rails doesn't have any specific support for service classes. For some extra reading on service classes (sometimes also called *service objects*), we recommend the following articles:

- "Service objects in Rails will help you design clean and maintainable code. Here's how." (https://netguru.co/blog/service-objects-in-rails-will-help)
- "7 Patterns to Refactor Fat ActiveRecord Models" (http://blog.codeclimate.com/blog/2012/10/17/7-ways-to-decompose-fat-activerecord-models/)

---

[1] The default setting for `delivery_method` is SMTP. This will direct Action Mailer to connect to an SMTP server running on `localhost`—that is, the machine Rails is running on.

The second of these articles is more generic, and it covers a lot more than just service objects.

You'll use a service class to create a comment and then send out notifications to all of the watchers of the ticket.

Why not just use callbacks in the model, or send the notifications from the `CommentsController`?

This is a bit of a tricky subject. It would be very easy to say to yourself, "I want to send out some email every time I create a comment, so I can write an `after_create` callback in the `Comment` model to do this, right?"

It would be easy to do that, and it would work, but it would also be a bad idea for a couple of reasons:

- *It violates the single-responsibility principle, and introduces tighter coupling.* A `Comment` object in this system has one purpose—managing the data that it holds, the content, the state, and so on. Introducing a callback that adds behavior unrelated to this purpose *couples* this model with the other objects you'd be referencing, such as the mailer. If you change something in the mailer, your model (which is just supposed to be saving data) could completely break in weird and wonderful ways.
- *It slows down your tests, and a lot of other things too.* This is more a side-effect of the first downside. Think of all of the possible times you might want to create a comment, but *not* send out these notification emails—when experimenting in the Rails console or when calling factories in tests, for example. Think of all the tests you've written that create comments—they would now have the added overhead of creating and trying to send emails that you really don't care about. There's only one time you really want to send them—when a comment is created through the Ticketee web interface.

Okay, so why not do this in the controller?

- *Controllers are notoriously difficult to test.* In an ideal world, you'd want to test this interaction—that when you save a comment in the web app, all these emails get triggered—and you'd want to test it easily. Controller testing isn't straightforward and typically requires a lot of fiddly mocking and stubbing because a controller touches all of the different parts of the Rails stack, from the request to the response—that's its job.
- *The logic isn't reusable if it's locked away in a controller.* Later on down the road you might want to use this notification logic elsewhere, such as if you write a Rake task that automatically closes tickets that haven't had any activity in a long time. You'd want to notify the watchers that the ticket was closed in this scenario too, meaning you'd have to duplicate all of the logic from the controller. If you encapsulate it in a service object, you can reuse it in your Rake task, or anywhere else you specifically decide you want to save and send notifications.

Now that you've decided that service objects are a good idea, how do you build them, and where do you put them? There's no predefined place to store them in a Rails application, but a services directory sounds like a logical place to put them. Make a new directory, app/services, and add a new file, app/services/comment_creator.rb:

```ruby
class CommentCreator
  attr_reader :comment

  def self.build(scope, current_user, comment_params)
    comment = scope.build(comment_params)
    comment.author = current_user

    new(comment)
  end

  def initialize(comment)
    @comment = comment
  end

  def save
    if @comment.save
      notify_watchers
    end
  end

  def notify_watchers
    (@comment.ticket.watchers - [@comment.author]).each do |user|
      CommentNotifier.created(@comment, user).deliver_now
    end
  end
end
```

This class is a simple PORO (plain old Ruby object) that wraps a `Comment` instance and lets you add a little bit of logic around `save` and `build` methods. Your main entry point to it is via the `build` method—you can call it with the association you want to build on, the author you're assigning to the comment, and the parameters you're building the comment with.

The save method in the `CommentCreator` not only saves the comment it builds, but it's also tasked with notifying the watchers of the ticket, but not the user who posted the comment.

The `CommentNotifier` referenced inside `save` is something you'll create in the next section. The `created` method for `CommentNotifier` will build an email for each of the users watching this ticket, and `deliver_now` will send it out immediately.

Why is the delivery method called `deliver_now`?

The `deliver_now` method used to be called `deliver` in all versions of Rails before version 4.2. So why the change? It changed because Rails 4.2 introduced a component called ActiveJob.

(continued)

ActiveJob serves as a proxy between Rails and job-queuing gems like Sidekiq (http://sidekiq.org/), Resque (https://github.com/resque/resque), and delayed_job (https://github.com/collectiveidea/delayed_job). These gems are designed to perform tasks outside of the request cycle, like sending emails. Imagine if your service class was going to send dozens or hundreds of emails when you created a comment—that's not something you want to happen while you're sitting and waiting to see if your comment was successfully posted.

If you wanted to queue up your email to send through one of these systems, you'd use the `deliver_later` method. This method would queue up the job in whatever system you had configured with ActiveJob, and then the email would be delivered when the workers for that system got around to it. But you don't have one of those systems, and so for now you'll use `deliver_now`.

You can use this new `CommentCreator` service in the `create` action of `CommentsController` by changing that action.

Listing 12.3   Replacing comment creation with the `CommentCreator` service class

```
class CommentsController < ApplicationController
  ...

  def create
    @creator = CommentCreator.build(@ticket.comments, current_user,
      sanitized_parameters)
    authorize @creator.comment, :create?

    if @creator.save
      flash[:notice] = "Comment has been created."
      redirect_to [@ticket.project, @ticket]
    else
      flash.now[:alert] = "Comment has not been created."
      @project = @ticket.project
      @comment = @creator.comment
      render "tickets/show"
    end
  end

  ...
```

You can see that the creation logic in the controller has been replaced with the new service class and its `build` method. It also unwraps the comment from the service class in the error case; you need to have the actual comment to display on the comment form, not the service class.

When you run `bundle exec rspec spec/features/ticket_notifications_spec.rb`, you're told this:

```
1) Users can receive notifications about ticket updates ticket authors
   automatically receive notifications
   Failure/Error: click_button "Create Comment"
   NoMethodError:
     undefined method `watchers' for #<Ticket:0x007fd68c582720>
   # ...
   # ./app/services/comment_creator.rb:22:in `notify_watchers'
```

In this `save` method in your service class, you call the `watchers` method to get at the watchers for this ticket. It fails because you haven't defined this association yet, so let's go ahead and do that now.

12.1.3 Defining the watchers association

The `watchers` method should return a collection of users who are watching a ticket, including (by default) the user who created the ticket in the first place. This means that in your feature, Alice (the author) receives the email triggered by Bob's comment.

Here you must do two things: first, define the `watchers` association, and second, add the ticket owner to the watchers list when the ticket is created.

You'll use a `has_and_belongs_to_many` association to define the `watchers` collection, this time in your `Ticket` model. To define it, put this code inside the `Ticket` model, along with the other `has_and_belongs_to_many` for tags.

> **Listing 12.4 Adding an association between a ticket and its watchers**

```
class Ticket < ActiveRecord::Base
  ...
  has_and_belongs_to_many :watchers, join_table: "ticket_watchers",
    class_name: "User", uniq: true
  ...
```

Here you pass the `:join_table` option to specify a custom table name for your `has_and_belongs_to_many`. If you didn't do this, the table name would be inferred by Rails to be `tickets users`,[2] which doesn't really explain the purpose of this table as much as `ticket_watchers` does. You pass another option too, `:class_name`, which tells your model that the objects from this association are `User` objects. If you left this option out, Active Record would infer that you wanted the `Watcher` class instead, which doesn't exist.

You can create a migration that will create this table with this command:

```
$ rails g migration create_join_table_ticket_watchers tickets users
```

That will create a migration that looks like the following listing.

---

[2] Rails generates the table name by putting the two joined table names together alphabetically, separated by an underscore.

Listing 12.5   db/migrate/[timestamp]_create_join_table_ticket_watchers.rb

```
class CreateJoinTableTicketWatchers < ActiveRecord::Migration
  def change
    create_join_table :tickets, :users do |t|
      # t.index [:ticket_id, :user_id]
      # t.index [:user_id, :ticket_id]
    end
  end
end
```

This is exactly what you did to create the join table between tickets and tags in chapter 11. You have just one minor change to make—Rails has picked up that you wanted a join table from the phrase `create_join_table` in the migration name, but it hasn't picked up the name you wanted for the table. You can specify the table name as an argument to the `create_join_table` method inside the migration as follows.

Listing 12.6   Specifying the table name

```
class CreateJoinTableTicketWatchers < ActiveRecord::Migration
  def change
    create_join_table :tickets, :users, table_name: :ticket_watchers
      do |t|
      ...
```

Save the modified migration, and then run it using `bundle exec rake db:migrate`.

That's ticket watchers taken care of. But when you run `bundle exec rspec spec/ features/ticket_notifications_spec.rb`, you'll see that the email still isn't being sent:

```
1) Users can receive notifications about ticket updates ticket authors
   automatically receive notifications
   Failure/Error: email = find_email!(alice.email)
   EmailSpec::CouldNotFindEmailError:
     Could not find email  in the mailbox for alice@example.com.
     Found the following emails:

     []
```

You haven't yet added the ticket author to the watchers list, so they're still not getting notified about updates. To fix this failure, you can add the author using an `after _create` callback on your `Ticket` model, like this:

```
class Ticket < ActiveRecord::Base
  ...
  after_create :author_watches_me
  ...
```

To define the `author_watches_me` method, put the following code at the bottom of the `Ticket` class definition:

```
class Ticket < ActiveRecord::Base
  ...
  private
```

```
def author_watches_me
  if author.present? && !self.watchers.include?(author)
    self.watchers << author
  end
end
...
```

This method will add the author of the ticket to the list of watchers for this ticket whenever the `after_create` callbacks are triggered. This means that each `Ticket` object will now have a list of users who are watching the ticket. Eventually it will be able to act on that list to send out notifications when comments get posted.

Now that you have some code to associate the author of the ticket as a watcher of that ticket, let's see what else needs doing. Running the test again will result in this exception:

```
1) Users can receive notifications about ticket updates ticket authors
   automatically receive notifications
   Failure/Error: click_button "Create Comment"
   NameError:
     uninitialized constant CommentCreator::CommentNotifier
   # ./app/services/comment_creator.rb:23:in ...
```

This time, your feature is failing because it can't find the constant `CommentNotifier`, which will be the class you use to send out the notifications of new activity to your users. To create this class, you'll use Action Mailer.

12.1.4 *Introducing Action Mailer*

You need to define the `CommentNotifier` mailer to send out ticket-update notifications using the `CommentCreator` service. You can generate this mailer by running the mailer generator.

A *mailer* is a class defined for sending out emails. To define your mailer, run this command:

```
$ rails g mailer comment_notifier
```

When you run this command, you'll see the following output:

```
create  app/mailers/comment_notifier.rb
create  app/mailers/application_mailer.rb
invoke  erb
create    app/views/comment_notifier
create    app/views/layouts/mailer.text.erb
create    app/views/layouts/mailer.html.erb
invoke  rspec
create    spec/mailers/comment_notifier_spec.rb
create    spec/mailers/previews/comment_notifier_preview.rb
```

The first thing the command generates is the `CommentNotifier` class itself, defining it in a new file at app/mailers/comment_notifier.rb. This is done to keep the models and mailers separate. In previous versions of Rails, mailers lived in the app/models directory, which led to clutter. With mailers separated out into their own folder, the codebase becomes easier to manage. Inside this class, you'll define (as methods) the different notifications that you'll send out, beginning with the comment-created notification. We'll get to that in just a minute.

The next file is app/mailers/application_mailer.rb. This file defines the `ApplicationMailer` class, which is what all mailers, such as `CommentNotifier`, inherit from. In app/mailers/application_mailer.rb, you'll see the following code.

Listing 12.7   The default `ApplicationMailer`

```
class ApplicationMailer < ActionMailer::Base
  default from: "from@example.com"
  layout 'mailer'
end
```

`ActionMailer::Base` defines a lot of helpful methods that you can use to configure and send your emails. The `default` method used here configures default options for this mailer, and it will set the From address on all emails to be the one specified. Change this to be your email address. The `layout` method determines what layout to use for all the emails that come from your application.

The next thing that's generated is the app/views/comment_notifier directory, which is used to store the templates for all emails belonging to the `CommentNotifier`. Each method in the `CommentNotifier` class will correspond to a different type of email sent out, and each type of email will have its templates in this directory.

The final thing that's generated is spec/mailers/comment_notifier_spec.rb, which you won't use right now because you've got your feature testing this notifier anyway.

Now that you have the `CommentNotifier` class defined, what happens when you run your feature? Run it using `bundle exec rspec spec/features/ticket_notifications _spec.rb` and find out:

```
1) Users can receive notifications about ticket updates ticket authors
   automatically receive notifications
   Failure/Error: click_button "Create Comment"
   NoMethodError:
     undefined method `created' for CommentNotifier:Class
   # ...
   # ./app/services/comment_creator.rb:23:in ...
```

In the `CommentNotifier` class, you need to define the `created` method, which will build an email to be sent out when a comment is created. This method needs to get the email address for all the watchers of the comment's ticket and send an email to each of them. You can define the method like this:

```
class CommentNotifier < ApplicationMailer
  def created(comment, user)
    @comment = comment
    @user = user
```

```
    @ticket = comment.ticket
    @project = @ticket.project

    subject = "[ticketee] #{@project.name} - #{@ticket.name}"
    mail(to: user.email, subject: subject)
  end
end
```

This may look wrong because you define it as an instance method, even though the error complains about a class method. Rest assured, this `created` method is truly the method that Action Mailer is looking for.

Action Mailer performs a little bit of magic for your benefit. The `created` method doesn't exist on the `CommentNotifier` class, but it does exist on the instances. So what happens here is that the call to that method is caught by `method_missing`, which then initializes a new instance of this class, and then, with some sleight of hand, it ends up calling your `created` method.

Metaprogramming with `method_missing`

`method_missing` is one of those special sauces that make Ruby such a wonderful programming language. It acts like a catch-all method in a class—if you call a method that the class doesn't know how to respond to, Ruby will first look for a `method_missing` method to handle this unexpected method call. If `method_missing` doesn't exist, then the typical `NoMethodError` will be raised.

With `method_missing`, you can truly create dynamic classes that respond to a wide variety of methods, based on things like database fields. Active Record uses `method_missing` extensively to define getter and setter methods for each of the fields in the model's database table.

For a contrived example of `method_missing` in the flesh, you could define a class like the following:

```
class StringLength
  def method_missing(arg)
    "'#{arg}' has #{arg.length} letters!"
  end
end
```

You could then interact with your class like so:

```
> StringLength.new.a_word
=> "'a_word' has 6 letters!"
> StringLength.new.something_long
=> "'something_long' has 14 letters!"
> StringLength.new.does_it_respond_to_anything?
=> "'does_it_respond_to_anything?' has 28 letters!"
```

You probably won't use `method_missing` extensively in your Rails apps, but it's good to know it exists, and what kinds of dynamic interfaces it can create.

When the `created` method is called in your `CommentNotifier`, it will attempt to render a plain-text template for the email, which should be found at app/views/comment_notifier/created.text.erb. (You'll define this template after you've got the method working.)

Mailers work like controller actions in that all instance variables are accessible to the rendered template, but local variables are not. You need to assign a set of variables as instance variables so you can use them in the content of the email. After assigning the variables, you can then use the `mail` method to generate a new email, passing the `to` and `subject` keys, which define where the email goes to as well as the subject for the email.

When you run `bundle exec rspec spec/features/ticket_notifications _spec.rb`, you'll see that the user now receives an email and therefore is able to open it, but the link you're looking for isn't there, which brings up this error:

```
1) Users can receive notifications about ticket updates ticket authors
   automatically receive notifications
   Failure/Error: click_button "Create Comment"
   ActionView::MissingTemplate:
     Missing template comment_notifier/created with "mailer". Searched
     in:
       * "comment_notifier"
```

Methods defined within an Action Mailer class need to have a corresponding template that defines the content of the email, much like actions in controllers have templates.

Let's define a template for the `CommentNotifier#created` mailer method now.

12.1.5 *An Action Mailer template*

Templates for Action Mailer classes go in app/views because they serve a purpose identical to the controller views: they display a final, dynamic result to users.

Once you have this template in place, the plain-text email a user receives will look like figure 12.1. As you can see, you'll need to mention who updated the ticket and what they updated it with, and you'll also need to provide a link to the ticket.

You can define a text template for your `created` method at app/views/comment _notifier/created.text.erb as follows.

> **Listing 12.8   app/views/comment_notifier/created.text.erb**

```erb
<%= project_ticket_url(@project, @ticket) %>
```

☆ **Ticketee to me**

Hello.

alice@ticketee.com has just updated the Release date ticket for TextMate 2. They wrote:

Posting a comment!

Figure 12.1   Your first email

Wait, text.erb? Yes! This is the template for the plain-text version of the email, after all. Remember, the format of a view in Rails is the first part of the file extension, with the latter part being the actual file type. Because you send a text-only email, you use the text format here.

This template is a little barren at the moment, but it's all that's required to get this feature working. You'll flesh it out in a little while.

When you run the test again, you'll see this error:

```
1) Users can receive notifications about ticket updates ticket authors
   automatically receive notifications
   Failure/Error: click_button "Create Comment"
   ActionView::Template::Error:
     Missing host to link to! Please provide the :host parameter, set
     default_url_options[:host], or set :only_path to true
   # ...
   # ./app/views/comment_notifier/created.text.erb:1:in ...
```

This is the line that you just added! This line is causing an error because the view wants to know the hostname to use to construct the full URL for a ticket, but you haven't told the app what that hostname is. In the controller context, the view knows which URL to use because it has a request to base this information on. Mailers don't have access to anything to do with the request, and this means that your mailer won't have that information.

You can fix this now by putting the following line in config/environments/test.rb, inside the `Rails.application.configure` block:

```
Rails.application.configure do
  ...
  config.action_mailer.default_url_options = {
    host: "ticketee.dev"
  }
  ...
```

The ticketee.dev domain is a made-up domain that you'll use for testing purposes. You'll want to set something in config/environments/production.rb too, but you'll do that in the next chapter when we look at a production deployment of the application.

When you run your tests again, they'll pass:

```
1 example, 0 failures
```

You've done quite a lot to get this simple little feature to pass.

In the beginning, you created a service class called `CommentCreator`. This service class wraps up all the logic around creating comments and notifying watchers of the ticket whenever that comment is saved.

That notification is done by the `CommentNotifier` class. `CommentNotifier` is an Action Mailer class that's responsible for sending out emails to the users of your application. In this file you defined the `created` method, which is responsible for collecting all the information to present to the mailer template, just like how an action in a controller collects all the information for a view.

You wouldn't know what notifications to send out if it weren't for the `watchers` association that you added to the `Ticket` model. This association currently tracks only the user who created the ticket, but eventually you'll change it so that anyone who comments on the ticket will automatically become a watcher too.

Finally, you defined the template for the `created` email at app/views/comment_notifier/created.text.erb and included the link that you click to complete the final step of your scenario. You also had to tell Action Mailer what host to use for its URL building.

This scenario completes the first steps of sending email notifications to your users. You should now run all your tests to make sure you didn't break anything, by running `bundle exec rspec`:

```
129 examples, 0 failures, 1 pending
```

Great to see everything still passing! The one pending spec is located in spec/mailers/comment_notifier_spec.rb, but rather than deleting that file, keep it and just delete the pending spec in it. You're going to use that file in the next section.

If you delete just the spec and rerun `bundle exec rspec`, you'll see this:

```
128 examples, 0 failures
```

You've added email ticket notifications to your application, so you should now make a commit saying just that and push it:

```
$ git add .
$ git commit -m "Added basic email ticket notifications"
$ git push
```

Now that you've got your application sending plain-text emails, you should flesh out the emails a bit more, giving them some content that tells the user why they're receiving the email, rather than having them contain only a link. To test that, you'll use the mailer spec that was generated along with the mailer.

12.1.6 *Testing with mailer specs*

Now you're going to get down into the nitty-gritty of exactly how your mailer works, with mailer specs. Mailer specs are generally contained within the files that are generated along with the mailer, and they test details about the mail that's sent out by those mailers, such as the body content.

In this section, you'll learn how to write a mailer spec—you'll write one that checks that the email contains specific content.

The spec that you'll write will make sure that when a user receives the email, it contains a phrase like "[user] has just updated the [ticket name] for [project name]," and the content for the comment. You may already be familiar with these types of emails from services such as Facebook. To test this, you'll first need to create a project, and then a ticket for that project that belongs to a user. The test itself will create a comment and then check the email that's just been sent to ensure that it's got the correct content.

Write the content from the following listing into spec/mailers/comment_notifier
_spec.rb.

Listing 12.9   spec/mailers/comment_notifier_spec.rb

```
require "rails_helper"

RSpec.describe CommentNotifier, type: :mailer do
  describe "created" do
    let(:project) { FactoryGirl.create(:project) }
    let(:ticket_owner) { FactoryGirl.create(:user) }
    let(:ticket) do
      FactoryGirl.create(:ticket,
        project: project, author: ticket_owner)
    end

    let(:commenter) { FactoryGirl.create(:user) }
    let(:comment) do
      Comment.new(ticket: ticket, author: commenter,
        text: "Test comment")
    end

    let(:email) do
      CommentNotifier.created(comment, ticket_owner)
    end

    it "sends out an email notification about a new comment" do
      expect(email.to).to include ticket_owner.email
      title = "#{ticket.name} for #{project.name} has been updated."
      expect(email.body.to_s).to include title
      expect(email.body.to_s).to include "#{commenter.email} wrote:"
      expect(email.body.to_s).to include comment.text
    end
  end
end
```

At the beginning of this test, a whole bunch of things are set up. First, the test needs a
project and a ticket. That part's easy. The ticket needs to have an author associated
with it so that there's someone to be notified when the comment notification goes
out. Next, there needs to be a comment so that the mailer can act on something. The
comment needs to have some text so that you can validate that it shows up in the
email that's sent out.

Inside the test itself, you create a new mail message by calling the created method
and passing it the comment and ticket_owner objects. The ticket owner is passed here
because that's the user that needs to be notified by this email. For the test, you assert
that the to address for the email contains the ticket owner's email, that the body contains a message saying that a ticket has been updated, and that the body also contains
the comment's text.

When you run this test with bundle exec rspec spec/mailers/comment_notifier
_spec.rb, you'll see that the email body doesn't contain that specialized message:

```
1) CommentNotifier created sends out an email notification about a new
   comment
   Failure/Error: expect(email.body.to_s).to include title
     expected "http://ticketee.dev/projects/257/tickets/169\n\n" to
     include "Example ticket for Example project has been updated."
     Diff:
     @@ -1,2 +1,2 @@
     -Example ticket for Example project has been updated.
     +http://ticketee.dev/projects/257/tickets/169

   # ./spec/mailers/comment_notifier_spec.rb:25:in ...
```

This failure is happening because you haven't yet put the correct message inside the email; all it contains is a link. To put that message in the email and make it look a whole lot nicer, replace the link inside app/views/comment_notifier/created.text.erb with this:

```
Hello!

<%= @ticket.name %> for <%= @project.name %> has been updated.

<%= @comment.author.email %> wrote:

<%= @comment.text %>

You can view this ticket online by going to:
<%= project_ticket_url(@project, @ticket) %>
```

When you rerun `bundle exec rspec spec/mailers/comment_notifier_spec.rb`, you'll see that this spec is now passing because the email contains the text that you're looking for:

```
1 example, 0 failures
```

Now that you've spruced up the text template for the email, users will receive relevant information about the comment notification, rather than just a link.

With that feature passing, this is a good spot for a commit. But first, run your tests with `bundle exec rspec`:

```
129 examples, 0 failures
```

All passing—excellent. Commit and push:

```
$ git add .
$ git commit -m "Give more details about the ticket in email body"
$ git push
```

In this section, you've learned how to generate a mailer and create a mailer method for it, and now you're going to look at how you can let people subscribe to these emails. You're currently only subscribing the ticket's author to the list of watchers associated with this ticket, but other people may also wish to be notified of ticket updates. You can do this in two separate ways: through a Watch button, and through automatic subscription when a user leaves a comment on a ticket.

12.2 Subscribing to updates

You want to provide other users with two ways to stay informed of ticket updates. The first approach will be very similar to the automatic subscription of the user who creates the ticket, but this time you'll automatically subscribe users who comment on a ticket. You'll reuse the same code that you used in the previous section to achieve this, but not in the way you might think.

The second approach will involve adding a Watch button on the ticket page, which will display either "Watch" or "Unwatch," depending on whether or not the user is watching the ticket, as shown in figure 12.2.

We'll first look at implementing the automatic subscription when a user posts a comment to a ticket.

| Watchers: | 👁 Watch |

Figure 12.2 The Watch button

12.2.1 Testing comment subscription

The first feature you need to add will automatically subscribe users to a ticket when they create a comment on it. This is useful because users will likely want to keep up to date with tickets they've commented on. Later on, you'll implement a way for these users to opt out.

To automatically subscribe a user to a ticket upon adding a comment, you'll use `after_create`, just as you did in the `Ticket` model for the author of that ticket. But first you need to ensure that this works!

You need to add another scenario to the ticket-notifications feature, but first let's consider the current flow with the help of a couple of diagrams. Consider figure 12.3. Here, Alice creates a ticket, and she will be subscribed for notification of any comments posted to it.

Next, Bob comes along and leaves a comment on the ticket, which should now subscribe Bob to these ticket updates (see figure 12.4). This is the feature that you'll code in a short while.

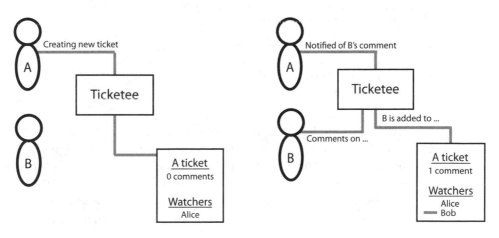

Figure 12.3 Alice creates a ticket   **Figure 12.4 Bob comments on the ticket**

After Bob has commented on the ticket, Alice receives a notification telling her that Bob has left a comment. Now that Bob is subscribed to the ticket, he should receive comment notifications every time somebody else—such as Alice—comments on the ticket, as shown in figure 12.5.

If Alice posts a comment, she shouldn't receive a notification about that, even though she's on the watchers list; only Bob should.

Now that you understand the scenario, you can write it in Capybara form at the bottom of the ticket-notifications feature. Add the scenario from the following listing inside the feature of spec/features/ticket_notifications _spec.rb.

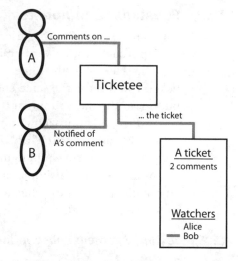

Figure 12.5　Alice comments on the ticket

Listing 12.10　Testing automatic comment subscription

```
RSpec.feature "Users can receive notifications about ticket updates" do
  ...

  scenario "comment authors are automatically subscribed to a ticket" do
    fill_in "Text", with: "Is it out yet?"
    click_button "Create Comment"
    click_link "Sign out"

    reset_mailer

    login_as(alice)
    visit project_ticket_path(project, ticket)
    fill_in "Text", with: "Not yet - sorry!"
    click_button "Create Comment"

    expect(page).to have_content "Comment has been created."
    expect(unread_emails_for(bob.email).count).to eq 1
    expect(unread_emails_for(alice.email).count).to eq 0
  end
end
```

In this scenario, you're already logged in as Bob (courtesy of the `before` block in this feature). With Bob, you create a comment on the ticket, and then sign out. Then you clear the email queue—Alice should have received one email when Bob commented, but you want to make sure she receives no more after this point. You then sign in as Alice and create a comment, which should trigger an email send to Bob, but not to Alice, because users shouldn't receive notifications of their own actions!

On the final lines for this scenario, you check the number of unread emails for each user—Bob should have one from Alice's comment, and Alice should have none because she shouldn't be notified about her own comment.

When you run this scenario using `bundle exec rspec spec/features/ticket _notifications_spec.rb`, you'll see that Bob never receives an email from that final comment left by Alice:

```
1) Users can receive notifications about ticket updates comment authors
   are automatically subscribed to a ticket
   Failure/Error: expect(unread_emails_for(bob.email).count).to eq 1

      expected: 1
           got: 0

   (compared using ==)
```

This is failing on the step that checks if Bob has an email. You can therefore determine that Bob isn't subscribed to receive comment update notifications, as he should have been when he posted a comment. You need to add any commenter to the watchers list when they post a comment, so that they're notified of ticket updates.

12.2.2 *Automatically adding the commenter to the watchers list*

To keep comment authors up to date with tickets, you'll automatically add them to the watchers list for that ticket when they post a comment. You currently do this when users create a new ticket, so you can apply the same logic to adding them to the list when they create a comment.

You can define another `after_create` callback in the `Comment` model by using this line:

```
class Comment < ActiveRecord::Base
  ...
  after_create :author_watches_ticket
  ...
```

Next, you need to define the method that this callback calls, which you can do by placing the following code at the bottom of your `Comment` model:

```
class Comment < ActiveRecord::Base
  ...
  def author_watches_ticket
    if author.present? && !ticket.watchers.include?(author)
      ticket.watchers << author
    end
  end
end
```

By using `<<` on the watchers association, you can add the creator of this comment to the watchers for this ticket. This should mean that when a comment is posted to this ticket, any user who has posted a comment previously, not only the ticket creator, will receive an email.

Now that a comment's owner is automatically added to a ticket's watchers list, that should be enough to get the new scenario to pass. Find out by rerunning `bundle exec rspec spec/features/ticket_notifications_spec.rb`.

```
2 examples, 0 failures
```

Perfect! Now users who comment on tickets are added to the watchers list automatically, and the user who posts the comment isn't notified if they are already on that list.

Did you break anything by implementing this change? Have a look-see by running `bundle exec rspec`:

```
130 examples, 0 failures
```

Every test that you have thrown at this application is still passing, which is a great thing to see. Commit this change:

```
$ git add .
$ git commit -m "Automatically subscribe users to a ticket when they
  comment on it"
$ git push
```

You now have automatic subscriptions for ticket notifications when a user creates a ticket or posts a comment to one, but currently there's no way to switch notifications off. To implement this, you'll add an Unwatch button that, when clicked, will remove the user from the list of watchers for that ticket.

12.2.3 Unsubscribing from ticket notifications

You need to add a button to the ticket page to unsubscribe users from future ticket notifications. When you're done here, the ticket page will look like figure 12.6.

Figure 12.6   The Unwatch button

Along with implementing the ability to turn off notifications by clicking this button, you'll also add a way for users to turn on notifications, using what will effectively be the same button with a different label. This button will toggle users' watching status, which will allow them to subscribe to ticket notifications without creating their own ticket or posting a comment.

You'll implement the on/off functionality simultaneously by writing a feature in a new file at spec/features/watching_tickets_spec.rb. Start with the code from the following listing.

Listing 12.11   Ticket-watching feature setup

```
require "rails_helper"

RSpec.feature "Users can watch and unwatch tickets" do
  let(:user) { FactoryGirl.create(:user) }
```

```
let(:project) { FactoryGirl.create(:project) }
let(:ticket) do
  FactoryGirl.create(:ticket, project: project, author: user)
end

before do
  assign_role!(user, "viewer", project)
  login_as(user)
  visit project_ticket_path(project, ticket)
end
end
```

In this example, you create a single user, a project, and a ticket. Because this user created the ticket, they're automatically subscribed to watching this ticket, so they should see the Unwatch button on the ticket page. You can test this by putting the scenario in the following listing underneath the before in this feature.

Listing 12.12 Ticket-watch toggling

```
RSpec.feature "Users can watch and unwatch tickets" do
  ...
  scenario "successfully" do
    within("#watchers") do
      expect(page).to have_content user.email
    end

    click_link "Unwatch"
    expect(page).to have_content "You are no longer watching this " +
      "ticket."

    within("#watchers") do
      expect(page).to_not have_content user.email
    end
  end
end
```

In this scenario, you check that a user is automatically subscribed to the ticket by asserting that their email address is visible in the #watchers element on the page. When that user clicks the Unwatch button, they'll be told that they're no longer watching the ticket, and their email will no longer be visible inside #watchers.

To begin to watch a ticket again, all the user has to do is click the Watch button, which you can also test by adding the following code to this scenario:

```
scenario "successfully" do
  ...
  click_link "Watch"
  expect(page).to have_content "You are now watching this ticket."

  within("#watchers") do
    expect(page).to have_content user.email
  end
end
```

See? That's how you'll test
the watching/not-watching
function simultaneously!
You don't need to post a

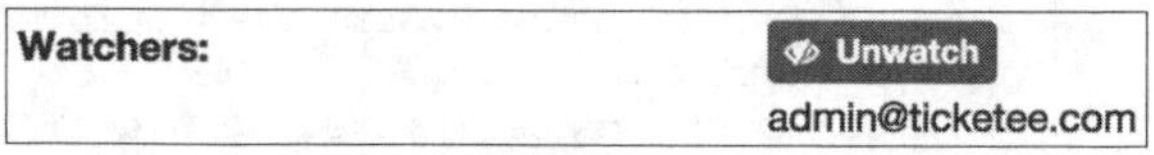

Figure 12.7   Who's watching

comment and test that a user is truly watching this ticket; you can instead check to see
if a user's name appears in a list of all the watchers on the ticket page, which will look
like figure 12.7.

As usual, you'll see what you need to code to get your feature on the road to passing by running `bundle exec rspec spec/features/watching_tickets_spec.rb`.
You'll see that it's actually the watchers list, indicated by Capybara telling you that it
can't find that element:

```
1) Users can watch and unwatch tickets successfully
   Failure/Error: within("#watchers") do
   Capybara::ElementNotFound:
     Unable to find css "#watchers"
```

You need to add this new element with ID `watchers`. You can add it to app/views/
tickets/show.html.erb at the bottom of the `attributes` table by using the code in the
following listing.

Listing 12.13   app/views/tickets/show.html.erb

```
<table id="attributes">
  ...

  <tr id="watchers">
    <th>Watchers:</th>
    <td>
      <%= @ticket.watchers.map(&:email).to_sentence %>
    </td>
  </tr>
</table>
```

You add another row to the table with the `id` attribute set to `watchers`, which is the
element that your scenario looks for. In this row, you collect all the watchers' emails
using `map`, and then you use `to_sentence` on that array. What this will do is turn the
array of user's emails into a proper sentence, such as "alice@example.com,
bob@example.com and corey@example.com."

When you have this element and you run your feature again with `bundle exec
rspec spec/features/watching_tickets_spec.rb`, you'll see that your feature gets
one step closer to passing by locating the user's email in the `#watchers` element. But
now it can't find the Unwatch button:

```
1) Users can watch and unwatch tickets successfully
   Failure/Error: click_link "Unwatch"
   Capybara::ElementNotFound:
     Unable to find link "Unwatch"
```

This button will toggle the current user's watching status for this ticket, and the text and appearance will differ depending on whether the user is or isn't currently watching this ticket. In both cases, however, the button will go to the same action. Because so much of the code will be duplicated for both buttons, you can add the buttons to the view by using a helper method, changing the first few lines of the element to this:

```
<tr id="watchers">
  <th>Watchers:</th>
  <td>
    <%= toggle_watching_button(@ticket) %><br />
    ...
```

This `toggle_watching_button` helper will only appear in views for the `Tickets-Controller`, so you should put the method definition in app/helpers/tickets _helper.rb inside the `TicketsHelper` module. Use the code from the following listing to define the method.

Listing 12.14 `toggle_watching_button` inside `TicketsHelper`

```
module TicketsHelper
  ...
  def toggle_watching_button(ticket)
    text = if ticket.watchers.include?(current_user)
      "Unwatch"
    else
      "Watch"
    end
    link_to text, watch_project_ticket_path(ticket.project, ticket),
      class: text.parameterize, method: :post
  end
end
```

On the last line of the helper, you use `link_to` to create an HTML link, but you specify that the `method` of the link is `:post`. This tells Rails to create a `POST` request when the link is clicked, rather than the standard `GET` request.

Inside the `link_to`, you use a new route helper that you haven't defined yet. When you run `bundle exec rspec spec/features/watching_tickets_spec.rb`, it will complain that this method is undefined when it tries to render the app/views/tickets/ show.html.erb page:

```
1) Users can watch and unwatch tickets successfully
   Failure/Error: visit project_ticket_path(project, ticket)
   ActionView::Template::Error:
     undefined method `watch_project_ticket_path' for #<#<Class:...
   # ./app/helpers/tickets_helper.rb:21:in `toggle_watching_button'
```

This route helper points to a specific action on a project's ticket. You can define it in config/routes.rb inside the `resources :tickets` block, which itself is nested inside the `resources :projects` block.

Listing 12.15 Adding `watch` route to `config/routes.rb`

```
Rails.application.routes.draw do
  ...
  resources :projects, only: [:index, :show, :edit, :update] do
    resources :tickets do
      collection do
        get :search
      end

      member do
        post :watch
      end
    end
  end
  ...
```

The purpose of `link_to` is to toggle the watch status of a single ticket, so you want to define a `member` route for your ticket resource. You put it inside the `tickets` resource, nested under the `projects` resource, because for your `watch` action you'll want to confirm that the person has permission to view this project. You define the route to the `watch` action with `post`, because `button_to` generates a form by default, and a form's HTTP method will default to POST.

When you run your feature again using `bundle exec rspec spec/features/watching_tickets_spec.rb`, it will complain now because there's no `watch` action for your button to go to:

```
1) Users can watch and unwatch tickets successfully
   Failure/Error: click_link "Unwatch"
   AbstractController::ActionNotFound:
     The action 'watch' could not be found for TicketsController
```

You're almost done! Defining this `watch` action is almost the last thing you have to do. This action will add the user who visits it to a specific ticket's watchers list if they aren't already watching it, or remove them if they are. To define this action, open app/controllers/tickets_controller.rb, and under the `search` action insert the code in the following listing.

Listing 12.16 `watch` action inside `TicketsController`

```
class TicketsController < ApplicationController
  ...
  def watch
    authorize @ticket, :show?
    if @ticket.watchers.exists?(current_user.id)
      @ticket.watchers.destroy(current_user)
      flash[:notice] = "You are no longer watching this ticket."
    else
      @ticket.watchers << current_user
      flash[:notice] = "You are now watching this ticket."
    end
```

```
    redirect_to project_ticket_path(@ticket.project, @ticket)
  end
  ...
```

The first thing you need to notice is that you don't define the @ticket variable before you use it on the first line of this method. That's because you can add this action to the list of actions that the before_action :set_ticket runs on by changing the call in your controller:

```
class TicketsController < ApplicationController
  ...
  before_action :set_ticket, only: [:show, :edit, :update, :destroy,
    :watch]
  ...
```

At the top of this action you need to check that the user is authorized to view this ticket. You don't want users being able to watch tickets that they're not permitted to view! If you didn't have this authorize! call in place, it wouldn't matter anyway, as Pundit would throw its Pundit::AuthorizationNotPerformedError exception.

In this action, you use exists?, which will check if the given user is in the list of watchers. If they are, you'll use watchers.destroy to remove the watcher from the list. If they aren't on the watchers list, you'll use watchers << to add them to the list of watchers.

The watch action now defines the behavior for a user to start and stop watching a ticket by clicking the button above the watchers list. When you run bundle exec rspec spec/features/watching_tickets_spec.rb, it will pass:

```
1 example, 0 failures
```

Great! Now you have a way for users to toggle their watch status on any given ticket. But when you load up a ticket's page in your browser, as shown in figure 12.8, it could be a bit prettier.

Figure 12.8 An unstyled Watch button

Let's spend a little bit of time making the button prettier, so it fits in with all of your other buttons and styles.

Because these styles will only be used on the ticket page, you should put them in app/asscts/stylesheets/ticket.scss. Open that file, and add the following code at the bottom.

Listing 12.17 Styling the Watch and Unwatch buttons

```
.watch, .unwatch {
  @extend .btn;
  @extend .btn-xs;
  font-weight: bold;

  &:before {
```

```
    font-family: "FontAwesome";
    padding-right: 0.5em;
  }
}

.watch {
  @extend .btn-success;

  &:before {
    @extend .fa-eye;
  }
}

.unwatch {
  @extend .btn-danger;

  &:before {
    @extend .fa-eye-slash;
  }
}
```

This code styles the Watch/Unwatch button with Bootstrap's `btn` and `btn-xs` styles, so that they look the same as the tags and states displayed in the `attributes` table. You also give the two buttons different styles and colors—the Watch button is green and has an icon of an eye, and the Unwatch button is red with a crossed-out eye.

When you refresh the page now, the buttons will be nicely styled, as shown in figure 12.9.

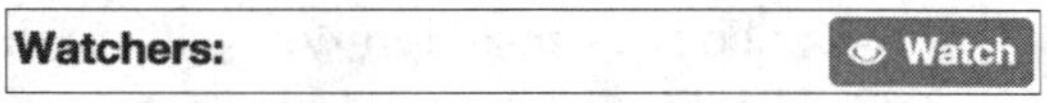

Figure 12.9   Much better!

Excellent! Make sure that everything else is still working by running `bundle exec rspec`. You should see the following output:

```
131 examples, 0 failures
```

Everything is still A-OK, which is good to see. Commit this change:

```
$ git add .
$ git commit -m "Add button so users can toggle watching on a ticket"
$ git push
```

You've now got a way for a user to start or stop watching a ticket. When watching a ticket, a user will receive an email when a comment is posted to the ticket.

You're doing great in theoretically testing email, but you haven't yet configured your application to send emails out to the real world. You'll see how to do that in the next chapter, when you deploy the application to a production environment.

12.3   Summary

In this chapter, you learned how to send out your own kind of emails. You also added two ways that users can subscribe to a ticket.

The first way was an automatic subscription that occurred when a user created a ticket. Every time a comment was posted to a ticket, the owner of the ticket was notified through a simple email message.

The second way was to allow users to click a button to subscribe to or unsubscribe from a ticket. This allowed all users, and not just those who created the ticket, to choose to receive emails when a comment is posted on the ticket. This way, all users can stay up to date on tickets they're interested in.

The next chapter involves deploying the application to a production environment and will build on some of the things you built in this chapter. You'll even be sending real emails!

13

Deployment

Developing applications is fun, but using them is more fun. Nobody can use your application until you deploy it to the public internet somewhere. In this chapter, we'll get you started on learning how to deploy Rails, and we'll talk about how to deploy your app when your tests are green.

Deployment is a big topic, enough for dedicated books on the subject alone.[1] This book can't possibly explain everything there is to know about deployment, so please think of this as an introduction.

---

[1] Books such as *Deploying Rails* by Tom Copeland and Anthony Burns (http://mng.bz/QwSU), or *Reliably Deploying Rails Applications* by Ben Dixon (https://leanpub.com/deploying_rails_applications).

One of the difficult things about deployment is that the process often relies on the details of how you've built your application. That means different projects have slightly different deployment processes. This book will show you what's needed to deploy Ticketee, but more complicated applications may have additional needs that we won't cover here.

A wealth of tooling exists to assist you with getting your application into production. This chapter will build up your understanding of deployment slowly, so that you can understand all the parts. Although it's true that deploying Rails involves a bit more than FTP-ing a few files to a remote server,[2] you'll have to confront these details eventually, no matter what your framework.

At the end of the chapter, you'll make your application send real-world emails using the features that you built in the last chapter, with a service called Mailgun.

13.1 What is deployment?

We saw a tweet the other day that said, "Broke production for the first time at my new job today." Someone else responded, "Now you truly work there. Congrats." Anyone who's worked as a web developer for a while knows that feeling. Sometimes development is just the beginning for your application. No code is ever truly perfect, even if it does have tests.

Deployment is the act of placing your application on the public web. There's an entire process involved in getting your application off your laptop and onto a server somewhere: setting up a server, transferring the code over, handling credentials and connections to other servers, and so on. But there are dedicated Platform as a Service (PaaS) options such as Heroku (http://heroku.com) that remove a lot of this pain.

You can also think of deployment as moving your application into a different environment. Remember your config/environments directory? It has files for three different environments: development, test, and production. You use the *development* environment when you're playing with your application using `rails server`. You use the *test* environment every time you run your tests with `bundle exec rspec`. But you haven't used the *production* environment yet. That's what this chapter is about.

Deploying to Heroku is as simple as `git push heroku master`. This pushes your code to Heroku rather than GitHub, and Heroku runs a series of steps in order to get your application ready for production. The production environment is special, because it's the only one that other people can use.[3] Your development and test environments aren't shared; they're for your eyes only. Also, they are generally used on your local machine, whereas production environments are used on a server somewhere else. Production environments are often configured for

---

[2] Like in other Pretty Highly Prominent languages.

[3] Some projects will also have a *staging* environment, for demonstrating new features to clients before they go into production. A staging environment is also usable by other people, but usually by a limited audience, not the general public. Staging should also have an identical configuration to production.

maximum speed, whereas development and test environments are configured for maximum convenience.

With that in mind, let's go ahead and get Ticketee out there for everyone to try.

13.2   Simple deployment with Heroku

Heroku is a company that specializes in handling all the details of deployment for you. How convenient! Heroku started off specializing in hosting Rails applications, and it eventually added support for many other languages and frameworks. Heroku still pays extra attention to Ruby, though; the company even pays Matz[4] and two other members of the Ruby core team to work on Ruby itself.

There is a catch, of course: that convenience comes at a cost. Heroku is more expensive than other hosting options. But for small apps, it has a service tier that is 100% free. That's what you'll use here. It's not a lot, but it's enough to get you going with your first few deployments.

13.2.1   Signing up

You need two things to get set up with Heroku: an account and the Heroku Toolbelt. Luckily, they're both easy to acquire. Getting an account with Heroku is this easy: go to https://www.heroku.com/, click the big Sign Up button, enter your name and email address, click Create Free Account, and then follow the instructions in the email you're sent. Once you're finished with that, it's time to get the Toolbelt.

Heroku distributes a bunch of command-line tools that you can use to interact with your Heroku account. These tools are called the Toolbelt. To get a copy, go to https://toolbelt.heroku.com/ and follow the instructions. Pretty easy, eh?

You need to do one last bit of setup: link together the Toolbelt and your account. There's an easy command-line way to do this:

```
$ heroku login
```

The heroku login command will ask you for the email and password you used to create the account on the website. It will then try to find your SSH keys. SSH stands for *Secure Shell*, and it's a program you'll use to log in to remote servers. If you haven't used SSH before, you won't have any keys, and heroku login will ask you if you want to generate some new ones. If it asks you this, click Yes. It will then upload the public half of your key to your Heroku account, allowing you to use the Toolbelt to the fullest extent.

13.2.2   Provisioning an app

The first part of any deployment process is called *provisioning*. Provisioning is the process of requesting some kind of resource from a provider of that resource. In this case, you want to provision a new application on Heroku. Doing so creates all the internal accounting needed to give you access, and then you can deploy your code to that application.

---

[4]   Remember, Yukihiro "Matz" Matsumoto is the creator of Ruby!

The Heroku Toolbelt gives you a simple way to provision a new application:

```
$ heroku apps:create
```

After running this command, you'll see some output that looks like this:

```
$ heroku apps:create
Creating stark-chamber-2017... done, stack is cedar-14
https://stark-chamber-2017.herokuapp.com/ |
  https://git.heroku.com/stark-chamber-2017.git
Git remote heroku added
```

The names will be a bit different, because they're random. Every Heroku application must have a unique name, so `heroku apps:create` generates a random one for you. In this example, the app was christened `stark-chamber-2017`.

The next line gives you two different URLs: one HTTP and one Git. The HTTP URL is a link that you can open in a web browser to view your application. When you open that URL, you'll see the page in figure 13.1.

> **OPENING YOUR HEROKU APP** If at any point you want to open your Heroku app, just run `heroku open` in the Ticketee application directory. This will automatically open your app in a browser for you.

The Git URL is a link to a Git repository that represents your application on Heroku. When you set up your local repository to push to GitHub, you set GitHub up as a remote branch of the repository (often just shortened to _remote_), named `origin`. Creating the Heroku app will automatically add another remote to your repository, named `heroku`. You can see this by running `git remote -v`:

```
$ git remote -v
heroku   git@heroku.com:stark-chamber-2017.git (fetch)
heroku   git@heroku.com:stark-chamber-2017.git (push)
origin   git@github.com:rubysherpas/r4ia_examples.git (fetch)
origin   git@github.com:rubysherpas/r4ia_examples.git (push)
```

Of course, you'll see your GitHub username and the random name Heroku generated, not the ones shown here.

Anyway, that's it for provisioning! If you visit your Heroku dashboard, you can see that you now have a new app: https://dashboard.heroku.com/apps. Next, we're going to dive a bit deeper into this app concept and you'll see how to best design your application for production.

Figure 13.1 The default generated Heroku app

13.3   *Twelve-factor apps*

There are many, many ways to build web applications. The number of options is overwhelming. After you deploy a few applications, you'll probably develop some opinions about how an application can best be designed for ease of use.

Designed your app for production? Yep, the design decisions that you make in development can also affect production. For example, if you allow file uploads, your production setup must be able to accept the files, save them somewhere, and serve them back to users. If you add a job queue that requires Redis—as you would by using the Resque or Sidekiq gems—your deployment strategy has to take Redis into account as well. In each case you can make good choices or bad choices. Good choices will make deployment a breeze. Bad choices will make it difficult, complex, and scary.

Cloud providers like Heroku offer a particular set of guidelines for building applications. These choices are based on lessons learned while scaling hundreds of Rails applications. Even if you don't use a provider like Heroku, the guidelines are still useful.

These suggestions can be boiled down to just 12 points, explained in *The Twelve-Factor App* (http://12factor.net/). The entire document is worth reading, because it makes a bunch of great points about deploying applications. We won't go over all 12 points here; the website does a good job of explaining itself. But we will go over a couple of them and show how they affect writing a Rails application.

13.3.1   *Configuration*

Part III of the twelve-factor app is about configuration. The rule is this: "The twelve-factor app stores config in environment variables." *Config* doesn't mean everything in your config directory; it means everything that varies between different deployments of an application.

How does this affect your Rails application? In the last chapter you added some code for sending out emails. If this code contained your email credentials, then anyone with access to the code would know the credentials. It's a much safer idea to store these credentials on a protected production server. This is an application of the twelve-factor configuration principle.

The config section in the twelve-factor document also has a good rule of thumb for testing this rule about storing config in environment variables: "A litmus test for whether an app has all config correctly factored out of the code is whether the codebase could be made open source at any moment, without compromising any credentials." This is a great way to think about this problem, because it shows the strength of making this choice outside of a deployment context, too—if someone were to leak your source code, would your data still be safe? If a new employee joins your team, do they need the keys to the production data store on their first day? Ideally, secrets should be as secret as possible, not saved in a place that everyone has access to.

13.3.2 *Processes*

Part VI, Processes, states this: "Twelve-factor processes are stateless and share-nothing." Huh?

Imagine that you had two servers, each running a copy of your application. If these servers had their own copy of the database locally, they'd have state and so would not be stateless. Also, they'd need to keep their data in sync, so you'd have to pass new data back and forth to keep everything consistent. Those are bad choices. If, instead, each of your servers saved no state of its own and wrote all of its state to a separate database server, you wouldn't need to share any data between copies of your application, and there would be no consistency complexity. You could change from 2 servers to 200 servers, and your application wouldn't care. You could make your database server grow with your data, yet keep your app servers lean and mean.

Heroku enforces this statelessness aspect, so your application needs to be designed to accommodate it. The first place this crops up in application design is often file uploads. Remember back in chapter 9, when you used CarrierWave? You saved those files locally. If you deployed two copies of your application, some files would be on one server, and other files would be on another server. You're back to shared, stateful servers. That's why CarrierWave provides an option to configure your application to use another backing store, such as Amazon S3 (Simple Storage Service).

The first thing you'll need is an Amazon S3 account. You can get one here: http://mng.bz/aj7W.

> **IT'S FREE, BUT...** You'll need a credit card to sign up to Amazon S3. You won't be charged anything for the first year of service. If you don't want to sign up with a credit card, you can still continue with this chapter. The only issue will be that file uploads won't persist between deploys for the Ticketee application.

After that, you need four bits of information: your *access key*, your *secret key*, your *bucket name*, and your *region*. You can get all of these credentials from your AWS dashboard. To create an access key, sign in to your Amazon AWS account, click your name, and then click Security Credentials. On this page, expand the Access Keys section and create a new access key. You'll be prompted to download the credentials. Do that, and your access key and secret key will be in that file.

> **CORRECT AS OF TIME OF WRITING!** These instructions are based on Amazon's S3 setup procedure at the time of writing. If the setup design has since changed, please consult Amazon's own documentation on how to set up your S3 account.

Now for the S3 bucket. An S3 bucket is where Ticketee's uploaded files will be stored. To create the bucket, go to the S3 Management console (https://console.aws.amazon.com/s3/home) and click Create Bucket; then give your bucket a name like "ticketee" so that you know what it's for. You can select whichever region you like, but typically you'd select a region close to your users so that the files will be served faster for them.

Once you've created the bucket, getting the AWS name of the region you selected is a little tricky. One way to do it on the S3 dashboard is to select your bucket, click Properties, and expand Static Website Hosting. The region you want is the part of the endpoint in "s3-website-[region_name].amazonaws.com"; for example, `us-east-1` or `ap-southeast-2`.

13.3.3 Combining Heroku and S3

Now that you have your S3 credentials and a bucket set up, you can use the Heroku Toolbelt command to configure those credentials in your environment:

```
$ heroku config:add S3_KEY=your_s3_access_key S3_SECRET=your_s3_secret \
  S3_BUCKET=your_s3_bucket S3_REGION=your_s3_region
```

`heroku config:add` makes new environment variables inside your Heroku application and sets them to some value. This is the "store config in the environment" part of the config rule.

> **MANAGING CONFIGURATION VARIABLES**   You can also manage these config vars from the Heroku dashboard. If you select your app in the list of Personal Apps and click Settings > Reveal Config Vars > Edit, you can edit the existing config vars or add any new ones.

Now you need to configure CarrierWave to use these variables when uploading your files. Open config/initializers/carrierwave.rb and change the configuration to match the following listing.

Listing 13.1   Using Amazon S3 in the production environment

```ruby
CarrierWave.configure do |config|
  config.root = Rails.root

  if Rails.env.production?
    config.storage = :fog
    config.fog_credentials = {
      provider: "AWS",
      aws_access_key_id: ENV["S3_KEY"],
      aws_secret_access_key: ENV["S3_SECRET"],
      region: ENV["S3_REGION"]
    }
    config.fog_directory = ENV["S3_BUCKET"]
  else
    config.storage = :file
  end
end
```

Easy. This code tells CarrierWave that if the application is running in production, go ahead and get the credentials out of the environment and upload to S3 by way of the

Fog gem. The Fog gem is built for talking to cloud services, including AWS's S3 and many others.

You need to add Fog to your Gemfile so that you can upload to S3:

```
gem "fog", "~> 1.29.0"
```

As usual, you need to bundle to update your bundle.

You also need to change your AttachmentUploader. In app/uploaders/ attachment_uploader.rb, there are some lines that look like this:

```
class AttachmentUploader < CarrierWave::Uploader::Base
  ...
  # Choose what kind of storage to use for this uploader:
  storage :file
  # storage :fog
  ...
```

Remove all three lines. You now have a global configuration setting for which kind of storage to use, so you don't want to override it in the uploader itself.

Once you've made these changes, go ahead and commit:

```
$ git add .
$ git commit -m "Configuring CarrierWave for 12factor"
```

That's it! CarrierWave will now work with Heroku.

You have another thing that needs to be configured, though: your database. SQLite, the database you've been using, stores your data into a file on disk. That's excellent for development, but it won't cut it in production. You can't have that shared state between servers. So rather than use SQLite, you'll use PostgreSQL for your production data store. Heroku comes with excellent PostgreSQL support.

Setting up PostgreSQL locally can be a pain, though. Wouldn't it be nice if you could use SQLite locally, but PostgreSQL on Heroku? If you guessed that that was a leading question, you'd be correct. All you need to do is configure your gems.

Find this line in your Gemfile,

```
# Use sqlite3 as the database for Active Record
gem "sqlite3"
```

and change it to this:

```
gem "sqlite3", group: [:development, :test]
gem "pg",      group: :production
```

> **USING DIFFERENT DATABASES IN DIFFERENT ENVIRONMENTS CONSIDERED HARMFUL** On any kind of serious production application, we highly recommend taking the time to set up PostgreSQL, along with the pg gem, in all environments. If you use different databases in the different environments, you may have a case where the code works locally but not on production, which can be disastrous. We've only configured this way for the sake of brevity.

We're not going to have you install the pg gem in the development environment for a couple of reasons:

- To install the pg gem locally, you need to have PostgreSQL installed—or at least its development header files. On Linux it's easy to install just the headers; on other operating systems, not so much.
- You're not going to be using PostgreSQL anyway!

To install only the gems you'll use in development (and test), you can tweak the bundle command slightly:

```
$ bundle install --without=production
```

You only have to do this once; future bundle commands will remember this preference. At the end of the output from running bundle, you'll see the following:

```
Bundle complete! 26 Gemfile dependencies, 113 gems now installed.
Gems in the group production were not installed.
Use `bundle show [gemname]` to see where a bundled gem is installed.
```

It's that easy! Commit these changes:

```
$ git add .
$ git commit -m "Add Postgres for our production data store"
$ git push
```

Now you've got PostgreSQL configured for your production database. You have one more thing to configure with regard to statelessness: assets.

A stateless app delegates things to a backing store as needed. Your application's assets—that is, its graphics and CSS and JavaScript files—are state. But they're not mutable state, in that you only mutate them when you make a new deploy.

The second thing about assets is that they don't require any application logic to serve; you want to give everyone access to them. By default, Rails assumes that all assets are public and therefore can be stored in an external, fast store, like Amazon S3. But if you remember, back in chapter 9 you added some application logic to hide images that users didn't upload themselves. You want your Heroku application to serve these assets, so you can protect them. It'll be slower, but your users value their privacy.

Another thing that is stateful is application logs. If two servers were each writing their own logs, they'd need to send them to each other to keep the logs in sync. By putting logs to standard output rather than to a file, external tools can send the logs along to an external logging service, which can aggregate logs from all of your servers.

Fixing this is pretty simple. Heroku provides a gem for Rails called rails_12factor that changes Rails' configuration settings to do both of these things. Installing it is easy; just add this line to your Gemfile:

```
gem "rails_12factor", group: :production
```

Then run bundle install. Your app will serve up assets and log to the correct place. Nice and easy!

Once you've made these changes, go ahead and commit:

```
$ git add .
$ git commit -m "Adding rails_12factor gem for logging and static
  assets"
$ git push
```

Your Rails app is finally twelve-factor compliant. That wasn't too bad! As we said before, make sure you check out all 12 points—they can teach you a lot about how things work under the hood. But enough talk; let's get your application into production.

13.4 Deploying Ticketee

After all that fuss with getting your application ready, you may be sweating bullets when thinking about finally deploying it. With all that setup, the final process must be hard, right? Don't worry, we'll get through this together.

We'll start with the first step: sending your code up to Heroku. You can do this with the new `heroku` Git remote that `heroku create` added for you:

```
$ git push heroku master
```

When you do this, you'll see a bunch of output, though it may take a minute or two to get going. It looks something like this:

```
Counting objects: 1256, done.
Delta compression using up to 4 threads.
Compressing objects: 100% (883/883), done.
Writing objects: 100% (1256/1256), 144.56 KiB | 0 bytes/s, done.
Total 1256 (delta 773), reused 527 (delta 315)
Compressing source files... done.
Building source:

-----> Ruby app detected
-----> Compiling Ruby/Rails
-----> Using Ruby version: ruby-2.0.0
-----> Installing dependencies using 1.7.12
       Running: bundle install --without development:test --path ...
       Fetching gem metadata from https://rubygems.org/........
       Fetching git://github.com/radar/searcher.git
       Installing CFPropertyList 2.3.1
       Installing i18n 0.7.0
       Installing rake 10.4.2
       Installing minitest 5.5.1
....
```

It goes on and on and on … and eventually you should see it succeed. It'll give you a couple of warnings though—let's look at resolving those first.

As part of the output, you'll see some text like the following:

```
###### WARNING:
       You have not declared a Ruby version in your Gemfile.
       To set your Ruby version add this line to your Gemfile:
       ruby '2.0.0'
       # See https://devcenter.heroku.com/articles/ruby-versions for
```

```
    # more information.

###### WARNING:
    No Procfile detected, using the default web server (webrick)
    https://devcenter.heroku.com/articles/ruby-default-web-server
```

These are both issues you can and should fix; you're not even using Ruby 2.0.0 in development!

13.4.1 *Fixing deployment issues*

You've successfully completed the first step of deployment to Heroku, but you received some warnings you can easily fix. Open up your Gemfile, and right at the top you can specify the version of Ruby you're using.

Listing 13.2   Specifying the version of Ruby in your Gemfile

```
source 'https://rubygems.org'
ruby "2.2.1"


...
```

The second issue is a little trickier—you haven't specified a web server to use. In development you've just been using `rails server`, which uses WEBrick by default. This isn't recommended for a production environment, so you're getting this error.

Follow the link in the warning, and read all about the pitfalls of using WEBrick in development. Okay, WEBrick bad. Puma good. Let's look at setting up your app with Puma.

You can start by adding Puma to your Gemfile for use in the production environment only.

Listing 13.3   Using `puma` in production

```
gem "puma", group: :production
```

Then `bundle` as always, to get the gem installed.

You don't need to do a lot of configuration for Puma, but you do need to create a new file called Procfile in the root of your Rails application. You can put the following configuration in it.

Listing 13.4   Defining a new Procfile

```
web: bundle exec puma -t 5:5 -p ${PORT:-3000}
  -e ${RACK_ENV:-development}
```

We've spread the code over two lines here, but in your Procfile it should only be a single line.

Commit these changes, and try deploying again:

```
$ git add .
$ git commit -m "Configure Ruby version and Puma for Heroku"
$ git push
$ git push heroku master
```

You'll see the same type of long Heroku output as before, with one small difference:

```
...
-----> Ruby app detected
-----> Compiling Ruby/Rails
-----> Using Ruby version: ruby-2.2.1
-----> Installing dependencies using 1.7.12
       Ruby version change detected. Clearing bundler cache.
       Old: ruby 2.0.0p643 (2015-02-25 revision 49749) [x86_64-linux]
       New: ruby 2.2.1p85 (2015-02-26 revision 49769) [x86_64-linux]
...
```

It's picked up your Ruby version change. Excellent! It's also read the Procfile you created:

```
-----> Discovering process types
       Procfile declares types -> web
       Default types for Ruby  -> console, rake, worker
```

And both of the warnings have gone! This is very good news.

Open the URL it gives you in your browser; it should look something like http://stark-chamber-2017.herokuapp.com/. Congratulations! Your application is now up and running. Check on it by running `heroku open`. You'll see something like figure 13.2. Oh dear! Your first production issue. What do you do in this case?

To start with, you can consult the Heroku logs. The logs are the first place that you should go looking whenever anything goes wrong in your application. Open them now with `heroku logs`. You'll get a lot of output that looks similar to what you see when you run `rails server` in your own terminal. Looking through them, you'll see this part:

```
...
[timestamp] app[web.1]: Started GET "/" for [IP address] at [timestamp]
[timestamp] app[web.1]:    Rendered projects/index.html.erb within
                           layouts/application (1.0ms)
[timestamp] app[web.1]:
[timestamp] app[web.1]: ActionView::Template::Error (PG::UndefinedTable:
                        ERROR:  relation "states" does not exist
[timestamp] app[web.1]: LINE 1: SELECT "states".* FROM "states"
...
```

> ### We're sorry, but something went wrong.
>
> If you are the application owner check the logs for more information.

Figure 13.2 If things are going well, you should never see this message. Things aren't going well.

This tells you that the states relation doesn't exist. In PostgreSQL, tables are called *relations*, so that would indicate that the states table is the thing that doesn't exist.

How would this come to be? It would seem that you've forgotten to run your migrations on your production environment! To run the migrations on Heroku, you can run this command:

```
$ heroku run rake db:migrate
```

When that's complete, refresh your application again. This time you'll see it running properly, as in figure 13.3.

In order to sign in to the application, you can use the admin credentials. Well, at least you could do that if that user existed in your production database. To get that user created on Heroku, you can run another Rake command:

Figure 13.3 Ticketee, running on Heroku!

```
$ heroku run rake db:seed
```

As you might have guessed by now, you can prefix your normal rake commands with heroku run to run them in your Heroku application. This command will create the users, projects, and states from the db/seeds.rb file of your application, which is just perfect for testing your application. Take a break and play around with it. You've come a long way.

13.4.2 *Fixing CarrierWave file uploads*

You might find, through your tinkering around with the system, that file uploads don't quite work in your production application. You can upload a file successfully, but then clicking the link to view it gives you that same old "We're sorry, something went wrong" error message. Not cool.

What's gone wrong? Check again with heroku logs.

Listing 13.5 The latest error message

```
[timestamp] app[web.1]: Started GET "/attachments/1" for [IP] at ...
[timestamp] app[web.1]:   User Load (3.1ms)  SELECT  "users".* FROM ...
[timestamp] app[web.1]:   Parameters: {"id"=>"1"}
[timestamp] app[web.1]: Processing by AttachmentsController#show as HTML
[timestamp] app[web.1]: Sent file uploads/attachment/file/1/cool.jpeg
[timestamp] app[web.1]: ActionController::MissingFile (Cannot read file
                        uploads/attachment/file/1/cool.jpeg):
[timestamp] app[web.1]: Completed 500 Internal Server Error in 24ms
```

That makes sense, because that path isn't where you're uploading files now—you're using Fog and uploading them to S3. You need to tell your app to send the file via its URL when you have a file at a remote URL, and via its path when you don't.

You can do this by tweaking your `AttachmentsController` to add the logic we just mentioned. Instead of blindly calling `send_file attachment.file.path`, you can do the following.

Listing 13.6   app/controllers/attachments_controller.rb

```
class AttachmentsController < ApplicationController
  ....
  def show
    ...
    send_file file_to_send(attachment), disposition: :inline
  end
  ...

  private

  def file_to_send(attachment)
    if URI.parse(attachment.file.url).scheme
      filename = "/tmp/#{attachment.attributes["file"]}"
      File.open(filename, "wb+") do |tf|
        tf.write open(attachment.file.url).read
      end
      filename
    else
      attachment.file.path
    end
  end
end
```

This uses `URI.parse`[5] to parse the URL that the file has—your files in development will have a generic URI, without a *scheme* (for example, http or https), whereas your files on S3 will have a scheme of https. You can use this to determine what kind of action you take.

If it's a generic file, you can do what you were doing before—just use `send_file` directly with the file path. But you need some fiddly code in there to deal with remote files—you read the contents of the file into an identically named *tempfile* stored on the Heroku server, and then you use `send_file` to send that temporary file to the browser. It's a little hacky, but it will get you going.

Commit this change:

```
$ git add .
$ git commit -m "Files are served correctly from S3 in production"
$ git push
```

Now you can redeploy your code to Heroku:

```
$ git push heroku master
```

When that's done, verify that your file uploads can now be downloaded again. Success!

---

[5] See the URI documentation for more info: http://ruby-doc.org/stdlib-2.2.1/libdoc/uri/rdoc/ URI.html#method-c-parse.

13.4.3 Deploying is hard

Deploying is a new step in your process. You run your tests, commit, push to GitHub, and then push to Heroku.

> **Listing 13.7   Sample deployment process**

```
$ bundle exec rspec
$ git add .
$ git commit -m "Some message"
$ git push origin
$ git push heroku
```

Isn't that kind of annoying? Six steps. Wouldn't it be nicer if you could just do this,

```
$ git add .
$ git commit -m "Some message"
$ git push origin
```

and then some magical *thing* would handle running your tests and pushing to Heroku? You can do this with a technique called continuous deployment. You'll do that with one of our favorite services: Travis CI. Read on!

13.5 *Continuous deployment with Travis CI*

Before we get into the details of Travis CI, let's talk about what *continuous deployment* means. In a nutshell, continuous deployment means that every time you commit code, it ends up going into production. If that sounds a little extreme, that's because it is. Many people prefer to have a discrete time when they deploy. But if you limit your deployments to only doing them by hand, it's easy to not automate them as much, because you're already doing the work anyway. Furthermore, once you have fully automatic deployments, you can do all kinds of neat things. Continuous deployment can be a useful strategy, given the right developer mentality.

Travis CI's claim to fame isn't deployment—it's testing. Travis CI is a service that, like Heroku, came out of the Ruby community and then grew to support a host of other languages and platforms. Here's the idea behind it: Every time you push to GitHub, Travis runs your tests. If your tests fail, Travis will notify you via email. It's that simple. It's impossible to forget to run your tests, because it's automatic. If you're building a library, Travis can also automatically run your tests against multiple versions of Ruby, including JRuby and Rubinius. Furthermore, Travis watches your pull requests and can tell you if a given pull request still passes all the tests after it's been merged. Travis is a powerful tool in any developer's arsenal. And like many services, it's free for open source projects.

13.5.1 Configuring Travis

Configuring Travis for your Rails app is pretty simple: just add a .travis.yml file to the root of your Ticketee project, and put this in it:

```
language: ruby
rvm: 2.2.1
script: bundle exec rspec
before_install:
  - export DISPLAY=:99.0
  - sh -e /etc/init.d/xvfb start
```

This tells Travis that you have a Ruby project, that you wish to use Ruby version 2.2.1 (rvm stands for *Ruby Version Manager*, which is the tool Travis uses to switch Ruby versions), and that you run your tests via bundle exec rspec. The last chunk is the before_install bit. Because you're using Selenium to test some JavaScript, you need to use xvfb, the X virtual frame buffer. This will let your browser operate in headless mode.

Commit this to your repository:

```
$ git add .
$ git commit -m "Adding support for Travis"
```

Don't push it to GitHub just yet. You need an account on the Travis site first.

Go to https://travis-ci.org/ and click "Sign In with GitHub" at the upper right. That's right, Travis works with your GitHub account. Once you've signed in, choose an account from the submenu under your name at the upper right, and you should see all of your GitHub repositories listed. Find your Ticketee repository, and click the slider so it says "On." Then you're ready to push:

```
$ git push origin
```

That's it! Check out your project on Travis. It will take a few minutes, but if you wait a while, you'll see a build happen and then pass. You'll get a nice green circle for your effort. That wasn't so bad!

A lot of the power of Travis comes from its ability to do things if your build passes or fails. One example is that when your build fails, Travis can email your entire team to let you know that something is wrong. Another example is that when your build passes, Travis can deploy the application to Heroku. Let's explore that now.

13.5.2 Deployment hooks

Travis can run any arbitrary script after a build passes or fails. One of the first things that people did when Travis was released was to write scripts that deploy things somewhere. This idea was popular enough that Travis eventually added full deployment support as an option.

Here's how it works. You take your Heroku API key, encrypt it, and give it to Travis. Then, after a successful build, Travis pushes to Heroku for you. If your tests fail, Travis won't push your code. It's so simple!

To do this, you first need your Heroku API key. You can find this on your account page, https://dashboard.heroku.com/account. Click Show API Key, enter your password, and copy the key onto your clipboard. It should look like a long string of letters and numbers, like 825dff5749744ffbac3cfb6815c703e7. Now, run this command from your terminal:

```
$ gem install travis
```

Like the Heroku Toolbelt, Travis includes a tool that you can use to interact with your application. Unlike the Toolbelt, Travis's tool is distributed via RubyGems. Because your application doesn't rely on the gem, you don't need to put it in your Gemfile; using gem install is enough.

Once the travis gem is installed, you need to authenticate with it. Travis authenticates via GitHub, so if you want to log in the normal way, you need to provide your GitHub username and password to the following command:

```
$ travis login
```

If you don't feel comfortable doing this, you can instead generate a GitHub personal access token, and use that to authenticate with Travis. To do this, visit the Settings menu in GitHub, and under Applications you can generate a new personal access token. The only permission you need to give it is public_repo, so you can uncheck the rest of the boxes. Make sure to copy the token after it's created—it's another long string of letters and numbers. Then you can log in with this token:

```
$ travis login --github-token=your_token_here
Successfully logged in as [your-username]!
```

Once you're logged in successfully, you can configure Travis for your Ticketee app:

```
$ travis setup heroku
```

travis setup asks you two questions. They default to Yes, and you should answer Yes. You'll see some output that looks like this:

```
$ travis setup heroku
Shell completion not installed. Would you like to install it now? |y| y
Detected repository as [you]/ticketee, is this correct? |yes| y
Deploy only from [you]/ticketee? |yes| yes
Encrypt API key? |yes| yes
```

That's it. Check out your .travis.yml, because it has been changed. Ours now looks like this:

```
language: ruby
rvm: 2.2.1
script: rspec
before_install:
- export DISPLAY=:99.0
- sh -e /etc/init.d/xvfb start
deploy:
  provider: heroku
  api_key:
    secure: ...
  app: r4ia-ticketee
  on:
    repo: rubysherpas/r4ia_examples
```

There's some new stuff there. These settings say, "Deploy rubysherpas/r4ia_examples to Heroku. The app name is r4ia-ticketee, and the API key is encrypted. Here it is." This is all the information Travis needs to deploy your code.

Commit this new config file:

```
$ git add .
$ git commit -m "Adding deploy support to Travis"
$ git push origin
```

If you check out the build on Travis, you should see your tests pass and then the deployment. Congratulations: you are now continuously deploying! Don't ever worry about deploying manually again; let other computers handle that for you. Simply push to GitHub, and your users will have your new features in a few minutes.

With this all up and running, why use anything else? Well, although Travis and Heroku are free for open source projects, Heroku can get pricey for bigger applications. Plus, even though twelve-factor apps are a good idea, you might find the rules a bit too constraining and want to build an application in a totally custom manner. To do so, you'll need to use your own custom server and deployment tooling. That's a topic for another book entirely.

13.6 Sending emails

The final thing that you need to do for your application in this chapter is to configure it to send out emails in the real world. You have the mailer code, and now what you need to do is add the email configuration. To get there, you'll use Heroku's addons feature to add a service called Mailgun to your application.

Mailgun is a service that lets users send emails either via traditional means (an SMTP server) or via HTTP. It also provides many other features, none of which you're going to use right now. You're more than welcome to experiment with those features after you're done this chapter.

Mailgun also provides a free plan on Heroku Addons, called Starter. To set up Mailgun with your Heroku account, all you need to do is run this command in the terminal:

```
$ heroku addons:add mailgun:starter
```

When that completes successfully, you'll see a message like this:

```
Adding mailgun:starter on stark-chamber-2017... done, v17 (free)
Use `heroku addons:docs mailgun` to view documentation.
```

The documentation is good, but there's no need to read it since we'll cover the important parts right here, right now. When you link Mailgun to Heroku, a Mailgun account is automatically set up for you, and its credentials are made available through environment variables in your application. If you run `heroku config` you can see them:

```
MAILGUN_API_KEY:          [redacted]
MAILGUN_SMTP_LOGIN:       [redacted]
MAILGUN_SMTP_PASSWORD:    [redacted]
MAILGUN_SMTP_PORT:        587
MAILGUN_SMTP_SERVER:      smtp.mailgun.org
```

You can use most of these environment variables to send emails through Mailgun by putting this code in config/environments/production.rb. Remember to specify your own application hostname as the host variable!

```
Rails.application.configure do
  ...
  ActionMailer::Base.delivery_method = :smtp

  host = "yourapp.herokuapp.com"

  ActionMailer::Base.smtp_settings = {
    port:           ENV['MAILGUN_SMTP_PORT'],
    address:        ENV['MAILGUN_SMTP_SERVER'],
    user_name:      ENV['MAILGUN_SMTP_LOGIN'],
    password:       ENV['MAILGUN_SMTP_PASSWORD'],
    domain:         host,
    authentication: :plain,
  }

  config.action_mailer.default_url_options = {
    host: host
  }
  ...
```

With this configuration, you tell Action Mailer that you want to deliver emails with SMTP, and that the settings for SMTP are going to use the MAILGUN_* environment variables, which are only available on Heroku for port, server, login, and password. The host variable should be the root URL of your application on Heroku. The default_url_options bit at the end will tell Action Mailer what URL to use when it decides it wants to create a link.

Push this configuration up now:

```
$ git add .
$ git commit -m "Add Mailgun configuration"
$ git push
```

Go over to Travis and wait for the build to complete. It will take a couple of minutes to run, but it's worth it for all it's doing.

To test this feature, you can do the following on your production Heroku application:

1 Create a new account on Ticketee with a real email address.
2 Sign out from that user.
3 Sign in as admin@ticketee.com and grant your email address "Manager" permissions on a project.
4 Sign out from admin@ticketee.com, and sign in again with your real email address.
5 Create a ticket on that project as your real email address.
6 Sign out, and then sign back in as admin@ticketee.com.
7 Leave a comment on the ticket that you created.

After doing this little dance, you should see an email arrive in your inbox from Ticketee. That's pretty great!

13.7 *Summary*

In this short chapter, we've shown how you can deploy Ticketee to Heroku by using either `git push` or Travis CI. The Travis path is better because it ensures that all your tests are passing beforehand and then does the pushing for you.

In the next chapter, we'll look at how you can create an API—a simple way to share part of Ticketee with other applications.

Designing an API

This chapter covers

- Creating JSON responses using ActiveModel::Serializers
- Creating an API namespace
- Request testing and using HTTParty for manually interacting with your API
- Responding appropriately to common API errors

It's becoming more and more apparent that if you have an application of any significance, you're going to need an *application programming interface*, or API. Some applications are only an API. ProgrammableWeb (www.programmableweb.com/), a blog that keeps track of the API space, has a directory of APIs, and at the time of writing, there are 13,628 being tracked. By the time you read this, there could be over 15,000 listed. That's a lot of APIs!

In this chapter, we'll compare a few different ways to build APIs, and then you'll build one. Let's get going.

468

14.1 An overview of APIs

For a very long time, it's been considered good practice in computer science to give your programs a deliberate structure. By "a very long time," we mean an eternity in computer years: since March 1968. Edsger Dijkstra wrote a paper for that month's edition of *Communications of the ACM*, titled "Go To Statement Considered Harmful," in which he, in his well-known style, declares that using structured programming is the only proper way to write good software. Since then, a great deal of computer science work has been predicated around the proper way to actually structure programs. One example is the MVC pattern that you've been applying throughout this book.

As the web became popular, it changed the structure of programs a bit. Before networking was prevalent, programs ran mostly on one computer. But when you build a web application, you're building a distributed system: part of the application runs on a server, and part of it runs in the client's browser. A common way to scale up a web application is to have an application server running your Rails code, as well as a database server running your database. Two servers plus a client browser is another sort of distributed system.

We bring this up because the simple way to think of an API is "We share some stuff about our application with you." But it's important to acknowledge that an API is more than that—APIs also allow others to build applications that use your component. This means that you're not only building a distributed system; you're building a system that you don't entirely control. That brings up a whole ton of issues that mostly involve coordinating development with an completely separate group of software developers.

This is a book about Rails, not a book about APIs. We won't get into all of the things that you should do to build a perfect API; we just want to get you started building them in Rails. But before we talk about the API project you'll build in this chapter, let's spend a moment talking about API formats.

The core idea of an API is that you expose part of your application to the world, and allow others to use that part in their own applications. There are two main ways to do this: you can expose your data, or you can expose your workflow. Once you've chosen which way you want to share your information with others, you then have to choose some kind of format. We call these formats *MIME types*. Some MIME types are better for data, and some are better for workflow.

Rails has historically supported the expose-your-data methodology well. This is generally called a *RESTful* API. The expose-your-workflow style is called a *hypermedia* or *web* API. This style is newer and a bit less well-known, so we won't discuss it further in this book, though we will hint at it from time to time.

Within the expose-your-data tradition, Rails originally shipped with one of the original best-practice API MIME types: XML. Later, a MIME type called JSON grew quite popular, so Rails supported it as well. Nowadays, most people prefer JSON—due to its simplicity compared with XML—so we won't talk about XML-based APIs in this chapter.

That's enough theory for now. Let's look at how a RESTful API might be implemented in Rails.

14.1.1 *A practical example*

Consider a simple `ProjectsController` that finds a particular `Project` model and displays it. You've written code like this as far back as chapter 3 and all the way through the book so far, and it looked like this:

```
class ProjectsController < ApplicationController
  def show
    authorize @project, :show?
    @tickets = @project.tickets
  end
end
```

This then loads up app/views/projects/show.html.erb. Let's explicitly add support for returning HTML, rather than implicitly relying on it:

```
class ProjectsController < ApplicationController
  def show
    authorize @project, :show?
    @tickets = @project.tickets
    respond_to do |format|
      format.html
    end
  end
end
```

This `respond_to` block shows all of the MIME types that the `show` action can return. In this case, you just have HTML. You can add a JSON format too:

```
class ProjectsController < ApplicationController
  def show
    authorize @project, :show?
    @tickets = @project.tickets
    respond_to do |format|
      format.html
      format.json
    end
  end
end
```

Now if you were to load up http://localhost:3000/projects/1.json, or make a request with a program like curl to http://localhost:3000/projects/1 with a `Content-Type` header set to `application/json` (which is JSON's full MIME type name), Rails would attempt to render app/views/posts/show.json.erb, instead of show.html.erb. An example of a curl request would be as follows:

```
curl http://localhost:3000/projects/1.json
# or
curl -H "Content-Type=application/json" http://localhost:3000/projects/1
```

> **CURL** curl is a program that lets you send HTTP requests, and it's available on most operating systems. If you don't have it already, install it with your operating system's package manager, or download it from http://curl.haxx.se/download.html.

Both of these curl examples do the same thing. By putting .json on the end of the URL, you request the resource in the *format* of JSON. By specifying the Content-Type header, you tell the server you expect to get back JSON. Rails supports either of these approaches for ease-of-use reasons.

If you switch over to not using the .json format, it will render the HTML view instead.

Easy! You can see how the format.html leads to show.html.erb and format.json leads to show.json.erb. The power of conventions!

But Rails also knows how to serialize your models, turning their data into JSON and XML. The serialization approach looks like this:

```
class ProjectsController < ApplicationController
  def show
    authorize @project, :show?
    @tickets = @project.tickets
    respond_to do |format|
      format.html
      format.json { render json: @project }
      format.xml { render xml: @project }
    end
  end
end
```

Now you don't load up a view. render :json and render :xml are two special calls to render that end up calling special methods on your model: .to_json and .to_xml, respectively. The controller then sets the proper headers to make sure that the client knows it's getting JSON or XML, and then sends the converted model data.

There are a number of formats more specialized than just plain XML or JSON. You'll be using one soon called JSON-API, which builds on top of JSON and is specifically great for APIs. You should also check out the many other approaches and the various gems that help you implement them with Rails. Here are some names to get you started: HAL, Collection+JSON, Siren, JSON-LD, and OData. Choosing a well-known format can help you reuse tooling that others have written, whereas if you go totally custom with your JSON, you'll have to write it all yourself.

Let's not build a totally custom solution. As with most tasks you need to accomplish in Rails, there's a gem for that: ActiveModel::Serializers.

14.2   *Using ActiveModel::Serializers*

To help turn your model objects into JSON, you can use a gem called Active-Model::Serializers, or AMS for short. We've already told you that Rails knows how to serialize models via to_json, so you might wonder why you need a gem.

Rails only provides you with the most basic of serialization options. As soon as your application becomes more complicated than "show me all of the data," the default implementation of to_json just isn't enough. For example, let's say that you have a simple model called Post you want to turn into JSON:

```
def show
  @post = Post.find(params[:id])
  render json: @post
end

# => {"id": 1, "title": "Rails is Omakase", "body": "..."}
```

And suppose you don't just want the data from your model, you want to add some metadata. You need to include a root element to scope the data with:

```
def show
  @post = Post.find(params[:id])
  ActiveRecord::Base.include_root_in_json = true
  render json: @post
end

# => {"post": {"id": 1, "title": "Rails is Omakase", "body": "..."}}
```

That's not very intuitive. And if you want to do that only for some models, you'll have to remember to turn the setting on and off for each one.

What if you want to show only the post title, and nothing else? Maybe based on a parameter that's passed in?

```
def show
  @post = Post.find(params[:id])
  ActiveRecord::Base.include_root_in_json = true

  if params[:summary]
    render json: @post.to_json(only: [:title])
  else
    render json: @post
  end

ensure
  ActiveRecord::Base.include_root_in_json = false
end
```

Yes, if you want to pass options to `to_json`, you must do it yourself. You can see how complex this is getting, and we haven't even introduced other common scenarios, like including a certain set of attributes if the `current_user` is an administrator or a regular user. You'll need something more powerful.

Enter AMS. With it, you define a serializer class, and it controls all of the serialization options. For each of the previous scenarios, the action code stays the same:

```
def show
  @post = Post.find(params[:id])

  render json: @post
end
```

In addition, you have a serializer, which would be stored at app/serializers/ post_serializer.rb and would look like this:

```
class PostSerializer < ActiveModel::Serializer
  attributes :id, :title, :body
end
```

This has the root style set by default. If you wanted to remove it for just this serializer, you'd do this:

```
class PostSerializer < ActiveModel::Serializer
  attributes :id, :title, :body

  self.root = false
end
```

And none of the other serializers would be affected.

This is the best approach for many reasons. First of all, it places all of the logic about how to serialize your model in one place, rather than dumping it in the controller or forcing you to write a model method (which mixes presentational requirements in with your business logic). Serializers are easy to test because they're plain old Ruby objects, nothing fancy. You can have a few different serializers for one model, which is nice if you have various serialization scenarios. And finally, serializers operate on one of Rails' core principles: convention over configuration.

By following AMS's defaults, you'll get nice behavior out of the box, and it'll be similar to other projects that use AMS out of the box as well. This means reusability, because standard tooling can be used to understand the AMS format. With all of these advantages, why is AMS not the default?

Originally, AMS was committed to core Rails, but then it was reverted by Rails' creator, David Heinemeier Hansson. David prefers to use his own library, JBuilder, which uses the *Builder* pattern to create JSON, rather than rely on convention over configuration. JBuilder is included by default with Rails 4. But just like you used RSpec over MiniTest and you turned Turbolinks off, the Rails defaults are not the only way to do things. We believe that AMS is the best option due to its convention-over-configuration approach, and luckily, you install different gems and build applications the way you want to.

With that said, let's serialize some models.

14.2.1 *Getting your hands dirty*

As with any Rails gem, you first need to add AMS to your Gemfile.

Listing 14.1　Adding AMS to your Gemfile

```
gem "active_model_serializers", "~> 0.9.3"
```

You should also undo the changes you made to your `ProjectsController` in this chapter, when you added the `respond_to` block (if you did). When you're done, it should look just like it did before.

Listing 14.2　Back to the old `ProjectsController` show action

```
class ProjectsController < ApplicationController
  ...
  def show
```

```
      authorize @project, :show?
      @tickets = @project.tickets
    end
    ...
end
```

Next, you need to actually install AMS. Once everything is set up, commit that to Git as well:

```
$ bundle
$ git add .
$ git commit -m "Adding ActiveModel::Serializers"
```

Now you can generate a serializer for your `Ticket` model. Try this command:

```
$ rails g serializer ticket
```

You'll see some output that shows it created app/serializers/ticket_serializer.rb. Let's examine that:

```
class TicketSerializer < ActiveModel::Serializer
  attributes :id
end
```

This looks mostly like the `PostSerializer` sample you saw earlier. Excellent!

Now that you have a serializer, you need to make sure your controller is using it. Open your app/controllers/tickets_controller.rb and change the `show` action to look like this:

```
class TicketsController < ApplicationController
  ...
  def show
    authorize @ticket, :show?
    @comment = @ticket.comments.build(state_id: @ticket.state_id)

    respond_to do |format|
      format.html
      format.json { render json: @ticket }
    end
  end
  ...
```

This uses the `respond_to` block we discussed earlier. In the case of an HTML request, this action will do the same thing it did before, which is render the app/views/tickets/show.html.erb view. In the case of JSON, the action will render some JSON instead.

Now that your controller is set up, you can test it in your browser. Start your server,

```
$ rails server
```

and visit a ticket's page. Go to the URL bar of your browser, add .json to the end, and then hit Enter. Our URL was http://localhost:3000/projects/1/tickets/1.json, but you may have a different project or ticket number. The JSON should look like the following.

Listing 14.3 A `Ticket` instance, rendered with the `TicketSerializer`

```
{
  "ticket": {
    "id": 1
  }
}
```

There you have it. Just one ticket with an ID.

Why just the ID? Well, that's what you put in your serializer. Go ahead and change app/serializers/ticket_serializer.rb to add more attributes:

```
class TicketSerializer < ActiveModel::Serializer
  attributes :id, :name, :description, :project_id, :created_at,
    :updated_at, :author_id, :state_id
end
```

If you refresh the JSON in your browser, you'll see the new attributes:

```
{
  "ticket": {
    "id": 1,
    "name": "Round and round and round it goes",
    "description": "Where it stops nobody knows",
    "project_id": 1,
    "created_at": "[timestamp]",
    "updated_at": "[timestamp]",
    "author_id": 1,
    "state_id": 1
  }
}
```

See how that `state_id` is 1? That's because states are an association. You just have the ID here. You can change your serializer to include the state information inline, instead of listing the `state_id` attribute:

```
class TicketSerializer < ActiveModel::Serializer
  attributes :id, :name, :description, :project_id, :created_at,
    :updated_at, :author_id

  has_one :state
end
```

Refresh it, and the JSON will look like this:

```
{
  "ticket": {
    "id": 1,
    "title": "Round and round and round it goes",
    "description": "Where it stops nobody knows",
    "project_id": 1,
    "created_at": "[timestamp]",
    "updated_at": "[timestamp]",
    "author_id": 1,
    "state": {
      "id": 1,
```

```
        "name": "New",
        "color": "#0066CC",
        "default": true
      }
    }
  }
}
```

HAS_ONE ASSOCIATION The actual `state` association in the `Ticket` model is a `belongs_to` association, but here you use `has_one` instead. As the AMS documentation explains, serializers are only concerned with multiplicity, and not ownership, so both `belongs_to` and `has_one` are simplified to just `has_one`.

The `has_one` method in serializers will include a JSON representation of the object passed in. To get that JSON representation, ActiveModel::Serializers will go looking for a serializer with that class's name. In this case, that would be `StateSerializer`. If that serializer existed, it would be used to generate the JSON for this `has_one` output for the serializer. It doesn't exist, though; instead `to_json` is called on the object and all the fields from the object are made available as JSON.

That's all you need to know about the basics. You now have a very small, very simple API. You allow users to see details about a ticket. If you'd like, you could also add serializers for comments, projects, and users. For now, though, we'll talk about another part of building APIs: authentication and authorization.

14.3 *API authentication and authorization*

As you learned earlier, you can simulate a real-life request to an API using curl, a program that lets you send HTTP requests. Open http://localhost:3000/projects/1/ tickets/1.json with `curl`, using the `-i` flag:

```
$ curl -i http://localhost:3000/projects/1/tickets/1.json
HTTP/1.1 302 Found
X-Frame-Options: SAMEORIGIN
X-Xss-Protection: 1; mode=block
X-Content-Type-Options: nosniff
Location: http://localhost:3000/
Content-Type: text/html; charset=utf-8
Cache-Control: no-cache
X-Request-Id: 7300a07b-5fa5-4df6-8cfb-2cc7f12d4b91
X-Runtime: 0.007952
Server: WEBrick/1.3.1 (Ruby/2.2.1/2015-02-26)
Date: [timestamp]
Content-Length: 88
Connection: Keep-Alive
Set-Cookie: _ticketee_session=MGZEZ...; path=/; HttpOnly

<html><body>You are being <a href="http://localhost:3000/">redirected
  </a>.</body></html>
```

CURL'S -i FLAG When you use the `-i` flag, you're asking `curl` to include extra information about the request in its output.

You can see here that you got a 302 Found response and then some HTML saying you've been ... redirected? What gives? You might have expected a 200 OK and some JSON.

This happened because you're not authenticated, and you only want people who have permission to see the tickets. The curl command has no knowledge of what's happening in the browser, so the request made by curl to the server is treated as though it was made by an anonymous source.

Making requests to the API requires some way of authenticating, and the way we'll discuss in this section is token-based authentication. With token-based authentication, you pass a token through in the request, and then the application checks if the token belongs to any user. If so, the application works out that the request must be coming from that user, so that user is then authenticated for that request.

You need to be careful, however. If you keep putting code in your Tickets-Controller to serve as an API, you run the risk of making that controller too complex; it would be serving both HTML and JSON. There will be some code in the controller specifically for the HTML response, and some code specifically for the JSON response, and it can end up as a big tangled mess.

Take the show action from TicketsController in its current incarnation as an example:

```
class TicketsController < ApplicationController
  ...
  def show
    authorize @ticket, :show?
    @comment = @ticket.comments.build(state_id: @ticket.state_id)

    respond_to do |format|
      format.html
      format.json { render json: @ticket }
    end
  end
  ...
```

The JSON response of this action doesn't need the @comment variable at all, since that's only needed for rendering the "New Comment" form in the HTML response. It only needs the @ticket variable, which is set up by the before_action called set_ticket. Rather than chucking everything in the one controller and calling it done, you should take the time to separate the JSON and HTML parts of your application. You can do this by introducing an API namespace.

14.3.1 *The API namespace*

Just as you added an admin namespace back in chapter 7, you'll add an API namespace here. This namespace will be used to separate the code that generates API responses from the code that generates HTML responses.

Before you go generating any new controllers, you should first write a new test to make sure that this feature will work as intended. In your test, you'll want to ensure that users can authenticate using a token when making a request to the API. To validate that the request is going through okay, you could assert that the response status is 200, but you can go another step further and validate the structure of the JSON as well. The API that you'll test is the new-tickets API.

Write this new test in spec/requests/api/tickets_spec.rb.

Listing 14.4   spec/requests/api/tickets_spec.rb

```
require "rails_helper"

RSpec.describe "Tickets API" do
  let(:user) { FactoryGirl.create(:user) }
  let(:project) { FactoryGirl.create(:project) }
  let(:state) { FactoryGirl.create(:state, name: "Open") }
  let(:ticket) do
    FactoryGirl.create(:ticket, project: project, state: state)
  end

  before do
    assign_role!(user, :manager, project)
    user.generate_api_key
  end

  context "as an authenticated user" do
    let(:headers) do
      { "HTTP_AUTHORIZATION" => "Token token=#{user.api_key}" }
    end

    it "retrieves a ticket's information" do
      get api_project_ticket_path(project, ticket, format: :json),
        {}, headers
      expect(response.status).to eq 200

      json = TicketSerializer.new(ticket).to_json
      expect(response.body).to eq json
    end
  end
end
```

We've put the test under spec/requests because you're going to test a request for your API.[1] You could also put the test in spec/controllers/api/tickets_controller_spec.rb, but you're testing the rendered response as well, which is out of the domain of a controller test.

CONTROLLER TESTS VS. REQUEST TESTS You can test rendered responses in controller tests (by using render_views and testing response.body), but this isn't good practice—"unit" tests should test one type of thing only, and that would be testing controllers *and* views. Request tests are higher-level tests that can test the entire stack, but from a code perspective, not from an interface perspective like feature tests.

---

[1] RSpec request specs are documented here: https://www.relishapp.com/rspec/rspec-rails/docs/request-specs/request-spec.

The test is at spec/requests/api because you may, in the future, have request specs that test other parts of your application, and not necessarily just the API.

In the test, you set up a project and link a ticket to it. You also set up a user and call a new method on that user called `generate_api_key`. This method will do what it says: generate an API key for the user. In the setup of the test, you set up an `HTTP_AUTHORIZATION` header to pass in to the request. This header is in a very specific format, and you'll see why when you implement the controller code to make this test pass.

In the body of the test, you make a `get` request to `api_project_ticket_path` with a `format` of JSON and the headers hash that you defined earlier. When the request runs, you'll expect to see a successful response and you'll also expect to see the ticket JSON that you saw earlier. Rather than writing out exactly what you expect it to be here, the test cheats a little and uses the `TicketSerializer` class to generate a serialized version.

Testing JSON

If you cared about the precise structure of this JSON, you'd probably write it all out by hand, like this:

```
expect(response.body).to eq(JSON.dump({
  "ticket" => {
    "id" => ticket.id,
    "title" => ticket.title
    ....
  }
}))
```

Doing it this way is useful in cases when you need to know that your API endpoints are returning *exactly* the correct structure. In this simple test, you don't care so much. In a large application, you might care a lot, and you might start writing specs specifically for your serializers to test all of the output cases.

When you run the test now with `bundle exec rspec spec/requests/api/tickets _spec.rb`, you'll see this error:

```
1) Tickets API as an authenticated user retrieves a ticket's information
   Failure/Error: user.generate_api_key
   NoMethodError:
     undefined method `generate_api_key' for #<User:0x007f9ca15ad580>
```

Ah, the `generate_api_key` method is missing! You can define this method now in your `User` model:

```ruby
class User < ActiveRecord::Base
  ...
  def generate_api_key
    self.update_column(:api_key, SecureRandom.hex(16))
  end
  ...
```

This method will generate a new API key for your users by using the `SecureRandom` class from Ruby's standard library. The `update_column` method used here will update just one column on your object in the database. The `update_column` method is typically used in cases where you want to update a column and you don't care about validations—it's perfect for this case.

The `api_key` field is what you'll use in your tests to authenticate your users. That field doesn't exist in your database right now, so you can add it by creating and running a migration. Create the migration with this command:

```
$ rails g migration add_api_key_to_users api_key:string:index
```

The migration will look like this:

```
class AddApiKeyToUsers < ActiveRecord::Migration
  def change
    add_column :users, :api_key, :string
    add_index :users, :api_key
  end
end
```

As you can see, the extra `index` part of the generator command will add a database index to the `api_key` field. This is a good idea because you'll use that field to look up users, so it should be optimized for that.

Run the migration with `bundle exec rake db:migrate`. When you rerun your test, it should be satisfied that the `generate_api_key` method on `User` objects is now present. The test will now error like this:

```
1) Tickets API as an authenticated user retrieves a ticket's information
   Failure/Error: get api_project_ticket_path(project, ticket, format...
   NoMethodError:
     undefined method 'api_project_ticket_path' for #<RSpec::...
```

You don't currently have a route defined for this path helper, which should route to a `TicketsController` within your very-soon-to-be-created `API` namespace. You can create all of this now in your config/routes.rb file, directly underneath the admin namespace.

Listing 14.5 Defining an `api` namespace

```
Rails.application.routes.draw do
  ...
  namespace :api do
    resources :projects, only: [] do
      resources :tickets
    end
  end
  ...
```

An alternative way of solving the problem would be to use a *scope* instead of a nested resource, as follows.

Listing 14.6 Defining a scope instead of a `projects` resource

```
namespace :api do
  scope path: "/projects/:project_id", as: "project" do
    resources :tickets
  end
end
```

The `scope` routing method is used here to create a path that you can nest your `tickets` resources under. You don't currently have a `projects` resource in your API, so this is a good workaround. But if you were to add some project-related routes later, you'd have to refactor and remove the scope, instead of just adding some action names to the `only` option.

The `as` option used in the `scope` adds the very important "project" part to the route helpers to make them `api_project_tickets_path` and the like. Without this, the routing helpers for the tickets resource in the API namespace would just be `api_tickets_path`. That would be no good for when you eventually *do* have a projects resource, as the routing helpers will change.

You now have the routes, and more importantly the routing helpers that your test requires. Run your tests again and see what happens next;

```
1) Tickets API as an authenticated user retrieves a ticket's information
   Failure/Error: get api_project_ticket_path(project, ticket, format...
   ActionController::RoutingError:
     uninitialized constant Api
```

Your code is looking for the constant `Api`, but it can't find it. This is happening because the routes are working and attempting to route to a `TicketsController` that exists within an `Api` module. The module name itself is a problem; it looks like a bad spelling of *happy* and not the proper form of *API*.

This isn't a hard problem to fix, because you only need to define an inflection rule for your application.

14.3.2 *A small tangent on inflections*

Inflections are Rails' way of knowing how to pluralize or singularize words. You can also define uncountable words, and Rails is smart enough already to know that you can't pluralize words like *news* and *sheep*. It also has some rules about irregulars, like where *person* becomes *people* when it's pluralized. The final thing that inflections can do in Rails is define acronyms, and that's what you'll use right now to change *Api* to *API* in your application.

Custom inflection rules for a Rails application are defined within config/initializers/inflections.rb, and currently that file looks like this:

```
# Be sure to restart your server when you modify this file.

# Add new inflection rules using the following format. Inflections
# are locale specific, and you may define rules for as many different
# locales as you wish. All of these examples are active by default:
```

```
# ActiveSupport::Inflector.inflections(:en) do |inflect|
#   inflect.plural /^(ox)$/i, '\1en'
#   inflect.singular /^(ox)en/i, '\1'
#   inflect.irregular 'person', 'people'
#   inflect.uncountable %w( fish sheep )
# end

# These inflection rules are supported but not enabled by default:
# ActiveSupport::Inflector.inflections(:en) do |inflect|
#   inflect.acronym 'RESTful'
# end
```

The `ActiveSupport::Inflector.inflections` method takes a two-letter locale code.
This is so you can define inflections for different languages. For instance, in German
the word for a child is *kind* but its plural form is *kinder*. In English, it's *child* and *children*.

At the very bottom of this file is an English acronym inflection that defines *RESTful*,
which is indeed an acronym. You can define a similar acronym inflection rule for *API*,
so that your module is called *API* and not the bad-spelling-of-happy *Api*.

Replace the final block in that file with the following.

Listing 14.7   config/initializers/inflections.rb

```
ActiveSupport::Inflector.inflections(:en) do |inflect|
  inflect.acronym "API"
end
```

When you run the test again, you'll see the correct constant:

```
1) Tickets API as an authenticated user retrieves a ticket's information
   Failure/Error: get api_project_ticket_path(project, ticket, format...
   ActionController::RoutingError:
     uninitialized constant API
```

There's one small drawback of making this inflection change—it means that everywhere you've previously referenced `Api` as a constant, you now need to reference `API`
instead, or it won't work anymore.

You haven't done this anywhere, but the generators you've used have done it in
one place—in the migration you created to add the `api_key` field to your `User` model.
It starts with the following line:

```
class AddApiKeyToUsers < ActiveRecord::Migration
```

You need to update that line. Open the file db/migrate/[timestamp]_add_api_key
_to_users.rb, and alter that line to reference `API` instead:

```
class AddAPIKeyToUsers < ActiveRecord::Migration
```

Now if you ever need to run this migration again (as you will when you deploy this
code to production), it will run without error.

And now you can continue on your journey to making this test pass.

14.3.3 *Getting back to your API*

You can now define the `API::TicketsController` that your routes are crying out for by running this command:

```
$ rails g controller api/tickets
```

This command will generate that new controller that your test needs. Now see what happens when you run the test again:

```
1) Tickets API as an authenticated user retrieves a ticket's information
   Failure/Error: get api_project_ticket_path(project, ticket, format...
   AbstractController::ActionNotFound:
      The action 'show' could not be found for API::TicketsController
```

It looks very much like you'll need to now define the show action of this controller.

Listing 14.8   app/controllers/api/tickets_controller.rb

```ruby
class API::TicketsController < ApplicationController
  before_action :set_project

  def show
    @ticket = @project.tickets.find(params[:id])
    authorize @ticket, :show?
    render json: @ticket
  end

  private

  def set_project
    @project = Project.find(params[:project_id])
  end
end
```

This is a stripped-down variant of what you had in `TicketsController`. There's no need to load the `@states` or `@comment` instance variables here because your response simply doesn't need them.

When you run the test again, you'll see this happening:

```
1) Tickets API as an authenticated user retrieves a ticket's information
   Failure/Error: expect(response.status).to eq 200

      expected: 200
           got: 302

   (compared using ==)
```

You're being redirected, but where to? If you look in log/test.log, you can see where:

```
Started GET "/api/projects/5/tickets/5.json" for [IP] at [timestamp]
Processing by API::TicketsController#show as JSON
  Parameters: {"project_id"=>"5", "id"=>"5"}
  Project Load (0.1ms)  SELECT "projects".* FROM "projects" WHERE ...
  Ticket Load (0.1ms)   SELECT  "tickets".* FROM "tickets" WHERE ...
```

```
Project Load (0.1ms)  SELECT "projects".* FROM "projects" WHERE ...
  Role Exists (0.2ms)  SELECT  1 AS one FROM "roles" WHERE ...
Redirected to http://www.example.com/
Completed 302 Found in 24ms (ActiveRecord: 0.5ms)
```

Your specs use http://www.example.com as the base path of your application, so you're being redirected back to the root path of your application, but why is that? This is probably happening in a controller, but because there's no code to redirect you in `API::TicketsController`, it must be happening farther up the chain. Farther up the chain is `ApplicationController`, which has these lines in it:

```
class ApplicationController < ActionController::Base
  ...
  rescue_from Pundit::NotAuthorizedError, with: :not_authorized

  ....

  def not_authorized
    redirect_to root_path, alert: "You aren't allowed to do that."
  end
end
```

This is a likely culprit. Pundit works by requesting `current_user` in your controllers, and using that to determine if the user making the request has authorization to perform the actions in your controllers. Because you're not accessing the API through a normal request, which would have a session, `current_user` is always going to be `nil`. To fix this, you can define a `current_user` method in `API::TicketsController`, which uses different logic for finding the user, in two parts.

The first part is a `before_action` callback that authenticates a user based on the token from the `HTTP_AUTHORIZATION` header:

```
class API::TicketsController < ApplicationController
  before_action :authenticate_user

  ...

  private

  def authenticate_user
    authenticate_with_http_token do |token|
      @current_user = User.find_by(api_key: token)
    end
  end
end
```

DON'T FORGET TO KEEP THINGS DRY! If you were building a larger API, you'd repeat this method a lot, so it would make sense to extract it out into a common `API::ApplicationController` and have all of your API controllers extend from that controller instead of `ApplicationController`. You did a similar thing when you wanted to add a common authorization check for all of the controller actions in your `admin` namespace.

The `authenticate_with_http_token` method comes from Rails and is used to authenticate users based on the `HTTP_AUTHORIZATION` token.

The second part defines the `current_user` method that Pundit is looking for. Because the method should just return the `@current_user` instance variable you've created, you can add this with an `attr_reader` at the top of your controller.

Listing 14.9   Defining the `current_user` method that Pundit needs

```
class API::TicketsController < ApplicationController
  attr_reader :current_user

  ...
```

Run your test one more time:

```
1 example, 0 failures
```

Hooray! It has passed. You've now got an API for tickets.

Now that this API exists, you don't need the `respond_to` block in the `show` action of your normal `TicketsController`, so you can remove these lines.

Listing 14.10   Cleaning up in app/controllers/tickets_controller.rb

```
respond_to do |format|
  format.html
  format.json { render json: @ticket }
end
```

Now run all your tests with `bundle exec rspec`. This is what you'll see:

```
133 examples, 0 failures, 1 pending
```

The one pending test is located at spec/helpers/api/tickets_helper_spec.rb, and you can delete this file because you're not using it at all. Now your tests will be all green:

```
132 examples, 0 failures
```

Commit this change:

```
$ git add .
$ git commit -m "Added basic Tickets API"
```

So far in this chapter, you've seen two ways of building an API. The first demonstrated that you can use `respond_to` in a controller's actions in order to respond differently depending on the request. That made things difficult, because sometimes in controller actions you can have code that only needs to run for a particular format. You ended up moving the code that handles the JSON requests for your application out to an `API` namespace.

The benefits of doing this are that you don't have unnecessary code being run in the actions, and the controller code is more single-purpose than it would otherwise be. You could also very easily rewrite the API component in some other language—as some developers choose to do these days, mainly for reasons of speed. If the code was all combined in the same controller, it would be harder to separate out the parts.

The next step would be to implement other actions of this API. As an example, you could allow users to create new tickets for a project and allow them to update tickets. You could also build an entirely new set of API endpoints for projects, and one for users that only admins could touch. That's an exercise best left for you, the reader. Consider it your homework for this section.

Now we'll move on to one way of using this API: the HTTParty gem.

14.4   *It's not a party without … HTTParty*

You've seen how to build an API and test it, but you haven't yet seen how to connect to it from outside of your application. That's what we'll look at now, using the HTTParty gem.

The HTTParty gem can be used to make HTTP requests, and it provides a neat API for doing so:

```
HTTParty.get("http://example.com/api/resource.json")
```

This code will return an `HTTParty::Response` object, which has a method called `parsed_response`; this is where the magic for HTTParty happens. HTTParty will inspect the response and see if it has a content type of `application/json`. If it does, HTTParty will parse the JSON into a hash using `JSON.parse`. You can then work with the hash object however you please, and you don't have to go around parsing JSON responses yourself.

You can now write some code to interact with your API using HTTParty. Rather than writing this code in your application, you'll put it in a new directory at the same path as the `ticketee` app with the extremely imaginative name of ticketee_api. Inside this directory, you'll create a file called tickets.rb, and in that file you'll put some code that will be used to pull down a ticket's info from the API.

Listing 14.11   ticketee_api/tickets.rb

```
require "httparty"

token = "YOUR_TOKEN_GOES_HERE"
url = "http://localhost:3000/api/projects/1/tickets/1.json"

response = HTTParty.get(url,
  headers: {
    "Authorization" => "Token token=#{token}"
  }
)

puts response.parsed_response
```

This code requires the HTTParty gem and then defines two variables that will be used in the request: a token and a URL. To make a `GET` request, you just need to call

HTTParty.get and pass in the URL and the Authorization header. This will make a request just like the API requests you were making earlier, but it will use data from your development database rather than the test database.

You'll need to install the httparty gem from the terminal:

```
$ gem install httparty
```

In the previous code, you've got YOUR_TOKEN_GOES_HERE where you should have a real token. In order to get that token, you'll need to run the generate_api_key method on one of your User objects. You can do that in the rails console:

```
$ rails console
Loading development environment (Rails 4.2.1)
irb(main):001:0> user = User.find_by(email: "admin@ticketee.com")
=> #<User id: 1, email: "admin@ticketee.com", ....
irb(main):002:0> user.generate_api_key
=> true
irb(main):003:0> user.api_key
=> [an alphanumeric string here]
```

The string returned by the final method is your API key. Replace YOUR_TOKEN_GOES _HERE in tickets.rb with that string.

You've now got all the parts to make this file work, and the only thing left to do is to run it. First, launch a Rails server (if you don't already have one running):

```
$ rails server
```

Now, to run tickets.rb, open a new terminal window and run this command inside the ticketee_api directory:

```
$ ruby tickets.rb
```

You should see a response like this:

```
{"ticket"=>{"id"=>1, ...}
```

This means that your code for accessing the API is now working!

HTTParty has other methods, like post, put, and delete. Again, we'll leave it to you to learn how to build the remainder of the tickets API and then connect it with HTTParty. Or, if you have a lot of JavaScript skills, you could build a JavaScript web app in something like AngularJS or Ember.js, and use AJAX to load data from the API for rendering.

Go on, give it a try!

14.5 Handling errors

Not every request to your API is going to end in happiness. Sometimes, other people and their programs might try to make a request to it using an invalid API token, or they might send data through that doesn't satisfy the validations defined in the model. In either case, you need to return messages to the people or programs that indicate that something has gone wrong and that they need to fix it.

Let's first take a look at how you can return an error message when the API is accessed with an invalid token. After that, we'll look at how you can return error messages from your API when the data passed to it doesn't pass muster.

14.5.1 *Authenticating with a blank token*

When an invalid or even blank token is passed to your API, it should respond in a way that's useful to the thing doing the requesting. Currently, it responds, but not in a nice way.

You can see what it does by running your usual `curl` command and not passing it an API key:

```
curl http://localhost:3000/api/projects/1/tickets/1.json
```

The response you'll get back from this is (in a slightly edited format) as follows:

```
<html>
  <body>
    You are being <a href="http://localhost:3000/">redirected</a>
  </body>
</html>
```

Hmmm. That isn't so helpful. What's happening here is that Pundit is detecting that you aren't authorized to access that particular project, so it's raising a `Pundit::NotAuthorizedError` and that's being rescued in `ApplicationController` and redirecting. Just as you saw earlier in this chapter.

What should be happening instead is that the request should respond with a `401 Unauthorized` HTTP status code, as well as a bit of JSON that tells the user that they're unauthorized. You can add a test for this now to the bottom of spec/requests/api/tickets_spec.rb:

```
RSpec.describe "Tickets API" do
  ...
  context "as an unauthenticated user" do
    it "responds with a 401" do
      get api_project_ticket_path(project, ticket, format: "json")
      expect(response.status).to eq 401
      error = { "error" => "Unauthorized" }
      expect(JSON.parse(response.body)).to eq error
    end
  end
end
```

You're not authenticating as anybody in this particular spec, so when you make the request, you expect your API to return a status of 401 with a JSON error message. It's currently doing neither of those, as you saw when you ran `curl` and as you'll see now if you run this test with `bundle exec rspec spec/requests/api/tickets_spec.rb`:

```
1) Tickets API as an unauthenticated user responds with a 401
   Failure/Error: expect(response.status).to eq 401

       expected: 401
            got: 302

       (compared using ==)
```

To fix this, you'll need to handle the case in `API::TicketsController` where `authenticate_with_http_token` doesn't even try to find your user, or it attempts to find your user but there are no users matching the token passed in. In either of those cases, the `@current_user` variable inside the block will either not be set or will be set to `nil`, which is the default value of instance variables anyway.

This makes it easy for you to check if that authentication has failed. If it has, then `@current_user` will be `nil`. When it's `nil`, you should return the unauthorized status. You can make your controller do this now by changing `authenticate_user` in `API::TicketsController` to this:

```
class API::TicketsController < ApplicationController
  ...
  def authenticate_user
    authenticate_with_http_token do |token|
      @current_user = User.find_by(api_key: token)
    end

    if @current_user.nil?
      render json: { error: "Unauthorized" }, status: 401
      return
    end
  end
  ...
```

When you call `render` with a blank `return` here, the filter chain will halt and the actions of the controller will not be run. The response will instead be a JSON hash containing an `error` key with a short message, and an HTTP status of 401 will be set on the request.

Run that test again. It should pass this time:

```
2 examples, 0 failures
```

Excellent! Now your API will return a useful error message to users who authenticate with an invalid or blank token.

For our next trick, we'll take a look at what you can do if a user doesn't have the right permissions to perform an action on a resource of your system.

14.5.2 *Permission denied*

When a user doesn't have permission to access a project on your application, you'll want to show them a very similar error as in the previous section. Rather than returning a 401 HTTP status code, you'll return a 403. A 403 response indicates that the request was forbidden.

Add a test for this to spec/requests/api/tickets_spec.rb inside the "as an authenticated user" block:

```
RSpec.describe "Tickets API" do
  ...
  context "as an authenticated user" do
    ...
```

```
    context "without permission to view the project" do
      before do
        user.roles.delete_all
      end

      it "responds with a 403" do
        get api_project_ticket_path(project, ticket, format: "json"),
          {}, headers
        expect(response.status).to eq 403
        error = { "error" => "Unauthorized" }
        expect(JSON.parse(response.body)).to eq error
      end
    end
  end
end
...
```

In the before block for this context, you delete the user's roles using .delete_all. This is a bit messy because it's running some code to create the user's role and then running some other code to delete it, which makes the initial action pointless. You could move the role assignment so it's used exclusively within a new context block that assigns the role. We'll do that after you get this test passing.

In the body of the test, you make a request in the same way as the one above it: you want to access a project's ticket and you're authenticating. But this time you expect to see a 403 HTTP status returned, with an error shown in the JSON.

When you run this test with bundle exec rspec spec/requests/api/tickets _spec.rb, this is what you'll see happening:

```
1) Tickets API as an authenticated user without permission to view the
   project responds with a 403
   Failure/Error: expect(response.status).to eq 403

     expected: 403
          got: 302

   (compared using ==)
```

You see a redirection happen again, and you know that this is being caused by the not_authorized method that's defined in ApplicationController. That particular method is called when the Pundit::NotAuthorized exception is raised. All of that is exactly what you want to happen, except for the redirect. In your API, it should be returning a 403 status code instead.

To override this behavior, you can simply redefine the not_authorized method in API::TicketsController.

Listing 14.12 Overwriting the not_authorized method

```
class API::TicketsController < ApplicationController
  ...
  def not_authorized
    render json: { error: "Unauthorized" }, status: 403
  end
end
```

This method employs a flow similar to the end of your `authenticate_user` request, where you render JSON and then return a status. In the `not_authorized` method, you don't need to have a `return` because you're not halting the request flow. The `not_authorized` is the end of the line.

With this tiny change to your controller, your test will now pass:

```
3 examples, 0 failures
```

Great! When `Pundit::NotAuthorized` exceptions are raised within actions of this controller, rather than redirecting to the `root_path`, your controller will now respond properly with an HTTP status of 403 and JSON data informing the user that they're making an unauthorized request.

Let's now take a look at how you can handle a different kind of error in your API: validation errors.

14.5.3 *Validation errors*

When users submit invalid data to your API, you want it to return an error similar to the case where they attempt to use an invalid token. In the case of invalid data, you'll return a `422 Unprocessable Entity` HTTP status code and a JSON hash like the following:

```
{ errors: ["Title can't be blank", "Description can't be blank"] }
```

Before you return any errors, you should first make sure that your API actually allows people to create tickets. To make sure your API allows that, you can write a short test for it in spec/requests/api/tickets_spec.rb, directly underneath the "retrieves a ticket's information" test:

```
RSpec.describe "Tickets API" do
  ...
  context "as an authenticated user" do
    ...
    it "can create a ticket" do
      params = {
        format: "json",
        ticket: {
          name: "Test Ticket",
          description: "Just testing things out."
        }
      }

      post api_project_tickets_path(project, params), {}, headers
      expect(response.status).to eq 201

      json = TicketSerializer.new(Ticket.last).to_json
      expect(response.body).to eq json
    end
    ...
```

In this test, you set up some parameters that will be passed to the `create` action in your controller, you put these parameters into a URL, and then you send a POST

request to your controller. The full URL would look something like /api/projects/
:project_id/tickets. From the response, you're expecting a 201 status code, and you're
expecting to see the ticket that you just created.

Run this spec now with `bundle exec rspec spec/features/api/tickets_spec.rb`
and see how far along it gets:

```
1) Tickets API as an authenticated user can create a ticket
   Failure/Error: post api_project_tickets_path(project, params), {},
   headers
   AbstractController::ActionNotFound:
     The action 'create' could not be found for API::TicketsController
```

It's not getting very far at all. The `create` action is missing from `API::Tickets-`
`Controller`, and your test is whining about not having it, so it's best to go and create it
now. Add it to the controller defined in app/controllers/api/tickets_controller.rb.

> **Listing 14.13 Adding a `create` action to `API::TicketsController`**

```
class API::TicketsController < ApplicationController
  ...
  def create
    @ticket = @project.tickets.build(ticket_params)
    authorize @ticket, :create?
    if @ticket.save
      render json: @ticket, status: 201
    end
  end
  ...
```

In this `create` action, you build a new ticket, authorize the user to create tickets within
a project, and then save the ticket. Once the ticket is saved, you respond with it in
JSON form—thanks to your `TicketSerializer` class—and an HTTP status of `201 Cre-`
`ated`, indicating that the action has proceeded successfully and that a resource has
been created by the request.

You need to define `ticket_params` here too. You'll only allow a name and a
description to be sent through in the API requests, just to keep things simple for now:

```
class API::TicketsController < ApplicationController
  ...
  private

  def ticket_params
    params.require(:ticket).permit(:name, :description)
  end
  ...
```

When you run your test again, all the pieces will be in place:

```
4 examples, 0 failures
```

Now that you've created the `create` action, it's time to handle the case where invalid
data is submitted. First, add a new test underneath the one you just wrote:

```
RSpec.describe "Tickets API" do
  ...
  context "as an authenticated user" do
    ...
    it "cannot create a ticket with invalid data" do
      params = {
        format: "json",
        ticket: {
          name: "", description: ""
        } }
      post api_project_tickets_path(project, params), {}, headers

      expect(response.status).to eq 422
      json = {
        "errors" => [
          "Name can't be blank",
          "Description can't be blank",
          "Description is too short (minimum is 10 characters)"
        ]
      }
      expect(JSON.parse(response.body)).to eq json
    end
    ...
```

With this test, you send through a blank title and a blank description. According to the rest of the test, when you do this you'll see a 422 response come back from your API and some errors reported in JSON.

When you run these tests again, they fail like this:

```
1) Tickets API as an authenticated user cannot create a ticket with
   invalid data
   Failure/Error: post api_project_tickets_path(project, params), {}...
   ActionView::MissingTemplate:
     Missing template api/tickets/create, ...
```

This happens because the request is falling through the action and out the other side. The `if` statement inside the request returns `false`, so the code inside of that doesn't get run at all.

To stop the request in its tracks and return the things you want your API to return, you need an `else` to go with that `if`:

```
class API::TicketsController < ApplicationController
  ...
  def create
    @ticket = @project.tickets.build(ticket_params)
    authorize @ticket, :create?
    if @ticket.save
      render json: @ticket, status: 201
    else
      render json: { errors: @ticket.errors.full_messages }, status: 422
    end
  end
  ...
```

The full_messages method called on errors here will return a list of error messages, just as your test expects. When you run that test again, you'll see it's now passing:

```
5 examples, 0 failures
```

You now have a create action in your API that allows users to create tickets within projects, and as an additional bonus it scolds them about invalid data.

You're almost done here. You've done the red and green parts of your development, and now it's time for the fun part: the refactoring.

14.6   *A small refactoring*

When you build out the rest of your API, you'll build controllers that use the same helpers that your TicketsController uses. The current_user, authenticate_user, and not_authorized methods can be used in other parts of your API too, so having them in API::TicketsController probably isn't the best way to do things.

Instead, you should move them to a class that all of your API controllers can inherit from. You can call this class API::ApplicationController and define it in app/controllers/api/application_controller.rb.

> **Listing 14.14   app/controllers/api/application_controller.rb**

```
class API::ApplicationController < ApplicationController
  attr_reader :current_user
  before_action :authenticate_user

  private

  def authenticate_user
    authenticate_with_http_token do |token|
      @current_user = User.find_by(api_key: token)
    end

    if @current_user.nil?
      render json: { error: "Unauthorized" }, status: 401
      return
    end
  end

  def not_authorized
    render json: { error: "Unauthorized" }, status: 403
  end
end
```

Then you can switch your API::TicketsController over to inherit from this controller:

```
class API::TicketsController < API::ApplicationController
```

You can remove the authenticate_user, current_user, not_authorized, and before_action :authenticate_user methods from API::TicketsController, too.

Did you break anything with these changes? Find out by running your tests using `bundle exec rspec spec/requests/api`:

```
5 examples, 0 failures
```

Nope! That's great. Double-check that none of the specs are broken by running the entire suite with `bundle exec rspec`:

```
136 examples, 0 failures
```

Perfect! Make a commit and push to wrap up your work here:

```
$ git add .
$ git commit -m "Fleshed out tickets API with creating tickets and responses
  for error conditions"
$ git push
```

14.7 Summary

There are whole books about how to design APIs, and, in fact, multiple books about multiple ways to build APIs. There are a lot of ways you can go from here, but this is enough to get you started.

First, you learned how to do API-first development. If you know you want to have an API, building it from the start can help you do it right. It's not too hard to build one after the fact in Rails, but just as TDD revolutionized the way you write code to make it easy to test, API-first development can change the way you build APIs.

Next, you found out about ActiveModel::Serializers and how convention over configuration can make it easy to generate JSON. ActiveModel::Serializers follows the same pattern that makes Rails so productive. All you need to do is make a serializer object, and let ActiveModel::Serializers build some excellent JSON.

Then you went down a path of adding a JSON response to `TicketsController` using a `respond_to` block, but you quickly discovered that this led to messy code in the controller action. Separating it out into a controller that serves HTML and another controller that serves JSON allowed you to keep each controller slim, but with the cost of some duplication.

Finally, you wrote a small piece of code to interact with the API that you built in this chapter. We are completely serious about our homework suggestions, by the way. You really should try building out the API some more, allowing projects to be managed by admins and allowing tickets to be created, updated, and deleted as well as read. Then refactor it. We can almost guarantee that you'll learn something during the process.

In the next chapter, the final chapter of the book, we'll showcase the foundational web server interface of Rails, called Rack, and explain how it's used to connect not just the different parts of Rails, but also other frameworks written in Ruby.

Rack-based applications

15

> **This chapter covers**
> - Learning how HTTP requests work under the hood with Rack
> - Mounting Rack applications inside a Rails application
> - Introduction to the Sinatra web framework
> - Intercepting requests with custom middleware

So far, this book has primarily focused on how to work with pieces of the Rails framework. In this chapter, we'll look at something lower-level than that: the Rack web server interface.

Rack is the underlying web server framework that powers the request/response cycle found in Rails, but it isn't a part of Rails itself. It's completely separate, with Rails requiring the parts of Rack it needs. When your application runs, it's run through a web server. When your web server receives a request, it will pass it off to Rack, as shown in figure 15.1.

Rack then determines where to route this request, and in this case it's chosen to route to a specific application stack. The request passes through a series of pieces called *middleware* (covered in the final section of this chapter) before arriving at the application itself. The application will then generate a response and pass it back up through the stack to Rack, and then Rack will pass it back to the server, which will finally pass it back to the browser. All of this happens in lightning-quick fashion.

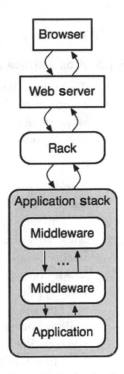

Separating Rack from Rails not only reduces bloat in the framework, but also provides a common interface that other frameworks can use. When you standardize the request/response cycle, applications that are built on top of Rack can interact with one another and with all web servers in a common format.

In this chapter, you'll see how you can do this by making your Rails application work with applications built using Rack, but not Rails. You'll build some Rack applications in this chapter that aren't Rails applications, but will work just as seamlessly. You'll learn how Rack provides the request/response cycle underneath Rails and other Ruby frameworks, and learn how to build your own small, lightweight, Rack-based applications.

With these lightweight applications crafted, you'll then create one more application that will re-implement the tickets API functionality you created in the last chapter using another Rack-based web framework called Sinatra. You'll

Figure 15.1   Application request through the stack

mount this Sinatra application inside your Rails application using methods that Rails provides. This will provide an example of how you can interact with classes from your Rails application from within a mounted Rack application.

Finally, we'll look at middleware within both the Rack and Rails stacks, and you'll learn how to use it to your advantage to manipulate requests coming into your application.

All Rack-based applications work the same way. You request a URL from the application, and it sends back a response. But what goes on between that request and the response is the most interesting part. Let's create a light Rack application now so that you can understand the basics.

15.1   Building Rack applications

Rack standardizes the way an application receives requests across all the Ruby frameworks. With this standardization, you know that any application purporting to be a Rack application will have a standard way for you to send requests to it, and a standard way of receiving responses.

You'll build a basic Rack application so that you can learn about the underlying architecture for requests and responses found in Rails and other Ruby frameworks. With this knowledge, you'll be able to build lightweight Rack applications that you can hook into your Rails stack, or even Rack middleware.

When you're content with the first application, you'll create another and then make them work together as one big application. First things first, though.

15.1.1   *A basic Rack application*

To build a basic Rack application, you only need to have an object in Ruby that responds to the call method. That call method needs to take one argument (the request) and also needs to return a three-element Array object. This array represents the response that will be given back to Rack, and it looks something like this:

```
[200, {"Content-Type" => "text/plain"}, ["Hello World"]]
```

The first element in this response array is the status code for your response. In this example, it's 200, which represents a successful response.

The second element in this array is a Hash containing the headers that will be sent back. These headers are used by the browser to determine how to deal with the response. In this case, the response will be rendered as is to the page because the Content-Type header is text/plain, indicating normal text with no formatting applied. Usually your Rack application would set this to text/html to indicate an HTML response.

The third element represents the response body, the content of the page. In a Rails application, this would be the complete HTML of the page to be rendered by the browser. Rack then compiles everything into a single HTTP response, which is sent back to where the request came from.

Let's see this in action. You'll create a light Rack application that responds with "OK" whenever it receives a request. This kind of application is often used to check whether a server is still up and responding to HTTP calls.

To get started, create a new file inside your Ticketee application's root folder called lib/heartbeat.ru (you're checking the "heartbeat" of the server), and fill it with this content:

```
run lambda { |env| [200, {"Content-Type" => "text/plain"}, ["OK"]] }
```

The .ru extension for this file represents a Rack configuration file, also known as a *Rackup* file. In it, you call the run method, which needs an object that responds to call. When Rack receives a request for this application, it calls the call method on the object passed to run, which then generates and returns a response back to the server. The object in this case is a lambda (or Proc) object, which automatically responds to call.

When the call method is called on this lambda, the code responds with the three-element array, completely ignoring the env object that is passed through. Inside this array, you have the three elements Rack needs: the HTTP status, the headers for the response, and the body to return.

To see your lib/heartbeat.ru in action, you can launch a Rack server by using the following command:

```
$ rackup lib/heartbeat.ru
```

> **You already have a Rackup file**
>
> Your Rails application has one of these .ru files, called config.ru, which is used by Rack-based servers to run your application. You can see this in action by running the `rackup config.ru` command, which will start up your application using the config.ru file's configuration.
>
> If you look in this file in the root folder of your application, you'll see these lines:
>
> ```
> # This file is used by Rack-based servers to start the application.
>
> require ::File.expand_path('../config/environment', __FILE__)
> run Rails.application
> ```
>
> The first line requires the config/environment.rb of the application, which is responsible for setting up the environment of the application. Then it uses the `run` method—just as you are—except it passes `Ticketee::Application`, which responds to `call`. Cool stuff!

This is now running a server on 9292 (the standard port for Rack) using the Thin HTTP server, as indicated by the server output you'll see:

```
>> Thin web server (v1.5.1 codename Straight Razor)
>> Maximum connections set to 1024
>> Listening on localhost:9292, CTRL+C to stop
```

You can now go to your browser and open http://localhost:9292 to make a request to this application. You'll get back "OK," and that's good. You can also make a request to any path at the http://localhost:9292 "application," such as http://localhost:9292/status, and it will respond in the same way.

What you've done here is write one of the simplest Rack applications possible. This application receives a response to any path using any method, and it always responds with "OK." This application will respond very quickly because it hasn't loaded anything, but at the cost of being a one-trick pony

15.1.2 *Let's increase the heartbeat*

You can make this little application respond differently in a number of ways. The easiest (and most fun!) would be to program it to change its response depending on the path it's given, like a Rails application does with its routes.

To do this, you can use the env object that we've been ignoring this whole time. First up, let's see what this env object gives you by changing your little script to do this:

```
require "yaml"

run lambda { |env| [200,
  {"Content-Type" => "text/plain"},
  [env.to_yaml]]
}
```

The to_yaml method provided by the YAML standard library file will transform your env object (spoiler: it's a Hash) into human-readable YAML output (like that found in config/database.yml in a Rails application).

To apply this new change, you can't refresh the page like you would in a Rails application; you have to stop the server and start it again. You can press Ctrl-C to stop it and rerun rackup lib/heartbeat.ru. This time when you go to your server, you'll see output that includes content like this:

```
GATEWAY_INTERFACE: CGI/1.1
PATH_INFO: /
QUERY_STRING: ""
REMOTE_ADDR: 127.0.0.1
REQUEST_METHOD: GET
REQUEST_URI: http://localhost:9292/
...
```

This output is the YAML-ized version of the env hash, which comes from Rack itself. Rack parses the incoming request and provides this env hash so that you can determine how you'd like to respond to the request. You can alter the behavior of the request using any one of the keys in this hash,[1] but in this case you'll keep it simple and use the PATH_INFO key.

A lambda is great for one-liners, but now your Rack application is going to become more complex, so you've probably outgrown the usefulness of a lambda. You don't have to use a lambda, though; you only need to pass run to an object that has a call method that responds with that three-element array. Your new code will be a couple of lines long, so it's probably best to define it as a method (called call) on an object, and what better object to define it on than a class?

A class object will allow you to define other methods and can be used to abstract chunks of the call method as well. For good measure, call this class Application and put it inside a module called Heartbeat, replacing the content of lib/heartbeat.ru.

Listing 15.1   A classy Rack application

```
module Heartbeat
  class Application
    def self.call(env)
      [200, {"Content-Type" => "text/plain"}, ["Classy!"]]
    end
  end
end


run Heartbeat::Application
```

Here you define Heartbeat::Application to have a call method, which once again returns a plain-text string for any request. On the final line, you call run and pass

---

[1] Yes, even the HTTP_USER_AGENT key to send users of a certain browser used for exploring the internet elsewhere.

in Heartbeat::Application, which will work like your first example because Heartbeat::Application has a call method defined on it.

If this looks familiar, it's because there's a similar-looking line in your application's config.ru file, which you saw earlier.

Listing 15.2　Part of config.ru

```
run Ticketee::Application
```

Your Rails application is actually a Rack-based application! Of course, there's a little bit more that goes on behind the scenes in your Rails application than in your Rack application at the moment, but the two are used identically. They both respond in nearly identical ways with the three-element response array. Your Rack application is nearly the simplest form you can have. If you restart it and make a request to it, you'll see it output "Classy!"

15.1.3　*You're not done yet*

You can now change your Heartbeat application to respond differently to different request paths by referencing the PATH_INFO key within env. Replace the code inside your call method with the following.

Listing 15.3　Experimenting with different paths

```
module Heartbeat
  class Application
    def self.call(env)
      default_headers = {"Content-Type" => "text/plain"}

      if env["PATH_INFO"] =~ /200/
        body = "Success!"
        status = 200
      else
        body = "Failure!"
        status = 500
      end

      [status, default_headers, ["#{env["PATH_INFO"]} == #{body}"]]
    end
  end
end
```

The env["PATH_INFO"] here returns the path that has been requested, and this is the same part of env that Rails' own router uses to determine the path requested. If you make a request like http://localhost:9292/books to your Rack application, this variable will return "/books." In this new call code, you compare this string to a regular expression using the =~ operator, and if it contains 200, you'll return "Success" in the body, along with an HTTP status of 200. For everything else, it's "Failure" with an HTTP status of 500.

Restart the server once again, and make a new request to http://localhost:9292. You'll see this output:

```
/ == Failure!
```

This is because for any request to this server that doesn't have 200 in it, you return this failure message. If you make a request to http://localhost:9292/200 or even http://localhost:9292/the/200/page, you'll see the success message instead:

```
/the/200/page == Success!
```

Also, if you look in the console, you'll see a single line for each request that's been served:

```
127.0.0.1 - - [[timestamp]] "GET / HTTP/1.1" 500 - 0.0004
127.0.0.1 - - [[timestamp]] "GET /200 HTTP/1.1" 200 - 0.0004
127.0.0.1 - - [[timestamp]] "GET /the/200/page HTTP/1.1" 200 - 0.0004
```

This output shows

- The IP address where the request came from
- The local time when the request happened
- The request itself
- The HTTP status contained within the response
- How long the page took to run

What you've done here is implement a basic router for your Rack application. If the route for a request contains "200," then you give back a successful response. Otherwise, you give back a 500 status, indicating an error. Rails implements a much more complex routing system than this, extracting the complexity away and leaving you with methods such as root and resources that you use in config/routes.rb. But the underlying theory is the same.

You've learned the basics of how a Rack application works and how your Rails application is a bigger version of the little application you've written. But there's much more to Rack than providing this abstraction for the underlying request/response cycle. For example, you can build more-complex apps with logic for one part of the application in one class and additional logic in another.

One other feature of Rack is that it allows you to build applications by combining smaller applications into a larger one. Let's see how you can do this.

15.2 Building bigger Rack applications

Your basic Rack application quickly outgrew the lambda shell you placed it in, so you moved its logic into a class and added some more. With the class, you're able to define a call method that then returns the response that Rack needs. The class allows you to cleanly write a more complex Rack application than a lambda would.

What happens if you outgrow a class? Well, you can abstract the function of your application into multiple classes and build a Rack application using those classes. The structure is not unlike the controller structure you have in a Rails application, because it will have separate classes that are responsible for different things.

In this new multiclass Rack application, you'll have two classes that perform separate tasks but still run on the same instance of the server. The first class will be your `Heartbeat::Application` class, and the second will provide two forms, each with one button: one for success and one for failure. These forms will then submit to the actions provided within the `Heartbeat::Application` class, demonstrating how you can get your classes to talk to each other.

15.2.1 *You're breaking up*

Now that your Rack application is getting more complex, you'll break it out into three files. The first file will be the `Heartbeat::Application` class, the second will be a new class called `Heartbeat::TestApplication`, and the third will be the Rackup file that will be responsible for combining these two classes into one glorious application.

You can begin by dividing your application and the Rackup file into two separate files. Remove the old lib/heartbeat.ru file you just created, and in a new lib/heartbeat directory, add the code shown in the following listing to lib/heartbeat/application.rb. This is the same `Heartbeat::Application` class you had previously in lib/heartbeat.ru.

Listing 15.4 lib/heartbeat/application.rb

```
module Heartbeat
  class Application
    def self.call(env)
      default_headers = {"Content-Type" => "text/plain"}

      if env["PATH_INFO"] =~ /200/
        body = "Success!"
        status = 200
      else
        body = "Failure!"
        status = 500
      end

      [status, default_headers, ["#{env["PATH_INFO"]} == #{body}"]]
    end
  end
end
```

Next, in lib/heartbeat/config.ru, add the code shown in the next listing.

Listing 15.5 lib/heartbeat/config.ru

```
heartbeat_root = File.expand_path(File.dirname(__FILE__))
require heartbeat_root + "/application"

run Heartbeat::Application
```

This new lib/heartbeat/config.ru file sets up a `heartbeat_root` variable so that you can require files relative to the root of the heartbeat directory without having to specify direct paths to them.

You could also use Ruby's `require_relative`. At the moment, this file still contains the run line from the old heartbeat.ru, but you'll change this shortly.

Before that change though, you need to add your second application class, `Heartbeat::TestApplication`, to a new file at lib/heartbeat/test_application.rb, using the content shown in the following listing.

Listing 15.6   **lib/heartbeat/test_application.rb**

```ruby
module Heartbeat
  class TestApplication
    def self.call(env)
      default_headers = {"Content-Type" => "text/html"}
      body = %Q{
        <!doctype html>
        <html>
          <head>
            <title>Success or FAILURE?!</title>
          </head>
          <body>
            <h1>Success or FAILURE?!</h1>
            <form action="/test/200">
              <input type="submit" value="Success!">
            </form>

            <form action="/test/500">
              <input type="submit" value="Failure!">
            </form>
          </body>
        </html>
      }

      [200, default_headers, [body]]
    end
  end
end
```

This file follows the same style as the file that defines `Heartbeat::Application`, but in this class the body returned as part of the Rack response consists of two forms, each with their own `submit` button. The first form goes to /test/200, which should give you the response of "Success!," and the second goes to /test/500, which should give you a "Failure!" response because the path doesn't include the number 200.

You may have noticed that you've nested the paths to the Heartbeat responses underneath a path called `test`. This is because when you build your combined class application, you'll make your `Heartbeat::Application` sit under the /test route. This is so that when you click the Submit button on those two forms from `Heartbeat::TestApplication`, the request will be sent to `Heartbeat::Application`. When do you do this? Right now!

15.2.2 *Running a combined Rack application*

You're now going to change the lib/heartbeat/config.ru file to create a Rack application that combines both of your Rack application classes. For this, you'll use the
Rack::Builder class's app method, which lets you build Rack applications from different parts. The result will effectively work much like how the routing and controllers
work within Rails.

Fill lib/heartbeat/config.ru with the content shown in the following listing.

> **Listing 15.7 Combining two Rack applications**

```
heartbeat_root = File.expand_path(File.dirname(__FILE__))
require heartbeat_root + "/application"
require heartbeat_root + "/test_application"

app = Rack::Builder.app do
  map "/test" do
    run Heartbeat::Application
  end

  map "/" do
    run Heartbeat::TestApplication
  end
end

run app
```

Rather than call run Heartbeat::Application here, you compile a multifaceted Rack
application using Rack::Builder.app. The run method you've been using all this
time is actually defined inside the Rack::Builder class. A *.ru file is usually evaluated
within the instance of a Rack::Builder object by the code the rackup command uses,
so you can use the run method without having to call Rack::Builder.new before it, or
wrapping your .ru code in a Rack::Builder.app block.

This time, you're being implicit and building a new Rack::Builder instance using
Rack::Builder.app. Inside this instance, you'll declare two routes using the map
method. Within a block given to each of your map calls, you're calling the run method
again, passing it one of your two application classes.

When a request comes into this application beginning with the path /test, it will
be served by the Heartbeat::Application class. All other requests will be served by
the Heartbeat::TestApplication class. This is not unlike the way requests in your
Rails application beginning with /tickets are routed to the TicketsController, and
others beginning with /projects go to the ProjectsController. In fact, the similarities are astounding.

Stop any other rackup servers you have running, and start this application and see
what it can do by running this command:

```
$ rackup lib/heartbeat/config.ru
```

Now remember, to make requests to the `Heartbeat::Application` class, you must prefix them with /test; otherwise they'll be served by `Heartbeat::TestApplication`. Keeping that in mind, try making a request to http://localhost:9292/test/200. You'll see something unusual: the path displayed on the page isn't /test/200 as you might expect, but rather it's /200. The `env["PATH_INFO"]` key doesn't need to contain the path where your application is mounted, because that's not important for routing requests within the application itself.

If you make a request to another path not beginning with the /test prefix (such as http://localhost:9292/foo/bar), you'll see the two buttons in forms provided by `Heartbeat::TestApplication`, as shown in figure 15.2.

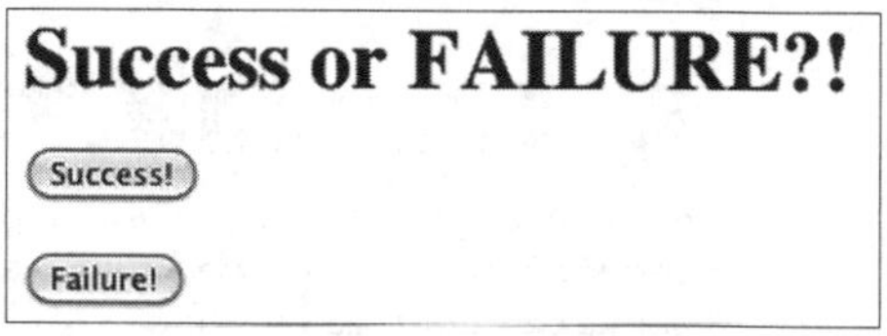

Success or FAILURE?!

Success!

Failure!

Figure 15.2 Success or FAILURE?!

When you click on the Success! button, you send a request to the /test/200 path, which will be served by the `Heartbeat::Application` class and will respond with a body that says "/200 == Success!" When you click the Back button in your browser and then the Failure! button, you see "/500 == Failure!"

This is the basic foundation for Rack applications, and it provides a lightweight demonstration of how routing in very basic Rack applications works. When you began, you were able to write `run Heartbeat::Application` to run a single class as your Rack application, but as it's grown more complex, you've split different pieces of the functionality out into different classes. To combine these classes into one super-application, you used the `Rack::Builder.app` method.

Now you should have a basic understanding of how you can build Rack applications that offer a lightweight way of creating dynamic responses. How does all of this apply to Rails? Well, in Rails you're able to mount a Rack application so that it can serve requests on a path (like you did with `Rack::Builder`), rather than having the request go through the entire Rails stack.

15.3   *Mounting a Rack application with Rails*

Sometimes, you'll want to serve requests in a lightning-fast fashion. Rails is great for serving super-dynamic requests quickly, but occasionally you'll want to forgo the heaviness of the Rails controller stack and have a piece of code that receives a request and responds quickly.

Previously, your Rack application did just that. But you might need access to parts of your Rails application, like your models, inside the Rack application. To achieve this, you can mount the Rack app _inside_ the Rails application, to get all the performance of the Rack application while still leveraging the parts of Rails you want. To test this out, you'll re-implement your tickets API as a Rack application, and mount it inside your main Ticketee app.

Let's do this.

This new API will be version 2 of your API (things move fast in this app!). It will be accessible at /api/v2/projects/:project_id/tickets/:id. As with your original API, it will require a token parameter to be passed through to your application. If the token matches a user, and that user has access to the requested project, you can send back the details of the ticket in JSON format. This is the same way that v1 of your API, which you built in the last chapter, worked.

But you'll add some new functionality: If the token sent through doesn't match a user, you'll send back a helpful error message explaining that. If the project requested isn't accessible by the authenticated user, you'll deny all knowledge of its existence by sending back a 404 response.

Before you get into any of that, though, you should probably look at how mounting works within Rails by using one of your basic applications first.

15.3.1 *Mounting Heartbeat*

Mounting a Rack application involves defining a route in your Rails application that basically says, "I want to put this application at this path." Back when you were creating a pure Rack application, you did this in the lib/heartbeat/config.ru file like this:

```
map "/test" do
  run Heartbeat::Application
end
```

Rails has a better place than that for routes: config/routes.rb. This location provides you with some lovely helpers for mounting your Rack applications.

In your Rails application, to do the same thing as you did in your Rack application, you'd need to first require the application by placing this line at the top of config/routes.rb:

```
require "heartbeat/application"

Rails.application.routes.draw do
  ...
```

Then inside the `routes` block of config/routes.rb, put this line:

```
Rails.application.routes.draw do
  mount Heartbeat::Application, at: "/heartbeat"
  ...
```

Once you've made these changes to your config/routes.rb file, stop any Rails servers you have running, and boot up a new one:

```
$ rails s
```

You should now be able to go to http://localhost:3000/heartbeat/200 and see the friendly "/200 == Success!" message. This means that your `Heartbeat::Application` is responding as you'd like it to, nestled within the confines of your Rails application.

Rails has been told to forward requests that go to /heartbeat to this Rack application, and it has done so diligently. Rather than initializing a new instance of a controller (which is what normally happens in a standard Rails request), a Rack class is much lighter and is perfect for serving high-intensity requests that don't require views, like the response from your `Heartbeat::Application` and the responses from your API.

It's time to commit your changes:

```
$ git add .
$ git commit -m "Mounted the Heartbeat Rack application inside Ticketee"
$ git push
```

Even though there isn't a lot to see, you've learned a lot so far in your experiments with Rack.

Now that you've learned how to mount your `Heartbeat::Application`, it's time to build a slightly more complex Rack application that will serve JSON API requests for tickets. To make sure everything works, you'll also write tests to cover the functionality, using helpers called `Rack::Test::Methods`.

Rather than writing this application as a standard Rack app, let's mix things up a bit and use another Ruby web framework called Sinatra, which uses the Rack architecture underneath, just like Rails.

15.3.2 *Introducing Sinatra*

Sinatra is an exceptionally lightweight Ruby web framework that's perfect for building small applications, such as those that serve an API. Like Rails, it's built on top of Rack, so you'll have no worries about using them together. You'll use it here to create version 2 of your API.

Building your app this way not only demonstrates the power of Sinatra, but also shows that there's more than one way to skin this particular cat.[2]

To install the sinatra gem, run this command:

```
$ gem install sinatra
```

You can make a small Sinatra script now by creating a file called sin.rb.

> **Listing 15.8   A sample basic Sinatra application**

```
require "sinatra"

get "/" do
  "Hello World"
end
```

This is the most basic Sinatra application that you can write. On the first line, you require the `sinatra` file, which gives you some methods you can use to define your application, such as the `get` method you use on the next line. This `get` method is used to define a root route for your application, which returns the string "Hello World" for GET requests to "/."

---

[2] Although why anybody would skin a cat these days is unknown to the authors.

You could also make it into a class, which is what you'll need to do for it to be mountable in your application.

> **Listing 15.9　A sample basic Sinatra application ... in a class!**

```
require "sinatra"

class Tickets < Sinatra::Base
  get "/" do
    "Hello World"
  end
end
```

By making it a class, you'll be able to mount it in your application using the `mount` method in config/routes.rb and specifying the class name. Once you mount this Sinatra application inside your Rails application, it will have access to all the classes from your Rails application, such as your models, which is precisely what you're going to need for this new version of your API. You won't use this code example right now, but it's handy to know that you can do this.

To use Sinatra with your application, you need to add it to the Gemfile with the following line.

> **Listing 15.10　Adding `sinatra` to your Gemfile**

```
gem "sinatra"
```

Then run `bundle`, just to make sure a compatible version of Sinatra is installed.

You can go ahead now and start building this API using Sinatra.[3]

15.3.3　*The API, by Sinatra*

Create a new file at spec/requests/api/v2/tickets_spec.rb to test your experimental new API. In this file, you want to set up a project that has at least one ticket, as well as a user that you can use to make requests to your API. After that, you want to make a request to /api/v2/tickets and check that you get back a proper response of tickets.

With this in mind, write a spec that looks like the code shown in the following listing.

> **Listing 15.11　spec/requests/api/v2/tickets_spec.rb**

```
require "rails_helper"

describe API::V2::Tickets do
  let(:project) { FactoryGirl.create(:project) }
  let(:user) { FactoryGirl.create(:user) }
  let(:ticket) { FactoryGirl.create(:ticket, project: project) }
  let(:url) { "/api/v2/projects/#{project.id}/tickets/#{ticket.id}" }
```

---

[3]　You can learn more about Sinatra at https://github.com/sinatra/sinatra/ and at http://sinatrarb.com/ intro.

```
let(:headers) do
  { "HTTP_AUTHORIZATION" => "Token token=#{user.api_key}" }
end

before do
  assign_role!(user, :manager, project)
  user.generate_api_key
end

context "successful requests" do
  it "can view a ticket's details" do
    get url, {}, headers

    expect(response.status).to eq 200
    json = TicketSerializer.new(ticket).to_json
    expect(response.body).to eq json
  end
end
end
```

This test looks remarkably like the one in spec/requests/tickets_spec.rb, except this time you're only testing for JSON responses, and you've changed the URL that you're requesting to api/v2/projects/:project_id/tickets/:id.

When you run this spec with bundle exec rspec spec/requests/api/v2/tickets_spec.rb, you'll see that it gives you this error:

```
.../ticketee/spec/requests/api/v2/tickets_spec.rb:3:in `<top
  (required)>': uninitialized constant API::V2 (NameError)
```

This is because you haven't yet defined the module for the API::V2 namespace. Create a new file at app/controllers/api/v2/tickets.rb that defines this module.

Listing 15.12 app/controllers/api/v2/tickets.rb

```
require "sinatra"

module API
  module V2
    class Tickets < Sinatra::Base
      before do
        headers "Content-Type" => "text/json"
      end

      get "/:id" do
        []
      end
    end
  end
end
```

Within this file, you define the API::V2::Tickets class that's described at the top of your spec, which will now make your spec run. This class inherits from Sinatra::Base, so you'll get the helpful methods that Sinatra provides, such as the `before` and `get` methods that you use here.

The `get` method takes a parameter, as indicated by `:id`. This will be available inside the block as `params[:id]`, just like parameters are available inside a Rails controller.

You've already seen what `get` can do, but `before` is new. This method is similar to `before_action` in Rails, and it'll execute the block before each request. In this block, you set the headers for the request using Sinatra's `headers` method, so that consumers of your API can correctly identify that the response will be valid JSON.

Why put this code inside app/controllers? Well, even though this "controller" is most definitely not a controller in the common Rails sense, it's still a class that's going to be handling requests and acting like a controller, so app/controllers is a perfectly good place for it.

Rerun the spec, and this time you'll see a new error:

```
1) API::V2::Tickets successful requests can view a ticket's details
   Failure/Error: get url, {}, headers
   ActionController::RoutingError:
     No route matches [GET] "/api/v2/projects/1/tickets/3"
```

This is a better start. Now your test is running and failing as it should, because you haven't defined the route for it yet. Your test is expecting to be able to do a `GET` request to /api/v2/projects/1/tickets/3, but it can't.

This route can be interpreted as /api/v2/projects/1/tickets, and you can use the `api` namespace already in config/routes.rb to act as a home for this route. Put the following code for v2 of your API inside this namespace now.

Listing 15.13   config/routes.rb

```ruby
Rails.application.routes.draw do
  ...
  namespace :api do
    namespace :v2 do
      mount API::V2::Tickets, at: "/projects/:project_id/tickets"
    end

    resources :projects, only: [] do
      resources :tickets
    end
  end
  ...
```

When you place this `mount` call inside the namespaces, the Rack application will be mounted at /api/v2/projects/:project_id/tickets rather than the /tickets URI that would result if you didn't have it nested.

Additionally, you've specified a dynamic parameter in the form of `:project_id` inside the `at` option for the `mount` call, which means you'll be able to access the requested project ID from inside your Rack application using a method very similar to the way you'd usually access parameters in a controller.

If you attempt to run your spec again, it will bomb out with another new error:

```
1) API::V2::Tickets successful requests can view a ticket's details
   Failure/Error: expect(response.body).to eq json

     expected: "{\"ticket\":{\"id\":1...
          got: ""

     (compared using ==)
```

This means that requests are able to get to your Rack app, and that the response you've declared is being served successfully. Now you need to fill this response with meaningful data.

To do this, you need to find the project that's being referenced in the URL by using the parameters passed through, finding it with the `params` method. Unfortunately, Sinatra doesn't load the parameters from your Rails application; it creates its own `params` hash based on the request data, so `params[:project_id]` is not going to be set.

Luckily, you can still get to the project ID through one of the keys in the environment hash, which is accessible through the `env` method in your Sinatra actions. When you built your pure Rack applications earlier, you saw this `env` method in action, when you tested `env["PATH_INFO"]` for success or failure. This time it will have a little more to it, because it's gone through the Rails request stack.

You can add some debugging code to your Sinatra action to see what options you have. Change the `get` action in tickets.rb to this:

```
get "/:id" do
  pp env.keys
  []
end
```

When you rerun your test, you'll see a nice list of all the available keys output at the top, with one of the keys being `action_dispatch.request.path_parameters`. This key stores the parameters discovered by Rails routing, and your `project_id` parameter should fall neatly into this category.

Find out by changing the `pp env.keys` line in your root route to `pp env["action_dispatch.request.path_parameters"]` and then rerunning your test. You should see something like this:

```
{:project_id=>"3"}
```

Okay, so you can access two parameter hashes—one from Sinatra and one from Rails—but you'll need to merge them if you're going to do anything useful with them.

You can merge them into a super `params` method by redefining the `params` method as a private method in your app. Underneath the `get` method definition in your `API::V2::Tickets` class, you can put this:

```
...
  private

  def params
    hash = env["action_dispatch.request.path_parameters"].merge!(super)
    HashWithIndifferentAccess.new(hash)
  end
end
```

By calling the super method here, you'll reference the params method in the super-class, Sinatra::Base. You want to access the keys in this hash using either symbols or strings as you can do in your Rails application, so you create a new HashWith-IndifferentAccess object, which is returned by this method. You'll remember HashWithIndifferentAccess from way back in chapter 3.

Now switch your route back to calling pp params instead of pp env["action_dispatch .request.path_parameters"]. When you run your test again, you should see that you finally have access to the project's ID.

```
{"project_id"=>"3", "splat"=>[], "captures"=>["4"], "id"=>"4"}
```

The extra splat and captures arguments come from Sinatra and can safely be ignored for now.

With these params, you'll be able to load the project and then the correct ticket for it. You'll also need to authorize access to this ticket.

You can do this in parts. First, you can add the set_project method as something to be called before every action in this controller. This is very similar to how you had before_action :set_project in your TicketsController:

```
class Tickets < Sinatra::Base
  before do
    headers "Content-Type" => "text/json"
    set_project
  end

  ...
```

You can then define the set_project method underneath the private keyword:

```
module API
  module V2
    class Tickets < Sinatra::Base
    ...
    private

    def set_project
      @project = Project.find(params[:project_id])
    end
    ...
```

So far so good. Now you need to find the user based on their API key. To do this, you can add a set_user method call to the before block, too:

```
class Tickets < Sinatra::Base
  before do
    headers "Content-Type" => "text/json"
    set_user
    set_project
  end
  ...
```

Then add the set_user method underneath the set_project method. This is just like a before_action :authenticate_user! call:

```
module API
  module V2
    class Tickets < Sinatra::Base
    ...
    private

    def set_user
      if env["HTTP_AUTHORIZATION"].present?
        auth_token = /Token token=(.*)/.match(env["HTTP_AUTHORIZATION"])[1]
        User.find_by!(api_key: auth_token)
      end
    end
    ...
```

It looks similar to the `authenticate_user` method you defined in version 1 of your API, except you have to do a bit of manual management of the `env["HTTP _AUTHORIZATION"]` value. You're able to reference the models from your Rails application inside your Sinatra application, and there's nothing special you have to configure to allow this.

You don't need to be too concerned with what happens if an invalid `params[:project_id]` or user token is passed through at the moment; you'll fix those up after you've got this first test passing.

With the project now found, you should be able to display a ticket's information in JSON form. Change your Sinatra route to return the JSON-ified ticket:

```
module API
  module V2
    class Tickets < Sinatra::Base
      ...
      get "/:id" do
        ticket = @project.tickets.find(params[:id])
        TicketSerializer.new(ticket).to_json
      end
      ...
```

Now this route will respond with a ticket's information, which is all that's required to have your test pass. Check if this is the case by running `bundle exec rspec spec/api/ v2/tickets_spec.rb`:

```
1 example, 0 failures
```

Great, this spec is now passing, which means that your Rack application is now serving a base for version 2 of your API. By making this a Rack application, you can serve requests in a more lightweight fashion than you could within Rails.

But you don't have basic error-checking in place yet for situations such as when an invalid token is provided (one that doesn't match a valid user record), or if a user accesses a project that they're not authorized to see. Before we move on, let's quickly add tests for these two issues.

15.3.4 *Basic error-checking*

To add the error-checking, open spec/requests/api/v2/tickets_spec.rb and add some tests inside the describe block in a new context block.

Listing 15.14   Adding API request specs for error handling

```
describe API::V2::Tickets do
  ...
  context "unsuccessful requests" do
    it "doesn't allow requests that don't pass through an API key" do
      get url
      expect(response.status).to eq 401
      expect(response.body).to include "Unauthenticated"
    end

    it "doesn't allow requests that pass an invalid API key" do
      get url, {}, { "HTTP_AUTHORIZATION" => "Token token=notavalidkey" }
      expect(response.status).to eql 401
      expect(response.body).to include "Unauthenticated"
    end

    it "doesn't allow access to a ticket that the user doesn't have
➥ permission to read"
      project.roles.delete_all
      get url, {}, headers
      expect(response.status).to eq 404
    end
  end
end
```

In the first test, you make a request without passing through a token, which should result in a 401 unauthorized status and a message telling you that the user is not authenticated. The second test is similar, except in this case you try authenticating with the token provided, but it's not valid. In the final test, you use the delete_all association method to remove all permissions for the user and then attempt to request tickets in a project that the user no longer has access to. This should result in a 404 response, which means your API will deny all knowledge of that project and its tickets.

To make your first test pass, you'll need to check that your set_user method actually returns a valid user; otherwise you'll return a 401 unauthorized response. The best place to do this would be inside the set_user method itself, turning it into this:

```
module API
  module V2
    class Tickets < Sinatra::Base
      ...
      def set_user
        if env["HTTP_AUTHORIZATION"].present?
          if auth_token = /Token token=(.*)/.match(env["HTTP_AUTHORIZATION"])
            @user = User.find_by(api_key: auth_token[1])
            return @user if @user.present?
          end
```

```
      end

    unauthenticated!
  end
  ...
```

You can quickly add the unauthenticated! method underneath it:

```
...
def unauthenticated!
  halt 401, {error: "Unauthenticated"}.to_json
end
...
```

If a user isn't found in this case, you'll call the unauthenticated! method, which calls Sinatra's halt method. The halt method here will stop a request dead in its tracks. In this case, it will return a 401 status code with the body being the string specified.

When you run your tests again with bundle exec rspec spec/requests/api/v2/ tickets_spec.rb, the first three should be passing, with the last one still failing:

```
1) API::V2::Tickets unsuccessful requests don't allow access to a ticket
   ➡ that the user doesn't have permission to read
   Failure/Error: expect(response.status).to eq 404

        expected: 404
             got: 200

      (compared using ==)
```

Now if a missing or invalid token is passed, you're behaving responsibly and returning a useful error message in JSON format. This error tells the API client that the token used is invalid and returns a 401 unauthorized status.

Finally, you'll need to send a 404 response if the user isn't allowed to read the ticket they've requested. To do this, you can add an authorization check inside your get method:

```
module API
  module V2
    class Tickets < Sinatra::Base
      ...
      get "/:id" do
        ticket = @project.tickets.find(params[:id])
        unless TicketPolicy.new(@user, ticket).show?
          halt 404, "The ticket you were looking for could not be found."
        end
        TicketSerializer.new(ticket).to_json
      end
      ...
```

Here, you call out directly to TicketPolicy, creating a new instance, and then call the show? method on that. This is similar to the code that gets run when you call authorize in a proper Rails controller.

When you run your tests for a final time with `bundle exec rspec spec/requests/ api/v2/tickets_spec.rb`, they should all pass:

```
4 examples, 0 failures
```

Awesome! This should give you a clear idea of how you could implement an API similar to the one you created back in the last chapter by using the lightweight framework of Sinatra. All of this is possible because Rails provides an easy way to mount Rack-based applications inside your Rails applications. You could go further with this API, but that's another exercise for you to undertake if you wish.

Make sure you haven't broken anything else in your app while you've been working on your Sinatra API by running `bundle exec rspec`:

```
140 examples, 0 failures
```

Perfect! Commit these changes.

```
$ git add .
$ git commit -m "Added V2 of our Tickets API using Rack and Sinatra"
```

So far in this chapter, you've learned how you can use Rack applications to serve as endpoints of requests, but you can also create pieces of code that hook into the middle of the request cycle, called *middleware*. Rails has a few of these already, and you saw the effects of one of them when you were able to access the `env["action_dispatch.request.path_parameters"]` key inside your Sinatra application. Without the middleware of the Rails stack, this parameter would be unavailable. In the next section, we'll look at middleware examples in the real world, including some found in the Rails stack, as well as at how you can build and use your own.

15.4 *Middleware*

When a request comes into a Rack application, it doesn't go straight to a single place that serves the request. Instead, it goes through a series of pieces known as *middleware*, which may process the request before it gets to the end of the stack (your application) or may modify it and pass it onward, as shown in figure 15.3.

You can run `bundle exec rake middleware` within your Rails application's directory to see the list of middleware currently in use by your Rails application.

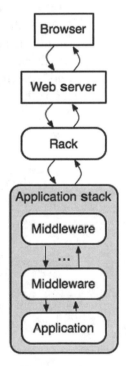

Figure 15.3   Full request stack, redux

Listing 15.15   An abbreviated list of middleware used by Ticketee

```
use Rack::Sendfile
use ActionDispatch::Static
use Rack::Lock
...
use Rack::ETag
use Warden::Manager
run Ticketee::Application.routes
```

Each of these middleware pieces performs its own individual function. For instance, the second piece of middleware, `ActionDispatch::Static`, intercepts requests for static files such as images, JavaScript files, or style sheets found in public and serves them immediately, without the request to them falling through to the rest of the stack. It's important to note that this middleware is only active in the development environment, since in production your web server (such as Nginx) is better suited for serving static assets.

Let's look at how `ActionDispatch::Static` works.

15.4.1 *Middleware in Rails*

In the case of the `ActionDispatch::Static` middleware, a response is returned if it finds a file to serve, and the request stops there. If no such file is found, then the request is modified and allowed to continue down the chain of middleware until it hits `Ticketee::Application.routes`, which will serve the request using the routes and code in your application. The process of `ActionDispatch::Static` can be seen in figure 15.4.

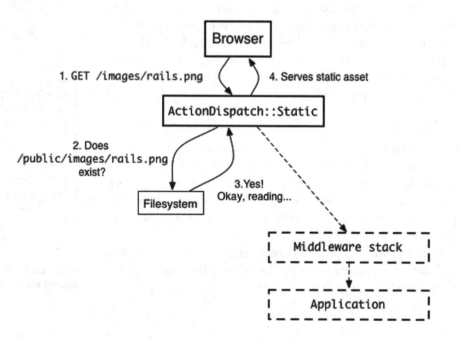

Figure 15.4   `ActionDispatch::Static` **request**

When a request is made to /images/rails.png, the middleware checks to see if the public/images/rails.png file exists. If it does, it's returned as the response to this request.

This middleware will also check for cached pages. If you make a request to /projects, Rails (by default) will first check to see if a public/projects.html file exists before sending the request to the rest of the stack.

In this request, the ActionDispatch::Static middleware first checks for the presence of public/projects.html, which would be there if you had cached the page. Because it's not there, the request goes through the rest of the middleware stack.

In order to see how middleware works in Rails, it's easy to craft your own. Let's do this now.

15.4.2 *Crafting middleware*

Soon you'll have your own piece of middleware that you can put into the middleware stack of a Rails or Rack application. This middleware will allow the request to run all the way down the chain to the application and then will modify the body, replacing specific letters in link text with other letters that you specify.

Create a new file for your middleware at lib/link_jumbler.rb and fill it with the content in the following listing.

Listing 15.16 lib/link_jumbler.rb

```ruby
require "nokogiri"

class LinkJumbler
  def initialize(app, letters)
    @app = app
    @letters = letters
  end

  def call(env)
    status, headers, response = @app.call(env)
    if headers['Content-Type'].include?("text/html")
      body = Nokogiri::HTML(response.body)
      body.css("a").each do |a|
        @letters.each do |find, replace|
          a.content = a.content.gsub(find.to_s, replace.to_s)
        end
      end
    else
      body = response.body
    end

    [status, headers, Rack::Response.new(body.to_s)]
  end
end
```

In this file you define the LinkJumbler class, which contains an initialize and a call method. The initialize method sets the stage, setting up the @app and @letters variables you'll use in your call method.

In the `call` method, you make a call down the middleware stack in order to set up your status, headers, and body values. You can do this because the `@app.call(env)` call will always return a three-element array. Each element of this array will be assigned to its respective variable.

In a Rails application's middleware stack, the third element isn't an array but rather an instance of `ActionDispatch::Response`. To get to the good part of this response, you can use the `body` method, like you do on the second line of your `call` method.

With this body, you use the `Nokogiri::HTML` method (provided by the `require "nokogiri"` line at the top of this file) to parse the body returned by the application into a `Nokogiri::HTML::Document` object. This will allow you to parse the page more easily than if you used regular expressions. With this object, you call the `css` method and pass it the `"a"` argument, which finds all a tags in the response body. You then iterate through each of these tags and go through all of your letters from `@letters`, using the keys of the hash as the find argument and the values as the replace argument. You then set the content of each of the a tags to be the substituted result.

Finally, you return a three-element array using your new body, resulting in links being jumbled.

To see this middleware in action, you'll need to add it to the middleware stack in your application. To do that, put these two lines inside the `Ticketee::Application` class definition in config/application.rb:

```
require "link_jumbler"
config.middleware.use LinkJumbler, { "e" => "a" }
```

15.4.3 *Using middleware*

The `config.middleware.use` method will add your middleware to the end of the middleware stack, making it the last piece of middleware to be processed before a request hits your application.

> **CONFIG.MIDDLEWARE METHODS** For more methods for `config.middleware`, look at the "Configuring Middleware" section of the official Configuring Rails Applications guide: http://guides.rubyonrails.org/configuring.html#configuring-middleware.

Any additional arguments passed to the `use` method will be passed as arguments to the `initialize` method for this middleware, so this hash you've passed will be the `letters` argument in your middleware. This means your `LinkJumbler` middleware will replace the letter *e* with *a* anytime it finds it in an a tag.

To see this middleware in action, fire up a server by running `rails s` in a terminal. When you go to http://localhost:3000, you should notice that something's changed, as shown in figure 15.5. As you can see, your links have had their *e*'s replaced with *a*'s, and any other occurrences, such as in the user's email address, has been left untouched.

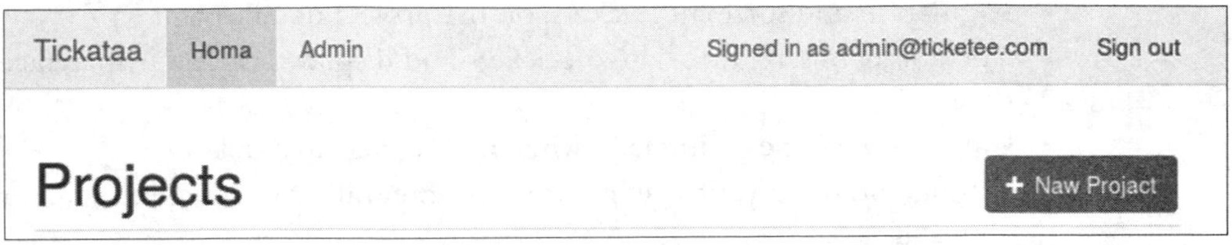

Figure 15.5 What's a Tickataa?!

This is one example of how you can use middleware to affect the outcome of a request within Rails; you could have modified anything or even sent a response back from the middleware itself. The opportunities are endless. This time, though, you've made a piece of middleware that finds all the a tags and jumbles up the letters based on what you tell it.

15.5 Summary

You've now seen a lot of what Rack, one of the core components of the Rails stack, can offer you. In the beginning of this chapter, you built a small Rack application that responded with "OK." You then fleshed out this application to respond differently based on the provided request. Then you built another Rack application that called this first Rack application, running both of these within the same instance by using the Rack::Builder class.

You saw how you could use these applications within the Rails stack by first mounting your initial Rack application and then branching out into something a little more complex, with a Sinatra-based application serving what could possibly be the beginnings of version 2 of Ticketee's API.

Finally, you saw a piece of standard Rails middleware: ActionDispatch::Static. You learned how it works so that you could use that knowledge to build your own middleware—a neat little piece that jumbles up the text on the link based on the options passed to it.

Congratulations! You've made it to the very end, and there was no monster at the end of the book. Well done!

We hope you've enjoyed your tour through the foundations of Rails. You've built and thoroughly tested a fully functional web application and deployed it to the internet for the world to see.

What should you do next? Build some more apps! It's one thing to follow a guide, carefully crafted to explain all of the concepts as you go along, but it's quite another to build something of your own. You could build a web forum, or a question-and-answer site, or your own miniversion of Twitter or Facebook. Or you could add some more features to Ticketee—other ideas that we wanted to cover (but ran out of space!) are things like these:

- The ability to log in using Twitter or Facebook, using OmniAuth
- Sending emails via background jobs, using Active Job

- Pagination and sorting of tickets, on the project details page
- The ability to set a due date on tickets and display a calendar interface for due dates
- Autocompleting existing tags, when adding tags to a ticket
- Setting and displaying avatars for users, integrating with an external service like Gravatar
- Deleting uploaded files on a ticket

And this is just a short list—the possibilities are endless!

If you're after more to read, we can recommend the following books to you, to expand both your Ruby and Rails horizons:

- *Practicing Rails* by Justin Weiss
- *Rails 4 Test Prescriptions* by Noel Rappin
- *Practical Object-Oriented Design in Ruby* by Sandi Metz
- *Confident Ruby* by Avdi Grimm

But above all else, have fun, and good luck!

appendix A
Installation guide

Before you can get started building Rails applications, you need to spend some time setting up your development environment. This means installing Ruby, and Rails, on your operating system of choice.

There are various tools you can use to do so, and there's no "best" or "perfect" solution. This guide covers the installation of our two preferred tools—ruby-install for installing different versions of Ruby from source, and chruby for switching your installed versions of Ruby easily. Then we'll look at using those tools to install Ruby and Rails, and then spin up a new working Rails app.

Windows

It's a bit tedious to set up Ruby and Rails on Windows. Windows doesn't have a package manager built in, and it doesn't have support for some native gems. But Ruby development is still possible, and for the purposes of this book, it's perfectly fine to use Windows.

> **TESTED WITH ...** This section has been verified with Windows 8.1, Ruby 2.1.6, and Rails 4.2.1.

We'll install Ruby via RubyInstaller, and then install DevKit, which enables you to build many of the C/C++ extensions available.

> **RUBY VERSIONS** Although RubyInstaller has a version that includes Ruby 2.2.2, many of the basic gems such as sqlite haven't been updated to be compatible with this newer version of Ruby under Windows. All of the code samples in this book will work just fine with Ruby 2.1, so if you're on a Windows machine, stick to using Ruby 2.1.

RubyInstaller

To start with, we'll show you how to install Ruby using RubyInstaller. Visit the Ruby-Installer website at http://rubyinstaller.org/downloads and grab the latest version for your operating system—we're using the Ruby 2.1.6 version.

Follow the instructions in RubyInstaller, making sure to tick the check box that says "Add Ruby executables to your path" on the final step before completing the installation process.

After installation, open the command prompt (which you can do by right-clicking on the Windows icon in the bottom-left corner, and clicking Command Prompt) and run ruby -v. You should see something like this:

```
ruby 2.1.6p336 (2015-04-13 revision 50298) [i386-mingw32]
```

Next, you need to install the Windows DevKit for Ruby.

DevKit

The DevKit (or Development Kit) is a toolkit that makes it easy to build and use native C/C++ extensions for Ruby on Windows. That might not mean much to you, but just know that you need it to install a lot of gems correctly, including some of Rails' dependencies.

DevKit is also accessible from the RubyInstaller downloads page, so visit http://rubyinstaller.org/downloads and download the latest version labeled "For use with Ruby 2.0 and 2.1." If you downloaded the x64 version of RubyInstaller, make sure you also grab the x64 version of DevKit. We're using the 32-bit version in this example.

When the file has downloaded, open it and extract it to C:\DevKit. After the extraction is complete, go back to your command prompt—you'll get familiar with it over the course of this book! Run the following commands, and you should see the following output:

```
$ cd C:\DevKit
$ ruby dk.rb init
[INFO] found RubyInstaller v2.1.6 at C:/Ruby21

Initialization complete! Please review and modify the auto-generated
'config.yml' file to ensure it contains the root directories to all
of the installed Rubies you want enhanced by the DevKit.

$ ruby dk.rb install
[INFO] Updating convenience notice gem override for 'C:/Ruby21'
[INFO] Installing 'C:/Ruby21/lib/ruby/site_ruby/devkit.rb'
```

Great, Ruby is all set up!

Rails

Now you have a working Ruby. What about Rails?

Ruby comes with its own package manager called RubyGems, and this is what you can use to install Rails. Gems are just little bundled-up packages of Ruby code, and Rails is a gem. You can install Rails with this command:

```
$ gem install rails -v 4.2.1
```

This will install the specified version of Rails, 4.2.1, and all of its dependencies. It'll take a while as it figures out the dependencies, installs the gems, and then parses and installs documentation. (You can skip the documentation install by running the command with`--no-document`; for example, `gem install rails --no-document`. But you might want it one day!)

> **IF INSTALLING RAILS DOESN'T WORK FOR YOU** You may have issues with the `gem install rails` command. If so, take a look at the "SSL upgrades on ruby-gems.org and RubyInstaller versions" discussion (https://gist.github.com/luislavena/f064211759ee0f806c88) to learn how to fix them, and run`gem install rails` again.

When it's done, verify the installation by running `rails -v`—it should tell you that it's using 4.2.1. Hooray!

STARTING A NEW RAILS APP

There are a couple more things you need to do before starting an app. These are minor gotchas that exist simply because Rails gives you a lot of choice in what libraries you use with your app.

One of those choices is which database library you'll use. By default, when generating an app, Rails will try to configure the app to use SQLite, a simple file-based database system. This is a decent choice for learning and will work out of the box on Windows.

But once you get going with the application, you may wish to switch to using a different database system, such as MySQL or PostgreSQL. These won't work out of the box on Windows—you'll need to fetch and install the database systems yourself.

If you want to use MySQL, you need to visit the MySQL website at http://mysql.com and go to the Downloads page. There, under MySQL Community Edition, you can click through and download the MySQL Community Server.

If you want to use PostgreSQL, you need to visit http://postgresql.org and download the Windows binary package from the Downloads page.

You also need to decide on which JavaScript runtime you want to use in your Rails application. Why do you need a *JavaScript* runtime to write *Ruby* apps? Well, way back when, in Rails 3.1, the Rails core team introduced a new feature called the *asset pipeline*. The asset pipeline, also known as "that blasted Sprockets thing," is a way to make your style sheets, JavaScript files, and other assets much more efficient. It includes support for preprocessors like CoffeeScript and Sass, automatic concatenation and minification of files, appending of file digests to filenames to prevent misbehaving browsers from caching things they shouldn't, and much, much more. To get the full power of the asset pipeline, you need a JavaScript runtime.

You can visit the ExecJS readme (https://github.com/sstephenson/execjs#execjs) to see a list of available runtimes. The most common is Node.js, which you can download from http://nodejs.org. We're using version 0.12.1. Once you've downloaded and installed it, you'll need to restart your computer to get your computer to pick up that it's installed.

Once all that setup is done, starting a new Rails app is trivial. Simply enter this in your terminal:

```
$ rails new my_awesome_app
```

This will create a new app using SQLite in the my_awesome_app directory of your current folder.

Once that's complete, you can start the Rails server:

```
$ cd my_awesome_app
$ rails server
```

Once WEBrick, the built-in Ruby web server, tells you it has loaded on port 3000, you can open up a browser and visit http://localhost:3000.

Welcome aboard! You're riding Ruby on Rails!

Mac OS X

OS X is the second-easiest of the three operating systems to install Ruby on. The reason it's in second place is that it doesn't come with a package manager like most flavors of Linux do. Instead, you must elect to install a tool called Homebrew to manage these packages.

> **TESTED WITH ...** This section has been verified with Mac OS X 10.10 but will *probably* work on earlier versions of OS X 10.x.

Homebrew

To start with, you'll install Homebrew (get it at Homebrew), which bills itself as "The missing package manager for OS X." The features that Homebrew provides, along with its ease of use, have helped it quickly gain status as *the* tool for managing packages on OS X.

Follow the installation instructions at the bottom of http://brew.sh to install Homebrew. The instructions say to run this command in Terminal:

```
$ ruby -e "$(curl -fsSL


https://raw.githubusercontent.com/Homebrew/install/master/install)"
```

Go ahead and do that now.

This command will pull down the Homebrew installation script and run it using the version of Ruby that comes standard with every modern OS X install. Follow the prompts and allow the Xcode tools to install. Once the Xcode tools are installed, press any key in the Terminal to finish setting up Homebrew.

ruby-install

The Ruby install that comes with OS X isn't as recent as it could be. In addition to this, the permissions for the default Ruby install aren't set up in a good way on the machine, and this Ruby version requires root access to install its gems. Therefore, we're going to use ruby-install to install a new version of Ruby.

You can see the version number of your system's default Ruby install, also known as the _system Ruby_, by running `ruby -v`. You'll see something like this:

```
ruby 2.0.0.p481 (2014-05-08 revision 45883) [universal.x86_64-darwin14]
```

The latest version of Ruby—at this time of writing—is Ruby 2.2.2, and that's what you'll install. `ruby-install` will download the Ruby source and associated dependencies, and compile it all neatly for you to use.

Ruby-install is open source on GitHub and can be found here: https://github.com/postmodern/ruby-install. The installation instructions (https://github.com/postmodern/ruby-install#install) say to use wget, but OS X doesn't have that installed by default. You can use Homebrew to install wget with this command:

```
$ brew install wget
```

With wget installed, you can run the installation instructions for ruby-install:

```
$ wget -O ruby-install-0.5.0.tar.gz https://github.com/

postmodern/ruby-install/archive/v0.5.0.tar.gz
$ tar -xzvf ruby-install-0.5.0.tar.gz
$ cd ruby-install-0.5.0/
$ sudo make install
```

You need to enter your password for sudo for that last step.

Once these installation steps have been completed, you can go up a directory and remove the ruby-install directory:

```
$ cd ..
$ rm -r ruby-install-*
```

With ruby-install installed, you can install Ruby 2.2.2 by running this command:

```
$ ruby-install ruby 2.2.2
```

With Ruby installed, you can now install and use chruby.

Chruby

Chruby is a simple shell tool used to manage your Ruby installations. Its main purpose is to switch between different versions of Ruby installed on your system and to handle all of the shell mess for you, so that running ruby will always run the correct interpreter. It can also be used to switch automatically to the Ruby version that you have just installed.

First, you need to install chruby:

```
$ wget -O chruby-0.3.9.tar.gz https://github.com/

postmodern/chruby/archive/v0.3.9.tar.gz
$ tar -xzvf chruby-0.3.9.tar.gz
$ cd chruby-0.3.9/
$ sudo make install
```

After that's done, you can safely delete this directory just like you did with ruby-install:

```
$ cd ..
$ rm -r chruby-*
```

Next, you can add chruby to your ~/.bash_profile file so that its features are loaded when you start a new terminal session. Open ~/.bash_profile in an editor and add these lines to that file:

```
source /usr/local/share/chruby/chruby.sh
source /usr/local/share/chruby/auto.sh
```

The auto.sh file will check the current directory for a .ruby-version file. If it exists, chruby will attempt to switch to that version of Ruby.

Create a ~/.ruby-version file now and specify that 2.2.2 is your default version of Ruby to use:

```
ruby-2.2.2
```

To have this configuration take effect, you need to open a new terminal window. Inside that new window, run `ruby -v`, and you should see the following:

```
ruby 2.2.2p95 (2015-04-13 revision 50295) [x86_64-darwin14]
```

Great! This means that Ruby has been set up correctly. Your next step is to set up Rails itself.

Rails

So now you have a working Ruby. What about Rails?

Ruby comes with its own package manager called RubyGems, and you can use it to install Rails. Gems are just little bundled-up packages of Ruby code, and Rails is a gem.

You can install Rails with this command:

```
$ gem install rails -v 4.2.1
```

This will install the specified version of Rails, 4.2.1, and all of its dependencies. It'll take a while as it figures out the dependencies, installs the gems, and then parses and installs documentation. (You can skip the documentation install by running the command with `--no-document`; for example, `gem install rails --no-document`. But hey, you might want it one day.)

STARTING A NEW RAILS APP

Starting a new Rails application on OS X is easier than in the other two operating systems this book covers. The SQLite 3 libraries that are used for the application's database come with OS X. A JavaScript runtime (used for compiling JavaScript files) also comes with OS X. (On Linux, for example, you might have to set both of these up.)

Starting a new application is as easy as running `rails new` and providing the application's name.

Once you get going with the application, you may wish to switch to using a different database system, such as MySQL or PostgreSQL. The gems for these are called mysql2 and pg respectively, and neither gem installs cleanly on the installation setup that you have so far.

If you run `gem install mysql2`, you'll see a big error that starts with this:

```
Fetching: mysql2-0.3.17.gem (100%)
Building native extensions.  This could take a while...
ERROR:  Error installing mysql2:
  ERROR: Failed to build gem native extension.

    /Users/<your username>/.rubies/ruby-2.2.2/bin/ruby extconf.rb
checking for ruby/thread.h... yes
....
```

Similarly, if you try to run `gem install pg`, you'll see this:

```
Fetching: pg-0.17.1.gem (100%)
Building native extensions.  This could take a while...
ERROR:  Error installing pg:
  ERROR: Failed to build gem native extension.

    /Users/<your username>/.rubies/ruby-2.2.2/bin/ruby extconf.rb
checking for pg_config... no
....
```

The gems are failing to install because they require libraries provided by their respective database systems. In order to develop for either of these database systems, you will first need to install them, which will install the libraries that these gems need. We recommend installing the database systems through Homebrew. You can choose to install one or the other, or both. You can always install the other at a later time if you need it.

To install MySQL, run this:

```
$ brew install mysql
```

To install PostgreSQL, run this:

```
$ brew install postgresql
```

Now when you try to install these gems with `gem install mysql2` and `gem install pg`, they will be installed without issue.

This appendix doesn't cover how to switch between the different database systems, but the book does. So go get cracking on setting up that Rails application!

LInux

Linux is perhaps the easiest of the three operating systems to get Ruby running on, but Rails is a little more difficult. All Linux flavors come with decent package management built in, so getting the necessary prerequisites is easy, safe, and guaranteed not to mess with software already installed on your system.

TESTED WITH ... This section has been verified with both Ubuntu 14.10 and Fedora 21, and presumes that your desktop is fully up to date, with all updates installed. There are no other installation prerequisites.

> ### For Fedora
> A basic Fedora install is a lot more bare-boned than Ubuntu, and as such, some really basic packages must be installed before you can install anything else. Installing Rails (actually, Nokogiri, a dependency of Rails) will require the patch library to be installed, so you'll need to install that first:
>
> ```
> $ sudo yum install -y patch
> ```

ruby-install

The first Linux tool we're going to look at is ruby-install.

WHAT IS IT?

Ruby-install is a tool used to download the Ruby source and associated dependencies and then compile it all neatly for you to use.

WHY DO WE USE IT?

Through a quirk of fate (or a disgruntled Debian package maintainer), the versions of Ruby available in the Ubuntu software repositories aren't quite up to scratch. Currently they contain different packages for Ruby 1.9.3p484 (called any of `ruby`, `ruby1.9.3`, and `ruby1.9.1`), Ruby 2.0.0p484 (named `ruby2.0`), and no Ruby 2.1. Although both 1.9.3 and 2.0 can be installed on your system, you can't have multiple patch-level versions of Ruby 2.0 (for example), or beta versions (such as 2.2.0-preview1), or older versions (such as 1.8.7). Ruby-install lets you install all of those things, as well as any other known version of Ruby, released or not.

Ruby-install is also easy to use! It just takes one line in your terminal to install any version of Ruby currently available. And keeping it separate from chruby means that you can update ruby-install only when necessary, to pull in new features or bug fixes, and doing so will have no other side effects (unlike some other all-in-one tools).

WHERE IS IT?

You can get ruby-install here: https://github.com/postmodern/ruby-install.

INSTALLATION

The latest version of ruby-install is 0.5.0, and you can install it like so:

```
# Download the zipped source for ruby-install
$ wget -O ruby-install-0.5.0.tar.gz \
  https://github.com/postmodern/ruby-install/archive/v0.5.0.tar.gz

# Unzip the source
$ tar -xzvf ruby-install-0.5.0.tar.gz

# Go into the directory we just unzipped
$ cd ruby-install-0.5.0/

# Install the software
$ sudo make install
```

```
# And clean up afterwards
$ cd ..
$ rm -r ruby-install-0.5.0/
```

Once it's installed, you can get a list of available stable rubies to install using the command `ruby-install`. It's not a complete list of all available rubies—just the currently known stable versions—but you can install any version just by specifying its name.

You can install a ruby by using `ruby-install <ruby type> <ruby version>`; for example,

```
# Install the following named ruby
$ ruby-install ruby 2.2.1
```

Ruby-install knows where to get the source code for Ruby 2.2.1, and also what dependencies are needed to compile it. It might ask for your sudo password, because it will use your package manager (apt-get or yum) to verify the dependencies, and then fetch and install any missing ones. For a brand new Fedora install, that's over 20 missing packages!

Once it's done all of that, it will start compiling Ruby, and you'll see lots and lots of random output as it checks a lot of things and then compiles all of the necessary files. There doesn't appear to be a built-in way to silence this output, but you can let it do its thing—go get a can of Diet Coke or something; it will take a few minutes.

When it's done, you'll see a nice happy message:

```
>>> Successfully installed ruby 2.2.1 into /home/<your username>/
  .rubies/ruby-2.2.1
```

You now have a ruby installed. How do you use it? The folder it installed to isn't part of your path, so calling `ruby` will have no effect. Enter chruby.

Chruby

Now that you have Ruby installed, how do you use it? Enter chruby.

WHAT IS IT?

Chruby is a simple shell tool used to manage your Ruby installations. Its main purpose is to switch between different versions of Ruby installed on your system and handle all of the shell mess for you, so that running `ruby` will always run the correct interpreter.

It's by the same author as ruby-install, so the two tools work very well together.

WHY DO WE USE IT?

There are tools already built into Linux to do things like this, such as update-alternatives, but they're not as convenient to use. They also don't have features like automatic Ruby switching when you change directories in your terminal, which is one of our favorite features.

WHERE IS IT?

You can get chruby here: https://github.com/postmodern/chruby.

INSTALLATION

The latest version of chruby is 0.3.9, and you can install it like so:

```
# Download the zipped source for chruby
$ wget -O chruby-0.3.9.tar.gz \
  https://github.com/postmodern/chruby/archive/v0.3.9.tar.gz

# Unzip the source
$ tar -xzvf chruby-0.3.9.tar.gz

# Go into the directory we just unzipped
$ cd chruby-0.3.9/

# Install the software
$ sudo make install
```

Once it's installed, you can configure it.

```
# Add this to your ~/.bashrc file or ~/.zshrc file
source /usr/local/share/chruby/chruby.sh

# Add this as well if you want to use chruby's switching behaviour,
# ie. so you can change Rubies automatically when changing into certain
# directories
source /usr/local/share/chruby/auto.sh
```

You can now set the Ruby you installed earlier as our default Ruby, like so:

```
# Add this to your ~/.bashrc or ~/.zshrc file like before, after the
# lines that load chruby
chruby 2.2.1
```

To get it working, you'll need to restart your terminal (closing it and re-opening it is easiest). If you run chruby, you should now see ruby-2.2.1 listed with a star next to it, meaning it's the currently active ruby. Running ruby -v will also confirm that you're using 2.2.1.

   If you have multiple rubies listed, you can switch between them using chruby <ruby>; for example, chruby 2.1.0. For now you likely just have the one, and that's just fine.

Rails

Now you have a working Ruby. What about Rails?

   Ruby comes with its own package manager called RubyGems, and you can use it to install Rails. Gems are just little bundled-up packages of Ruby code, and Rails is a gem. You can install Rails with this command:

```
$ gem install rails -v 4.2.1
```

This will install the specified version of Rails, 4.2.1, and all of its dependencies. It'll take a while as it figures out the dependencies, installs the gems, and then parses and installs documentation. (You can skip the documentation install by running the command with --no-document; for example, gem install rails --no-document. But hey, you might want it one day.)

When it's done, verify the installation by running `rails -v`—it should tell you that it's using 4.2.1. Hooray!

STARTING A NEW RAILS APP

There are a couple more things you need to do before starting an app. These are minor gotchas that exist because Rails gives you a lot of choice in what libraries you use with your app.

One of those choices is which database library you'll use. By default, when generating an app, Rails will try to configure the app to use SQLite, a simple file-based database system. This is a decent choice, but it requires that you already have both the sqlite package and its corresponding development headers installed.

If you don't have the headers installed when you generate a new app, you'll get a big error that includes the following:

```
Gem::Installer::ExtensionBuildError: ERROR: Failed to build gem native extens
    ion.

        /home/<your username>/.rubies/ruby-2.2.1/bin/ruby extconf.rb
checking for sqlite3.h... no
sqlite3.h is missing. Try 'port install sqlite3 +universal',
'yum install sqlite-devel' or 'apt-get install sqlite3-dev'
and check your shared library search path (the
location where your sqlite3 shared library is located).
*** extconf.rb failed ***
Could not create Makefile due to some reason, probably lack of necessary
libraries and/or headers. Check the mkmf.log file for more details. You may
need configuration options.
```

If you were generating a new app using an alternative database library such as MySQL or PostgreSQL (using `-d mysql` or `-d postgresql`), you'd get a similar error, but for a different header file.

The fix for this is to make sure you have the relevant development headers installed for the database library you want to use, before creating your Rails app:

```
# To use sqlite in Ubuntu
$ sudo apt-get install libsqlite3-dev

# To use PostgreSQL in Ubuntu
$ sudo apt-get install libpq-dev

# To use MySQL in Ubuntu
$ sudo apt-get install libmysqlclient-dev

# To use sqlite in Fedora
$ sudo yum install -y sqlite-devel

# To use PostgreSQL in Fedora
$ sudo yum install -y postgresql-devel

# To use MariaDB (a drop-in replacement for MySQL) in Fedora
$ sudo yum install -y mariadb-devel
```

Once you have the relevant package installed, you can rerun the `rails new` command, overwriting files where necessary.

You also need to decide on which JavaScript runtime you want to use in your Rails application. Why do you need a *JavaScript* runtime to write *Ruby* apps? Well, way back when, in Rails 3.1, the Rails core team introduced a new feature called the *asset pipeline*. The asset pipeline, also known as "that blasted Sprockets thing," is a way to make your style sheets, JavaScript files, and other assets much more efficient. It includes support for preprocessors like CoffeeScript and Sass, automatic concatenation and minification of files, appending of file digests to filenames to prevent misbehaving browsers from caching things they shouldn't, and much, much more. To get the full power of the asset pipeline, you need a JavaScript runtime.

You can visit the ExecJS readme (https://github.com/sstephenson/execjs#execjs) to see a list of available runtimes. One of the two most common is nodejs, which is installable from your package manager:

```
# To install nodejs in Ubuntu
$ sudo apt-get install nodejs

# To install nodejs in Fedora
$ sudo yum install -y nodejs
```

The other is therubyracer, which is installable as a gem. To get that installed for your app, open the Gemfile in the root of your application, and uncomment the line (remove the # in front of the text) `gem 'therubyracer'`. Once you've done that, you can run `bundle install` to get the gem installed.

Pick *one* of the two runtimes and install it. When you have it installed, your `rails server` should start without argument. Once WEBrick, the built-in Ruby web server, tells you it has loaded on port 3000, you can open up a browser and visit http://localhost:3000.

Welcome aboard! You're riding Ruby on Rails!

appendix B
Why Rails?

Two common questions from newcomers to the Ruby on Rails community are "Why Ruby?" and "Why Rails?" This appendix answers these questions with several key points about why people should be using Ruby on Rails over other frameworks, covering such things as the culture and community standards.

Ruby is an exceptionally powerful language that can be used for anything from short scripts to full-featured web applications, such as those built with Ruby on Rails. Its clean syntax and focus on making programmers happy are two of the many advantages that have generated a large community of users. There are hobbyists who use it just for the sake of it, and hardcore programmers who swear by it.

Ruby and—by extension—Rails should not be used as "golden hammers." Not all problems can be solved by Ruby or Rails, but the chance of running into one of those problems is extremely low. People who have used other languages before coming to Ruby suggest that "Ruby just makes more sense."[1]

The speed at which you can develop applications using Ruby on Rails is demonstrably faster than with other languages. An application that takes four months to build in Java could be done in three weeks in Rails, for example. This has been proven again and again. Rails even claims on http://rubyonrails.org that "Ruby on Rails is optimized for programmer happiness and *sustainable productivity.*"

The Ruby and Rails communities have a consistent focus on self-improvement. Over the last couple of years, we've seen developments such as the improvements from Rails 2 to Rails 3 to Rails 4, Ruby 2, the asset pipeline, and more. All of these have vastly improved the ease of development that is intrinsic to Ruby. Other developments have focused on other areas, such as RSpec and Capybara,

---

[1] Quote attributed to Sam Shaw from RailsConf 2011.

featured prominently in this book.[2] Through consistent improvements, things are becoming easier for Ruby developers every year.

Along the same vein of self-improvement is an almost zealous focus on testing—on code that tests other code. While this may seem silly to begin with, it helps us make fewer silly mistakes and provides the groundwork for testing the fixes for any bugs that come up in a system. Ruby, just like every other language, is no good at preventing buggy code. Such errors are a human trait that is unavoidable.

The shift away from SVN to the wonderful world of distributed version control was also a major milestone, with GitHub (a Rails application!) being created in early 2008. Services such as GitHub have made it easier than ever for Ruby developers to collaborate on code across cultures. As an example, you only need to look at the commits on the Rails project to see the wide gamut of authors.

Don't just take it from us. Here's a direct quote from somebody who had only been using Rails for a few days:

> *When I am programming with Ruby I think I'm making magic.*
>
> —New person

While Ruby isn't quite the magic of fairy tales, you'll find young and old, experienced and not-so-experienced people all claiming that it's a brilliant language to work with. As Yukihiro Matsumoto (the creator of the language) says, Ruby is designed to make programmers happy. Along the same lines, the Rails claim to be "optimized for programmer happiness and sustainable productivity" is not smoke and mirrors, either. You can be extremely happy and productive while using Rails, compared with other frameworks.

Let's dive a little deeper into the reasons why Rails (the framework) and Ruby (the language) are so great.

Reason #1: The sense of community

The Rails community is like none other on the planet. There is a large sense of togetherness in the community, with people freely sharing ideas and code through services such as GitHub and RubyGems (see reason #2). An example of this is the vibrant community on the Freenode IRC network (irc.freenode.net), where the main #rubyonrails channel is primarily used for asking questions about Rails. Anybody can come into the channel and ask a question and receive a response promptly from one of the other people who visit the channel. There's no central support authority; it's a group of volunteers who offer their time to help strangers with problems, without asking for money or expecting anything else in return.

There's also a large support community around Stack Overflow (http://stackoverflow.com) and other locations such as the Ruby on Rails Talk mailing list (http://groups .google.com/group/rubyonrails-talk) and Rails Forum (https://railsforum.com/). There's also the RailsBridge (http://railsbridge.org) organization, which aims to bridge the gap between newbies and experienced developers.

---

[2] A quick nod to the aruba gem (http://github.com/aslakhellesoy/aruba), which is used extensively to test RSpec and Cucumber's CLI (command-line interfaces), but can also be used to test other CLIs.

All of these different areas of the internet share a common goal: being nice to the people who are asking for help. One mantra in the Ruby community is "Matz is nice always, so we are nice," often abbreviated to "MINASWAN." People in the Ruby and Rails communities are incredibly nice to everyone.

Another example of the excellent community around Ruby on Rails is the number of conferences and gatherings held worldwide. The smallest of them are the intimate hack sessions where people work together on applications and share ideas in a room. Slightly bigger and more organized than those are the events such as Rails Camps (http://railscamps.org), which have about 150 people attending and run from Friday to Monday, with interesting talks given on Saturdays and Sundays. The largest, however, is RailsConf (http://railsconf.com/), which has about 2,000 people in attendance.

There are hundreds of thousands, if not millions of people using Ruby on Rails today, building great web applications with it and building the best web framework community on the planet.

Reason #2: The speed and ease of development

The speed with which you can develop a Ruby on Rails application is definitely one of the main reasons that people gravitate toward (and stick with) the framework.

One documented case involves a team that had developed an application using a Java-based framework, which took four months. When that application became difficult to maintain, alternative languages and frameworks were sought, with Ruby and Ruby on Rails fitting the bill adequately. The team re-implemented *all* the features of the original Java-based application within three weeks, with less code that was more beautiful.

Ruby on Rails follows a paradigm known as "convention over configuration." This paradigm has been adopted not only by Rails, but also by other modern web frameworks. Rails is designed in such a way that it takes care of the normal configuration that you might have to do in other frameworks, leaving you to get down to coding *real features* for your application.

One example of convention over configuration is the mapping between classes designed to interact with the database and the tables related to these classes. If the class is called `Project`, then it can be assumed by Rails (and the people coding the application) that the related table is going to be called `projects`. If that table name isn't desired for some reason, the name can be configured using a setting in the class.

Reason #3: RubyGems

This third point is more about a general boon to the Ruby community, but RubyGems plays a key role in developing Rails applications.

As we stated before, the culture of the Rails community is one of self-improvement. There are people who are consistently thinking of new ways to make other people's lives better. One of these ways is the RubyGems system, which allows people to share libraries in a common format. By installing a gem, a user is able to use its code along with their own code. For example, there's the json gem, which is used for parsing JSON data, the nokogiri gem for parsing XML, and of course the Rails suite of gems.

Previously, gems were hosted on a system known as RubyForge, which was unstable at times. In July 2009, Nick Quaranto, a prominent Rubyist, created the RubyGems site we know today: http://rubygems.org. This is now the primary nexus for hosting and downloading gems for the Ruby community, with RubyForge now playing second fiddle. The site Nick created provides an easy way for people to host gems that other people can use, freely. Isn't that just awesome?

Working with gems on a project used to be tough. To identify what gems a project used, they had to be listed somewhere, and there were often times when the tools used to install these gems caused problems, either installing the wrong gems or simply refusing to work at all. Then along came Bundler. The Bundler gem provides a standardized way across all Ruby projects for managing gem dependencies. It's a gem that manages the gems projects use. You can list the gems you want your project to use in a special file known as the Gemfile. Bundler then interprets (when `bundle install` is run) the special syntax in this file to figure out what gems (and dependencies) need to be installed, and it then goes about doing it. Bundler solves the gem dependency hell previously witnessed in Ruby and Rails in a simple fashion.

Similarly, having different Ruby versions running on the same machine used to be difficult and involved a lot of hacking around. Then another prominent Rubyist, Wayne E. Seguin, created a gem called RVM (Ruby Version Manager), which allows for simplistic management of the different versions. Later, other such versioning managers were built, such as rbenv, rbfu, and chruby (which we use in this book).

All in all, RubyGems and its ecosystem are very well thought out and sustainable. RubyGems provides an accessible way for people to share their code freely, and it serves as one of the foundations of the Ruby language. All of this work has been done by the exceedingly great community, which is made up of many different kinds of people, perhaps one day even including you.

Reason #4: The emphasis on testing

Within the Ruby and Rails communities, there's a huge focus on writing great, maintainable code. To help with this process, there's also a strong focus on test-driven development, and on the mantra "red-green-refactor." This mantra describes the process of test-driven development: we write tests that fail (usually indicated by the color red); we write the code that makes those tests pass (indicated by green); and then we clean up (refactor) the code in order to make it easier for people to know what it's doing. We cover this process in chapter 2.

Because Ruby is interpreted rather than compiled like other languages, you can't rely on compilers to pick up errors in your code. Instead, you write tests that describe functionality before it's implemented. Those tests will fail initially, but when you write that functionality, those tests will pass. In some situations (such as tests written using the Cucumber gem), these tests can be read by people who requested a feature, and they can be used as a set of instructions explaining exactly how this feature works. This is a great way to verify that the feature is precisely what was requested.

As you write tests for the application, you provide a safety net for when things go wrong. This collection of tests is referred to as a *test suite*. When you develop a new feature, you have the tests you wrote *before* the feature to prove that it's still working as you originally thought it should. If you want to make sure that the code is working at some point in the future, you have the test suite to fall back on.

If something does go wrong and it's not tested, you've got that base to build upon. You can write a test for an unanticipated situation—a process known as *regression testing*—and always have that test in the future to ensure that the problem doesn't crop up again.

index

Symbols

_ (underscore) 91
* (asterisk) 76, 102
//= directives prefix 315
<% %> tags 11, 56
<< association 395
~> approximate version
    constraint operator 49
$ function 321

A

absolute positioning 106, 118
acceptance testing 31
accepts_nested_attributes_for
    helper 298
access control
  admins
    adding admin field to users
      table 172–173
    creating admin user
      173–174
    overview 171–172
  API
    API namespace 477–481,
      483–486
    authenticating with invalid
      token 488–489
    permission denied
      error 489–491
    token-based
      authentication
      476–486
    for comment form 334–342

CRUD based on namespaces
  archiving users 205–210
  create action 196–197
  creating admin users
    197–199
  editing users 199–205
  index action 193–194
  listing users 194–195
  new action 195–196
  overview 191–193
  preventing archived users
    from signing in
    211–214
  preventing archiving
    oneself 210–211
ensuring authorization for all
  actions 266–269
handling authorization
  errors 230–232
hiding links
  delete link 189–191
  new project link 187–189
  overview 187
namespaced controllers
  creating 174–176
  moving functionality
    into 180–186
  overview 174
  testing 177–180
project-update permission
  hiding edit project
    link 240–241
  implementing
    authorization 238–239
  testing 236–238

project-viewing permission
  assigning viewer role in
    specs 217–219
  checking user roles with
    exists? method
    224–227
  creating Role model
    219–220
  creating tickets 227–228
  deleting tickets 228–229
  editing projects 229–230
  Pundit gem 220–223
  testing 223–224
  testing for authorization of
    displayed links
    232–236
  viewing tickets 228–229
for tags 396–402
ticket-creation permission
  hiding "New Ticket"
    link 254–256
  implementing
    authorization 252–254
  testing 250–252
ticket-destroying permission
  hiding "Delete Ticket"
    link 264–266
  implementing
    authorization 264
  testing 262–263
ticket-updating permission
  hiding "Edit Ticket"
    link 259–262
  implementing
    authorization 258–259
  testing 256–258

access control *(continued)*
  ticket-viewing permission
    custom RSpec
      matcher 243–246
    metaprogramming magic
      in 249–250
    testing 246–249
    ticket policy overview
      242–250
  user roles page
    Bootstrap styling 276–277
    building list of projects in
      select box 271–276
    displaying user roles
      277–278
    feature spec 270–271
    processing submitted role
      data 278–280
    roles screen 271
    saving roles of new
      users 280–282
action attribute 18, 63
Action Mailer
  overview 429–432
  templates for 432–434
  :test option 423
ActionDispatch::Static
  middleware 518–519
Active Record 132–133, 225
active_for_authentication?
  method 211
ActiveJob component 426
ActiveModel::Serializers
  generating serializer for
    Ticket model 473–476
  overview 471–473
admins
  adding admin field to users
    table 172–173
  creating admin user 173–174
  CRUD based on namespaces
    archiving users 205–210
    create action 196–197
    creating admin users
      197–199
    editing users 199–205
    index action 193–194
    listing users 194–195
    new action 195–196
    overview 191–193
    preventing archived users
      from signing in
      211–214
    preventing archiving
      oneself 210–211

hiding links
  delete link 189–191
  new project link 187–189
  overview 187
  moving functionality into
    admin namespace 180–186
  overview 171–172
after_action method 268
after_create method 348, 355,
  394–395
after_destroy method 348
after_save method 348
after_update method 348
after_validation method 348
Agile development 39
AJAX 408
allow method 179
Amazon S3 (Simple Storage
  Service) 454–457
APIs (application programming
  interfaces)
  ActiveModel::Serializers
    generating serializer for
      Ticket model 473–476
    overview 471–473
  authentication
    API namespace 477–481,
      483–486
    token-based 476–486
  error handling
    authenticating with invalid
      token 488–489
    permission denied 489–491
    validation errors 491–494
  example of 470–471
  HTTParty gem 486–487
  moving common helpers to
    ApplicationController
    494–495
  overview 468–469
  Sinatra
    API using 509–514
    error handling with
      515–517
    overview 508–509
append method 321
application programming
  interfaces. *See* APIs
application/json type 470
applications
  committing changes 74
  configuration
    BDD 49–50
    database 50–51
    Gemfile 47–49

  creating 6–7, 41–42
  deleting from database 21–23
  DRY code 77–78
  ERB files 11
  forms
    form_for helper 11–12
    submitting 12–14
  helpers 76–77
  migrations 9–10
  naming 7
  routing 17–18
  scaffolding 8–9
  setting page title 74–75
  starting 7–8
  styling
    Bootstrap 103–104
    buttons 104–106
    links 106–107
    navigation bar 117–119
    page header style 104–106
    responsive 120–123
    Simple Form gem 102–103,
      113–117
  styling, semantic
    for buttons 107–111
    for flash messages 111–113
    overview 107
  twelve-factor apps
    configuration 452
    defined 452
    processes 453–454
  updating database 18–21
  user stories
    application layout 70–73
    building form 63–64
    controller create action
      65–67
    defining controller 55–57
    overview 41
    resource creation 52–55
    RESTful routing 57–60
    routing of migrations
      61–63
    routing of models 60
    strong parameters 67–70
    validations 78–83
  validations
    overview 14–15
    show action 16–17
  version control
    configuring Git client
      44–46
    overview 42–43
    using GitHub 43–44
archiving users 205–210

arrange, act, assert form 89
aruba gem 536
assertions 28, 30, 340
asset pipeline 71
assets directory 5, 315
association methods 129
associations
    belongs_to association
        163, 219, 476
    has_and_belongs_to_many
        association 387, 427
    has_many association
        129–131, 296, 298
    has_one association 476
asynchronous requests
    appending content to
        form 320–322
    overview 317–320
    purpose of 408
    sending parameters for
        322–324
attaching files
    many files
        creating spec for 293–294
        implementing feature
            294–298
        nested attributes 298–302
        overview 293
    serving files through control-
    ler
        permissions for
            attachments 304–306
        private attachments
            308–310
        public attachments
            307–308
        showing attachments
            306–307
        testing existing
            functionality 303–304
    single file
        CarrierWave gem 286–287
        creating spec for 285–286
        implementing feature
            287–290
        overview 284
        persisting uploads when
            redisplaying form
            290–292
    using JavaScript
        attaching more files
            316–317
        disabling database transac-
            tions for tests 312–314
        jQuery 314–315

overview 310
testing 310–312
Turbolinks gem 315–316
attr_accessible feature 68
attr_accessor method 36, 385
attributes, virtual 385
authenticate_user! method 179
authenticate_with_http_token
    method 485
authentication
    API
        API namespace 477–481,
            483–486
        authenticating with invalid
            token 488–489
        permission denied
            error 489–491
        token-based 476–486
    defined 170
    Devise gem
        overview 149–151
        styling views for 159–161
    linking tickets to users
        161–168
    sign-in 154–157
    sign-out 157–159
    sign-up page 152–154
authenticity_token
    parameter 67
authorization
    for comment form 334–342
    defined 170
    ensuring for all actions
        266–269
    handling errors 230–232
    saving to database and
        253, 258
    for tags 396–402
    whitelist vs. blacklist 216
Authorization header 486

B

Basecamp 2
BDD (behavior-driven
    development)
    advantages of 26
    configuration 49–50
    overview 31
    RSpec 31–32
    running specs 33–34
    test example 34–37
    using Factory Girl gem 85–87
    writing specs 32–33
before method 511

&:before rule 108
before_action method
    101, 201, 266
before_create method
    348, 355, 395
before_destroy method 348
before_save method 348
before_update method 348
before_validation method 348
behavior-driven development.
    See BDD
belongs_to association
    163, 219, 476
Bitbucket 43
blacklist authorization 216
blink tag 285
Bootstrap 103–104, 121,
    176, 446
browser testing 49
btn class 104
btn-success class 105
buckets, S3 453
builder pattern 473
Bundler 47, 538
button_to method 444
buttons
    semantic styling for 107–111
    styling 104–106

C

C/C++ extensions 524
cache 290–291
call method 498, 500
callbacks
    defined 348
    when to avoid 424
Capybara 41, 49, 310, 340
CarrierWave gem
    configuring upload
        folder 308
    fixing file uploads for
        deployment 460–461
    overview 286–287
Cascading Style Sheets. *See* CSS
character encoding 51
check boxes 198
Chrome 378
chruby installation
    Linux 531–532
    Mac OS X 527–528
class_name option 163, 333, 427
classes
    abstracting Rack applications
        into

classes *(continued)*
    overview 502–504
    running application
        505–506
    inheritance 335
code
    smell 226
    writing better 26
CoffeeScript 54, 72, 320–322
collection method 411
collection routes 206
Collection+JSON 471
comment form
    authorization for 334–342
    controller for 332–333
    model for 329–332
    overview 326–328
    security for
        change_state
            permission 375–376
        hacking forms 376–378
        hiding select box 373–374
        ignoring parameters
            378–381
comments 391–395
committing changes 74
community 536–537
compiling assets 98
config.middleware methods 520
configuration
    BDD 49–50
    database 50–51
    Gemfile 47–49
    twelve-factor apps and 452
confirmable module 150
consider_all_requests_local
    setting 97
console 79
content_for method 76
content_tag helper 358
Content-Type header 470, 498
context blocks 188
continuous deployment
    configuration 462–463
    deployment hooks 463–465
    overview 462
controllers
    avoiding notifications sent
        from 424
    for comment form 332–333
    consistent order of CRUD
        actions 200
    create action in 65–67
    creating 55–57
    destroy action 94, 96

directory for 4
edit action 88–92
handling uploaded files
    permissions for
        attachments 304–306
    private attachments
        308–310
    public attachments
        307–308
    showing attachments
        306–307
    testing existing
        functionality 303–304
namespace
    creating 174–176
    moving functionality
        into 180–186
    overview 174
    testing 177–180
namespace, CRUD based on
    archiving users 205–210
    create action 196–197
    creating admin users
        197–199
    editing users 199–205
    index action 193–194
    listing users 194–195
    new action 195–196
    overview 191–193
    preventing archived users
        from signing in
        211–214
    preventing archiving
        oneself 210–211
update action
    failure to update
        behavior 93–94
    implementing 92–93
convention over
    configuration 2, 46, 537
Coordinated Universal Time. *See*
    UTC
coupling, tight 424
create_table method 61–62
create! method 80
created_at attribute 80
cross-site request forgery. *See*
    CSRF
CRUD (create, read, update,
    delete)
    based on namespaces
        archiving users 205–210
        create action 196–197
        creating admin users
            197–199

editing users 199–205
    index action 193–194
    listing users 194–195
    new action 195–196
    overview 191–193
    preventing archived users
        from signing in
        211–214
    preventing archiving
        oneself 210–211
consistent order of actions in
    controllers 200
creating tickets
    adding section for 124–126
    controller for 127–128
    finding tickets scoped by
        project 133–134
    has_many associations
        129–131
    nested routing
        helpers 126–127
    overview 131–133
    URL placeholders 128–129
    validations 135–136
defined 51
deleting projects 94–97
deleting tickets
    for deleted projects
        139–141
    individual tickets 145–147
editing projects
    edit action 88–92
    update action 92–93
    update failure behavior
        93–94
editing tickets
    creating spec for 141–143
    edit action 144
    update action 144–145
exception handling
    handling RecordNotFound
        exception 99–101
    serving static error
        page 98–99
viewing all projects 85, 87–88
viewing tickets
    listing all 138–139
    overview 136–138
CSRF (cross-site request
    forgery) 72
csrf_meta_tags method 72
CSS (Cascading Style Sheets)
    5, 98
Cucumber 26

curl
　defined 470
　-i flag 476
custom RSpec matchers 245

D

:data option 95–96
data truncation 312
data-params attribute 322–323
Database Cleaner gem 312–313
database_authenticatable
　　module 150
databases
　configuration 50–51
　controllers and 4
　indexing 344, 388
　join tables 382
　rolling back changes 173
　transactions 279
　using different for develop-
　　ment and production 455
debugging 253
default attribute 368, 430
delayed_job gem 426
delegation 336
DELETE method 58
:delete option 405
deliver_later method 426
deliver_now method 425–426
delivery_method setting 423
:dependent option 141
deployment
　continuous deployment with
　　Travis CI
　　configuration 462–463
　　deployment hooks 463–465
　　overview 462
　Heroku
　　correcting warnings
　　　458–460
　　fixing CarrierWave file
　　　uploads 460–461
　　overview 450
　　process overview 462
　　provisioning apps 450–451
　　signing up 450
　　using Git 457–458
　　using S3 with 454–457
　overview 449–450
　sending emails using
　　Mailgun 465–467
　twelve-factor apps
　　configuration 452
　　defined 452
　　processes 453–454

describe block 32
destroy action 94, 96, 146
development environment
　　48, 72
Devise gem
　overview 149–151
　sign_in helper 400
　sign_in method 379
　styling views for 159–161
DevKit 524
disposition option 307
domain logic 4
DRY (Don't Repeat
　Yourself!) 77–78
DSL (domain-specific
　language) 31

E

edit action 88–92
editor role 216
Elasticsearch 409
email
　sending ticket notifications
　　Action Mailer
　　　overview 429–432
　　Action Mailer
　　　templates 432–434
　　automatically watching
　　　tickets 421–423
　　defining watchers
　　　association 427–429
　　testing 423, 434–436
　　using service classes
　　　423–427
　sending using Mailgun
　　465–467
　subscribing to update
　　notifications
　　automatically adding
　　　commenter as
　　　watcher 439–440
　　testing 437–439
　　unsubscribing 440–446
Email Spec gem 421
engines 151, 159
environments 48
ERB (Embedded Ruby) 4, 11
error handling
　API
　　authenticating with invalid
　　　token 488–489
　　permission denied 489–491
　　validation errors 491–494
　　authorization errors 230–232

handling RecordNotFound
　exception 99–101
helper methods for 82–83
serving static error page
　98–99
using Sinatra 515–517
errors object 494
:except option 101, 184
ExecJS 525, 534
exists? method 225
@extend directive 108, 110

F

fa_icon helper 105
Facebook 150
Factory Girl gem
　overview 85–87
　traits 171
fadeOut() function 408
falsey values 35, 172
Fedora 530
fields_for helper 296–297
fields, database 9
file_cache field 300
find method 133
find_by method 75, 276
find_email! method 422
Firefox 378
flash messages
　defined 14
　flash vs. flash.now 81
　passing flash to redirect_to 66
　rendering all 73
　semantic styling for 111–113
Fog gem 454
Font Awesome project 105
foreign key support 130, 164
form_for method 411
form_tag helper 411
forms
　creating user story for 63–64
　form_for helper 11–12, 63
　hacking 376–378
　Simple Form gem
　　Boolean values in 198
　　Bootstrap and 276
　　overview 102–103, 113–117
　　simple_fields_for
　　　helper 296
　submitting 12–14
:full_error component 116
full_messages method 494

G

g command 50
Gemfile 47–49, 414, 458
gems
  defined 47
  overview 3–4
GET method 53
get method 369, 511
Git
  checkout command 74
  commit command 44, 290
  configuring client 44–46
  deploying to Heroku
    using 457–458
  push command 45
  remote add command 45
  stash command 74
GitHub
  Ruby on Rails usage 5, 536
  setting up for application
    43–44
global support loading 218

H

hacking forms 376–378
halt method 516
handlers 55
has_and_belongs_to_many
    association 382, 387, 427
has_content? method 340
has_many association 129–131,
    296, 298, 330
has_one association 476
hashing passwords 204
<header> tag 110
–help option 42
helpers 5, 76–77
Heroku
  checking logs 460
  continuous deployment with
    Travis CI
      configuration 462–463
      deployment hooks 463–465
      overview 462
  correcting warnings 458–460
  fixing CarrierWave file
    uploads 460–461
  overview 450
  process overview 462
  provisioning apps 450–451
  signing up 450
  using Git 457–458
  using S3 with 454–457

Homebrew 526
HTTP (Hypertext Transfer
    Protocol)
  PATCH method 20
  RESTful routing 58
HTTP_AUTHORIZATION
    token 485
HTTParty gem 486–487
Hulu 1
hypermedia 469

I

i18n (internationalization) 212
@import directive 103, 105
inactive_message method 212
include method 158
index action 55, 85
index option 344, 388
inflection 481–482
inheritance 337
  for classes 335
  for templates 201–202
initialize method 520
initializers 149
installation
  chruby
    on Linux 531–532
    on Mac OS X 527–528
  DevKit 524
  Homebrew 526
  Rails
    on Linux 532–533
    on Mac OS X 528
    on Windows 524–525
  RSpec 31
  Ruby on Rails 6
  ruby-install
    on Linux 530–531
    on Mac OS X 526–527
  RubyInstaller 524
integration testing 49
internationalization. See i18n
IRC channel 536
it syntax 243

J

JavaScript
  runtime for 525, 534
  uploading files using
    attaching more files
      316–317

disabling database transac-
    tions for tests 312–314
  jQuery 314–315
  overview 310
  testing 310–312
  Turbolinks gem 315–316
JavaScript Object Notation. See
    JSON
javascript_include_tag
    method 72
JBuilder library 473
join tables 382
:join_table option 427
joins method 235
jQuery 314–315
jquery_ujs file 96, 314
js:true option 310
JSON (JavaScript Object
    Notation) 469
JSON-API format 471
JSON-LD format 471

L

label method 64
label_tag helper 272, 411
layout method 430
layout option 319
lazy-loading 142
let blocks 416
let method 142, 188
Lighthouse 395
line breaks 134
link_to method
  caution when using 139
  :method option 95, 443
  overview 11, 19, 57
  :remote option 316, 405
links
  hiding
    delete link 189–191
    new project link 187–189
    overview 187
  styling 106–107
Linux
  chruby installation 531–532
  installing Rails 6, 532–533
  overview 529–530
  ruby-install 530–531
  starting new Rails app
    533–534
list_item method 367, 404
lockable module 150
login_as method 157, 162
logs, Heroku 460

M

Mac OS X
  chruby installation 527–528
  Homebrew 526
  installing Rails 6, 528
  ruby-install 526–527
  starting new Rails app
    528–529
mailers directory 5
Mailgun 465–467
manager role 216
Markdown 3
marquee tag 285
master branch 45
media queries 120
member routes 206
meta tags 120
metaprogramming
  249–250, 431
method attribute 18
method option 95, 443
method_missing method 431
middleware
  ActionDispatch::Static
    middleware 518–519
  creating 519–520
  overview 517–518
  using 520–521
migrations
  overview 9–10
  rolling back changes 173
  routing for 61–63
  running 10
MIME types 469
MiniTest
  overview 28–29
  test example 29–31
  writing tests 27–29
model-view-controller. See MVC
models
  for comment form 329–332
  directory for 4
  importance of 60
  routing for 60
  for tags 387–388
  when to avoid using
    callbacks 424
mount method 509
MVC (model-view-
  controller) 4–5
MySQL 50, 164, 525, 528–529

N

namespaces
  controller
    creating namespaced
      controller 174–176
    moving functionality into
      admin
      namespace 180–186
    overview 174
    testing namespaced
      controller 177–180
  CRUD based on
    archiving users 205–210
    create action 196–197
    creating admin users
      197–199
    editing users 199–205
    index action 193–194
    listing users 194–195
    new action 195–196
    overview 191–193
    preventing archived users
      from signing in
      211–214
    preventing archiving
      oneself 210–211
  root 175
navigation bar 117–119
nested resources
  creating tickets
    adding section for 124–126
    controller for 127–128
    finding tickets scoped by
      project 133–134
    has_many associations
      129–131
    nested routing
      helpers 126–127
    overview 131–133
    URL placeholders 128–129
    validations 135–136
  deleting tickets
    for deleted projects
      139–141
    individual tickets 145–147
  editing tickets
    creating spec for 141–143
    edit action 144
    update action 144–145
  viewing tickets
    listing all 138–139
    overview 136–138
new command 42
nil value 75, 172

Node.js 525, 534
not_authorized method 232
notifications
  emailing for ticket updates
    Action Mailer
      overview 429–432
    Action Mailer
      templates 432–434
    automatically watching
      tickets 421–423
    defining watchers
      association 427–429
    testing 423, 434–436
    using service classes
      423–427
  subscribing to
    automatically adding
      commenter as
      watcher 439–440
    testing 437–439
    unsubscribing 440–446
:nullify option 140
number_to_human_size
  helper 289

O

OData 471
OmniAuth 150
:only option 101, 184
origin repository 45
overriding methods 199

P

PaaS (Platform as a Service) 449
page-header class 104
parameterize method 347
params data attribute 322–323
params method 66, 512
parent() function 408
parsed_response method 486
partials
  defined 90
  template inheritance and 202
password hashing 204
PATCH method 20, 58, 207
PATH_INFO key 501
pg gem 455
placeholders, URL 128–129
plain old Ruby object. See PORO
Platform as a Service. See PaaS
policies, Pundit 220
policy view helper 341, 373
polymorphic routing 132

PORO (plain old Ruby object) 425
:post option 443
PostgreSQL 50, 164, 455, 525, 528–529
presence validation 79
primary key 344
production environment 48, 98, 449
ProgrammableWeb 468
provisioning apps 450
Pry gem 253
Puma 458
Pundit gem
  overview 220–221
  policy view helper 341, 373
  spec helpers 221–223
PUT method 58

R

race conditions 150–151
Rack applications
  abstracting into classes
    overview 502–504
    running application 505–506
  middleware
    ActionDispatch::Static middleware 518–519
    creating 519–520
    overview 517–518
    using 520–521
  mounting with Rails
    API using Sinatra 509–514
    error handling 515–517
    overview 506–508
    Sinatra overview 508–509
  overview 496–498
  responding to different requests 499–502
  simple example 498–499
Rackup files 498–499
Rails
  advantages of
    community 536–537
    emphasis on testing 538–539
    overview 2–3, 535–536
    RubyGems 537–538
    speed of development 537
  gems 3–4
  GitHub example 5
  history of 2
  inflection 481–482

installation
  Linux 532–533
  Mac OS X 528
  Windows 524–525
  terminology 4–5
Rails Camps 537
rails command 6, 8, 41
Rails Lighthouse 395
Rails Rumble event 2
rails_12factor gem 456
RAILS_ENV environment variable 98
RailsBridge 536
RailsConf 537
Rake middleware 62, 517
ready method 321
RecordNotFound exception 99–101
recoverable module 150
red-green-refactor process 26, 538
redirect_to method 65–66, 133
refactoring 92
registerable module 150
regression testing 27, 40, 539
relative positioning 106
remberable module 150
remote option 316, 405
render method 11, 92
Representational State Transfer. See REST
request tests 478
require method 68
require_relative 504
require_tree method 315
resolve method 233
resource routes 57
resources
  creating tickets
    adding section for 124–126
    controller for 127–128
    finding tickets scoped by project 133–134
    has_many associations 129–131
    nested routing helpers 126–127
    overview 131–133
    URL placeholders 128–129
    validations 135–136
  defined 17, 51
  deleting tickets
    for deleted projects 139–141
    individual tickets 145–147

editing tickets
  creating spec for 141–143
  edit action 144
  update action 144–145
viewing tickets
  listing all 138–139
  overview 136–138
respond_to 470
responsive styling 119–123
Resque gem 426
REST (Representational State Transfer)
  RESTful apps 469
  routing
    of migrations 61–63
    of models 60
    overview 57–60
  terminology explained 5
:restrict_with_error option 140
:restrict_with_exception option 140
role_on method 272, 275
roles, user
  Bootstrap styling 276–277
  building list of projects in select box 271–276
  displaying user roles 277–278
  feature spec 270–271
  processing submitted role data 278–280
  roles screen 271
  saving roles of new users 280–282
rolling back changes 173
root namespace 175
root route 53
routes.rb file 17
routing
  member routes vs. collection routes 206
  migrations 61–63
  models 60
  nested routing helpers 126–127
  overview 17–18, 57–60
  polymorphic 132
  root route 53
RSpec
  custom matcher 243–246
  let method 142
  overview 31–32
  request specifications 478
  running specs 33–34
  test example 34–37
  writing specs 32–33

Ruby
    emphasis on testing 538–539
    overview 535–536
    RubyGems 537–538
Ruby Version Manager. *See* RVM
ruby-install tool
    Linux 530–531
    Mac OS X 526–527
RubyInstaller tool 524
RVM (Ruby Version
        Manager) 463, 538

S

Safari 378
sanitized_parameters
        method 397
SASS (Syntactically Awesome
        Stylesheets) 71
scaffold generator 8–9, 25, 40
scoping, defined 209
SCSS 54, 71
Searcher gem 409, 414
searching
    displaying all tickets with
        tag 417–419
    overview 409
    by state 416–417
    by tags 412–415
    testing 409–412
SECRET_KEY_BASE option 99
secure shell. *See* SSH
security
    change_state permission
        375–376
    hacking forms 376–378
    hiding select box 373–374
    ignoring parameters 378–381
seed data 173
select_tag helper 272
Selenium 311, 313
self. prefix 36
semantic styling
    for buttons 107–111
    for flash messages 111–113
    overview 107
send_file method 307
sequence method 155
serialization
    generating serializer for
        Ticket model 473–476
    overview 471–473
server command 7
service classes 423–427
serving static resources 98–99

set_project method 101
show action 16–17, 69
Sidekiq gem 426
sign_in helper 379, 400
Simple Form gem
    advantages of 345
    automatically selected
        values 352
    Boolean values in 198
    Bootstrap and 276
    overview 102–103, 113–117
    simple_fields_for helper 296
Simple Mail Transfer Protocol.
        See SMTP
Simple Storage Service.
        See Amazon S3
Sinatra
    API using 509–514
    error handling with 515–517
    overview 508–509
single-responsibility
        principle 424
Siren 471
skip_after_action method 268
SMTP (Simple Mail Transfer
        Protocol) 465
spec helpers, Pundit 221–223
specs
    concise way for writing policy
        specs 243–246
    let method 142
    running 33–34
    test example 34–37
    view 180
    writing 32–33
Sprockets gem 70, 72, 119,
        315, 525
SQLite3 10, 50, 164
SSH (secure shell) 43
Stack Overflow 536
staging area 44
staging environment 449
state
    adding states 361–366
    changing 342–343, 345–352
    comment form
        authorization for 334–342
        controller for 332–333
        model for 329–332
        overview 326–328
    defining default 367–371
    searching by 416–417
    security for
        change_state
            permission 375–376

    hacking forms 376–378
    hiding select box 373–374
    ignoring parameters
        378–381
    seeding 352–353, 373
    setting default 352, 371–372
    State model 343–344
    tracking changes
        before_create
            callback 355–356
        displaying changes
            356–358
        overview 353
        recording changes 353–355
        styling states 358–361
statelessness 453
static resources 98–99
store_dir method 308
story-driven development 40
strong parameters 13, 67–70
stubbing 177–178
stylesheet_link_tag method 70
styling
    Bootstrap 103–104
    buttons 104–106
    Devise gem views 159–161
    links 106–107
    navigation bar 117–119
    page header style 104–106
    responsive 120–123
    semantic
        for buttons 107–111
        for flash messages 111–113
        overview 107
    Simple Form gem 102–103,
        113–117
subject method 224
submit method 64
submit_tag helper 411
super method 513
support loading 218
SVN (Subversion) 536
Syntactically Awesome
        Stylesheets. *See* SASS

T

tags
    adding through
        comments 391–395
    creating 384–386
    deleting
        adding link for 404–408
        overview 402–403

tags *(continued)*
   removing tag from
      page 408–409
   testing 403–404
   displaying 386–391
   has_and_belongs_to_many
      association 387
   model for 387–388
   restricting use of 396–402
   searching
      displaying all tickets with
         tag 417–419
      overview 409
      by state 416–417
      by tags 412–415
      testing 409–412
TDD (test-driven development)
   advantages of 26
   MiniTest 28–29
   overview 27
   test example 29–31
   writing tests 27–29
templates
   inheritance for 201–202
   partials 90
   setting page title 74–75
test environment 48
test fixtures 27
:test option 423
test-driven development. *See*
   TDD
Test::Unit 27
testing
   BDD
      advantages of 26
      overview 31
      RSpec 31–32
      running specs 33–34
      test example 34–37
      writing specs 32–33
   browser 49
   controllers 424
   emphasis on 538–539
   Factory Girl gem 85
   importance of 25–26
   namespaced controller
      177–180
   stubbing 178
   subject method 224
   TDD
      advantages of 26
      MiniTest 28–29
      overview 27
      test example 29–31
      writing tests 27–29
   views 260

text_field_tag helper 411
text/html type 498
Textile 3
time_ago_in_words helper 163
timeoutable module 150
timestamps 61–62, 387
:title option 405
title, page 74–75
titleize helper 274
to_a method 350
to_json method 471–472
to_s method 199
to_yaml method 500
token-based
   authentication 476–486
Toolbelt 450
top-down design 128
trackable module 150
tracking changes
   before_create callback
      355–356
   displaying changes 356–358
   overview 353
   recording changes 353–355
   styling states 358–361
traits, Factory Girl 171
transactions, database 279
transient attributes 304
Travis CI
   configuration 462–463
   deployment hooks 463–465
   overview 462
troubleshooting
   delete functionality 96
   link_to method 139
truthy values 172
try method 189, 226
Turbolinks gem 315–316
twelve-factor apps
   configuration 452
   defined 452
   processes 453–454
Twitter 1, 150

U

unauthenticated! method 516
Uniform Resource Locators. *See*
   URLs
uniqueness validation 79, 387
update action
   failure to update
      behavior 93–94
   implementing 92–93
update_column method 480

updated_at attribute 80
uploading files
   asynchronous requests
      appending content to
         form 320–322
      overview 317–320
      sending parameters
         for 322–324
   attaching many files
      creating spec for 293–294
      implementing feature
         294–298
      nested attributes 298–302
      overview 293
   attaching single file
      CarrierWave gem 286–287
      creating spec for 285–286
      implementing feature
         287–290
      overview 284
      persisting uploads when
         redisplaying form
         290–292
   fixing uploads for
      deployment 460–461
   serving files through control-
      ler
      permissions for
         attachments 304–306
      private attachments
         308–310
      public attachments
         307–308
      showing attachments
         306–307
      testing existing
         functionality 303–304
   using JavaScript
      attaching more files
         316–317
      disabling database transac-
         tions for tests 312–314
      jQuery 314–315
      overview 310
      testing 310–312
      Turbolinks gem 315–316
Urban Dictionary 1
url method 288
:url option 405
URLs (Uniform Resource
   Locators) 128–129
use method 520
use_transactional_fixtures
   option 313